Mapping the Social Landscape

Readings in Sociology

Seventh Edition

SUSAN J. FERGUSON
Grinnell College

Mc Graw Hill

Connect
Learn
Succeed™

Connect
Learn
Succeed™

MAPPING THE SOCIAL LANDSCAPE: READINGS IN SOCIOLOGY, SEVENTH EDITION

Published by McGraw-Hill, a business unit of The McGraw-Hill Companies, Inc., 1221 Avenue of the Americas, New York, NY 10020. Copyright 2013 by The McGraw-Hill Companies, Inc. All rights reserved. Printed in the United States of America. Previous editions © 2010, 2008, 2005. No part of this publication may be reproduced or distributed in any form or by any means, or stored in a database or retrieval system, without the prior written consent of The McGraw-Hill Companies, Inc., including, but not limited to, in any network or other electronic storage or transmission, or broadcast for distance learning.

Some ancillaries, including electronic and print components, may not be available to customers outside the United States.

This book is printed on acid-free paper.

2 3 4 5 6 7 8 9 0 DOC/DOC 1 0 9 8 7 6 5 4 3

ISBN 978-0-07-8026799
MHID 0-07-8026792

Vice President & Editor in Chief: *Michael Ryan*
Executive Director of Development: *Lisa Pinto*
Managing Director: *Gina Boedeker*
Editorial Coordinator: *Adina Lonn*
Marketing Specialist: *Alexandra Schultz*
Managing Development Editor: *Amy Mittelman*
Project Manager: *Judi David*
Buyer: *Jennifer Pickel*
Media Project Manager: *Sridevi Palani*
Cover Designer: *Studio Montage, St. Louis, MO*
Cover Image: © PhotoAlto/SuperStock, ©Andersen Ross/Blend Images LLC, © Paul Burns/Corbis
Composition: *MPS Limited*
Typeface: *10/12 Palatino*
Printer: *RR Donnelley*

All credits appearing on page or at end of the book are considered to be an extension of the copyright page.

Library of Congress Cataloging-in-Publication Data
Mapping the social landscape : readings in sociology / [edited by] Susan J. Ferguson.—7th ed.
    p. cm.
    ISBN 978-0-07-802679-9 (alk. paper)
  1. Social institutions.   2. Socialization.   3. Equality.   4. Social change.   5. Sociology.
I. Ferguson, Susan J.

HM826.M36 2013
301—dc23

2012027919

The Internet addresses listed in the text were accurate at the time of publication. The inclusion of a Web site does not indicate an endorsement by the authors or McGraw-Hill, and McGraw-Hill does not guarantee the accuracy of the information presented at these sites.

www.mhhe.com

With love to my grandmother, Edna Catherine Clark, who always believed that an education would open the doors of the world to me.
She was right.

Preface

As the title suggests, *Mapping the Social Landscape* is about exploration and discovery. It means taking a closer look at a complex, ever-changing social world in which locations, pathways, and boundaries are not fixed. Because sociology describes and explains our social surroundings, it enables us to understand this shifting landscape. Thus, sociology is about discovering society and discovering ourselves. The purpose of this anthology is to introduce the discipline of sociology and to convey the excitement and the challenge of the sociological enterprise.

Although a number of readers in introductory sociology are already available for students, I have yet to find one that exposes students to the broad diversity of scholarship, perspectives, and authorship that exists within the field of sociology. This diversity goes beyond recognizing gender, racial-ethnic, and social class differences to acknowledging a plurality of voices and views within the discipline. Like other anthologies, this one includes classic works by authors such as Karl Marx, Max Weber, C. Wright Mills, Kingsley Davis, Philip Zimbardo, and Wilbert Moore; in addition, however, I have drawn from a wide range of contemporary scholarship, some of which provides newer treatments of traditional concepts. This diversity of viewpoints and approaches should encourage students to evaluate and analyze the sociological ideas and research findings presented.

In addition, because I find it invaluable in my own teaching to use examples from personal experiences to enable students to see the connection between "private troubles and public issues," as C. Wright Mills phrased it, I have included in this collection a few personal narratives to help students comprehend how social forces affect individual lives. Thus, this anthology includes classic as well as contemporary writings, and the voices of other social scientists who render provocative sociological insights. The readings also exemplify functionalist, conflict, and symbolic interactionist perspectives and different types of research methodology. Each article is preceded by a brief headnote that sets the context within which the reader can seek to understand the sociological work. Thus, the selections communicate an enthusiasm for sociology while illustrating sociological concepts, theories, and methods.

During the past 30 years, sociology has benefited from a rich abundance of creative scholarship, but many of these original works have not been adequately presented in textbooks or readers. I believe an introductory anthology needs to reflect the new questions concerning research and theory within the discipline. Moreover, I find that students enjoy reading the actual words and research of sociologists. This anthology, therefore, includes many cutting-edge pieces of sociological scholarship and some very recent publications by recognized social analysts. Current issues are examined, including childhood school cliques, tourism in Hawaii, working at McDonald's, the effects of globalization, racism in the United States, socialization in law school, race and home ownership, elite college admissions, health care, poverty, sexual assault on college campuses, working in a slaughterhouse, military boot camps, teen suicide, eating disorders, prison riots, and the media in Iraq. In essence, I have attempted, not to break new ground, but, rather, to compile a collection that provides a fresh, innovative look at the discipline of sociology.

Changes to the Seventh Edition

With this seventh edition, I have selected readings that will invite students into the fascinating discipline of sociology. Most of the readings are by top scholars in the field of sociology, many of whom have high name recognition or are award-winning scholars. In fact, only 5 of the 58 readings are not authored by sociologists or social scientists, but instead are written by investigative journalists, such as Barbara Ehrenreich and Charlie LeDuff. I also maintain a critical balance of classical (14 percent) and contemporary readings (86 percent). In addition to many of the classic pieces that appeared in the sixth edition, I have added some new classics, including Howard S. Becker's "Culture: A Sociological View." All of the eight classic pieces are insightful readings, and they lay the groundwork for enhanced sociological understanding. Other changes I have made include adding a separate section on sociological theory to the first part of the book, and after providing an overview reading, I moved the classic readings by Karl Marx and Friedrich Engels, "The Manifesto of the Communist Party," and David L. Rosenhan's "On Being Sane in Insane Places," to this new section. I also have thoroughly updated several other sections of the anthology, including the section on the media, government and politics, medicine and health care, and race and ethnicity.

Overall, I have added twenty new selections (more than a third) to this edition of *Mapping the Social Landscape* to keep this collection cutting-edge with contemporary sociological research that illustrates timely analyses of social issues and the intersections between race, social class, and gender. These new selections examine gender socialization in children, the new global elites, poor women and motherhood, black male nurses and the glass escalator, the failure of health care during Katrina, the military control of the media in Iraq, female sexual slavery in Thailand, the admission policies of elite colleges, Muslims in America, gender and televised sports, and race, wealth, and home ownership. Among these readings are some selections that I consider to be contemporary classics in that they provide an overview of the discipline of sociology or a specific content area. These readings include the research by Matthew Desmond and Mustafa Emirbayer on racial domination; Debra Van Ausdale and Joe Feagin on preschool children's understandings of race; Evelyn Nakano Glenn's compelling research on skin lighteners and the racialized beauty ideal; and an essay from Dalton Conley's collection *Everywhere USA*, in which he discusses the changes in the relationships between individuals and groups in society. Based on the reviewers' comments, I also have added five readings that have a global emphasis, and at least seven readings in the anthology address sexuality.

One significant change is that I have brought back the piece by Kathryn Edin and Maria Kefalas from *Promises I Could Keep: Why Poor Women Put Motherhood Before Marriage*. So many reviewers and faculty who have used this anthology wanted to see Edin and Kefalas' research returned. Every time I revise an edition, I have to cut some pieces that I think are excellent, but do not review well with other teachers or because the permission costs have become prohibitive. I know these changes can be frustrating for some of you, but I think the students will find the newer pieces in this edition to be more accessible and interesting. Of course, for all of the readings, I have tried to choose selections that are compelling to students but also demonstrate well the diversity within the discipline of sociology in terms of sociological theory, research methods, or area of research. I am still looking for excellent contemporary pieces that illustrate C. Wright Mills' concept of the sociological imagination and appreciate any suggestions you may have for it or other potential readings for future editions. Please note that I welcome feedback from professors and students on this edition of *Mapping the Social Landscape*. You can e-mail me at Grinnell College. My e-mail address is fergusos@grinnell.edu.

Supplemental Learning Materials

An accompanying test bank contains numerous examination and discussion questions for each reading. Instructors can access this password-protected test bank on the Web site that accompanies the seventh edition of *Mapping the Social Landscape* at www.mhhe.com/ferguson7. Student resources, including extensive discussion questions and self-quizzes, are available on the student side of the same Web site.

Acknowledgments

The completion of this book involved the support and labor of many people. I would like to begin by acknowledging my former sociology editor, Serina Beauparlant of Mayfield Publishing Company, who challenged me, almost 18 years ago, to take on this project. Much of Serina's vision is contained within the structure of this book. Over the years we spent many hours on the telephone debating the strengths and weaknesses of various readings. Serina, if I am a clutch hitter, then you are the phenomenal batting coach. I could not have asked for a more thoughtful and attentive sociology editor. Thank you for initiating this project with me.

I also am indebted to my student research assistants at Grinnell College, Lizzie Buehler and Amelia Rudberg, for copying material and carrying innumerable pounds of books between my office and the library.

Over the past eighteen years, over 86 sociologists have reviewed earlier drafts of the manuscript and provided me with valuable observations concerning the readings and teaching introductory sociology. First and foremost, I want to acknowledge the early insights of Agnes Riedmann, who suggested several key pieces in the first draft. I also appreciate the suggestions for selections made by Joan Ferrante, Annette Lareau, and Michael Messner.

My special thanks go to Arnold Arluke, Northeastern University; Joanne M. Badagliacco, University of Kentucky; Gary L. Brock, Southwest Missouri State University; Tom Gerschick, Illinois State University; Thomas B. Gold, University of California at Berkeley; Jack Harkins, College of DuPage; Paul Kamolnick, East Tennessee State University; Peter Kivisto, Augustana College; Fred Kniss, Loyola University; Diane E. Levy, University of North Carolina at Wilmington; Peter Meiksins, Cleveland State University; Roslyn Arlin Mickelson, University of North Carolina at Charlotte; and Carol Ray, San Jose State University, for their feedback on the first edition of the manuscript. As a team of reviewers, your detailed comments were enormously helpful in the tightening and refining of the manuscript. Moreover, your voices reflect the rich and varied experiences with teaching introductory sociology.

For the second edition, I would like to thank the following team of reviewers: Angela Danzi, State University of New York at Farmingdale; Diane Diamond, State University of New York at Stony Brook; Yvonne Downs, State University of New York at Fredonia; Kay Forest, Northern Illinois University; Bob Granfield, University of Denver; Susan Greenwood, University of Maine; Kate Hausbeck, University of Nevada at Las Vegas; Arthur J. Jipson, Miami University; James Jones, Mississippi State University; Carolyn A. Kapinus, Penn State University; J. Richard Kendrick, Jr., State University of New York at Cortland; Mary Kris Mcilwaine, University of Arizona; Kristy McNamara, Furman University; Tracy Ore, University of Illinois at Urbana; Denise Scott, State University of New York at Geneseo; Maynard Seider, Massachusetts College of Liberal Arts; Thomas Soltis, Westmoreland County Community College; Martha Thompson, Northeastern Illinois University; Huiying Wei-Arthus, Weber State University; Adam S. Weinberg, Colgate University; Amy S. Wharton, Washington State University; and John Zipp, University of Wisconsin at Milwaukee.

For the third edition, I would like to thank the following reviewers: Stephen Adair, Central Connecticut State University; Javier Auyero, State University of New York, Stony Brook; David K. Brown, University of Illinois at Urbana-Champaign; Kay B. Forest, Northern Illinois University; Angela J. Hattery, Wake Forest University; Karen Honeycutt, University of Michigan; Neal King, Belmont University; Judith N. Lasker, Lehigh University; Rosemary F. Powers, Eastern Oregon University; Melissa Riba, Michigan State University; Deirdre Royster, University of Massachusetts, Amherst; James T. Salt, Lane Community College; H. Lovell Smith, Loyola College in Maryland; and Thomas Soltis, Westmoreland County Community College.

For the fourth edition, I would like to thank the following reviewers: Kevin J. Delaney, Temple University; Patricia L. Gibbs, Foothill College; Rebecca Klatch, University of California, San Diego; David Rohall, University of New Hampshire; Patricia Shropshire, Michigan State University; Thomas Soltis, Westmoreland County Community College; Kevin A. Tholin, Indiana University, South Bend; and several anonymous reviewers. All of your comments were extremely helpful to me during the revision process.

For the fifth edition, I would like to thank the following reviewers: Thomas Brignall III, Tennessee Tech University; Kenneth Colburn, Butler University; Susan A. Dumais, Louisiana State University; Colleen R. Greer, Bemidji State University; Joseph A. Kotarba, University of Houston; Heather Laube, University of Michigan, Flint; Philip Manning, Cleveland State University; David Schweingruber, Iowa State University; and Mohammad H. Tamdgidi, University of Massachusetts, Boston.

For the sixth edition, I would like to thank the following reviewers: Wendy Cadge, Brandeis University; Patricia E. Carson, Suffolk County Community College—Eastern Campus; Margo DeMelio, Central New Mexico Community College; Bruce K. Friesen, University of Tampa; Cheryl Maes, University of Nevada, Reno; Rodney A. McDanel, Ivy Tech Community College—Lafayette; David Miyahara, Azusa Pacific University; Michelle Petrie, Spring Hill College; Ken Spring, Belmont University; Patricia Gibbs Stayte, Foothill College; Raymond Swisher, Bowling Green State University; and Erica Ryu Wong, Loyola University Chicago.

For the seventh edition, I would like to thank the following reviewers: Gretchen Arnold, St. Louis University; ReAnne M. Ashlock, Rogers State University; Anne Eisenberg, SUNY-Geneseo; Kelly Mosel-Talavera, Texas State University-San Marcos; Patricia O'Brien, Elgin Community College; Julie A. Raulli, Wilson College; Tracy Scott, Emory University; Karrie Ann Snyder, Northwestern University; and Patricia Gibbs Stayte, Foothill College.

Finally, at McGraw-Hill Companies, I would like to recognize the creative and patient efforts of several individuals, including my development editor, Nicole Bridge. I also want to acknowledge the detailed work of the permissions editor, Sheri Gilbert, and the production editor, Vicki Moran. Thank you all for whipping my manuscript into shape!

About the Editor

Susan Ferguson is a professor of sociology at Grinnell College, where she has taught for almost 20 years. Ferguson regularly teaches Introduction to Sociology, and her critically acclaimed anthology, *Mapping the Social Landscape: Readings in Sociology* (McGraw-Hill, 2013) is used in introductory classes around the country. Ferguson also teaches courses on the family, medical sociology, the sociology of the body, and a new seminar on social inequality and identity. Ferguson has published in all of these areas, including the research collection, *Breast Cancer: Society Shapes an Epidemic* (with co-editor Anne Kasper, Palgrave, 2000); *Shifting the Center: Understanding Contemporary Families* (McGraw-Hill, 2011); and most recently, *Race, Gender, Sexuality, and Social Class: Dimensions of Inequality* (Sage, 2013). In addition, Ferguson is the General Editor for "Contemporary Family Perspectives," which is a series of research monographs and short texts on the family (Sage Publications).

Ferguson, who grew up in a working-class family in Colorado, still considers the Rocky Mountains to be her spiritual home. A first-generation college student, Ferguson was able to attend college with the help of scholarships, work study, and financial loans. She majored in political science and Spanish and also completed certificates of study in women's studies and Latin American studies. After working for a couple of years for a large biotechnology research grant sponsored by the United States Agency for International Development, Ferguson entered graduate school and completed her master's degree in sociology at Colorado State University and her Ph.D. in sociology at the University of Massachusetts at Amherst. Her areas of study are gender, family, women's health, and pedagogy, but her primary enthusiasm is for teaching.

Contents

Preface   v

Part I   THE SOCIOLOGICAL PERSPECTIVE   1

1. C. Wright Mills
   THE PROMISE   1
   —*classic piece on the sociological imagination*

2. Donna Gaines
   TEENAGE WASTELAND: Suburbia's Dead-End Kids   7
   —*applying the sociological imagination to teen suicide*

3. Mary Romero
   AN INTERSECTION OF BIOGRAPHY AND HISTORY:
   My Intellectual Journey   19
   —*applying the sociological imagination to domestic service*

THEORY

4. Chris Hunter and Kent McClelland
   THEORETICAL PERSPECTIVES IN SOCIOLOGY   33
   —*an introduction to the primary theories used in sociology*

5. Karl Marx and Friedrich Engels
   MANIFESTO OF THE COMMUNIST PARTY   43
   —*classic piece on the relationship between the capitalists
   and the workers*

6. David L. Rosenhan
   ON BEING SANE IN INSANE PLACES   48
   —*classic piece on labeling and social deviance*

SOCIAL RESEARCH

7. Michael Schwalbe
FINDING OUT HOW THE SOCIAL WORLD WORKS   59
    —*a summary of what it means to be sociologically mindful*

8. Craig Haney, W. Curtis Banks, and Philip G. Zimbardo
INTERPERSONAL DYNAMICS IN A SIMULATED PRISON   69
    —*classic piece on the research design of Zimbardo's
    famous experiment*

9. Meika Loe
WORKING AT BAZOOMS: The Intersection of
Power, Gender, and Sexuality   79
    —*an investigation of gender, sexuality, and power in
    the work place*

Part II   CULTURE   95

10. Howard S. Becker
CULTURE: A SOCIOLOGICAL VIEW   95
    —*classic piece that provides a theory of culture*

11. Barry Glassner
THE CULTURE OF FEAR: Why Americans Are Afraid
of the Wrong Things   105
    —*one perspective of American culture*

12. Haunani-Kay Trask
LOVELY HULA HANDS: Corporate Tourism and the
Prostitution of Hawaiian Culture   113
    —*an examination of cultural commodification and exploitation*

Part III   SOCIALIZATION   121

13. Emily W. Kane
"NO WAY MY BOYS ARE GOING TO BE LIKE THAT!":
Parents' Responses to Children's Gender Nonconformity 121
    —*how parents socialize children to gender norms*

14. Debra Van Ausdale and Joe R. Feagin
USING RACIAL AND ETHNIC CONCEPTS: The Critical
Case of Very Young Children   134
    —*a study of preschool children's understandings of race and
    ethnicity*

15. Robert Granfield
MAKING IT BY FAKING IT: Working-Class Students in
an Elite Academic Environment   145
   —working class identity and law school socialization

16. Gwynne Dyer
ANYBODY'S SON WILL DO   158
   —resocialization into the total institution of the military

Part IV   GROUPS AND SOCIAL STRUCTURE   169

17. Dalton Conley
THE BIRTH OF THE INTRAVIDUAL   169
   —an analysis of the individual and groups in society

18. Patricia A. Adler and Peter Adler
PEER POWER: Clique Dynamics among School Children   179
   *—a study of the structure and interactional dynamics
   among school children's groups*

19. Christine L. Williams
SHOPPING AS SYMBOLIC INTERACTION:
Race, Class, and Gender in the Toy Store   194
   —an example of secondary group relationships and interaction

Part V   DEVIANCE, CRIME, AND SOCIAL CONTROL   205

20. Penelope A. McLorg and Diane E. Taub
ANOREXIA NERVOSA AND BULIMIA: The Development of
Deviant Identities   205
   —the social construction of deviant identities

21. A. Ayres Boswell and Joan Z. Spade
FRATERNITIES AND COLLEGIATE RAPE CULTURE:
Why Are Some Fraternities More Dangerous Places for Women? 216
   —the social organization of crime

22. Mark Colvin
DESCENT INTO MADNESS:
The New Mexico State Prison Riot   229
   —an example of social structure breaking down

Part VI   SOCIAL INEQUALITY   243

SOCIAL CLASS

23. Kingsley Davis and Wilbert E. Moore with a
    Response by Melvin Tumin
    SOME PRINCIPLES OF STRATIFICATION   243
        —*classic piece on the functions of social stratification*

24. G. William Domhoff
    WHO RULES AMERICA?: The Corporate Community
    and the Upper Class   253
        —*the lifestyles and social institutions of the upper class*

25. Thomas M. Shapiro
    RACE, HOMEOWNERSHIP, AND WEALTH   266
        —*an examination of racial differences in wealth and assets*

26. Barbara Ehrenreich
    NICKEL-AND-DIMED: On (Not) Getting By in America   278
        —*an exploration of the lives of the working poor*

GENDER

27. Barbara Risman
    GENDER AS STRUCTURE   291
        —*a review of four theories that explain sex and gender*

28. Betsy Lucal
    WHAT IT MEANS TO BE GENDERED ME: Life on the
    Boundaries of a Dichotomous Gender System   301
        —*one woman's narrative of gender identity and performance*

29. C. J. Pascoe
    "DUDE, YOU'RE A FAG?": Adolescent Male Homophobia   315
        —*an examination of masculinity and homophobia in high schools*

30. Kevin Bales
    BECAUSE SHE LOOKS LIKE A CHILD   324
        —*an exploration of female sexual slavery in Thailand*

RACE AND ETHNICITY

31. Matthew Desmond and Mustafa Emirbayer
    WHAT IS RACIAL DOMINATION?   338
        —*an introduction to the study of race and racism*

32. Charlie LeDuff
    AT A SLAUGHTERHOUSE, SOME THINGS NEVER DIE   354
        —*an examination of the racial dynamics at one work place site*

33. Katherin M. Flower Kim
OUT OF SORTS: Adoption and (Un)Desirable Children 364
—how race and racism influence adoption decisions

34. Evelyn Nakano Glenn
YEARNING FOR LIGHTNESS: Transnational Circuits
in the Marketing and Consumption of Skin Lighteners 377
—how racism influences beauty ideals around the world

Part VII   SOCIAL INSTITUTIONS 391

POWER AND POLITICS

35. C. Wright Mills
THE POWER ELITE 391
—classic piece on the power elite

36. Richard L. Zweigenhaft and G. William Domhoff
THE IRONIES OF DIVERSITY 398
—a study of which minorities become the power elite

37. Chrystia Freeland
THE RISE OF THE NEW GLOBAL ELITE 413
—how the global economy is creating a new power elite

MASS MEDIA

38. Eric Klinenberg
CONVERGENCE: News Production in a Digital Age 423
—an in-depth investigation of one major news organization

39. Michael A. Messner and Cheryl Cooky
GENDER IN TELEVISED SPORTS: News and Highlights
Shows, 1989–2009 437
—an empirical investigation of gender in sports reporting

40. Andrew M. Lindner
CONTROLLING THE MEDIA IN IRAQ 453
—how the military has influenced journalism during wartime

THE ECONOMY AND WORK

41. Robin Leidner
OVER THE COUNTER: McDonald's 464
—an ethnographic study of routinization in work

42. Adia Harvey Wingfield
    RACIALIZING THE GLASS ESCALATOR: Reconsidering
    Men's Experiences with Women's Work   479
        —*a study of the race and gender dimensions of work*

43. Arlie Russell Hochschild
    THE TIME BIND: When Work Becomes Home and
    Home Becomes Work   491
        —*how individuals combine their work and home lives*

RELIGION

44. Max Weber
    THE PROTESTANT ETHIC AND THE SPIRIT
    OF CAPITALISM   502
        —*classic piece on the influence of religion on the economy*

45. Steven P. Dandaneau
    RELIGION AND SOCIETY: Of Gods and Demons   509
        —*a sociological overview of the institution of religion*

46. Jen'nan Ghazal Read
    MUSLIMS IN AMERICA   519
        —*an empirical examination of one religious group*

HEALTH AND MEDICINE

47. Jill Quadagno
    INSTITUTIONS, INTEREST GROUPS, AND IDEOLOGY: An
    Agenda for the Sociology of Health Care Reform   527
        —*how social structure affects the organization of health care*

48. Lillian B. Rubin
    SAND CASTLES AND SNAKE PITS   539
        —*an examination of how deinstitutionalization increased the
        numbers of mentally ill among the homeless*

49. Keith Wailoo
    A SLOW, TOXIC DECLINE: Dialysis Patients, Technological
    Failure, and the Unfulfilled Promise of Health in America   547
        —*an example of how U.S. health care is not working*

EDUCATION

50. Mary Crow Dog with Richard Erdoes
CIVILIZE THEM WITH A STICK   557
    —*education as an institution of social control*

51. Mitchell L. Stevens
A SCHOOL IN A GARDEN   564
    —*how college admissions at elite schools reinforce social class*

52. Ann Arnett Ferguson
BAD BOYS: Public Schools in the Making of Black Masculinity 578
    —*racial and gender stereotyping in American schools*

THE FAMILY

53. Andrew J. Cherlin
THE DEINSTITUTIONALIZATION OF AMERICAN
MARRIAGE   586
    —*an examination of the weakening of social norms in the
    institution of marriage*

54. Kathryn Edin and Maria Kefalas
UNMARRIED WITH CHILDREN   598
    —*the changing meaning of marriage and motherhood*

55. Annette Lareau
INVISIBLE INEQUALITY: Social Class and Childrearing
in Black Families and White Families   606
    —*an examination of social class differences in parenting and
    child rearing in African American and white families*

Part VIII   SOCIAL CHANGE   623

56. D. Stanley Eitzen
THE ATROPHY OF SOCIAL LIFE   623
    —*how social isolation is affecting society*

57. Elijah Anderson
THE COSMOPOLITAN CANOPY   631
    —*an ethnographic account of how urban spaces can transform
    race relations*

58. Duane F. Alwin
GENERATIONS X, Y AND Z: Are They Changing America?   644
    —*an examination of factors affecting social change*

Tell me the landscape in which you live, and I will tell you who you are.

José Ortega y Gasset

PART I

The Sociological Perspective

1

THE PROMISE

C. WRIGHT MILLS

The initial three selections examine the sociological perspective. The first of these is written by C. Wright Mills (1916–1962), a former professor of sociology at Columbia University. During his brief academic career, Mills became one of the best known and most controversial sociologists. He was critical of the U.S. government and other social institutions where power was unfairly concentrated. He also believed that academics should be socially responsible and speak out against social injustice. The excerpt that follows is from Mills' acclaimed book *The Sociological Imagination.* Since its original publication in 1959, this text has been required reading for most introductory sociology students around the world. Mills' sociological imagination perspective not only compels the best sociological analyses but also enables the sociologist and the individual to distinguish between "personal troubles" and "public issues." By separating these phenomena, we can better comprehend the sources of and solutions to social problems.

Nowadays men often feel that their private lives are a series of traps. They sense that within their everyday worlds, they cannot overcome their troubles, and in this feeling, they are often quite correct: What ordinary men are directly aware of and what they try to do are bounded by the private orbits in which they live; their visions and their powers are limited to the close-up scenes of job, family, neighborhood; in other milieux, they move vicariously and remain spectators. And the more aware they become, however vaguely, of ambitions and of threats which transcend their immediate locales, the more trapped they seem to feel.

Underlying this sense of being trapped are seemingly impersonal changes in the very structure of continent-wide societies. The facts of contemporary history are also facts about the success and the failure of

This article was written in 1959 before scholars were sensitive to gender inclusivity in language. The references to masculine pronouns and men are, therefore, generic to both males and females and should be read as such. Please note that I have left the author's original language in this selection and other readings.—*Editor* individual men and women. When a society is industrialized, a peasant becomes a worker; a feudal lord is liquidated or becomes a businessman. When classes rise or fall, a man is employed or unemployed; when the rate of investment goes up or down, a man takes new heart or goes broke. When wars happen, an insurance salesman becomes a rocket launcher; a store clerk, a radar man; a wife lives alone; a child grows up without a father. Neither the life of an individual nor the history of a society can be understood without understanding both.

Yet men do not usually define the troubles they endure in terms of historical change and institutional contradiction. The well-being they enjoy, they do not usually impute to the big ups and downs of the societies in which they live. Seldom aware of the intricate connection between the patterns of their own lives and the course of world history, ordinary men do not usually know what this connection means for the kinds of men they are becoming and for the kinds of history making in which they might take part. They do not possess the quality of mind essential to grasp the interplay of man and society, of biography and history, of self and world. They cannot cope with their personal troubles in such ways as to control the structural transformations that usually lie behind them.

Surely it is no wonder. In what period have so many men been so totally exposed at so fast a pace to such earthquakes of change? That Americans have not known such catastrophic changes as have the men and women of other societies is due to historical facts that are now quickly becoming "merely history." The history that now affects every man is world history. Within this scene and this period, in the course of a single generation, one-sixth of mankind is transformed from all that is feudal and backward into all that is modern, advanced, and fearful. Political colonies are freed; new and less visible forms of imperialism installed. Revolutions occur; men feel the intimate grip of new kinds of authority. Totalitarian societies rise and are smashed to bits—or succeed fabulously. After two centuries of ascendancy, capitalism is shown up as only one way to make society into an industrial apparatus. After two centuries of hope, even formal democracy is restricted to a quite small portion of mankind. Everywhere in the underdeveloped world, ancient ways of life are broken up and vague expectations become urgent demands. Everywhere in the overdeveloped world, the means of authority and of violence become total in scope and bureaucratic in form. Humanity itself now lies before us, the super-nation at either pole concentrating its most coordinated and massive efforts upon the preparation of World War Three.

The very shaping of history now outpaces the ability of men to orient themselves in accordance with cherished values. And which values? Even when they do not panic, men often sense that older ways of feeling and thinking have collapsed and that newer beginnings are ambiguous to the point of moral stasis. Is it any wonder that ordinary men feel they cannot cope with the larger worlds with which they are so suddenly confronted? That they cannot understand the meaning of their epoch for their own lives? That—in defense of selfhood—they become morally insensible, trying to remain altogether private men? Is it any wonder that they come to be possessed by a sense of the trap?

––––––––

It is not only information that they need—in this Age of Fact, information often dominates their attention and overwhelms their capacities to assimilate it. It is not only the skills of reason that they need—although their struggles to acquire these often exhaust their limited moral energy.

What they need, and what they feel they need, is a quality of mind that will help them to use information and to develop reason in order to achieve lucid summations of what is going on in the world and of what may be happening within themselves. It is this quality, I am going to contend, that journalists and scholars, artists and publics, scientists and editors are coming to expect of what may be called the sociological imagination.

––––––––

The sociological imagination enables its possessor to understand the larger historical scene in terms of its meaning for the inner life and the external career of a variety of individuals. It enables him to take into account how individuals, in the welter of their daily experience, often become falsely conscious of their social positions. Within that welter, the framework of modern society is sought, and within that framework the psychologies of a variety of men and women are formulated. By such means the personal uneasiness of individuals is focused upon explicit troubles and the indifference of publics is transformed into involvement with public issues.

The first fruit of this imagination—and the first lesson of the social science that embodies it—is the idea that the individual can understand his own experience and gauge his own fate only by locating himself within his period, that he can know his own chances in life only by becoming aware of those of all individuals in his circumstances. In many ways it is a terrible lesson; in many ways a magnificent one. We do not know the limits of man's capacities for supreme effort or willing degradation, for agony or glee, for pleasurable brutality or the sweetness of reason. But in our time we have come to know that the limits of "human nature" are frighteningly broad. We have come to know that every individual lives, from one generation to the next, in some society; that he lives out a biography, and that he lives it out within some historical sequence. By the fact of his living he contributes, however minutely, to the shaping of this society and to the course of its history, even as he is made by society and by its historical push and shove.

The sociological imagination enables us to grasp history and biography and the relations between the two within society. That is its task and its promise. To recognize this task and this promise is the mark of the classic social analyst. It is characteristic of Herbert Spencer—turgid, polysyllabic, comprehensive; of E. A. Ross—graceful, muckraking, upright; of Auguste Comte and Emile Durkheim; of the intricate and subtle Karl Mannheim. It is the quality of all that is intellectually excellent in Karl Marx; it is the clue to Thorstein Veblen's brilliant and ironic insight, to Joseph Schumpeter's many-sided constructions of reality; it is the basis of the psychological sweep of W. E. H. Lecky no less than of the profundity and clarity of Max

Weber. And it is the signal of what is best in contemporary studies of man and society.

No social study that does not come back to the problems of biography, of history and of their intersections within a society, has completed its intellectual journey. Whatever the specific problems of the classic social analysts, however limited or however broad the features of social reality they have examined, those who have been imaginatively aware of the promise of their work have consistently asked three sorts of questions:

1. What is the structure of this particular society as a whole? What are its essential components, and how are they related to one another? How does it differ from other varieties of social order? Within it, what is the meaning of any particular feature for its continuance and for its change?
2. Where does this society stand in human history? What are the mechanics by which it is changing? What is its place within and its meaning for the development of humanity as a whole? How does any particular feature we are examining affect, and how is it affected by, the historical period in which it moves? And this period—what are its essential features? How does it differ from other periods? What are its characteristic ways of history making?
3. What varieties of men and women now prevail in this society and in this period? And what varieties are coming to prevail? In what ways are they selected and formed, liberated and repressed, made sensitive and blunted? What kinds of "human nature" are revealed in the conduct and character we observe in this society in this period? And what is the meaning for "human nature" of each and every feature of the society we are examining?

Whether the point of interest is a great power state or a minor literary mood, a family, a prison, a creed—these are the kinds of questions the best social analysts have asked. They are the intellectual pivots of classic studies of man in society—and they are the questions inevitably raised by any mind possessing the sociological imagination. For that imagination is the capacity to shift from one perspective to another—from the political to the psychological; from examination of a single family to comparative assessment of the national budgets of the world; from the theological school to the military establishment; from considerations of an oil industry to studies of contemporary poetry. It is the capacity to range from the most impersonal and remote transformations to the most intimate features of the human self—and to see the relations between the two. Back of its use there is always the urge to know the social and historical meaning of the individual in the society and in the period in which he has his quality and his being.

That, in brief, is why it is by means of the sociological imagination that men now hope to grasp what is going on in the world, and to understand what is happening in themselves as minute points of the intersections of biography and history within society. In large part, contemporary man's self-conscious view of himself as at least an outsider, if not a permanent stranger, rests upon an absorbed realization of social relativity and of the transformative power of history. The sociological imagination is the most fruitful form of this self-consciousness. By its use men whose mentalities have swept only a series of limited orbits often come to feel as if suddenly awakened in a house with which they had only supposed themselves to be familiar. Correctly or incorrectly, they often come to feel that they can now provide themselves with adequate summations, cohesive assessments, comprehensive orientations. Older decisions that once appeared sound now seem to them products of a mind unaccountably dense. Their capacity for astonishment is made lively again. They acquire a new way of thinking, they experience a transvaluation of values: in a word, by their reflection and by their sensibility, they realize the cultural meaning of the social sciences.

———————

Perhaps the most fruitful distinction with which the sociological imagination works is between "the personal troubles of milieu" and "the public issues of social structure." This distinction is an essential tool of the sociological imagination and a feature of all classic work in social science.

Troubles occur within the character of the individual and within the range of his immediate relations with others; they have to do with his self and with those limited areas of social life of which he is directly and personally aware. Accordingly, the statement and the resolution of troubles properly lie within the individual as a biographical entity and within the scope of his immediate milieu—the social setting that is directly open to his personal experience and to some extent his willful activity. A trouble is a private matter: Values cherished by an individual are felt by him to be threatened.

Issues have to do with matters that transcend these local environments of the individual and the range of his inner life. They have to do with the organization of many such milieux into the institutions of a historical society as a whole, with the ways in which various milieux overlap and interpenetrate to form the larger structure of social and historical life. An issue is a public matter: Some value cherished by publics is felt to be threatened. Often there is a debate about what that value really is and about what it is that really threatens it. This debate is often without focus if only because it is the very nature of an issue, unlike even widespread trouble, that it cannot very well be defined in terms of the immediate and everyday environments of ordinary men. An issue, in fact, often involves a crisis in institutional arrangements, and often too it involves what Marxists call "contradictions" or "antagonisms."

———————

In these terms, consider unemployment. When, in a city of 100,000, only one man is unemployed, that is his personal trouble, and for its relief we properly look to the character of the man, his skills, and his immediate opportunities. But when in a nation of 50 million employees, 15 million men are unemployed, that is an issue, and we may not hope to find its solution within the range of opportunities open to any one individual. The very structure of opportunities has collapsed. Both the correct statement of the problem and the range of possible solutions require us to consider the economic and political institutions of the society, and not merely the personal situation and character of a scatter of individuals.

Consider war. The personal problem of war, when it occurs, may be how to survive it or how to die in it with honor; how to make money out of it; how to climb into the higher safety of the military apparatus; or how to contribute to the war's termination. In short, according to one's values, to find a set of milieux and within it to survive the war or make one's death in it meaningful. But the structural issues of war have to do with its causes; with what types of men it throws up into command; with its effects upon economic and political, family and religious institutions, with the unorganized irresponsibility of a world of nation-states.

Consider marriage. Inside a marriage a man and a woman may experience personal troubles, but when the divorce rate during the first four years of marriage is 250 out of every 1,000 attempts, this is an indication of a structural issue having to do with the institutions of marriage and the family and other institutions that bear upon them.

Or consider the metropolis—the horrible, beautiful, ugly, magnificent sprawl of the great city. For many upper-class people, the personal solution to "the problem of the city" is to have an apartment with a private garage under it in the heart of the city, and forty miles out, a house by Henry Hill, garden by Garrett Eckbo, on a hundred acres of private land. In these two controlled environments—with a small staff at each end and a private helicopter connection—most people could solve many of the problems of personal milieux caused by the facts of the city. But all this, however splendid, does not solve the public issues that the structural fact of the city poses. What should be done with this wonderful monstrosity? Break it all up into scattered units, combining residence and work? Refurbish it as it stands? Or, after evacuation, dynamite it and build new cities according to new plans in new places? What should those plans be? And who is to decide and to accomplish whatever choice is made? These are structural issues; to confront them and to solve them requires us to consider political and economic issues that affect innumerable milieux.

Insofar as an economy is so arranged that slumps occur, the problem of unemployment becomes incapable of personal solution. Insofar as war is inherent in the nation-state system and in the uneven industrialization of the world, the ordinary individual in his restricted milieu will be powerless—with or without psychiatric aid—to solve the troubles this system or lack of system imposes upon him. Insofar as the family as an institution turns women into darling little slaves and men into their chief providers and unweaned dependents, the problem of a satisfactory marriage remains incapable of purely private solution. Insofar as the overdeveloped megalopolis and the overdeveloped automobile are built-in features of the overdeveloped society, the issues of urban living will not be solved by personal ingenuity and private wealth.

———

What we experience in various and specific milieux, I have noted, is often caused by structural changes. Accordingly, to understand the changes of many personal milieux we are required to look beyond them. And the number and variety of such structural changes increase as the institutions within which we live become more embracing and more intricately connected with one another. To be aware of the idea of social structure and to use it with sensibility is to be capable of tracing such linkages among a great variety of milieux. To be able to do that is to possess the sociological imagination.

2

TEENAGE WASTELAND
Suburbia's Dead-End Kids

DONNA GAINES

This reading by Donna Gaines is excerpted from her internationally acclaimed book *Teenage Wasteland: Suburbia's Dead-End Kids* (1990). *Rolling Stone* declared *Teenage Wasteland* "the best book on youth culture" and it is a required reading for university course lists in several disciplines. Gaines is a journalist, cultural sociologist, and New York State certified social worker. An international expert on youth violence and culture, Gaines has been interviewed extensively in newspapers, for documentaries, on radio and on television. Professor Gaines also has taught sociology at Barnard College of Columbia University and at the Graduate Faculty of New School University.

This excerpt is an example of sociological research that employs C. Wright Mills' sociological imagination and, specifically, his distinction between personal troubles and public issues. As Gaines illustrates, when one teenager commits suicide it is a personal tragedy, but when groups of teenagers form a suicide pact and successfully carry it out, suicide becomes a matter of public concern. In order to explain adequately why this incident occurred, Gaines examines both the history and the biography of suburban teens.

In Bergenfield, New Jersey, on the morning of March 11, 1987, the bodies of four teenagers were discovered inside a 1977 rust-colored Chevrolet Camaro. The car, which belonged to Thomas Olton, was parked in an unused garage in the Foster Village garden apartment complex, behind the Foster Village Shopping Center. Two sisters, Lisa and Cheryl Burress, and their friends, Thomas Rizzo and Thomas Olton, had died of carbon monoxide poisoning.

Lisa was 16, Cheryl was 17, and the boys were 19—they were suburban teens, turnpike kids like the ones in the town I live in. And thinking about them made me remember how it felt being a teenager too. I was horrified that it had come to this. I believed I understood why they did it, although it wasn't a feeling I could have put into words.

You could tell from the newspapers that they were rock and roll kids. The police had found a cassette tape cover of AC/DC's *If You Want Blood, You've Got It* near the bodies. Their friends were described as kids who listened to thrash metal, had shaggy haircuts, wore lots of black and leather. "Dropouts," "druggies," the papers called them. Teenage suburban rockers whose lives revolved around their favorite bands and their friends. Youths who barely got by in school and at home and who did not impress authority figures in any remarkable way. Except as fuck-ups.

My friends, most of whom were born in the 1950s, felt the same way about the kids everyone called "burnouts." On the weekend following the suicides, a friend's band, the Grinders, were playing at My Father's Place, a Long Island club. That night the guys dedicated a song, "The Kids in the Basement," to the four teens from Bergenfield: *This is for the suicide kids.* In the weeks following the suicide pact, a number of bands in the tri-state area also dedicated songs to them. Their deaths had hit close to home. . . .

A week or two after the suicide pact, *The Village Voice* assigned me to go to Bergenfield. Now this was not a story I would've volunteered for. . . . But one day my editor at the *Voice* called to ask if I wanted to go to Bergenfield. She knew my background—that I knew suburbia, that I could talk to kids. By now I fully embraced the sociologist's ethical commitment to the "rights of the researched," and the social worker's vow of client confidentiality. As far as suicidal teenagers were concerned, I felt that if I couldn't help them, I didn't want to bother them.

But I was really pissed off at what I kept reading. How people in Bergenfield openly referred to the four kids as "troubled losers." Even after they were dead, nobody cut them any slack. "Burnouts," "druggies," "dropouts." Something was wrong. So I took the opportunity.

From the beginning, I believed that the Bergenfield suicides symbolized a tragic defeat for young people. Something was happening in the larger society that was not yet comprehended. Scholars spoke ominously of "the postmodern condition," "societal upheaval," "decay," "anomie." Meanwhile, American kids kept losing ground, showing all the symptoms of societal neglect. Many were left to fend for themselves, often with little success. The news got worse. Teenage suicides continued, and still nobody seemed to be getting the point.

Now, in trying to understand this event, I might have continued working within the established discourse on teenage suicide. I might have carried on the tradition of obscuring the bigger picture, psychologizing the Bergenfield suicide pact, interviewing the parents of the four youths, hounding their friends for the gory details. I might have spent my time probing school records, tracking down their teachers and shrinks for insights, focusing on their personal histories and intimate relationships. I might have searched out the individual motivations behind the words left in the note written and signed by each youth on the brown paper bag found with their bodies on March 11. But I did not.

Because the world has changed for today's kids. We also engaged in activities that adults called self-destructive. But for my generation, "doing it" meant having sex; for them, it means committing suicide.

"Teenage suicide" was a virtually nonexistent category prior to 1960. But between 1950 and 1980 it nearly tripled, and at the time of the Bergenfield suicide pact it was described as the second leading cause of death among America's young people; "accidents" were the first. The actual suicide rate among people aged 15 to 24—the statistical category for teenage suicide—is estimated to be even higher, underreported because of social stigma. Then there are the murky numbers derived from drug overdoses and car crashes, recorded as accidents. To date, there are more than 5,000 teen suicides annually, accounting for 12 percent of youth mortalities. An estimated 400,000 adolescents attempt suicide each year. While youth suicide rates leveled off by 1980, by mid-decade they began to increase again. Although they remained lower than adult suicide rates, the acceleration at which youth suicide rates increased was alarming. By 1987, we had books and articles detailing "copycat" and "cluster" suicides. Teenage suicide was now described as an epidemic.

Authors, experts, and scholars compiled the lists of kids' names, ages, dates, and possible motives. They generated predictive models: Rural and suburban white kids do it more often. Black kids in America's urban teenage wastelands are more likely to kill each other. Increasingly, alcohol and drugs are involved. In some cases, adults have tried to identify the instigating factor as a lyric or a song—Judas Priest, Ozzy Osbourne. Or else a popular film about the subject—the suicide of a celebrity; too much media attention or not enough.

Some kids do it violently: drowning, hanging, slashing, jumping, or crashing. Firearms are still the most popular. Others prefer to go out more peacefully, by gas or drug overdose. Boys do it more than girls, though girls try it more often than boys. And it does not seem to matter if kids are rich or poor.

Throughout the 1980s, teenage suicide clusters appeared across the country—six or seven deaths, sometimes more, in a short period of time in a single community. In the boomtown of Plano, Texas. The fading factory town of Leominster, Massachusetts. At Bryan High School in a white, working-class suburb of Omaha, Nebraska. A series of domino suicides among Arapaho Indian youths at the Wind River Reservation in Wyoming. Six youth suicides in the county of Westchester, New York, in 1984; five in 1985 and seven in 1986.

Sometimes they were close friends who died together in pacts of two. In other cases, one followed shortly after the other, unable to survive apart. Then there were strangers who died alone, in separate incidents timed closely together.

The Bergenfield suicide pact of March 11 was alternately termed a "multiple-death pact," a "quadruple suicide," or simply a "pact," depending on where you read about it. Some people actually called it a *mass* suicide because the Bergenfield case reminded them of Jonestown, Guyana, in 1978, where over 900 followers of Jim Jones poisoned themselves, fearing their community would be destroyed.

As experts speculated over the deaths in Bergenfield, none could recall a teenage suicide pact involving four people dying together; *it was historically unique.*

I wondered, did the "burnouts" see themselves as a community under siege? Like Jim Jones' people, or the 960 Jews at Masada who jumped to their deaths rather than face defeat at the hands of the Romans? Were the "burnouts" of Bergenfield choosing death over surrender? Surrender to what? Were they martyrs? If so, what was their common cause?

Because the suicide pact was a *collective act*, it warrants a social explanation—a portrait of the "burnouts" in Bergenfield as actors within a particular social landscape.

For a long time now, the discourse of teenage suicide has been dominated by atomizing psychological and medical models. And so the larger picture of American youth as members of a distinctive generation with a unique collective biography, emerging at a particular moment in history, has been lost.

The starting-off point for this research, then, is a teenage suicide pact in an "upper-poor" white ethnic suburb in northern New Jersey. But, of course, the story did not begin and will not end in Bergenfield.

Yes, there were specific sociocultural patterns operating in Bergenfield through which a teenage suicide pact became objectively possible. Yes, there were particular conditions which influenced how the town reacted to the event. Yes, there were reasons—that unique constellation of circumstances congealed in the lives of the four youths in the years, weeks, and days prior to March 11—that made suicide seem like their best alternative.

Given the four youths' personal histories, their losses, their failures, their shattered dreams, the motivation to die in this way seems transparent. Yet, after the suicide pact, in towns across the country, on television and in the press, people asked, "Why did they do it?" But I went to Bergenfield with other questions.

This was a suicide pact that involved close friends who were by no accounts obsessed, star-crossed lovers. What would make four people want to die together? Why would they ask, in their collective suicide note, to be waked and buried together? Were they part of a suicide cult?

If not, what was the nature of the *social* bond that tied them so closely? What could be so intimately binding that in the early morning hours of March 11 not one of them could stop, step back from the pact they had made to say, "Wait, I can't do this"? Who were these kids that everybody called "burnouts"?

"Greasers," "hoods," "beats," "freaks," "hippies," "punks." From the 1950s onward, these groups have signified young people's refusal to cooperate. In the social order of the American high school, teens are expected to do what they are told—make the grade, win the prize, play the game. Kids who refuse have always found something else to do. Sometimes it kills them; sometimes it sets them free.

In the 1980s, as before, high school kids at the top were the "preps," "jocks," or "brains," depending on the region. In white suburban high schools in towns like Bergenfield, the "burnouts" are often the kids near the bottom—academically, economically, and socially.

To outsiders, they look tough, scruffy, poor, wild. Uninvolved in and unimpressed by convention, they create an alternative world, a retreat, a refuge. Some burnouts are proud; they "wave their freak flags high." They call themselves burnouts to flaunt their break with the existing order, as a form of resistance, a statement of refusal.

But the meaning changes when "burnout" is hurled by an outsider. Then it hurts. It's an insult. Everyone knows you don't call somebody a burnout to their face unless you are looking for a fight. At that point, the word becomes synonymous with "troubled loser," "druggie"—all the things the press and some residents of the town called the four kids who died together in Tommy Olton's Camaro.

How did kids in Bergenfield *become* "burnouts," I wondered. At what point were they identified as outcasts? Was this a labeling process or one of self-selection? What kinds of lives did they have? What resources were available for them? What choices did they have? What ties did these kids have to the world outside Bergenfield? Where did their particular subculture come from? Why in the 1980s, the Reagan years, in white, suburban America?

What were their hopes and fears? What did heavy metal, Satan, suicide and long hair mean to them? Who were their heroes, their gods? What saved them and what betrayed them in the long, cold night?

And what was this "something evil in the air" that people spoke about? Were the kids in Bergenfield "possessed"? Was the suicide pact an act of cowardice by four "losers," or the final refuge of kids helplessly and hopelessly trapped? How different was Bergenfield from other towns?

Could kids be labeled to death? How much power did these labels have? I wanted to meet other kids in Bergenfield who were identified as "burnouts" to find out what it felt like to carry these labels. I wanted to understand the existential situation they operated in—not simply as hapless losers, helpless victims, or tragic martyrs, but also as *historical actors* determined in their choices, resistant, defiant.

Because the suicide pact in Bergenfield seemed to be a symptom of something larger, a metaphor for something more universal, I moved on from there to other towns. For almost two years I spent my time reading thrash magazines, seeing shows, and hanging out with "burnouts" and "dirtbags" as well as kids who slip through such labels. . . .

From the beginning, I decided I didn't want to dwell too much on the negatives. I wanted to understand how alienated kids survived, as well as how they were defeated. How did they maintain their humanity against what I now felt were impossible odds? I wondered. What keeps young people together when the world they are told to trust no longer seems to work?

What motivates them to be decent human beings when nobody seems to respect them or take them seriously? . . .

Joe's[1] been up for more than a day already. He's fried, his clothes are getting crusty, and he points to his armpits and says he smells (he doesn't). He's broke, he misses his girlfriend. He says he can't make it without someone. His girlfriend dumped him last year. He's gone out with other girls, but it's not the same. And he knows he can't win in this town. He's got a bad name. What's the use. He's tried it at least six times. Once he gashed at his vein with an Army knife he picked up in Times Square. He strokes the scars.

Tonight, he says, he's going to a Bible study class. Some girl he met invited him. Shows me a God pamphlet, inspirational literature. He doesn't want anyone to know about this, though. He thought the Jesus girl was nice. He's meeting her at seven. Bobby comes back in the room with Nicky, looking for cigarettes.

Later in the living room Joe teases Doreen. Poking at her, he gets rough. Bobby monitors him: *Calm down, Joe.* We are just sitting around playing music, smoking cigarettes. Fooling around. Did you see those Jesus freaks down at Cooper's Pond the other day? Randy laughs. Nicky tells Joe to forget it. Jesus chicks won't just go with you; you have to date them for a long time, pretend you're serious about them. They don't fuck you right away: *It's not worth the bother.*

Suicide comes up again. Joan and Susie have razor scars. The guys make Susie show me her freshly bandaged wrists. I look at her. She's such a beautiful girl. She's sitting there with her boyfriend, Randy, just fooling around. I ask her quietly: *Why are you doing this?* She smiles at me seductively. She doesn't say anything. What the fuck is this, erotic? Kicks? Romantic? I feel cold panic.

Nicky slashed his wrists when his old girlfriend moved out of state. His scars are much older. I motion to him about Susie. Discreetly he says: *It's best just to ignore it, don't pay too much attention.* Throughout the afternoon I try every trick I know to get Susie to talk to me. She won't. She's shy, quiet; she's all inside herself.

And I really don't want to push too hard. The kids say they're already going nuts from all the suicide-prevention stuff. You can't panic. But I have to figure out if this is a cult, a fad, a hobby, or something I'm supposed to report to the police. I'm afraid to leave.

I wonder, do they know the difference between vertical and horizontal cuts? Don't their parents, their teachers, the cops, and neighbors see this shit going on? Maybe they feel as confused as I do. Maybe this is why they didn't see it coming here, and in the other towns. You can't exactly go around strip-searching teenagers to see if they have slash wounds. . . .

After the suicide pact, parents complained that the kids really did need somewhere to go when school let out. The after-school activities were limited to academics, sports, or organized school clubs. Even with part-time after-school jobs, a number of the town's young people did not find the conventional activities offered by the town particularly intriguing.

But according to established adult reasoning, if you didn't get absorbed into the legitimate, established routine of social activity, you'd be left to burn out on street corners, killing time, getting wasted. It was impossible for anyone to imagine any autonomous activity that nonconforming youth en masse might enjoy that would not be self-destructive, potentially criminal, or meaningless.

Parents understood that the lack of "anything to do" often led to drug and alcohol abuse. Such concerns were aired at the volatile meeting in the auditorium of Bergenfield High School. It was agreed that the kids' complaint of "no place to go" had to be taken seriously. Ten years ago, in any suburban town, teenagers' complaints of "nothing to do" would have been met with adult annoyance. But not anymore.

In Bergenfield, teenage boredom could no longer be dismissed as the whining of spoiled suburban kids. Experts now claimed that national rates of teenage suicide were higher in suburbs and rural areas because of teen isolation and boredom. In Bergenfield, adults articulated the fact that many local kids did hang out on street corners and in parks looking for drugs because things at home weren't too good.

Youngsters have always been cautioned by adults that the devil would make good use of their idle hands. But now they understood something else: boredom led to drugs, and boredom could kill. Yet it was taken for granted that if you refused to be colonized, if you ventured beyond the boundaries circumscribed by adults, you were "looking for trouble." But in reality, it was adult organization of young people's social reality over the last few hundred years that had *created* this miserable situation: one's youth as wasted years. Being wasted and getting wasted. Adults often wasted kids' time with meaningless activities, warehousing them in school; kids in turn wasted their own time on drugs. Just to have something to do.

So by now whenever kids hang out, congregating in some unstructured setting, adults read *dangerousness.* Even if young people are talking about serious things, working out plans for the future, discussing life, jobs, adults just assume they are getting wasted. They are. . . .

For the duration of my stay, in almost every encounter, the outcast members of Bergenfield's youth population would tell me these things: The cops are dicks, the school blows, the jocks suck, Billy Milano (lead singer of now defunct S.O.D.—Stormtroopers of Death) was from a nearby town, and Iron Maiden had dedicated "Wasted Years" to the Burress sisters the last time the band played Jersey. These were their cultural badges of honor, unknown to the adults.

Like many suburban towns, Bergenfield is occupationally mixed. Blue-collar aristocrats may make more money than college professors, and so one's local class identity is unclear. Schools claim to track kids in terms of "ability," and cliques are determined by subculture, style, participation, and refusal.

Because the myth of a democratized mass makes class lines in the suburbs of the United States so ambiguous to begin with, differences in status become the critical lines of demarcation. And in the mostly white, mainly

Christian town of Bergenfield, where there are neither very rich nor very poor people, this sports thing became an important criterion for determining "who's who" among the young people.

The girls played this out, too, as they always have, deriving their status by involvement in school (as cheerleaders, in clubs, in the classroom). And just as important, by the boys they hung around with. They were defined by who they were, by what they wore, by where they were seen, and with whom.

Like any other "Other," the kids at the bottom, who everybody here simply called burnouts, were actually a conglomerate of several cliques— serious druggies, Deadheads, dirtbags, skinheads, metalheads, thrashers, and punks. Some were good students, from "good" families with money and prestige. In any other setting all of these people might have been bitter rivals, or at least very separate cliques. But here, thanks to the adults and the primacy of sports, they were all lumped together—united by virtue of a common enemy, the jocks. . . .

For a bored, ignored, lonely kid, drug oblivion may offer immediate comfort; purpose and adventure in the place of everyday ennui. But soon it has a life of its own—at a psychic and a social level, the focus of your life becomes *getting high* (or *well* as some people describe it). Ironically, the whole miserable process often begins as a positive act of self-preservation.

Both the dirts and the burnt may understand how they are being fucked over and by whom. And while partying rituals may actually celebrate the refusal to play the game, neither group has a clue where to take it beyond the parking lot of 7-Eleven.

So they end up stranded in teenage wasteland. They devote their lives to their bands, to their friends, to partying; they live in the moment. They're going down in flames, taking literally the notion that "rust never sleeps," that it is "better to burn out than fade away." While left-leaning adults have valorized the politically minded punks and right-wing groups have engaged some fascistic skins, nobody really thinks too much about organizing dirts or burnouts. Law enforcement officials, special education teachers, and drug treatment facilities are the adults who are concerned with these kids.

Such wasted suburban kids are typically not politically "correct," nor do they constitute an identifiable segment of the industrial working class. They are not members of a specific racial or ethnic minority, and they have few political advocates. Only on the political issues of abortion and the death penalty for minors will wasted teenage girls and boys be likely to find adults in their corner.

Small in numbers, isolated in decaying suburbs, they aren't visible on any national scale until they are involved in something that really horrifies us, like a suicide pact, or parricide, or incest, or "satanic" sacrifice. For the most part, burnouts and dirtbags are anomic small-town white boys and girls, just trying to get through the day. Their way of fighting back is to have enough fun to kill themselves before everything else does. . . .

In the scheme of things, average American kids who don't have rich or well-connected parents have had these choices: Play the game and try to get ahead. Do what your parents did—work yourself to death at a menial job and find solace in beer, God, or family. Or take risks, cut deals, or break the law. The Reagan years made it hard for kids to "put their noses to the grindstone" as their parents had. Like everyone, these people hoped for better lives. But they lived in an age of inflated expectations and diminishing returns. Big and fast money was everywhere, and ever out of reach. America now had an economy that worked sort of like a cocaine high—propped up by hot air and big debt. The substance was absent. People's lives were like that too, and at times they were crashing hard.

In the meantime, wherever you were, you could still dream of becoming spectacular. A special talent could be your ticket out. Long Island kids had role models in bands like the Crumbsuckers, Ludichrist, Twisted Sister, Steve Vai, and Pat Benatar. North Jersey was full of sports celebrities and rock millionaires—you grew up hoping you'd end up like Mike Tyson or Jon Bon Jovi. Or like Keith Richards, whose father worked in a factory; or Ozzy, who also came from a grim English factory town, a hero who escaped the drudge because he was spectacular. This was the hip version of the American dream.

Kids who go for the prize now understand there are only two choices— rise to the top or crash to the bottom. Many openly admit that they would rather end it all now than end up losers. The nine-to-five world, corporate grunt life, working at the same job for 30 years, that's not for them. They'd prefer to hold out until the last possibility and then just piss on it all. The big easy or the bottomless pit, but never the everyday drone. And as long as there are local heroes and stories, you can still believe you have a chance to emerge from the mass as something larger than life. You can still play the great lottery and dream.

Schools urge kids to make these choices as early as possible, in a variety of ways. In the terse words of the San Francisco hardcore band MDC: *There's no such thing as cheating in a loser's game.* Many kids who start out as nobody from nowhere with nothing will end up that way. Nevertheless, everyone pretends that everything is possible if you give it your best shot. We actually believe it. While educators hope to be as efficient as possible in figuring out where unspectacular students can plug into the workforce, kids try to play at being one in a million, some way of shining, even if it's just for a while. . . .

Girls get slightly different choices. They may hope to become spectacular by virtue of their talents and their beauty. Being the girlfriend of a guy in a band means you might get to live in his mansion someday if you stick it out with him during the lean years. You might just end up like Bon Jovi's high school sweetheart, or married to someone like Cinderella's lead singer—he married his hometown girlfriend and helped set her up in her own business. These are suburban fairy tales.

Around here, some girls who are beautiful and talented hope to become stars, too, like Long Island's local products Debbie Gibson and Taylor Dayne. Some hope to be like actress Heather Locklear and marry someone really hot like Motley Crüe's drummer, Tommy Lee. If you could just get to the right place at the right time.

But most people from New Jersey and Long Island or anywhere else in America don't end up rich and famous. They have some fun trying, though, and for a while life isn't bad at all.

Yet, if you are unspectacular—not too book-smart, of average looks and moderate creative ability—there have always been places for you. Much of your teachers' efforts will be devoted to your more promising peers, and so will your nation's resources. But your parents will explain to you that this is the way it is, and early on, you will know to expect very little from school.

There are still a few enclaves, reservations. The shop and crafting culture of your parents' class of origin is one pocket of refuge. In the vocational high school, your interests are rewarded, once you have allowed yourself to be dumped there. And if the skills you gather there don't really lead to anything much, there's always the military.

Even though half the kids in America today will never go to college, the country still acts as if they will. At least, most schools seem to be set up to prepare you for college. And if it's not what you can or want to do, their attitude is tough shit, it's your problem.

And your most devoted teachers at vocational high school will never tell you that the training you will get from them is barely enough to get your foot in the door. You picture yourself getting into something with a future only to find that your skills are obsolete, superficial, and the boss prefers people with more training, more experience, more promise. So you are stuck in dead-end "youth employment jobs," and now what?

According to the William T. Grant Commission on Work, Family and Citizenship, 20 million people between the ages of 16 and 24 are not likely to go to college. The "forgotten half," as youth advocates call them, will find jobs in service and retail. But the money is bad, only half that of typical manufacturing jobs. The good, stable jobs that don't require advanced training have been disappearing rapidly. From 1979 to 1985 the U.S.A. suffered a net loss of 1.7 million manufacturing jobs. What's left?

In my neighborhood, the shipping and warehousing jobs that guys like the Grinders took, hedging their bets against rock stardom, are now seen as "good jobs" by the younger guys at Metal 24. I am regularly asked to . . . "find out if they're hiring" down at [the] shipping company. Dead-end kids around here who aren't working with family are working "shit jobs."

The skills used in a typical "shit job" . . . involve slapping rancid butter on stale hard rolls, mopping the floor, selling Lotto tickets, making sure shelves and refrigerators are clean, sorting and stacking magazines, taking delivery on newspapers, and signing out videos. They are also advised to look out for shoplifters, to protect the register, and to be sure that the surveillance camera is running. Like most kids in shit jobs, they are most skilled at getting over on the boss and in developing strategies to ward off boredom. It is not unusual to see kids at the supermarket cash register or the mall clothing shop standing around with a glazed look in their eyes. And you will often hear them complain of boredom, tiredness, or whine: *I can't wait to get out of here.* Usually, in shit jobs this is where it begins and ends. There aren't many alternatives.

Everywhere, such kids find getting into a union or having access to supervisory or managerial tracks hard to come by. Some forms of disinvestment are more obvious than others. In a company town, you will be somewhat clear about what is going on. At the end of the 1980s, the defense industry of Long Island seemed threatened; people feared that their lives would soon be devastated.

But the effect of a changing economic order on most kids only translates into scrambling for a new safety zone. It is mostly expressed as resentment against entrepreneurial foreigners (nonwhites) and as anomie—a vague sense of loss, then confusion about where they might fit in. . . .

So where are we going? Some people fear we are polarizing into a two-class nation, rich and poor. More precisely, a privileged knowledge-producing class and a low-paid, low-status service class. It is in the public high school that this division of labor for an emergent postindustrial local economy is first articulated. At the top are the kids who will hold jobs in a highly competitive technological economic order, who will advance and be respected if they cooperate and excel.

At the bottom are kids with poor basic skills, short attention spans, limited emotional investment in the future. Also poor housing, poor nutrition, bad schooling, bad lives. And in their bad jobs they will face careers of unsatisfying part-time work, low pay, no benefits, and no opportunity for advancement.

There are the few possibilities offered by a relative—a coveted place in a union, a chance to join a small family business in a service trade, a spot in a small shop. In my neighborhood, kids dream of making a good score on the cop tests, working up from hostess to waitress. Most hang out in limbo hoping to get called for a job in the sheriff's department, or the parks, or sanitation. They're on all the lists, although they know the odds for getting called are slim. The lists are frozen, the screening process is endless.

Meantime they hold jobs for a few months here and there, or they work off the books, or at two bad jobs at once. . . .

When he gave the eulogy at his godson's funeral, Tommy Olton's uncle Richard was quoted as saying: *When I held you in my arms at your baptism, I wanted it to be a fresh start, for you to be more complete than we had ever been ourselves, but I wonder if we expected too much. In thinking only of ourselves, maybe we passed down too great a burden.*

Trans-historically, cross-culturally, humans have placed enormous burdens on their young. Sometimes these burdens have been primarily economic: The child contributes to the economy of the family or tribe. Sometimes the burden has been social—the child is a contribution to the immortality of our creed. Be fruitful and multiply.

But the spiritual burden we pass on to the child may be the most difficult to bear. We do expect them to fulfill an incompleteness in ourselves, in our world. Our children are our vehicle for the realization of unfulfilled human dreams: our class aspirations, our visions of social justice and world peace, of a better life on earth.

Faith in the child, in the next generation, helps get us through this life. Without this hope in the future *through the child* we could not endure slavery, torture, war, genocide, or even the ordinary, everyday grind of a "bad life." The child-as-myth is an empty slate upon which we carve our highest ideals. For human beings, the child is God, utopia, and the future incarnate. The Bergenfield suicide pact ruptured the sacred trust between the generations. It was a negation.

After I had been to Bergenfield, people asked me: *Why did they do it?* People want to know in 25 words or less. But it's more complicated than that. I usually just say: *They had bad lives,* and try to explain why these lives ended where, when, and how they did. But I still wonder, at what point are people pushed over the line?

On the surface the ending of the four kids' bad lives can be explained away by the "case history" approach. Three of the four had suicidal or self-destructive adult role models: the suicide of Tommy Olton's father, the drug-related death of the Burress sisters' father. Tommy Rizzo, along with his three friends, had experienced the recent loss of a beloved friend, Joe Major. Before Joe, the death of three other local "burnouts." Then there was the chronic drug and alcohol abuse, an acknowledged contributing factor in suicide. Families ruptured by divorce, death, estrangement. Failure at school.

But these explanations alone would not add up to a suicide pact among four kids. If they did, the teenage suicide rate would be much, much higher. The personal problems experienced by the four kids were severe, painful, but by the 1980s, they were no longer remarkable.

For a while I wondered if the excessive labeling process in Bergenfield was killing off the "burnouts." Essentially, their role, their collective identity in their town was that of the "nigger" or "Jew." Us and Them, the One and the Other. And once they were constituted as "burnouts" by the town's hegemonic order, the kids played out their assigned role as self-styled outcasts with irony, style, and verve.

Yes, Bergenfield was guilty of blaming the victim. But only slightly more guilty than any other town. Labeling, blaming the victim, and conferring rewards on more cooperative kids was cruel, but also not remarkable in the eighties.

As I felt from the beginning, the unusually cloying geography of Bergenfield seemed somehow implicated in the suicide pact. The landscape appeared even more circumscribed because of the "burnouts'" lack of legitimate space in the town: they were too old for the [roller skating] Rink, and the Building [an abandoned warehouse taken over by the teens] was available for criminal trespass only. Outcast, socially and spatially, for years the "burnouts" had been chased from corner to parking lot, and finally, to the garage bays of Foster Village. They were nomads, refugees in the town of their birth. *There was no place for them.* They felt unloved, unwanted, devalued, disregarded, and discarded.

But this little town, not even two miles long from north to south, was just a dot on a much larger map. It wasn't the whole world. Hip adults I know, friends who grew up feeling like outcasts in their hometown, were very sympathetic to the plight of the "burnouts." Yet even they often held out one last question, sometimes contemptuously: *Why didn't they just leave?* As if the four kids had failed even as outcasts. My friends found this confusing: *No matter how worthless the people who make the rules say you are, you don't have to play their game. You can always walk and not look back,* they would argue. People who feel abject and weird in their hometown simply move away.

But that has always been a class privilege. The townies are the poor kids, the wounded street warriors who stay behind. And besides, escape was easier for everyone 20 years ago. American society had safety nets then that don't exist now—it's just not the same anymore.

During the eighties, dead-end kids—kids with personal problems and unspectacular talents living in punitive or indifferent towns with a sense of futility about life—became more common. There were lots of kids with bad lives. They didn't all commit suicide. But I believe that in another decade, Tommy Rizzo, Cheryl Burress, Tommy Olton, and Lisa Burress would not have "done it." They might have had more choices, or choices that really meant something to them. Teenage suicide won't go away until kids' bad lives do. Until there are other ways of moving out of bad lives, suicide will remain attractive.

ENDNOTE

[1] As I promised the kids I met hanging out on the streets of Bergen County and on Long Island, "No names, no pictures." Names such as "Joe," "Eddie," and "Doreen" are fictitious, changed to protect their privacy.

3

AN INTERSECTION OF BIOGRAPHY AND HISTORY
My Intellectual Journey

MARY ROMERO

This selection by Mary Romero is another example of C. Wright Mills' sociological imagination. Romero is a professor in the School of Justice and Social Inquiry at Arizona State University, where she teaches sociology and Chicano studies. In this excerpt, Romero explains how biography and history influenced her investigation of domestic service work done by

Chicanas. In particular, she describes her research process, which involved reinterpreting her own and others' domestic service experiences within the larger work history of Mexican Americans and the devaluation of housework. Thus, this selection is from the introduction to Romero's 1992 book, *Maid in the U.S.A.*, a study of domestic work and the social interactions between domestics and their employers.

When I was growing up many of the women whom I knew worked cleaning other people's houses. Domestic service was part of my taken-for-granted reality. Later, when I had my own place, I considered housework something you did before company came over. My first thought that domestic service and housework might be a serious research interest came as a result of a chance encounter with live-in domestics along the U.S.–Mexican border. Before beginning a teaching position at the University of Texas at El Paso, I stayed with a colleague while apartment hunting. My colleague had a live-in domestic to assist with housecleaning and cooking. Asking around, I learned that live-in maids were common in El Paso, even among apartment and condominium dwellers. The hiring of maids from Mexico was so common that locals referred to Monday as the border patrol's day off because the agents ignored the women crossing the border to return to their employers' homes after their weekend off. The practice of hiring undocumented Mexican women as domestics, many of whom were no older than 15, seemed strange to me. It was this strangeness that raised the topic of domestic service as a question and made problematic what had previously been taken for granted.

I must admit that I was shocked at my colleague's treatment of the 16-year-old domestic whom I will call Juanita. Only recently hired, Juanita was still adjusting to her new environment. She was extremely shy, and her timidity was made even worse by constant flirting from her employer. As far as I could see, every attempt Juanita made to converse was met with teasing so that the conversation could never evolve into a serious discussion. Her employer's sexist, paternalistic banter effectively silenced the domestic, kept her constantly on guard, and made it impossible for her to feel comfortable at work. For instance, when she informed the employer of a leaky faucet, he shot her a look of disdain, making it clear that she was overstepping her boundaries. I observed other encounters that clearly served to remind Juanita of her subservient place in her employer's home.

Although Juanita was of the same age as my colleague's oldest daughter and but a few years older than his two sons, she was treated differently from the other teenagers in the house. She was expected to share her bedroom with the ironing board, sewing machine, and other spare-room types of objects.[1] More importantly, she was assumed to have different wants and needs. I witnessed the following revealing exchange. Juanita was poor. She had not brought toiletries with her from Mexico. Since she had not yet been paid, she had to depend on her employer for necessities. Yet instead of offering her a small advance in her pay so she could purchase the items herself and giving her a ride to the nearby supermarket to select her own toiletries, the employer handled Juanita's request for toothbrush, toothpaste, shampoo, soap, and the like in the following manner. In the presence of all the family and the houseguest, he made a list of the things she needed. Much teasing and joking accompanied the encounter. The employer shopped for her and purchased only generic brand items, which were a far cry from the brand-name products that filled the bathroom of his 16-year-old daughter. Juanita looked at the toothpaste, shampoo, and soap with confusion; she may never have seen generic products before, but she obviously knew that a distinction had been made.

One evening I walked into the kitchen as the employer's young sons were shouting orders at Juanita. They pointed to the dirty dishes on the table and pans in the sink and yelled: *WASH! CLEAN!* Juanita stood frozen next to the kitchen door, angry and humiliated. Aware of possible repercussions for Juanita if I reprimanded my colleague's sons, I responded awkwardly by reallocating chores to everyone present. I announced that I would wash the dishes and the boys would clear the table. Juanita washed and dried dishes alongside me, and together we finished cleaning the kitchen. My colleague returned from his meeting to find us in the kitchen washing the last pan. The look on his face was more than enough to tell me that he was shocked to find his houseguest—and future colleague—washing dishes with the maid. His embarrassment at my behavior confirmed my suspicion that I had violated the normative expectations of class behavior within the home. He attempted to break the tension with a flirtatious and sexist remark to Juanita which served to excuse her from the kitchen and from any further discussion.

The conversation that followed revealed how my colleague chose to interpret my behavior. Immediately after Juanita's departure from the kitchen, he initiated a discussion about "Chicano radicals" and the Chicano movement. Although he was a foreign-born Latino, he expressed sympathy for *la causa*. Recalling the one Chicano graduate student he had known to obtain a Ph.D. in sociology, he gave several accounts of how the student's political behavior had disrupted the normal flow of university activity. Lowering his voice to a confidential whisper, he confessed to understanding why Marxist theory has become so popular among Chicano students. The tone of his comments and the examples that he chose made me realize that my "outrageous" behavior was explained, and thus excused, on the basis of my being one of those "Chicano radicals." He interpreted my washing dishes with his maid as a symbolic act; that is, I was affiliated with *los de abajo*.

My behavior had been comfortably defined without addressing the specific issue of maids. My colleague then further subsumed the topic under the rubric of "the servant problem" along the border. (His reaction was not unlike the attitude employers have displayed toward domestic service in the United States for the last hundred years.)[2] He began by providing me with chapter and verse about how he had aided Mexican women from Juarez by helping them cross the border and employing them in his home. He took further credit for introducing them to the appliances found in an

American middle-class home. He shared several funny accounts about teaching country women from Mexico to use the vacuum cleaner, electric mixer, and microwave (remember the maid scene in the movie *El Norte*?) and implicitly blamed them for their inability to work comfortably around modern conveniences. For this "on-the-job training" and introduction to American culture, he complained, his generosity and goodwill had been rewarded by a high turnover rate. As his account continued, he assured me that most maids were simply working until they found a husband. In his experience they worked for a few months or less and then did not return to work on Monday morning after their first weekend off. Of course it never dawned on him that they may simply have found a job with better working conditions.

The following day, Juanita and I were alone in the house. As I mustered up my best Spanish, we shared information about our homes and families. After a few minutes of laughter about my simple sentence structure, Juanita lowered her head and in a sad, quiet voice told me how isolated and lonely she felt in this middle-class suburb literally within sight of Juarez. Her feelings were not the consequence of the work or of frustrations with modern appliances, nor did she complain about the absence of Mexican people in the neighborhood; her isolation and loneliness were in response to the norms and values surrounding domestic service. She described the situation quite clearly in expressing puzzlement over the social interactions she had with her employer's family: Why didn't her employer's children talk to her or include her in any of their activities when she wasn't working? Her reaction was not unlike that of Lillian Pettengill, who wrote about her two-year experience as a domestic in Philadelphia households at the turn of the century: "I feel my isolation alone in a big house full of people."[3]

Earlier in the day, Juanita had unsuccessfully tried to initiate a conversation with the 16-year-old daughter while she cleaned her room. She was of the same age as the daughter (who at that moment was in bed reading and watching TV because of menstrual cramps—a luxury the maid was not able to claim). She was rebuffed and ignored and felt that she became visible only when an order was given. Unable to live with this social isolation, she had already made up her mind not to return after her day off in Juarez. I observed the total impossibility of communication. The employer would never know why she left, and Juanita would not know that she would be considered simply another ungrateful Mexican whom he had tried to help.

After I returned to Denver, I thought a lot about the situations of Juanita and the other young undocumented Mexican women living in country club areas along the border. They worked long days in the intimacy of American middle-class homes but were starved for respect and positive social interaction. Curiously, the employers did not treat the domestics as "one of the family," nor did they consider themselves employers. Hiring a domestic was likely to be presented within the context of charity and good works; it was considered a matter of helping "these Mexican women" rather than recognized as a work issue.

undocumented workers are norm
ignoring unless needed.

I was bothered by my encounter along the border, not simply for the obvious humanitarian reasons, but because I too had once worked as a domestic, just as my mother, sister, relatives, and neighbors had. As a teenager, I cleaned houses with my mother on weekends and vacations. My own working experience as a domestic was limited because I had always been accompanied by my mother or sister instead of working alone. Since I was a day worker, my time in the employer's home was limited and I was able to return to my family and community each day. In Juanita's situation as a live-in domestic, there was no distinction between the time on and off work. I wondered whether domestic service had similarly affected my mother, sister, and neighbors. Had they too worked beyond the agreed-upon time? Did they have difficulty managing relationships with employers? I never worked alone and was spared the direct negotiations with employers. Instead, I cooperated with my mother or sister in completing the housecleaning as efficiently and quickly as possible.

I could not recall being yelled at by employers or their children, but I did remember anger, resentment, and the humiliation I had felt at kneeling to scrub other people's toilets while they gave step-by-step cleaning instructions. I remember feeling uncomfortable around employers' children who never acknowledged my presence except to question where I had placed their belongings after I had picked them up off the floor to vacuum. After all, my experience was foreign to them; at the age of 14 I worked as a domestic while they ran off to swimming, tennis, and piano lessons. Unlike Juanita, I preferred to remain invisible as I moved around the employer's house cleaning. Much later, I learned that the invisibility of workers in domestic service is a common characteristic of the occupation. Ruth Schwartz Cowan has commented on the historical aspect of invisibility:

> The history of domestic service in the United States is a vast, unresolved puzzle, because the social role "servant" so frequently carries with it the unspoken adjective *invisible*. In diaries and letters, the "invisible" servant becomes visible only when she departs employment ("Mary left today"). In statistical series, she appears only when she is employed full-time, on a live-in basis; or when she is willing to confess the nature of her employment to a census taker, and (especially since the Second World War) there have frequently been good reasons for such confessions to go unmade.[4]

Although I remained invisible to most of the employers' family members, the mothers, curiously enough, seldom let me move around the house invisibly, dusting the woodwork and vacuuming carpets. Instead, I was subjected to constant supervision and condescending observations about "what a good little girl I was, helping my mother clean house." After I had moved and cleaned behind a hide-a-bed and Lazy-boy chair, vacuumed three floors including two sets of stairs, and carried the vacuum cleaner up and downstairs twice because "little Johnny" was napping when I was cleaning the bedrooms—I certainly didn't feel like a "little girl helping mother." I felt like a domestic worker!

There were employers who attempted to draw parallels between my adolescent experience and their teenagers' behavior: they'd point to the messy bedrooms and claim: *Well, you're a teenager, you understand clothes, books, papers, and records on the floor.* Even at 14, I knew that being sloppy and not picking up after yourself was a privilege. I had two brothers and three sisters. I didn't have my own bedroom but shared a room with my sisters. Not one of us would think of leaving our panties on the floor for the others to pick up. I didn't bother to set such employers straight but continued to clean in silence, knowing that at the end of the day I would get cash and confident that I would soon be old enough to work elsewhere.

Many years later, while attending graduate school, I returned to domestic service as an "off-the-record" means to supplement my income. Graduate fellowships and teaching assistantships locked me into a fixed income that frequently was not enough to cover my expenses.[5] So once again I worked alongside my mother for seven hours as we cleaned two houses. I earned about 50 dollars for the day. Housecleaning is strenuous work, and I returned home exhausted from climbing up and down stairs, bending over, rubbing, and scrubbing.

Returning to domestic service as a graduate student was awkward. I tried to reduce the status inconsistency in my life by electing to work only in houses from which families were absent during the day. If someone appeared while I worked, I ignored their presence as they did mine. Since working arrangements had been previously negotiated by my mother, I had limited face-to-face interactions with employers. Most of the employers knew I was a graduate student, and fortunately, most seemed reluctant to ask me too many questions. Our mutual silence served as a way to deal with the status inconsistency of a housewife with a B.A. hiring an ABD to clean her house.

I came to El Paso with all of these experiences unquestioned in my memory. My presuppositions about domestic service were called into question only after observing the more obviously exploitative situation in the border town. I saw how vulnerable undocumented women employed as live-in domestics are and what little recourse they have to improve their situation, short of finding another job. Experiencing Juanita's shame and disgust at my colleague's sons' behavior brought back a flood of memories that eventually influenced me to study the paid housework that I had once taken for granted. I began to wonder professionally about the Chicanas employed as domestics that I had known throughout my own life: how vulnerable were they to exploitation, racism, and sexism? Did their day work status and U.S. citizenship provide protection against degradation and humiliation? How did Chicanas go about establishing a labor arrangement within a society that marked them as racial and cultural inferiors? How did they deal with racial slurs and sexist remarks within their employers' homes? How did Chicanas attempt to negotiate social interactions and informal labor arrangements with employers and their families?

An Exploratory Study

The Research Process

Intending to compare my findings with the research on U.S. minority women employed as domestics, I chose to limit my study to Chicanas, that is, women of Mexican descent born and raised in the United States. Although many women born in Mexico and living in the United States consider themselves Chicanas, my sample did not include women born outside the United States. My major concern in making this distinction was to avoid bringing into the analysis immigration issues that increase the vulnerability of the women employed as domestics. I wanted to keep conditions as constant as possible to make comparisons with the experiences Judith Rollins, Bonnie Thornton Dill, and Soraya Moore Coley report among African American women and with Evelyn Nakano Glenn's study of Japanese American women.[6] In order to duplicate similar residential and citizenship characteristics of these studies, I restricted my sample to Chicanas living in Denver whose families had migrated from rural areas of New Mexico and Colorado. All of the women interviewed were U.S. citizens and lived in Denver most of their adult lives.

I began the project by soliciting the cooperation of current and former domestics from my own family. I relied on domestics to provide entree into informal networks. These networks turned out to be particularly crucial in gaining access to an occupation that is so much a part of the underground economy. My mother, sister, and sister-in-law agreed to be interviewed and to provide names of relatives, friends, and neighbors. I also identified Chicana domestics in the community with the assistance of outreach workers employed by local churches and social service agencies. The snowball sampling was achieved by asking each interviewee to recommend other Chicana domestics as potential interviewees.

The women were extremely cautious about offering the names of friends and relatives. In most cases, they contacted the person first and only then gave me the name and telephone number. This actually turned out to be quite helpful. Potential interviewees had already heard about my study from someone who had been interviewed. They had a general idea of the questions I was going to ask and in some cases a little background information about who I was. However, on three occasions, I called women to ask for an interview and was confronted with resistance and shame. The women expressed embarrassment at being identified by their work—as a "housekeeper" or "cleaning lady." I responded by sharing my research interests in the occupation and in the relationship between work and family. I also shared my previous experience as a domestic.[7] One woman argued with me for 20 minutes about conducting research on an occupation that was low status, suggesting instead that I study Chicana lawyers or doctors, that is, "another occupation that presents our people in a more positive light." Another woman denied ever having worked as a domestic even though several women, including her sister-in-law, had given me her name as someone currently employed as a domestic.

domestic- seemed by some as low and embarassing.

The stigma of domestic service was a problem during the interviews as well. From the outset, it was very important for each woman to establish herself as someone more than a private household worker. Conducting non-structured, free-flowing, and open-ended interviews allowed the women to establish multiple identities, particularly diffuse family and community roles.

The interviews were conducted in the women's homes, usually while sitting in the living room or at the dining room table with the radio or television on in the background. Although family members peeked in, for the most part there were few interruptions other than an occasional telephone call. From time to time, the women called to their husbands in the other room to ask the name of a street where they had once lived or the year the oldest son had been born in order to figure out when they had left and returned to work. The average interview lasted two hours, but I often stayed to visit and chat long after the interview was over. They told me about their church activities and plans to remodel the house and asked me for my opinion on current Chicano politics. Some spread out blankets, tablecloths, and pillow covers to exhibit their needlework. They showed me pictures of their children and grandchildren, giving me a walking tour of living rooms and bedrooms where wedding and high school portraits hung. As each one was identified, I learned more about their lives.

I conducted 25 open-ended interviews with Chicanas living and working in the greater Denver metropolitan area. The most visible Chicano communities in Denver are in the low-income neighborhood located in the downtown area or in one of two working-class neighborhoods in the northern and western areas of the city. I interviewed women from each of these communities. I asked them to discuss their overall work histories, with particular emphasis on their experiences as domestics. I probed for detailed information on domestic work, including strategies for finding employers, definitions of appropriate and inappropriate tasks, the negotiation of working conditions, ways of doing housework efficiently, and the pros and cons of domestic service. The accounts included descriptions of the domestics' relationships with white middle-class mistresses and revealed Chicanas' attitudes toward their employers' lifestyles.

All of the interviewees' families of orientation were from northern New Mexico or southern Colorado, where many of them had lived and worked on small farms. Some of the women had arrived in Denver as children with their parents, others as young brides, and still others as single women to join siblings and cousins in Denver's barrios. Several women recalled annual migrations to northern Colorado to pick sugar beets, prior to their permanent relocation to Denver. In some cases, the women's entire families of orientation had migrated to Denver; in others, parents and siblings had either remained behind or migrated to other cities. Many older women had migrated with their husbands after World War II, and several younger women interviewed had arrived at the same time, as children. Women who had migrated as single adults typically had done so in the last 10 or 15 years. Now they were married and permanently living in Denver. . . .

Historical Background

After the Mexican-American War, Mexicans were given the option to maintain their Mexican citizenship and leave the country or become U.S. citizens.
Many reluctantly chose the latter in order to keep their homes. Although the
Treaty of Guadalupe Hidalgo was supposed to guarantee land grant provisions to those who chose to remain in occupied territory, legal and illegal
maneuvers were used to eliminate communal usage of land and natural resources. Between 1854 and 1930, an estimated 2,000,000 acres of private land
and 1,700,000 acres of communal land were lost.[8] In the arid Southwest,
small plots were insufficient to continue a subsistence-based farming economy, thus the members of the Hispano community were transformed
from landowners to wage laborers. Enclosure of the common lands forced
Mexicans from their former economic roles, "freed" Mexicans for wage labor,
and established a racially stratified labor force in the Southwest.

As early as 1900, the Hispano farming and ranching communities of
northern New Mexico and southern Colorado began to lose their population. A combination of push-pull factors conspired to force rural Hispanos
off the land and attracted them to urban areas like Denver. Rural northern
New Mexico and southern Colorado experienced drastic depopulation as
adults left to find jobs. During the Depression, studies conducted in cooperation with the Works Progress Administration (WPA) noted the desperate
situation:

> The Tewa Basin Study by the U.S. Department of Agriculture showed
> that in 11 Spanish-American villages containing 1,202 families, an aver-
> age of 1,110 men went out of the villages to work for some part of each
> year prior to 1930. In 1934, only 157 men out of 1,202 families had found
> outside work.[9]

Migration in search of jobs became a way of life for many families. New
Mexicans and southern Coloradans joined the migratory farm labor stream
from Texas, California, and Mexico. World War II further depopulated the
rural villages as people flocked to the cities in response to job openings in defense plants and related industries. Postwar migration from New Mexico
was estimated to be one-fifth of the 1940 rural Chicano population.[10] This
pattern continued in the following decades. For instance, Thomas Malone
found that during the decade of the 1950s, only one of seven northern counties in New Mexico had not experienced a decrease in its former predominantly Spanish-speaking population.[11] By 1960, 61 percent of the population
had been urbanized,[12] and between 1950 and 1960, an additional 24 percent
left their rural communities.[13]

Perhaps because research on population movement among Chicanos has
been so overwhelmingly concerned with emigration from Mexico, this type
of internal population movement among Chicanos has not been well studied. What research is available has focused primarily on male workers and
the relationship between urbanization and acculturation.[14] Chicanas have
been either ignored or treated simply as family members—mothers, daughters, or wives, accompanying male relatives in search of work—rather than

as wage earners in their own right. Nevertheless, for many women migration to an urban area made it necessary that they enter the labor market. Domestic service became a significant occupation in the experience.

Profile of Chicana Household Workers

Only the vaguest statistical data on Chicana private household workers are available; for the most part these workers remain a doubly hidden population. The reasons are themselves instructive. Domestic workers tend to be invisible because paid domestic work has not been one of the occupations recorded in social science surveys, and the U.S. Census Bureau uses a single code lumping together all private household workers, including launderers, cooks, housekeepers, child-care workers, cleaners, and servants. Even when statistics on domestics can be teased out of the census and labor data bases, they are marred by the common practice of underreporting work in the informal sector. Unlike some of the private household workers in the East, Chicana domestics are not unionized and remain outside the "counted" labor force. Many private household workers are not included in the statistics collected by the Department of Labor. The "job" involves an informal labor arrangement made between two people, and in many cases payment is simply a cash transaction that is never recorded with the Internal Revenue Service (IRS).

Governmental undercounting of Chicanos and Mexican immigrants in the United States further adds to the problem of determining the number of Chicanas and Mexicanas employed as private household workers. For many, domestic service is part of the underground economy, and employing undocumented workers is reported neither to the IRS nor to the Immigration and Naturalization Service (INS), thus making another source of statistical information unreliable. Chicanos continue to be an undercounted and obscure population. Problems with the categorization of domestics have been still further complicated by changing identifiers for the Mexican American population: Mexican, Spanish-speaking, Hispanic, Spanish-surnamed, and the like make it impossible to segment out the Chicano population.

The 25 Chicanas whom I interviewed included welfare recipients as well as working-class women, ranging in age from 29 to 68. Thirteen of the 25 women were between 29 and 45 years old. The remaining 12 were over 52 years old. All the women had children, and the older women also had grandchildren. The smallest family consisted of one child, and the largest family had seven children. The average was three children. All but one of the women had been married. Five of the women were single heads of households, two of them were divorced, and the other three were single, separated, or widowed. The married women were currently living with husbands employed in blue-collar positions, such as construction and factory work. At the time of the interview, the women who were single heads of households were financially supporting no more than two children.

Educational backgrounds ranged from no schooling to completion of high school. Six women had completed high school, and seven had no high school experience, including one who had never attended school at all. The remaining 12 had at least a sixth-grade education. Although the least educated were the older women, eight of the women under 42 had not completed high school. The youngest woman with less than an eighth-grade education was 53 years old. The 12 women over 50 averaged eight years of schooling. Three of the high school graduates were in their early thirties, two were in their early forties, and one was 57 years old. Although one woman preferred to be interviewed in Spanish, all the women spoke English.

Work experience as a private household worker ranged from five months to 30 years. Women 50 years and older had worked in the occupation from eight to 30 years, while four of the women between the ages of 33 and 39 had worked as domestics for 12 years. Half of the women had worked for more than 10 years as private household workers. Only three women had worked as domestics prior to marriage; each of these women had worked in live-in situations in rural areas in Colorado. Several years later, after marriage and children, they returned as day workers. All the other women, however, had turned to nonresidential day work in response to a financial crisis; in the majority of cases, it was their first job after marriage and having children. Some of the women remained domestics throughout their lives, but others moved in and out of domestic work. Women who returned to domestic service after having other types of jobs usually did so following a period of unemployment.

The work histories revealed that domestic service was only one of several low-paying, low-status jobs the women had held during their lives. They had been hired as waitresses, laundresses, janitors, farmworkers, nurse's aides, fast-food servers, cooks, dishwashers, receptionists, school aides, cashiers, baby-sitters, salesclerks, factory workers, and various types of line workers in poultry farms and car washes. Almost half of the women had worked as janitors in hospitals and office buildings or as hotel maids. About one-fourth of the women had held semiskilled and skilled positions such as beauticians, typists, and medical-record clerks. Six of the women had worked only as domestics.

Paid and Unpaid Domestic Work

In describing their daily routine activities, these Chicanas drew my attention to the interrelationship between paid and unpaid housework. As working women, Chicana private household workers face the "double day" or "second shift," but in their case both days consisted of the same types of tasks. Paid housework done for an employer was qualitatively different from housework done for their own families.

In the interviews, Chicanas described many complexities of domestic service. They explained how they used informal networks to find new employers for themselves and for relatives and friends. As they elaborated on the advantages and disadvantages of particular work arrangements and their reasons for refusing certain household tasks, I soon realized that these women not only knew a great deal about cleaning and maintaining homes, but they understood the influence of social relationships on household tasks. Analysis of the extensive planning and negotiation involved in the informal and underground arrangements of domestic service highlighted the significance of the social relationships surrounding housework.

Their work histories included detailed explanations of beginning, returning to, and continuing in domestic service. In the discussions, I began to understand the paradox of domestic service: On the one hand, cleaning houses is degrading and embarrassing; on the other, domestic service can be higher paying, more autonomous, and less dehumanizing than other low-status, low-skilled occupations. Previous jobs in the beet fields, fast-food restaurants, car washes, and turkey farms did not offer annual raises, vacations, or sick leave. Furthermore, these jobs forced employees to work long hours and to keep rigid time schedules, and they frequently occurred outside or in an unsafe work environment. Unlike the other options available, domestic service did have the potential for offering flexible work schedules and autonomy. In most cases, domestic service also paid much more. Although annual raises, vacation, and Social Security were not the norm for most Chicanas in domestic service, there remained the possibility that such benefits could be negotiated with employers. Furthermore, as former farmworkers, laundresses, and line workers, the women found freedom in domestic work from exposure to dangerous pesticides, poor ventilation, and other health risks. This paradox foreshadowed a critical theoretical issue, the importance of understanding the social process that constructs domestic service as a low-status occupation.

Stigma as a perceived occupational hazard of domestic service emerged during the initial contact and throughout most of the interviews. The stigma attached to domestic service punctuated the interviews. I knew that many women hid their paid household labor from the government, but I did not realize that this secrecy encompassed neighbors, friends, and even extended family members. Several women gave accounts that revealed their families' efforts to conceal their employment as domestics. Children frequently stated that their mothers "just did housework," which was ambiguous enough to define them as full-time homemakers and not necessarily as domestics.

Faced with limited job opportunities, Chicanas selected domestic service and actively sought to make the most of the situation. In comparison with other jobs they had held, domestic service usually paid more and offered greater flexibility in arranging the length of the workday and workweek. Although other jobs did not carry the stigma of servitude, workers were under constant supervision, and the work was similarly low status. Therefore, the women who chose domestic service over other low-paying, low-status jobs based their selection on the occupation that offered some possibility of control. Their challenge was to structure the work so as to reap the most benefits: pay, work hours, labor, and autonomy. Throughout the interviews, the women emphasized job flexibility as the major advantage of domestic service over previous jobs. Nonrigid work schedules allowed time to do their own housework and fulfill family obligations, such as caring for sick children or attending school functions. By stressing the benefits gained by doing day work, Chicanas diffused the low status in their work identities and emphasized their family and community identities. The ways in which they arranged both work and family revealed coping strategies used to deal with the stigma, and this drew me to analyze housework as a form of labor having both paid and unpaid manifestations.

The conventional social science separation of work and family is an analytical construct and is not found in the lived reality of Chicana domestics. Invariably the interviewees mixed and intertwined discussions of work and family. Moreover, the actual and practical relationships between work and family were explicit in their descriptions of daily activities: The reasons for seeking employment included the family's financial situation and the desire to raise its standard of living; earning extra money for the household was viewed as an extension of these women's roles as mothers and wives; arranging day work involved planning work hours around the children's school attendance, dentist and doctor appointments, and community and church activities; in some cases, young mothers even took their preschool-age children with them to work. The worlds of paid and unpaid housework were not disconnected in the lives of these women.

Attending to the importance of the relationship between paid and unpaid domestic work led me to ponder new questions about the dynamics of buying and selling household labor. How does housework differ when it is paid work? How does the housewife role change when part of her work is allocated to another woman? What is the range of employer–employee relationships in domestic service today? And is there a difference in the type of relationships developed by employed and unemployed women buying household labor?

The importance of attending to both paid and unpaid housework in researching domestic service became more apparent as I began presenting my research to academic audiences. When I read papers on the informal labor market or on family and community networks used to find work, some of my colleagues responded as women who employed domestics. Frequently, question-and-answer sessions turned into a defense of such practices as hiring undocumented workers, not filing income taxes, or gift giving in lieu of raises and benefits. Although I was aware that as working women, many academics employed someone to clean their houses, I was not prepared for scholars and feminists to respond to my scholarly work as housewives or employers. I was also surprised to discover that many of the maternalistic practices traditionally found in domestic service were common practices in their homes. The recurring responses made me realize that my feminist colleagues had never considered their relationships with the "cleaning woman" on the same plane as those with secretaries, waitresses, or janitors; that is, they thought of the former more or less in terms of the mistress–maid relationship. When, through my research, I pointed out the contradiction, many still had difficulty thinking of their homes—the haven from the cruel academic world—as someone's workplace. Their overwhelming feelings of discomfort, guilt, and resentment, which sometimes came out as hostility, alerted me to the fact that something more was going on. . . .

Domestic service must be studied because it raises a challenge to any feminist notion of "sisterhood." A growing number of employed middle- and upper-middle-class women escape the double-day syndrome by hiring poor women of color to do housework and child care. David Katzman underscored the class contradiction:

> Middle-class women, the employers, gained freedom from family roles and household chores and assumed or confirmed social status by the employment of a servant. . . . The greater liberty of these middle-class women, however, was achieved at the expense of working-class women, who, forced to work, assumed the tasks beneath, distasteful to, or too demanding for the family members.[15]

Housework is ascribed on the basis of gender, and it is further divided along class lines and, in most cases, by race and ethnicity. Domestic service accentuates the contradiction of race and class in feminism, with privileged women of one class using the labor of another woman to escape aspects of sexism.

ENDNOTES

[1] The conditions I observed in El Paso were not much different from those described by D. Thompson in her 1960 article, "Are Women Bad Employers of Other Women?" *Ladies' Home Journal:* "Quarters for domestic help are usually ill placed for quiet. Almost invariably they open from pantry or kitchen, so that if a member of the family goes to get a snack at night he wakes up the occupant. And the live-in maid has nowhere to receive a caller except in the kitchen or one [of] those tiny rooms." "As a general rule anything was good enough for a maid's room. It became a catchall for furniture discarded from other parts of the house. One room was a cubicle too small for a regular-sized bed." Cited in Linda Martin and Kerry Segrave, *The Servant Problem: Domestic Workers in North America* (Jefferson, NC: McFarland, 1985), p. 25.

[2] David Katzman addresses the "servant problem" in his historical study of domestic service, *Seven Days a Week: Women and Domestic Service in Industrializing America* (Chicago: University of Illinois Press, 1981). Defined by middle-class housewives, the problem includes both the shortage of servants available and the competency of women willing to enter domestic service. Employers' attitudes about domestics have been well documented in women's magazines. Katzman described the topic as "the bread and butter of women's magazines between the Civil War and World War I"; moreover, Martin and Segrave, *The Servant Problem,* illustrate the continuing presence of articles on the servant problem in women's magazines today.

[3] Lillian Pettengill's account *Toilers of the Home: The Record of a College Woman's Experience As a Domestic Servant* (New York: Doubleday, 1903) is based on two years of employment in Philadelphia households.

[4] Ruth Schwartz Cowan, *More Work for Mother: The Ironies of Household Technology from the Open Hearth to the Microwave* (New York: Basic Books, 1983), p. 228.

[5] Earning money as domestic workers to pay college expenses not covered by scholarships is not that uncommon among other women of color in the United States. Trudier Harris interviewed several African American women public school and university college teachers about their college-day experiences in domestic service. See *From Mammies to Militants: Domestics in Black American Literature* (Philadelphia: Temple University Press, 1982), pp. 5–6.

[6] Judith Rollins, *Between Women: Domestics and Their Employers* (Philadelphia: Temple University Press, 1985); Bonnie Thornton Dill, "Across the Boundaries of Race and Class: An Exploration of the Relationship between Work and Family among Black Female Domestic Servants" (Ph.D. dissertation, New York University, 1979); Judith Rollins, "'Making Your Job Good Yourself': Domestic Service and the Construction of Personal Dignity," in *Women and the Politics of Empowerment,* ed. Ann Bookman and Sandra Morgen (Philadelphia: Temple University Press, 1988), pp. 33–52; Soraya Moore Coley, "'And Still I Rise': An Exploratory Study of Contemporary Black Private Household Workers" (Ph.D. dissertation, Bryn Mawr College, 1981); Evelyn Nakano Glenn, *Issei, Nisei, War Brides: Three Generations of Japanese American Women in Domestic Service* (Philadelphia: Temple University Press, 1986).

[7] In some cases, it was important to let women know that my own background had involved paid housework and that my mother and sister were currently employed full-time as private

household workers. Sharing this information conveyed that my life had similarities to theirs and that I respected them. This sharing of information is similar to the concept of "reciprocity" (R. Wax, "Reciprocity in Field Work," in *Human Organization Research: Field Relationships and Techniques,* ed. R. N. Adams and J. J. Preiss [New York: Dorsey, 1960], pp. 90–98).

[8] Clark Knowlton, "Changing Spanish-American Villages of Northern New Mexico," *Sociology and Social Research* 53 (1969): 455–75.

[9] Nancie Gonzalez, *The Spanish-Americans of New Mexico* (Albuquerque: University of New Mexico Press, 1967), p. 123.

[10] William W. Winnie, "The Hispanic People of New Mexico" (Master's thesis, University of Florida, 1955).

[11] Thomas J. Malone, "Recent Demographic and Economic Changes in Northern New Mexico," *New Mexico Business* 17 (1964): 4–14.

[12] Donald N. Barrett and Julian Samora, *The Movement of Spanish Youth from Rural to Urban Settings* (Washington, DC: National Committee for Children and Youth, 1963).

[13] Clark Knowlton, "The Spanish Americans in New Mexico," *Sociology and Social Research* 45 (1961): 448–54.

[14] See Paul A. Walter, "The Spanish-Speaking Community in New Mexico," *Sociology and Social Research* 24 (1939): 150–57; Thomas Weaver, "Social Structure, Change and Conflict in a New Mexico Village" (Ph.D. dissertation, University of California, 1965); Florence R. Kluckhohn and Fred L. Stodtbeck, *Variations in Value Orientations* (Evanston, IL: Row, Peterson, 1961); Frank Moore, "San Jose, 1946: A Study in Urbanization" (Master's thesis, University of New Mexico, 1947); Donald N. Barrett and Julian Samora, *The Movement of Spanish Youth* (Washington, DC: National Committee for Children and Youth, 1963).

[15] David Katzman, *Seven Days a Week* (Chicago: University of Illinois Press, 1981), pp. 269–70.

THEORY

4

THEORETICAL PERSPECTIVES IN SOCIOLOGY

CHRIS HUNTER • KENT McCLELLAND

This reading, "Theoretical Perspectives in Sociology," is the first of three to introduce sociological theories. Theories are different explanations of social phenomena; they provide a lens or a perspective to help us understand our social world. Some scholars distinguish between grand theories (large theoretical frameworks like Marxism, feminism, etc.) and others focus on what is called the mid-range theory or theories that addresses one particular social finding. Sociological theory both drives research and can be generated from research, and like scholars in other disciplines, sociologists debate different theoretical approaches to their work. This reading succinctly summarizes the three main theoretical perspectives: functionalism or structural functionalism, conflict theory, and symbolic interactionism. It also

"Theoretical Perspectives in Sociology" by Chris Hunter and Kent McClelland. Unpublished manuscript, reprinted by permission of the authors.

introduces a number of contemporary theories that are often used in sociological research. The authors, Chris Hunter and Kent McClelland, both professors of sociology at Grinnell College, designed this reading as a handout
for introductory sociology students. Note that key concepts related to each
theoretical perspective are in bold.

Functionalism

Functionalism was for decades the dominant theoretical perspective in sociology and many other social sciences. This perspective is built upon twin emphases: application of the scientific method to the objective social world and
use of an analogy between the individual organism and society.

The emphasis on scientific method leads to the assertion that one can
study the social world in the same ways as one studies the physical world.
Thus, functionalists see the social world as "objectively real," as observable
with such techniques as social surveys and interviews. Furthermore, their
positivistic view of social science assumes that study of the social world can
be **value-free**, in that the investigator's values will not necessarily interfere
with the disinterested search for social laws governing the behavior of social
systems. Many of these ideas go back to Emile Durkheim (1858-1917), the
great French sociologist whose writings form the basis for functionalist theory (see Durkheim 1915, 1964); Durkheim was himself one of the first sociologists to make use of scientific and statistical techniques in sociological
research (1951).

The second emphasis, on the organic unity of society, leads functionalists
to speculate about needs which must be met for a **social system** to exist, as
well as the ways in which social institutions satisfy those needs. A functionalist might argue, for instance, that every society will have a religion, because
religious institutions have certain **functions** that contribute to the survival of
the social system as a whole, just as the organs of the body have functions
that are necessary for the body's survival.

This analogy between society and an organism focuses attention on the
homeostatic nature of social systems: social systems work to maintain
equilibrium and to return to it after external shocks disturb the balance
among social institutions. Such social equilibrium is achieved, most importantly, through the **socialization** of members of the society into the basic
values and **norms** of that society, so that **consensus** is reached. Where
socialization is insufficient for some reason to create conformity to culturally appropriate roles and socially supported norms, various **social control
mechanisms** exist to restore conformity or to segregate the nonconforming
individuals from the rest of society. These social control mechanisms range
from **sanctions** imposed informally—sneering and gossip, for example—to
the activities of certain formal organizations, like schools, prisons, and
mental institutions.

You might notice some similarities between the language used by
functionalists and the jargon of "systems theorists" in computer science or

biology. Society is viewed as a system of interrelated parts, a change in any part affecting all the others. Within the boundaries of the system, **feedback** loops and exchanges among the parts ordinarily lead to homeostasis. Most changes are the result of natural growth or of **evolution**, but other changes occur when outside forces impinge upon the system. A thorough-going functionalist, such as Talcott Parsons, the best-known American sociologist of the 1950s and 1960s, conceptualizes society as a collection of systems within systems: the personality system within the small-group system within the community system within society (Parsons 1951). Parsons (1971) even viewed the whole world as a system of societies.

Functionalist analyses often focus on the individual, usually with the intent to show how individual behavior is molded by broader social forces. Functionalists tend to talk about individual actors as decision-makers, although some critics have suggested that functionalist theorists are, in effect, treating individuals either as puppets, whose decisions are a predictable result of their location in the **social structure** and of the norms and **expectations** they have internalized, or sometimes as virtual prisoners of the explicit social control techniques society imposes. In any case, functionalists have tended to be less concerned with the ways in which individuals can control their own destiny than with the ways in which the limits imposed by society make individual behavior scientifically predictable.

Robert Merton, another prominent functionalist, has proposed a number of important distinctions to avoid potential weaknesses and clarify ambiguities in the basic perspective (see Merton 1968). First, he distinguishes between **manifest** and **latent** functions: respectively, those which are recognized and intended by actors in the social system and hence may represent motives for their actions, and those which are unrecognized and, thus, unintended by the actors. Second, he distinguishes among consequences that are positively functional for a society (sometimes termed eufunctions), consequences that injure the society (**dysfunctions**), and consequences that are neither. Third, he distinguishes between levels of society, that is, the specific social units for which regularized patterns of behavior are functional or dysfunctional. Finally, he concedes that the particular social structures, which satisfy functional needs of society, are not indispensable, but that **structural alternatives** may exist which can also satisfy the same functional needs.

Functionalist theories have very often been criticized as **teleological,** that is, reversing the usual order of cause and effect by explaining things in terms of what happens afterward, not what went before. A strict functionalist might explain certain religious practices, for instance, as being functional by contributing to a society's survival; however, such religious traditions will usually have been firmly established long before the question is finally settled of whether the society as a whole will actually survive. Bowing to this kind of criticism of the basic logic of functionalist theory, most current sociologists have stopped using any explicitly functionalistic explanations of social phenomena, and the extreme version of functionalism expounded by Talcott Parsons has gone out of fashion. Nevertheless, many sociologists continue to expect that by careful, objective scrutiny of social phenomena they will eventually be able to discover the general laws of social behavior, and this hope still serves as the motivation for a great deal of sociological thinking and research.

Symbolic Interactionism

Symbolic interactionism, or interactionism for short, is one of the major theoretical perspectives in sociology. This perspective has a long intellectual history, beginning with the German sociologist and economist, Max Weber (1864–1920) and the American philosopher, George H. Mead (1863–1931), both of whom emphasized the **subjective meaning** of human behavior, the social process, and pragmatism. Although there are a number of versions of interactionist thought, some deriving from phenomenological writings by philosophers, the following description offers a simplified amalgamation of these ideas, concentrating on points of convergence. Herbert Blumer, who studied with Mead at the University of Chicago, is responsible for coining the term, "symbolic interactionism," as well as for formulating the most prominent version of the theory (Blumer 1969).

Interactionists focus on the subjective aspects of social life, rather than on objective, macro-structural aspects of social systems. One reason for this focus is that interactionists base their theoretical perspective on their image of humans, rather than on their image of society (as the functionalists do). For interactionists, humans are **pragmatic actors** who continually must adjust their behavior to the actions of other actors. We can adjust to these actions only because we are able to **interpret** them, i.e., to denote them symbolically and treat the actions and those who perform them as symbolic objects. This process of adjustment is aided by our ability to **imaginatively rehearse** alternative lines of action before we act. The process is further aided by our ability to think about and to react to our own actions and even our **selves** as symbolic objects. Thus, the interactionist theorist sees humans as active, creative participants who construct their social world, not as passive, conforming objects of socialization.

For the interactionist, society consists of organized and patterned interactions among individuals. Thus, research by interactionists focuses on easily observable face-to-face interactions rather than on macro-level structural relationships involving social institutions. Furthermore, this focus on interaction and on the meaning of events to the participants in those events (the **definition of the situation**) shifts the attention of interactionists away from stable norms and values toward more changeable, continually readjusting **social processes.** Whereas for functionalists socialization creates stability in the social system, for interactionists **negotiation** among members of society creates temporary, socially constructed relations, which remain in constant flux, despite relative stability in the basic framework governing those relations.

These emphases on symbols, negotiated reality, and the social construction of society lead to an interest in the **roles** people play. Erving Goffman (1958), a prominent social theorist in this tradition, discusses roles **dramaturgically,** using an analogy to the theater, with human social behavior seen as more or less well **scripted** and with humans as role-taking actors. **Role-taking** is a key mechanism of interaction, for it permits us to take the other's perspective, to see what our actions might mean to the other actors with whom we interact. At other times, interactionists emphasize the **improvisational** quality of roles, with human social behavior seen as poorly scripted and with humans as role-making improvisers. **Role-making,** too, is a key mechanism of interaction, for all situations and roles are inherently ambiguous, thus requiring us to create those situations and roles to some extent before we can act.

Ethnomethodology, an offshoot of symbolic interactionism, raises the question of how people who are interacting with each other can create the illusion of a shared social order even when they don't understand each other fully and in fact have different points of view. Harold Garfinkel, a pioneer in these investigations, demonstrated the problem by sending his students out to perform "experiments in trust," called **breaching experiments,** in which they brought ordinary conversations to an abrupt halt by refusing to take for granted that they knew what the other person was saying, and so demanded explanations and then explanations of the explanations (Garfinkel 1967). More recently, ethnomethodologist researchers have performed minutely detailed analyses of ordinary conversations in order to reveal the methods by which turn-taking and other conversational maneuvers are managed.

Interactionists tend to study social interaction through **participant observation,** rather than surveys and interviews. They argue that close contact and immersion in the everyday lives of the participants is necessary for understanding the meaning of actions, the definition of the situation itself, and the process by which actors construct the situation through their interaction. Given this close contact, interactionists could hardly remain free of value commitments, and, in fact, interactionists make explicit use of their values in choosing what to study but strive to be objective in the conduct of their research.

Symbolic interactionists are often criticized by other sociologists for being overly impressionistic in their research methods and somewhat unsystematic in their theories. These objections, combined with the fairly narrow focus of interactionist research on small-group interactions and other social psychological issues, have relegated the interactionist camp to a minority position among sociologists, although a fairly substantial minority.

Conflict Theory

The several social theories that emphasize **social conflict** have roots in the ideas of Karl Marx (1818–1883), the great German theorist and political activist. The Marxist, conflict approach emphasizes a materialist interpretation of history, a dialectical method of analysis, a critical stance toward existing social arrangements, and a political program of revolution or, at least, reform.

The **materialist** view of history starts from the premise that the most important determinant of social life is the work people are doing, especially work that results in provision of the basic necessities of life, food, clothing, and shelter. Marx thought that the way the work is socially organized and the technology used in production will have a strong impact on every other aspect of society. He maintained that everything of value in society results from human labor. Thus, Marx saw working men and women as engaged in making society, in creating the conditions for their own existence.

Marx summarized the key elements of this materialist view of history as follows:

> In the social production of their existence, men inevitably enter into definite relations, which are independent of their will, namely relations of production appropriate to a given stage in the development of their material forces of production. The totality of these relations of production constitutes the economic structure of society, the real foundation, on which arises a legal and political superstructure and to which correspond definite forms of social consciousness. The mode of production of material life conditions the general process of social, political and intellectual life. It is not the consciousness of men that determines their existence, but their social existence that determines their consciousness (Marx 1971:20).

Marx divided history into several stages, conforming to broad patterns in the **economic structure** of society. The most important stages for Marx's argument were **feudalism, capitalism,** and **socialism.** The bulk of Marx's writing is concerned with applying the materialist model of society to capitalism, the stage of economic and social development that Marx saw as dominant in 19th century Europe. For Marx, the central institution of capitalist society is **private property,** the system by which **capital** (that is, money, machines, tools, factories, and other material objects used in production) is controlled by a small minority of the population. This arrangement leads to two opposed **classes,** the owners of capital (called the **bourgeoisie**) and the workers (called the **proletariat**), whose only property is their own labor time, which they have to sell to the capitalists.

Owners are seen as making profits by paying workers less than their work is worth and, thus, **exploiting** them. (In Marxist terminology, **material forces of production** or **means of production** include capital, land, and labor, whereas **social relations of production** refers to the division of labor and implied class relationships.)

Economic exploitation leads directly to political **oppression,** as owners make use of their economic power to gain control of the state and turn it into a servant of bourgeois economic interests. Police power, for instance, is used to enforce property rights and guarantee unfair contracts between capitalist and worker. Oppression also takes more subtle forms: religion serves capitalist interests by pacifying the population; intellectuals, paid directly or indirectly by capitalists, spend their careers justifying and rationalizing the existing social and economic arrangements. In sum, the economic structure of society molds the **superstructure,** including ideas (e.g., morality, ideologies, art, and literature) and the social institutions that support the class structure of society (e.g., the state, the educational system, the family, and religious institutions). Because the dominant or **ruling class** (the bourgeoisie) controls the social relations of production, the dominant **ideology** in capitalist society is that of the ruling class. Ideology and social institutions, in turn, serve to **reproduce** and perpetuate the economic class structure. Thus, Marx viewed the exploitative economic arrangements of capitalism as the real foundation upon which the superstructure of social, political, and intellectual consciousness is built. (Figure 4.1 depicts this model of historical materialism.)

Marx's view of history might seem completely cynical or pessimistic, were it not for the possibilities of change revealed by his method of dialectical analysis. (The Marxist **dialectical** method, based on Hegel's earlier idealistic dialectic, focuses attention on how an existing social arrangement, or **thesis,** generates its social opposite, or **antithesis,** and on how a qualitatively different social form, or **synthesis,** emerges from the resulting struggle.) Marx was an optimist. He believed that any stage of history based on exploitative economic arrangements generated within itself the seeds of its own destruction. For instance, feudalism, in which land owners exploited the peasantry, gave rise to a class of town-dwelling merchants, whose dedication to making profits eventually led to the **bourgeois revolution** and the modern capitalist era. Similarly, the class relations of capitalism will lead inevitably to the next stage, **socialism.** The class relations of capitalism embody a **contradiction**: capitalists need workers, and vice versa, but the economic interests of the two groups are fundamentally at odds. Such contradictions mean inherent conflict and instability, the **class struggle.** Adding to the instability of the capitalist system are the inescapable needs for ever-wider markets and ever-greater investments in capital to maintain the profits of capitalists. Marx expected that the resulting economic cycles of expansion and contraction, together with tensions that will build as the working class gains greater understanding of its exploited position (and thus attains **class consciousness**), will eventually culminate in a socialist revolution.

Despite this sense of the unalterable logic of history, Marxists see the need for social criticism and for political activity to speed the arrival of socialism, which, not being based on private property, is not expected to involve as many contradictions and conflicts as capitalism. Marxists believe that social theory and political practice are dialectically intertwined, with theory enhanced by political involvement and with political practice necessarily guided by theory. Intellectuals ought, therefore, to engage in **praxis,** to combine political criticism and political activity. Theory itself is seen as necessarily critical and value-laden, since the prevailing social relations are based upon **alienating** and **dehumanizing** exploitation of the labor of the working classes.

Marx's ideas have been applied and reinterpreted by scholars for over a hundred years, starting with Marx's close friend and collaborator, Friedrich Engels (1825–1895), who supported Marx and his family for many years from the profits of the textile factories founded by Engels' father, while Marx shut himself away in the library of the British Museum. Later, Vladimir I. Lenin

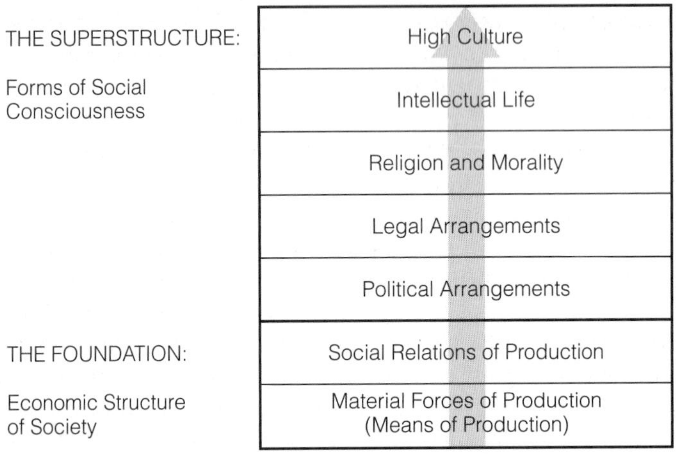

THE SUPERSTRUCTURE:	High Culture
Forms of Social Consciousness	Intellectual Life
	Religion and Morality
	Legal Arrangements
	Political Arrangements
THE FOUNDATION:	Social Relations of Production
Economic Structure of Society	Material Forces of Production (Means of Production)

FIGURE 4.1   Marx Used the Metaphor of a Building to Describe Society.
The upper stories (superstructure) rest upon a foundation of economic arrangements. When the foundation shifts, the whole house moves. The arrow shows the main direction of causality.

(1870–1924), leader of the Russian revolution, made several influential contributions to Marxist theory. In recent years Marxist theory has taken a great variety of forms, notably the world-systems theory proposed by Immanuel Wallerstein (1974, 1980) and the comparative theory of revolutions put forward by Theda Skocpol (1980). Marxist ideas have also served as a starting point for many of the modern feminist theorists. Despite these applications, Marxism of any variety is still a minority position among American sociologists.

Other Current Theories

Feminism, though not a unified theory, is among the most influential of current theoretical perspectives. Focusing their analyses on gender inequalities and on the institution of patriarchy, feminists have sought to understand society from the standpoint of women. Feminists have criticized all three of the traditionally dominant theoretical perspectives—functionalism, symbolic interactionism, and conflict theory—as biased toward male points of view. However, the feminist movement has also had its limitations. Most feminists have been white middle-class women, and feminist literature from the early days of the movement (1965–1985) often neglected the concerns of working-class women and women of color. In recent years, however, some feminists have begun to analyze the ways that race, class, and gender inequalities intersect. For instance, Patricia Hill Collins in her book, *Black Feminist Thought* (1990), argues that the common experiences of African American women have given them a unique perspective on social theory. Feminists come in a variety of theoretical stripes. Early feminists divided themselves up into liberal, radical, or socialist camps, depending on their political points of view. Today, many feminist sociologists continue to draw heavily on the conflict theory tradition, while many others have been influenced by symbolic interactionism. A few even call themselves functionalists or rational choice theorists (see below and see England 1993).

Another perspective gaining popularity in recent years is known as **rational choice theory.** Sociologists in this tradition have drawn heavily on the work of economists and political scientists in their analyses of the ways that economic incentives and other material considerations affect the choices people make. Some of the earliest sociological work of this type was known as **exchange theory,** exemplified in the works of George Homans and Peter Blau. More recently, James S. Coleman, with his monumental book, *Foundations of Social Theory* (1990), emerged as the leading sociologist in the field. Despite the name "rational choice," much of the sociological work in this tradition has focused on probing the limits of rationality and on devising mathematical models of the conditions needed for maintaining trust and solidarity within a social group.

Yet another approach to sociological theory, which has been gaining in popularity, is **phenomenology.** The approach is based on the ideas of German philosopher Edmund Husserl, who insisted that the phenomena we encounter in sensory perceptions are the ultimate source of all knowledge. His perspective was brought to the United States by sociologist Alfred Schutz and then was developed further by Harold Garfinkel, whose work on **ethnomethodology** was described in the section on symbolic interactionism above. Another important development in phenomenological thinking can be found in the works of Peter Berger and Thomas Luckmann, whose landmark book, *The Social Construction of Reality* (1966), has been widely influential, especially among contemporary feminists. Prominent theorist Dorothy Smith draws heavily on **social construction theory,** and also the ideas of Garfinkel and others, in her presentation of **feminist standpoint theory,** arguing that sociological theory as constructed by men gives a distorted picture of women's experiences, and that any theory which ignores the perspectives of women (and of other excluded groups) is necessarily incomplete.

Finally, **poststructuralism** and **postmodernism,** perspectives developed on the French intellectual scene, have had considerable influence on American sociologists in recent years (as well as on scholars in many other fields, especially literary studies). Derived from (but largely rejecting) both the Marxist tradition and the works of anthropologist Claude Lévi-Strauss— who developed a "structuralist" theory of culture—these theoretical schools seek to account for the apparent disintegration of modern culture over the past several decades. Among the tradition's major figures, such as Jacques Derrida and Jean Baudrillard, perhaps the best known is Michel Foucault, a historian and philosopher. Tracing the historical changes in societal attitudes toward punishment, mental illness, and sexuality, among other topics, he argued that knowledge and power have become inextricably entwined.

Foucault stressed the disciplinary nature of power, and argued that (social) scientific discourse as one such discipline may itself need to be questioned. Sociologists in this tradition seek not only to study the world differently, but to make the production of sociological knowledge, and thus our own situatedness within structures of knowledge and power, part of the study. American sociologists influenced by this tradition sometimes call their work **discourse analysis** or **cultural studies.**

Not mentioned in this quick review of the current sociological theories are some major theorists with their own influential perspectives. Jürgen Habermas, a leading German sociologist, Anthony Giddens, a leading British sociologist, and American sociologist Randall Collins are all noted for having constructed theories, which synthesize ideas drawn from several theoretical traditions. For introductory students, the point is not to memorize all these names, but to be aware of the multiple points of view and the often contentious theoretical differences among contemporary sociologists. Sociology is in a theoretical ferment, as sociologists seek new ways to understand the formidable complexity of the social world.

REFERENCES

Blumer, Herbert. 1969. *Symbolic Interactionism: Perspective and Method.* Englewood Cliffs, NJ: Prentice-Hall.

Coleman, James S. 1990. *Foundations of Social Theory.* Cambridge, MA: Belknap Harvard.

Collins, Patricia Hill. 1990. *Black Feminist Thought.* Boston: Unwin Hyman.

Durkheim, Emile. 1915. *The Elementary Forms of the Religious Life: A Study in Religious Sociology.* Translated by Joseph Ward Swain. New York: Macmillan.

_____. [1897] 1951. *Suicide: A Study in Sociology.* Tr. John A. Spaulding and George Simpson. Glencoe, IL: Free Press.

_____. [1893] 1964. *The Division of Labor in Society.* Tr. George Simpson. New York: Free Press.

England, Paula, ed. 1993. *Theory on Gender/Feminism on Theory.* New York: Aldine de Gruyter.

Garfinkel, Harold. 1967. *Studies in Ethnomethodology.* Englewood Cliffs, NJ: Prentice-Hall.

Goffman, Erving. 1958. *The Presentation of Self in Everyday Life.* Edinburgh: University of Edinburgh, Social Sciences Research Centre.

Marx, Karl. 1971. Preface to *A Contribution to the Critique of Political Economy.* Tr. S. W. Ryanzanskaya, edited by M. Dobb. London: Lawrence & Whishart.

Merton, Robert K. 1968. *Social Theory and Social Structure.* New York: Free Press.

Parsons, Talcott. 1951. *The Social System.* Glencoe, IL: Free Press.

_____. 1971. *The System of Modern Societies.* Englewood Cliffs, NJ: Prentice-Hall.

Skocpol, Theda. 1980. *States and Social Revolutions: A Comparative Analysis of France, Russia, and China.* New York: Cambridge University Press.

Wallerstein, Immanuel M. 1974. *The Modern World-System: Capitalist Agriculture and the Origins of the European World-Economy in the Sixteenth Century.* New York: Academic Press.

_____. 1980. *The Modern World-System II: Mercantilism and the Consolidation of the European World-Economy, 1600-1750.* New York: Academic Press.

5

MANIFESTO OF THE COMMUNIST PARTY

KARL MARX • FRIEDRICH ENGELS

This second selection in this section on theory is an excerpt from the classic "Manifesto of the Communist Party," written by Karl Marx and Friedrich Engels in 1848. Karl Marx's influence on sociological theory was discussed in the previous reading (Reading 4). Students often are surprised to discover the currency of many of the topics discussed by Marx (1818–1883) and Engels (1820–1895). Specifically, Marx and Engels foresaw the rise of global capitalism. They also accurately described exploitive industrial conditions and the oppositional interests of workers and capitalists. Even though Marx and Engels are criticized for not foreseeing the rise of other social agents (such as the middle class, the government, and unions) in mediating the conflict between capitalists and workers, their theory of class struggle and revolution is still provocative and a source for worldwide social change.

The history of all hitherto existing society is the history of class struggles.

Freeman and slave, patrician and plebeian, lord and serf, guild-master and journeyman, in a word, oppressor and oppressed, stood in constant opposition to one another, carried on an uninterrupted, now hidden, now open fight, a fight that each time ended, either in a revolutionary reconstitution of society at large, or in the common ruin of the contending classes.

In the earlier epochs of history, we find almost everywhere a complicated arrangement of society into various orders, a manifold gradation of social rank. In ancient Rome we have patricians, knights, plebeians, slaves; in the Middle Ages, feudal lords, vassals, guild-masters, journeymen, apprentices, serfs; in almost all of these classes, again, subordinate gradations.

The modern bourgeois society that has sprouted from the ruins of feudal society has not done away with class antagonisms. It has but established new classes, new conditions of oppression, new forms of struggle in place of the old ones.

Our epoch, the epoch of the bourgeoisie, possesses, however, this distinctive feature: It has simplified the class antagonisms. Society as a whole is more and more splitting up into two great hostile camps, into two great classes directly facing each other: Bourgeoisie and Proletariat.

Karl Marx and Friedrich Engels, "The Manifesto of the Communist Party," translated by Friedrich Engels (1888).

From the serfs of the Middle Ages sprang the chartered burghers of the earliest towns. From these burgesses the first elements of the bourgeoisie were developed.

The discovery of America, the rounding of the Cape, opened up fresh ground for the rising bourgeoisie. The East-Indian and Chinese markets, the colonization of America, trade with the colonies, the increase in the means of exchange and in commodities generally, gave to commerce, to navigation, to industry, an impulse never before known, and thereby, to the revolutionary element in the tottering feudal society, a rapid development.

The feudal system of industry, under which industrial production was monopolized by closed guilds, now no longer sufficed for the growing wants of the new markets. The manufacturing system took its place. The guild-masters were pushed on one side by the manufacturing middle class; division of labour between the different corporate guilds vanished in the face of division of labour in each single workshop.

Meantime the markets kept ever growing, the demand ever rising. Even manufacture no longer sufficed. Thereupon, steam and machinery revolutionized industrial production. The place of manufacture was taken by the giant, Modern Industry, the place of the industrial middle class, by industrial millionaires, the leaders of whole industrial armies, the modern bourgeois.

Modern industry has established the world-market, for which the discovery of America paved the way. This market has given an immense development to commerce, to navigation, to communication by land. This development has, in its turn, reacted on the extension of industry; and in proportion as industry, commerce, navigation, railways extended, in the same proportion the bourgeoisie developed, increased its capital, and pushed into the background every class handed down from the Middle Ages.

We see, therefore, how the modern bourgeoisie is itself the product of a long course of development, of a series of revolutions in the modes of production and of exchange.

Each step in the development of the bourgeoisie was accompanied by a corresponding political advance of that class. An oppressed class under the sway of the feudal nobility, an armed and self-governing association in the mediaeval commune; here independent urban republic (as in Italy and Germany), there taxable "third estate" of the monarchy (as in France), afterwards, in the period of manufacture proper, serving either the semi-feudal or the absolute monarchy as a counterpoise against the nobility, and, in fact, corner-stone of the great monarchies in general, the bourgeoisie has at last, since the establishment of Modern Industry and of the world-market, conquered for itself, in the modern representative State, exclusive political sway. The execution of the modern State is but a committee for managing the common affairs of the whole bourgeoisie.

The bourgeoisie, historically, has played a most revolutionary part.

The bourgeoisie, wherever it has got the upper hand, has put an end to all feudal, patriarchal, idyllic relations. It has pitilessly torn asunder the motley feudal ties that bound man to his "natural superiors," and has left remaining no other nexus between man and man than naked self-interest, than callous "cash payment." It has drowned the most heavenly ecstasies of religious fervor, of chivalrous enthusiasm, of philistine sentimentalism, in the icy water of egotistical calculation. It has resolved personal worth into exchange value and, in place of the numberless indefeasible chartered freedoms, has set up that single, unconscionable freedom—Free Trade. In one word, for exploitation, veiled by religious and political illusions, it has substituted naked, shameless, direct, brutal exploitation.

The bourgeoisie has stripped of its halo every occupation hitherto honored and looked up to with reverent awe. It has converted the physician, the lawyer, the priest, the poet, the man of science, into its paid wagelabourers.

The bourgeoisie has torn away from the family its sentimental veil, and has reduced the family relation to a mere money relation.

The bourgeoisie has disclosed how it came to pass that the brutal display of vigor in the Middle Ages, which Reactionists so much admire, found its fitting complement in the most slothful indolence. It has been the first to show what man's activity can bring about. It has accomplished wonders far surpassing Egyptian pyramids, Roman aqueducts, and Gothic cathedrals; it has conducted expeditions that put in the shade all former Exoduses of nations and crusades.

The bourgeoisie cannot exist without constantly revolutionizing the instruments of production, and thereby the relations of production, and with them the whole relations of society. Conservation of the old modes of production in unaltered form, was, on the contrary, the first condition of existence for all earlier industrial classes. Constant revolutionizing of production, uninterrupted disturbance of all social conditions, everlasting uncertainty and agitation distinguish the bourgeois epoch from all earlier ones. All fixed, fastfrozen relations, with their train of ancient and venerable prejudices and opinions, are swept away, all new-formed ones become antiquated before they can ossify. All that is solid melts into air, all that is holy is profaned, and man is at last compelled to face with sober senses, his real conditions of life, and his relations with his kind.

The need of a constantly expanding market for its products chases the bourgeoisie over the whole surface of the globe. It must nestle everywhere, settle everywhere, establish connections everywhere.

The bourgeoisie has through its exploitation of the world-market given a cosmopolitan character to production and consumption in every country. To the great chagrin of Reactionists, it has drawn from under the feet of industry the national ground on which it stood. All old-established national industries have been destroyed or are daily being destroyed. They are dislodged by new industries, whose introduction becomes a life and death question for all civilized nations, by industries that no longer work up indigenous raw material, but raw material drawn from the remotest zones; industries whose products are consumed, not only at home, but in every quarter of the globe. In place of the old wants, satisfied by the productions of the country, we find new wants, requiring for their satisfaction the products of distant lands and climes. In place of the old local and national seclusion and self-sufficiency, we have intercourse in every direction, universal inter-dependence of nations. And as in material, so also in intellectual production. The intellectual creations of individual nations become common property. National one-sidedness and narrow-mindedness become more and more impossible, and from the numerous national and local literatures, there arises a world literature.

The bourgeoisie, by the rapid improvement of all instruments of production, by the immensely facilitated means of communication, draws all, even the most barbarian, nations into civilization. The cheap prices of its commodities are the heavy artillery with which it batters down all Chinese walls, with which it forces the barbarians' intensely obstinate hatred of foreigners to capitulate. It compels all nations, on pain of extinction, to adopt the bourgeois mode of production; it compels them to introduce what it calls civilization into their midst, *i.e.*, to become bourgeois themselves. In one word, it creates a world after its own image.

The bourgeoisie has subjected the country to the rule of the towns. It has created enormous cities, has greatly increased the urban population as compared with the rural, and has thus rescued a considerable part of the population from the idiocy of rural life. Just as it has made the country dependent on the towns, so it has made barbarian and semi-barbarian countries dependent on the civilized ones, nations of peasants on nations of bourgeois, the East on the West.

The bourgeoisie keeps more and more doing away with the scattered state of the population, of the means of production, and of property. It has agglomerated population, centralized means of production, and has concentrated property in a few hands. The necessary consequence of this was political centralization. Independent, or but loosely connected provinces, with separate interests, laws, governments and systems of taxation, became lumped together into one nation, with one government, one code of laws, one national class-interest, one frontier and one customs-tariff.

The bourgeoisie, during its rule of scarce one hundred years, has created more massive and more colossal productive forces than have all preceding generations together. Subjection of Nature's forces to man, machinery, application of chemistry to industry and agriculture, steam-navigation, railways, electric telegraphs, clearing of whole continents for cultivation, canalization of rivers, whole populations conjured out of the ground—what earlier century had even a presentiment that such productive forces slumbered in the lap of social labour?

We see then: the means of production and of exchange, on whose foundation the bourgeoisie built itself up, were generated in feudal society. At a certain stage in the development of these means of production and of exchange, the conditions under which feudal society produced and exchanged, the feudal organization of agriculture and manufacturing industry, in one word, the feudal relations of property became no longer compatible with the already developed productive forces; they became so many fetters. They had to be burst asunder; they were burst asunder.

Into their place stepped free competition, accompanied by a social and political constitution adapted to it, and by the economical and political sway of the bourgeois class.

A similar movement is going on before our own eyes. Modern bourgeois society with its relations of production, of exchange and of property, a society that has conjured up such gigantic means of production and of exchange, is like the sorcerer, who is no longer able to control the powers of the nether world whom he has called up by his spells. For many a decade past the history of industry and commerce is but the history of the revolt of modern productive forces against modern conditions of production, against the property relations that are the conditions for the existence of the bourgeoisie and of its rule. It is enough to mention the commercial crises that by their periodical return put on its trial, each time more threateningly, the existence of the entire bourgeois society. In these crises a great part not only of the existing products, but also of the previously created productive forces, are periodically destroyed. In these crises there breaks out an epidemic that, in all earlier epochs, would have seemed an absurdity—the epidemic of over-production. Society suddenly finds itself put back into a state of momentary barbarism; it appears as if a famine, a universal war of devastation had cut off the supply of every means of subsistence; industry and commerce seem to be destroyed; and why? Because there is too much civilization, too much means of subsistence, too much industry, too much commerce. The productive forces at the disposal of society no longer tend to further the development of the conditions of bourgeois property; on the contrary, they have become too powerful for these conditions, by which they are fettered, and so soon as they overcome these fetters, they bring disorder into the whole of bourgeois society, endanger the existence of bourgeois property. The conditions of bourgeois society are too narrow to comprise the wealth created by them. And how does the bourgeoisie get over these crises? On the one hand, by enforced destruction of a mass of productive forces; on the other, by the conquest of new markets, and by the more thorough exploitation of the old ones. That is to say, by paving the way for more extensive and more destructive crises, and by diminishing the means whereby crises are prevented.

The weapons with which the bourgeoisie felled feudalism to the ground are now turned against the bourgeoisie itself.

But not only has the bourgeoisie forged the weapons that bring death to itself; it has also called into existence the men who are to wield those weapons—the modern working class—the proletarians.

In proportion as the bourgeoisie, *i.e.*, capital, is developed, in the same proportion is the proletariat, the modern working class, developed—a class of labourers, who live only so long as they find work and who find work only so long as their labour increases capital. These labourers, who must sell themselves piece-meal, are a commodity, like every other article of commerce, and are consequently exposed to all the vicissitudes of competition, to all the fluctuations of the market.

Owing to the extensive use of machinery and to division of labour, the work of the proletarians has lost all individual character and, consequently, all charm for the workman. He becomes an appendage of the machine, and it is only the most simple, most monotonous, and most easily acquired knack that is required of him. Hence, the cost of production of a workman is restricted, almost entirely, to the means of subsistence that he requires for his maintenance and for the propagation of his race. But the price of a commodity, and therefore also of labour, is equal to its cost of production. In proportion, therefore, as the repulsiveness of the work increases, the wage decreases. Nay more, in proportion as the use of machinery and division of labour increases, in the same proportion the burden of toil also increases, whether by prolongation of the working hours, by increase of the work exacted in a given time, or by increased speed of the machinery, etc.

Modern industry has converted the little workshop of the patriarchal master into the great factory of the industrial capitalist. Masses of labourers, crowded into the factory, are organised like soldiers. As privates of the industrial army they are placed under the command of a perfect hierarchy of officers and sergeants. Not only are they slaves of the bourgeois class and of the bourgeois State; they are daily and hourly enslaved by the machine, by the over-looker, and, above all, by the individual bourgeois manufacturer himself. The more openly this despotism proclaims gain to be its end and aim, the more petty, the more hateful and the more embittering it is.

The less the skill and exertion of strength implied in manual labour, in other words, the more modern industry becomes developed, the more is the labour of men superseded by that of women. Differences of age and sex have no longer any distinctive social validity for the working class. All are instruments of labour, more or less expensive to use, according to their age and sex.

No sooner is the exploitation of the labourer by the manufacturer, so far, at an end, that he receives his wages in cash, than he is set upon by the other portions of the bourgeoisie, the landlord, the shopkeeper, the pawnbroker, etc.

6

ON BEING SANE IN INSANE PLACES

DAVID L. ROSENHAN

The third and final reading in this introduction to sociological theory is a classic piece by David L. Rosenhan on the social construction of illness and mental health. In this selection, which was originally published in 1973, Rosenhan explores the social deviance of mental illness and the consequences

David L. Rosenhan, "On Being Sane in Insane Places" from *Science* 179 (1973): 250–258. Copyright © 1973 by the American Association for the Advancement of Science. Reprinted with permission.

of labeling people "sane" or "insane." Symbolic interactionists claim that deviance is relative depending on the situation and which person is perceiving the act of social deviance. Thus, according to *labeling theory,* people label certain acts as deviant and others as normal. Rosenhan uses symbolic interactionism and labeling theory to inform his research, and he designs a field experiment in which he sends pseudopatients into mental institutions to test the consistency of mental health illness labels. This piece informs sociological theory, sociological research methods, and the study of social deviance. Rosenhan is currently a professor emeritus of psychology and law at Stanford University.

I f sanity and insanity exist . . . how shall we know them? The question is neither capricious nor itself insane. However much we may be personally convinced that we can tell the normal from the abnormal, the evidence is simply not compelling. It is commonplace, for example, to read about murder trials wherein eminent psychiatrists for the defense are contradicted by equally eminent psychiatrists for the prosecution on the matter of the defendant's sanity. More generally, there is a great deal of conflicting data on the reliability, utility, and meaning of such terms as *sanity, insanity, mental illness,* and *schizophrenia.*[1] Finally, as early as 1934, Benedict suggested that normality and abnormality are not universal.[2] What is viewed as normal in one culture may be seen as quite aberrant in another. Thus, notions of normality and abnormality may not be quite as accurate as people believe they are.

To raise questions regarding normality and abnormality is in no way to question the fact that some behaviors are deviant or odd. Murder is deviant. So, too, are hallucinations. Nor does raising such questions deny the existence of the personal anguish that is often associated with "mental illness." Anxiety and depression exist. Psychological suffering exists. But normality and abnormality, sanity and insanity, and the diagnoses that flow from them may be less substantive than many believe them to be.

At its heart, the question of whether the sane can be distinguished from the insane (and whether degrees of insanity can be distinguished from each other) is a simple matter: Do the salient characteristics that lead to diagnoses reside in the patients themselves or in the environments and contexts in which observers find them? From Bleuler, through Kretchmer, through the formulations of the recently revised [1968] *Diagnostic and Statistical Manual* of the American Psychiatric Association, the belief has been strong that patients present symptoms, that those symptoms can be categorized, and, implicitly, that the sane are distinguishable from the insane. More recently, however, this belief has been questioned. Based in part on theoretical and anthropological considerations, but also on philosophical, legal, and therapeutic ones, the view has grown that psychological categorization of mental illness is useless at best and downright harmful, misleading, and pejorative at worst. Psychiatric diagnoses, in this view, are in the minds of the observers and are not valid summaries of characteristics displayed by the observed.[3, 4, 5]

Gains can be made in deciding which of these is more nearly accurate by getting normal people (that is, people who do not have, and have never suffered, symptoms of serious psychiatric disorders) admitted to psychiatric hospitals and then determining whether they were discovered to be sane and, if so, how. If the sanity of such pseudopatients were always detected, there would be *prima facie* evidence that a sane individual can be distinguished from the insane context in which he is found. Normality (and presumably abnormality) is distinct enough that it can be recognized wherever it occurs, for it is carried within the person. If, on the other hand, the sanity of the pseudopatients were never discovered, serious difficulties would arise for those who support traditional modes of psychiatric diagnosis. Given that the hospital staff was not incompetent, that the pseudopatient had been behaving as sanely as he had been outside of the hospital, and that it had never been previously suggested that he belonged in a psychiatric hospital, such an unlikely outcome would support the view that psychiatric diagnosis betrays little about the patient but much about the environment in which an observer finds him.

This article describes such an experiment. Eight sane people gained secret admission to twelve different hospitals.[6] Their diagnostic experiences constitute the data of the first part of this article; the remainder is devoted to a description of their experiences in psychiatric institutions. Too few psychiatrists and psychologists, even those who have worked in such hospitals, know what the experience is like. They rarely talk about it with former patients, perhaps because they distrust information coming from the previously insane. Those who have worked in psychiatric hospitals are likely to have adapted so thoroughly to the settings that they are insensitive to the impact of that experience. And while there have been occasional reports of researchers who submitted themselves to psychiatric hospitalization,[7] these researchers have commonly remained in the hospitals for short periods of time, often with the knowledge of the hospital staff. It is difficult to know the extent to which they were treated like patients or like research colleagues. Nevertheless, their reports about the inside of the psychiatric hospital have been valuable. This article extends those efforts.

Pseudopatients and Their Settings

The eight pseudopatients were a varied group. One was a psychology graduate student in his 20s. The remaining seven were older and "established." Among them were three psychologists, a pediatrician, a psychiatrist, a painter, and a housewife. Three pseudopatients were women, five were men. All of them employed pseudonyms, lest their alleged diagnoses embarrass them later. Those who were in mental health professions alleged another occupation in order to avoid the special attentions that might be accorded by staff, as a matter of courtesy or caution, to ailing colleagues.[8] With the exception of myself (I was the first pseudopatient and my presence was known to the hospital administrator and chief psychologist and, so far as I can tell, to them alone), the presence of pseudopatients and the nature of the research program were not known to the hospital staffs.[9]

The settings were similarly varied. In order to generalize the findings, admission into a variety of hospitals was sought. The 12 hospitals in the sample were located in five different states on the East and West coasts. Some were old and shabby, some were quite new. Some were research-oriented, others not. Some had good staff-patient ratios, others were quite understaffed. Only one was a strictly private hospital. All of the others were supported by state or federal funds or, in one instance, by university funds.

After calling the hospital for an appointment, the pseudopatient arrived at the admissions office complaining that he had been hearing voices. Asked what the voices said, he replied that they were often unclear, but as far as he could tell they said "empty," "hollow," and "thud." The voices were unfamiliar and were of the same sex as the pseudopatient. The choice of these symptoms was occasioned by their apparent similarity to existential symptoms. Such symptoms are alleged to arise from painful concerns about the perceived meaninglessness of one's life. It is as if the hallucinating person were saying, "My life is empty and hollow." The choice of these symptoms was also determined by the *absence* of a single report of existential psychoses in the literature.

Beyond alleging the symptoms and falsifying name, vocation, and employment, no further alterations of person, history, or circumstances were made. The significant events of the pseudopatient's life history were presented as they had actually occurred. Relationships with parents and siblings, with spouse and children, with people at work and in school, consistent with the aforementioned exceptions, were described as they were or had been. Frustrations and upsets were described along with joys and satisfactions. These facts are important to remember. If anything, they strongly biased the subsequent results in favor of detecting sanity, since none of their histories or current behaviors were seriously pathological in any way.

Immediately upon admission to the psychiatric ward, the pseudopatient ceased simulating *any* symptoms of abnormality. In some cases, there was a brief period of mild nervousness and anxiety, since none of the pseudopatients really believed that they would be admitted so easily. Indeed, their shared fear was that they would be immediately exposed as frauds and greatly embarrassed. Moreover, many of them had never visited a psychiatric ward; even those who had, nevertheless had some genuine fears about what might happen to them. Their nervousness, then, was quite appropriate to the novelty of the hospital setting, and it abated rapidly.

Apart from that short-lived nervousness, the pseudopatient behaved on the ward as he "normally" behaved. The pseudopatient spoke to patients and staff as he might ordinarily. Because there is uncommonly little to do on a psychiatric ward, he attempted to engage others in conversation. When asked by the staff how he was feeling, he indicated that he was fine, that he no longer experienced symptoms. He responded to instructions from attendants, to calls for medication (which was not swallowed), and to dining-hall instructions. Beyond such activities as were available to him on the admissions ward, he spent his time writing down his observations about the ward, its patients, and the staff. Initially these notes were written "secretly," but as it soon became clear that no one much cared, they were subsequently written on standard tablets of paper in such public places as the dayroom. No secret was made of these activities.

The pseudopatient, very much as a true psychiatric patient, entered a hospital with no foreknowledge of when he would be discharged. Each was told that he would have to get out by his own devices, essentially by convincing the staff that he was sane. The psychological stresses associated with hospitalization were considerable, and all but one of the pseudopatients desired to be discharged almost immediately after being admitted. They were, therefore, motivated not only to behave sanely, but to be paragons of cooperation. That their behavior was in no way disruptive is confirmed by nursing reports, which have been obtained on most of the patients. These reports uniformly indicate that the patients were "friendly," "cooperative," and "exhibited no abnormal indications."

The Normal Are Not Detectably Sane

Despite their public "show" of sanity, the pseudopatients were never detected. Admitted, except in one case, with a diagnosis of schizophrenia,[10] each was discharged with a diagnosis of schizophrenia "in remission." The label "in remission" should in no way be dismissed as a formality, for at no time during any hospitalization had any question been raised about any pseudopatient's simulation. Nor are there any indications in the hospital records that the pseudopatient's status was suspect. Rather, the evidence is strong that, once labeled schizophrenic, the pseudopatient was stuck with that label. If the pseudopatient was to be discharged, he must naturally be "in remission"; but he was not sane, nor, in the institution's view, had he ever been sane.

The uniform failure to recognize sanity cannot be attributed to the quality of the hospitals, for, although there were considerable variations among them, several are considered excellent. Nor can it be alleged that there was simply not enough time to observe the pseudopatients. Length of hospitalization ranged from 7 to 52 days, with an average of 19 days. The pseudopatients were not, in fact, carefully observed, but this failure clearly speaks more to the traditions within psychiatric hospitals than to lack of opportunity.

Finally, it cannot be said that the failure to recognize the pseudopatients' sanity was due to the fact that they were not behaving sanely. While there was clearly some tension present in all of them, their daily visitors could detect no serious behavioral consequences—nor, indeed, could other patients. It was quite common for the patients to "detect" the pseudopatients' sanity. During the first three hospitalizations, when accurate counts were kept, 35 of a total of 118 patients on the admissions ward voiced their suspicions, some vigorously. "You're not crazy. You're a journalist, or a professor [referring to the continual note-taking]. You're checking up on the hospital." While most of the patients were reassured by the pseudopatient's insistence that he had been sick before he came in but was fine now, some continued to believe that the pseudopatient was sane throughout his hospitalization.[11] The fact that the patients often recognized normality when staff did not raises important questions.

Failure to detect sanity during the course of hospitalization may be due to the fact that physicians operate with a strong bias toward what statisticians call the type 2 error.[12] This is to say that physicians are more inclined to call a healthy person sick (a false positive, type 2) than a sick person healthy (a false negative, type 1). The reasons for this are not hard to find: It is clearly more dangerous to misdiagnose illness than health. Better to err on the side of caution, to suspect illness even among the healthy.

But what holds for medicine does not hold equally well for psychiatry. Medical illnesses, while unfortunate, are not commonly pejorative. Psychiatric diagnoses, on the contrary, carry with them personal, legal, and social stigmas.[13] It was therefore important to see whether the tendency toward diagnosing the sane insane could be reversed. The following experiment was arranged at a research and teaching hospital whose staff had heard these findings but doubted that such an error could occur in their hospital. The staff was informed that at some time during the following three months, one or more pseudopatients would attempt to be admitted into the psychiatric hospital. Each staff member was asked to rate each patient who presented himself at admissions or on the ward according to the likelihood that the patient was a pseudopatient. A 10-point scale was used, with a 1 and 2 reflecting high confidence that the patient was a pseudopatient.

Judgments were obtained on 193 patients who were admitted for psychiatric treatment. All staff who had had sustained contact with or primary responsibility for the patient—attendants, nurses, psychiatrists, physicians, and psychologists—were asked to make judgments. Forty-one patients were alleged, with high confidence, to be pseudopatients by at least one member of the staff. Twenty-three were considered suspect by at least one psychiatrist. Nineteen were suspected by one psychiatrist and one other staff member. Actually, no genuine pseudopatient (at least from my group) presented himself during this period.

The experiment is instructive. It indicates that the tendency to designate sane people as insane can be reversed when the stakes (in this case, prestige and diagnostic acumen) are high. But what can be said of the 19 people who were suspected of being "sane" by one psychiatrist and another staff member? Were these people truly "sane," or was it rather the case that in the course of avoiding the type 2 error the staff tended to make more errors of the first sort—calling the crazy "sane"? There is no way of knowing. But one thing is certain: Any diagnostic process that lends itself so readily to massive errors of this sort cannot be a very reliable one.

The Stickiness of Psychodiagnostic Labels

Beyond the tendency to call the healthy sick—a tendency that accounts better for diagnostic behavior on admission than it does for such behavior after a lengthy period of exposure—the data speak to the massive role of labeling in psychiatric assessment. Having once been labeled schizophrenic, there is nothing the pseudopatient can do to overcome the tag. The tag profoundly colors others' perceptions of him and his behavior.

From one viewpoint, these data are hardly surprising, for it has long been known that elements are given meaning by the context in which they occur. Gestalt psychology made this point vigorously, and Asch[14] demonstrated that there are "central" personality traits (such as "warm" versus "cold") which are so powerful that they markedly color the meaning of other information in forming an impression of a given personality.[15] "Insane," "schizophrenic," "manic-depressive," and "crazy" are probably among the most powerful of such central traits. Once a person is designated abnormal, all of his other behaviors and characteristics are colored by that label. Indeed, that label is so powerful that many of the pseudopatients' normal behaviors were overlooked entirely or profoundly misinterpreted. Some examples may clarify this issue.

Earlier I indicated that there were no changes in the pseudopatient's personal history and current status beyond those of name, employment, and, where necessary, vocation. Otherwise, a veridical description of personal history and circumstances was offered. Those circumstances were not psychotic. How were they made consonant with the diagnosis of psychosis? Or were those diagnoses modified in such a way as to bring them into accord with the circumstances of the pseudopatient's life, as described by him?

As far as I can determine, diagnoses were in no way affected by the relative health of the circumstances of a pseudopatient's life. Rather, the reverse occurred: The perception of his circumstances was shaped entirely by the diagnosis. A clear example of such translation is found in the case of a pseudopatient who had had a close relationship with his mother but was rather remote from his father during his early childhood. During adolescence and beyond, however, his father became a close friend, while his relationship with his mother cooled. His present relationship with his wife was characteristically close and warm. Apart from occasional angry exchanges, friction was minimal. The children had rarely been spanked. Surely there is nothing especially pathological about such a history. Indeed, many readers may see a similar pattern in their own experiences, with no markedly deleterious consequences. Observe, however, how such a history was translated in the psychopathological context, this from the case summary prepared after the patient was discharged.

> This white 39-year-old male . . . manifests a long history of considerable ambivalence in close relationships, which begins in early childhood. A warm relationship with his mother cools during adolescence. A distant relationship to his father is described as becoming very intense. Affective stability is absent. His attempts to control emotionality with his wife and children are punctuated by angry outbursts and, in the case of the children, spankings. And while he says that he has several good friends, one senses considerable ambivalence embedded in those relationships also.

The facts of the case were unintentionally distorted by the staff to achieve consistency with a popular theory of the dynamics of schizophrenic reaction.[16] Nothing of an ambivalent nature had been described in relations with parents, spouse, or friends. To the extent that ambivalence could be inferred, it was probably not greater than is found in all human relationships. It is true the pseudopatient's relationships with his parents changed over time, but in the ordinary context that would hardly be remarkable—indeed, it might very well be expected. Clearly, the meaning ascribed to his verbalizations (that is, ambivalence, affective instability) was determined by the diagnosis: schizophrenia. An entirely different meaning would have been ascribed if it were known that the man was "normal."

All pseudopatients took extensive notes publicly. Under ordinary circumstances, such behavior would have raised questions in the minds of observers, as, in fact, it did among patients. Indeed, it seemed so certain that the notes would elicit suspicion that elaborate precautions were taken to remove them from the ward each day. But the precautions proved needless. The closest any staff member came to questioning these notes occurred when one pseudopatient asked his physician what kind of medication he was receiving and began to write down the response. "You needn't write it," he was told gently. "If you have trouble remembering, just ask me again."

If no questions were asked of the pseudopatients, how was their writing interpreted? Nursing records for three patients indicate that the writing was seen as an aspect of their pathological behavior. "Patient engages in writing behavior" was the daily nursing comment on one of the pseudopatients who was never questioned about his writing. Given that the patient is in the hospital, he must be psychologically disturbed. And given that he is disturbed, continuous writing must be a behavioral manifestation of that disturbance, perhaps a subset of the compulsive behaviors that are sometimes correlated with schizophrenia.

One tacit characteristic of psychiatric diagnosis is that it locates the sources of aberration within the individual and only rarely within the complex of stimuli that surrounds him. Consequently, behaviors that are stimulated by the environment are commonly misattributed to the patient's disorder. For example, one kindly nurse found a pseudopatient pacing the long hospital corridors. "Nervous, Mr. X?" she asked. "No, bored," he said.

The notes kept by pseudopatients are full of patient behaviors that were misinterpreted by well-intentioned staff. Often enough, a patient would go "berserk" because he had, wittingly or unwittingly, been mistreated by, say, an attendant. A nurse coming upon the scene would rarely inquire even cursorily into the environmental stimuli of the patient's behavior. Rather, she assumed that his upset derived from his pathology, not from his present interactions with other staff members. Occasionally, the staff might assume that the patient's family (especially when they had recently visited) or other patients had stimulated the outburst. But never were the staff found to assume that one of themselves or the structure of the hospital had anything to do with a patient's behavior. One psychiatrist pointed to a group of patients who were sitting outside the cafeteria entrance half an hour before lunchtime. To a group of young residents he indicated that such behavior was characteristic of the oral-acquisitive nature of the syndrome. It seemed not to occur to him that there were very few things to anticipate in the psychiatric hospital besides eating.

A psychiatric label has a life and an influence of its own. Once the impression has been formed that the patient is schizophrenic, the expectation is that he will continue to be schizophrenic. When a sufficient amount of time has passed, during which the patient has done nothing bizarre, he is considered to be in remission and available for discharge. But the label endures beyond discharge, with the unconfirmed expectation that he will behave as a schizophrenic again. Such labels, conferred by mental health professionals, are as influential on the patient as they are on his relatives and friends, and it should not surprise anyone that the diagnosis acts on all of them as a self-fulfilling prophecy. Eventually, the patient himself accepts the diagnosis, with all of its surplus meanings and expectations, and behaves accordingly.[17]

The inferences to be made from these matters are quite simple. Much as Zigler and Phillips have demonstrated that there is enormous overlap in the symptoms presented by patients who have been variously diagnosed,[18] so there is enormous overlap in the behaviors of the sane and the insane. The sane are not "sane" all of the time. We lose our tempers "for no good reason." We are occasionally depressed or anxious, again for no good reason. And we may find it difficult to get along with one or another person—again for no reason that we can specify. Similarly, the insane are not always insane. Indeed, it was the impression of the pseudopatients while living with them that they were sane for long periods of time—that the bizarre behaviors upon which their diagnoses were allegedly predicated constituted only a small fraction of their total behavior. If it makes no sense to label ourselves permanently depressed on the basis of an occasional depression, then it takes evidence that is presently available to label all patients insane or schizophrenic on the basis of bizarre behaviors or cognitions. It seems more useful, as Mischel[19] has pointed out, to limit our discussions to *behaviors*, the stimuli that provoke them, and their correlates.

It is not known why powerful impressions of personality traits, such as "crazy" or "insane," arise. Conceivably, when the origins of and stimuli that give rise to a behavior are remote or unknown, or when the behavior strikes us as immutable, trait labels regarding the *behavior* arise. When, on the other hand, the origins and stimuli are known and available, discourse is limited to the behavior itself. Thus, I may hallucinate because I am sleeping, or I may hallucinate because I have ingested a peculiar drug. These are termed sleep-induced hallucinations, or dreams, and drug-induced hallucinations, respectively. But when the stimuli to my hallucinations are unknown, that is called craziness, or schizophrenia—as if that inference were somehow as illuminating as the others.

The Consequences of Labeling and Depersonalization

Whenever the ratio of what is known to what needs to be known approaches zero, we tend to invent "knowledge" and assume that we understand more than we actually do. We seem unable to acknowledge that we simply don't know. The needs for diagnosis and remediation of behavioral and emotional problems are enormous. But rather than acknowledge that we are just embarking on understanding, we continue to label patients "schizophrenic," "manic-depressive," and "insane," as if in those words we had captured the essence of understanding. The facts of the matter are that we have known for a long time that diagnoses are often not useful or reliable, but we have nevertheless continued to use them. We now know that we cannot distinguish insanity from sanity. It is depressing to consider how that information will be used.

Not merely depressing, but frightening. How many people, one wonders, are sane but not recognized as such in our psychiatric institutions? How many have been needlessly stripped of their privileges of citizenship, from the right to vote and drive to that of handling their own accounts? How many have feigned insanity in order to avoid the criminal consequences of their behavior, and conversely, how many would rather stand trial than live interminably in a psychiatric hospital—but are wrongly thought to be mentally ill? How many have been stigmatized by well-intentioned, but nevertheless erroneous, diagnoses? On the last point, recall again that a "type 2 error" in psychiatric diagnosis does not have the same consequences it does in medical diagnosis. A diagnosis of cancer that has been found to be in error is cause for celebration. But psychiatric diagnoses are rarely found to be in error. The label sticks, a mark of inadequacy forever.

ENDNOTES

[1] P. Ash, *Journal of Abnormal and Social Psychology* 44 (1949): 272; A. T. Beck, *American Journal of Psychiatry* 119 (1962): 210; A. T. Boisen, *Psychiatry* 2 (1938): 233; J. Kreitman, *Journal of Mental Science* 107 (1961): 876; N. Kreitman, P. Sainsbury, J. Morrisey, J. Towers, and J. Scrivener, *Journal of Mental Science* 107 (1961): 887; H. O. Schmitt and C. P. Fonda, *Journal of Abnormal Social Psychology* 52 (1956): 262; W. Seeman, *Journal of Nervous Mental Disorders* 118 (1953): 541. For analysis of these artifacts and summaries of the disputes, see J. Zubin, *Annual Review of Psychology* 18 (1967): 373; L. Phillips and J. G. Draguns, *Annual Review of Psychology* 22 (1971): 447.

[2] R. Benedict, *Journal of General Psychology* 10 (1934): 59.

[3] See in this regard Howard Becker, *Outsiders: Studies in the Sociology of Deviance* (New York: Free Press, 1963); B. M. Braginsky, D. D. Braginsky, and K. Ring, *Methods of Madness: The Mental Hospital As a Last Resort* (New York: Holt, Rinehart and Winston, 1969); G. M. Crocetti and P. V. Lemkau, *American Sociological Review* 30 (1965): 577; Erving Goffman, *Behavior in Public Places* (New York: Free Press, 1964); R. D. Laing, *The Divided Self: A Study of Sanity and Madness* (Chicago: Quadrangle, 1960); D. L. Phillips, *American Sociological Review* 28 (1963): 963; T. R. Sarbin, *Psychology Today* 6 (1972): 18; E. Schur, *American Journal of Sociology* 75 (1969): 309; Thomas Szasz, *The Myth of Mental Illness: Foundations of a Theory of Mental Illness* (New York: Hoeber Harper, 1963). For a critique of some of these views, see W. R. Gave, *American Sociological Review* 35 (1970): 873.

[4] Erving Goffman, *Asylums* (Garden City, NY: Doubleday, 1961).

[5] T. J. Scheff, *Being Mentally Ill: A Sociological Theory* (Chicago: Aldine, 1966).

[6] Data from a ninth pseudopatient are not incorporated in this report because, although his sanity went undetected, he falsified aspects of his personal history, including his marital status and parental relationships. His experimental behaviors therefore were not identical to those of the other pseudopatients.

[7] A. Barry, *Bellevue Is a State of Mind* (New York: Harcourt Brace Jovanovich, 1971); I. Belknap, *Human Problems of a State Mental Hospital* (New York: McGraw-Hill, 1956); W. Caudill, F. C. Redlich, H. R. Gilmore, and E. B. Brody, *American Journal of Orthopsychiatry* 22 (1952): 314; A. R. Goldman, R. H. Bohr, and T. A. Steinberg, *Professional Psychology* 1 (1970): 427; *Roche Report* 1, no. 13 (1971): 8.

[8] Beyond the personal difficulties that the pseudopatient is likely to experience in the hospital, there are legal and social ones that, combined, require considerable attention before entry. For example, once admitted to a psychiatric institution, it is difficult, if not impossible, to be discharged on short notice, state law to the contrary notwithstanding. I was not sensitive to these difficulties at the outset of the project, nor to the personal and situational emergencies that can arise, but later a writ of habeas corpus was prepared for each of the entering pseudopatients and an attorney was kept "on call" during every hospitalization. I am grateful to John Kaplan and Robert Bartels for legal advice and assistance in these matters.

[9] However distasteful such concealment is, it was a necessary first step to examining these questions. Without concealment, there would have been no way to know how valid these experiences were; nor was there any way of knowing whether whatever detections occurred were a tribute to the diagnostic acumen of the staff or to the hospital's rumor network. Obviously, since my concerns are general ones that cut across individual hospitals and staffs, I have respected their anonymity and have eliminated clues that might lead to their identification.

[10] Interestingly, of the 12 admissions, 11 were diagnosed as schizophrenic and one, with the identical symptomatology, as manic-depressive psychosis. This diagnosis has a more favorable prognosis, and it was given by the only private hospital in our sample. On the relations between social class and psychiatric diagnosis, see A. B. Hollinghead and F. C. Redlich, *Social Class and Mental Illness: A Community Study* (New York: Wiley, 1958).

[11] It is possible, of course, that patients have quite broad latitudes in diagnosis and therefore are inclined to call many people sane, even those whose behavior is patently aberrant. However, although we have no hard data on this matter, it was our distinct impression that this was not the case. In many instances, patients not only singled us out for attention, but came to imitate our behaviors and styles.

[12] Scheff, *Being Mentally Ill.*

[13] J. Cumming and E. Cumming, *Community Mental Health* 1 (1965): 135; A. Farina and K. Ring, *Journal of Abnormal Psychology* 40 (1965): 47; H. E. Freeman and O. G. Simmons, *The Mental Patient Comes Home* (New York: Wiley, 1963); W. J. Johannsen, *Mental Hygiene* 53 (1969): 218; A. S. Linsky, *Social Psychology* 5 (1970): 166.

[14] S. E. Asch, *Abnormal Social Psychology* 41 (1946): 258; S. E. Asch, *Social Psychology* (New York: Prentice-Hall, 1952).

[15] See also I. N. Mensch and J. Wishner, *Journal of Personality* 16 (1947): 188; J. Wishner, *Psychological Review* 67 (1960): 96; J. S. Bruner and K. R. Tagiuri in *Handbook of Social Psychology*, vol. 2, ed. G. Lindzey (Cambridge, MA: Addison-Wesley, 1954), pp. 634–54; J. S. Bruner, D. Shapiro, and R. Tagiuri in *Person Perception and Interpersonal Behavior*, ed. R. Tagiuri and L. Petrullo (Stanford, CA: Stanford University Press, 1958), pp. 277–88.

[16] For an example of a similar self-fulfilling prophecy, in this instance dealing with the "central" trait of intelligence, see R. Rosenthal and L. Jacobson, *Pygmalion in the Classroom* (New York: Holt, Rinehart and Winston, 1968).

[17] Scheff, *Being Mentally Ill.*

[18] E. Zigler and L. Phillips, *Journal of Abnormal and Social Psychology* 63 (1961): 69. See also R. K. Freudenberg and J. P. Robertson, *A.M.A. Archives of Neurological Psychiatry* 76 (1956): 14.

[19] W. Mischel, *Personality and Assessment* (New York: Wiley, 1968).

7

FINDING OUT HOW
THE SOCIAL WORLD WORKS

MICHAEL SCHWALBE

Most sociologists agree that the best way to learn about research is through hands-on experience gained by conducting a study. The research process, examined in the next three readings, often turns up new questions and challenges for the researcher. The first reading is by Michael Schwalbe, a professor of sociology at North Carolina State University, and is excerpted from his 1998 book, *The Sociologically Examined Life: Pieces of the Conversation.* In this selection, Schwalbe explains the advantages of utilizing systematic research to study the social world. Schwalbe also summarizes the kinds of questions sociologists often ask and argues that it is important to be "sociologically mindful" whenever addressing social research.

Without looking up any statistics, can you say whether there are more poor black people or poor white people in the United States? A common mistake, because blacks are often represented as being poor, is to say that there are more poor black people than poor white people. But blacks make up only about 12 percent of the U.S. population. And even though the rate of poverty is higher among blacks (about 30 percent) than among whites (about 15 percent), there are so many more white people in the United States that whites still make up the majority of those living in poverty. . . . A few facts and a bit of logic make this easy to figure out.

So logical deduction is one way to know things, or to find out the implications of what we know. Much of what we know comes straight from others. It is passed on to us by parents, teachers, friends, and so on. We can also know things from personal experience or observation, from systematic research, and from mystical revelation. It is possible, too, that some knowledge is instinctive, as, for example, when an infant "knows" that it should suck on whatever is put in its mouth.

It is interesting to think about where our knowledge comes from. What usually concerns us more, however, is how to be sure that our knowledge is valid and reliable. Each source of knowledge has limitations in these respects. Part of being sociologically mindful is being aware of these limitations.

Logical deduction, for instance, is a fine way to elaborate our knowledge—except that if our *premises* are wrong, then our conclusions will also be wrong; we will simply reason our way to further ignorance. One strength of logical deduction, however, is that others can check up on our assumptions and our reasoning, and thus correct us if we go astray.

Relying on what others tell us is necessary and is often a good way to learn, but how do we know that what others tell us is right? Surely you have had the experience of being told—by a parent, teacher, or mentor— something that later turned out to be wrong. Then there is the problem of deciding between different versions of the truth that come to us from sources that seem equally credible. How do we decide who is right?

Personal experience and observation are good sources of knowledge, except that it is easy to misjudge and overgeneralize from these sources. For example, your own observations might tell you that the sun revolves around the earth, or that all Lithuanians are slobs because both of the Lithuanians you've met in your life were a bit slobby, or that there is no ruling class in the United States because you've never seen it gathered in one place, or that crime is rising because you were just robbed. The problem in each case is not that you don't know what you've seen, but that what you've seen isn't enough to support the conclusion you reached. . . .

Advantages of Systematic Research

Careful research is perhaps the best way to create valid and reliable knowledge about the state of the social world and how it works. It is the best way for several reasons. First, by using standard, widely accepted means of finding things out, we can control personal biases. If we can do this, we are less likely to mistake what we would like to be true for what is really true.

Suppose, for example, I believe that democratic work organizations are better than authoritarian ones and would therefore like to believe that they are also more efficient. My bias would be to look only for evidence that supports my belief. But if I use a standard method of assessing efficiency, and use it carefully and fairly to compare democratic and authoritarian work organizations, I will have to accept whatever I find. My bias would thus be canceled out, or at least controlled.

Second, research can get us beyond personal experience and casual observation, because to re-*search* is to look beyond what is obvious to us from where we stand. It is to look for ideas and information that might challenge the common sense that gets us through daily life. It means considering the quality and correctness of knowledge created by others, even if we find their knowledge irritating. All this can be difficult, because our usual habit is to settle comfortably into believing that we already know what is right.

A third reason for doing research is that it lets us check up on each other. If we use methods that others agree are proper, they can look at our results and say, "Hmmm, yes, you did it right; these results must be correct." Or they can say, "Ah, you went astray here at this point, so your conclusions are not trustworthy." We can make the same judgments when others offer us knowledge they have created. In this way, by working together, we can do better at dispelling illusions and, in the long run, creating knowledge that is valid and reliable.

Perhaps you noticed that I had only good things to say about knowledge that comes from research. Does this mean that one should accept as true whatever is published in a scientific or scholarly journal? No. Knowledge from any source should be critically interrogated. Careful research is just a way to avoid problems that are common when knowledge is created in other ways. And if research is not done properly, it can yield as much foolishness as any other method.

The larger point here is that we should be mindful, to the extent we can, of where our own knowledge comes from. We can be mindful in this way by asking ourselves how we know what we claim to know. Is some piece of knowledge a result of logical deduction? (If so, have we reasoned correctly? How do we know that our premises are correct?) Is some piece of knowledge a hand-me-down from others? (If so, where did *their* knowledge come from? How can we be sure it is correct?) Is some piece of knowledge a result of personal experience or observation? (If so, are we claiming to know more than our personal experience can warrant? Is it possible that we have observed only what we want to believe is true, or that our observations have been limited in some crucial way?)

The point of asking ourselves these questions is not to arrive at a paralyzing state of doubt about what we know, but to more wisely decide how much faith to put in what we know. If we can do this, we can open ourselves to new knowledge without fear of surrendering our minds to yet another fishy belief system. Being sociologically mindful, we can get a better view of what is coming at us by way of new knowledge and where it is coming from. We can also see what is worth catching.

The Kinds of Questions We Can Ask

All attempts to create knowledge are responses to questions, and knowledge must be created in a way that suits the question. For example, if you asked, "How much does this book weigh?" the proper way to get an answer is to weigh it. How many words does it contain? Count them. Will it fly like a boomerang? Give it the right kind of throw and observe the result. These are *empirical* questions, which means that they are answerable by measuring, counting, or looking to see what happens.

But suppose you asked, "Is the cover of this book beautiful?" What then? You could ask ten artists for their opinions. What if seven said it was ugly, two were ambivalent, and one thought it was beautiful? In this case no measuring stick will settle the matter, because you have asked an *aesthetic* question—a question about what is subjectively pleasing to the senses—and aesthetic questions are not answerable with data. We can try to say why something strikes us as ugly or beautiful, tasteful or crass, but no evidence or logic will prove us right and others wrong.

Here is another kind of question: Was it worthwhile for me to write this [article], considering that I might have been doing other useful things with my time? Again, this is not an empirical question, since there is no way to get an answer by measuring, counting, or observing. It is a *moral* question, since it calls for a judgment about what is right to do. I could say why it seemed to me a good thing to write this [article], but my reasons would be based on moral precepts and on my sense of how the future is likely to unfold. There is no data I can show, no standard analysis, to prove that my answer is right. All I can do is to offer reasonable arguments.

There are also questions of *interpretation,* the most simple of which is "What does this thing mean?" Such questions often arise when we confront works of art. We might look at a painting or read a novel and wonder what the writer or artist wanted us to understand. But any fact, object, gesture, phrase, or behavior—anything that has meaning—can raise a question of interpretation.

Sometimes we can get an answer by asking for clarification. Perhaps the writer or artist can tell us what s/he meant (although writers and artists can't always fully explain what their work means). Or perhaps there is expert opinion available to help us make sense of things. Other times there might be so much ambiguity that no clear interpretation can be nailed down. All anyone can do then is to give reasons to support the plausibility of a particular interpretation.

You can perhaps see now that research is better suited to answering some questions than others. It is a good way to answer empirical questions. It can also be useful for answering interpretive questions, because we can sometimes dig up evidence that supports the plausibility of an interpretation. And although it is wise to search for ideas and information to help guide our moral and aesthetic judgments, research will not tell us which judgments are correct.

It is good to be mindful of the kind of question we are facing. Sometimes we get into fruitless debates because we are not clear about this. There is no point, for example, in trading opinions about the correct answer to a simple empirical question. Are crime rates rising? Go to the library and look up the best answer you can find. If it is the answer to an empirical question that is in dispute, we should stop disputing and go get the answer.

Interpreting the Answers to Empirical Questions

Sometimes the answer to an empirical question can create a great deal of interpretive trouble. For example, to ask "What are the rates of poverty among blacks and whites living in the United States?" is to ask an empirical question. We can look up the answers because someone else (the U.S. Census Bureau) has already done the counting and the arithmetic. As I noted earlier, the poverty rate among blacks is about 30 percent and among whites it is about 15 percent (these figures fluctuate somewhat and can also vary depending on how poverty is defined). But what do these figures mean? How can we interpret them?

I once presented these figures during a discussion of racial inequality. The class suddenly got quiet. No one wanted to comment on the meaning of the percentages. When I pressed for some reaction, a white student said, "I think no one is talking because the figures are embarrassing." Did he mean that the figures were embarrassing because they pointed out a failure to overcome racial inequality? I wasn't sure, so I asked him to be more explicit. "The figures are embarrassing," he said with some hesitation, "to black students." I was baffled by this.

After further conversation, it became clear that the student who spoke about the figures being "embarrassing to black students" saw the figures as evidence of black inferiority. His presumption was that the poverty rate of a group was an indicator of the capability of people in that group. I saw the figures as evidence of racism and discrimination. In this case, the facts about poverty rates were clear, but they did not speak for themselves. The same facts lent themselves to nearly opposite interpretations.

To support my interpretation, I might have said that in the United States, millions of people, black and white, are poor because they can't find jobs that pay a decent wage, or they can't find jobs at all. Sometimes the jobs available in an area don't match people's skills. Or else the jobs disappear when employers move factories to foreign countries where they can pay workers less. And so people can end up poor, or very nearly poor, even though they are able and willing to work.

I might have added that the higher poverty rate among blacks is a result of factories being closed down in inner cities in the North, where a lot of the black population is concentrated. It's a result of schools that do not serve black children well. It's a result of discrimination in hiring and network advantages enjoyed by whites. In some cases, part of the problem is a lack of marketable skills, but that's because access to education and training is limited, not because people's natural abilities are limited.

I might have said all this—and probably did—but was it enough to establish my interpretation as correct? Although I am sure that my statement helped some people see why the white student's interpretation was wrong, others who preferred to hold onto that interpretation could point out, correctly, that I had not really *proven*—by anything I'd said or any evidence I'd shown—that blacks were not inferior to whites. All I had done was to suggest that "black inferiority" was not a plausible explanation—if other things were taken into account, if those other things were true, and if no significant counterevidence was being overlooked.

My interpretation was not, however, a matter of opinion. My interpretation was based on previously answered empirical questions. Have jobs disappeared in areas heavily populated by blacks? Do employers discriminate against blacks? Do whites enjoy network advantages when it comes to getting jobs? Do schools serve black kids as well as they serve white kids? Is there a lack of access to education and job training? With knowledge of the answers to these empirical questions, we can determine which interpretation of the poverty-rate figures is most likely to be correct. . . .

Mindful Skepticism

Once, during a discussion of the benefits of education, a black woman said she was outraged to learn that, on the average, a high-school diploma was likely to yield higher earnings (by mid-life) for a white man than a college degree was likely to yield for a black woman. When she said this, another student, a white male said, "I don't believe it. How can you possibly know that?" Before she could answer, I said, "She probably read the article that was assigned for today. If you look on page 34 in the text, you'll see a table that shows what she's referring to." He paged through his book and found the table. After studying it for a few moments, he harumphed and said, "Well, anybody can make up numbers."

As a teacher, I was irritated by this response, because it meant this: "No matter what information I am presented with, if it does not suit my prior beliefs, if it does not make me comfortable, I will discount it, so I can continue to believe what I want to believe." An attitude like this leaves little room for education to make a dent. I wondered why this student would bother to study anything at all, or read any books at all, if he was so intent on being unchanged.

And yet I could not say that his attitude was entirely foolish. Numbers are often cooked up to mislead us, and numbers can be wrong because of honest mistakes, so it is reasonable to be skeptical of numbers, whatever the source. Is there any way to tell which numbers are right? Yes, it can be done; it just requires training. Since most people do not have such training, however, it is understandable that they might say, "I can't tell what's right or wrong, so I'm going to treat all statistics as hogwash."

This is clearly not a mindful response to the situation. It is like saying, "I can't read, so I am going to treat all books as hogwash." It would be better to learn to read and to learn also what is necessary to distinguish the hog from the wash. This is hard but not impossible. What helps is being mindfully, rather than indiscriminately, skeptical of new information.

One of the difficulties in learning about the social world is that we must rely on information created and filtered by others. We can't check out everything for ourselves, even if we know how. This being the case, we must pay attention to how information (in the form of words or numbers) is created, by whom, for what purposes. We must ask, Who stands to benefit if this information is accepted as true? Being mindful in these ways puts us on alert against fraud, yet it does not cut us off from learning.

We should also seek alternative views, since this can help us see the limits of our own knowledge. A bit of conventional knowledge—that "Columbus discovered America," for instance—seems simple and true until an alternative is suggested: "Columbus launched a brutal invasion of an already populated continent." This is not just a different way to describe the same events, but a different way of seeing what those events were. If we try out this alternative view, we can look at what passes for conventional knowledge and see that it is, at the very least, contestable.

What is conventional and what is alternative depends, of course, on where you stand. A view that you consider alternative might seem conventional to someone else. Recognizing this relativity of perspectives is part of being sociologically mindful. But there is more to it. Being sociologically mindful, we can also see that these alternative perspectives create the possibility of understanding the world more fully, because they give us more angles from which to view it.

Perhaps by looking for and seriously considering alternative views—and there are always multiple alternatives—we will eventually get closer to a better version of the truth. That is something to aim for. In the meantime, it is wise to consider alternative views because doing so can help us see how competing versions of the truth are created. In this way we can learn more about how others see the world, how we have come to see the world, and what more we might see if we are willing to suffer a bit of uncertainty.

Partial Truth and Inevitable Uncertainty

The student who said, "Anyone can make up numbers," did not want to suffer uncertainty. Perhaps he was afraid that if he let go of what he already believed, he would end up lost, not knowing what to believe. He did not know how to be mindfully skeptical.

Part of what we fear is losing what we think is the truth. If we are sociologically mindful, however, we know that we never possess the absolute, complete truth. What we have is a head full of humanly-created images, representations, and accounts that seem to pretty well make sense of the world as we know it. Why not stand ready, as we see and experience more of the world, to invent or borrow new ways of making sense?

If we can admit that there is more to the world than we have yet seen or experienced—and more than we could see and experience in a lifetime—perhaps we can also say to ourselves, "In anticipation of learning more about the world, as I surely will do, I will treat my current beliefs as provisional and explore alternative ways of making sense of things, because one of these ways might come in handy some day."

To adopt this stance toward knowledge does not mean flitting from one belief to another. It is like the deliberate movement of wading upstream in a river. To move ahead you must take gentle steps, making sure of your footing before you shift your weight forward. You must stay flexible and lean into the current. If you rush or lose concentration, you will end up all wet. So you pay attention, moving mindfully when it makes sense to move.

Being sociologically mindful, we know that we never get to the whole truth about the social world. All the truths that we invent or borrow—all the images, representations, and accounts we come upon—are partial views of a whole that is unknowable because it is always changing in ways that run ahead of our ability to understand. We thus need not fear that new ideas and information will wrest the truth from us. They might, however, give us a larger, more complex, and unruly truth to contend with, and that can be unsettling.

For some people it is scary to think of never being sure of having it right. Imagining that one has it right, now and forever, is comforting. The problem, however, is that other people see things differently, and when conflicts arise, others will neither happily conform to the version of truth that comforts us nor lay down their knowledge to embrace ours. And so, if we want to understand and get along with others, we must be willing to seriously consider their perspectives and to tolerate the uncertainty that comes with this openness.

Perpetual Inquiry and Conversation

I have been recommending a mindful skepticism toward all knowledge—that which we already possess and that which strikes us as new and strange. In this way we can avoid the dead ends of nihilism ("There is no truth. Anyone can make up numbers. You might as well believe what you want.") and fanaticism ("There is only one truth and my people know it! All other beliefs are false or insane!"). These are dead ends because they make conversation pointless and offer no hope of resolving conflict.

A mindful skepticism toward knowledge keeps us inquiring, observing, and trying to make better sense of things; it keeps us trying to create more accurate, complete, and useful representations; it keeps us open to new information; and it keeps us connected to others as we try to do all this. Conversation is both a means to this end and an end in itself—at least it is if we believe that it is better to try to understand others than to ignore or to hurt them. Be mindfully skeptical, then, of all knowledge, including that which I have offered in this [article]. After fair consideration, take and use what is helpful for making sense and for keeping the conversation going.

Curiosity, Care, and Hope

If you could live forever, would life get boring? Some people might say, "Yes, because it would be the same old thing, day after day, forever." But here is another possibility: Life would get more *interesting* because as one learned more about the world, one would see more complexities, more mysteries, more problems to be solved, and more things to be done. Why might some people see life as holding such great promise? I think it is because they are full of curiosity, care, and hope.

If there is no curiosity about the nature of things and how they work, then the world will seem like a drab backdrop against which life is endured until it is over. If there is no care about anything outside one's self or beyond one's time, then it will seem pointless to worry about things that don't matter for getting through the day. Without hope, it will seem pointless to invest much effort in analyzing the social world. So it seems that we need curiosity, care, and hope to spark a desire to pay attention to the social world, to try to understand it as it is, and to use this awareness to pursue change.

Sometimes the conditions of people's lives do not inspire much curiosity, care, or hope. There might be so much day-to-day hardship and sameness, and so few prospects for change, that people limit their attention to each day's tasks and fleeting amusements. Other people might be so comfortable that they too lose interest in critically examining the world beyond their cocoon of privilege. Under these conditions, people are not likely to develop much sociological mindfulness. Then again, perhaps the process can be turned around. Perhaps a lesson in mindfulness can spark curiosity, care, and hope.

Being mindful that the world is a complex and mysterious place, and that penetrating these mysteries is satisfying, ought to arouse our curiosity. Being mindful of how our actions affect others' experiences of joy and suffering ought to encourage feelings of care. And being mindful of how human action creates the world ought to give us hope that we can make the world a better place. Obviously these are expressions of my own wishes, yet I have tried to do more than put them forth as wishes.

I have tried to show how much there is to be curious about: the many connections, patterns, contingencies, appearances, and interdependencies that constitute the social world; all the ways that people try to solve problems together and end up creating cultural habits; the ways that some people create social arrangements to benefit themselves at the expense of others; and all the ways that people create the images, accounts, and representations that make up our knowledge of social reality. We could study these matters forever and always be learning something new.

I have also shown that sociological mindfulness gives us reasons for caring. The more we pay attention to and understand connections, interdependencies, and contingencies, the better we can see how *our* ways of thinking and acting affect *others'* chances for good lives. We can see, too, that what others think and do affects us as well. Being sociologically mindful helps us see how this is true in a way that goes beyond what is obvious in everyday life as we interact with others who are close to us.

And just as we care about the others who are close to us, we can, if we are sociologically mindful, come to care about the distant others whose lives are intertwined with ours. At the least, we can thus see new reasons for caring about the social arrangements that bind us to others, for better or worse.

Perhaps you are thinking, "What about hope? It seems that 'being sociologically mindful' just makes us aware of how messed up the social world is. How is *that* supposed to inspire hope?" Actually, mere awareness of problems—inequalities, exploitation, the suffering of others—is not supposed to inspire hope. It is supposed to inspire outrage and a desire to change things. Unfortunately, when awareness of problems is combined with feelings of powerlessness, the result is often despair.

Being sociologically mindful, however, we know that the social world is, for all its seeming solidity, a social construction. All the ideas, habits, arrangements, and so on that make up the social world are human creations. We know, too, that the social world keeps going as it does because of the beliefs people share and because of how they keep doing things together on an everyday basis. If we are mindful of all this, we can see that the problems that exist now need not exist forever; they are all within our power to overcome.

Of course it will not be easy, because many powerful people benefit from the arrangements that cause problems for so many others. There is also the problem of changing the arrangements that are devised to keep things from changing. Yet the possibility of change always exists, if only people can organize to make it happen, and that is a good reason for hope.

Mindfulness can get us out of the rut of despair by reminding us that we cannot change a society overnight by ourselves. It is silly to say, "I failed to bring about a revolution this week, even though I tried very hard. That proves it's hopeless. I guess I'll give up and just march along with everyone else." Yet many people fall into this kind of trap. The way out is through awareness that change requires working with others to challenge existing arrangements and to create new ones. We cannot do it alone.

There is no point in despairing because we cannot single-handedly change the world. Of course we can't. We can, however, try to find or organize others who recognize a need for change and are willing to work for it. It is amazing how being in community with others can help alleviate the despair that arises from failed dreams of heroism.

Sociological mindfulness also reminds us that we *can* change a small part of the social world single-handedly. If we treat others with more respect and compassion, if we refuse to participate in re-creating inequalities even in little ways, if we raise questions about official representations of reality, if we refuse to work in destructive industries, then we are making change. We do not have to join a group or organize a protest to make these kinds of changes. We can make them on our own, by deciding to live differently.

Perhaps our modest efforts will reverberate with others and inspire them to live differently. Or perhaps no one will notice, or they will notice but think we are strange. And so you might think, "If no one is going to notice that I am a superior moral being, then what is the point? Why bother to be different and risk ridicule?" That is one way to look at it. Being sociologically mindful, however, suggests a different thought: "I cannot be sure that *anything* I do will change things for the better, yet I can be sure that if I do not at least *try,* then I will fail to do what I think is right and will be contributing to keeping things the same. Therefore I will opt to do what is right, whether much or little comes of it."

In the end, sociological mindfulness must be about more than studying how the social world works. It must also do more than inspire curiosity, care, and hope—although these we cannot do without. If it is to be worth practicing, sociological mindfulness must help us change ourselves and our ways of doing things together so that we can live more peacefully and productively with others, without exploitation, disrespect, and inequality. Sociological mindfulness is a way to see where we are and what needs to be done. It is a path to heartful membership in a conversation that ought to have no end.

RELATED READINGS

Kuhn, Thomas. 1970. *The Structure of Scientific Revolutions.* 2d ed. Chicago: University of Chicago Press.

Lofland, John and Lyn H. Lofland. 1995. *Analyzing Social Settings.* 3d ed. Belmont, CA: Wadsworth.

Maxwell, Nicholas. 1984. *From Knowledge to Wisdom.* New York: Basil Blackwell.

O'Hear, Anthony. 1989. *An Introduction to the Philosophy of Science.* New York: Oxford University Press.

Thomas, Jim. 1993. *Doing Critical Ethnography.* Newbury Park, CA: Sage.

Winch, Peter. 1958. *The Idea of a Social Science and Its Relations to Philosophy.* London: Routledge and Kegan Paul.

8

INTERPERSONAL DYNAMICS IN A SIMULATED PRISON

CRAIG HANEY • W. CURTIS BANKS
• PHILIP G. ZIMBARDO

Ethical questions concerning social research are a rather recent discussion in the history of social science. It was not until the 1960s and early 1970s that we began to question research protocols and the effects of social experiments on humans. This second reading in the social research section, by Craig Haney, W. Curtis Banks, and Philip G. Zimbardo, reviews the research methodology used in Zimbardo's famous prison study conducted in 1971. Zimbardo, a professor emeritus of psychology at Stanford University, was fascinated with the social dynamics of prisons, especially the social interaction that takes place between guards and prisoners. The selection below takes us inside the research world of the prison environment and reveals many ethical and logistical concerns about using social experiments to study human behavior.

Although we have passed through many periods of so-called prison "reform," in which physical conditions within prisons have improved and in which the rhetoric of rehabilitation has replaced the language of punitive incarceration, the social institution of prison has continued to fail. On purely pragmatic grounds, there is substantial evidence that prisons really

Craig Haney, W. Curtis Banks, and Philip G. Zimbardo, "Interpersonal Dynamics in a Simulated Prison" [abridged] from *International Journal of Criminology and Penology* 1 (1973): 69–97. Reprinted with the permission of Craig Haney.

neither "rehabilitate" nor act as a deterrent to future crime—in America, recidivism rates upwards of 75 percent speak quite decisively to these criteria. And, to perpetuate what is additionally an economic failure, American taxpayers alone must provide an expenditure for "corrections" of 1.5 billion dollars annually. On humanitarian grounds as well, prisons have failed: our mass media are increasingly filled with accounts of atrocities committed daily, man against man, in reaction to the penal system or in the name of it.

Attempts at explaining the deplorable condition of our penal system, and its dehumanizing effects upon prisoners and guards, characteristically focus upon what can be called the *dispositional hypothesis*. Rarely expressed explicitly, it is central to a prevalent nonconscious ideology: The state of the social institution of prison is due to the "nature" of the people who administrate it, or the "nature" of the people who populate it, or both. The dispositional hypothesis has been embraced by the proponents of the prison status quo (blaming violence on the criminal dispositions of prisoners), as well as by its critics (attributing brutality of guards and staff to their sadistic personality structures). The appealing simplicity of this proposition localizes the source of prison riots, recidivism, and corruption in these "bad seeds" and not in the conditions of the "prison soil." The system itself goes on essentially unchanged, its basic structure unexamined and unchallenged.

A critical evaluation of the dispositional hypothesis, however, cannot be made directly through observation in existing prison settings, since such naturalistic observation necessarily confounds the acute effects of the environment with the chronic characteristics of the inmate and guard populations. To partial out the situational effects of the prison environment per se from those attributable to a priori dispositions of its inhabitants requires a research strategy in which a "new" prison is constructed, comparable in its fundamental social-psychological milieu to existing prison systems but entirely populated by individuals who are undifferentiated in all essential dimensions from the rest of society.

Such was the approach taken in the present empirical study, namely, to create a prisonlike situation in which the guards and inmates were initially comparable and characterized as being "psychologically healthy," and then to observe the patterns of behavior which resulted and to record the cognitive, emotional, and attitudinal reactions that emerged.

No specific hypotheses were advanced other than the general one that assignment to the treatment of "guard" or "prisoner" would result in significantly different reactions on behavioral measures of interaction, emotional measures of mood state and pathology, and attitudes toward self, as well as other indices of coping and adaptation to this extreme situation.

Method

The effects of playing the role of "guard" or "prisoner" were studied in the context of an experimental simulation of a prison environment. The research design was a relatively simple one, involving as it did only a single treatment variable, the random assignment to either a "guard" or "prisoner" condition. These roles were enacted over an extended period of time (nearly one week) within an environment which had been physically constructed to closely resemble a prison. Central to the methodology of creating and maintaining the psychological state of imprisonment was the functional simulation of significant properties of "real prison life" (established through information from former inmates, correctional personnel, and texts).

Subjects

The 22 subjects who participated in the experiment were selected from an initial pool of 75 respondents who answered a newspaper ad asking for male volunteers to participate in a psychological study of "prison life," in return for payment of $15 per day. Those who responded to the notice completed an extensive questionnaire concerning their family background, physical and mental health history, prior experience, and attitudinal propensities with respect to any possible sources of psychopathology (including their involvements in crime). Each respondent who completed the background questionnaire was interviewed by one of two experimenters. Finally, the 24 subjects who were judged to be *most stable* (physically and mentally) were selected to participate in the study. On a random basis, half of the subjects were assigned the role of "guard," half were assigned to the role of "prisoner."

The subjects were normal, healthy males attending colleges throughout the United States who were in the Stanford [University] area during the summer. They were largely of middle-class background and Caucasians (with the exception of one Asian subject). Initially they were strangers to each other, a selection precaution taken to avoid the disruption of any preexisting friendship patterns and to mitigate against any transfer of previously established relationships or patterns of behavior into the experimental situation.

Procedure

Role Instructions All subjects had been told that they would be randomly assigned either the guard or the prisoner role, and all had voluntarily agreed to play either role for $15 per day for up to two weeks. They signed a contract guaranteeing a minimally adequate diet, clothing, housing, and medical care, as well as the financial remuneration, in return for their stated "intention" of serving in the assigned role for the duration of the study.

It was made explicit in the contract that those assigned to be prisoners should expect to be under surveillance (have little or no privacy) and to have some of their basic civil rights suspended during their imprisonment. They were aware that physical abuse was explicitly prohibited. Subjects were given no other information about what to expect and no instructions about behavior "appropriate" for the prisoner role. Those actually assigned to this treatment were informed by phone to be available at their place of residence on a given Sunday, when we would start the experiment.

The subjects assigned to be guards attended an orientation meeting on the day prior to the induction of the prisoners. At this time they were introduced to the principal investigators, the "superintendent" of the prison (P.G.Z.) and an undergraduate research assistant who assumed the administrative role of "warden." They were told that we were attempting to simulate a prison environment within the limits imposed by pragmatic and ethical considerations. Their assigned task was to "maintain the reasonable degree of order within the prison necessary for its effective functioning," although the specifics of how this duty might be implemented were not explicitly detailed. To involve the subjects in their roles even before the first prisoner was incarcerated, the guards assisted in the final phases of completing the prison complex—putting the cots in the cells, posting signs on the walls, setting up the guards' quarters, and moving furniture, water coolers, and refrigerators.

The guards generally believed that we were interested primarily in studying the behavior of prisoners. Of course, we were also concerned with effects which enacting the role of guard in this environment would have on their behavior and subjective states. For this reason, they were given few explicit instructions on what it meant to be a guard and were left to "fill in" their own definitions of the role. A notable exception was the explicit and categorical prohibition against the use of physical punishment or aggression, which we emphasized from the outset of the study.

The prisoner subjects remained in the mock prison 24 hours a day for the duration of the study. Three were arbitrarily assigned to each of the three cells, and two others were on standby call at their homes. The guard subjects worked on three-man, eight-hour shifts, remaining in the prison environment only during their work shifts and going about their usual routines at other times. The one subject assigned to be a standby guard withdrew just before the simulation phase began. Final data analysis, then, is based on 11 prisoners and 10 guards.

Physical Aspects of the Prison   The prison was built in a 35-foot section of a basement corridor in the psychology building at Stanford University. It was partitioned by two fabricated walls, one of which was fitted with the only entrance door to the cell block; the other contained a small observation screen. Three small cells (6 × 9 feet) were made from converted laboratory rooms by replacing the usual doors with steel-barred doors painted black and removing all furniture. A cot (with mattress, sheet, and pillow) for each prisoner was the only furniture in the cells. A small closet across from the cells served as a solitary confinement facility; its dimensions were extremely small (2 × 2 × 7 feet), and it was unlit.

In addition, several rooms in an adjacent wing of the building were used as guards' quarters (to change in and out of uniform or for rest and relaxation), a bedroom for the "warden" and "superintendent," and an interview-testing room. Concealed video recording equipment was located in the testing room and behind the observation screen at one end of the "yard," where there was also sufficient space for several observers.

Uniforms   In order to promote feelings of anonymity in the subjects, each group was issued uniforms. For the guards, this consisted of plain khaki shirts and trousers, a whistle, a police nightstick (wooden baton), and reflecting sunglasses which made eye contact impossible. The prisoners' uniforms were loosely fitting muslin smocks with an identification number on front and back. A light chain and lock were placed around one ankle. On their feet they wore rubber sandals, and their hair was covered with a nylon stocking made into a cap. Each prisoner was also issued a toothbrush, soap, soapdish, towel, and bed linen. No personal belongings were allowed in the cells. The outfitting of both prisoners and guards in this manner served to enhance group identity and reduce individual uniqueness within the two groups.

Induction Process   With the cooperation of the Palo Alto City Police Department, all of the subjects assigned to the prisoner treatment were unexpectedly "arrested" at their residences. A police officer charged them with either suspicion of burglary or armed robbery, advised them of their legal rights, handcuffed them, thoroughly searched them (often as curious neighbors looked on), and carried them off to the police station in the rear of the police car. At the station they went through the standard booking routines of being fingerprinted, having an identification file prepared, and then being placed in a detention cell. Subsequently, each prisoner was blindfolded and driven by one of the experimenters and a subject-guard to our mock prison. Throughout the entire arrest procedure, the police officers involved maintained a formal, serious attitude, avoiding answering any questions of clarification as to the relation of this "arrest" to the mock prison study.

Upon arrival at our experimental prison, each prisoner was stripped, sprayed with a delousing preparation (deodorant spray), and made to stand alone, naked, in the cell yard before being outfitted. After being given their uniforms and having an I.D. picture ("mug shot") taken, each prisoner was put in his cell.

Administrative Routine   When all the cells were occupied, the warden greeted the prisoners and read them the rules of the institution (developed the previous day by the guards and the warden). They were to be memorized and to be followed. Prisoners were to be referred to only by the number of their uniforms, in a further effort to depersonalize them.

The prisoners were served three bland meals per day, were allowed three supervised toilet visits, and were given two hours daily for the privilege of reading or letter writing. Work assignments were issued for which the prisoners were to receive an hourly wage to constitute their $15 daily payment. Two visiting periods per week were scheduled, as were movie rights and exercise periods. Three times a day all prisoners were lined up for a "count" (one on each guard work-shift). The initial purpose of the count was to ascertain that all prisoners were present and to test them on their knowledge of the rules and of their I.D. numbers. The first perfunctory counts lasted only about 10 minutes, but on each successive day (or night) they were spontaneously increased in duration by the guards until some lasted several hours. Many of the preestablished features of administrative routine were modified or abandoned by the guards, and some privileges were forgotten by the staff over the course of study.

Data Collection: Dependent Measures

The exploratory nature of this investigation and the absence of specific hypotheses led us to adopt the strategy of surveying as many behavioral and psychological manifestations of the prison experience on the guards and the prisoners as was possible. The dependent measures were of two general types: (1) transactions between and within each group of subjects, recorded on video- and audiotape as well as directly observed, and (2) individual reactions on questionnaires, mood inventories, personality tests, daily guard shift reports, and postexperimental interviews.

Data collection was organized around the following sources:

1. *Videotaping*   Using the concealed video equipment, about 12 hours of recordings were made of daily, regularly occurring events such as the counts and meals, as well as unusual interactions such as a prisoner rebellion; visits from a priest, a lawyer, and parents; parole board meetings; and others.

2. *Audio recording*   Concealed microphones recorded over 30 hours of verbal interactions between guards and prisoners in the prison yard, as well as some within the cells and in the testing-interview room.

3. *Rating scales*   Mood adjective checklists and sociometric measures were administered on several occasions to assess emotional changes in affective state and interpersonal dynamics among the guard and prisoner groups.

4. *Individual difference scales*   Prior to the start of the simulation, all subjects had completed a series of paper-and-pencil personality tests selected to provide dispositional indicators of interpersonal behavior styles—the F scale of Authoritarian Personality (Adorno, Frenkel-Brunswik, Levinson, and Sanford 1950) and the Machiavellianism Scale (Christie and Geis 1970)—and to isolate areas of possible personality pathology through the newly developed Comrey Personality Scale (Comrey 1970).

5. *Personal observations*   The guards made daily reports of their observations after each shift, the experimenters kept informal diaries, and all subjects completed postexperimental questionnaires of their reactions to the experience about a month after the study was over.

Data Analysis: Video Recordings

Special analyses were required only of the video and audio material. The other data sources were analyzed following established scoring procedures.

Since the present discussion is based primarily on the videotaped material, details of this analysis are outlined here.

There were 25 relatively discrete incidents identifiable on the tapes of prisoner–guard interactions. Each incident or scene was scored for the presence of nine behavioral (and verbal) categories by two judges who had not been involved with the simulation study. These categories were defined as follows:

- ▾ *Question*   All questions asked, requests for information or assistance (excluding rhetorical questions).
- ▾ *Command*   An order to commence or abstain from a specific behavior, directed to either individuals or groups. Also generalized orders; e.g., "Settle down."
- ▾ *Information*   A specific piece of information proffered by anyone, whether requested or not, dealing with any contingency of the simulation.
- ▾ *Individuating reference*   Positive: use of a person's real name, nickname, or allusion to special positive physical characteristics. Negative: use of prison number, title, generalized "you," or reference to derogatory characteristic.
- ▾ *Threat*   Verbal statement of contingent negative consequences of a wide variety; e.g., no meal, long count, pushups, lock-up in hole, no visitors.
- ▾ *Deprecation/insult*   Use of obscenity, slander, malicious statement directed toward individuals or groups, e.g., "You lead a life of mendacity," "You guys are really stupid."
- ▾ *Resistance*   Any physical resistance, usually prisoners to guards, such as holding onto beds, blocking doors, shoving guard or prisoner, taking off stocking caps, refusing to carry out orders.
- ▾ *Help*   Person physically assisting another (excludes verbal statements of support); e.g., guard helping another to open door, prisoner helping another prisoner in cleanup duties.
- ▾ *Use of instruments*   Use of any physical instrument to either intimidate, threaten, or achieve specific end; e.g., fire extinguisher, batons, whistles.

Results

The results of the present experiment support many commonly held conceptions of prison life and validate anecdotal evidence supplied by articulate exconvicts. The environment of arbitrary custody had great impact upon *the affective states* of both guards and prisoners as well as upon *the interpersonal processes* between and within those role-groups.

In general, guards and prisoners showed a marked decrease in positive affect or emotion, and their overall outlook became increasingly negative. As the experiment progressed, prisoners expressed intentions to do harm to others more frequently. For both prisoners and guards, self-evaluations were more deprecating as the experience of the prison environment became internalized.

Overt behavior was generally consistent with the subjective self-reports and affective expressions of the subjects. While guards and prisoners were essentially free to engage in any form of interaction (positive or negative, supportive or affrontive, etc.), the characteristic nature of their encounters tended to be negative, hostile, affrontive, and dehumanizing. Prisoners immediately adopted a generally passive style of responding, while guards assumed a very active initiative role in all interactions. Throughout the experiment, commands were the most frequent form of verbal behavior and, generally, verbal exchanges were strikingly impersonal, with few references to individual identity. Although it was clear to all subjects that the experimenters would not permit physical violence to take place, varieties of less direct aggressive behavior were observed frequently (especially on the part of guards). In fact, varieties of verbal affronts became the most frequent form of interpersonal contact between guards and prisoners.

The most dramatic evidence of the impact of the mock prison upon the participants was seen in the gross reactions of five prisoners who had to be released from the study because of extreme emotional depression, crying, rage, or acute anxiety. The pattern of symptoms was quite similar in four of the subjects and began as early as the second day of imprisonment. The fifth subject was released after being treated for a psychosomatic rash which covered portions of his body. Of the remaining prisoners, only two said they were unwilling to forfeit all the money they had earned in return for being "paroled" from the study. When the experiment was terminated prematurely after only six days, all the remaining prisoners were delighted by their unexpected good fortune; in contrast, most of the guards seemed to be distressed by the decision to stop the experiment. It appeared to us that the guards had become sufficiently involved in their roles so that they now enjoyed the extreme control and power they exercised and were reluctant to give it up. One guard, who did report being personally upset at the suffering of the prisoners, claimed to have considered asking to change his role to become one of them— but never did so. None of the guards ever failed to come to work on time for their shift, and indeed, on several occasions guards remained on duty voluntarily and uncomplainingly for extra hours—without additional pay.

The extreme reactions which emerged in both groups of subjects provide clear evidence of the power of the social forces operating in this pathological setting. There were, however, individual differences observed in *styles* of coping with this stressful experience, as well as varying degrees of success in adaptation to it. While all were somewhat adversely affected by it, half the prisoners did "endure" the oppressive atmosphere—at least in the sense that they remained until the study was completed. Not all of the guards resorted to the overt and inventive forms of hostility employed by others. Some guards were tough but fair ("played by the rules"), some went far beyond their roles to engage in cruelty and harassment, while a few were passive and rarely instigated any coercive control over the prisoners. It is important to emphasize, however, that at some time during the six days *all* guards participated in what could be characterized as sadistic treatment of prisoners. . . .

Representative Personal Statements

Much of the flavor and impact of this prison experience has been unavoidably lost in the relatively formal, objective analyses outlined in [other papers]. The following quotations taken from interviews, conversations, and question-naires provide a more personal view of what it was like to be a prisoner or guard in the "Stanford County Prison" experiment.

GUARDS' COMMENTS

They [the prisoners] seemed to lose touch with the reality of the experiment—they took me so seriously.

I didn't interfere with any of the guards' actions. Usually if what they were doing bothered me, I would walk out and take another duty.

. . . looking back, I am impressed by how little I felt for them.

They [the prisoners] didn't see it as an experiment. It was real and they were fighting to keep their identity. But we were always there to show them just who was boss.

I was tired of seeing the prisoners in their rags and smelling the strong odors of their bodies that filled the cells. I watched them tear at each other, on orders given by us.

Acting authoritatively can be fun. Power can be a great pleasure.

During the inspection, I went to cell 2 to mess up a bed which the prisoner had made and he grabbed me, screaming that he had just made it, and he wasn't going to let me mess it up. He grabbed my throat, and although he was laughing I was pretty scared. I lashed out with my stick and hit him in the chin (although not very hard) and when I freed myself I became angry.

PRISONERS' COMMENTS

The way we were made to degrade ourselves really brought us down, and that's why we all sat docile toward the end of the experiment.

I realize now (after it's over) that no matter how together I thought I was inside my head, my prison behavior was often less under my control than I realized. No matter how open, friendly, and helpful I was with other prisoners I was still operating as an isolated, self-centered person, being rational rather than compassionate.

I began to feel I was losing my identity, that the person I call _____ , the person who volunteered to get me into this prison (because it was a prison to me, it still is a prison to me, I don't regard it as an experiment or a simulation . . .) was distant from me, was remote until finally I wasn't that person, I was 416. I was really my number and 416 was really going to have to decide what to do.

I learned that people can easily forget that others are human.

Debriefing Encounter Sessions

Because of the unexpectedly intense reactions (such as the above) generated by this mock prison experience, we decided to terminate the study at the end of six days rather than continue for the second week. Three separate encounter sessions were held, first for the prisoners, then for the guards, and finally for all participants together. Subjects and staff openly discussed their reactions, and strong feelings were expressed and shared. We analyzed the moral conflicts posed by this experience and used the debriefing sessions to make explicit alternative courses of action that would lead to more moral behavior in future comparable situations.

Follow-ups on each subject over the year following termination of the study revealed that the negative effects of participation had been temporary, while the personal gain to the subjects endured.

Conclusions and Discussion

It should be apparent that the elaborate procedures (and staging) employed by the experimenters to ensure a high degree of "mundane realism" in this mock prison contributed to its effective functional simulation of the psychological dynamics operating in "real" prisons. We observed empirical relationships in the simulated prison environment which were strikingly isomorphic to the internal relations of real prisons, corroborating many of the documented reports of what occurs behind prison walls. Most dramatic and distressing to us were the ease with which sadistic behavior could be elicited from individuals who were not "sadistic types" and the frequency with which acute emotional breakdowns could occur in persons selected precisely for their emotional stability.

Authors' Note: This research was funded by an ONR grant: N00014-67-A-0112-0041 to Professor Philip G. Zimbardo.

The ideas expressed in this paper are those of the authors and do not imply endorsement of ONR or any sponsoring agency. We wish to extend our thanks and appreciation for the contributions to this research by David Jaffe who served as "warden" and pretested some of the variables in the mock prison situation. In addition, Greg White provided invaluable assistance during the data reduction phase of this study. Many others (most notably Carolyn Burkhart, Susie Phillips, and Kathy Rosenfeld) helped at various stages of the experiment, with the construction of the prison, prisoner arrest, interviewing, testing, and data analysis—we extend our sincere thanks to each of these collaborators. Finally, we especially wish to thank Carlo Prescott, our prison consultant, whose personal experience gave us invaluable insights into the nature of imprisonment.

REFERENCES

Adorno, T. W., E. Frenkel-Brunswik, D. J. Levinson, and R. N. Sanford. 1950. *The Authoritarian Personality.* New York: Harper.
Christie, R., and F. L. Geis, eds. 1970. *Studies in Machiavellianism.* New York: Academic Press.
Comrey, A. L. 1970. *Comrey Personality Scales.* San Diego, CA: Educational and Industrial Testing Service.

9

WORKING AT BAZOOMS
The Intersection of Power, Gender, and Sexuality

MEIKA LOE

Social research is concerned with the definition and assessment of social phenomena. Many social phenomena in day-to-day interaction are taken for granted, such as riding on a city bus, the daily routine inside a beauty salon, and children playing on a playground. Social researchers enable us to get inside these diverse social settings and discover what social forces are at work in creating social life. This selection, written by Meika Loe, an associate professor of sociology, anthropology, and women's studies at Colgate University, takes us inside the social world of waitressing. The award-winning study excerpted here was written by Loe when she was an undergraduate. It utilizes in-depth interviews and participant observation to reveal how gender and sexuality affect one workplace culture.

This [reading] is an investigation into power, gender, and sexuality in the workplace. This research is based on six months of participant observation and interviews at a restaurant I will call "Bazooms."[1] Bazooms is an establishment that has been described both as "a family restaurant" and as "a titillating sports bar."[2] The name of this restaurant, according to the menu, is a euphemism for "what brings a gleam into men's eyes everywhere besides beer and chicken wings and an occasional winning football team." Breasts, then, form the concept behind the name.

The purpose of this [reading] is to examine the dynamics of power, gender, and sexuality as they operate in Bazooms' workplace. This is a setting in which gender roles, sexuality, and job-based power dynamics are all being constructed and reconstructed through customer, management, and waitress interactions. The first half of the [reading] describes how power, gender, and sexuality shape, and are concurrently shaped by, Bazooms' management and customers. The second half deals specifically with how Bazooms waitresses attempt to reshape these dynamics and to find strategies for managing the meaning and operation of gender, power, and sexuality. By using Bazooms waitresses as examples, I hope to show that women are not merely "objectified victims" of sexualized workplaces, but are also active architects of gender, power, and sexuality in such settings.

Meika Loe, "Working at Bazooms: The Intersection of Power, Gender, and Sexuality" from *Sociological Inquiry* 66, No. 4 (November 1996): 399–421. Copyright © John Wiley and Sons. Reprinted with permission.

The Bazooms Workplace Environment

Bazooms is the fastest-growing restaurant chain in the nation. . . .

When I applied for a job at Bazooms in the winter of 1994, the first thing I was told was: *The 'Bazooms girl' is what this restaurant revolves around; she is a food server, bartender, hostess, table busser, promo girl, and more.* At the job interview I was shown a picture of a busty blonde in a tight top and short shorts leaning seductively over a plateful of buffalo wings and was asked if I would be comfortable wearing the Bazooms uniform. Then I was told that the managers try to make the job "fun," by supplying the "girls" with "toys" like hula hoops to play with in between orders. Finally, I was asked to sign Bazooms' official sexual harassment policy form, which explicitly states: "In a work atmosphere based upon sex appeal, joking and innuendo are commonplace."

Sixty "lucky" women were chosen to be "Bazooms girls" out of about eight hundred applications. Most of the "new hires" were local college students, ranging in age from eighteen to twenty-eight years, and as I found out later, more than several were mothers. The hiring process was extremely competitive owing to the fact that Bazooms hired minors and inexperienced waitresses. Also, everyone had been told that working at Bazooms could be quite lucrative. The general "Bazooms girl type" seemed to be white, thin, with blonde or brown hair, although there were several black, Chicana, and Asian American women in the bunch.[3] We all went through full-time training together (which included appearance training, menu workshops, song learning, alcohol and food service licensing, and reviewing the employee manual), and eventually were placed in a new location opened in Southern California.

Women work at Bazooms for a variety of reasons. No one in management ever asked me why I was applying, and I never told them, but the fact is that I applied for a position as a Bazooms girl because I wanted to know more about how the women who worked there experienced and responded to a highly sexualized workplace. I worked there for six months, during which I "became the phenomenon" (Mehan and Wood 1975).[4]

During my six months of participant observation and interviews with coworkers, I explained that I was interviewing people in my place of work as part of a class research project.[5] I made no attempt to construct a random sample of Bazooms girls to interview; rather, I interviewed those whom I felt closest to, and worked regularly with, and who I thought would feel comfortable responding honestly to my questions. The waitresses I interviewed for the most part were very committed to their jobs. Some were upset with their conditions of employment, and their voices may stand out for the reader. But I should emphasize that others, whose voices may not attract notice, expressed general contentment with the job. In the pages that follow I will present their views and my observations about the ways in which power, gender, and sexuality are constructed and negotiated in the sexualized workplace of a Bazooms restaurant.

Job-Based Power

Formal Power

Gender and power at Bazooms are reflected in its management structure. In this restaurant, four men manage more than 100 employees working various shifts: 60 Bazooms girls and 40 kitchen guys. In addition, both the franchise owners and the founders are all male. This is not rare. According to Catherine MacKinnon (1980:60), countless studies have shown that "women are overwhelmingly in positions that other people manage, supervise, or administer. Even in 'women's jobs' the managers are men." As in most workplace environments, formal authority and power are concentrated in management positions at Bazooms. In everything from scheduling to paychecks, floor assignments, and breaks, managers have the last word. In this way, Bazooms girls are placed in a subordinate position. This is not an unusual finding. MacKinnon contends that as "low-prestige" workers, women are often placed in positions of dependence upon men for economic security, hiring, retention, and advancement.

In these dependent situations, a woman's job is literally on the line all the time. One waitress whom I interviewed described management procedures for getting a worker fired at a Colorado Bazooms as follows:

> *All of a sudden, we would have menu tests and we were told that if we missed too many we would be fired. Now, I know I missed about twenty. These girls they wanted to fire missed less than that, I'm sure. They were fired right away because they missed some . . . but they didn't say a thing to me. Or, if they really wanted to get rid of certain people, they would put up one schedule, then put a different copy up with different hours (the "real" one) after the girls left. The girls wouldn't know, so they were fired for not showing up to their shifts.*

Disciplinary action based upon "company rules" is one of management's most common exertions of power. Before every shift, managers hold "jump start" which, in theory, is supposed to motivate the workers to "get out there and have fun." Instead, it becomes an ideal time for management to assert authority. Each waitress is quickly checked for uniform cleanliness, "natural" yet "styled" hair, make-up, and so forth. Then the group is counseled on "proper" Bazooms girl behavior and attitude. Sometimes "pop quizzes" are given to each woman, with questions about proper Bazooms girl service and responsibilities. At other times, lectures are given reiterating rules that have been ignored or broken earlier in the week. The practice of "jump start," at the beginning of each shift, operates in a way that makes power relations explicit. . . .

In short, male management's right to exercise veto power over each worker's appearance, attitude, and so forth reflects gendered power relations at Bazooms.

Informal Power

Besides having the ultimate say in formal matters such as scheduling, hiring, and firing, male managers sustain dominance at Bazooms in other, more subtle, ways. Eleanor LaPointe (1992:382) identifies a number of "interactional techniques" often used by men to sustain dominance and maintain the inferior status of women. At Bazooms such power was exercised by the use of derogatory terms of address, disciplinary actions, direct orders, threats, general avoidance of waitresses' concerns, cynicism, and even humiliation. For instance, the fact that female employees between the ages of eighteen and thirty are called girls by Bazooms managers and customers alike is an example of such an "interactional technique" used to sustain dominance. Everyone knows that the managers (all men in their twenties and thirties) are not to be called boys (neither are the "kitchen guys" to be called boys). Yet, by seeing and addressing the "low-status" employees as girls (based upon the "Bazooms girl" concept), one can retain dominance as a manager or customer (since waitresses are referred to by all as Bazooms girls) and maintain the subordinate status of female employees. Humiliating comments during the work shift about personal appearance from managers is another example of an interactional technique causing Bazooms girls to feel that they aren't respected or that they are treated poorly. In the words of one (Trina): *[The management] has no respect for any of us waitresses. No respect.*

Gender

It has already been established that Bazooms is a "gendered workplace," where, according to MacKinnon (1980), women "tend to be employed in occupations that are considered 'for women,' to be men's subordinates on the job and to be paid less than men both on the average and for the same work."

Behavior Rules

Management codes and guidelines shape gendered identities in work environments. At Bazooms, women work as "girls." According to one Bazooms manager: *What differentiates us from every other restaurant in the marketplace are the Bazooms girls. That's the reason that there's a Bazooms concept, that's the reason that we're successful. . . .*

The following are Bazooms girl guidelines selected from the employee handbook:

- ▾ Wholesome-looking, All American cheerleading types (the kind you would be proud to take home to mother). Prom-like appearance.
- ▾ Hair should always be styled. The girls are always "on stage" and should be camera ready at all times.
- ▾ Make-up needs to be worn. It should not be excessive, and at the same time it needs to highlight her natural features.
- ▾ Always smiling, extremely friendly and courteous.

▾ Always should appear to be having a great time.

▾ Extremely attentive to all customers. . . .

Simultaneously she is "the girl next door," the "cheerleader," the "actress" (always camera ready), the "good daughter" (attentive, subservient), the "prom queen," and the shining, happy personality. One waitress said matter-of-factly: *It's like they [managers] have an ideal image in their heads of us* (Katy). With all of these demands placed upon her, the Bazooms girl is constantly in the process of learning how to adapt to the company's expectations, and acting out her gender (according to men's rules).

Appearance Rules

It is clear from these guidelines that the "Bazooms girl" role embodies what are seen as traditionally "feminine" (in this case, many "girlish") qualities. One way gender is symbolized is through uniform style, which, according to LaPointe (1992), "incorporates a gendered meaning into the work" (p. 382).[6] The uniforms, short shorts, and choice of tight tank top, crop, or tight T-shirt, may be part of the popular "beach theme," which Bazooms likes to accentuate, but it carries gendered meaning as well. Few men, if any, work in what is considered a "neighborhood restaurant" wearing a size too small dolphin shorts and a shirt showing off his midriff and chest.[7] But for a woman this is "beach wear," revealing her truly feminine characteristics.

Barbara Reskin and Patricia Roos (1987:9) argue that the "sexual division of labor is grounded in stereotypes of innate sex differences in traits and abilities, and maintained by gender-role socialization and various social control mechanisms." . . . The director of training at Bazooms advised new hires to *look like you are going on a date. You were chosen because you all are pretty. But I say makeup makes everyone look better. Push-up bras make everyone look better. And we all want to look our best.* These "feminine ideals" not only define "the perfect" Bazooms girl, but are used by management to constantly reify femininity in the workplace through the dissemination of "rules" and the use of discipline to uphold these rules. In this way, through interaction, not only power relations but gender roles are constantly being defined and redefined in the workplace.

Emotional Labor

The gendered workplace demands more than manipulation of behavior and appearance. Arlie Hochschild's (1979) ethnography of flight attendants introduces another type of labor that is common in female-dominated occupations, which she dubs "emotional labor." Emotional labor requires one to *induce or suppress feeling* in order to sustain an outward countenance that produces the desired state of mind in others (Hochschild 1983:7). Thus, emotion workers must always "display" an image that is determined by management, and "over time 'display' comes to assume a certain relation to feeling" (p. 90). Hochschild found that emotion workers, over time, may become estranged from their true feelings, which are ignored, disguised, or created in order to achieve a desired image.[8]

Hochschild's notion of "display" and manipulation of feeling can be found at Bazooms, especially among the female employees. According to management, the Bazooms girl, when on the floor, is expected to "perform as if [she] is on stage." This means embodying a specific image, sustaining an outward countenance, and behaving in specific ways. One manager with whom I spoke put it this way:

> *Well, after working eight years I can pretty much tell who will be perfect for the job and who won't. [By looking at them?] Well, by talking with them and seeing what type of personality they have. You know, they must be performers as Bazooms girls. Nobody can be bubbly that long, but when you're working you put on an act.*

As Greta Paules (1991:160) put it, "By furnishing the waitress with a script, a costume, and a backdrop of a servant, the restaurant is encouraging her to become absorbed in her role—to engage in deep acting." . . .

The corporate image that Bazooms projects of happy, sexy, eager-to-serve workers is what sells. What became clear to me on one of my first days on the job was that emotional labor is demanded not only by management, but by customers as well. For instance, one afternoon I approached a table full of marines without a smile or a "Can I help you?" look on my face. Their first words to me were, "You look pissed." I felt I had to make excuses for what I realized was poor emotion management on my part.

Deference is a large portion of emotion work, according to Hochschild. "Ritualized deference is always involved when one is in a subordinate position" (Reskin and Roos 1987:8). Clearly, in the service industry, employees (the majority women) are expected to have been trained in "niceness" from an early age (girls are made of sugar and spice and everything nice). So "working as women" (or girls) naturally assumes that "a friendly and courteous manner" will be incorporated into the job. During training at Bazooms, new hires were instructed to "kill them [rude customers] with kindness and class." In other words, suppress any desire to yell or lecture rude customers, and instead, defer to the old maxim "the customer always is right," and treat them only with kindness. In this case, emotion work entails being at the service of others to the point of devaluing oneself and one's own emotions. Because of their subordination and vulnerable positioning, women become easy targets of verbal abuse, and of others' (managers', customers', even colleagues') displaced feelings. When kindness is not effective enough in handling rude customers, Bazooms asks their waitresses to defer to the management. "Problems" are then handled by the men, who must also manage their emotions, but they are more allowed to wield anger, since they have been socialized to express "negative" emotions from an early age (Hochschild 1983:163). . . .

The Sexualized Workplace

It is beyond my—my mental capacity to understand how anyone could walk into a [Bazooms] restaurant and apply for a job and look at the sign and look at the—the concept and look at the uniform and not understand that female sex appeal is an essential ingredient in the concept.

—Mr. McNeil, Manager of Bazooms, Minnesota

At the turn of the century Emma Goldman suggested, "Nowhere is woman treated according to the merit of her work but rather as a sex. . . . She must assert herself as a personality, not as a sex commodity" (1970:7,12). Close to a century later, Catherine MacKinnon (1980) related a similar point in her book *Sexual Harassment of Working Women:* "Most women perform the jobs they do because of their gender, with the element of sexuality pervasively explicit" (p. 60). According to Goldman, MacKinnon, and other feminist theorists, women not only work "as women" but as *sexualized* women.

Bazooms makes no secret about sexuality as a part of its key to success. The employee manual states in its sexual harassment policy that employees should be aware that they are employed in an establishment "based upon female sex appeal." As Mr. McNeil pointed out, everything right down to the waitresses' uniforms and the name of the restaurant connotes sex appeal. The slang term *bazooms* is usually used in the context of male desire and breast fetishism; it is a term that treats one part of the female body as an object of sexual desire. Tanya, director of training for Bazooms, answered a new hire's question about the term *bazooms* in this way:

> So what if [Bazooms] means "tits." That doesn't offend me. It's all in fun . . . just six guys in Florida trying to be goofy. They used to want us to hide the fact that it means breasts. But now we figure, Why be ashamed of it? You girls should never be ashamed of where you work. And if anyone asks you what it means, you just say, "Whatever you want it to mean."

Why is female sex appeal such a great marketing success? Probably because it appeals to male fantasy. Customers (roughly eighty-five percent male at my workplace) buy into the commodified Bazooms girl, which they hear about everywhere. Since "no publicity is bad publicity" to Bazooms, Bazooms girls have been highlighted in popular magazines such as *Playboy.* In a leading national business magazine, Bazooms is described as a place with "food, folks, and fun, and a little bit of sex appeal." In fact, according to this magazine, the idea for Bazooms came from a Florida football player/contractor in 1983 who wanted "a mildly profitable excuse for swilling beer and ogling blondes." Thus, Bazooms is premised on women's bodies and their presence in male fantasies. . . .

Comments that customers made to me reflect the "titillating" nature of Bazooms, and the expectations they have about what the waitresses symbolize. One man said he didn't want to embarrass himself, but he thought that I was "too wholesome" to work at Bazooms. Answering my question about why he didn't think I fit in, he whispered to me, "You are not slutty enough." Another male customer called me over to remark, "I've been watching you all night and I think you have to be the most innocent-looking girl here. This means that you must have a wild side and I like that." Both of these comments encapsulate this male fantasy of the virgin/whore. I was obviously too much "virgin" for both of them, but the second man made up for this by fantasizing that I had a "wild side" (the "whore" was simply latent or hidden away).

Further comments and behaviors reflected the sexualized expectations of customers. I asked one man who looked interested in buying a shirt, "Can I show you something?" pointing to the merchandise counter. The customer responded, "I'll tell you what I want to see . . ." and tossed a dollar my way. . . .

It is in this sexually charged workplace catering to male fantasy that "masculine culture" emerges. A major newspaper describes Bazooms as "a lot of men's idea of big fun." With women (Bazooms girls) "acting out" feminine roles (pet, mother, sex object), men (customers) perform as well. At Bazooms, customers perform masculinity rituals, often in groups. One might encounter groups of male customers engaging in a number of masculine "acts." These generally include flirting with waitresses and vying for their attention, joking about body parts and other publicly taboo subjects, challenging each other in the area of alcohol consumption, setting each other up with waitresses, making requests for hula-hooping, and so on. For example, comments such as, "You give good head," can be heard among groups of males when a waitress is pouring beer. One man asked, "Why don't you wear the low-cut tank top?" while another said, "My friend wants to meet that girl over there. Can you get her to come over?" . . .

Socialized through interaction with customers, Bazooms girls learn to "manage feeling" in order to keep the customers as happy as possible. "The masculinity rituals [in the bar] would not be effective without the cooperation of the waitress. She has learned to respond demurely to taunts, invitations, and physical invasions of her personal space. . . . The cultural expectations are clear: she should remain dependent and passive" (Spradley and Mann 1975:133). In this way, gendered sexual identities, expectations, and roles are shaped through customer interaction. As the "audience, marginal participant, and sex object," the Bazooms girl is there to "enhance" masculine culture (add to the eroticism by playing out visual and interactive elements of male fantasy) and at the same time, enjoy the attention she gets as "the object" (p. 133).

The fact that Bazooms is male-identified is well illustrated by the feelings of intimidation experienced by female customers. The most common question asked by a female customer upon entering the restaurant is "Am I the only woman in here?" Although there are between six and fourteen Bazooms girls within the restaurant at any given time, the "men's club" atmosphere is quite obvious. . . .

Sexual Harassment and "Sex Joking"

. . . In her study of sex in the workplace, Gutek (1985:144) found that of a random national sample of 827 "traditionally employed women . . . 75% said that sexual jokes and comments were common in their places of work."

Similarly, Spradley and Mann (1975:95) found joking to be a powerful force in the work environment they studied. The "joking relationship" was essential to establishing the "masculine atmosphere" of Bradys' Bar, "centering on insults made in jest, direct references to sexual behavior, comments about anatomical features with sexual meanings, and to related topics normally taboo for conversations between men and women."

I observed numerous examples of this sort of sexual harassment or "sex joking" at Bazooms. Comments made by customers such as "You give good head," or "Your lips would be so nice to kiss," or "I wish I were in the shower with all of you," are not common at Bazooms, but they also are not taboo. I was warned by one Bazooms girl when I went to apply for the job: "You do have to put up with a lot of shit."

A national business magazine reports that "appropriate activities among [Bazooms] customers include winking, leering, nudging and smirking." According to Bazooms girl Sheri, there's something about the Bazooms environment that permits behaviors one wouldn't find at another restaurant: *What makes it different is that Bazooms customers are a little more open because of the atmosphere. They [customers] are a lot more forward—instead of waiting a couple of times to establish themselves as regulars until they attempt to ask you something. . . .*

What a sexually permissive environment allows for is room for degrading comments, sexist behaviors, and "insults made in jest." As a consequence, women working at Bazooms reported feelings of hurt, embarrassment, and humiliation. . . .

Kanja felt embarrassed and upset about behavior that occurred at Bazooms:

> *The worst experience was when this rock station was in the restaurant and they were asking me and another Bazooms girl about which actresses had real or fake boobs. The last question was whether I had real or fake boobs. I just sat there silent, I was so upset. And then they started asking bra sizes at one of the tables. That just makes me so mad.*

In restaurants subtle yet pervasive forms of sex joking and sexual harassment are used as social distancing techniques that reinforce a waitress's vulnerable position and maintain her inferiority (LaPointe 1992:388; MacKinnon 1980:60). The joking relationship is asymmetrical; so, while women may "marginally participate," they must be careful not to say things that would appear coarse or crude. Thus, insults operate mostly one-way, initiated and followed up on by men (Spradley and Mann 1975:97).

Some Bazooms girls mentioned that they wished they knew how to "manage" better when it came to uncomfortable comments, sex joking, and innuendo. . . .

While Bazooms' management espouses an open-door policy for all workers, Bazooms girl Jeni describes management's ideal Bazooms girl:

> *What they want is the ones who can deal with people and shit and don't complain. They don't want you there if you are going to stick up for yourself.*

Gutek found that women working in female-dominated occupations (i.e., "traditionally female jobs") are less likely to report and view sexual harassment as a problem, because it is "part of the job" (1985:136). The idea that sexual harassment is part of the job at Bazooms came up constantly in subtle ways during my interviews. The fact that these women expected to have to learn to deal with sex joking and sexist behaviors from customers or managers is a commentary on what women are willing to put up with in the nineties workplace. . . . Bazooms' sexual harassment policy states specifically: "Sexual harassment does not refer to occasional compliments of a socially acceptable nature. It does not refer to mutually acceptable joking or teasing. It refers to behavior which is unwelcome, that is personally offensive, that debilitates morale, and that, therefore, interferes with work effectiveness" (Bazooms Employee Handbook).

The part that managers play in the "elimination" of sexual harassment at Bazooms has been criticized severely in sexual discrimination and harassment lawsuits in at least three states. A leading law journal charged recently that Bazooms' managers are breaking their own sexual harassment policies, and "promoting misogyny and inflicting it on their own employees and inviting the public to come in and inflict it on the employees. . . ."

Agency

What is missing so far in this analysis is women's responses to these dynamics. There is no question that by following workplace rules of dress and demeanor, Bazooms girls were participants in the interplay of power, gender, and sexuality in the Bazooms workplace. Some waitresses dressed and behaved in ways that emphasized their sexuality and encouraged male patrons' attention—strategies that were seen to result in bigger tips. The financial bottom line no doubt underlay most Bazooms girls' calculations about the trade-off between sometimes demeaning dress and behavior expectations and the wages and tips they could expect to receive. There were limits, however, to how much unwelcome attention or harassment the waitresses would tolerate. When these limits were reached, Bazooms girls resisted and manipulated their gendered and sexualized workplace role in a variety of ways. . . .

At Bazooms, waitresses work within and against the constraints imposed by these factors in at least three ways: (1) They attempt to undermine or otherwise challenge the power structure, (2) they manipulate gender to preserve self-image, and (3) they both co-opt and counteract sexualized identities.

Undermining and Challenging the Power Structure

At Bazooms, formal power can be undermined by informal means. Challenges to the established power structure at Bazooms mainly take the form of gossip. Waitresses often expressed negative sentiments and shared complaints about management's constant exercise of authority.[9] During any given shift, one may overhear comments made by waitresses such as: *They always pick out the bad instead of rewarding or encouraging us on the good stuff*

(Lori), or *You know we aren't respected at all* (Trina), or *I've never been in a restaurant where the workers are so badly treated* (Kelly), or *They are on a total power trip. Especially since they are in control of a lot of girls, and because they are men, they are taking that authority a bit too far* (Teri). Thus, by coming together and sharing grievances, gossip can be a form of resistance.

In some cases at Bazooms, waitresses have been known to challenge managers directly on their policies. One waitress, after being denied a break for eight hours, let one of the managers know how she was feeling: *I was so mad I was pretty much crying and he said, "Get in the office. What's wrong with you?" I said, "You know, you have no respect for any of us waitresses." He said, "You know, I should just send you home for good." Then I shut up* (Trina). This was a clear use of the interactional technique of threatening a waitress with the loss of her job to sustain the established power structure at Bazooms (classical management dominance and waitress subordination). . . .

Another waitress became defensive and upset when she was told that her hair wasn't styled enough. In talking back, this waitress challenged authority and used informal power to get her way. (The manager on that particular day decided it was not worth arguing about and let her keep her hair the way it was.) In both of these cases, established power boundaries were consciously tested by management and waitress alike.

It is clear that even after indirect and direct challenges to the established power hierarchy by waitresses, management retains its ultimate power over workers. Direct challenges to authority generally are squelched, as reflected in Teri's statement: *You can't talk back or you will get fired or written up. It's a power play.* Bazooms wouldn't be Bazooms without the established power hierarchy (males on top). Nonetheless it is important to note that the women who work at Bazooms do not simply accept these power relations. They struggle to create solidarity and actively resist the passivity management wants from them.

Gender-Based Strategies

Just as waitresses attempt to resist the power structure at Bazooms, they also resist and manipulate gender roles to fit their needs. As one would expect, not all of the women hired at Bazooms were comfortable with the Bazooms girl role they were supposed to embody on the job. Much of the controversy about taking a job at Bazooms centers around the uniforms. About half of my interviewees described initial nervousness and insecurity about the uniforms. But at the time of most of the interviews (two to three months after the interviewees had started work), these thoughts had changed. . . .

> *The only thing I hate about the Bazooms uniform is that they tie the knots [on the back of the tank top] so tight that I can't breathe. And the nylons, they are always running and I have to buy new ones. They tried to get me to wear XX small shorts and I minded that. They made me try it on and I'm, like, "I'm not wearing this!" But the X small isn't bad. . . .*

Each waitress went through a socializing process that often began with feeling nervous, even opposing the uniform. Waitresses then went through a period of adjustment based upon the fact that each wore the same thing as her coworkers did. Thus, as the definition of *normal* was revised, the nervous comments and complaints tended to subside. Yet, not everyone wears the same thing in the same ways. As their comments suggest, waitresses make choices about what to wear, and how to wear their outfits. The women made these choices based upon how comfortable they felt with the Bazooms girl image and their calculations about the financial utility of various style choices. Choices about whether to show cleavage, to wear a T-shirt (seen as more conservative by not highlighting the breasts) or a tank, to hike up the shorts, and so forth are also examples of negotiating the Bazooms girl's sexualized image. In other words, through manipulation of uniforms, these women manipulated the Bazooms girl concept to fit their own self-images and goals. . . .

But dress codes aren't the only thing that waitresses actively negotiate. Along with the dress codes come other pressures associated with "femaleness," especially in terms of appearance. [Trina] stated that appearance-based insecurities often became obsessions:

> *A lot of the girls are obsessed with the way they look. I know with our society looks are so important. I care about how I look. And there's not one girl in there who isn't really pretty. But I walk in there and people are talking about losing weight and stuff. It's too much based upon looks. I tell them, "I can tell you how to lose fat, and I can do it if I want, but I like eating what I eat. . . ."*

By being aware of pressures to be thin and pretty, and counseling [her] coworkers on resisting these pressures, Trina [was] actively redefining gender ideals in the workplace.

Counteracting and Co-opting Sexual Identities

Women who dress to get attention, to show off their bodies, to look or feel "sexy" in our society, often end up getting labeled "whore," or "slut," and may be seen as "asking for it." Many of the Bazooms waitresses were concerned that their provocative outfits would force them into one of these sexualized roles. In response to a sexual slogan printed on the back of every T-shirt and tank, one Bazooms girl stated: *My hair covers the slogan, and we're not those kind of girls anyway.* Nonetheless, Bazooms girls are associated with "those kind of girls," that is, sex workers or prostitutes working in a sexually charged environment where sex appeal is part of the product commodified and sold in the marketplace to men. The girls I worked with became aware of these associations early on, and they spent much time sharing and reacting to these negative associations. . . .

Some of the women who work at Bazooms attempt to counteract these negative associations. One Bazooms girl remarked: *We need to educate men. Just because you are wearing this uniform doesn't mean that you are asking for anything, doesn't mean that you want anything more than a job.* Several Bazooms girls made a point of telling customers that they were college students, or mothers, waitressing in order to save up money for education or family expenses. In this way the "girls" challenge the Bazooms girl (ditzy, sexual pawn) image most customers have and try to make the role more personal and respectable by sharing their own stories.

Some of the women, on the other hand, do not resist the negative associations but use them to achieve their own ends. In co-opting the "bad girl" role, some hope to appeal to customers by using sex appeal to their advantage, hoping to get bigger tips (or more attention) this way. To Katy, "learning to deal with people more sexually" is to be able to control the situation in order to avoid embarrassment. Although it is harder to get people to admit to using the sexualized image for their own ends, once in a while stories fly among customers and waitresses about "what some [Bazooms] girls will do for money." Playing up the sexualized Bazooms girl role can be a serious money-making strategy:

> *I've seen girls hula-hoop and get money thrown at them. Then they lean over and give the cleavage shot to the men. And at the downtown store the girls do things with pitchers of beer to make it look like a wet T-shirt contest. These things just do not work for me at all. . . .*

There appears to be a split among these women: those who try to resist the Bazooms girl role, downplaying the sexualized, flirty image, and those who co-opt it, embellishing it as their own. One employee rejects the company's expectation; another turns it to her own ends. . . .

Negotiation of Sexuality and Sexual Harassment

There are times when the Bazooms game goes too far. What may be fun and games to one woman may be sexual harassment to another. Responses to crudeness or to offensive comments or actions by customers take many different forms at Bazooms. Katy says that when customers deal "sexually" with her: *I just get so embarrassed and walk away. But if they said something that offended me, I'd just go to the managers. I wouldn't even hesitate.* Trina concurs, saying: *We don't have to put up with jack. I won't take [offensive remarks]. It's not worth my pride. I give customers the gnarliest looks.* Kristy's response to offensive remarks is different: *I usually just laugh and walk away.* As illustrated in these differing instances, women are responding in varied ways to the sexualized nature of the job, and to offensiveness from customers. . . .

Harassment is taken for granted as part of the job at Bazooms. By defining abuse as part of the job, waitresses can continue to work without necessarily internalizing or accepting the daily hassles and degradations as aspects of their self-definitions or sense of self-worth (LaPointe 1992:391). In other words, if women enter into a waitressing job expecting crude remarks, degrading uniforms, and unnecessary management-based power plays, they may prepare themselves for the worst by setting personal boundaries, with conditions attached.

The waitress (Christine) who had her "butt grabbed" made a decision to deal with the harassment in a way that she thought would bring a higher tip. And it did. Another waitress, Twayla, made a decision to react quite differently in a similar circumstance: *I turned right around and told him, "You will not do these things to me."* These two women weighed personal priorities and dealt with similar sexual behavior in different ways. Christine decided to allow a man to cross a particular boundary—but for a price, turning the incident to her advantage. Twayla made clear her boundary would not be crossed. . . .

For others, self-esteem is more undermined than affirmed by the sexualization of the workplace, and the tips are not worth the price. *Bazooms is kind of degrading sometimes,* says Trina. *[Customers] refer to us as if we are stupid. It's hard to explain, the way they talk . . . they are talking down to us.* Of course, contempt sometimes goes the other way. Trina goes on to add that the waitresses don't respect the customers either: *I think the waitresses kind of look down on the men. Because all of them—it's like they are dirty old men.*

Conclusion

Bazooms is a good deal more than a "family" restaurant or a place where men can "swill beer and ogle blondes." It is a theater in which dramas of power, gender, and sexuality are played out. Within this drama, women play an explicitly subordinate role. As MacKinnon, LaPointe, Reskin and Roos, and Hochschild point out, their behaviors are severely constrained by the realities of employment in the service sector. Women are hired to put on a specific performance, and at Bazooms they are constrained by the formal script that Bazooms encourages its employees to follow. Furthermore, women are limited greatly by the assumptions men make about the appropriate and desirable place for women, especially in a sexually charged atmosphere. In the Bazooms environment, it is easy to classify these women as objects.

Yet, women are also actively shaping their own experiences at Bazooms. The constraints on their actions are severe, but within them women struggle to retain their self-esteem, exercise power, and affirm the identities they value. . . .

Bazooms girls are not helpless performers. They are women struggling to find ways to alter their roles, rewrite the script, and refashion the nature of the drama. . . . Women sometimes also turn the play to their own advantage, finding opportunities to increase tips, support their kids, and even find some affirmation of self-worth.

In sum, the waitress is not a passive casualty of the hardships of her work. Within the structure of the job, she has developed an arsenal of often subtle but undeniably effective tactics to moderate the exploitive elements of her occupation and secure attention to her own needs (Paules 1991:171). Few people passively watch their lives go by. The notion of agency suggests that workers in all fields, regardless of their formal options, actively take at least some control of their own destinies. In the voices of Trina, Katy, Christine, and others we can hear women responding to their circumstances and asserting themselves as agents within the Bazooms drama.

ENDNOTES

[1] For reasons of confidentiality, all names used in this paper have been changed. Identifying traits (of this establishment) have been removed and identifying references are not included. This [research] was cleared through the University of California Human Subjects Committee as a student project.

[2] Bazooms' management likes to characterize their establishment as catering to families, probably in order to counter the sexy, bachelor-pad reputation that the local media assign to the establishment.

[3] Interestingly, only about half of the chosen group would be considered "busty" by society's standards.

[4] This falls under the category of opportunistic research or "auto-ethnography," in which the researcher becomes a participant in the setting so as not to alter the flow of interaction unnaturally, as well as to immerse oneself and grasp the depth of the subjectively lived experience (Denzin and Lincoln 1994).

[5] I am aware that covert research has come under significant attack from social scientists. The issue seems to be that of disguise: misrepresentation of self in order to enter a new or forbidden domain, and deliberate misrepresentation of the character of research one is engaged in (Denzin and Lincoln 1994). These issues do not apply to my project, since I did not disguise myself in any way in order to get "in" at Bazooms. The management did not ask why I was applying and I therefore did not volunteer the information. Furthermore, I was up front with my subjects about "doing a school project," upon interviewing them. Finally, with names and identities changed throughout, I cannot see this report inflicting harm in any way. All quotes (from waitresses) are based upon recorded interviews.

[6] LaPointe argues that requiring employees to wear degrading uniforms emphasizes their "low status" and distinguishes them from their superiors.

[7] Recent news coverage did report that, based upon a four-year investigation, Bazooms is being charged $22 million by the Equal Employment Opportunity Commission for sex discrimination in hiring. Yet, amid recent controversy over the EEOC's decision, Bazooms Company took out full-page ads in major national newspapers to insist that men do not belong as servers at Bazooms. Each ad featured a picture of a brawny man ludicrously dressed in a Bazooms girl uniform.

[8] It must be mentioned that, like women, males are also often required to do "emotional labor" in the workplace. Nonetheless, as Hochschild points out, females hold the majority of responsibility for emotion work. According to Hochschild:

> With the growth of large organizations calling for skills in personal relations, the womanly art of status enhancement and the emotion work that it requires has been made more public, more systematized, more standardized. It is performed by mostly middle-class women in largely public-contact jobs. Jobs involving emotional labor comprise over a third of all jobs. But they form only a quarter of all jobs that men do, and over half of all the jobs that women do (1983:171).

[9] It is important to add that some of the waitresses believe "management is just doing their job," and don't complain.

REFERENCES

Denzin, N. K. and Y. S. Lincoln. 1994. *Handbook of Qualitative Research*. Thousand Oaks, CA: Sage.
Goldman, Emma. 1970. *The Traffic in Women*. Ojai, CA: Times Change Press.
Gutek, Barbara. 1985. *Sex and the Workplace*. San Francisco: Jossey-Bass.
Hochschild, Arlie. 1979. "Emotion Work, Feeling Rules, and Social Structure." *American Journal of Sociology* 85(3):551–72.
———. 1983. *The Managed Heart*. Berkeley: University of California Press.
LaPointe, Eleanor. 1992. "Relationships with Waitresses: Gendered Social Distance in Restaurant Hierarchies." *Qualitative Sociology* 15(4):377–93.

MacKinnon, Catherine. 1980. "Women's Work," and "Sexual Harassment Cases." Pp. 59–66 and 111–13 in *Sexuality in Organizations,* edited by D. A. Neugarten and J. M. Shafritz. Oak Park, IL: Moore Publishing.

Paules, Greta. 1991. *Dishing It Out: Power and Resistance among Waitresses in a New Jersey Restaurant.* Philadelphia: Temple University Press.

Reskin, B. F. and P. A. Roos. 1987. "Status Hierarchies and Sex Segregation." Pp. 3–22 in *Ingredients for Women's Employment Policy.* New York: State University of New York Press.

Spradley, James P. and Brenda J. Mann. 1975. *The Cocktail Waitress, Woman's Work in a Man's World.* New York: Wiley.

PART II
Culture

10

CULTURE: A SOCIOLOGICAL VIEW

HOWARD S. BECKER

Culture is defined as the shared ways of a human social group. This definition includes the ways of thinking, understanding, and feeling that have
been gained through common experience in social groups and are passed on
from one generation to another. Thus, culture reflects the social patterns of
thought, emotions, and practices that arise from social interaction within a
given society. In this reading, the first of three to explore culture, Howard S.
Becker, a professor emeritus of sociology, provides an overview of the concept of culture. This classic piece, published in *The Yale Review* in 1982, helps
the reader to understand why this concept is so central to the discipline of
sociology. Becker introduces not only the content of the sociological study of
culture but also many of the key scholars who have studied it.

I was for some years what is called a Saturday night musician, making myself available to whoever called and hired me to play for dances and parties in groups of varying sizes, playing everything from polkas through
mambos, jazz, and imitations of Wayne King. Whoever called would tell me
where the job was, what time it began, and usually would tell me to wear a
dark suit and a bow tie, thus ensuring that the collection of strangers he was
hiring would at least look like a band because they would all be dressed
more or less alike. When we arrived at work we would introduce
ourselves—the chances were, in a city the size of Chicago (where I did much
of my playing), that we were in fact strangers—and see whom we knew in
common and whether our paths had ever crossed before. The drummer
would assemble his drums, the others would put together their instruments
and tune up, and when it was time to start the leader would announce the
name of a song and a key—"Exactly Like You" in B flat, for instance—and we
would begin to play. We not only began at the same time, but also played
background figures that fit the melody someone else was playing and, perhaps most miraculously, ended together. No one in the audience ever
guessed that we had never met until twenty minutes earlier. And we kept
that up all night, as though we had rehearsed often and played together for

Howard S. Becker, "Culture: A Sociological View." *The Yale Review,* Vol. 71, Summer 1982:
pp. 513–528. Copyright © 1982 John Wiley and Sons. Reprinted with permission.

years. In a place like Chicago, that scene might be repeated hundreds of times during a weekend.

What I have just described embodies the phenomenon that sociologists have made the core problem of their discipline. The social sciences are such a contentious bunch of disciplines that it makes trouble to say what I think is true, that they all in fact concern themselves with one or another version of this issue—the problem of collective action, of how people manage to act together. I will not attempt a rigorous definition of collective action here, but the story of the Saturday night musicians can serve as an example of it. The example might have concerned a larger group—the employees of a factory who turn out several hundred automobiles in the course of a day, say. Or it might have been about so small a group as a family. It needn't have dealt with a casual collection of strangers, though the ability of strangers to perform together that way makes clear the nature of the problem. How do they do it? How do people act together so as to get anything done without a great deal of trouble, without missteps and conflict?

We can approach the meaning of a concept by seeing how it is used, what work it is called on to do. Sociologists use the concept of *culture* as one of a family of explanations for the phenomenon of concerted activity; I will consider some of the others below, in order to differentiate culture from them. Robert Redfield defined culture as "conventional understandings made manifest in act and artifact." The notion is that the people involved have a similar idea of things, understand them in the same way, as having the same character and the same potential, capable of being dealt with in the same way; they also know that this idea is shared, that the people they are dealing with know, just as they do, what these things are and how they can be used. Because all of them have roughly the same idea, they can all act in ways that are roughly the same, and their activities will, as a result, mesh and be coordinated. Thus, because all those musicians understood what a Saturday night job at a country club consisted of and acted accordingly, because they all knew the melody and harmony of "Exactly Like You" and hundreds of similar songs, because they knew that the others knew this as they knew it, they could play that job successfully. The concept of culture, in short, has its use for sociologists as an explanation of those musicians and all the other forms of concerted action for which they stand.

I said that culture was not the only way sociologists explain concerted action. It often happens, for example, even in the most stable groups and traditional situations, that things happen which are not fully or even partly covered by already shared understandings. That may be because the situation is unprecedented—a disaster of a kind that has never occurred before—or because the people in the group come from such a variety of backgrounds that, though they all have some idea about the matter at hand and all speak a common language, they do not share understandings. That can easily happen in stratified societies, in ethnically differentiated societies, in situations where different occupational groups meet. Of course, people in such situations will presumably share some understandings which will form the basis of discussion and mediation as they work out what to do. If the Saturday night musicians had not shared as much knowledge as they did, they would have sat down to discuss what kind of music they would play, sketched out parts, and so on. They would have had to negotiate, a process I will consider more fully below.

Culture, however, explains how people act in concert when they do share understandings. It is thus a consequence (in this kind of sociological thinking) of the existence of a group of acting people. It has its meaning as one of the resources people draw on in order to coordinate their activities. In this it differs from most anthropological thinking in which the order of importance is reversed, culture leading a kind of independent existence as a system of patterns that make the existence of larger groups possible.

Most conceptions of culture include a great deal more than the spare definition I offered above. But I think, for reasons made clear later, that it is better to begin with a minimal definition and then to add other conditions when that is helpful.

Many people would insist that, if we are to call something culture, it must be traditional, of long standing, passed on from generation to generation. That would certainly make the concept unavailable as an explanation of the Saturday night musician. While we might conceivably say that these men were engaging in a traditional cultural activity, since a tradition of musicians playing for the entertainment of others goes back centuries and the American tradition of professional musicians playing for dances and parties is decades old, they were not doing it the way people who play for peasant parties in Greece or Mexico do, playing songs their grandparents played, perhaps on the same instruments. No, they were playing songs no more than twenty or thirty years old, songs their grandfathers never knew; in fact, few of their grandfathers had been musicians in whatever countries they came from, and, by becoming musicians themselves, these men were doing something untraditional in their families (and usually something not desired by their families either). They, of course, had learned to do many of the things they were doing from others who were slightly older, as I had learned many of the tricks of being a weekend musician when I was fifteen from people as old as seventeen or eighteen, who had in turn learned them from still older people. But, still, they did not know how to do what they were doing because it was traditional.

Many other people would insist that, if we are to call something culture, it must be part of a larger *system*, in which the various parts not only cohere in the sense of being noncontradictory, but, more than that, harmonize in the sense of being different versions of the same underlying themes. Such people would not use the term "culture" to describe the patterns of cooperation of the weekend musicians unless those patterns were also reflected in the music they played, the clothing they wore, the way they spent their leisure time, and so on. But none of that was true because they were not just musicians, and much of what they did reflected understandings they had acquired by participating in other social arenas in which the musicians' culture was irrelevant and vice versa. Nor, in any event, did they play what they might have played if they had been free to express their cultural understandings, for what they played was largely what they were paid to play (polkas on Friday, mambos on Saturday).

And many people would insist that my example is misleading to begin with, for the kinds of coherence that constitute "real" culture occur only at the level of the whole society. But if we connect culture to activities people carry on with one another, then we have to ask what all the members of a whole society do, or what they all do together, that requires them to share these general understandings. There are such things, but I think they tend to be rather banal and not at the level usually meant in discussions of general cultural themes. Thus, we all use the money of our society and know how many of the smaller units make one of the larger ones. Less trivially, we probably share understandings about how to behave in public, the things Edward T. Hall and Erving Goffman have written about—how close to stand to someone when we talk or how much space someone is entitled to in a public place, for example. But, even if for the sake of the argument we imagine that some substantial body of such materials exists, as it might in a relatively undifferentiated or rural society, that would not help us understand how the weekend musicians did their trick, and we would need some other term for what they were able to do and the web of shared understandings they used to do it.

Other people have other requirements for what can be called culture, all of which can be subjected to similar criticisms. Some think that culture, to be "really" culture, must be built in some deep way into the personalities of the people who carry it; others require that culture consist of "basic values," whatever might be meant by that. In neither case would the activities of the Saturday night musicians qualify as culture, however, if those definitional requirements were observed.

Normally, of course, we can define terms any way we want, but in the case of culture, several things seem to limit our freedom. The two most important are the quasi ownership of the term by anthropologists and the ambiguity of the word with respect to the problem of "high culture," to which I will return later. Anthropologists, and most other people, regard culture as anthropology's key concept and assume that the discipline is therefore entitled to make the definition. But anthropologists do not agree on a definition of culture; indeed, they differ spectacularly among themselves, as a famous compendium by Alfred Kroeber and Clyde Kluckhohn demonstrates. That did not dissuade Kroeber and Talcott Parsons from signing a jurisdictional agreement (like those by which the building trades decide how much of the work carpenters can do and where electricians must take over) giving "culture" to anthropology and "society" to sociology. But the social sciences, unlike the building trades, have not respected the deal their leaders made.

Which of these additional criteria, if any, should be incorporated into the definition of culture I have already given? Do we need any of them? Do we lose anything by using the most minimal definition of culture, as the shared understandings that people use to coordinate their activities? I think not. We have an inclusive term which describes not only the Saturday night musicians and the way they accomplish their feat of coordination, but all the other combinations of attributes that turn up in real life, raising questions about when they go together and when they do not.

Much depends on what kind of archetypal case you want the definition to cover, since a small Stone Age tribe living at the headwaters of the Amazon, which has never been in contact with European civilization, is obviously quite different from such typical products of twentieth-century urban America as the weekend musicians. The kinds of collective action required in the two situations differ enormously and, consequently, the kinds of shared understandings participants can rely on vary concomitantly. Many anthropologists have a kind of temperamental preference for the simplicity, order, and predictability of less complicated societies, in which everyone knows what everyone else is supposed to do, and in which there is a "design for living." If you share that preference, then you can turn culture into an honorific term by denying it to those social arrangements which do not "deserve" it, thereby making a disguised moral judgment about those ways of life. But that leaves a good part of modern life, not just the Saturday night musicians, out of the culture sphere altogether.

How does culture—shared understanding—help people to act collectively? People have ideas about how a certain kind of activity might be carried on. They believe others share these ideas and will act on them if they understand the situation in the same way. They believe further that the people they are interacting with believe that they share these ideas too, so everyone thinks that everyone else has the same idea about how to do things. Given such circumstances, if everyone does what seems appropriate, action will be sufficiently coordinated for practical purposes. Whatever was under way will get done—the meal served, the child dealt with, the job finished, all well enough so that life can proceed.

The cultural process, then, consists of people doing something in line with their understanding of what one might best do under the given circumstances. Others, recognizing what was done as appropriate, will then consult their notions of what might be done and do something that seems right to them, to which others in return will respond similarly, and so on. If everyone has the same general ideas in mind, and does something congruent with that image or collection of ideas, then what people do will fit together. If we all know the melody and harmony of "Exactly Like You," and improvise accordingly, whatever comes out will sound reasonable to the players and listeners, and a group of perfect strangers will sound like they know what they are doing.

Consider another common situation. A man and woman meet and find each other interesting. At some stage of their relationship, they may consider any of a variety of ways of organizing their joint activities. Early on, one or the other might propose that they "have a date." Later, one or the other might, subtly or forthrightly, suggest that they spend the night together. Still later, they might try "living together." Finally, they might decide to "get married." They might skip some of these stages and they might not follow that progression, which in contemporary America is a progression of increasingly formal commitment. In other societies and at other times, of course, the stages and the relationships would differ. But, whatever their variety, insofar as there are names for those relationships and stages, and insofar as most or all of the people in a society know those names and have an idea of what they imply as far as continuing patterns of joint activity are concerned, then the man and woman involved will be able to organize what they do by referring to those guideposts. When one or the other suggests one of these possibilities, the partner will know, more or less, what is being suggested without requiring that every item be spelled out in detail, and the pair can then organize their daily lives, more or less, around the patterns suggested by these cultural images.

What they do from day to day will of course not be completely covered by the details of that imagery, although they will be able to decide many details by consulting it together and adapting what it suggests to the problem at hand. None of these images, for instance, really establishes who takes the garbage out or what the details of their sexual activity may be, but the images do, in general, suggest the kind of commitments and obligations involved on both sides in a wide range of practical matters.

That is not the end of the matter, though. Consider a likely contemporary complication: the woman, divorced, has small children who live with her. In this case, the couple's freedom of action is constrained, and no cultural model suggests what they ought to do about the resulting difficulties. The models for pairing and for rearing children suggest incompatible solutions, and the partners have to invent something. They have to improvise.

This raises a major problem in the theory of culture I am propounding. Where does culture come from? The typical cultural explanation of behavior takes the culture as given, as preexisting the particular encounter in which it comes into play. That makes sense. Most of the cultural understandings we use to organize our daily behavior are there before we get there and we do not propose to change them or negotiate their details with the people we encounter. We do not propose a new economic system every time we go to the grocery store. But those understandings and ways of doing things have not always been there. Most of us buy our food in supermarkets today, and that requires a different way of shopping from the corner grocery stores of a generation ago. How did the new culture of supermarkets arise?

One answer is that the new culture was imposed by the inventors of the concept, the owners of the new stores which embodied it. They created the conditions under which change was more or less inevitable. People might have decided not to shop in supermarkets and chain stores, but changing conditions of urban life caused so many of them to use the new markets that the corner grocery, the butcher shop, the poultry and fish stores disappeared in all but a few areas. Once that happened, supermarkets became the only practical possibility left, and people had to invent new ways of serving themselves.

So, given new conditions, people invent culture. The way they do it was suggested by William Graham Sumner a century ago in *Folkways*. We can paraphrase him in this way. A group finds itself sharing a common situation and common problems. Various members of the group experiment with possible solutions to those problems and report their experiences to their fellows. In the course of their collective discussion, the members of the group arrive at a definition of the situation, its problems and possibilities, and develop a consensus as to the most appropriate and efficient ways of behaving. This consensus thenceforth constrains the activities of individual members of the group, who will probably act on it, given the opportunity. In other words, new situations provoke new behavior. But people generally find themselves in company when dealing with these new situations, and since they arrive at their solutions collectively, each assumes that the others share them. The beginnings of a new shared understanding thus come into play quickly and easily.

The ease with which new cultural understandings arise and persist varies. It makes a difference, for one thing, how large a group is involved in making the new understandings. At one extreme, as I have noted, every mating couple, every new family, has to devise its own culture to cover the contingencies of daily interaction. At the other, consider what happens during industrialization when hundreds of thousands—perhaps millions—of people are brought from elsewhere to work in the new factories. They have to come from elsewhere because the area could not support that many people before industrialization. As a result, the newcomers differ in culture from the people already there, and they differ as well in the role they play in the new industries, usually coming in at the bottom. When industrialization takes place on a large scale, not only does a new culture of the workplace have to be devised but also a new culture of the cities in which they all end up living—a new experience for everyone involved.

The range of examples suggests, as I mean it to, that people create culture continuously. Since no two situations are alike, the cultural solutions available to them are only approximate. Even in the simplest societies, no two people learn quite the same cultural material; the chance encounters of daily life provide sufficient variation to ensure that. No set of cultural understandings, then, provides a perfectly applicable solution to any problem people have to solve in the course of their day, and they therefore must remake those solutions, adapt their understandings to the new situation in the light of what is different about it. Even the most conscious and determined effort to keep things as they are would necessarily involve strenuous efforts to remake and reinforce understandings so as to keep them intact in the face of what was changing.

There is an apparent paradox here. On the one hand, culture persists and antedates the participation of particular people in it: indeed, culture can be said to shape the outlooks of people who participate in it. But cultural understandings, on the other hand, have to be reviewed and remade continually, and in the remaking they change.

This is not a true paradox, however: the understandings last *because* they change to deal with new situations. People continually refine them, changing some here and some there but never changing all of them at once. The emphasis on basic values and coherence in the definition of culture arises because of this process. In making the new versions of the old understandings, people naturally rely on what they already have available, so that consciously planned innovations and revolutions seem, in historical perspective, only small variations on what came before.

To summarize, how culture works as a guide in organizing collective action and how it comes into being are really the same process. In both cases, people pay attention to what other people are doing and, in an attempt to mesh what they do with those others, refer to what they know (or think they know) in common. So culture is always being made, changing more or less, acting as a point of reference for people engaged in interaction.

What difference does it make that people continually make culture in the way I have described? The most important consequence is that they can, as a result, cooperate easily and efficiently in the daily business of life, without necessarily knowing each other very well.

Most occupations, for example, operate on the premise that the people who work in them all know certain procedures and certain ways of thinking about and responding to typical situations and problems, and that such knowledge will make it possible to assemble them to work on a common project without prior team training. Most professional schools operate on the theory that the education they offer provides a basis for work cooperation among people properly trained anywhere. In fact, people probably learn the culture which makes occupational cooperation possible in the workplace itself. It presents them with problems to solve that are common to people in their line of work, and provides a group of more experienced workers who can suggest solutions. In some occupations, workers change jobs often and move from workplace to workplace often (as do the weekend musicians), and they carry what they have learned elsewhere with them. That makes it easy for them to refine and update their solutions frequently, and thus to develop and maintain an occupational culture. Workers who do not move but spend their work lives in one place may develop a more idiosyncratic work culture, peculiar to that place and its local problems—a culture of IBM or Texas Instruments or (because the process is not limited to large firms) Joe's Diner.

At a different level of cooperative action, Goffman has described cultural understandings which characterize people's behavior in public. For instance, people obey a norm of "civil inattention," allowing each other a privacy which the material circumstances of, say, waiting for a bus do not provide. Since this kind of privacy is what Americans and many others find necessary before they can feel comfortable and safe in public (Hall has shown how these rules differ in other cultures), these understandings make it possible for urban Americans to occupy crowded public spaces without making each other uneasy. The point is not trivial, because violations of these rules are at least in part responsible for the currently common fear that some public areas are "not safe," quite apart from whatever assaults have taken place in them. Most people have no personal knowledge of the alleged assaults, but they experience violation of what might be called the "Goffman rules" of public order as the prelude to danger and do not go to places which make them feel that way.

Cultural understandings, if they are to be effective in the organization of public behavior, must be very widely held. That means that people of otherwise varying class, ethnic, and regional cultures must learn them routinely, and must learn them quite young, because even small children can disrupt public order very effectively. That requires, in turn, substantial agreement among people of all segments of the society on how children should be brought up. If no such agreement exists or if some of the people who agree in principle do not manage to teach their children the necessary things, public order breaks down, as it often does.

In another direction, cultural understandings affect and "socialize" the internal experiences people have. By applying understandings they know to be widely accepted to their own perhaps inchoate private experiences, people learn to define those internal experiences in ways which allow them to mesh their activities relevant to those topics with those of others with whom they are involved. Consider the familiar example of falling in love. It is remarkable that one of the experiences we usually consider private and unique—falling in love—actually has the same character for most people who experience it. That is not to say that the experience is superficial, but rather that when people try to understand their emotional responses to others, one available explanation of what they feel is the idea, common in Western culture, of romantic love. They learn that idea from a variety of sources, ranging from the mass media to discussion with their peers, and they learn to see their own experiences as embodiments of it. Because most people within a given culture learn to experience love in the same way from the same sources, two people can become acquainted and successfully fall in love with each other—not an easy trick.

Because shared cultural understandings make it easy to do things in certain ways, moreover, their existence favors those ways of doing things and makes other ways of achieving the same end, which might be just as satisfactory to everyone involved, correspondingly less likely. Random events, which might produce innovations desirable to participants, occur infrequently. In fact, even when the familiar line of activity is not exactly to anyone's liking, people continue it simply because it is what everyone knows and knows that everyone else knows, and thus is what offers the greatest likelihood of successful collective action. Everyone knows, for instance, that it would be better to standardize the enormous variety of screw threads in this country, or to convert the United States to the metric system. But the old ways are the ones we know, and, of course, in this instance, they are built into tools and machines which would be difficult and costly to change. Many activities exhibit that inertia, and they pose a problem that sociologists have been interested in for many years: which elements of a society or culture are most likely to change? William Fielding Ogburn, for instance, proposed sixty years ago that material culture (screw threads) changed more quickly than social organization, and that the resultant "lag" could be problematic for human society.

A final consequence: the existence of culture makes it possible for people to plan their own lives. We can plan most easily for a known future, in which the major organizational features of society turn out to be what we expected them to be and what we made allowances for in our planning. We need, most importantly, to predict the actions of other people and of the organizations which consist of their collective actions. Culture makes those actions, individual and collective, more predictable than they would otherwise be. People in traditional societies may not obey in every detail the complex marriage rules held out to them, but those rules supply a sufficiently clear guide for men and women to envision more or less accurately when they will marry, what resources will be available to them when they do, and how the course of their married life will proceed.

In modern industrial societies, workers can plan their careers better when they know what kinds of work situations they will find themselves in and what their rights and obligations at various ages and career stages will be. Few people can make those predictions successfully in this country any more, which indicates that cultural understandings do not always last the twenty or thirty years necessary for such predictability to be possible. When that happens, people do not know how to prepare themselves for their work lives and do not receive the benefits of their earlier investments in hard work. People who seemed to be goofing off or acting irrationally, for example, sometimes make windfall profits as the work world comes to need just those combinations of skills and experiences that they acquired while not following a "sensible" career path. As technical and organizational innovations make new skills more desirable, new career lines open up which were not and could not have been predicted ten years earlier. The first generation of computer programmers benefited from that kind of good luck, as did the first generation of drug researchers, among others.

In every society, some of the understandings we have been talking about are thought to be more important, more noble, more imbued with the highest aspirations or achievements of that society. For hundreds of years, Western societies have given that kind of privileged position to what some regard as "high culture" and what others regard as "culture" without a qualifying adjective—art, reflective thought, philosophy. These pursuits are generally opposed to more manual occupations and to those connected with industry and commerce, although the growth of science and the commercialization of art in more recent times have created substantial areas of ambiguity. It seems obvious, without Thorstein Veblen to point it out, that these judgments reflect the relative prestige of those segments of society which more often engage in or patronize those pursuits. They are the hobbies, the playthings of political and religious leaders as well as of people of power and privilege in general, and it is a good sociological question whether they receive their *mana* from the power of those interested in them or whether they lend some portion of that *mana* to those supporters.

How do these areas of cultural understanding differ from the more mundane examples I addressed earlier? They have a better reputation, of course, but is the basis for that reputation discernible in them or could any set of concerns and activities achieve that special estate? That is an enormously complicated question which I am not going to answer in a few words. It is enough to ask, from the point of view assumed here, what kinds of activities, pursued by whom, follow from the existence of these understandings. Who can do what together as a result of their existence?

One answer is that, in Western societies originally at least, culturally reputable activities are carried on by specialists who make a profession of them. Those professions gather around them a special world—a network of people who collaborate in the production, distribution, and celebration of "high" culture—and that collaboration is made possible by the kinds of cultural understandings I have been discussing throughout this paper.

In addition, the people who cooperate in these ventures regard the work they do as having special value. "Art" is an honorific category, a word applied to productions that a society decides to treat as especially valuable. A great deal of work that seems to share the observable qualities of what comes to be called high art never earns that distinction, and that suggests that the difference does not lie in the *work* so honored but rather in the process of *honoring*. We can easily observe, furthermore, that the same objects and events earn the label of "art" on some occasions and not others, often migrating back and forth across the dividing line as fashions change. (I have discussed these matters at length in *Art Worlds*.)

High culture, then, consists of work recognized as belonging to an honored category of cultural understandings by the people who have the power to make that determination and to have it accepted by others. We may be able to devise systematic criteria that will identify work of superior quality, but it is unlikely that the work we can distinguish in that way will be the same as the work legitimated as high culture by the institutions that make that decision for any society.

Thinking of high culture this way suggests the levelling impulse contained in most systematic sociological analysis. Basic social processes, such as the development of common ways of looking at things, usually cross the honorific lines drawn in a society. Discussing culture in this fashion may seem awkward or impudent, but the warrant for doing it comes from the increased understanding the procedure gives us of the processes that lie under all our activities, honorable and otherwise.

11

THE CULTURE OF FEAR
Why Americans Are Afraid of the Wrong Things

BARRY GLASSNER

Sociologists are interested in how culture limits our free choice and shapes social interaction. Because each of us is born into a particular culture that has certain norms and values, our personal values and life expectations are profoundly influenced by our culture. For example, what are the values of American culture? Many scholars agree that some dominant U.S. values are

---

This chapter was written in the 1990s before the 2008 economic recession and high unemployment rates. While some economic data may have changed since this chapter was written, the argument is still sound.

achievement, Judeo-Christian morals, material comfort, patriotism, and individualism. In this reading, the second of three to explore culture, Barry Glassner examines one aspect of American culture, which he labels *the culture of fear*. Glassner, professor of sociology at the University of Southern California, raises interesting questions about our culture and the implications of living in a culture of fear. This excerpt is taken from Glassner's 1999 award-winning book of the same name, *The Culture of Fear: Why Americans Are Afraid of the Wrong Things*.

W hy are so many fears in the air, and so many of them unfounded? Why, as crime rates plunged throughout the 1990s, did two-thirds of Americans believe they were soaring? How did it come about that by mid-decade 62 percent of us described ourselves as "truly desperate" about crime—almost twice as many as in the late 1980s, when crime rates were higher? Why, on a survey in 1997, when the crime rate had already fallen for a half dozen consecutive years, did more than half of us disagree with the statement "This country is finally beginning to make some progress in solving the crime problem"?[1]

In the late 1990s the number of drug users had decreased by half compared to a decade earlier; almost two-thirds of high school seniors had never used any illegal drugs, even marijuana. So why did a majority of adults rank drug abuse as the greatest danger to America's youth? Why did nine out of ten believe the drug problem is out of control, and only one in six believe the country was making progress?[2]

Give us a happy ending and we write a new disaster story. In the late 1990s the unemployment rate was below 5 percent for the first time in a quarter century. People who had been pounding the pavement for years could finally get work. Yet pundits warned of imminent economic disaster. They predicted inflation would take off, just as they had a few years earlier—also erroneously—when the unemployment rate dipped below 6 percent.[3]

We compound our worries beyond all reason. Life expectancy in the United States has doubled during the twentieth century. We are better able to cure and control diseases than any other civilization in history. Yet we hear that phenomenal numbers of us are dreadfully ill. In 1996 Bob Garfield, a magazine writer, reviewed articles about serious diseases published over the course of a year in the *Washington Post*, the *New York Times*, and *USA Today*. He learned that, in addition to 59 million Americans with heart disease, 53 million with migraines, 25 million with osteoporosis, 16 million with obesity, and 3 million with cancer, many Americans suffer from more obscure ailments such as temporomandibular joint disorders (10 million) and brain injuries (2 million). Adding up the estimates, Garfield determined that 543 million Americans are seriously sick—a shocking number in a nation of 266 million inhabitants. "Either as a society we are doomed, or someone is seriously double-dipping," he suggested.[4]

Garfield appears to have underestimated one category of patients: for psychiatric ailments his figure was 53 million. Yet when Jim Windolf, an editor of the *New York Observer*, collated estimates for maladies ranging from borderline personality disorder (10 million) and sex addiction (11 million) to less well-known conditions such as restless leg syndrome (12 million) he came up with a figure of 152 million. "But give the experts a little time," he advised. "With another new quantifiable disorder or two, everybody in the country will be officially nuts."[5]

Indeed, Windolf omitted from his estimates new-fashioned afflictions that have yet to make it into the *Diagnostic and Statistical Manual of Mental Disorders* of the American Psychiatric Association: ailments such as road rage, which afflicts more than half of Americans, according to a psychologist's testimony before a congressional hearing in 1997.[6] . . .

Killer Kids

When we are not worrying about deadly diseases we worry about homicidal strangers. Every few months for the past several years it seems we discover a new category of people to fear: government thugs in Waco, sadistic cops on Los Angeles freeways and in Brooklyn police stations, mass-murdering youths in small towns all over the country. A single anomalous event can provide us with multiple groups of people to fear. After the 1995 explosion at the federal building in Oklahoma City, first we panicked about Arabs. "Knowing that the car bomb indicates Middle Eastern terrorists at work, it's safe to assume that their goal is to promote free-floating fear and a measure of anarchy, thereby disrupting American life," a *New York Post* editorial asserted. "Whatever we are doing to destroy Mideast terrorism, the chief terrorist threat against Americans, has not been working," wrote A. M. Rosenthal in the *New York Times*.[7]

When it turned out that the bombers were young white guys from middle America, two more groups instantly became spooky: right-wing radio talk show hosts who criticize the government—depicted by President Bill Clinton as "purveyors of hatred and division"—and members of militias. No group of disgruntled men was too ragtag not to warrant big, prophetic news stories.[8] . . .

The more things improve the more pessimistic we become. Violence-related deaths at the nation's schools dropped to a record low during the 1996–97 academic year (19 deaths out of 54 million children), and only one in ten public schools reported *any* serious crime. Yet *Time* and *U.S. News & World Report* both ran headlines in 1996 referring to "Teenage Time Bombs." In a nation of "Children Without Souls" (another *Time* headline that year), "America's beleaguered cities are about to be victimized by a paradigm shattering wave of ultraviolent, morally vacuous young people some call 'the superpredators,'" William Bennett, the former Secretary of Education, and John DiIulio, a criminologist, forecast in a book published in 1996.[9]

Instead of the arrival of superpredators, violence by urban youths continued to decline. So we went looking elsewhere for proof that heinous behavior by young people was "becoming increasingly more commonplace in America" (CNN). After a sixteen-year-old in Pearl, Mississippi, and a fourteen-year-old in West Paducah, Kentucky, went on shooting sprees in late

1997, killing five of their classmates and wounding twelve others, these isolated incidents were taken as evidence of *an epidemic of seemingly depraved adolescent murderers* (Geraldo Rivera). Three months later, in March 1998, all sense of proportion vanished after two boys ages eleven and thirteen killed four students and a teacher in Jonesboro, Arkansas. No longer, we learned in *Time*, was it "unusual for kids to get back at the world with live ammunition." When a child psychologist on NBC's *Today* show advised parents to reassure their children that shootings at schools are rare, reporter Ann Curry corrected him: *But this is the fourth case since October*, she said.[10]

Over the next couple of months young people failed to accommodate the trend hawkers. None committed mass murder. Fear of killer kids remained very much in the air nonetheless. In stories on topics such as school safety and childhood trauma, reporters recapitulated the gory details of the killings. And the news media made a point of reporting every incident in which a child was caught at school with a gun or making a death threat. In May, when a fifteen-year-old in Springfield, Oregon, did open fire in a cafeteria filled with students, killing two and wounding twenty-three others, the event felt like a continuation of a "disturbing trend" (*New York Times*). The day after the shooting, on National Public Radio's *All Things Considered*, the criminologist Vincent Schiraldi tried to explain that the recent string of incidents did not constitute a trend, that youth homicide rates had declined by 30 percent in recent years, and more than three times as many people were killed by lightning than by violence at schools. But the show's host, Robert Siegel, interrupted him: *You're saying these are just anomalous events?* he asked, audibly peeved. The criminologist reiterated that *anomalous* is precisely the right word to describe the events, and he called it "a grave mistake" to imagine otherwise. . . .

Roosevelt Was Wrong

We had better learn to doubt our inflated fears before they destroy us. Valid fears have their place; they cue us to danger. False and overdrawn fears only cause hardship. . . .

I do not contend, as did President Roosevelt in 1933, that *the only thing we have to fear is fear itself*. My point is that we often fear the wrong things. In the 1990s middle-income and poorer Americans should have worried about unemployment insurance, which covered a smaller share of workers than twenty years earlier. Many of us have had friends or family out of work during economic downturns or as a result of corporate restructuring. Living in a nation with one of the largest income gaps of any industrialized country, where the bottom 40 percent of the population is worse off financially than their counterparts two decades earlier, we might also have worried about income inequality. Or poverty. During the mid- and late-1990s, 5 million elderly Americans had no food in their homes, more than 20 million people used emergency food programs each year, and one in five children lived in poverty—more than a quarter million of them homeless. All told, a larger proportion of Americans were poor than three decades earlier.[11]

One of the paradoxes of a culture of fear is that serious problems remain widely ignored even though they give rise to precisely the dangers that the populace most abhors. Poverty, for example, correlates strongly with child abuse, crime, and drug abuse. Income inequality is also associated with adverse outcomes for society as a whole. The larger the gap between rich and poor in a society, the higher its overall death rates from heart disease, cancer, and murder. Some social scientists argue that extreme inequality also threatens political stability in a nation such as the United States, where we think of ourselves not as "haves and have nots" but as "haves and will haves." "Unlike the citizens of most other nations, Americans have always been united less by a shared past than by the shared dreams of a better future. If we lose that common future," the Brandeis University economist Robert Reich has suggested, "we lose the glue that holds our nation together."[12]

The combination of extreme inequality and poverty can prove explosive. In an insightful article in *U.S. News & World Report* in 1997 about militia groups, reporters Mike Tharp and William Holstein noted that people's motivations for joining these groups are as much economic as ideological. The journalists argued that the disappearance of military and blue-collar jobs, along with the decline of family farming, created the conditions under which a new breed of protest groups flourished. "What distinguishes these antigovernment groups from, say, traditional conservatives who mistrust government is that their anger is fueled by direct threats to their livelihood, and they carry guns," Tharp and Holstein wrote.[13]

That last phrase alludes to a danger that by any rational calculation deserves top billing on Americans' lists of fears. So gun crazed is this nation that Burger King had to order a Baltimore franchise to stop giving away coupons from a local sporting goods store for free boxes of bullets with the purchase of guns. We have more guns *stolen* from their owners—about 300,000 annually—than many countries have gun owners. In Great Britain, Australia, and Japan, where gun ownership is severely restricted, no more than a few dozen people are killed each year by handguns. In the United States, where private citizens own a quarter-billion guns, around 15,000 people are killed, 18,000 commit suicide, and another 1,500 die accidentally from firearms. American children are twelve times more [likely] to die from gun injuries than are youngsters in other industrialized nations.[14]

Yet even after tragedies that could not have occurred except for the availability of guns, their significance is either played down or missed altogether. Had the youngsters in the celebrated schoolyard shootings of 1997–98 not had access to guns, some or all of the people they killed would be alive today. Without their firepower those boys lacked the strength, courage, and skill to commit multiple murders. Nevertheless, newspapers ran editorials with titles such as "It's Not Guns, It's Killer Kids" (*Fort Worth Star-Telegram*) and "Guns Aren't the Problem" (*New York Post*), and journalists, politicians, and pundits blathered on endlessly about every imaginable cause of youthful rage, from "the psychology of violence in the South" to satanism to fights on *Jerry Springer* and simulated shooting in Nintendo games.[15]. . .

In Praise of Journalists

Any analysis of the culture of fear that ignored the news media would be patently incomplete, and of the several institutions most culpable for creating and sustaining scares the news media are arguably first among equals. They are also the most promising candidates for positive change. Yet, by the same token, critiques such as Stolberg's presage a crucial shortcoming in arguments that blame the media. Reporters not only spread fears, they also debunk them and criticize one another for spooking the public. A wide array of groups, including businesses, advocacy organizations, religious sects, and political parties, promote and profit from scares. News organizations are distinguished from other fearmongering groups because they sometimes bite the scare that feeds them.

A group that raises money for research into a particular disease is not likely to negate concerns about that disease. A company that sells alarm systems is not about to call attention to the fact that crime is down. News organizations, on the other hand, periodically allay the very fears they arouse to lure audiences. Some newspapers that ran stories about child murderers, rather than treat every incident as evidence of a shocking trend, affirmed the opposite. After the schoolyard shooting in Kentucky the *New York Times* ran a sidebar alongside its feature story with the headline "Despite Recent Carnage, School Violence Is Not on Rise." Following the Jonesboro killings they ran a similar piece, this time on a recently released study showing the rarity of violent crimes in schools.[16]

Several major newspapers parted from the pack in other ways. *USA Today* and the *Washington Post*, for instance, made sure their readers knew that what should worry them is the availability of guns. *USA Today* ran news stories explaining that easy access to guns in homes accounted for increases in the number of juvenile arrests for homicide in rural areas during the 1990s. While other news outlets were respectfully quoting the mother of the thirteen-year-old Jonesboro shooter, who said she did not regret having encouraged her son to learn to fire a gun (*It's like anything else, there's some people that can drink a beer, and not become an alcoholic*), *USA Today* ran an op-ed piece proposing legal parameters for gun ownership akin to those for the use of alcohol and motor vehicles. And the paper published its own editorial in support of laws that require gun owners to lock their guns or keep them in locked containers. Adopted at that time by only fifteen states, the laws had reduced the number of deaths among children in those states by 23 percent.[17]

Morality and Marketing

Why do news organizations and their audiences find themselves drawn to one hazard rather than another? . . .

In the first half of the 1990s, U.S. cities spent at least $10 billion to purge asbestos from public schools, even though removing asbestos from buildings posed a greater health hazard than leaving it in place. At a time when about one-third of the nation's schools were in need of extensive repairs, the money might have been spent to renovate dilapidated buildings. But hazards posed by seeping asbestos are morally repugnant. A product that was supposed to protect children from fires might be giving them cancer. By directing our worries and dollars at asbestos, we express outrage at technology and industry run afoul.[18] . . .

Within public discourse fears proliferate through a process of exchange. It is from crosscurrents of scares and counterscares that the culture of fear swells ever larger. Even as feminists disparage large classes of men, they themselves are a staple of fearmongering by conservatives. To hear conservatives tell it, feminists are not only "anti-child and anti-family" (Arianna Huffington) but through women's studies programs on college campuses they have fomented an "anti-science and anti-reason movement" (Christina Hoff Sommers).[19]

Conservatives also like to spread fears about liberals, who respond in kind. Among other pet scares, they accuse liberals of creating "children without consciences" by keeping prayer out of schools—to which liberals rejoin with warnings that right-wing extremists intend to turn youngsters into Christian soldiers.[20]

Samuel Taylor Coleridge was right when he claimed, "In politics, what begins in fear usually ends up in folly." Political activists are more inclined, though, to heed an observation from Richard Nixon: "People react to fear, not love. They don't teach that in Sunday school, but it's true." That principle, which guided the late president's political strategy throughout his career, is the sine qua non of contemporary political campaigning. Marketers of products and services ranging from car alarms to TV news programs have taken it to heart as well.[21]

The short answer to why Americans harbor so many misbegotten fears is that immense power and money await those who tap into our moral insecurities and supply us with symbolic substitutes.

ENDNOTES

[1] Crime data here and throughout are from reports of the Bureau of Justice Statistics unless otherwise noted. Fear of crime: Esther Madriz, *Nothing Bad Happens to Good Girls* (Berkeley: University of California Press, 1997), ch. 1; Richard Morin, "As Crime Rate Falls, Fears Persist," *Washington Post* National Edition, 16 June 1997, p. 35; David Whitman, "Believing the Good News," *U.S. News & World Report*, 5 January 1998, pp. 45–46.

[2] Eva Bertram, Morris Blachman et al., *Drug War Politics* (Berkeley: University of California Press, 1996), p. 10; Mike Males, *Scapegoat Generation* (Monroe, ME: Common Courage Press, 1996), ch. 6; Karen Peterson, "Survey: Teen Drug Use Declines," *USA Today*, 19 June 1998, p. A6; Robert Blendon and John Young, "The Public and the War on Illicit Drugs," *Journal of the American Medical Association* 279 (18 March 1998): 827–32. In presenting these statistics and others I am aware of a seeming paradox: I criticize the abuse of statistics by fearmongering politicians, journalists, and others but hand down precise-sounding numbers myself. Yet to eschew all estimates because some are used inappropriately or do not withstand scrutiny would be as foolhardy as ignoring all medical advice because some doctors are quacks. Readers can be assured I have interrogated the statistics presented here as factual. As notes make clear, I have tried to rely on research that appears in peer-reviewed scholarly journals. Where this was not possible or sufficient, I traced numbers back to their sources, investigated the research methodology utilized to produce them, or conducted searches of the popular and scientific literature for critical commentaries and conflicting findings.

[3] Bob Herbert, "Bogeyman Economics," *New York Times*, 4 April 1997, p. A15; Doug Henwood, "Alarming Drop in Unemployment," *Extra*, September 1994, pp. 16–17; Christopher Shea, "Low Inflation and Low Unemployment Spur Economists to Debate 'Natural Rate' Theory," *Chronicle of Higher Education*, 24 October 1997, p. A13.

[4] Bob Garfield, "Maladies by the Millions," *USA Today*, 16 December 1996, p. A15.

[5] Jim Windolf, "A Nation of Nuts," *Wall Street Journal*, 22 October 1997, p. A22.

[6] Andrew Ferguson, "Road Rage," *Time*, 12 January 1998, pp. 64–68; Joe Sharkey, "You're Not Bad, You're Sick. It's in the Book," *New York Times*, 28 September 1997, pp. N1, 5.

[7] Jim Naureckas, "The Jihad That Wasn't," *Extra*, July 1995, pp. 6–10, 20 (contains quotes). See also Edward Said, "A Devil Theory of Islam," *Nation*, 12 August 1996, pp. 28–32.

[8] Lewis Lapham, "Seen but Not Heard," *Harper's*, July 1995, pp. 29–36 (contains Clinton quote). See also Robin Wright and Ronald Ostrow, "Illusion of Immunity Is Shattered," *Los Angeles Times*, 20 April 1995, pp. A1, 18; Jack Germond and Jules Witcover, "Making the Angry White Males Angrier," column syndicated by Tribune Media Services, May 1995; and articles by James Bennet and Michael Janofsky in the *New York Times*, May 1995.

[9] Statistics from "Violence and Discipline Problems in U.S. Public Schools: 1996–97," National Center on Education Statistics, U.S. Department of Education, Washington, DC, March 1998; CNN, "Early Prime," 2 December 1997; and Tamar Lewin, "Despite Recent Carnage, School Violence Is Not on Rise," *New York Times*, 3 December 1997, p. A14. Headlines: *Time*, 15 January 1996; *U.S. News & World Report*, 25 March 1996; Margaret Carlson, "Children Without Souls," *Time*, 2 December 1996, p. 70; William J. Bennett, John J. DiIulio, and John Walters, *Body Count* (New York: Simon & Schuster, 1996).

[10] CNN, "Talkback Live," 2 December 1997; CNN, "The Geraldo Rivera Show," 11 December 1997; Richard Lacayo, "Toward the Root of Evil," *Time*, 6 April 1998, pp. 38–39; NBC, "Today," 25 March 1998. See also Rick Bragg, "Forgiveness, After 3 Die in Shootings in Kentucky," *New York Times*, 3 December 1997, p. A14; Maureen Downey, "Kids and Violence," 28 March 1998, *Atlanta Journal and Constitution*, p. A12.

[11] "The State of America's Children," report by the Children's Defense Fund, Washington, DC, March 1998; "Blocks to Their Future," report by the National Law Center on Homelessness and Poverty, Washington, DC, September 1997; reports released in 1998 from the National Center for Children in Poverty, Columbia University, New York; Douglas Massey, "The Age of Extremes," *Demography*, 33 (1996): 395–412; Trudy Lieberman, "Hunger in America," *Nation*, 30 March 1998, pp. 11–16; David Lynch, "Rich Poor World," *USA Today*, 20 September 1996, p. B1; Richard Wolf, "Good Economy Hasn't Helped the Poor," *USA Today*, 10 March 1998, p. A3; Robert Reich, "Broken Faith," *Nation*, 16 February 1998, pp. 11–17.

[12] Inequality and mortality studies: Bruce Kennedy et al., "Income Distribution and Mortality," *British Medical Journal* 312 (1996): 1004–7; Ichiro Kawachi and Bruce Kennedy, "The Relationship of Income Inequality to Mortality," *Social Science and Medicine* 45 (1997): 1121–27. See also Barbara Chasin, *Inequality and Violence in the United States* (Atlantic Highlands, NJ: Humanities Press, 1997). Political stability: John Sloan, "The Reagan Presidency, Growing Inequality, and the American Dream," *Policy Studies Journal* 25 (1997): 371–86 (contains Reich quotes and "will haves" phrase). On both topics see also Philippe Bourgois, *In Search of Respect: Selling Crack in El Barrio* (Cambridge: Cambridge University Press, 1996); William J. Wilson, *When Work Disappears* (New York, Knopf, 1996); Richard Gelles, "Family Violence," *Annual Review of Sociology* 11 (1985): 347–67; Sheldon Danziger and Peter Gottschalk, *America Unequal* (Cambridge, MA: Harvard University Press, 1995); Claude Fischer et al., *Inequality by Design* (Princeton, NJ: Princeton University Press, 1996).

[13] Mike Tharp and William Holstein, "Mainstreaming the Militia," *U.S. News & World Report*, 21 April 1997, pp. 24–37.

[14] Burger King: "Notebooks," *New Republic*, 29 April 1996, p. 8. Statistics from the FBI's Uniform Crime Reports, Centers for Disease Control reports, and Timothy Egan, "Oregon Freeman Goes to Court," *New York Times*, 23 May 1998, pp. A1, 8.

[15] Bill Thompson, "It's Not Guns, It's Killer Kids," *Fort Worth Star-Telegram*, 31 March 1998, p. 14; "Guns Aren't the Problem," *New York Post* 30 March 1998 (from *Post* Web site); "Arkansas Gov. Assails 'Culture of Violence,'" *Reuters*, 25 March 1998; Bo Emerson, "Violence Feeds 'Redneck,' Gun-Toting Image," *Atlanta Journal and Constitution*, 29 March 1998, p. A8; Nadya Labi, "The Hunter and the Choir Boy," *Time*, 6 April 1998, pp. 28–37; Lacayo, "Toward the Root of Evil."

[16] Lewin, "More Victims and Less Sense"; Tamar Lewin, "Study Finds No Big Rise in Public-School Crimes," *New York Times*, 25 March 1998, p. A18.

[17] "Licensing Can Protect," *USA Today,* 7 April 1998, p. A11; Jonathan Kellerman, "Few Surprises When It Comes to Violence," *USA Today,* 27 March 1998, p. A13; Gary Fields, "Juvenile Homicide Arrest Rate on Rise in Rural USA," *USA Today,* 26 March 1998, p. A11; Karen Peterson and Glenn O'Neal, "Society More Violent, So Are Its Children," *USA Today,* 25 March 1998, p. A3; Scott Bowles, "Armed, Alienated and Adolescent," *USA Today,* 26 March 1998, p. A9. Similar suggestions about guns appear in Jonathan Alter, "Harnessing the Hysteria," *Newsweek,* 6 April 1998, p. 27.

[18] Mary Douglas and Aaron Wildavsky, *Risk and Culture* (Berkeley: University of California Press, 1982), see esp. pp. 6–9; Mary Douglas, *Risk and Blame* (London: Routledge, 1992). See also Mary Douglas, *Purity and Danger* (New York: Praeger, 1966). Asbestos and schools: Peter Cary, "The Asbestos Panic Attack," *U.S. News & World Report,* 20 February 1995, pp. 61–64; Children's Defense Fund, "State of America's Children."

[19] CNN, "Crossfire," 27 August 1995 (contains Huffington quote); Ruth Conniff, "Warning: Feminism Is Hazardous to Your Health," *Progressive,* April 1997, pp. 33–36 (contains Sommers quote). See also Susan Faludi, *Backlash* (New York: Crown, 1991); Deborah Rhode, "Media Images, Feminist Issues," *Signs* 20 (1995): 685–710; Paula Span, "Did Feminists Forget the Most Crucial Issues?" *Los Angeles Times,* 28 November 1996, p. E8.

[20] See Katha Pollitt, "Subject to Debate," *Nation,* 26 December 1994, p. 788, and 20 November 1995, p. 600.

[21] Henry Nelson Coleridge, ed., *Specimens of the Table Talk of the Late Samuel Taylor Coleridge* (London: J. Murray, 1935), entry for 5 October 1930. Nixon quote cited in William Safire, *Before the Fall* (New York: Doubleday, 1975), Prologue.

12

LOVELY HULA HANDS
Corporate Tourism and the Prostitution
of Hawaiian Culture

HAUNANI-KAY TRASK

Many U.S. racial-ethnic groups, including Native Americans, Latina/os, and African Americans, have experienced cultural exploitation. Exploitation occurs when aspects of a subculture, such as its beliefs, rituals, and social customs, are commodified and marketed without the cultural group's permission. This selection by Haunani-Kay Trask explores the cultural commodification and exploitation of Hawaiian culture. Trask, a descendant from the Pi'ilani line of Maui and the Kahakumakaliua line of Kaua'i, is a professor of Hawaiian Studies at the University of Hawai'i at Manoa. In this excerpt, taken from her 1993 book, *From a Native Daughter: Colonialism and Sovereignty in Hawai'i,* Trask argues that several aspects of Polynesian and Hawaiian cultures, including their language, dress, and dance forms, have been marketed as products for the mass consumption of tourists.

I am certain that most, if not all, Americans have heard of Hawai'i and have wished, at some time in their lives, to visit my native land. But I doubt that the history of how Hawai'i came to be territorially incorporated, and economically, politically, and culturally subordinated to the United States is known to most Americans. Nor is it common knowledge that Hawaiians have been struggling for over 20 years to achieve a land base and some form of political sovereignty on the same level as American Indians. Finally, I would imagine that most Americans could not place Hawai'i or any other Pacific island on a map of the Pacific. But despite all this appalling ignorance, five million Americans will vacation in my homeland this year *and* the next, and so on into the foreseeable capitalist future. Such are the intended privileges of the so-called American standard of living: ignorance of, and yet power over, one's relations to native peoples.

Thanks to postwar American imperialism, the ideology that the United States has no overseas colonies and is, in fact, the champion of self-determination the world over holds no greater sway than in the United States itself. To most Americans, then, Hawai'i is *theirs:* to use, to take, and, above all, to fantasize about long after the experience.

Just five hours away by plane from California, Hawai'i is a thousand light-years away in fantasy. Mostly a state of mind, Hawai'i is the image of escape from the rawness and violence of daily American life. Hawai'i—the word, the vision, the sound in the mind—is the fragrance and feel of soft kindness. Above all, Hawai'i is "she," the Western image of the native "female" in her magical allure. And if luck prevails, some of "her" will rub off on you, the visitor.

This fictional Hawai'i comes out of the depths of Western sexual sickness which demands a dark, sin-free native for instant gratification between imperialist wars. The attraction of Hawai'i is stimulated by slick Hollywood movies, saccharine Andy Williams music, and the constant psychological deprivations of maniacal American life. Tourists flock to my native land for escape, but they are escaping into a state of mind while participating in the destruction of a host people in a native place.

To Hawaiians, daily life is neither soft nor kind. In fact, the political, economic, and cultural reality for most Hawaiians is hard, ugly, and cruel.

In Hawai'i, the destruction of our land and the prostitution of our culture are planned and executed by multinational corporations (both foreign-based and Hawai'i-based), by huge landowners (like the missionary-descended Castle and Cooke—of Dole Pineapple fame—and others) and by collaborationist state and county governments. The ideological gloss that claims tourism to be our economic savior and the "natural" result of Hawaiian culture is manufactured by ad agencies (like the state-supported Hawai'i Visitors' Bureau) and tour companies (many of which are owned by the airlines), and spewed out to the public through complicitous cultural engines like film, television and radio, and the daily newspapers. As for the local labor unions, both rank and file and management clamor for more tourists while the construction industry lobbies incessantly for larger resorts. . . .

My use of the word *tourism* in the Hawai'i context refers to a mass-based, corporately controlled industry that is both vertically and horizontally integrated such that one multinational corporation owns an airline, the tour buses that transport tourists to the corporation-owned hotel where they eat in a corporation-owned restaurant, play golf and "experience" Hawai'i on corporation-owned recreation areas, and eventually consider buying a second home built on corporation land. Profits, in this case, are mostly repatriated back to the home country. In Hawai'i, these "home" countries are Japan, Taiwan, Hong Kong, Canada, Australia, and the United States. . . .

With this as a background on tourism, I want to move now into the area of cultural prostitution. "Prostitution" in this context refers to the entire institution which defines a woman (and by extension the "female") as an object of degraded and victimized sexual value for use and exchange through the medium of money. The "prostitute" is then a woman who sells her sexual capacities and is seen, thereby, to possess and reproduce them at will, that is, by her very "nature." The prostitute and the institution which creates and maintains her are, of course, of patriarchal origin. The pimp is the conduit of exchange, managing the commodity that is the prostitute while acting as the guard at the entry and exit gates, making sure the prostitute behaves as a prostitute by fulfilling her sexual–economic functions. The victims participate in their victimization with enormous ranges of feeling, including resistance and complicity, but the force and continuity of the institution are shaped by men.

There is much more to prostitution than my sketch reveals but this must suffice for I am interested in using the largest sense of this term as a metaphor in understanding what has happened to Hawaiian culture. My purpose is not to exact detail or fashion a model but to convey the utter degradation of our culture and our people under corporate tourism by employing "prostitution" as an analytic category.

Finally, I have chosen four areas of Hawaiian culture to examine: our homeland, or *one hānau* that is Hawai'i, our lands and fisheries, the outlying seas and the heavens; our language and dance; our familial relationships; and our women.

Nā Mea Hawai'i—Things Hawaiian

The *mo'ōlelo,* or history of Hawaiians, is to be found in our genealogies. From our great cosmogonic genealogy, the *Kumulipo,* derives the Hawaiian identity. The "essential lesson" of this genealogy is "the interrelatedness of the Hawaiian world, and the inseparability of its constituent parts." Thus, "the genealogy of the land, the gods, chiefs, and people intertwine one with the other, and with all aspects of the universe."[1]

In the *mo'ōlelo* of Papa and Wākea, earth-mother and sky-father, our islands are born: Hawai'i, Maui, O'ahu, Kaua'i, and Ni'ihau. From their human offspring came the *taro* plant and from the taro came the Hawaiian people. The lessons of our genealogy are that human beings have a familial relationship to land and to the *taro,* our elder siblings or *kua'ana.*

In Hawai'i, as in all of Polynesia, younger siblings must serve and honor elder siblings who, in turn, must feed and care for their younger siblings. Therefore, Hawaiians must cultivate and husband the land which will feed and provide for the Hawaiian people. This relationship of people to land is called *mālama 'āina* or *aloha 'āina*, care and love of the land.

When people and land work together harmoniously, the balance that results is called *pono*. In Hawaiian society, the *ali'i* or chiefs were required to maintain order, abundance of food, and good government. The *maka'āinana* or common people worked the land and fed the chiefs; the *ali'i* organized production and appeased the gods.

Today, *mālama 'āina* is called stewardship by some, although that word does not convey spiritual and genealogical connections. Nevertheless, to love and make the land flourish is a Hawaiian value. *'Āina*, one of the words for land, means *that which feeds*. *Kama'āina*, a term for native-born people, means *child of the land*. Thus is the Hawaiian relationship to land both familial and reciprocal.

Our deities are also of the land: Pele is our volcano, Kāne and Lono our fertile valleys and plains, Kanaloa our ocean and all that lives within it, and so on with the 40,000 and 400,000 gods of Hawai'i. Our whole universe, physical and metaphysical, is divine.

Within this world, the older people or *kūpuna* are to cherish those who are younger, the *mo'opuna*. Unstinting generosity is a value and of high status. Social connections between our people are through *aloha*, simply translated as love but carrying with it a profoundly Hawaiian sense that is, again, familial and genealogical. Hawaiians feel *aloha* for Hawai'i whence they come and for their Hawaiian kin upon whom they depend. It is nearly impossible to feel or practice *aloha* for something that is not familial. This is why we extend familial relations to those few non-natives whom we feel understand and can reciprocate our *aloha*. But *aloha* is freely given and freely returned; it is not and cannot be demanded, or commanded. Above all, *aloha* is a cultural feeling and practice that works among the people and between the people and their land.

The significance and meaning of *aloha* underscores the centrality of the Hawaiian language or *'ōlelo* to the culture. *'Ōlelo* means both language and tongue; *mo'ōlelo*, or history, is that which comes from the tongue, that is, a story. *Haole* or white people say we have oral history, but what we have are stories passed on through the generations. These are different from the *haole* sense of history. To Hawaiians in traditional society, language had tremendous power, thus the phrase, *i ka 'ōlelo ke ola; i ka 'ōlelo ka make*—in language is life, in language is death.

After nearly 2,000 years of speaking Hawaiian, our people suffered the near extinction of our language through its banning by the American-imposed government in 1896. In 1900, Hawai'i became a territory of the United States. All schools, government operations, and official transactions were thereafter conducted in English, despite the fact that most people, including non-natives, still spoke Hawaiian at the turn of the century.

Since 1970, *'ōlelo Hawai'i*, or the Hawaiian language, has undergone a tremendous revival, including the rise of language immersion schools. The state of Hawai'i now has two official languages, Hawaiian and English, and the call for Hawaiian language speakers and teachers grows louder by the day.[2]

Along with the flowering of Hawaiian language has come a flowering of Hawaiian dance, especially in its ancient form, called *hula kahiko*. Dance academies, known as *hālau*, have proliferated throughout Hawai'i as have *kumu hula,* or dance masters, and formal competitions where all-night presentations continue for three or four days to throngs of appreciative listeners. Indeed, among Pacific Islanders, Hawaiian dance is considered one of the finest Polynesian art forms today.

Of course, the cultural revitalization that Hawaiians are now experiencing and transmitting to their children is as much a *repudiation* of colonization by so-called Western civilization in its American form as it is a *reclamation* of our past and our own ways of life. This is why cultural revitalization is often resisted and disparaged by anthropologists and others: they see very clearly that its political effect is decolonization of the mind. Thus our rejection of the nuclear family as the basic unit of society and of individualism as the best form of human expression infuriates social workers, the churches, the legal system, and educators. Hawaiians continue to have allegedly "illegitimate" children, to *hānai* or adopt both children and adults outside of sanctioned Western legal concepts, to hold and use land and water in a collective form rather than a private property form, and to proscribe the notion and the value that one person should strive to surpass and therefore outshine all others.

All these Hawaiian values can be grouped under the idea of *'ohana,* loosely translated as family, but more accurately imagined as a group of both closely and distantly related people who share nearly everything, from land and food to children and status. Sharing is central to this value since it prevents individual decline. Of course, poverty is not thereby avoided, it is only shared with everyone in the unit. The *'ohana* works effectively when the *kua'ana* relationship (elder sibling/younger sibling reciprocity) is practiced.

Finally, within the *'ohana,* our women are considered the lifegivers of the nation, and are accorded the respect and honor this status conveys. Our young women, like our young people in general, are the *pua,* or flower of our *lāhui,* or our nation. The renowned beauty of our women, especially their sexual beauty, is not considered a commodity to be hoarded by fathers and brothers but an attribute of our people. Culturally, Hawaiians are very open and free about sexual relationships, although Christianity and organized religion have done much to damage these traditional sexual values.

With this understanding of what it means to be Hawaiian, I want to move now to the prostitution of our culture by tourism.

Hawai'i itself is the female object of degraded and victimized sexual value. Our *'āina,* or lands, are not any longer the source of food and shelter, but the source of money. Land is now called real estate, rather than our mother, *Papa.* The American relationship of people to land is that of exploiter to exploited. Beautiful areas, once sacred to my people, are now expensive resorts; shorelines where net fishing, seaweed gathering, and crabbing occurred are more and more the exclusive domain of recreational activities:

sunbathing, windsurfing, jet skiing. Now, even access to beaches near hotels is strictly regulated or denied to the local public altogether.

The phrase *mālama 'āina*—to care for the land—is used by government officials to sell new projects and to convince the locals that hotels can be built with a concern for "ecology." Hotel historians, like hotel doctors, are stationed in-house to soothe the visitors' stay with the pablum of invented myths and tales of the "primitive."

High schools and hotels adopt each other and funnel teenagers through major resorts for guided tours from kitchens to gardens to honeymoon suites in preparation for postsecondary jobs in the lowest-paid industry in the state. In the meantime, tourist appreciation kits and movies are distributed through the state department of education to all elementary schools. One film, unashamedly titled *What's in It for Me?*, was devised to convince locals that tourism is, as the newspapers never tire of saying, "the only game in town."

Of course, all this hype is necessary to hide the truth about tourism, the awful exploitative truth that the industry is the major cause of environmental degradation, low wages, land dispossession, and the highest cost of living in the United States.

While this propaganda is churned out to local residents, the commercialization of Hawaiian culture proceeds with calls for more sensitive marketing of our native values and practices. After all, a prostitute is only as good as her income-producing talents. These talents, in Hawaiian terms, are the *hula*; the generosity, or *aloha*, of our people; the *u'i* or youthful beauty of our women and men; and the continuing allure of our lands and waters, that is, of our place, Hawai'i.

The selling of these talents must produce income. And the function of tourism and the state of Hawai'i is to convert these attributes into profits.

The first requirement is the transformation of the product, or the cultural attribute, much as a woman must be transformed to look like a prostitute, that is, someone who is complicitous in her own commodification. Thus *hula* dancers wear clownlike make-up, don costumes from a mix of Polynesian cultures, and behave in a manner that is smutty and salacious rather than powerfully erotic. The distance between the smutty and the erotic is precisely the distance between Western culture and Hawaiian culture. In the hotel version of the *hula*, the sacredness of the dance has completely evaporated while the athleticism and sexual expression have been packaged like ornaments. The purpose is entertainment for profit rather than a joyful and truly Hawaiian celebration of human and divine nature.

But let us look at an example that is representative of literally hundreds of images that litter the pages of scores of tourist publications. From an Aloha Airlines booklet—shamelessly called the "Spirit of Aloha"—there is a characteristic portrayal of commodified *hula* dancers, one male and one female. The costuming of the female is more South Pacific—the Cook Islands and Tahiti—while that of the male is more Hawaiian. (He wears a Hawaiian loincloth called a *malo*.) The ad smugly asserts the hotel dinner service as a *lū'au*, a Hawaiian feast (which is misspelled) with a continuously open bar, lavish "island" buffet, and "thrilling" Polynesian revue. Needless to say, Hawaiians did not drink alcohol, eat "island" buffets, or participate in "thrilling" revues before the advent of white people in our islands.

But back to the advertisement. Lahaina, the location of the resort and once the capital of Hawai'i, is called "royal" because of its past association with our *ali'i*, or chiefs. Far from being royal today, Lahaina is sadly inundated by California yuppies, drug addicts, and valley girls.

The male figure in the background is muscular, partially clothed, and unsmiling. Apparently, he is supposed to convey an image of Polynesian sexuality that is both enticing and threatening. The white women in the audience can marvel at this physique and still remain safely distant. Like the black American male, this Polynesian man is a fantasy animal. He casts a slightly malevolent glance at our costumed maiden whose body posture and barely covered breasts contradict the innocent smile on her face.

Finally, the "wondrous allure" referred to in the ad applies to more than just the dancers in their performances; the physical beauty of Hawai'i "alive under the stars" is the larger reference.

In this little grotesquerie, the falseness and commercialism fairly scream out from the page. Our language, our dance, our young people, even our customs of eating are used to ensnare tourists. And the price is only a paltry $39.95, not much for two thousand years of culture. Of course, the hotel will rake in tens of thousands of dollars on just the *lū'au* alone. And our young couple will make a pittance.

The rest of the magazine, like most tourist propaganda, commodifies virtually every part of Hawai'i: mountains, beaches, coastlines, rivers, flowers, our volcano goddess, Pele, reefs and fish, rural Hawaiian communities, even Hawaiian activists.

The point, of course, is that everything in Hawai'i can be yours, that is, you the tourist, the non-native, the visitor. The place, the people, the culture, even our identity as a "native" people is for sale. Thus, the magazine, like the airline that prints it, is called *Aloha*. The use of this word in a capitalist context is so far removed from any Hawaiian cultural sense that it is, literally, meaningless.

Thus, Hawai'i, like a lovely woman, is there for the taking. Those with only a little money get a brief encounter; those with a lot of money, like the Japanese, get more. The state and counties will give tax breaks, build infrastructure, and have the governor personally welcome tourists to ensure they keep coming. Just as the pimp regulates prices and guards the commodity of the prostitute, so the state bargains with developers for access to Hawaiian land and culture. Who builds the biggest resorts to attract the most affluent tourists gets the best deal: more hotel rooms, golf courses, and restaurants approved. Permits are fast-tracked, height and density limits are suspended, new groundwater sources are miraculously found.

Hawaiians, meanwhile, have little choice in all this. We can fill up the unemployment lines, enter the military, work in the tourist industry, or leave Hawai'i. Increasingly, Hawaiians are leaving, not by choice but out of economic necessity.

Our people who work in the industry—dancers, waiters, singers, valets, gardeners, housekeepers, bartenders, and even a few managers—make between $10,000 and $25,000 a year, an impossible salary for a family in Hawai'i. Psychologically, our young people have begun to think of tourism as the only employment opportunity, trapped as they are by the lack of alternatives. For our young women, modeling is a "cleaner" job when compared to waiting on tables, or dancing in a weekly revue, but modeling feeds on tourism and the commodification of Hawaiian women. In the end, the entire employment scene is shaped by tourism.

Despite their exploitation, Hawaiians' participation in tourism raises the problem of complicity. Because wages are so low and advancement so rare, whatever complicity exists is secondary to the economic hopelessness that drives Hawaiians into the industry. Refusing to contribute to the commercialization of one's culture becomes a peripheral concern when unemployment looms.

Of course, many Hawaiians do not see tourism as part of their colonization. Thus tourism is viewed as providing jobs, not as a form of cultural prostitution. Even those who have some glimmer of critical consciousness don't generally agree that the tourist industry prostitutes Hawaiian culture. To me, this is a measure of the depth of our mental oppression: We can't understand our own cultural degradation because we are living it. As colonized people, we are colonized to the extent that we are unaware of our oppression. When awareness begins, then so too does decolonization. Judging by the growing resistance to new hotels, to geothermal energy and manganese nodule mining which would supplement the tourist industry, and to increases in the sheer number of tourists, I would say that decolonization has begun, but we have many more stages to negotiate on our path to sovereignty.

My brief excursion into the prostitution of Hawaiian culture has done no more than give an overview. Now that you have heard a native view, let me just leave this thought behind. If you are thinking of visiting my homeland, please don't. We don't want or need any more tourists, and we certainly don't like them. If you want to help our cause, pass this message on to your friends.

ENDNOTES

Author's Note: "Lovely Hula Hands" is the title of a famous and very saccharine song written by a *haole* who fell in love with Hawai'i in the pre-statehood era. It embodies the worst romanticized views of *hula* dancers and Hawaiian culture in general.

[1]Lilikalā Kame'eleihiwa, *Native Land and Foreign Desires* (Honolulu: Bishop Museum Press, 1992), p. 2.

[2]See Larry Kimura, 1983. "Native Hawaiian Culture," in *Native Hawaiians Study Commission Report*, Vol. 1 (Washington, DC: U.S. Department of the Interior), pp. 173–97.

13

"NO WAY MY BOYS ARE GOING TO BE LIKE THAT!"
Parents' Responses to Children's Gender Nonconformity

EMILY W. KANE

In this and the following three selections, we examine socialization, the process of learning cultural values and norms. *Socialization* refers to these social processes through which an individual becomes integrated into a social group by learning the group's culture and his or her roles in that group. It is largely through this process that an individual's concept of self is formed. Thus, socialization teaches us the cultural norms, values, and skills necessary to survive in society. Socialization also enables us to form social identities and to develop an awareness about ourselves as individuals. We construct our social identities through social interaction with others, including members of our families, our peers, teachers, and employers. The following reading by Emily Kane, a professor of sociology at Bates College, is taken from a 2002 article in *Gender & Society* of the same name. Here, Kane examines socialization and how we learn our gender identities following birth.

Parents begin gendering their children from their very first awareness of those children, whether in pregnancy or while awaiting adoption. Children themselves become active participants in this gendering process by the time they are conscious of the social relevance of gender, typically before the age of two. I address one aspect of this process of parents doing gender, both for and with their children, by exploring how parents respond to gender nonconformity among preschool-aged children. As West and Zimmerman (1987: 136) note, "to 'do' gender is not always to live up to normative conceptions of femininity or masculinity; it is to engage in behavior *at the risk of gender assessment*." I argue that many parents make efforts to stray from and thus expand normative conceptions of gender. But for their sons in particular, they balance this effort with conscious attention to producing a

Emily W. Kane, "No Way My Boys Are Going to Be Like That!": Parents' Responses to Children's Gender Nonconformity." *Gender & Society*, Vol. 20, No. 2, April 2006, pp. 149–176. Copyright © 2006 Sociologists for Women in Society. Reprinted by permission of Sage Publications, Inc.

masculinity approximating hegemonic ideals. This balancing act is evident across many parents I interviewed regardless of gender, race/ethnicity, social class, sexual orientation, and partnership status. But I also argue that within that broader pattern are notable variations. Heterosexual fathers play a particularly central role in accomplishing their sons' masculinity and, in the process, reinforce their own as well. Their expressed motivations for that accomplishment work often involve personal endorsement of hegemonic masculinity. Heterosexual mothers and gay parents, on the other hand, are more likely to report motivations that invoke accountability to others for crafting their sons' masculinity in accordance with hegemonic ideals.

Three bodies of literature provide foundations for this argument. Along with the body of work documenting parental behaviors in relation to gendering children, I draw on interactionist approaches that view gender as a situated accomplishment and scholarship outlining the contours of normative conceptions of masculinity. These latter two literatures offer a framework for understanding the significance of the patterns evident in my analysis of interview data.

Parents and the Social Construction of Gender

Scholars of gender and childhood are increasingly interested in the role of peers in the process of gendering children, viewing children themselves as active agents rather than passive recipients of adult influence. However, they also continue to recognize parents as important in the gendering of children (Coltrane and Adams 1997; Maccoby 1998). Lytton and Romney's (1991) meta-analysis of the substantial quantitative and experimental literature on gender and parents' behavior toward their sons and daughters documents that parents do not always enforce gendered expectations for their children, nor do they consistently treat sons and daughters differently. Some researchers have highlighted subgroups of parents who actively seek to disrupt traditional gendered expectations for their children. . . . But as a whole, the literature documents definite parental tendencies toward gendered treatment of children. These tendencies are evident beginning at birth and in the early childhood years. For example, the literature indicates differential treatment of sons and daughters in terms of parental selection of toys . . . clothing . . . and décor for children's rooms . . . as well as parental emphasis on emotions versus autonomy in family stories. Across this literature, gender typing by parents is well documented, as are two patterns within that gender typing. First, fathers appear to engage in more differential treatment of sons and daughters and more enforcement of gender boundaries than do mothers; second, for both mothers and fathers, such boundary maintenance appears to be more evident in the treatment of sons than daughters (. . . Coltrane and Adams 1997; Maccoby 1998).

The large literature on gender typing by parents is predominantly quantitative and often based on experiments, closed-ended surveys, and/or counting the frequency of various parental behaviors. This literature is valuable in documenting the role that parents play in gendering their children. However, it does less to explore the nuances of how parents make meaning around gender, to document in detail what kinds of attributes and behaviors are accepted and sanctioned by parents of young children, to reveal what motivates parents as they participate in the social construction of their children's gender, or to illuminate how aware parents are of their role in these processes. Parents are clearly gendering their children, but what are the subtleties of the gendered outcomes they seek to construct, why do they seek to construct those, and how aware are they of that construction process?

Doing Gender: Accomplishment and Accountability

The interactionist approach to gender as accomplishment (West and Fenstermaker 1993, 1995; West and Zimmerman 1987) provides a powerful framework for understanding what I heard about gender nonconformity in my interviews with parents of young children. This approach allows us to view parents not simply as agents of gender socialization but rather as actors involved in a more complex process of accomplishing gender with and for their children. Along with the notion of gender as accomplished, equally central is the concept of accountability. Accountability is relevant not only when people are doing gender in accordance with the expectations of others but also when they resist or stray from such expectations. . . . Fenstermaker and West (2002) . . . note that their focus on the process by which gender is accomplished places activity, agency, and the possibility of resistance in the foreground. But the accomplishment of such change takes place within the context of, and is constrained by, accountability to gendered assessment. . . .

While accomplishment and accountability are key concepts framing my analysis of parents' responses to their children's gender nonconformity, it is also crucial to note the importance of normative conceptions. . . . Normative conceptions of appropriate masculine conduct are particularly relevant to my analysis, and to explore that domain, I turn briefly to scholarship on the history of masculinity as a social construct.

Normative Conceptions of Masculinity: Hegemonic Masculinity

Connell (1995: 77) has argued persuasively that "at any given time, one form of masculinity rather than others is culturally exalted." This hegemonic masculinity is cross-culturally and historically variable and offers a clear example of a locally specific normative conception of gender. It stands as a normative conception to which men are accountable, a form of masculinity in relation to which subordinated masculinities, as well as femininities, are defined. Connell (1987: 187) argues that there is no need for a concept of hegemonic femininity, because the fundamental purpose of hegemonic masculinity is to legitimate male domination. The subordination of non-hegemonic masculinities is crucial as well, as it allows hegemonic masculinity to legitimate not only male privilege but also race, class, and sexual orientation–based privileges as well.

Several elements of Connell's theory are especially relevant to my analysis of how parents think about their preschool sons' gender nonconformity. He argues that among the features of hegemonic masculinity in this particular time and place are aggression, limited emotionality, and heterosexuality. In addition, he and other scholars interested in the social construction of masculinity emphasize its relational meaning: "'masculinity' does not exist except in contrast with 'femininity'" (Connell 1995: 68). As Kimmel notes, the "notion of anti-femininity lies at the heart of contemporary and historical constructions of manhood, so that masculinity is defined more by what one is not rather than who one is" (1994: 119). Passivity and excessive emotionality, as well as more material adornments of femininity, are precisely what must be avoided in this hegemonic version of masculinity. Both Connell and Kimmel view homophobia as central to this rejection of femininity. Connell (1987: 186) states this bluntly when he notes that "the most important feature of contemporary hegemonic masculinity is that it is heterosexual. . . . Contempt for homosexuality and homosexual men . . . is part of the ideological package of hegemonic masculinity."

Data and Method

Participants and Interviewing

The analyses presented here are based on data from 42 interviews with a diverse sample of parents, each of whom has at least one preschool-aged child (three to five years old). Interviews focused on parents' perceptions of their children's gendered attributes and behaviors. The preschool age range is emphasized because this is the period when most children begin to develop a clear understanding of the gender expectations around them, as evidenced in the development of gender identity and the tendency to engage in more gender-typed patterns of behavior (Maccoby 1998; Weinraub et al. 1984).

Interviews were conducted primarily in southern and central Maine (with a small number conducted elsewhere in New England), over a period ranging from the summer of 1999 to the fall of 2002. Participants were recruited through postings in local child care centers, parents' resource organizations, community colleges, local businesses, and public housing projects and through personal networks (though none of the participants were people I knew prior to the interviews). Recruiting materials included general reference to "parents' experiences raising sons and daughters" and did not emphasize gender conformity or nonconformity. . . .

The 42 interviewees include 24 mothers and 18 fathers. Four of the fathers are married to women interviewed for the study as mothers. Although geographically specific primarily to northern New England, interviewees come from a relatively diverse range of family types (single-parent and two-parent families, with some of the latter being blended families), class locations (ranging from those self-identifying as poor/low income to upper middle class), racial/ethnic groups (including white, Asian American, and African American interviewees), and sexual orientations (including heterosexual and gay parents). These parents' children include biological children, adopted children, step-children, and foster children. Interviewees' educational backgrounds range from having completed less than a high school education to holding a doctorate, with the average years of formal schooling falling between high school graduate and college graduate. Ages range from 23 to 49 years, with the average age at 35 years. All of the men interviewed work outside the home for pay; among those in heterosexual partnerships, their female partners were roughly equally split among full-time homemakers, those employed part-time in the paid labor force, and those employed full-time. Among the mothers interviewed, about one in three are full-time homemakers, with the remainder employed part-time or full-time in the paid labor force. Interviewees average 2.5 children (with the mode being 2) and are split among those having only daughters (11), only sons (12), or at least one of each (23). The focal children on whom interviews focused include 22 sons and 20 daughters. . . .

Responses to Gender Nonconformity

Mothers and fathers, across a variety of social locations, often celebrated what they perceived as gender nonconformity on the part of their young daughters. They reported enjoying dressing their daughters in sports-themed clothing, as well as buying them toy cars, trucks, trains, and building toys. Some described their efforts to encourage, and pleased reactions to, what they considered traditionally male activities such as t-ball, football, fishing, and learning to use tools. Several noted that they make an effort to encourage their young daughters to aspire to traditionally male occupations and commented favorably on their daughters as "tomboyish," "rough and tumble," and "competitive athletically." These positive responses were combined with very little in the way of any negative response. The coding of each interviewee for the combination of positive/neutral and negative responses summarizes this pattern clearly: Among parents commenting about daughter(s), the typical combination was to express only positive responses. For example, a white, middle-class, heterosexual mother noted approvingly that her five-year-old daughter *does a lot of things that a boy would do, and we encourage that,* while a white, upper-middle-class, lesbian mother reported that she and her partner intentionally *do [a lot] of stuff that's not stereotypically female* with their daughter. Similarly, a white, upper-middle-class, heterosexual father indicated with relief that his daughter is turning out to be somewhat "boyish": *I never wanted a girl who was a little princess, who was so fragile. . . . I want her to take on more masculine characteristics.* An African American, working-class, heterosexual father also noted this kind of preference: *I don't want her just to color and play with dolls, I want her to be athletic. . . .*

In stark contrast to the lack of negative response for daughters, 23 of 31 parents of sons expressed at least some negative responses, and 6 of these offered only negative responses regarding what they perceived as gender nonconformity. Of 31 parents, 25 did indicate positive responses as well, but unlike references to their daughters, they tended to balance those positive feelings and actions about sons with negative ones as well. The most common combination was to indicate both positive and negative responses.

Domestic Skills, Nurturance, and Empathy

Parents accepted, and often even celebrated, their sons' acquisition of domestic abilities and an orientation toward nurturance and empathy. Of the 25 parents of sons who offered positive/neutral responses, 21 did so in reference to domestic skills, nurturance, and/or empathy. For example, they reported allowing or encouraging traditionally girl toys such as dolls, doll houses, kitchen centers, and tea sets, with that response often revolving around a desire to encourage domestic competence, nurturance, emotional openness, empathy, and nonviolence as attributes they considered nontraditional but positive for boys. These parents were reporting actions and sentiments oriented toward accomplishing gender in what they considered a less conventional manner. One white, low-income, heterosexual mother taught her son to cook, asserting that *I want my son to know how to do more than boil water, I want him to know how to take care of himself.* Another mother, this one a white, working-class, heterosexual parent, noted that she makes a point of talking to her sons about emotions: *I try to instill a sense of empathy in my sons and try to get them to see how other people would feel.* And a white, middle-class, heterosexual father emphasized domestic competence when he noted that it does not bother him for his son to play with dolls at his cousin's house: *How then are they going to learn to take care of their children if they don't?* This positive response to domestic activities is consistent with recent literature on parental coding of toys as masculine, feminine, or neutral, which indicates that parents are increasingly coding kitchens and in some cases dolls as neutral rather than exclusively feminine (Wood, Desmarais, and Gugula 2002).

In my study, mothers and fathers expressed these kinds of efforts to accomplish gender differently for their sons with similar frequency, but mothers tended to express them with greater certainty, while fathers were less enthusiastic and more likely to include caveats. For example, this mother described her purchase of a variety of domestic toys for her three-year-old son without ambivalence: *One of the first big toys [I got him] was the kitchen center . . . . We cook, he has an apron he wears . . . . He's got his Dirt Devil vacuum and he's got his baby [doll]. And he's got all the stuff to feed her and a highchair* (white, low-income, heterosexual mother).

Some mothers reported allowing domestic toys but with less enthusiasm, such as a white, low-income, heterosexual mother who said, regarding her three-year-old son, *He had been curious about dolls and I just said, you know, usually girls play with dolls, but it's okay for you to do it too.* But this kind of caution or lack of enthusiasm, even in a response coded as positive or neutral due to its allowance of gender-atypical behavior, was more evident among fathers, as the following quote illustrates: *Occasionally, if he's not doing something, I'll encourage him to maybe play with his tea cups, you know, occasionally. But I like playing with his blocks better anyway* (white, middle-class, heterosexual father).

Thus, evident among both mothers and fathers, but with greater conviction for mothers, was widespread support among parents for working to "undo" gender at the level of some of their sons' skills and values. However, this acceptance was tempered for many parents by negative responses to any interest in what I will refer to as iconic feminine items, attributes, or activities, as well as parental concern about homosexuality.

Icons of Femininity

A range of activities and attributes considered atypical for boys were met with negative responses, and for a few parents (3 of 31 parents of sons) this even included the kind of domestic toys and nurturance noted above. But more common were negative responses to items, activities, or attributes that could be considered icons of femininity. This was strikingly consistent with Kimmel's (1994: 119) previously noted claim that the "notion of anti-femininity lies at the heart of contemporary and historical constructions of manhood," and it bears highlighting that this was evident among parents of very young children. Parents of sons reported negative responses to their sons' wearing pink or frilly clothing; wearing skirts, dresses, or tights; and playing dress up in any kind of feminine attire. Nail polish elicited concern from a number of parents too, as they reported young sons wanting to have their fingernails or toenails polished. Dance, especially ballet, and Barbie dolls were also among the traditionally female activities often noted negatively by parents of sons. Of the 31 parents of sons, 23 mentioned negative reactions to at least one of these icons.

In relation to objects such as clothing and toys, the following responses are typical of the many concerns raised and the many indications of actions parents had taken to accomplish gender with and for their sons:

> *He's asked about wearing girl clothes before, and I said no. . . . He likes pink, and I try not to encourage him to like pink just because, you know, he's not a girl. . . . There's not many toys I wouldn't get him, except Barbie, I would try not to encourage that.* (white, low-income, heterosexual mother)

> *If we go into a clothing store . . . I try to shy my son away from the Powerpuff Girls shirt or anything like that. . . . I would steer him away from a pink shirt as opposed to having him wear a blue shirt.* (Asian American, middle-class, heterosexual father)

These quotes are typical of many instances in which parents not only specify the items that strike them as problematic but clearly indicate the actions they take in accomplishing gender. In the first quote, the mother indicates her actions in encouraging and discouraging various outcomes, while in the second, the father reports "shying away" and "steering" his young son.

Playing with nail polish and makeup, although tolerated by some parents, more often evoked negative responses like this one, from a white, upper-middle-class, gay father, speaking about his four-year-old son's use of nail polish: *He put nail polish on himself one time, and I said "No, you can't do that, little girls put nail polish on, little boys don't."*

Barbie dolls are an especially interesting example in that many parents reported positive responses to baby dolls, viewing these as encouraging nurturance and helping to prepare sons for fatherhood. Barbie, on the other hand, an icon of femininity, struck many parents of sons as more problematic. Barbie was often mentioned when parents were asked whether their child had ever requested an item or activity more commonly associated with the other gender. Four parents—three mothers and one father—-indicated that they had purchased a Barbie at their son's request, but more often parents of sons noted that they would avoid letting their son have or play with Barbie dolls. Sometimes this negative response was categorical, as in the quote above in which a mother of a three-year-old son noted that *there's not many toys I wouldn't get him, except Barbie.* A father offers a similar negative reaction to Barbie in relation to his two young sons: *If they asked for a Barbie doll, I would probably say no, you don't want [that], girls play with [that], boys play with trucks* (white, middle-class, heterosexual father). . . .

Along with material markers of femininity, many parents expressed concern about excessive emotionality (especially frequent crying) and passivity in their sons. For example, a white, upper-middle-class, heterosexual father, concerned about public crying, said about his five-year-old son, *I don't want him to be a sissy . . . . I want to see him strong, proud, not crying like a sissy.* Another father expressed his frustration with his four-year-old son's crying over what the father views as minor injuries and indicated action to discourage those tears: *Sometimes I get so annoyed, you know, he comes [crying], and I say, "you're not hurt, you don't even know what hurt is yet," and I'm like "geez, sometimes you are such a little wean," you know?* (white, middle-class, heterosexual father).

Passivity was also raised as a concern, primarily by fathers. For example, one white, middle-class, heterosexual father of a five-year-old noted that he has told his son to *stop crying like a girl,* and also reported encouraging that son to fight for what he wants: *You just go in the corner and cry like a baby, I don't want that. If you decide you want [some] thing, you are going to fight for it, not crying and acting like a baby and hoping that they're going to feel guilty and give it to you.*

A mother who commented negatively about passivity even more directly connected her concern to how her son might be treated: *I do have concerns. . . . He's passive, not aggressive. . . . He's not the rough and tumble kid, and I do worry about him being an easy target* (white, working-class, heterosexual mother).

Taken together, these various examples indicate clearly the work many parents are doing to accomplish gender with and for their sons in a manner that distances those sons from any association with femininity. This work was not evident among all parents of sons. But for most parents, across racial, class, and sexual orientation categories, it was indeed evident.

Homosexuality

Along with these icons of feminine gender performance, and arguably directly linked to them, is the other clear theme evident among some parents' negative responses to perceived gender nonconformity on the part of their sons: fear that a son either would be or would be perceived as gay. Spontaneous connections of gender nonconformity and sexual orientation were not evident in parents' comments about daughters, nor among gay and lesbian parents, but arose for 7 of the 27 heterosexual parents who were discussing sons. The following two examples are typical of responses that invoked the possibility of a son's being gay, with explicit links to performance of femininity and to the parents' own role in accomplishing heterosexuality:

> *If he was acting feminine, I would ask and get concerned on whether or not, you know. I would try to get involved and make sure he's not gay.* (white, low-income, heterosexual mother)

> *There are things that are meant for girls, but why would it be bad for him to have one of them? I don't know, maybe I have some deep, deep, deep buried fear that he would turn out, well, that his sexual orientation may get screwed up.* (white, middle-class, heterosexual father)

The first comment explicitly indicates that feminine behavior, even in a three-year-old boy, might be an indicator of an eventual nonheterosexual orientation. The second comment raises another possibility: that playing with toys "that are meant for girls" might not indicate but rather shape the son's eventual sexual orientation. In both cases, though, the parent is reporting on actions, either actual or hypothetical, taken to discourage homosexuality and accomplish heterosexuality. Another quote from a father raises a similar concern and further exemplifies parental responsibility for the accomplishment of masculinity as linked to heterosexuality. This father had noted throughout the interview that his five-year-old son tends to show some attributes he considers feminine. At one point, he mentioned that he sometimes wondered if his son might be gay, and he explained his reaction to that possibility in the following terms: *If [he] were to be gay, it would not make me happy at all. I would probably see that as a failure as a dad . . ., as a failure because I'm raising him to be a boy, a man* (white, upper-middle-class, heterosexual father). This comment suggests that the parent does not view masculinity as something that naturally unfolds but rather as something he feels responsible for crafting, and he explicitly links heterosexual orientation to the successful accomplishment of masculinity.

The fact that the connection between gender performance and sexual orientation was not raised for daughters, and that fear of homosexuality was not spontaneously mentioned by parents of daughters whether in connection to gender performance or not, suggests how closely gender conformity and heterosexuality are linked within hegemonic constructions of masculinity. Such connections might arise more by adolescence in relation to daughters, as I noted previously regarding other aspects of parental responses to gender nonconformity. But for sons, even among parents of very young children, heteronormativity appears to play a role in shaping parental responses to gender nonconformity. . . .

This implicit assumption appears to motivate at least some parental gender performance management among heterosexual parents, even for children as young as preschool age. Given the connections between male heterosexuality and the rejection of femininity noted previously as evident in theories of hegemonic masculinity, the tendency for parents to associate gender performance and sexual orientation for sons more than daughters may also reflect a more general devaluation of femininity.

Mothers versus Fathers in the Accomplishment of Masculinity

In documenting parental work to accomplish masculinity with and for young sons, I have focused on the encouragement of domestic skills, nurturance, and empathy; discouragement of icons of femininity; and heterosexual parents' concerns about homosexuality. Within all three of these arenas, variation by parental gender was evident. Although both mothers and fathers were equally likely to express a combination of positive and negative responses to their sons' perceived gender nonconformity, with domestic skills and empathy accepted and icons of femininity rejected, the acceptance was more pointed for mothers, and the rejection was more pointed for fathers. More fathers (11 of 14) than mothers (12 of 17) of sons indicated negative reactions to at least one of the icons discussed. Fathers also indicated more categorically negative responses: 7 of the 14 fathers but only 2 of the 17 mothers reported simply saying "no" to requests for things such as Barbie dolls, tea sets, nail polish, or ballet lessons, whether actual requests or hypothetical ones. Although fewer parents referred to excessive emotionality and passivity as concerns, the 6 parents of sons who did so included 4 fathers and 2 mothers, and here too, the quotes indicate a more categorical rejection by fathers.

Another indication of more careful policing of icons of femininity by fathers is evident in comments that placed age limitations on the acceptability of such icons. Four fathers (but no mothers) commented with acceptance on activities or interests that they consider atypical for boys but went on to note that these would bother them if they continued well past the preschool age range. The following quote from a father is typical of these responses. After noting that his four-year-old son sometimes asks for toys he thinks of as "girl toys," he went on to say, *I don't think it will ruin his life at this age but . . . if he was 12 and asking for it, you know, My Little Pony or Barbies, then I think I'd really worry* (white, middle-class, heterosexual father). While comments like this one were not coded as negative responses, since they involved acceptance, I mention them here as they are consistent with the tendency for fathers to express particular concern about their sons' involvement with icons of femininity.

Three of 15 heterosexual mothers and 4 of 12 heterosexual fathers of sons responded negatively to the possibility of their son's being, or being perceived as, gay. These numbers are too small to make conclusive claims comparing mothers and fathers. But this pattern is suggestive of another arena in which fathers—especially heterosexual fathers—may stand out, especially taken together with another pattern. Implicit in the quotes offered above related to homosexuality is a suggestion that heterosexual fathers may feel particularly responsible for crafting their sons' heterosexual orientation. In addition, in comparison to mothers, their comments are less likely to refer to fears for how their son might be treated by others if he were gay and more likely to refer to the personal disappointment they anticipate in this hypothetical scenario. . . .

Parental Motivations for the Accomplishment of Masculinity

The analysis I have offered thus far documents that parents are aware of their role in accomplishing gender with and for their sons. Although some parents did speak of their sons as entirely "boyish" and "born that way," many reported efforts to craft a hegemonic masculinity. Most parents expressed a very conscious awareness of normative conceptions of masculinity (whether explicitly or implicitly). Many, especially heterosexual mothers and gay parents, expressed a sense that they felt accountable to others in terms of whether their sons live up to those conceptions. In numerous ways, these parents indicated their awareness that their sons' behavior was at risk of gender assessment, an awareness rarely noted with regard to daughters. Parents varied in terms of their expressed motivations for crafting their sons' masculinity, ranging from a sense of measuring their sons against their own preferences for normative masculinity (more common among heterosexual fathers) to concerns about accountability to gender assessment by peers, other adults, and society in general (more common among heterosexual mothers and gay parents, whether mothers or fathers).

Conclusion

The interviews analyzed here, with New England parents of preschool-aged children from a diverse array of backgrounds, indicate a considerable endorsement by parents of what they perceive as gender nonconformity among both their sons and their daughters. This pattern at first appears encouraging in terms of the prospects for a world less constrained by gendered expectations for children. Many parents respond positively to the idea of their children's experiencing a greater range of opportunities, emotions, and interests than those narrowly defined by gendered stereotypes, with mothers especially likely to do so. However, for sons, this positive response is primarily limited to a few attributes and abilities, namely, domestic skills, nurturance, and empathy. And it is constrained by a clear recognition of normative conceptions of masculinity (Connell 1987, 1995). Most parents made efforts to accomplish, and either endorsed or felt accountable to, an ideal of masculinity that was defined by limited emotionality, activity rather than passivity, and rejection of material markers of femininity. Work to accomplish this type of masculinity was reported especially often by heterosexual fathers; accountability to approximate hegemonic masculinity was reported especially often by heterosexual mothers, lesbian mothers, and gay fathers. Some heterosexual parents also invoked sexual orientation as part of this conception of masculinity, commenting with concern on the possibility that their son might be gay or might be perceived as such. No similar pattern of well-defined normative expectations or accountability animated responses regarding daughters, although positive responses to pursuits parents viewed as more typically masculine may well reflect the same underlying devaluation of femininity evident in negative responses to gender nonconformity among sons.

In the broader study from which this particular analysis was drawn, many parents invoked biology in explaining their children's gendered tendencies. Clearly, the role of biological explanations in parents' thinking about gender merits additional investigation. But one of the things that was most striking to me in the analyses presented here is how frequently parents indicated that they took action to craft an appropriate gender performance with and for their preschool-aged sons, viewing masculinity as something they needed to work on to accomplish. . . . I began this project expecting that parents accept with little question ideologies that naturalize gender difference. Instead, the results I have presented here demonstrate that parents are often consciously aware of gender as something that they must shape and construct, at least for their sons. This argument extends the literature on the routine accomplishment of gender in childhood by introducing evidence of conscious effort and awareness by parents as part of that accomplishment. This awareness also has implications for efforts to reduce gendered constraints on children. Recognition that parents are sometimes consciously crafting their children's gender suggests the possibility that they could be encouraged to shift that conscious effort in less gendered directions.

In addition to documenting this parental awareness, I am also able to extend the literature by documenting the content toward which parents' accomplishment work is oriented. The version of hegemonic masculinity I have argued underlies parents' responses is one that includes both change and stability. Parental openness to domestic skills, nurturance, and empathy as desirable qualities in their sons likely represents social change, and the kind of agency in the accomplishment of gender to which Fenstermaker and West (2002) refer. As Connell (1995) notes, hegemonic masculinity is historically variable in its specific content, and the evidence presented in this article suggests that some broadening of that content is occurring. But the clear limits evident within that broadening suggest the stability and power of hegemonic conceptions of masculinity. The parental boundary maintenance work evident for sons represents a crucial obstacle limiting boys' options, separating boys from girls, devaluing activities marked as feminine for both boys and girls, and thus bolstering gender inequality and heteronormativity.

Finally, along with documenting conscious awareness by parents and the content toward which their accomplishment work is oriented, my analysis also contributes to the literature by illuminating the process motivating parental gender accomplishment. The heterosexual world in general, and heterosexual fathers in particular, play a central role in that process. This is evident in the direct endorsement of hegemonic masculinity many heterosexual fathers expressed and in the accountability to others (presumably heterosexual others) many heterosexual mothers, lesbian mothers, and gay fathers expressed. Scholarly investigations of the routine production of gender in childhood, therefore, need to pay careful attention to the role of heterosexual fathers as enforcers of gender boundaries and to the role of accountability in the process of accomplishing gender. At the same time, practical efforts to loosen gendered constraints on young children by expanding their parents' normative conceptions of gender need to be aimed at parents in general and especially need to reach heterosexual fathers in particular. The concern and even fear many parents—especially heterosexual mothers, lesbian mothers, and gay fathers—expressed about how their young sons might be treated if they fail to live up to hegemonic conceptions of masculinity represent a motivation for the traditional accomplishment of gender. But those reactions could also serve as a motivation to broaden normative conceptions of masculinity and challenge the devaluation of femininity, an effort that will require participation by heterosexual fathers to succeed.

REFERENCES

Coltrane, Scott, and Michele Adams. 1997. Children and Gender. In *Contemporary Parenting*, edited by Terry Arendell. Thousand Oaks, CA: Sage.

Connell, R. W. 1987. *Gender and Power*. Stanford, CA: Stanford University Press.

———. 1995. *Masculinities*. Berkeley: University of California Press.

Fenstermaker, Sarah, and Candace West, eds. 2002. *Doing Gender, Doing Difference*. New York: Routledge.

Kimmel, Michael S. 1994. Masculinity as Homophobia. In *Theorizing Masculinities*, edited by Harry Brod. Thousand Oaks, CA: Sage.

Lytton, Hugh, and David M. Romney. 1991. Parents' Differential Socialization of Boys and Girls. *Psychological Bulletin* 109:267–96.

Maccoby, Eleanor E. 1998. *The Two Sexes: Growing Up Apart, Coming Together*. Cambridge, MA: Harvard University Press.

Weinraub, Marsha, Lynda P. Clemens, Alan Sockloff, Teresa Ethridge, Edward Gracely, and Barbara Myers. 1984. The Development of Sex Role Stereotypes in the Third Year. *Child Development* 55:1493–1503.

West, Candace, and Sarah Fenstermaker. 1993. Power, Inequality and the Accomplishment of Gender. In *Theory on Gender/Feminism on Theory*, edited by Paula England. New York: Aldine de Gruyter.

———. 1995. Doing Difference. *Gender & Society* 9:8–37.

West, Candace, and Don Zimmerman. 1987. Doing Gender. *Gender & Society* 1:124–51.

Wood, Eileen, Serge Desmarais, and Sara Gugula. 2002. The Impact of Parenting Experience on Gender Stereotyped Toy Play of Children. *Sex Roles* 47:39–49.

14

USING RACIAL AND ETHNIC CONCEPTS:
The Critical Case of Very Young Children

DEBRA VAN AUSDALE • JOE R. FEAGIN

Many of the readings in this volume use *ethnographic fieldwork*, which involves scholars spending time observing or interviewing the research population, as Mary Romero did in her study of Chicana domestics (Reading 3) or Meika Loe did in her study of waitresses (Reading 9). While the first reading in this section on socialization did ethnographic research on parents and the gender identity of their children, this selection uses ethnographic research to observe young children and their understandings of race and ethnicity. The reading excerpted here, from a 1996 article in the *American Sociological Review*, is by Debra Van Ausdale and Joe Feagin. Van Ausdale and Feagin, both sociologists, observe preschool children and their conceptualizations of race and ethnicity. Contrary to what most people think, Van Ausdale and Feagin find that children as young as three to five years old already are using racial and ethnic concepts to define others and shape their social interactions with other children.

Since the 1930s social science has examined children's attitudes toward race. Research has focused on situations in which race has meaning for children and on how children form racial identities (Clark and Clark 1939; Spencer, Brookins, and Allen 1985), create in-group racial and ethnic orientations (Aboud 1977; Cross 1987; Spencer 1987), form attitudes toward others (Williams and Morland 1976), and use race in friend selection (Schofield and Francis 1982). The literature clearly demonstrates that racial identification and group orientation are salient issues for children (Ramsey 1987).

Cognitive development theories propose stage models to explain children's acquisition of racial and ethnic knowledge (Aboud 1977; Porter 1971). These models assume an age-related progression in children's ability to interpret racial and ethnic information, usually depicting children as proceeding in linear fashion toward cognitively mature adulthood. Most research focuses on children over five years of age; very young children are rarely studied. . . .

Researchers have rarely sought children's views directly, beyond recording brief responses to tests. Few have interviewed children or made in-depth, long-term observations to assess social attitudes, limiting the ability to investigate more fully the nature of children's lives. Children's abilities

Debra Van Ausdale and Joe R. Feagin, "Using Racial and Ethnic Concepts: The Critical Case of Very Young Children." *American Sociological Review*, 1996, Vol. 61 (October: 779–793). Copyright © 1996 by the American Sociological Association. Reprinted with the permission of the authors and the American Sociological Association.

have been seriously underestimated by reliance on techniques that do not make real-life sense to children (Donaldson 1978). Investigations often have assumed that young children are incapable of using abstract concepts (Holmes 1995). An emphasis on psychological testing is often coupled with the notion that children have limited understandings of race and ethnicity (Goodman 1964; Katz 1976; Porter 1971). Children are typically assumed to have temporary or naive views about social concepts until at least age seven. Prior to that age, children's use of concepts differs from that of adults in form and content.

Little attention has been devoted to how children create and assign meaning for racial and ethnic concepts. . . .

We provide data indicating that racial concepts are employed with ease by children as young as age three. Research based on the conception of children as incapable of understanding race (Menter 1989) presents an incorrect image of children's use of abstractions. Drawing on Willis (1990) and Thorne (1993), we suggest that notions of race and ethnicity are employed by young children as integrative and symbolically creative tools in the daily construction of social life.

The Research Approach

We gathered experiential data on how children use racial and ethnic understandings in everyday relationships. Influenced by Dunn's (1991) approach, we made unstructured field observations and recorded everyday behaviors. Our data come from extensive observations of 58 three-, four-, and five-year-old children in a large preschool in a southern city. The school employed a popular antibias curriculum (Derman-Sparks 1989). Over an 11-month period in 1993, we systematically observed everyday interactions in one large classroom containing a very diverse group of children. The center's official data on the racial and ethnic backgrounds of children in the classroom are: White = 24, Asian = 19, Black = 4, biracial = 3, Middle Eastern = 3, Latino = 2, and other = 3. . . .

Like the children and teachers, the senior author (hereafter Debi), a White woman, was usually in the classroom all day for five days a week. As observer and playmate, Debi watched the children and listened to them in their free play and teacher-directed activities. Over 11 months Debi observed 370 significant episodes involving a racial or ethnic dimension, about 1 to 3 episodes per day. When children mentioned racial or ethnic matters, Debi noted what they said, to whom they spoke, and the context of the incident. Extensive field notes were entered immediately on a computer in another room when the children were otherwise occupied. This was done to preserve the details of any conversations and the accuracy of the data. . . .

We began with the assumption that very young children would display no knowledge of racial or ethnic concepts and that any use of these concepts would be superficial or naive. Our data contradicted these expectations.

Using Racial and Ethnic Concepts to Exclude

Using the playhouse to bake pretend muffins, Rita (3.5: White/Latina) and Sarah (4: White) have all the muffin tins. Elizabeth (3.5: Asian/Chinese), attempting to join them, stands at the playhouse door and asks if she can play. Rita shakes her head vigorously, saying, *No, only people who can speak Spanish can come in.* Elizabeth frowns and says, *I can come in.* Rita counters, *Can you speak Spanish?* Elizabeth shakes her head no, and Rita repeats, *Well, then you aren't allowed in.*

Elizabeth frowns deeply and asks Debi to intercede by telling her: *Rita is being mean to me.* Acting within the child-initiated framework, Debi asks Rita, *If only people who speak Spanish are allowed, then how come Sarah can play? Can you speak Spanish, Sarah?* Sarah shakes her head no. *Sarah can't speak Spanish and she is playing,* Debi says to Rita, without suggesting she allow Elizabeth in. Rita frowns, amending her statement: *OK, only people who speak either Spanish or English. That's great!* Debi responds, *because Elizabeth speaks English and she wants to play with you guys.* Rita's frown deepens. *No,* she says. Debi queries, *But you just said people who speak English can play. Can't you decide?* Rita gazes at Debi, thinking hard. *Well,* Rita says triumphantly, *only people who speak two languages.*

Elizabeth is waiting patiently for Debi to make Rita let her play, which Debi has no intention of doing. Debi then asks Rita: *Well, Elizabeth speaks two languages, don't you, Elizabeth?* Debi looks at Elizabeth, who now is smiling for the first time. Rita is stumped for a moment, then retorts, *She does not. She speaks only English.* Debi smiles at Rita: *She does speak two languages—English and Chinese. Don't you?* Debi invites Elizabeth into the conversation. Elizabeth nods vigorously. However, Rita turns away and says to Sarah, *Let's go to the store and get more stuff.*

Language was the ethnic marker here. Rita defined rules for entering play on the basis of language—she was aware that each child not only did not look like the others but also spoke a different language. From a traditional Piagetian perspective, Rita might be seen as egocentric and strongly resistant to alternative views. However, here we see the crucial importance of the social-cultural context, in particular the development of racial and ethnic concepts in a collaborative and interpersonal context. Defending her rules, Rita realized her attempts to exclude Elizabeth by requiring two languages had failed. This three-year-old child had created a social rule based on a significant understanding of ethnic markers. The final "two languages" rule did not acknowledge the fact that Sarah only spoke English. Rita's choice of language as an exclusionary device was directed at preventing Elizabeth from entering, not at maintaining a bilingual play space. . . .

Using Racial and Ethnic Concepts to Include

The children also used racial and ethnic understandings and concepts to include others—to engage them in play or teach them about racial and ethnic identities.

Ling (5: Asian/Chinese) has a book that teaches the Chinese language. She announces to Debi that her grandmother has given her the book and that she is learning Chinese. Debi asks if she is making progress. *Oh yes,* Ling says happily, *I have already learned many characters. They're called characters, you know.* She points out several. *What does that say?* Debi asks, pointing to one. *Cat!* Ling beams. Debi and Ling spend some time reading from Ling's book, then Ling leaves to show off her reading prowess to another child.

Over several weeks, Ling's behavior underscores for the observer how racial and ethnic understandings develop in social contexts. Ling engages numerous others in reading Chinese with her. Carrying the book everywhere, she earnestly tries to teach others to read and write Chinese characters. Chinese characters appear on other children's drawings and on the playground. Other children actively embrace these new characters and concepts and incorporate them into their activities, a clear indication of how children learn ethnic ideas from each other. Ling's efforts demonstrate that she is aware that non-Chinese, including adults, do not know how to read Chinese. Clearly she is aware that Chinese is distinct from the experience of most people around her, and she recognizes this even though she herself is just learning to read Chinese. . . .

Using Racial and Ethnic Concepts to Define Oneself

The use of racial and ethnic concepts to include or exclude others is often coupled with the use of these concepts to describe and define oneself. For most children, racial and/or ethnic identity is an important aspect of themselves, and they demonstrate this in insightful ways in important social contexts.

Renee (4.5: White), a very pale little girl, has been to the beach over the weekend and comes to school noticeably tanned. Linda (4: White) and Erinne (5: biracial) engage her in an intense conversation. They discuss whether her skin would stay that color or get darker until she became, as Linda says, *an African American, like Charles* (another child). Renee denies she could become Black, but this new idea, planted in her head by interaction with the other children, distresses her. On her own initiative, she discusses the possibility with Debi and her mother, both of whom tell her the darker color is temporary.

Renee was unconvinced and commented on her racial identity for weeks. She brought up the issue with other children in many contexts. This linking of skin color with racial identity is found in much traditional literature on children's racial understandings (Clark and Clark 1940). But this racial marking was more than a fleeting interest, unlike the interest mainstream cognitive theorists might predict for such a young child. Renee reframed the meaning of skin color by questioning others on their thoughts and comparing her skin to others'.

Corinne (4: African/White) displays an ability to create meaning by drawing from her personal world. Corinne's mother is Black and is from an African country; her father is a White American. Corinne speaks French and English and is curious about everything at the center. She is a leader and often initiates activities with other children. Most children defer to her. One day

Corinne is examining a rabbit cage on the playground. A teacher is cleaning out the cage and six baby bunnies are temporarily housed in an aluminum bucket that Corinne is holding. Three bunnies are white, two are black, and one is spotted black and white.

As Corinne is sitting at a table, Sarah (4: White) stuck her head into the bucket. *Stop that!* Corinne orders. Sarah complies and asks, *Why do you have the babies? I'm helping Marie* [teacher], says Corinne. *How many babies are there?* Sarah asks Corinne. *Six!* Corinne announces. *Three boys and three girls. How can you tell if they're boys or girls?* Sarah questions. *Well,* Corinne begins, *my daddy is white, so the white ones are boys. My mommy is Black, so the black ones are girls.* Sarah counts: *That's only five.* The remaining bunny is black and white. *Well, that one is like me, so it's a girl,* Corinne explains gently. She picks up the bunny and says, *See, this one is both, like me!* Sarah then loses interest, and Corinne returns to cooing over the bunnies.

This four-year-old's explanation incorporates an interesting combination of color, race, and gender. While her causal reasoning was faulty, she constructed what for her was a sophisticated and reasonable view of the bunnies' sexes. She displayed an understanding of the idea that an offspring's color reflects the colors of its parents, a knowledge grounded in her experience as a biracial child. Strayer (1986) underscores how children develop appropriate attributions regarding situational determinants. Corinne's use of parental gender to explain the unknown gender of the bunnies was an appropriate explanation of how bunnies got certain colors. Skin color was a salient part of her identity, and it was reasonable in her social world to assume that it would be salient for the identity of others, even animals. . . .

In another setting, Corinne (4: African/White) provides an example of the complexity of young children's racial understandings: She refines the nature of racial identity during a handpainting activity. The children have taken a field trip and are asked to make a thank-you poster for their host, a poster constructed of a large sheet of paper featuring handprints of the children. Children are asked by the teacher to choose a color that "looks just like you do." The paints are known as "People Colors," and are common at daycare centers concerned with diversity issues. The activity was designed to increase appreciation of differences in color among the children (Derman-Sparks 1989).

The six paints ranged from dark brown to pale pink. The handprint poster activity is familiar to the children, and the teacher asks Debi to help. Debi accepts but keeps her involvement to a minimum. Several children wait in line to participate in this desirable activity. Each chooses paint according to the teacher's criterion, has Debi apply the paint to the palm of one hand, and then presses the painted hand onto the poster. Debi then writes the child's name next to the handprint. Some children point out how closely the paint matches their skin color or ask Debi if she thought the choice was "right."

Corinne approaches the table, and Debi says, *OK, which color is the most like you? Which color matches your skin?* Corinne looks over the bottles carefully and chooses pale brown. *This one for one hand,* she replies, continuing to scan the bottles, *and this one for the other hand,* she concludes, choosing a second, dark brown color. When Debi asks if that color matches her skin,

Corinne calmly replies, *I have two colors in my skin.* Debi smiles and paints one of her palms pale brown and the other dark brown. Corinne places both hands on the poster, making two prints. Debi then writes Corinne's name between the two handprints. *Perfect!* Corinne says.

This four-year-old chose appropriately for her understanding of the situation. That the paints she picked did not exactly match her skin color was not important to her because she was thinking in terms of her parents' different racial identities. Corinne insisted that she be allowed to choose two colors to reflect her biracial origin. For her, choosing two colors is not an example of cognitive confusion or inconsistency (as a mainstream analysis might see it), but rather her innovative way of recognizing that her mother is dark brown ("Black") and her father is pale brown ("White"). These examples show that children's abilities exceed what would be predicted from the mainstream research perspective.

Using Racial and Ethnic Concepts to Define Others

We observed many examples of children exploring the complex notions of skin color, hair differences, and facial characteristics. They often explore what these things mean and make racial and/or ethnic interpretations of these perceived differences. Mindy (4: White) insists that Debi is Indian. When queried, Mindy replies that it is because Debi is wearing her long dark hair in a braid. When Debi explains that she is not Indian, the child remarks that maybe Debi's mother is Indian.

These statements show not only awareness of the visible characteristics of race and ethnicity but also insight into how visible markers are passed from generation to generation. They demonstrate a child's ability to grasp salient characteristics of a racial and/or ethnic category not her own and apply them to others in a collaborative and evolving way.

In another episode, Taleshia (3: Black) approaches the handpainting table. Asked if she wants to make a handprint, she nods shyly. A child with dark brown skin, Taleshia scans the paint bottles and points to pale pink. Curious about her preference, Debi asks, *Taleshia, is this the color that looks like you?* Taleshia nods and holds out her hand. Behind her, Cathie (3.5: White) objects to Taleshia's decision. *No, no,* Cathie interjects. *She's not that color. She's brown.* Cathie moves to the table. *You're this color,* Cathie says and picks out the bottle of dark brown paint. Cathie is interested in helping Taleshia correct her apparent mistake about skin color. *Do you want this color?* Debi asks Taleshia. *No,* she replies, *I want this one,* touching the pink bottle. Regarding Taleshia with amazement, Cathie exclaims, *For goodness sake, can't you see that you aren't pink? Debi,* Cathie continues to insist, *you have to make her see that she's brown.* Cathie is exasperated and takes Taleshia by the arm. *Look,* she instructs, *you are brown! See?* Cathie holds Taleshia's arm next to her own. *I am pink, right?* Cathie looks to Debi for confirmation. *Sure enough,* Debi answers, *you are pink. Now,* Cathie continues, looking relieved, *Taleshia needs to be brown.* Debi looks at Taleshia, who is now frowning, and asks her, *Do you want to be brown?* She shakes her head vigorously and points to pale pink. *I want that color.*

Cathie is frustrated, and trying to be supportive, Debi explains that *Taleshia can choose any color she thinks is right.* Cathie again objects, but Taleshia smiles, and Debi paints her palm pink. Then Taleshia makes her handprint. Cathie stares, apparently convinced that Taleshia and Debi have lost touch with reality. As Taleshia leaves, Cathie takes her place, remarking to Debi, *I just don't know what's the matter with you. Couldn't you see that* she is brown! Cathie gives up and chooses pale pink for herself, a close match. Cathie makes her handprint and says to Debi. *See, I am* not *brown.*

Taleshia stuck to her choice despite Cathie's insistence. Both three-year-olds demonstrate a strong awareness of the importance of skin color, and their views are strongly held. This example underscores the importance of child-centered research. A traditional conceptualization of this Black child's choice of skin color paint might suggest that the child is confused about racial identity. If she chose pink in the usual experimental setting (Clark and Clark 1940; Porter 1971), she would probably be evaluated as rejecting herself for a preferred whiteness. Debi had several other interactions with Taleshia. The three-year-old had, on other occasions, pointed out how pale Debi was and how dark her own skin was. She had explained to Debi that she was Black, that she thought she was pretty, and that pink was her favorite color. One possible explanation for her choice of pink for her skin color in the handpainting activity relies on Debi's knowledge of Taleshia's personality, family background, and previous interactions with others. Taleshia may have chosen pink because it is her favorite color, but this does not mean that she is unaware that most of her skin is dark. Another explanation for Taleshia's choice of skin color representation is that, like other African Americans, Taleshia's palms are *pink* while most of her skin is very dark. Perhaps she was choosing a color to match the color of her palms, a reasonable choice because the task was to paint the palms for handprints. The validity of this interpretation is reinforced by another episode at the center. One day Taleshia sat down and held Debi's hands in hers, turning them from top to bottom. Without uttering a word, she repeated this activity with her own hands, drawing Debi's attention to this act. The three-year-old was contrasting the pink-brown variations in her skin color with Debi's pinkish hand color. This explanation for the child's paint choice might not occur to a researcher who did not pay careful attention to the context and the child's personal perspective. Taleshia's ideas, centered in observations of herself and others, were more important to her than another child's notions of appropriate color. Far from being confused about skin color, she was creating meaning for color based on her own evaluations.

Using Racial Concepts to Control

The complex nature of children's group interactions and their solo behaviors demonstrates that race and ethnicity are salient, substantial aspects of their lives. They understand racial nuances that seem surprisingly sophisticated, including the power of race. How children use this power in their relationships is demonstrated in further episodes. . . .

In another encounter, this time among three children, a White child demonstrates her knowledge of broader race relations, demonstrating her grasp of race-based power inequalities. During play time Debi watches Renee (4: White) pull Ling-mai (3: Asian) and Jocelyn (4.5: White) across the playground in a wagon. Renee tugs away enthusiastically. Suddenly, Renee drops the handle, which falls to the ground, and she stands still, breathing heavily. Ling-mai, eager to continue this game, jumps from the wagon and picks up the handle. As Ling-mai begins to pull, Renee admonishes her, *No, no. You can't pull this wagon. Only* White Americans *can pull this wagon.* Renee has her hands on her hips and frowns at Ling-mai. Ling-mai tries again, and Renee again insists that only "White Americans" are permitted to do this task.

Ling-mai sobs loudly and runs to a teacher, complaining that *Renee hurt my feelings. Did you hurt Ling-mai's feelings?* the teacher asks Renee, who nods, not saying a word. *I think you should apologize,* the teacher continues, *because we are all friends here and friends don't hurt each other's feelings. Sorry,* mutters Renee, looking at Ling-mai, *I didn't do it on purpose. OK,* the teacher finishes, *can you guys be good friends now?* Both girls nod without looking at each other and quickly move away.

This interaction reveals several layers of meaning. Both children recognized the implications of Renee's harsh words and demands. Renee accurately underscored the point that Ling-mai, the child of Asian international students, was neither White nor American. Her failure to be included in these two groups, according to Renee's pronouncement, precluded her from being in charge of the wagon. Ling-mai responded, not by openly denying Renee's statements, but by complaining to the teacher that Renee had hurt her feelings. Both children seem knowledgeable about the structure of the U.S. and global racial hierarchy and accept the superior position accorded to Whites. The four-year-old child exercised authority as a White American and controlled the play with comments and with her stance and facial expressions. Our findings extend previous research on young children's knowledge of status and power (Corsaro 1979; Damon 1977) by showing that children are aware of the power and authority granted to Whites. The children were not confused about the meanings of these harsh racial words and actions.

Adult Misperceptions

Children's use of racial and ethnic concepts often goes unnoticed, even by adults in daily contact with them. This is illustrated by the responses of classroom teachers and the center director to preliminary reports on our research. Debi wrote two research reports, one for the classroom teachers and one for the director. After reading the reports, the teachers insisted to Debi that she must have been observing *some other children* and that *these are not our kids.* The director seemed determined to "guess" the identity of children whose incidents Debi described at a meeting. Throughout the episodes Debi described, he interrupted with remarks like *I'll bet that's Sarah you're talking about, isn't it?* His determination to attach names to the children revealed his investment in "curing" racism. He seemed determined to discover the culprits so unlearning might begin.

Adults' strong need to deny that children can use racial and ethnic concepts is also revealed in the next account. Here two children are engaged in a discussion of "what" they are. Debi is sitting with all the children on the steps to the deck playing "Simon Says." "Simon," a child selected by teachers to lead the game, directs the main action, while Debi observes that Rita (3.5: White/Latina) and Louis (4: Black) are engaged in their own private side activity. While the game continues, Rita and Louis discuss what they are. *What are you?* Louis asks Rita, and without waiting for her reply announces, *I'm Black and you're White. No,* she retorts, correcting him, *I'm not White, I'm mixed.* Louis regards her curiously, but at this moment Joanne, the lone Black teacher in the classroom, intervenes. *You're not mixed, Rita, you're Spanish,* she informs the child. *What race am I?* Joanne continues, trying to get the children to change the subject and glancing over at me anxiously. Rita replies, *Mixed. Mixed!?* Joanne, laughing, responds, *Mixed with what? Blue,* Rita says, looking only at her hands. Joanne is wearing a solid blue outfit. *Oh no, honey,* Joanne says, *I'm Black too, like Louis, not mixed. What an interesting conversation you guys are having.* Rita says nothing in response, and Louis remains silent throughout Joanne's attempt at dialogue. Suddenly, "Simon Says" ends and the kids run to the playground, escaping Joanne's questions. Joanne smiles and remarks to Debi, *Boy, it's really amazing what they pick up, isn't it?*

When Joanne intervened, Rita and Louis had to refocus their attention from a discussion between themselves about what they "are" to responding to Joanne's questioning. The adult interruption silenced Louis completely and made Rita defensive and wary. As other research has demonstrated, adult involvement in children's discourse can result in changes in the nature of the children's relations (Danielewicz, Rogers, and Noblit 1996). Rita realized that she must avoid sanctions when Joanne introduced her own racial identity into the game, attempting to distract the children from what Joanne perceived as an argument based on racial differences. However, the children were engaged in an appropriate discussion about their origins. Rita is indeed a "mixed" Latina, for her mother is from one Latin American country and her father is from another Latin American country. Rita understood this and had on other occasions described trips to visit her father's home. Louis is indeed Black and views Rita as White. Rita seemed to be trying to extend the concept beyond skin color and thus to educate Louis, until the teacher interrupted. Joanne's assumption seemed to be twofold: that Rita was confused and that as a teacher Joanne must act preventively. Here the teacher focused on quashing prejudice rather than seizing an opportunity to listen to the children and discuss their racial and ethnic perspectives. Adults tend to control children's use of racial and ethnic concepts and interpret children's use of these concepts along prejudice-defined lines. Clearly, the social context of children's learning, emphasized in the interpretive approach, includes other children and adults, but our accounts also demonstrate the way in which children's sophisticated understandings are developed without adult collaboration and supervision. . . .

Conclusion

Through extensive observation, this study has captured the richness of children's racial and ethnic experiences. The racial nature of children's interactions becomes fully apparent only when their interactions are viewed over time and in context. Close scrutiny of children's lives reveals that they are as intricate and convoluted as those of adults.

Blumer (1969:138) suggests that any sociological variable is, on examination, "an intricate and inner-moving complex." Dunn (1993) notes that children's relationships are complex and multidimensional, even within their own families. . . . By exploring the use of racial concepts in the child's natural world, instead of trying to remove the child or the concepts from that world, we glean a more complete picture of how children view and manipulate racial and ethnic concepts and understandings.

For most children, racial and ethnic issues arise forcefully within the context of their interaction with others. Most of the children that we observed had little or no experience with people from other racial or ethnic groups outside of the center. For these very young children, who are having their first extensive social experiences outside the family, racial and ethnic differences became powerful identifiers of self and other. Whether this is also true for children who do not experience such a diverse range of exposure to racial and ethnic concepts is beyond the scope of this project. However, over the 11 months we observed dozens of slowly evolving transformations in these children's racial and ethnic explorations and understandings. For many children, racial and ethnic awareness increased. Some, like Taleshia, regularly explored racial identities by comparing their skin color with that of others. Others, like Renee, faced crises over identity. For still others, racial and/or ethnic matters arose intermittently, but these matters did not seem to be central to the children's explorations. Children varied in how often they expressed or indicated racial or ethnic understandings, but we were unable to observe each child constantly and cannot make a more detailed judgment on this issue.

To fully understand the importance of children's racial and/or ethnic understandings, the nuanced complexity and interconnected nature of their thinking and behavior must be accepted and recognized. Measures of racial and ethnic awareness should consider not only children's cognitive abilities but also the relationships that children develop in social situations. . . .

Regarding the racial and ethnic hierarchy, young children understand that in U.S. society higher status is awarded to White people. Many understand that simply by virtue of their skin color, Whites are accorded more power, control, and prestige. Very young children carry out interactions in which race is salient. Racial knowledge is situational, and children can interact in a race-based or race-neutral manner, according to their evaluations of appropriateness. In children's worlds race emerges early as a tool for social interaction and quickly becomes a complex and fluid component of everyday interaction.

The behaviors of the children in this preschool setting are likely to be repeated in other diverse settings. The traditional literature accepts that children display prejudice by the time they arrive at school, but offers no explanation about the acquisition of this prejudice beyond it being an imitation of parental behavior. We expect continuity of children's racial and ethnic categories across settings, for children reveal a readiness to use their knowledge of race and ethnicity.

The observed episodes underscore problems in traditional theories of child development. When children fail cognitive tasks framed in terms of principles such as conservation and reciprocity, researchers often conclude that children lack the cognitive capability to understand race. However, surveys and observations of children in natural settings demonstrate that three-year-old children have constant, well-defined, and negative biases toward racial and ethnic others (Ramsey 1987). Rather than insisting that young children do not understand racial or ethnic ideas because they do not reproduce these concepts on adult-centered cognitive tests, researchers should determine the extent to which racial and ethnic concepts—as used in daily interaction—are salient definers of children's social reality. Research on young children's use of racial and gender concepts demonstrates that the more carefully a research design explores the real life of children, the more likely that research can answer questions about the nature of race and ethnicity in children's everyday lives.

REFERENCES

Aboud, Frances E. 1977. "Interest in Ethnic Information: A Cross-Cultural Developmental Study." *Canadian Journal of Behavioral Science* 9:134–46.

Clark, Kenneth B. and Mamie P. Clark. 1939. "The Development of Consciousness of Self and the Emergence of Racial Identification in Negro Preschool Children." *Journal of Social Psychology,* SPSSI Bulletin 10:591–99.

———. 1940. "Skin Color as a Factor in Racial Identification and Preference in Negro Children." *Journal of Negro Education* 19:341–58.

Corsaro, William A. 1979. "We're Friends, Right?" *Language in Society* 8:315–36.

Cross, William E., Jr. 1987. "A Two-Factor Theory of Black Identity: Implications for the Study of Identity Development in Minority Children." Pp. 117–33 in *Children's Ethnic Socialization: Pluralism and Development,* edited by J. S. Phinney and M. J. Rotheram. Newbury Park, CA: Sage.

Damon, William. 1977. *The Social World of the Child.* San Francisco, CA: Jossey-Bass.

Danielewicz, Jane M., Dwight L. Rogers, and George Noblit. 1996. "Children's Discourse Patterns and Power Relations in Teacher-Led and Child-Led Sharing Time." *Qualitative Studies in Education* 9:311–31.

Derman-Sparks, Louise. 1989. *Anti-Bias Curriculum: Tools for Empowering Young Children.* Washington, DC: National Association for the Education of Young Children.

Donaldson, Margaret. 1978. *Children's Minds.* London, England: Fontana.

Dunn, Judy. 1993. "Young Children's Understanding of Other People: Evidence from Observations within the Family." Pp. 97–114 in *Young Children's Close Relationships: Beyond Attachment,* edited by J. Dunn. Newbury Park, CA: Sage.

Goodman, Mary E. 1964. *Race Awareness in Young Children.* New York: Crowell-Collier.

Holmes, Robyn M. 1995. *How Young Children Perceive Race.* Thousand Oaks, CA: Sage.

Katz, Phyllis A. 1976. "The Acquisition of Racial Attitudes in Children." Pp. 125–54 in *Towards the Elimination of Racism,* edited by P. A. Katz. New York: Pergamon.

Menter, Ian. 1989. "'They're Too Young to Notice': Young Children and Racism." Pp. 91–104 in *Disaffection from School? The Early Years,* edited by G. Barrett. London, England: Falmer.

Porter, Judith D. R. 1971. *Black Child, White Child: The Development of Racial Attitudes.* Cambridge, MA: Harvard University.

Ramsey, Patricia A. 1987. "Young Children's Thinking about Ethnic Differences." Pp. 56–72 in *Children's Ethnic Socialization: Pluralism and Development,* edited by J. S. Phinney and M. J. Rotheram. Newbury Park, CA: Sage.

Schofield, Janet W. and William D. Francis. 1982. "An Observational Study of Peer Interaction in Racially-Mixed 'Accelerated' Classrooms." *Journal of Educational Psychology* 74:722–32.

Spencer, Margaret B. 1987. "Black Children's Ethnic Identity Formation: Risk and Resilience of Castelike Minorities." Pp. 103–16 in *Children's Ethnic Socialization: Pluralism and Development,* edited by J. S. Phinney and M. J. Rotheram. Newbury Park, CA: Sage.

Spencer, Margaret B., Geraldine K. Brookins, and Walter R. Allen. 1985. *Beginnings: Social and Affective Development of Black Children.* New York: Erlbaum.

Strayer, Janet. 1986. "Children's Attributions Regarding the Situational Determinants of Emotion in Self and Others." *Developmental Psychology* 22:649–54.

Thorne, Barrie. 1993. *Gender Play: Girls and Boys in School.* New Brunswick, NJ: Rutgers University Press.

Williams, John E. and John K. Morland. 1976. *Race, Color, and the Young Child.* Chapel Hill, NC: University of North Carolina Press.

Willis, Paul. 1990. *Common Culture: Symbolic Work at Play in the Everyday Cultures of the Young.* Buckingham, England: Open University Press.

15

MAKING IT BY FAKING IT
Working-Class Students in an Elite Academic Environment

ROBERT GRANFIELD

An important point about socialization is that societal values, identities, and social roles are learned, *not* instinctual. We have to learn the social norms and behaviors our society expects from us. We also learn or are socialized into different identities—our gender identity, our racial-ethnic identity, and our social class identity—among several others. In this reading, published in 1991, Robert Granfield examines how the working-class identities of some law students are challenged during their years at elite law schools. Law students experience an intense period of professional socialization during their graduate-school years that not only teaches them their occupation, but also changes their values, identities, and social roles. Granfield, an associate professor of sociology at the University of Buffalo, argues that this intense socialization has consequences not only for the individual students but also for the legal profession.

Robert Granfield, "Making It by Faking It: Working-Class Students in an Elite Academic Environment" from *Journal of Contemporary Ethnography* (formerly *Urban Life*) 20, no. 3 (October 1991): 331–351. Copyright © 1991 by Sage Publications, Inc. Reprinted with the permission of Sage Publications, Inc.

R esearch on stigma has generated significant insights into the complex relationship between self and society. The legacy of Goffman's
(1963) seminal work on the subject can be found in studies on alco-
holism, mental illness, homosexuality, physical deformities, and juvenile
delinquency. Even the literature on gender and racial inequality has benefited
from an emphasis on stigma. Goffman's attention to the social processes of
devaluation and the emerging self-concepts of discredited individuals not
only created research opportunities for generations of sociologists but contributed to a humanistic ideology that viewed stigma assignment and its
effects as unjust.

One of the most vibrant research programs that emerged from Goffman's
classic work has been in the area of stigma management. A host of conceptual
terms have been employed to describe the process through which discreditable individuals control information about themselves so as to manage their
social identity. Concepts such as passing, deviance disavowal, accounts, dis-
claimers, and covering have often been used in analyzing accommodations
and adjustments to deviance, as Pfuhl's (1986) review shows. These tactics,
while offering rewards associated with being seen as normal, frequently contribute to psychological stress. Possessing what Goffman (1963:5) referred to
as "undesired differentness" often has significant consequences for one's personal identity as well as for available life chances. . . .

In this article, I focus on class stigma by examining a group of highly successful, upwardly mobile, working-class students who gained admission to
a prestigious Ivy League law school in the East. While upward mobility from
the working class occurs far less often within elite branches of the legal profession (Heinz and Laumann 1982; Smigel 1969) or corporate management
(Useem and Karabel 1986), a certain amount of this type of mobility does
take place. Working-class aspirants to the social elite, however, must accumulate cultural capital (Bourdieu and Passeron 1990; Cookson and Persell
1985) before they are able to transcend their status boundaries.

First, this article examines the ways in which working-class students experience a sense of differentness and marginality within the law school's elite
environment. Next, I explore how these students react to their emerging class
stigma by managing information about their backgrounds. I then demonstrate that the management strategies contribute to identity ambivalence and
consider the secondary forms of adjustment students use to resolve this
tension. Finally, I discuss why an analysis of social class can benefit from the
insights forged by Goffman's work on stigma.

Setting and Methodology

The data analyzed for this article were collected as part of a much larger
project associated with law school socialization (Granfield 1989). The subjects consist of students attending a prestigious, national law school in the
eastern part of the United States. The school has had a long reputation of
training lawyers who have become partners in major Wall Street law firms,

Supreme Court judges, United States presidents and other politicians, heads of foundations, and . . . [have assumed many] other eminent leadership positions. Throughout the school's history, it has drawn mostly on the talents of high-status males. It was not until the second half of the twentieth century that women, minorities, and members of the lower classes were allowed admission into this esteemed institution (Abel 1989).

Most of the students attending the university at the time the study was being conducted were white and middle class.[1] The overwhelming majority are the sons and daughters of the professional-managerial class. Over 70 percent of those returning questionnaires had Ivy League or other highly prestigious educational credentials. As one would expect, fewer working-class students possessed such credentials.

A triangulated research design (Fielding and Fielding 1986) was used to collect the data. The first phase consisted of extensive fieldwork at the law school from 1985 to 1988, during which time I became a "peripheral member" (Adler and Adler 1987) in selected student groups. My activities while in the field consisted of attending classes with students, participating in their Moot Court[2] preparations, studying with students on campus, and at times, in their apartments, lunching with them, becoming involved in student demonstrations over job recruiting and faculty hiring, attending extracurricular lectures presented on campus, and participating in orientation exercises for first-year students. Throughout the entire fieldwork phase, I assumed both overt and covert roles. During the observation periods in classrooms, I recorded teacher–student interactions that occurred.

To supplement these observations, I conducted in-depth interviews with 103 law students at various stages in their training. Both personal interviews and small-group interviews with three or four students were recorded. The interviews lasted approximately two hours each and sought to identify the lived process through which law students experience legal training.

Finally, I administered a survey to 50 percent of the 1,540 students attending the law school. The survey examined their backgrounds, motives for attending law school, subjective perceptions of personal change, expectations about future practice, and evaluations of various substantive areas of practice. Over half (391) of the questionnaires were returned—a high rate of response for a survey of six pages requiring approximately 30 minutes of the respondent's time.

For this article, a subset of working-class students was selected for extensive analysis. Of the 103 students interviewed for the larger study, 23 came from working-class backgrounds, none of these from either the labor aristocracy or the unstable sectors of the working class. Typical parental occupations include postal worker, house painter, factory worker, fireman, dock worker, and carpenter. Many of these students were interviewed several times during their law school career. Many of the students selected for interviews were identified through questionnaires, while others were selected through the process of snowball sampling (Chadwick, Bahr, and Albrecht 1984).

Feeling Out of Place

Working-class students entered this elite educational institution with a great deal of class pride. This sense of class pride is reflected in the fact that a significantly larger proportion of working-class students reported entering law school for the purposes of contributing to social change than their non-working-class counterparts (see Granfield and Koenig 1990). That these students entered law school with the desire to help the downtrodden suggests that they identified with their working-class kin. In fact, students often credited their class background as being a motivating factor in their decision to pursue a career in social justice. One third-year student, whose father worked as a postal worker, recalled her parental influence:

> *I wanted a career in social justice. It seemed to me to be a good value for someone who wanted to leave this world a little better than they found it. My parents raised me with a sense that there are right things and wrong things and that maybe you ought to try to do some right things with your life.*

A second-year student said that he was influenced by the oppressive experiences that his father endured as a factory laborer. Coming to law school to pursue a career in a labor union, this student explained, *I was affected by my father, who had a job as a machinist. My father believes that corporations have no decency. I would term it differently, but we're talking about the same thing.* Identifying with their working-class heritage produced not only a sense of pride but a system of values and ideals that greatly influenced their initial career objectives.

However, identification with the working class began to diminish soon after these students entered law school. Not long after arriving, most working-class students encountered an entirely new moral career. Although initially proud of their accomplishments, they soon came to define themselves as different and their backgrounds a burden. Lacking the appropriate cultural capital (Bourdieu 1984) associated with their more privileged counterparts, working-class students began to experience a crisis in competency. Phrases such as "the first semester makes you feel extremely incompetent," "the first year is like eating humble pie," and "I felt very small, powerless, and dumb" were almost universal among these working-class students. Some students felt embarrassed by their difficulty in using the elaborated speech codes (Bernstein 1977) associated with the middle class. One working-class woman said that she was very aware of using "proper" English, adding that *it makes me self-conscious when I use the wrong word or tense. I feel that if I had grown up in the middle class, I wouldn't have lapses. I have difficulty expressing thoughts while most other people here don't.*

The recognition of their apparent differentness is perhaps best noted by examining the students' perception of stress associated with the first year of studies. Incoming working-class students reported significantly higher levels of personal stress than did their counterparts with more elite backgrounds.

Much of this anxiety came from fears of academic inadequacy. Despite generally excellent college grades and their success in gaining admission to a nationally ranked law school, these students often worried that they did not measure up to the school's high standards. Nearly 62 percent of the first-year working-class students reported experiencing excessive grade pressure, compared to only 35 percent of those students from higher social class backgrounds.

In the words of Sennett and Cobb (1973), this lack of confidence is a "hidden injury of class," a psychological burden that working-class students experienced as they came to acquire the "identity beliefs" associated with middle-class society. While most students experience some degree of uncertainty and competency crisis during their first year, working-class students face the additional pressure of being cultural outsiders. Lacking manners of speech, attire, values, and experiences associated with their more privileged counterparts, even the most capable working-class student felt out of place:

> I had a real problem my first year because law and legal education are based on upper-middle-class values. The class debates had to do with profit maximization, law and economics, atomistic individualism. I remember in class we were talking about landlords' responsibility to maintain decent housing in rental apartments. Some people were saying that there were good reasons not to do this. Well, I think that's bullshit because I grew up with people who lived in apartments with rats, leaks, and roaches. I feel really different because I didn't grow up in suburbia.

Another student, a third-year working-class woman, felt marginalized because even her teachers assumed class homogeneity:

> I get sensitive about what professors have to say in class. I remember in a business class the professor seemed to assume that we all had fathers that worked in business and that we all understood about family investments. He said, "You're all pretty much familiar with this because of your family background." I remember thinking, doesn't he think there's any people in this law school who come from a working-class background?

Such experiences contributed to a student's sense of living in an alien world. The social distance these students experienced early in their law school career produced considerable discomfort.

This discomfort grew more intense as they became increasingly immersed into this new elite world. Within a short span of time, these students began to experience a credential gap vis-à-vis other students who possessed more prestigious academic credentials. A first-year male student who attended a state school in the Midwest explained:

> I'm not like most people here. I didn't go to prestigious schools. I'm a bit of a minority here because of that. When I got here I was really intimidated by the fact of how many Yale and Harvard people there were here.

At times, working-class law students were even embarrassed by their spouse's lower status. One first-year student described how her husband's credential gap caused her some anxiety:

> *People would ask me what my husband did and I would say he works for Radio Shack. People would be surprised. That was hard. Lately, we haven't done as much with [law school] people.*

Thus, students sometimes pruned contacts that would potentially result in stigma disclosure. In general, then, as working-class students progressed through law school, they began to adopt a view of themselves as different. The recognition of this difference subsequently led them to develop techniques of adjusting to their perceived secondary status.

Faking It

The management of identity has critical strategic importance not only for group affiliation and acceptance but for life chances. Stigma limits one's opportunities to participate in social life as a complete citizen, particularly so for those possessing gender or racial stigmas. However, because of the visibility of these stigmas, a person's adjustment to second-class citizenship is accomplished typically through either role engulfment in which a person accepts a spoiled identity (Schur 1971) or through direct confrontation where assignment of secondary status is itself challenged (Schur 1980). Rarely are these groups able to employ the concealment tactics typical among those groups whose stigma is not overtly visible.

Unlike gender or racial stigma, however, individuals often adjust to class stigma by learning to conceal their uniqueness. The practice of concealing one's class background, for instance, is not unusual. Certainly, members of the elite frequently learn that it is in "bad taste" to flaunt their privileged background and that it is more gracious to conceal their eminent social status (Baltzell 1958). Similarly, individuals who experience downward mobility often attempt to maintain their predecline image by concealing loss of status. Camouflaging unemployment in the world of management by using such terms as "consultant" and by doctoring résumés are ways that downwardly mobile executives "cover" their spoiled status (Newman 1988). Concealing one's social class circumstances and the stigma that may be associated with it assist individuals in dealing with any rejection and ostracism that may be forthcoming were the person's actual status known.

Initially, students who took pride in having accomplished upward mobility openly displayed a working-class presentation of self. Many went out of their way to maintain this presentation. One first-year student who grew up in a labor union family in New York explained that: *I have consciously maintained my working-class image. I wear work shirts or old flannel shirts and blue jeans every day.* During his first year, this student flaunted his working-class background, frequently also donning an old army jacket, hiking boots, and a wool hat. Identifying himself as part of the "proletarian left," he tried to remain isolated from what he referred to as the "elitist" law school community.

This attempt to remain situated in the working class, however, not only separated these students from the entire law school community but alienated them from groups that shared their ideological convictions. While much of the clothing worn by non-working-class students suggests resistance to being identified as a member of the elite, working-class students become increasingly aware of their differentness. Although these students identify with the working class, others, despite their appearance, possess traits and lifestyles that are often associated with more privileged groups (see Lurie 1983; Stone 1970). One first-year woman who described herself as "radical" complained that the other law school radicals were really "a bunch of upper-class white men." Subsequently, working-class students must disengage from their backgrounds if they desire to escape feeling discredited.

Working-class students disengaged from their previous identity by concealing their class backgrounds. Just as deviants seek to manage their identity by "passing" as nondeviants (Goffman 1963), these working-class law students often adopted identities that were associated with the more elite social classes.[3] Concealment allowed students to better participate in the culture of eminence that exists within the law school and reap available rewards.

This concealment meant, for instance, that students needed to acquire new dress codes. As Stone (1970) illustrated, appearance signifies identity and exercises a regulatory function over the responses of others. Such cultural codes pertaining to appearance often are used to exclude individuals from elite social positions (Bourdieu 1984; Jackell 1988; Lamont and Lareau 1988). Although working-class students lacked the cultural capital of higher social classes, they began to realize that they could successfully mimic their more privileged counterparts. Like undistinguished prep school students (Cookson and Persell 1985), working-class law students learned how to behave in an upper-class world, including how to dress for a new audience whose favorable appraisal they must cultivate. One second-year male discussed this process:

> *I remember going to buy suits here. I went to Brooks Brothers for two reasons. One, I don't own a suit. My father owns one suit, and it's not that good. Second, I think it's important to look good. A lot of my friends went to Brooks Brothers, and I feel it's worth it to do it right and not to have another hurdle to walk in and have the wrong thing on. It's all a big play act. . . . During my first year, I had no luck with interviews. I was in my own little world when I came here. I wished I had paid more attention to the dressing habits of second- and third-year students.*

Being in their own "working-class world" forced these students to begin recognizing the importance of different interpersonal skills. A second-year woman commented that:

> *I have really begun to see the value of having good social skills. I think that is one of the ways that law firms weed out people. In order to get jobs you have to have those social skills. I'm real conscious of that when I go out on interviews now.*

The recognition among working-class students that they were able to imitate upper-class students increasingly encouraged them to conceal their backgrounds. One second-year student, whose father worked as a house painter, boasted of his mastery of "passing":

> *I generally don't tell people what my father does or what my mother does. I notice that I'm different, but it's not something other people here notice because I can fake it. They don't notice that I come from a blue-collar background.*

Paying attention to the impression that one presents becomes extremely important for the upwardly mobile working-class student.

These students were sometimes assisted in their performances by professional career counselors employed by the law school. These professionals gave students instructions on how to present themselves as full-fledged members of this elite community. Students were taught that unless they downplayed their social class background, the most lucrative opportunities would be denied them. A third-year woman from a working-class area in Boston recalled learning this new norm of presentation:

> *I'm sort of proud that I'm from South Boston and come from a working-class background. During my second year, however, I wasn't having much luck with my first interviews. I went to talk with my adviser about how to change my résumé a bit or how to present myself better. I told my adviser that on the interviews I was presenting myself as a slightly unusual person with a different background. We talked about that, and he told me that it probably wasn't a good idea to present myself as being a little unusual. I decided that he was right and began to play up that I was just like them. After that, the interviews and offers began rolling in. I began to realize that they [interviewers] really like people who are like themselves.*

Recognizing that job recruiters seek homogeneity is an important lesson that upwardly mobile working-class students must learn if they are to gain admission into high status and financially rewarding occupations.[4] Kanter (1977) demonstrated, for instance, that managers come to reward those who resemble themselves. More recently, Jackell (1988) documented how the failure of managers to "fit in" resulted in suspicion and subsequent exclusion from advancement. Fitting in is particularly important in prestigious law firms which tend to resemble the high-status clients they represent (Abel 1989). During interviews, however, working-class law students faced a distinct disadvantage, as the interviewers who actively pursued new recruits rarely posed questions about the student's knowledge of law.[5] Most seemed intent on finding students who fit into the law firm's corporate structure. The entire recruitment process itself, from the initial interview to "fly out," represents ceremonial affirmation of these students' elite status in which they need only demonstrate their "social" competence. Working-class students typically found such interactions stressful. One third-year student explained her experiences:

> *They [the recruiters] didn't test my knowledge of law. They were interested in finding out what kind of person I was and what my background was. I tried*

to avoid talking about that and instead stressed the kind of work I was inter-
ested in. I think that most firms want a person who they can mold, that fits
into their firm.

Some of the most successful working-class students enjoyed the accolades
bestowed on them because of their hard work and natural abilities. In speaking of her success, a third-year student on law review said that when she entered law school, it never occurred to her that she would clerk for the Supreme
Court and then work for a major Wall Street law firm, adding that *once you*
begin doing well and move up the ladder and gain a whole new set of peers, then you
begin to think about the possibilities. However, such success comes at a price,
particularly for working-class students of color. Although having achieved
success, many of these students continued to feel like outsiders. One such
student, a third-year black male, reflected on what he considered the unfortunate aspects of affirmative action programs:

> *I have mixed feelings about the law review because of its affirmative action poli-*
> *cies. On the one hand, I think it's good that minorities are represented on the law*
> *review. On the other hand, there's a real stigma attached to it. Before law school,*
> *I achieved by my own abilities. On law review, I don't feel I get respect. I find*
> *myself working very hard and getting no respect. Other students don't work as*
> *hard. I spend a lot of time at the review because I don't want to turn in a bad*
> *assignment. I don't want them [other law review members] to think that I don't*
> *have what it takes.*

Students who perceived themselves as outsiders frequently overcompen-
sated for their failings because they felt judged by the "master status" associated with their social identity. This reaction to class stigma is typical among
working-class students in educational institutions. In addition to developing
their educational skills, working-class students are confronted with learning
social skills as well. This makes succeeding particularly difficult for these
students and is a task fraught with the fear of being discovered as incompetent (Sennett and Cobb 1973).

Ambivalence

Despite their maneuvers, these working-class students had difficulty transcending their previous identity. The attempt by these students to manage
their stigma resulted in what Goffman (1963:107) termed "identity ambivalence." Working-class students who sought to exit their class background
could neither embrace their group nor let it go. This ambivalence is often
felt by working-class individuals who attain upward mobility into the
professional-managerial class (Steinitz and Solomon 1986). Many experience
the "stranger in paradise" syndrome, in which working-class individuals feel
like virtual outsiders in middle-class occupations (Ryan and Sackrey 1984).
Such experiences frequently lead to considerable identity conflict among working-class individuals who attempt to align themselves with the middle class.

The working-class law students in my sample typically experienced identity conflicts on their upward climb. Not only did they feel deceptive in their adjustment strategies, but many felt the additional burden of believing they had "sold out" their own class and were letting their group down. Like other stigmatized individuals who gain acceptance among dominant groups (Goffman 1963), these students often felt they were letting down their own group by representing elite interests. One third-year female student ruefully explained:

> My brother keeps asking me whether I'm a Republican yet. He thought that after I finished law school I would go to work to help people, not work for one of those firms that do business. In a way, he's my conscience. Maybe he's right. I've got a conflict with what I'm doing. I came from the working class and wanted to do public interest law. I have decided not to do that. It's been a difficult decision for me. I'm not completely comfortable about working at a large firm.

Another student, who grew up on welfare, expressed similar reservations about his impending career in law:

> I'm not real happy about going to a large firm. I make lots of apologies. I'm still upset about the fact that my clients are real wealthy people, and it's not clear as to what the social utility of that will be.

Like the previous example, this student experienced a form of self-alienation as a result of his identity ambivalence. Students often experience a sense of guilt as they transcend their working-class backgrounds. Such guilt, however, needs to be abated if these students are to successfully adjust to their new reference group and reduce the status conflict they experience. For these working-class students, making the primary adjustment to upward mobility required strategies of accommodation in personal attitudes regarding their relationship to members of less privileged social classes. Secondary identity adjustments were therefore critical in helping students mitigate the ambivalence they experienced over their own success and subsequent separation from the working class.

Resolving Ambivalence

Although accommodation strategies were typical throughout the entire student body,[6] working-class students at this law school were more likely to employ particular types of strategies to help manage their identity. Students sought to manage their ambivalence by remaining "ideologically" distanced from the very social class their elite law school credential had facilitated alignment with. Many of these students became deliberate role models, unreservedly immersing themselves in higher social classes for that specific purpose. Such adjustments might be thought of as political since they were intended to directly challenge the domination of social elites. A black working-class student described how his actions would benefit the less fortunate:

> I get slammed for being a corporate tool. People feel that I have sold out. I'm irritated by that. For years, blacks have been treated as slaves, sharecroppers, or

> porters. So I think that whether I want to be a partner at Cravath or to be an
> NAACP defense attorney, either of these positions are politically correct. We
> need black people with money and power. I think that I can make significant con-
> tributions to black causes.

For many students who experienced ambivalence, working in elite law firms
was seen as the best way to help those they left behind. Other students redefined the value of large corporate law firms for the opportunities that such
positions offered in contributing to social change. One third-year student
suggested:

> I used to think that social change would come about by being an activist. That's
> why I originally wanted to do public interest law. But you really can't accom-
> plish much by doing this. The hiring partner at [a major New York law firm]
> convinced me that this is the only way to get things done. He served as the under
> secretary of state in the [former president's] administration. He made sense
> when he told me that if I wanted to contribute to social change I had to become
> an important person.

Students became less convinced that directly serving the less-privileged
social classes would effectively resolve the problems that concerned them.
A third-year student explained how disenchanted she had become with public interest law:

> I used to think that you could do good things for people. . . . I don't think that
> anymore. I'm no longer troubled by the idea of being a corporate lawyer as
> opposed to a public interest one. I'm still concerned about social problems like
> poverty or poor housing, but I'm not sure that being a public interest attorney is
> the way to resolve those things. The needs of the people that public interest
> lawyers serve are just beyond what I can do as an attorney. I think I can do more
> good for people if I commit myself to working with community groups or activi-
> ties in the bar during my spare time.

The offering of such accounts helps students resolve the contradiction they
experience by choosing a large law firm practice, as does the practical
planning to use one's spare time (e.g., to do community activities). Unfortunately, given the structure of contemporary large law firms, spare time is
a rarity (Nelson 1988; Spangler 1986). Adopting these new definitions regarding the pursuit of effective social change means that working-class
students need not feel penitent over their upward mobility. Such strategies, of course, are attractive, as they suggest that the student is becoming
elite not solely because he or she is striving for personal reward and success but as a means to best pursue the noble ideals of public service and
social activism.

A more drastic accommodation involved avoidance of those who
reminded working-class students of their social obligations toward helping
the less fortunate. Just associating with individuals whose career path was
geared toward helping the downtrodden caused considerable uneasiness
in working-class students who had decided to enter large law firms. One

third-year student said that he had begun to avoid law students who had retained their commitment to work with the poor:

> It's taken for granted here that you can work for a large firm and still be a good person. The people who don't reinforce that message make me uncomfortable now. Frankly, that's why I'm not hanging out with the public interest people. They remind me of my own guilt.

In some cases, avoidance turned into open hostility. Another third-year student described how she now saw other students who remained committed to their ideals of helping the less fortunate: *They're so single-minded at times and I think a little naive. They've really pushed me away from wanting to do public interest work as a full-time occupation.* Condemning her condemners helped this student neutralize the guilt she felt over working for a corporate law firm.

Conclusion

Upwardly mobile working-class students in this study, as well as in others, interpret and experience their social class from the perspective of stigma. However, since the stigma of being a member of the lower classes is thought to be just, upwardly mobile working-class students frequently construct identities in which they seek to escape the taint associated with their affiliation. Overcoming this stigma is therefore considered an individual rather than a collective effort. As was demonstrated in this study, such efforts often involve managing one's identity in the ways that Goffman outlined. Research that explores identity struggles as they relate to class could offer further extensions of Goffman's comments on stigma. Such research also has potential value in contributing to our understanding of working-class movements in the United States. Indeed, exploring the experience of class from the perspective of stigma and its management could offer great insight into the social psychology of working-class disempowerment.

ENDNOTES

Author's Note: Partial funding for this research was provided by the Woodrow Wilson Foundation.

[1] The following are the percentage distributions of social class background on the random sample of questionnaire returnees I collected for the larger project: upper class (2.8), upper-middle (44.6), middle (30.0), lower-middle (8.0), working (13.1), and lower (0.5).

[2] This is a first-year exercise in which students select a case to argue in front of a three-person panel consisting of a law professor, a third-year student, and an invited guest from the legal community. First-year students prepare their cases for several months in advance before formally presenting their oral argument.

[3] Similar findings were reported by Domhoff and Zweigenhaft (1991) in which they described the experiences of black students who were enrolled in elite prep schools as a result of affirmative action.

[4] Students are actively pursued. During the 1987 recruitment seasons at the law school, an average of 44 recruiters from commercial law firms conducted interviews with students each day. This represents nearly one law firm for each law student eligible to interview. In most cases, law firms are looking to hire more than one student.

[5]A study of hiring policies among large law firms found that "personal characteristics" ranked second among the criteria for selecting new lawyers (see Buller and Beck-Dudley 1990).

[6]Many students are confronted with identity conflicts that stem from the separation of personal values from professional roles. This is felt most among those students who entered law school with social activist ideals (for further discussion of this, see Granfield 1986, 1989, 1992).

REFERENCES

Abel, R. 1989. *American Lawyers.* New York: Oxford University Press.

Adler, P. and P. Adler. 1987. *Membership Roles in Field Research.* Newbury Park, CA: Sage.

Baltzell, E. D. 1958. *Philadelphia Gentlemen.* New York: Free Press.

Bernstein, B. 1977. *Class Codes and Control.* Vol. 3, *Towards a Theory of Educational Transmission.* London: Routledge & Kegan Paul.

Bourdieu, P. 1984. *Distinction: A Social Critique of the Judgment of Taste.* Cambridge, MA: Harvard University Press.

Bourdieu, P. and J. C. Passeron. 1990. *Reproduction in Education, Society and Culture.* London: Routledge & Kegan Paul.

Buller, P. and C. Beck-Dudley. 1990. "Performance, Policies and Personnel." *American Bar Association Journal* 76:94.

Chadwick, B., H. Bahr, and S. Albrecht. 1984. *Social Science Research Methods.* Englewood Cliffs, NJ: Prentice-Hall.

Cookson, P. and C. Persell. 1985. *Preparing for Power: America's Elite Boarding Schools.* New York: Basic Books.

Domhoff, G. W. and R. Zweigenhaft. 1991. *Blacks in the White Establishment: A Study of Race and Class in America.* New Haven, CT: Yale University Press.

Fielding, N. and J. Fielding. 1986. *Linking Data.* Beverly Hills, CA: Sage.

Goffman, E. 1963. *Stigma: Notes on the Management of Spoiled Identity.* Englewood Cliffs, NJ: Prentice-Hall.

Granfield, R. 1986. "Legal Education As Corporate Ideology: Student Adjustment to the Law School Experience." *Sociological Forum* 1:514–23.

———. 1989. "Making the Elite Lawyer: Culture and Ideology in Legal Education." Ph.D. dissertation, Northeastern University, Boston.

———. 1992. *Making Elite Lawyers.* New York: Routledge, Chapman & Hall.

Granfield, R. and T. Koenig. 1990. "From Activism to Pro Bono: The Redirection of Working Class Altruism at Harvard Law School." *Critical Sociology* 17:57–80.

Heinz, J. and E. Laumann. 1982. *Chicago Lawyers: The Social Structure of the Bar.* New York: Russell Sage.

Jackell, R. 1988. *Moral Mazes: The World of the Corporate Manager.* New York: Oxford University Press.

Kanter, R. 1977. *Men and Women of the Corporation.* New York: Basic Books.

Lamont, M. and A. Lareau. 1988. "Cultural Capital: Allusions, Gaps and Glissandos in Recent Theoretical Development." *Sociological Theory* 6:153–68.

Lurie, A. 1983. *The Language of Clothes.* New York: Vintage.

Nelson, R. 1988. *Partners with Power: The Social Transformation of the Large Law Firm.* Berkeley: University of California Press.

Newman, K. 1988. *Falling from Grace: The Experience of Downward Mobility in the American Middle Class.* New York: Free Press.

Pfuhl, E. 1986. *The Deviance Process.* Belmont, CA: Wadsworth.

Ryan, J. and C. Sackrey. 1984. *Strangers in Paradise: Academics from the Working Class.* Boston: South End Press.

Schur, E. 1971. *Labeling Deviant Behavior.* New York: Harper & Row.

———. 1980. *The Politics of Deviance.* Englewood Cliffs, NJ: Prentice-Hall.

Sennett, R. and R. Cobb. 1973. *The Hidden Injuries of Class.* New York: Random House.

Smigel, E. 1969. *The Wall Street Lawyer.* Bloomington: Indiana University Press.

Spangler, E. 1986. *Lawyers for Hire: Salaried Professionals at Work.* New Haven, CT: Yale University Press.

Steinitz, V. and E. Solomon. 1986. *Starting Out: Class and Community in the Lives of Working Class Youth.* Philadelphia: Temple University Press.

Stone, G. 1970. "Appearance and the Self." Pp. 394–414 in *Social Psychology through Symbolic Interaction,* edited by G. Stone and H. Farberman. New York: Wiley.

Useem, M. and J. Karabel. 1986. "Paths to Corporate Management." *American Sociological Review* 51:184–200.

16
_____

ANYBODY'S SON WILL DO

GWYNNE DYER

An important point about socialization is that if culture is learned, it also can be unlearned. Sociologists call this process *resocialization*. This situation occurs when an individual gives up one way of life and one set of values for another. Examples of resocialization include the experience of new immigrants, of a person changing careers, of someone joining a feminist consciousness-raising group, or of an individual undergoing a religious conversion, such as a woman entering a convent to become a nun or a person being initiated into a cult. The following reading by journalist Gwynne Dyer is from his 1985 book, *War: Past, Present, and Future.* Here, Dyer focuses on the intense resocialization civilians experience during military basic training.

You think about it and you know you're going to have to kill but you don't understand the implications of that, because in the society in which you've lived murder is the most heinous of crimes . . . and you are in a situation in which it's turned the other way round. . . . When you do actually kill someone the experience, my experience, was one of revulsion and disgust. . . .

I was utterly terrified—petrified—but I knew there had to be a Japanese sniper in a small fishing shack near the shore. He was firing in the other direction at Marines in another battalion, but I knew as soon as he picked off the people there—there was a window on our side—that he would start picking us off. And there was nobody else to go . . . and so I ran towards the shack and broke in and found myself in an empty room. . . .

There was a door which meant there was another room and the sniper was in that—and I just broke that down. I was just absolutely gripped by the fear that this man would expect me and would shoot me. But as it turned out he was in a sniper harness and he couldn't turn around fast enough. He was entangled in the harness so I shot him with a .45, and I felt remorse and shame. I can remember whispering foolishly, "I'm sorry" and then just throwing up. . . . I threw up all over myself. It was a betrayal of what I'd been taught since a child.

—WILLIAM MANCHESTER

Yet he did kill the Japanese soldier, just as he had been trained to—the revulsion only came afterward. And even after Manchester knew what it was like to kill another human being, a young man like himself, he went on trying to kill his "enemies" until the war was over. Like all the other tens of millions of soldiers who had been taught from infancy that killing was wrong, and had then been sent off to kill for their countries, he was almost helpless to disobey, for he had fallen into the hands of an institution so powerful and so subtle that it could quickly reverse the moral training of a lifetime.

The whole vast edifice of the military institution rests on its ability to obtain obedience from its members even unto death—and the killing of others. It has enormous powers of compulsion at its command, of course, but all authority must be based ultimately on consent. The task of extracting that consent from its members has probably grown harder in recent times, for the gulf between the military and the civilian worlds has undoubtedly widened: Civilians no longer perceive the threat of violent death as an everyday hazard of existence, and the categories of people whom it is not morally permissible to kill have broadened to include (in peacetime) the entire human race. Yet the armed forces of every country can still take almost any young male civilian and turn him into a soldier with all the right reflexes and attitudes in only a few weeks. Their recruits usually have no more than twenty years' experience of the world, most of it as children, while the armies have had all of history to practice and perfect their techniques.

> *Just think of how the soldier is treated. While still a child he is shut up in the barracks. During his training he is always being knocked about. If he makes the least mistake he is beaten, a burning blow on his body, another on his eye, perhaps his head is laid open with a wound. He is battered and bruised with flogging. On the march . . . they hang heavy loads round his neck like that of an ass.*
>
> —Egyptian, circa 1500 b.c.[1]

> *The moment I talk to the new conscripts about the homeland I strike a land mine. So I kept quiet. Instead, I try to make soldiers of them. I give them hell from morning to sunset. They begin to curse me, curse the army, curse the state. Then they begin to curse together, and become a truly cohesive group, a unit, a fighting unit.*
>
> —Israeli, circa a.d. 1970[2]

All soldiers belong to the same profession, no matter what country they serve, and it makes them different from everybody else. They have to be different, for their job is ultimately about killing and dying, and those things are not a natural vocation for any human being. Yet all soldiers are born civilians. The method for turning young men into soldiers—people who kill other people and expose themselves to death—is basic training. It's essentially the same all over the world, and it always has been, because young men everywhere are pretty much alike.

Human beings are fairly malleable, especially when they are young, and in every young man there are attitudes for any army to work with: the inherited values and postures, more or less dimly recalled, of the tribal warriors who were once the model for every young boy to emulate. Civilization did not involve a sudden clean break in the way people behave, but merely the progressive distortion and redirection of all the ways in which people in the old tribal societies used to behave, and modern definitions of maleness still contain a great deal of the old warrior ethic. The anarchic machismo of the primitive warrior is not what modern armies really need in their soldiers, but it does provide them with promising raw material for the transformation they must work in their recruits.

Just how this transformation is wrought varies from time to time and from country to country. In totally militarized societies—ancient Sparta, the samurai class of medieval Japan, the areas controlled by organizations like the Eritrean People's Liberation Front today—it begins at puberty or before, when the young boy is immersed in a disciplined society in which only the military values are allowed to penetrate. In more sophisticated modern societies, the process is briefer and more concentrated, and the way it works is much more visible. It is, essentially, a conversion process in an almost religious sense—and as in all conversion phenomena, the emotions are far more important than the specific ideas. . . .

Armies know this. It is their business to get men to fight, and they have had a long time to work out the best way of doing it. All of them pay lip service to the symbols and slogans of their political masters, though the amount of time they must devote to this activity varies from country to country. . . . Nor should it be thought that the armies are hypocritical—most of their members really do believe in their particular national symbols and slogans. But their secret is that they know these are not the things that sustain men in combat.

What really enables men to fight is their own self-respect, and a special kind of love that has nothing to do with sex or idealism. Very few men have died in battle, when the moment actually arrived, for the United States of America or for the sacred cause of Communism, or even for their homes and families; if they had any choice in the matter at all, they chose to die for each other and for their own vision of themselves. . . .

The way armies produce this sense of brotherhood in a peacetime environment is basic training: a feat of psychological manipulation on the grand scale which has been so consistently successful and so universal that we fail to notice it as remarkable. In countries where the army must extract its recruits in their late teens, whether voluntarily or by conscription, from a civilian environment that does not share the military values, basic training involves a brief but intense period of indoctrination whose purpose is not really to teach the recruits basic military skills, but rather to change their values and their loyalties. "I guess you could say we brainwash them a little bit," admitted a U.S. Marine drill instructor, "but you know they're good people."

The duration and intensity of basic training, and even its major emphases, depend on what kind of society the recruits are coming from, and on what sort of military organization they are going to. It is obviously quicker to train men from a martial culture than from one in which the dominant values are civilian and commercial, and easier to deal with volunteers than with reluctant conscripts. Conscripts are not always unwilling, however; there are many instances in which the army is popular for economic reasons. . . .

It's easier if you catch them young. You can train older men to be soldiers; it's done in every major war. But you can never get them to believe that they like it, which is the major reason armies try to get their recruits before they are 20. There are other reasons too, of course, like the physical fitness, lack of dependents, and economic dispensability of teenagers, that make armies prefer them, but the most important qualities teenagers bring to basic training are enthusiasm and naiveté. Many of them actively want the discipline and the closely structured environment that the armed forces will provide, so there is no need for the recruiters to deceive the kids about what will happen to them after they join.

> *There is discipline. There is drill. . . . When you are relying on your mates and they are relying on you, there's no room for slackness or sloppiness. If you're not prepared to accept the rules, you're better off where you are.*
> —BRITISH ARMY RECRUITING ADVERTISEMENT, 1976

> *People are not born soldiers, they become soldiers. . . . And it should not begin at the moment a new recruit is enlisted into the ranks, but rather much earlier, at the time of the first signs of maturity, during the time of adolescent dreams.*
> —*RED STAR* (SOVIET ARMY NEWSPAPER), 1973

Young civilians who have volunteered and have been accepted by the Marine Corps arrive at Parris Island, the Corps's East Coast facility for basic training, in a state of considerable excitement and apprehension: Most are aware that they are about to undergo an extraordinary and very difficult experience. But they do not make their own way to the base; rather, they trickle in to Charleston airport on various flights throughout the day on which their training platoon is due to form, and are held there, in a state of suppressed but mounting nervous tension, until late in the evening. When the buses finally come to carry them the 76 miles to Parris Island, it is often after midnight—and this is not an administrative oversight. The shock treatment they are about to receive will work most efficiently if they are worn out and somewhat disoriented when they arrive.

The basic training organization is a machine, processing several thousand young men every month, and every facet and gear of it has been designed with the sole purpose of turning civilians into Marines as efficiently as possible. Provided it can have total control over their bodies and their environment for approximately three months, it can practically guarantee converts. Parris Island provides that controlled environment, and the recruits do not set foot outside it again until they graduate as Marine privates 11 weeks later.

> *They're allowed to call home, so long as it doesn't get out of hand—every three weeks or so they can call home and make sure everything's all right, if they haven't gotten a letter or there's a particular set of circumstances. If it's a case of*

an emergency call coming in, then they're allowed to accept that call; if not, one of my staff will take the message. . . .

In some cases I'll get calls from parents who haven't quite gotten adjusted to the idea that their son had cut the strings—and in a lot of cases that's what they're doing. The military provides them with an opportunity to leave home but they're still in a rather secure environment.

—Captain Brassington, USMC

For the young recruits, basic training is the closest thing their society can offer to a formal rite of passage, and the institution probably stands in an unbroken line of descent from the lengthy ordeals by which young males in precivilized groups were initiated into the adult community of warriors. But in civilized societies it is a highly functional institution whose product is not anarchic warriors, but trained soldiers.

Basic training is not really about teaching people skills; it's about changing them so that they can do things they wouldn't have dreamt of otherwise. It works by applying enormous physical and mental pressure to men who have been isolated from their normal civilian environment and placed in one where the only right way to think and behave is the way the Marine Corps wants them to. The key word the men who run the machine use to describe this process is *motivation.*

I can motivate a recruit and in third phase, if I tell him to jump off the third deck, he'll jump off the third deck. Like I said before, it's a captive audience and I can train that guy; I can get him to do anything I want him to do. . . . They're good kids and they're out to do the right thing. We get some bad kids, but you know, we weed those out. But as far as motivation—here, we can motivate them to do anything you want, in recruit training.

—USMC Drill Instructor, Parris Island

The first three days the raw recruits spend at Parris Island are actually relatively easy, though they are hustled and shouted at continuously. It is during this time that they are documented and inoculated, receive uniforms, and learn the basic orders of drill that will enable young Americans (who are not very accustomed to this aspect of life) to do everything simultaneously in large groups. But the most important thing that happens in "forming" is the surrender of the recruits' own clothes, their hair—all the physical evidence of their individual civilian identities.

During a period of only 72 hours, in which they are allowed little sleep, recruits lay aside their former lives in a series of hasty rituals (like being shaven to the scalp) whose symbolic significance is quite clear to them even though they are quite deliberately given absolutely no time for reflection, or any hint that they might have the option of turning back from their commitment. The men in charge of them know how delicate a tightrope they are walking, though, because at this stage the recruits are still newly caught civilians who have not yet made their ultimate inward submission to the discipline of the Corps.

Forming Day One makes me nervous. You've got a whole new mob of recruits, you know, 60 or 70 depending, and they don't know anything. You don't know what kind of a reaction you're going to get from the stress you're going to lay on them, and it just worries me the first day. . . .

Things could happen, I'm not going to lie to you. Something might happen. A recruit might decide he doesn't want any part of this stuff and maybe take a poke at you or something like that. In a situation like that it's going to be a spur-of-the-moment thing and that worries me.

—USMC Drill Instructor

But it rarely happens. The frantic bustle of forming is designed to give the recruit no time to think about resisting what is happening to him. And so the recruits emerge from their initiation into the system, stripped of their civilian clothes, shorn of their hair, and deprived of whatever confidence in their own identity they may previously have had as 18-year-olds, like so many blanks ready to have the Marine identity impressed upon them.

The first stage in any conversion process is the destruction of an individual's former beliefs and confidence, and his reduction to a position of helplessness and need. It isn't really as drastic as all that, of course, for three days cannot cancel out 18 years; the inner thoughts and the basic character are not erased. But the recruits have already learned that the only acceptable behavior is to repress any unorthodox thoughts and to mimic the character the Marine Corps wants. Nor are they, on the whole, reluctant to do so, for they *want* to be Marines. From the moment they arrive at Parris Island, the vague notion that has been passed down for a thousand generations that masculinity means being a warrior becomes an explicit article of faith, relentlessly preached: To be a man means to be a Marine.

There are very few 18-year-old boys who do not have highly romanticized ideas of what it means to be a man, so the Marine Corps has plenty of buttons to push. And it starts pushing them on the first day of real training: The officer in charge of the formation appears before them for the first time, in full dress uniform with medals, and tells them how to become men.

The United States Marine Corps has 205 years of illustrious history to speak for itself. You have made the most important decision in your life . . . by signing your name, your life, your pledge to the Government of the United States, and even more importantly, to the United States Marine Corps—a brotherhood, an elite unit. In 10.3 weeks you are going to become a member of that history, those traditions, this organization—if you have what it takes. . . .

All of you want to do that by virtue of your signing your name as a man. The Marine Corps says that we build men. Well, I'll go a little bit further. We develop the tools that you have—and everybody has those tools to a certain extent right now. We're going to give you the blueprints, and we are going to show you how to build a Marine. **You've** *got to build a Marine—you understand?*

—Captain Pingree, USMC

The recruits, gazing at him in awe and adoration, shout in unison, "Yes, sir!" just as they have been taught. They do it willingly, because they are volunteers—but even conscripts tend to have the romantic fervor of volunteers if they are only 18 years old. Basic training, whatever its hardships, is a quick way to become a man among men, with an undeniable status, and beyond the initial consent to undergo it, it doesn't even require any decisions.

> *I had just dropped out of high school and I wasn't doing much on the street except hanging out, as most teenagers would be doing. So they gave me an opportunity—a recruiter picked me up, gave me a good line, and said that I could make it in the Marines, that I have a future ahead of me. And since I was living with my parents, I figured that I could start my own life here and grow up a little.*
>
> —USMC Recruit, 1982

> *I like the hand-to-hand combat and . . . things like that. It's a little rough going on me, and since I have a small frame I would like to become deadly, as I would put it. I like to have them words, especially the way they've been teaching me here.*
>
> —USMC Recruit (from Brooklyn), Parris Island, 1982

The training, when it starts, seems impossibly demanding physically for most of the recruits—and then it gets harder week by week. There is a constant barrage of abuse and insults aimed at the recruits, with the deliberate purpose of breaking down their pride and so destroying their ability to resist the transformation of values and attitudes that the Corps intends them to undergo. At the same time, the demands for constant alertness and for instant obedience are continuously stepped up, and the standards by which the dress and behavior of the recruits are judged become steadily more unforgiving. But it is all carefully calculated by the men who run the machine, who think and talk in terms of the stress they are placing on the recruits: *We take so many c.c.'s of stress and we administer it to each man—they should be a little bit scared and they should be unsure, but they're adjusting.* The aim is to keep the training arduous but just within most of the recruits' capability to withstand. One of the most striking achievements of the drill instructors is to create and maintain the illusion that basic training is an extraordinary challenge, one that will set those who graduate apart from others, when in fact almost everyone can succeed.

There has been some preliminary weeding out of potential recruits even before they begin basic training, to eliminate the obviously unsuitable minority, and some people do "fail" basic training and get sent home, at least in peacetime. The standards of acceptable performance in the U.S. armed forces, for example, tend to rise and fall in inverse proportion to the number and quality of recruits available to fill the forces to the authorized manpower levels. (In 1980, about 15% of Marine recruits did not graduate from basic training.) But there are very few young men who cannot be turned into passable soldiers if the forces are willing to invest enough effort in it.

Not even physical violence is necessary to effect the transformation, though it has been used by most armies at most times.

It's not what it was 15 years ago down here. The Marine Corps still occupies the po-sition of a tool which the society uses when it feels like that is a resort that they have to fall to. Our society changes as all societies do, and our society felt that through enlightened training methods we could still produce the same product—and when you examine it, they're right. . . . Our 100 c.c.'s of stress is really all we need, not two gallons of it, which is what used to be. . . . In some cases with some of the younger drill instructors it was more an initiation than it was an acute test, and so we introduced extra officers and we select our drill instructors to "fine-tune" it.

—Captain Brassington, USMC

There is, indeed, a good deal of fine-tuning in the roles that the men in charge of training any specific group of recruits assume. At the simplest level, there is a sort of "good cop–bad cop" manipulation of recruits' atti-tudes toward those applying the stress. The three younger drill instructors with a particular serial are quite close to them in age and unremittingly harsh in their demands for ever higher performance, but the senior drill instructor, a man almost old enough to be their father, plays a more benevolent and un-derstanding part and is available for individual counseling. And generally offstage, but always looming in the background, is the company commander, an impossibly austere and almost godlike personage.

At least these are the images conveyed to the recruits, although of course all these men cooperate closely with an identical goal in view. It works: In the end they become not just role models and authority figures, but the focus of the recruits' developing loyalty to the organization.

I imagine there's some fear, especially in the beginning, because they don't know what to expect. . . . I think they hate you at first, at least for a week or two, but it turns to respect. . . . They're seeking discipline, they're seeking someone to take charge, 'cause at home they never got it. . . . They're looking to be told what to do and then someone is standing there enforcing what they tell them to do, and it's kind of like the father-and-son game, all the way through. They form a fatherly image of the DI whether they want to or not.

—Sergeant Carrington, USMC

Just the sheer physical exercise, administered in massive doses, soon has recruits feeling stronger and more competent than ever before. Inspections, often several times daily, quickly build up their ability to wear the uniform and carry themselves like real Marines, which is a considerable source of pride. The inspections also help to set up the pattern in the recruits of un-questioning submission to military authority: Standing stock-still, staring straight ahead, while somebody else examines you closely for faults is about as extreme a ritual act of submission as you can make with your clothes on.

But they are not submitting themselves merely to the abusive sergeant making unpleasant remarks about the hair in their nostrils. All around them are deliberate reminders—the flags and insignia displayed on parade, the military music, the marching formations and drill instructors' cadenced calls—of the idealized organization, the "brotherhood" to which they will be admitted as full members if they submit and conform. Nowhere in the armed forces are the military courtesies so elaborately observed, the staffs' uniforms so immaculate (some DIs change several times a day), and the ritual aspects of military life so highly visible as on a basic training establishment.

Even the seeming inanity of close-order drill has a practical role in the conversion process. It has been over a century since mass formations of men were of any use on the battlefield, but every army in the world still drills its troops, especially during basic training, because marching in formation, with every man moving his body in the same way at the same moment, is a direct physical way of learning two things a soldier must believe: that orders have to be obeyed automatically and instantly, and that you are no longer an individual, but part of a group.

The recruits' total identification with the other members of their unit is the most important lesson of all, and everything possible is done to foster it. They spend almost every waking moment together—a recruit alone is an anomaly to be looked into at once—and during most of that time they are enduring shared hardships. They also undergo collective punishments, often for the misdeed or omission of a single individual (talking in the ranks, a bed not swept under during barracks inspection), which is a highly effective way of suppressing any tendencies toward individualism. And, of course, the DIs place relentless emphasis on competition with other "serials" in training: There may be something infinitely pathetic to outsiders about a marching group of anonymous recruits chanting, "Lift your heads and hold them high, 3313 is a-passin' by," but it doesn't seem like that to the men in the ranks.

Nothing is quite so effective in building up a group's morale and solidarity, though, as a steady diet of small triumphs. Quite early in basic training, the recruits begin to do things that seem, at first sight, quite dangerous: descend by ropes from 50-foot towers, cross yawning gaps hand-over-hand on high wires (known as the Slide for Life, of course), and the like. The common denominator is that these activities are daunting but not really dangerous: The ropes will prevent anyone from falling to his death off the rappelling tower, and there is a pond of just the right depth—deep enough to cushion a falling man, but not deep enough that he is likely to drown—under the Slide for Life. The goal is not to kill recruits, but to build up their confidence as individuals and as a group by allowing them to overcome apparently frightening obstacles.

> *You have an enemy here at Parris Island. The enemy that you're going to have at Parris Island is in every one of us. It's in the form of cowardice. The most rewarding experience you're going to have in recruit training is standing on line every evening, and you'll be able to look into each other's eyes, and you'll be able to say to each other with your eyes: "By God, we've made it one more day! We've defeated the coward."*
>
> —Captain Pingree, USMC

Number on deck, sir, 45 . . . highly motivated, truly dedicated, rompin', stompin', bloodthirsty, kill-crazy United States Marine Corps recruits, SIR!

—MARINE CHANT, PARRIS ISLAND, 1982

If somebody does fail a particular test, he tends to be alone, for the hurdles are deliberately set low enough that most recruits can clear them if they try. In any large group of people there is usually a goat: someone whose intelligence or manner or lack of physical stamina marks him for failure and contempt. The competent drill instructor, without deliberately setting up this unfortunate individual for disgrace, will use his failure to strengthen the solidarity and confidence of the rest. When one hapless young man fell off the Slide for Life into the pond, for example, his drill instructor shouted the usual invective—*Well, get out of the water. Don't contaminate it all day*—and then delivered the payoff line: *Go back and change your clothes. You're useless to your unit now.*

"Useless to your unit" is the key phrase, and all the recruits know that what it means is "useless *in battle*." The Marine drill instructors at Parris Island know exactly what they are doing to the recruits, and why. They are not rear-echelon people filling comfortable jobs, but the most dedicated and intelligent NCOs [non-commissioned officers] the Marine Corps can find; even now, many of them have combat experience. The Corps has a clear-eyed understanding of precisely what it is training its recruits for—combat—and it ensures that those who do the training keep that objective constantly in sight.

The DIs [drill instructors] stress the recruits, feed them their daily ration of synthetic triumphs over apparent obstacles, and bear in mind all the time that the goal is to instill the foundations for the instinctive, selfless reactions and the fierce group loyalty that is what the recruits will need if they ever see combat. They are arch-manipulators, fully conscious of it, and utterly unashamed. These kids have signed up as Marines, and they could well see combat; this is the way they have to think if they want to live.

I've seen guys come to Vietnam from all over. They were all sorts of people that had been scared—some of them had been scared all their life and still scared. Some of them had been a country boy, city boys—you know, all different kinds of people— but when they got in combat they all reacted the same—99 percent of them reacted the same. . . . A lot of it is training here at Parris Island, but the other part of it is survival. They know if they don't conform—conform I call it, but if they don't react in the same way other people are reacting, they won't survive. That's just it. You know, if you don't react together, then nobody survives.

—USMC DRILL INSTRUCTOR, PARRIS ISLAND, 1982

When I went to boot camp and did individual combat training, they said if you walk into an ambush what you want to do is just do a right face—you just turn right or left, whichever way the fire is coming from, and assault. I said, "Man, that's crazy. I'd never do anything like that. It's stupid." . . .

The first time we came under fire, on Hill 1044 in Operation Beauty Canyon in Laos, we did it automatically. Just like you look at your watch to see what time it is. We done a right face, assaulted the hill—a fortified position with concrete bunkers emplaced, machine guns, automatic weapons—and we took it. And we killed—I'd estimate probably 35 North Vietnamese soldiers in the assault, and we only lost three killed. I think it was about two or three, and about eight or ten wounded. . . .

But you know, what they teach you, it doesn't faze you until it comes down to the time to use it, but it's in the back of your head, like, What do you do when you come to a stop sign? It's in the back of your head, and you react automatically.

—USMC Sergeant, 1982

Combat is the ultimate reality that Marines—or any other soldiers, under any flag—have to deal with. Physical fitness, weapons training, battle drills, are all indispensable elements of basic training, and it is absolutely essential that the recruits learn the attitudes of group loyalty and interdependency which will be their sole hope of survival and success in combat. The training inculcates or fosters all of those things, and even by the halfway point in the 11-week course, the recruits are generally responding with enthusiasm to their tasks. . . .

In basic training establishments, . . . the malleability is all one way: in the direction of submission to military authority and the internalization of military values. What a place like Parris Island produces when it is successful, as it usually is, is a soldier who will kill because that is his job.

ENDNOTES

[1]Leonard Cottrell, *The Warrior Pharaohs* (London: Evans Brothers, 1968).
[2]Samuel Rolbart, *The Israeli Soldier* (New York: A. S. Barnes, 1970), p. 206.

PART IV

Groups and Social Structure

17

THE BIRTH OF THE INTRAVIDUAL

DALTON CONLEY

The following three selections explore groups and social structure. The basic components of social structure are the roles and social statuses of individuals. Over the course of a lifetime, people occupy numerous statuses and roles. A *status* is a social position an individual holds within a group or a social system. A *role* is a set of expectations about the behavior assigned to a particular social status. Each role helps to define the nature of interaction with others and contributes to social organization by creating patterns of interpersonal and group relationships. Because we modify social roles more than we do our social statuses, roles are the dynamic aspect of social status. In this first reading by Dalton Conley, a professor of sociology and Senior Vice Provost at New York University, Conley examines how the self and our identities have changed greatly in relationship to groups in the larger social structure of society. These radical changes at the individual level of society are a result of large-scale changes in our economy, technology, and urbanization, among others. This excerpt is taken from Conley's compelling 2009 book, *Elsewhere, U.S.A.: How We Got from the Company Man, Family Dinners and the Affluent Society to the Home Office, BlackBerry Moms and Economic Anxiety.*

All along I have been describing how modern boundaries that we once took for granted have given way, crumbling under the force of family, economic, and technological change. Perhaps the most fundamental line that has been breached is that between the "self" and the "other." The interpenetration of the social world into our daily consciousness—our orientation to elsewhere—has the ultimate effect of colonizing and fragmenting not just our attentions but our very identities. The result is often a competing cacophony of multiple selves all jostling for pole position in our mind.

These resulting intraviduals whom I have alluded to throughout [my research] are the various horcruxes—to borrow the language of *Harry Potter*—that together would theoretically make a complete self. I try to imply the fragmentation of the individual by instead using the prefix *intra*, meaning "within." The irony, of course, is that the intravidual is just as much an "intervidual" (*inter* meaning "between"), since it is the networked nature of our new, Elsewhere economy and the penetration of others into us that shatters the individual.[1]

When you grow up in a divorced family, shuttling between two houses, you know instinctively (if that were not an oxymoron in this context) that you are really two (or more) different people: one with your mom during the week and the other on weekends with your dad. If you speak two languages, you know that you can literally have two different personalities in the respective countries or cultures. Traders and other such figures have long occupied niches between communities and have even spanned entire societies. But today we can *all* occupy that ambivalent position to group society that Georg Simmel called "the stranger" a hundred years ago.

Before the intravidual could come about in social history, however, the individual had to arrive on the scene. With the movement of large masses of people to cities, the undifferentiated mass of collective consciousness was said to have begun to fragment. Encountering many strangers—different folks from many walks of life—the urban resident encountered a hitherto unknown freedom. This is when, supposedly, we learned to think for ourselves, becoming modern individuals. But many urban sociologists believe that there was a price to pay for this in the form of a blasé attitude among city dwellers. Such an attitude was necessary to protect the self from the constant stimulation of fast-paced urban life. While disaffected, the city dweller was not disconnected. In fact, this new individualism, paradoxically, results from groups.

According to Georg Simmel, premodern society (what used to be known as primitive society) is characterized by concentric group affiliations. That means that everyone in my family lives in my village; everyone in my village lives under the same king; everyone in the kingdom shares the same ethnicity, religion, and so on and so forth. Russian nesting dolls provide an adequate metaphor. By contrast, modern society is characterized by sets of overlapping affiliations that may be unique to each person. Our town and our family may not coincide, for example, if our sister has moved to another state. Nor might our nation and our religion, if we happen to be part of a minority group that got "trapped" in a state that was founded on a single religion model. (Think Iranian Jews, for example.) In fact, not everyone in a given family may even share citizenship (my kids are Australian even though I am American). If any one of us were to list all of our affiliations, we'd probably find out that we are unique: voilà—the birth of the individual. Through membership in many disparate groups, we become individuated. This individualism was supposedly born sometime around 1789, in Paris, and was blamed for the disintegration of French society in the wake of the ancien régime. In the English-speaking world, the term didn't come into usage until 1835, but certainly the underlying concept was present right through the Scottish Enlightenment.

Recently, something has changed about this traditional formula: Namely, the networked economy and society has made us intraviduals by breaking down physical barriers to group affiliation. In the modern city, the individual emerged from these overlapping affiliations, which were located in a unitary social place: the person. All interaction had to take place face-to-face. As such, while membership in a guild or a religious order may have linked the person to a wider, "imagined community," that larger group was always beyond the social horizon. What made up social interaction, and thus identity, was the interaction with the local representatives of the various larger groups to which I nominally belonged: Interacting in my apartment block, I meet my Catholic neighbor; at the office, I encounter a Scottish colleague, and our conversation makes me acutely aware of being American; at the green market in Union Square I meet farmers from rural Vermont, who make me self-conscious about being a jaded New Yorker; and of course, I never feel my race as acutely as when I enter a predominantly black church on a Sunday. The sum total of these—as well as many other—experiences creates my uniqueness as an individual.

The creation of the individual self in this process was a two-way street. I choose to affiliate with certain groups: my professional society, perhaps; my church; the PTA at my children's school; my bowling league; and so on. But to the extent that those groups are pervasive—everyone I know belongs to them—they do little to distinguish me as an individual (for example, someone may live in a city that is all Muslim, and thus while her own Islamic identity may play a big part in her life, it obviously does not make her unique). Similarly, if there is difference in a given community—for example, there are Protestants and Catholics; whites and non-whites; managers and workers; Republicans and Democrats—but if all the proverbial sticks fall on either side of some symbolic line, then this fails to create individuals as well. In other words, if all the Protestants are white Republican managers and all the Catholics are non-white Democratic workers, then the collective consciousness is probably pretty strong and individualism does not emerge.

It is only when the groups don't match up—when we are confronted with difference and when those differences are multifaceted—that the individual emerges. In this way, it is not a choice. It's not all about voluntary association. It's also about differences that are noted by others about us. We may feel like a woman inside, for example, but look like a man to everyone else—to take the case of gender. These disjunctures mean that we need to see ourselves as others see us in our social calculations—something that every kid learns to do, with the notable exception of many children on the autistic spectrum. Self-reflectiveness—and thus individualism and the social self—arises from creating an *objective* view of ourselves when we are forced into the exercise of seeing us as others who don't share our identities see us.

The number of affiliations I could have was generally limited by the demands of face time. Slowly, however, modern telecommunications have eroded that looking-glass aspect of confronting the other in the modern metropolis. We can now belong to—affiliate with—groups with which we have little physical contact and/or lack any common organizing theme or totem. In premodern society, the groups to which we belonged were not only concentrically organized, they were also ascriptive—that is, based on conditions of birth over which we had little control. We were born into a certain ethnic group, a certain religion, a certain feudal estate or social caste. These groups penetrated every aspect of our lives and consciousnesses. And, for the most part, we had little choice about those group memberships; we could not change them any more than we could change our physical bodies. In modern society, group membership shifted to include many seemingly voluntary associations. We ostensibly choose our church, our occupation, our place of residence, our spouse (as compared to the arranged marriages that dominated the prior epoch), and our bowling league. Of course, we still live with many ascriptive identities—hence the continued power of race and gender in the United States.

In positing that the modern individual came from the unique intersection of affiliations with myriad groups, Simmel faces a paradox of sorts. What is driving the selection of group memberships if not a preexisting individual with preferences? But where do preferences come from if not from the socialization of groups? Of course, there must be some preexisting self that throws off the chains of ascription. Hence, the phrase, "finding oneself"—the modern imperative to discover the natural or biological tendencies and preferences and to fashion our social world (our choice of partner, of job, of place to live, and so on) so that it is in accordance with the supposed underlying natural (and whole) self.

In the postmodern or information economy, those restraints have been totally removed. You can join as many groups as you want, deploying multiple aliases while you are at it. Members of stigmatized groups have always experienced the phenomenon of multiple selves: macho black men who seek gay sex on the down low, for instance; Communists during the McCarthy era; or even politicians today who happen to be atheists but dare not admit it. The difference is that today there is no need for *anyone* to reconcile the many facets of their identities. They can just create a new e-mail account for that gay affair, that membership in the online Wicca group, or that Dungeons & Dragons user group that the CEO finds too embarrassing to own up to in the presence of work colleagues.

Ever since the time of de Tocqueville, America has been known as a land of "joiners." What we lacked in voter turnout, we made up for in our rich civic life. Americans attended more meetings of voluntary associations than did any other population on the planet. However, something interesting has happened as of late: We are joining more but participating less, in the words of the Harvard political scientist Theda Skocpol.[2] We still have higher rates of affiliation than any other nation (in fact, higher than ever), but we now typically write checks or click on a Web site rather than get together and spend our precious time. And in some cases, it isn't really possible to "get together." The Internet has allowed for all sorts of geographically dispersed associations based on common interests or characteristics—the National Association of Left-Handed Golfers is just one example.

At least all of the above examples are social affiliations that have some content. The irony of the online social networking craze is that Web 2.0 sites like Orkut, Friendster, Facebook, and MySpace are all group and no beef. The broader the networks reach—and many of these try to connect the whole world—the less meaningful they necessarily have to be. That's because content = exclusivity.

Now when we log on to Facebook, we see not just our friends, but who our friends' friends are, and which networks are most common among them. We can then ask to be friends with those folks, too. On the lower-brow MySpace, we don't even need to be friends—that is, approved by someone—for us to go nosing around their social network or personal profile. And we can ask total strangers to be our buddies with little more to go on than how they look and what answers they've plugged into a series of prescripted questions intended to reveal their inner world. While there remains the possibility of being rejected as a "friend," blocked by a user, or even taken down off the site by the administrator if s/he deems your content offensive, for the most part the boundaries of social groups on these online networks has become so diluted as to lose all exclusivity. And with no exclusivity, there is no meaning to the group. No meaning to the group, then no identity. No identity, then no self. We can look at everyone, but we see right through them to their own "friends," and so on, ad infinitum, in a hall of one-way social mirrors.

At the same time, this new, networked economy erodes any sense of the private—all in the name of being connected. Netflix is the largest online movie distributor. Like Amazon.com for books, it provides recommendations to users based on past transactions. But Netflix goes beyond Amazon in allowing—in fact, encouraging—users to rate as many films as possible in order to get a sense of one's preferences. These preferences are then used to filter recommendations. They may be based on directors, genres, or actors you seem to prefer. But the newest aspect of the system is the use of social networks in the recommendation process: Specifically, my recommendations arise primarily from the list of movies I haven't seen but which others, who tend to like what I have also rated highly, have seen and enjoyed. There are, of course, adjustments for individuals' tendencies to be tough or easy critics, for the degree of overlap, for the variation in preferences, and so on. The core of the system, however, remains the notion that I will like what others who have similar tastes have recommended.

Sometimes this system works extremely well. The other night, my children and I watched what my Netflix compatriots thought would be a wonderful film—*Ring of Bright Water*—about a man who adopts an otter as his pet and as a result quits the hustle and bustle of London for the quiet life of coastal Scotland. Had I trekked down to my local video store, there is no doubt that they would not have carried this obscure movie due to limited shelf space. Not only would my local video store not have been able to afford the shelf space to stock *Ring of Bright Water*, but the issue more germane to the present discussion is that I would have never even known to ask for it. In fact, short of some chance encounter of a recommendation at a dinner party, I would have never even known that this 1969 British film existed. The fact that I now know it exists can be attributed to the network basis of the Netflix recommendation system.

The connected economy, then, does not merely facilitate sameness and the diffusion of hits. It can encourage niche consumption (as Chris Anderson celebrates in *The Long Tail*). But as wonderful as it is to have a computer recommend a sleeper film that even the slacker clerks at my neighborhood video store wouldn't be able to name, there is a subtle cost to this form of knowledge diffusion. If Amazon had told me that "other white men between ages 35 and 45" also bought Ian McEwan's latest novel and Joan Didion's memoir, I might find it offensive. As modernists, we don't take well to the salience of ascriptive categories. They feel reductive and demeaning of our individuality. If Amazon instead said, "Professors and social scientists who enjoy travel and live in urbanized settings" also enjoyed *The End of Poverty* by Jeffrey Sachs, then we might find it a little strange as well, even though it's based on my achieved—or affiliational—characteristics. We may bristle at being reduced to a half-dozen cultural, occupational, or lifestyle characteristics, as the character Allison does in *Annie Hall* when Alvy Singer (Woody Allen's role) says: "You, you, you're like New York, Jewish, left-wing, liberal, intellectual, Central Park West, Brandeis University, the socialist summer camps and the, the father with the Ben Shahn drawings, right, and the really, y'know, strike-oriented kind of, red diaper, stop me before I make a complete imbecile of myself."

"No," she replies sarcastically, "that was wonderful. I love being reduced to a cultural stereotype."

Simmel claimed, after all, that our individuality comes from the unique intersection of groups that we embody. When it doesn't feel so unique anymore—thanks to Amazon or Woody Allen—our very selfhood is diminished.

Yet when Amazon tells us that we might also enjoy the *Captain Underpants* series since we just purchased another children's graphic novel that was bought, in turn, by folks who got *Captain Underpants,* we say thanks. But this is just as powerful a form of social assignment. (Why not offer random selections from the millions of books or DVDs in the library?) And while not making social connections based on explicit identities, the computer applets are reducing the complexity of near-infinite choice by creating implicitly defined groups. In many ways such network-based categorizations are more insidious than the hackneyed groupings based on race, class, gender, religion, or any other demographic characteristic: The rules of assignment are not made explicit; there is no totem; and the group is, in fact, a group-less group.

This first point is fairly straightforward: Although the programmers in Palo Alto *may* know the formulas that go into the recommendation process, we certainly don't.* In fact, the Amazon (or Google pagerank) formula may even be beyond the knowledge of any single programmer in the same way that a modern, industrial machine such as the automobile is too complicated for any single line worker or engineer to fathom in its entirety.

Second, there is no totem to these groups. Ironically, by tailoring our consumer choices so narrowly to our previous preferences (as they align with the preferences of others), we create a situation of a group of one—myself—in which my uniqueness fails to create an individual because it is not created from the overlap of meaningful groups of "others" but rather

---

*Much the same issue is at work in the construction of what is arguably the most important number in your life: your credit score. Credit scores are calculated based on a proprietary equation that is unknown not only to the rated but also to many of the consumers of the output such as banks and credit card companies. What's more, they have been shown to be poor and biased predictors of actual loan repayment capability.

from a formula based on purchases recommending purchases. Like looking up a word in the dictionary and then the words in that definition and so on, it ultimately yields a self-referential loop unanchored to anything else.

Users often strike back, of course, creating common interest groups on the Internet. This is, essentially, an effort to upload a modernist, offline notion of the group onto the social network platform in much the same way one might import a bunch of songs from a physical CD into an iTunes library. In this way, the modern and postmodern can peacefully commingle. Yet sometimes when these two distinct forms of social interaction are merged together, the result is not pretty. I agreed to list my co-worker—who I obviously know in a meaningful offline context—as a friend on Netflix. As in almost any networked site, the choice had to be mutual. Once we had both agreed, however, we then had full access to each other's movie-viewing activity. I knew which films she was currently watching; she, in turn, knew which were on my list. The ostensible benefits of being able to take and make recommendations from a trusted (offline) friend were more than outweighed by the icky sense that my private viewing habits had been made a matter of semi-public concern (even though I hadn't even been nominated to the Supreme Court).

But I was bringing a modernist conception of privacy to the online world. Privacy as we knew it was predicated on a certain division between "front stage" and "back stage" (to use the phrases of the 1950s sociologist Erving Goffman). The front stage is where we present ourselves according to a certain script and where everyone knows and expects social life to follow a patterned structure. Back stage, in short, is where we can be ourselves, where we may let others peek in once in a while to see the "real" us—the authentic self. However, in a world where identities are not anchored within a single body— at the intersection of those group affiliations—there is no "authenticity" to act as lodestone for a private self. When we can have multiple selves with the click of a mouse and the creation of a new online identity, there is no single core to protect from public view. Self-protection is not achieved by withholding; rather, it is accomplished by offering up more and more information and identities until each identity is everywhere in the social house of mirrors and we cannot know from "authentic" anymore. We hide in plain sight.

Thus, the quintessential group of our epoch is not the Sikh student association that happens to maintain an online presence; rather, it is the ungroup, the Escher-like social network that is finite, yet boundless (as is our view of the universe itself). We have gone from the rigid, embedded group memberships of premodern societies, to the affiliational ones of the modern individual, to the porous, nominal ungroups of the current age. There are no boundaries. If you click on one of the books that Amazon recommended to you when you bought this one, then you are connected to yet another group of books to which that book belonged, perhaps ad infinitum. (I personally have never hit a dead end or gotten trapped in a loop when I have followed the hyperlinks of Amazon recommendations.)

In this way, the book is now the node in the network and the invisible user (or purchaser) is now the tie between objects. The collection of monetary interest was seen as immoral by the medieval Church, since the creation of money through lending it to another individual subjugated that individual to the money by making the social relationship between bank accounts and the individual the mere link between past and future amounts. (Islam still forbids the charging of interest on loans.) Had Facebook or Amazon existed back then, perhaps they would have been outlawed as well, since now the person is just the tie to another set of individuals (in the case of MySpace) or another collection of objects (in the case of Netflix).

The result for the user is the relational equivalent of the BlackBerry-induced Elsewhere Society: social relations for the sake of gaining additional social relations. Knowing people for the sake of who they connect us to. When I was a freshman in college at Berkeley, I was stunned by how students interacted with each other on Sproul Plaza—the main drag on campus. First of all, almost everyone wore sunglasses. I suppose this was to be expected in California, where the sun literally appeared to shine more brightly than it did back East—bouncing off shiny, metallic objects with an almost piercing glare. Still, for a New Yorker accustomed to intense eye contact, it was certainly disconcerting to be in a place where I couldn't tell whether or not the person was looking at me. Soon, however, I discovered that I could occasionally see through the Rayban wraparounds. My interlocutors were not, in fact, looking at me as they conversed. They were looking elsewhere. Further observation revealed that I should not have necessarily taken it personally: When almost everyone interacted with everyone else, they were looking askance, as in the famous Renoir painting *The Boating Party*. There might be a more enticing social encounter just beyond the corner of one's eye, so better to keep scanning, like a social searchlight.

This feeding frenzy for more and more social connections is driven by the sociological and business books that tell us that it's not what you know, it's who you know. The theory is actually based on solid, if outdated, research. Back in 1967, Stanley Milgram, an American psychologist, set up an experiment to test an idea that had been circulating for a while, namely, that every individual could be connected to another individual through a relatively small number of mutual acquaintances. Milgram recruited participants in Omaha, Nebraska, and gave them a letter that they were instructed to give, by hand, to someone they knew (either directly or a "friend of a friend"). The goal was to get the letter to a stockbroker in Sharon, Massachusetts, 1,452 miles away.[3] The results of this experiment formed the basis of our common-day notion of "six degrees of separation"—the idea that any two people in the world can be connected through only six people (at most). (Research on this theory has continued, and it looks like the true number of links is probably closer to eight or nine.) If not quite marking the birth of the coming network society, certainly Milgram's experiment inaugurated the science of networks that would be needed to study such a hyperlinked society. Although the experiment had actually been preceded by much network research during the 1950s and even earlier, the Milgram study gave us one of the two tropes or ethics that have come to dominate the network society: the notion of small worlds that are totally interconnected. More recent work by sociologist Duncan Watts has refined the "small world" hypothesis, finding that it works because particular individuals act as connectors across huge swaths of social (and geographical) space, thereby making social networks "scale free."

That is all well and nice, but the clincher came a few years after the original Milgram study, in 1972, when another sociologist, Mark Granovetter, gave us the second ethic of the network society in an article that would become a classic in social science and beyond. In "The Strength of Weak Ties," Granovetter argued that, ironically, it is often relatively *weak ties*—connections to folks you don't know all that well and that are not reinforced by other indirect pathways—that turn out to be quite valuable because they bring new information. The strength of weak ties has been found to be especially useful for job (and romantic) searches. In a densely connected network, all the individuals probably know the same people, hear of the same job openings, have the same contacts, and so on. By contrast, your next-door neighbor from childhood, whom you only see once in a while when you go home to visit your parents and aren't close friends with but think is generally a nice person, probably has a completely different set of connections. The irony is that this weak tie provides the most opportunities.[4]

For his landmark study, Granovetter interviewed professionals in Boston. He discovered that among his fifty-four respondents who found their employment via personal network ties, more than half saw this contact "occasionally" (less than once a week but more than once a year). Perhaps even more surprising was the fact that the runner-up to this category was not folks who the responders saw "often" (once a week or more); it was those they saw "rarely" (once a year or less) by a factor of almost 2 to 1. All of a sudden deep human relationships are found wanting; the real payoff is in knowing lots of folks who don't know one another. Perhaps, then, it is no longer rude *not* to introduce your friends to each other. Each "structural hole" (gap between people or groups) in our personal social network is worth money and power. It's a simple law of arbitrage: The more information that has to flow through you—since there are no other pathways for it to get from one part of the network to the other—the more you can profit from the information gap. This is what traders do, essentially, and real estate brokers (who try to create a gap through exclusive agreements).

In the networked economy, however, we face a paradox of small worlds and weak ties. It is the increased interconnectedness that makes a single bound from Peoria to Manila possible. But it is the easy connecting nature of the Internet that makes those structural holes (and the accompanying social power) all the more difficult to hold on to, since it is quite easy to Google someone ourselves. As it turns out, in certain circumstances weak ties aren't all that they're cracked up to be. According to recent research by sociologist Damon Centola, when we want to change our behavior in ways that aren't so easy—say, go on a diet, learn calculus, or train for a marathon—it is the strong ties that matter. Better to go to WeightWatchers with your lifelong friends. Better study for the SATs with the other soldiers from your foxhole. And better kick heroin with your drug gang. Behavioral messages that work the best are those that come from folks we know deeply and whose relationship to us is reinforced through many indirect ties.[5] Hence the concept of the intervention, where all that strong social capital is brought to bear on a deviant individual (alcoholic, drug addict, compulsive shoplifter) in one hard blow.

But an economy that favors movement and motion, one that needs weak ties to reach faraway markets in distant lands, a service economy where our customers, clients, and colleagues (not to mention investors) are drawn from the electronic Rolodex—this is an economy that favors the weak tie over the strong one. So we go from tribes, where we have little control over whom we interact with and where our identity stems from ascriptive affiliations that are matters of luck, to modern mobile families, where individuals are born through the unique intersections of their chosen (achieved) group affiliations, to globalized, amorphous clouds of network nodes (ungroups) on Facebook, where how we know someone is trivial compared to the fact that we do know them. In the process, however, we somehow have managed to lose our selves. Maybe the key moment was when we stopped looking at each other in the eye. Or maybe it happened the first time that someone created a second e-mail account. Or maybe it ocurred when Google trumped the sorting of Web pages by content with its site rankings by number of referring links.

ENDNOTES

[1]We can see this devolution of the self into conflicting parts in the way we talk about theories of the self—both mind and body. In neuroscience, for instance, examination of neurons and particular areas of the brain has largely been trumped by the now hotter approach of looking at neural networks in which memories, thoughts, and mental processes don't happen in specific places (i.e., neurons or sulcuses) but rather exist in the network of connections. The network is not reducible to the sum of its parts. Evidently, that goes for our own minds.

[2]Theda Skocpol, "Civic Transformation and Inequality in the Contemporary United States," in *Social Inequality,* ed. Kathryn M. Neckerman (New York: Russell Sage Foundation, 2004), pp. 729–68.

[3]Stanley Milgram, "The Small World Problem," *Psychology Today,* May 1967, pp. 60–67.

[4]Mark S. Granovetter, "The Strength of Weak Ties," *American Journal of Sociology* 78, no. 6 (May 1973):1360–80.

[5]Damon Centola, Robb Willer, and Michael Macy, "The Emperor's Dilemma: A Computational Model of Self-Enforcing Norms," *American Journal of Sociology* 110, no. 4 (January 2005): 1009–40.

18

PEER POWER
Clique Dynamics among School Children

PATRICIA A. ADLER • PETER ADLER

This selection by Patricia Adler, a professor of sociology at the University of Colorado at Boulder, and Peter Adler, a professor of sociology at the University of Denver, investigates the social roles and social statuses children hold in social cliques. The Adlers conducted ethnographic research of elementary school children to understand better how these friendship groups function in the social structure. Of particular interest to the Adlers is how social hierarchies are formed and how power is distributed among the friendship groups of third- to sixth-grade students. Thus, this study examines an aspect of social structure called primary groups. A *primary group* is a small, intimate, informal group of people like a family, a friendship clique, or a small group of work colleagues. Urban gangs and combat units also can be primary groups if the relationships and communication are deep and personal. Thus, primary groups emerge when people live or work closely together.

A dominant feature of children's lives is the clique structure that organizes their social world. The fabric of their relationships with others, their levels and types of activity, their participation in friendships, and their feelings about themselves are tied to their involvement in, around, or outside the cliques organizing their social landscape. Cliques are, at their base, friendship circles, whose members tend to identify each other as mutually connected.[1] Yet they are more than that; cliques have a hierarchical structure, being dominated by leaders, and are exclusive in nature, so that not all individuals who desire membership are accepted. They function as bodies of power within grades, incorporating the most popular individuals, offering the most exciting social lives, and commanding the most interest and attention from classmates (Eder and Parker 1987). As such, they represent a vibrant component of the preadolescent experience, mobilizing powerful forces that produce important effects on individuals.[2] . . .

In this [reading] we look at these dynamics and their association, at the way clique leaders generate and maintain their power and authority (leadership, power/dominance), and at what it is that influences followers to comply so readily with clique leaders' demands (submission). These interactional dynamics are not intended to apply to all children's friendship groups, only those (populated by one-quarter to one-half of the children) that embody the exclusive and stratified character of cliques.

Techniques of Inclusion

The critical way that cliques maintained exclusivity was through careful membership screening. Not static entities, cliques irregularly shifted and evolved their membership, as individuals moved away or were ejected from the group and others took their place. In addition, cliques were characterized by frequent group activities designed to foster some individuals' inclusion (while excluding others). Cliques had embedded, although often unarticulated, modes for considering and accepting (or rejecting) potential new members. These modes were linked to the critical power of leaders in making vital group decisions. Leaders derived power through their popularity and then used it to influence membership and social stratification within the group. This stratification manifested itself in tiers and subgroups within cliques composed of people who were hierarchically ranked into levels of leaders, followers, and wannabes. Cliques embodied systems of dominance, whereby individuals with more status and power exerted control over others' lives.

Recruitment

. . . Potential members could be brought to the group by established members who had met and liked them. The leaders then decided whether these individuals would be granted a probationary period of acceptance during which they could be informally evaluated. If the members liked them, the newcomers would be allowed to remain in the friendship circle, but if they rejected them, they would be forced to leave.

Tiffany, a popular, dominant girl, reflected on the boundary maintenance she and her best friend Diane, two clique leaders, had exercised in fifth grade:

> Q: Who defines the boundaries of who's in or who's out?
>
> Tiffany: *Probably the leader. If one person might like them, they might introduce them, but if one or two people didn't like them, then they'd start to get everyone up. Like in fifth grade, there was Dawn Bolton and she was new. And the girls in her class that were in our clique liked her, but Diane and I didn't like her, so we kicked her out. So then she went to the other clique, the Emily clique.*

Timing was critical to recruitment. The beginning of the year, when classes were being reconstructed and people formed new social configurations, was the major time when cliques considered additions. Once these alliances were set, cliques tended to close their boundaries once again and stick to socializing primarily within the group. Kara, a fifth-grade girl, offered her view: *In the fall, right after school starts, when everyone's lining up and checking each other out, is when people move up, but not during the school year. You can move down during the school year, if people decide they don't like you, but not up. . . .*

Most individuals felt that invitation to membership in the popular clique represented an irresistible offer. They repeatedly asserted that the popular group could get anybody they wanted to join them. One of the strategies used was to try to select new desirables and go after them. This usually meant separating the people from their established friends. Melody, an unpopular fourth-grade girl, described her efforts to hold on to her best friend who was being targeted for recruitment by the popular clique:

> *She was saying that they were really nice and stuff. I was really worried. If she joined their group, she would have to leave me. She was over there, and she told me that they were making fun of me, and she kind of sat there and went along with it. So I kind of got mad at her for doing that. "Why didn't you stick up for me?" She said, "Because they wouldn't like me anymore."*

Melody subsequently lost her friend to the clique.

When clique members wooed someone to join them, they usually showed only the better side of their behavior. It was not until they had the new person firmly committed to the group that the shifts in behavior associated with leaders' dominance and status stratification activities began. Diane recalled her inclusion into the popular clique and its aftermath:

> *In fifth grade I came into a new class and I knew nobody. None of my friends from the year before were in my class. So I get to school, a week late, and Tiffany comes up to me and she was like, "Hi Diane, how are you? Where were you? You look so pretty." And I was like, wow, she's so nice. And she was being so nice for like two weeks, kiss-ass major. And then she started pulling her bitch moves. Maybe it was for a month that she was nice. And so then she had clawed me into her clique and her group, and so she won me over that way, but then she was a bitch to me once I was inside it, and I couldn't get out because I had no other friends. 'Cause I'd gone in there and already been accepted into the popular clique, so everyone else in the class didn't like me, so I had nowhere else to go.*

Eder (1985) also notes that popular girls are often disliked by unpopular people because of their exclusive and elitist manner (as befits their status).

Application

A second way for individuals to gain initial membership into a clique occurred through their actively seeking entry (Blau 1964). . . . According to Rick, a fifth-grade boy who was in the popular clique but not a central member, application for clique entry was more easily accomplished by individuals than groups. He described the way individuals found routes into cliques:

> *It can happen any way. Just you get respected by someone, you do something nice, they start to like you, you start doing stuff with them. It's like you just kind of follow another person who is in the clique back to the clique, and he says, "Could this person play?" So you kind of go out with the clique for a while and*

you start doing stuff with them, and then they almost like invite you in. And then soon after, like a week or so, you're actually in. It all depends. . . . But you can't bring your whole group with you, if you have one. You have to leave them behind and just go in on your own.

Successful membership applicants often experienced a flurry of immediate popularity. Because their entry required clique leaders' approval, they gained associational status.

Friendship Realignment

Status and power in a clique were related to stratification, and people who remained more closely tied to the leaders were more popular. Individuals who wanted to be included in the clique's inner echelons often had to work regularly to maintain or improve their position.

Like initial entry, this was sometimes accomplished by people striving on their own for upward mobility. In fourth grade, Danny was brought into the clique by Mark, a longtime member, who went out of his way to befriend him. After joining the clique, however, Danny soon abandoned Mark when Brad, the clique leader, took an interest in him. Mark discussed the feelings of hurt and abandonment this experience left him with:

I felt really bad, because I made friends with him when nobody knew him and nobody liked him, and I put all my friends to the side for him, and I brought him into the group, and then he dumped me. He was my friend first, but then Brad wanted him. . . . He moved up and left me behind, like I wasn't good enough anymore.

The hierarchical structure of cliques, and the shifts in position and relationships within them, caused friendship loyalties within these groups to be less reliable than they might have been in other groups. People looked toward those above them and were more susceptible to being wooed into friendship with individuals more popular than they. When courted by a higher-up, they could easily drop their less popular friends.

Cliques' stratification hierarchies might motivate lower-echelon members to seek greater inclusion by propelling themselves toward the elite inner circles, but membership in these circles was dynamic, requiring active effort to sustain. More popular individuals had to put repeated effort into their friendship alignments as well, to maintain their central positions relative to people just below them, who might rise up and gain in group esteem. Efforts to protect themselves from the potential incursions of others took several forms, among them co-optation, position maintenance, follower realignment, and membership challenge, only some of which draw upon inclusionary dynamics.

Follower realignment involved the perception that other clique members were gaining in popularity and status and might challenge leaders' position. But instead of trying to hold them in place (position maintenance) or exclude them from the group (membership challenge), leaders shifted their base of support; they incorporated lesser but still loyal members into their activities, thereby replacing problematic supporters with new ones. . . .

Co-optation involved leaders diminishing others' threats to their position by drawing them into their orbit, increasing their loyalty, and diminishing their independence. Clique members gaining in popularity were sometimes given special attention. At the same time, leaders might try to cut out their rivals' independent base of support from other friends.

Darla, a fourth grader, had occupied a second-tier leadership position with Kristy, her best friend. She explained what happened when Denise, the clique leader, came in and tore their formerly long-standing friendship apart:

> *Me and Kristy used to be best friends, but she [Denise] hated that. 'Cause even though she was the leader, we were popular and we got all the boys. She didn't want us to be friends at all. But me and Kristy were, like, getting to be a threat to her, so Denise came in the picture and tore me and Kristy apart, so we weren't even friends. She made Kristy make totally fun of me and stuff. And they were so mean to me. . . .*

. . . Hence, friendship realignment involved clique members' abandoning previous friendships or plowing through existing ones in order to assert themselves into relationships with those in central positions. These actions were all geared toward improving instigators' positions and thus their inclusion. Their outcome, whether anticipated or not, was often the separation of people and the destruction of their relationships.

Ingratiation

Currying favor with people in the group, like previous inclusionary endeavors, can be directed either upward (supplication) or downward (manipulation). Addressing the former, Dodge et al. (1983) note that children often begin their attempts at entry into groups with low-risk tactics; they first try to become accepted by more peripheral members, and only later do they direct their gaze and inclusion attempts toward those with higher status. The children we observed did this as well, making friendly overtures toward clique followers and hoping to be drawn by them into the center.

The more predominant behavior among group members, however, involved currying favor with the leader to enhance their popularity and attain greater respect from other group members. One way they did this was by imitating the style and interests of the group leader. Marcus and Adam, two fifth-grade boys, described the way borderline people would fawn on their clique and its leader to try to gain inclusion:

> Marcus: *Some people would just follow us around and say, "Oh yeah, whatever he says, yeah, whatever his favorite kind of music is, is my favorite kind of music."*

> Adam: *They're probably in a position where they want to be more **in** because if they like what we like, then they think more people will probably respect them. Because if some people in the clique think this person likes their favorite group, say it's REM, or whatever, so it's say Bud's [the clique leader's], this person must know what we like in music and what's good and what's not, so let's tell him that he can come up and join us after school and do something.*

Fawning on more popular people not only was done by outsiders and peripherals but was common practice among regular clique members, even those with high standing. Darla, the second-tier fourth-grade girl mentioned earlier, described how, in fear, she used to follow the clique leader and parrot her opinions:

> *I was never mean to the people in my grade because I thought Denise might like them and then I'd be screwed. Because there were some people that I hated that she liked and I acted like I loved them, and so I would just be mean to the younger kids, and if she would even say, "Oh she's nice," I'd say, "Oh yeah, she's really nice!"*

Clique members, then, had to stay abreast of the leader's shifting tastes and whims if they were to maintain status and position in the group. Part of their membership work involved a regular awareness of the leader's fads and fashions, so that they could accurately align their actions and opinions with the current trends in a timely manner. (See also Eder and Sanford 1986.)

Besides outsiders supplicating to insiders and insiders supplicating to those of higher standing, individuals at the top had to think about the effects of their actions on their standing with those below them. While leaders did not have to explicitly imitate the style and taste of their followers, they did have to act in a way that held their adulation and loyalty. This began with people at the top making sure that those directly below them remained firmly placed where they could count on them. Any defection, especially by the more popular people in a clique, could seriously threaten their standing.

Leaders often employed manipulation to hold the attention and loyalty of clique members.[3] Another manipulative technique involved acting different ways toward different people. Rick recalled how Brad, the clique leader in fifth grade, used this strategy to maintain his position of centrality: *Brad would always say that Trevor is so annoying. "He is such an idiot, a stupid baby," and everyone would say, "Yeah, he is so annoying. We don't like him." So they would all be mean to him. And then later in the day, Brad would go over and play with Trevor and say that everyone else didn't like him, but that he did. That's how Brad maintained control over Trevor.* Brad employed similar techniques of manipulation to ensure that all the members of his clique were similarly tied to him. Like many leaders, he would shift his primary attention among the different clique members, so that everyone experienced the power and status associated with his favor. Then, when they were out of favor, his followers felt relatively deprived and strove to regain their privileged status. This ensured their loyalty and compliance.

To a lesser degree, clique members curried friendship with outsiders. Although they did not accept them into the group, they sometimes included them in activities and tried to influence their opinions. While the leaders had their in-group followers, lower-status clique members, if they cultivated them well, could look to outsiders for respect, admiration, and imitation. This attitude and behavior were not universal, however; some popular cliques were so disdainful and mean to outsiders that nonmembers hated them. Diane, Tiffany, and Darla, three popular girls who had gone to two different elementary schools, reflected on how the grade school cliques to which they had belonged displayed opposing relationships with individuals of lesser status:

> Darla: *We hated it if the dorks didn't like us and want us to be with them. 'Cause then we weren't the popularest ones 'cause we always had to have them look up to us, and when they wouldn't look up to us, we would be nice to them.*
>
> Diane: *The medium people always hated us.*
>
> Tiffany: *They hated us royally, and we hated them back whenever they started.*
>
> Darla: *Sometimes we acted like we didn't care, but it bothered me.*
>
> Tiffany: *We always won, so it didn't matter.*

Thus, while there were notable exceptions (see Eder 1985), many popular clique members strove to ingratiate themselves with people less popular than they, from time to time, to ensure that their dominance and adulation extended beyond their own boundaries, throughout the grade.

Techniques of Exclusion

Although inclusionary techniques reinforced individuals' popularity and prestige while maintaining the group's exclusivity and stratification, they failed to contribute to other essential clique features such as cohesion and integration, the management of in-group and out-group relationships, and submission to clique leadership. These features are rooted, along with further sources of domination and power, in cliques' exclusionary dynamics.

Out-Group Subjugation

When they were not being nice to try to keep outsiders from straying too far from their realm of influence, clique members predominantly subjected outsiders to exclusion and rejection.[4] They found sport in picking on these lower-status individuals. As one clique follower remarked: *One of the main things is to keep picking on unpopular kids because it's just fun to do.* Eder (1991) notes that this kind of ridicule, where the targets are excluded and not enjoined to participate in the laughter, contrasts with teasing, where friends make fun of each other in a more lighthearted manner but permit the targets to remain included in the group by also jokingly making fun of themselves. Diane, a clique leader in fourth grade, described the way she acted toward outsiders: *Me and my friends would be mean to the people outside of our clique. Like, Eleanor Dawson, she would always try to be friends with us, and we would be like, "Get away, ugly."*

Interactionally sophisticated clique members not only treated outsiders badly but managed to turn others in the clique against them. Parker and

Gottman (1989) observe that one of the ways people do this is through gossip. Diane recalled the way she turned all the members of her class, boys as well as girls, against an outsider:

> *I was always mean to people outside my group like Crystal, and Sally Jones; they both moved schools. . . . I had this gummy bear necklace, with pearls around it and gummy bears. She [Crystal] came up to me one day and pulled my necklace off. I'm like, "It was my favorite necklace," and I got all of my friends, and all the guys even in the class, to revolt against her. No one liked her. That's why she moved schools, because she tore my gummy bear necklace off and everyone hated her. They were like, "That was mean. She didn't deserve that. We hate you."*

Turning people against an outsider served to solidify the group and to assert the power of the strong over the vulnerability of the weak. Other classmates tended to side with the dominant people over the subordinates, not only because they admired their prestige but also because they respected and feared the power of the strong.

Insiders' ultimate manipulation in leading the group to pick on outsiders involved instigating the bullying and causing others to take the blame. Davey, the fifth-grade clique follower mentioned earlier, described, with some mystery and awe, the skilled maneuvering of Joe, his clique leader: *He'd start a fight and then he would get everyone in it, 'cause everyone followed him, and then he would get out of it so he wouldn't get in trouble.*

Q: How'd he do that?

Davey: *One time he went up to this kid Morgan, who nobody liked, and said, "Come on Morgan, you want to talk about it?" and started kicking him, and then everyone else started doing it. Joe stopped and started watching, and then some parapro[fessional] came over and said, "What's going on here?" And then everyone got in trouble except for him.*

Q: Why did he pick on Morgan?

Davey: *'Cause he couldn't do anything about it, 'cause he was a nerd.*

Getting picked on instilled outsiders with fear, grinding them down to accept their inferior status and discouraging them from rallying together to challenge the power hierarchy.[5] In a confrontation between a clique member and an outsider, most people sided with the clique member. They knew that clique members banded together against outsiders, and that they could easily become the next target of attack if they challenged them. Clique members picked on outsiders with little worry about confrontation or repercussion. They also knew that their victims would never carry the tale to teachers or administrators (as they might against other targets; see Sluckin 1981) for fear of reprisal. As Mike, a fifth-grade clique follower, observed: *They know if they tell on you, then you'll "beat them up," and so they won't tell on you, they just kind of take it in, walk away.*

In-Group Subjugation

Picking on people within the clique's confines was another way to exert dominance. More central clique members commonly harassed and were mean to those with weaker standing.[6] Many of the same factors prompting the ill treatment of outsiders motivated high-level insiders to pick on less powerful insiders. Rick, a fifth-grade clique follower, articulated the systematic organization of downward harassment:

> Basically the people who are the most popular, their life outside in the playground is picking on other people who aren't as popular, but are in the group. But the people just want to be more popular so they stay in the group, they just kind of stick with it, get made fun of, take it. . . . They come back everyday, you do more ridicule, more ridicule, more ridicule, and they just keep taking it because they want to be more popular, and they actually like you but you don't like them. That goes on a lot, that's the main thing in the group. You make fun of someone, you get more popular, because insults is what they like, they like insults.

The finger of ridicule could be pointed at any individual but the leader. It might be a person who did something worthy of insult, it might be someone who the clique leader felt had become an interpersonal threat, or it might be someone singled out for no apparent reason (see Eder 1991). Darla, the second-tier fourth grader discussed earlier, described the ridicule she encountered and her feelings of mortification when the clique leader derided her hair:

> Like I remember, she embarrassed me so bad one day. Oh my God, I wanted to kill her! We were in music class and we were standing there and she goes, "Ew! what's all that shit in your hair?" in front of the whole class. I was so embarrassed, 'cause, I guess I had dandruff or something.[7]

Often, derision against insiders followed a pattern, where leaders started a trend and everyone followed it. This intensified the sting of the mockery by compounding it with multiple force. Rick analogized the way people in cliques behaved to the links on a chain:

> Like it's a chain reaction, you get in a fight with the main person, then the person right under him will not like you, and the person under him won't like you, and et cetera, and the whole group will take turns against you. A few people will still like you because they will do their own thing, but most people will do what the person in front of them says to do, so it would be like a chain reaction. It's like a chain; one chain turns, and the other chain has to turn with them or else it will tangle.

Compliance

Going along with the derisive behavior of leaders or other high-status clique members could entail either active or passive participation. Active participation occurred when instigators enticed other clique members to pick on their friends. For example, leaders would often come up with the idea of placing phony phone calls to others and would persuade their followers to do the dirty work. They might start the phone call and then place followers on the line to finish it, or they might pressure others to make the entire call, thus keeping one step distant from becoming implicated, should the victim's parents complain.

Passive participation involved going along when leaders were mean and manipulative, as when Trevor submissively acquiesced in Brad's scheme to convince Larry that Rick had stolen his money. Trevor knew that Brad was hiding the money the whole time, but he watched while Brad whipped Larry into a frenzy, pressing him to deride Rick, destroy Rick's room and possessions, and threaten to expose Rick's alleged theft to others. It was only when Rick's mother came home, interrupting the bedlam, that she uncovered the money and stopped Larry's onslaught. The following day at school, Brad and Trevor could scarcely contain their glee. As noted earlier, Rick was demolished by the incident and cast out by the clique; Trevor was elevated to the status of Brad's best friend by his co-conspiracy in the scheme.

Many clique members relished the opportunity to go along with such exclusive activities, welcoming the feelings of privilege, power, and inclusion. Others were just thankful that they weren't the targets. This was especially true of new members, who, as Sanford and Eder (1984) describe, often feel unsure about their standing in a group. Marcus and Adam, two fifth-grade clique followers introduced earlier, expressed their different feelings about such participation:

Q: What was it like when someone in your group got picked on?

Marcus: *If it was someone I didn't like or who had picked on me before, then I liked it. It made me feel good.*

Adam: *I didn't really enjoy it. It made me feel better if they weren't picking on me. But you can't do too much about it, so you sort of get used to it.*

Like outsiders, clique members knew that complaining to persons in authority did them no good. Quite the reverse, such resistance tactics made their situation worse, as did showing their vulnerabilities to the aggressors.[8] Kara, a popular fifth-grade girl, explained why such declarations had the opposite effect from that intended: *Because we knew what bugged them, so we could use it against them. And we just did it to pester 'em, aggravate 'em, make us feel better about ourselves. Just to be shitty.*

When people saw their friends in tenuous situations, they often reacted in a passive manner. Popular people who got in fights with other popular people might be able to count on some of their followers for support, but most people could not command such loyalty. Jeff, a fifth-grade boy, explained why people went along with hurtful behavior:

It's a real risk if you want to try to stick up for someone because you could get rejected from the group or whatever. Some people do, and nothing happens because they're so high up that other people listen to them. But most people would just find themselves in the same boat. And we've all been there before, so we know what that's like.

Clique members thus went along with picking on their friends, even though they knew it hurt, because they were afraid (see also Best 1983). They became accustomed to living within a social world where the power dynamics could be hurtful, and accepted it.

Stigmatization

Beyond individual incidents of derision, clique insiders were often made the focus of stigmatization for longer periods of time. Unlike outsiders who commanded less enduring interest, clique members were much more involved in picking on their friends, whose discomfort more readily held their attention. Rick noted that the duration of this negative attention was highly variable: *Usually at certain times, it's just a certain person you will pick on all the time, if they do something wrong. I've been picked on for a month at a time, or a week, or a day, or just a couple of minutes, and then they will just come to respect you again.* When people became the focus of stigmatization, as happened to Rick, they were rejected by all their friends. The entire clique rejoiced in celebrating their disempowerment. They would be made to feel alone whenever possible. Their former friends might join hands and walk past them through the play yard at recess, physically demonstrating their union and the discarded individual's aloneness.

Worse than being ignored was being taunted. Taunts ranged from verbal insults to put-downs to singsong chants. Anyone who could create a taunt was favored with attention and imitated by everyone (see Fine 1981). Even outsiders, who would not normally be privileged to pick on a clique member, were able to elevate themselves by joining in on such taunting (see Sanford and Eder 1984).

The ultimate degradation was physical. Although girls generally held themselves to verbal humiliation of their members, the culture of masculinity gave credence to boys' injuring each other (Eder and Parker 1987; Oswald et al. 1987; Thorne 1993). Fights would occasionally break out in which boys were punched in the ribs or stomach, kicked, or given black eyes. When this happened at school, adults were quick to intervene. But after hours or on the school bus, boys could be hurt. Physical abuse was also heaped on people's homes or possessions. People spit on each other or others' books or toys, threw eggs at their family's cars, and smashed pumpkins in front of their house.

Expulsion

While most people returned to a state of acceptance following a period of severe derision (see Sluckin 1981 for strategies children use to help attain this end), this was not always the case. Some people became permanently excommunicated from the clique. Others could be cast out directly, without undergoing a transitional phase of relative exclusion. Clique members from any stratum of the group could suffer such a fate, although it was more common among people with lower status.

When Davey, mentioned earlier, was in sixth grade, he described how expulsion could occur as a natural result of the hierarchical ranking, where a person at the bottom rung of the system of popularity was pushed off. He described the ordinary dynamics of clique behavior:

Q: How do clique members decide who they are going to insult that day?

Davey: *It's just basically everyone making fun of everyone. The small people making fun of smaller people, the big people making fun of the small people. Nobody is really making fun of people bigger than them because they can get rejected, because then they can say, "Oh yes, he did this and that, this and that, and we shouldn't like him anymore." And everybody else says, "Yeah, yeah, yeah," 'cause all the lower people like him, but all the higher people don't. So the lowercase people just follow the highercase people. If one person is doing something wrong, then they will say, "Oh yeah, get out, good-bye."*

Being cast out could result either from a severely irritating infraction or from individuals standing up for their rights against the dominant leaders. Sometimes expulsion occurred as a result of breakups between friends or friendship realignments leading to membership challenges (mentioned earlier), where higher-status people carried the group with them and turned their former friends into outcasts. . . .

On much rarer occasions, high-status clique members or even leaders could be cast out of the group (see Best 1983). One sixth-grade clique leader, Tiffany, was deposed by her former lieutenants for a continued pattern of petulance and self-indulgent manipulations:

Q: Who kicked you out?

Tiffany: *Robin and Tanya. They accepted Heidi into their clique, and they got rid of me. They were friends with her. I remember it happened in one blowup in the cafeteria. I asked for pizza and I thought I wasn't getting enough attention anymore, so I was pissed and in a bitchy mood all the time and stuff, and so I asked them for some, so she [Robin] said like, "Wait, hold on, Heidi is taking a bite," or something, and I got so mad I said, "Give the whole fuckin' thing to Heidi," and something like that, and they got so sick of me right then, and they said like, "Fuck you."*

When clique members get kicked out of the group, they leave an established circle of friends and often seek to make new ones. Some people have a relatively easy time making what Davies (1982) calls "contingency friends" (temporary replacements for their more popular friends), and, according to one fifth-grade teacher, they are "hot items" for the unpopular crowd. . . .

Many cast-outs found new friendships harder to establish, however. They went through a period where they kept to themselves, feeling rejected, stigmatized, and cut off from their former social circle and status. Because of their previous behavior and their relations with other classmates, they had trouble being accepted by unpopular kids. Others had developed minimum acceptability thresholds for friends when they were in the popular crowd, and had difficulty stooping to befriend unpopular kids. When Mark was ejected from his clique in fifth grade, he explained why he was unsuccessful in making friends with the unpopular people: *Because there was nobody out there I liked. I just didn't like anybody. And I think they didn't like me because when I was in the popular group we'd make fun of everyone, I guess, so they didn't want to be around me, because I had been too mean to them in the past.*

Occasionally, rejects from the popular clique had trouble making friends among the remainder of the class due to the interference of their former friends. If clique members got angry at one of their friends and cast him or her out, they might want to make sure that nobody else befriended that individual. By soliciting friendship with people outside the clique, they could influence outsiders' behavior, causing their outcast to fall beyond the middle crowd to the status of pariah, or loner. Darla explained why and how people carried out such manipulations:

Q: Have you ever seen anyone cast out?

Darla: *Sure, like, you just make fun of them. If they don't get accepted to the medium group, if they see you like, "Fuck, she's such a dork," and like you really don't want them to have any friends, so you go to the medium group, and you're like, "Why are you hanging out with THAT loser, she's SUCH a dork, we HATE her," and then you be nice to them so they'll get rid of her so she'll be such a dork. I've done that just so she'll be such a nerd that no one will like her. You're just getting back at them. And then they will get rid of her just 'cause you said to, so then, you've done your way with them. If you want something, you'll get it.*

People who were cast out of their group often kept to themselves, staying in from the playground at recess and coming home after school alone. They took the bus to school, went to class, did what they had to do, but didn't have friends. Their feelings about themselves changed, and this was often reflected in the way they dressed and carried themselves. Being ejected from the clique thus represented the ultimate form of exclusion, carrying with it severe consequences for individuals' social lives, appearance, and identity.

The techniques of inclusion and exclusion represent the means by which the behavioral dynamics of cliques are forged. As such, they offer the basis for a generic model of clique functioning that interweaves these processes with the essential clique features of exclusivity, power and dominance, status stratification, cohesion and integration, popularity, submission, and in-group and out-group relations. . . .

These two dynamics work hand in hand. The inclusionary dynamic is central to cliques' foundation of attraction. Cliques' boundary maintenance makes them exclusive. They can recruit the individuals they want, wooing them from competing friendships, and reject the supplications of others they evaluate as unworthy. The popularity of their membership (with leaders to lend status and followers to lend power) strengthens their position at the center of activity. Upheavals and friendship realignments within cliques keep the hierarchical alignment of prestige and influence fluid, giving those successful at maneuvering toward and staying near the top the greatest esteem among their peers. The systematic upward ingratiation of individuals toward the leading members, and leading members' ability to easily ingratiate themselves downward with others, thereby securing the favors they desire, enhance the attractiveness of inclusion in the clique.

The exclusionary dynamic is central to cliques' bases of cohesion. Clique members solidify together in disparaging outsiders, learning that those in the in-group can freely demean out-group members, only to have their targets return for renewed chances at acceptance. They learn sensitivity toward changes in group boundaries, acting one way toward insiders and another way toward outsiders. This lesson manifests itself not only at the group's outer edges but within the clique, as individuals move in and out of relative favor and have to position themselves carefully to avoid the stigma of association with the disfavored. They learn the hierarchy of group positions and the perquisites of respect and influence that go with those roles, submitting to the dominance of clique leaders in order to earn a share of their reflected status and position. The periodic minicyclings of exclusion serve to manipulate followers into dependence and subservience, at the same time enhancing leaders' centrality and authority. The ultimate sanction of expulsion represents a dramatic example of the effects of exclusion, weakening or bringing down potential rivals from positions of power while herding other group members into cohesion. The dynamic of inclusion lures members into cliques, while the dynamic of exclusion keeps them there.[9]

ENDNOTES

[1]See Hallinan (1979), Hubbell (1965), Peay (1974), and Varenne (1982) for a discussion of cliques' sociometric characteristics.

[2]They are primary groups, offering individuals the opportunity to select close friendships of their own choosing (Elkin and Handel 1989), to learn about society, to practice their behavior, and to evolve their selves and identities. Autonomous from the world of adults (Fine 1981), they are often forged in opposition to adult values (Elkin and Handel 1989), with a culture of resistance to adult standards (Corsaro 1985). They thus encompass a robust form of children's peer culture that is both unique in its own right yet at the same time a staging ground for future adult behavior.

[3]Oswald, Krappmann, Chowdhuri, and von Salisch (1987) note that one way children assert superiority over others and indebt them with loyalty is to offer them "help," either materially or socially.

[4]Hogg and Abrams (1988) find that denigrating out-group members enhances a group's solidarity and improves the group status of people participating in such denigration. This tendency is particularly strong where two groups perceive themselves to be in conflict or competition.

[5]Eder and Sanford (1986) and Merten (1994) note the same tendency among adolescent peer groups in middle school.

[6]Eder (1991) also notes that when insiders pick on other members of their clique, this can have good-natured overtones, indicating that they like them.

[7]Eder and Sanford (1986) and Eder and Parker (1987) discuss the importance of physical appearance, particularly hair, in adhering to group norms and maintaining popularity.

[8]Merten (1994, 1996) discusses the dilemma faced by children who are picked on, who would like to report the problem to a teacher but cannot do so out of fear that the teacher's intervention would incur the wrath of others. He notes the consequences for one boy whose mother

complained to other parents about the way their children treated her son: when these others came to school the next day, they ridiculed the boy even more, taunting and deriding him for being a tattletale.

[9]Bigelow, Tesson, and Lewko (1996) also note this "Lord of the Flies" phenomenon.

REFERENCES

Best, Raphaela. 1983. *We've All Got Scars.* Bloomington: Indiana University Press.

Bigelow, Brian J., Geoffrey Tesson, and John H. Lewko. 1996. *Learning the Rules.* New York: Guilford Press.

Blau, Peter M. 1964. *Exchange and Power in Social Life.* New York: Wiley.

Corsaro, William A. 1985. *Friendship and Peer Culture in the Early Years.* Norwood, NJ: Ablex.

Davies, Bronwyn. 1982. *Life in the Classroom and Playground: The Accounts of Primary School Children.* London: Routledge and Kegan Paul.

Dodge, Kenneth A., David C. Schlundt, Iris Schocken, and Judy D. Delugach. 1983. "Social Competence and Children's Sociometric Status: The Role of Peer Group Entry Strategies." *Merrill-Palmer Quarterly* 29:309–36.

Eder, Donna. 1985. "The Cycle of Popularity: Interpersonal Relations among Female Adolescents." *Sociology of Education* 58:154–65.

———. 1991. "The Role of Teasing in Adolescent Peer Group Culture." Pp. 181–97 in *Sociological Studies of Child Development,* vol. 1, edited by P. A. Adler and P. Adler. Greenwich, CT: JAI Press.

Eder, Donna and Stephen Parker. 1987. "The Cultural Production and Reproduction of Gender: The Effect of Extracurricular Activities on Peer-Group Culture." *Sociology of Education* 60:200–213.

Eder, Donna and Stephanie Sanford. 1986. "The Development and Maintenance of Interactional Norms among Early Adolescents." Pp. 283–300 in *Sociological Studies of Child Development,* vol. 1, edited by P. A. Adler and P. Adler. Greenwich, CT: JAI Press.

Elkin, Frederick and Gerald Handel. 1989. *The Child and Society.* 5th ed. New York: Random House.

Fine, Gary Alan. 1981. "Friends, Impression Management, and Preadolescent Behavior." Pp. 29–52 in *The Development of Children's Friendships,* edited by S. Asher and J. Gottman. New York: Cambridge University Press.

Hallinan, Maureen. 1979. "Structural Effects on Children's Friendships and Cliques." *Social Psychology Quarterly* 42:43–54.

Hogg, Michael A. and Dominic Abrams. 1988. *Social Identifications.* New York: Routledge.

Hubbell, Charles H. 1965. "An Input-Output Approach to Clique Identification." *Sociometry* 28:377–99.

Merten, Don E. 1994. "The Cultural Context of Aggression: The Transition to Junior High School." *Anthropology and Education Quarterly* 25:29–43.

———. 1996. "Visibility and Vulnerability: Responses to Rejection by Nonaggressive Junior High School Boys." *Journal of Early Adolescence* 16:5–26.

Oswald, Hans, Lothar Krappmann, Irene Chowdhuri, and Maria von Salisch. 1987. "Gaps and Bridges: Interactions between Girls and Boys in Elementary School." Pp. 205–23 in *Sociological Studies of Child Development,* vol. 1, edited by P. A. Adler and P. Adler. Greenwich, CT: JAI Press.

Parker, Jeffrey G. and John M. Gottman. 1989. "Social and Emotional Development in a Relational Context." Pp. 95–131 in *Peer Relationships in Child Development,* edited by T. J. Berndt and G. W. Ladd. New York: Wiley.

Peay, Edmund R. 1974. "Hierarchical Clique Structures." *Sociometry* 37:54–65.

Sanford, Stephanie and Donna Eder. 1984. "Adolescent Humor during Peer Interaction." *Social Psychology Quarterly* 47:235–43.

Sluckin, Andy. 1981. *Growing Up in the Playground.* London: Routledge and Kegan Paul.

Thorne, Barrie. 1993. *Gender Play.* New Brunswick, NJ: Rutgers University Press.

Varenne, Herve. 1982. "Jocks and Freaks: The Symbolic Structure of the Expression of Social Interaction among American Senior High School Students." Pp. 210–35 in *Doing the Ethnography of Schooling,* edited by G. Spindler. New York: Holt, Rinehart, and Winston.

19

SHOPPING AS SYMBOLIC INTERACTION
Race, Class, and Gender
in the Toy Store

CHRISTINE L. WILLIAMS

This reading by Christine Williams, a professor of sociology at the University of Texas at Austin, is taken from Williams' 2006 book, *Inside Toyland: Working, Shopping, and Social Inequality.* As part of her research on the social organization of toy stores, Williams worked as an employee in two toy stores, where she examined the social relationships and social interaction between clerks and customers. Thus, this excerpt illustrates well the social interaction found in secondary relationships. *Secondary relationships* tend to be temporal, less intimate, and more formal than primary relationships. Moreover, secondary relationships are often utilitarian in that they serve some function. Williams discovered that these secondary relationships also reflect and reproduce social inequalities based on race, gender, and social class.

Erving Goffman (1967, 1977) claimed that face-to-face public encounters with strangers typically rely on ritualized scripts to make them go smoothly. In service work, this insight has been transformed into a maxim. Visit McDonald's and you are likely to encounter the "six steps of counter service" (Leidner 1993), beginning with the question "May I take your order please?" and until recently ending with "Do you want to super-size that?" Usually, this scripted server–customer interaction comes off without a hitch. When it does not, the result is often conflict. If customers linger too long over their food order or request some special item not on the menu, they will likely face disapproval, mostly from the customers behind them. Workers who refuse to say their lines will likely be fired.

This approach to understanding service work has been enormously popular and fruitful, especially in the gender literature where the "doing gender" approach (West and Zimmerman 1987), which was influenced by Goffman's theory, has become practically hegemonic. I would argue, however, that Goffman's perspective is limited for reasons that Herbert Blumer (1969) identified years ago. The meanings of these rituals are not self-evident. It is only through a process of symbolic interaction among active, creative, knowledgeable participants that the meanings and consequences of these rituals emerge. This [reading] focuses on the rituals of toy shopping. But it also

Christine L. Williams, "Shopping as Symbolic Interaction: Race, Class and Gender in the Toy Store" from *Symbolic Interaction* 28, No. 4 (2005): 459–472. Copyright © 2005, Society for the Study of Symbolic Interaction. Reprinted by permission of John Wiley and Sons.

examines the ongoing innovations, negotiations, and reinterpretations of shopping from the perspective of salesclerks.

I was employed for three months, a total of more than 300 hours, in two large stores that were parts of national chains. One of these stores, which I call Toy Warehouse (all store names have been changed for this [reading]), was a "big box" toy store located in a low-income redevelopment zone. I was one of four white women who worked on the staff of about seventy; most of my coworkers were African American women and men. The other store, which I call Diamond Toys, was in an urban, upscale shopping district that catered to high-income shoppers and tourists. At that store, most of the workers were white; only three African Americans (all women) worked on the staff of about seventy. Latina/os and Asian Americans also worked at these stores, making up about 20 percent of the workforce. This [reading] examines interactions between clerks and customers and discusses the relevance of symbolic interactionism for understanding labor processes.

The [reading] first describes the "rules" governing salesclerks in their interactions with customers at the two toy stores. These "official" rules are formulated by the corporations that own the toy store chains. Second, the [reading] discusses the "ropes," the informal rules that employees devise and follow to ensure order and preserve their self-respect in their interactions with customers. I argue that both the "rules" and the "ropes" take into account the race, gender, and class characteristics of the clerk and the customer. Finally, the [reading] discusses what happens when these formal and informal rules are not followed and interactions break down into conflict. Whether an interaction can be repaired depends on race, class, and gender: because different groups have different resources to draw on to assert their will in the toy store, the resolution of any particular conflict is shaped by social inequality and the creative efforts of the individuals involved.

The Rules: Corporate Culture in Toy Stores

. . . The corporation that owned the Toy Warehouse wanted its stores to create a fun, family-oriented atmosphere. Sales workers were expected to demonstrate a high degree of spirited enthusiasm. We were required to hand out balloons and stickers to children and sing to them on their birthdays. The name badge I wore proclaimed that I had been "delighting guests since 2001." Like all new employees, I was required on my first morning shift to hula-hoop in front of the staff. All clerks were required to form a gauntlet around the front door when the store opened and applaud the customers as they entered the store, much to their bewilderment.

In giant retail stores, corporate culture is usually communicated to new hires through perfunctory training sessions that last no more than one day. At the Toy Warehouse, our training consisted of watching nine 20-minute videotapes on everything from handling returns to selling the new Game Boy. One videotape showed executives, on stage at a corporate event, leading store directors in group singing and rousing cheers.

Whereas the Toy Warehouse aspired to present an image as an exciting playground for children and their families, Diamond Toys portrayed itself as a high-end specialty store oriented toward meeting the needs of discriminating adult shoppers. The store aimed to flatter the sophisticated tastes of the elite or those who would like to be elite. The very set-up of the store encouraged this aura. Diamond Toys resembled a fancy department store, not a warehouse. A door attendant out front greeted customers. Inside were lavish displays of giant toys with mechanical moving parts. A theme song played in a continuous loop, making me at times feel trapped inside a ride at Disneyland. The store also seemed to have the theme park effect on the many adults and children who stood in awe and marveled at the displays.

We did not have to watch videos during our training at Diamond Toys. Instead, we were issued an employee handbook. The personnel manager, Leslie, took the three new hires to a seminar room and read the entire 30-page document to us. We were invited to interrupt the presentation at any time to ask questions.

Much was said about the dress code. We were required to wear the company-issued maroon polo shirt tucked into belted chino slacks or skirt. Belts had to be black, tan, cordovan, or brown. No outside stitching or pockets were allowed, as this conveyed the look of jeans, which were forbidden. Leslie showed us where the ironing board and iron were kept "just in case" we needed them. We were allowed only two earrings per ear and a single nose stud. No visible tattoos and no unconventional hair color were allowed.

The corporate instruction we received as salesclerks was summed up in the "Five Is of Customer Service." These were: initiate, inquire, inform, include, and into the register. We were told we must initiate contact within thirty seconds with each customer who wandered into our section. . . . After a successful initiation, we were instructed to try to determine the customer's needs with open-ended questions or remarks, such as "Tell me about the kind of party you are planning." At the "inform" stage we were to match the customer's needs with product features . . . , and at the "include" stage we were to recommend accessories to complement the main purchase. . . . Our goal was to sell a minimum of two UPTs (units per transaction). We received a printout three times per shift showing us how we were doing.

Thus, the corporate board of Diamond Toys imagined a sales staff of Jeeves-like butlers. Correspondingly, their ideal customer was a member of the bourgeoisie in need of professional consultation on his or her purchases. Oddly, this customer was never shown in the instructional materials. There were no people in the toy catalogs, either; the focus was always on the "special" merchandise we offered.

The Toy Warehouse, on the other hand, was quite explicit about what its ideal customer looks like: she was a middle-class white mother. Several of the videos featured this woman and demonstrated the ways we were supposed to serve her. She usually knew what she wanted (a Game Boy, for instance), but she might need to be told that it required game cartridges, batteries, and a light worm. She did not like to be kept waiting, so we were supposed to work quickly to accommodate her (no lingering over party decorations). My manager, Olive, urged me to treat every woman in the store as if she were my mother. Mothers made the purchasing decisions, she said, so they got the special treatment. Olive said that the average child has $20,000 spent on toys for them before they are eighteen, and the Toy Warehouse wanted to be the place where most of that money was spent.

Advertising displayed in the Toy Warehouse was directed to middle-class families. The store "sponsored" National Day for Children, for example. This was celebrated by posting signs that read "National Day for Children" and putting out a stack of leaflets on a card table that gave "10 reasons to celebrate your child!" Also offered were a college savings plan (which put a small percentage of any purchase in a special account for college tuition), a parenting newsletter, and a summer camp program at which children could be dropped off for a two-hour activity on weekday mornings.

The "child" imagined by the Toy Warehouse's corporate office was thus middle-class and college-bound, from a traditional family where the mother did not work for pay but did all the shopping. Children were expected to have their own ideas about what they want. The store sold "gift cards" to give to children for their birthdays and special occasions. The equivalent of gift certificates, these were little plastic cards that look like credit cards. They were packaged in greeting-card envelopes with a space to write in the child's name and the dollar amount of the gift. At Diamond Toys, in contrast, children were much less central to the marketing agenda. Although they were the intended consumers of most of the merchandise, they were treated more as pampered and coddled pets than as willing and engaged buyers. At Diamond Toys, adults were our primary focus; it was to them that we directed our expert knowledge and solicitous attention. Leslie told us that people came to our store and were willing to pay more because we were "the ultimate toy experts." (In contrast, the Toy Warehouse considered kids to be the ultimate toy experts.) At Diamond Toys, we did not strive to make the shopping experience fun for families; rather, the mood we aspired to set was one of careful and quiet deliberation to assist adults in making a suitable purchase.

How did these corporate expectations play out in practice? In the most obvious sense, they selected for different kinds of customers. Shoppers at the Toy Warehouse represented all levels of the stratification system. I would often marvel at how our "guests" (as we were required to call them) were from every racial-ethnic group and every social class. Rich women with huge diamond rings shopped next to very poor families who were shabbily dressed. Recent immigrants from Africa, India, and Central America were also there, some in traditional clothes. Diamond Toys attracted a more upper-class clientele. It was like a gated community for rich whites. Although the doors opened onto diverse and chaotic urban streets, only the wealthy or the tourist class entered.

But what impact did the corporate rules have on actual interactions between clerks and customers? Retail workers were expected to conform to the corporate culture, but they often developed their own rules for dealing with customers that sometimes clashed with that agenda. I call those rules "the ropes."

The "Ropes": Shop Floor Culture

New hires learned the ropes from observing experienced workers on the shopping floor. One of the first lessons I learned at the Toy Warehouse was that middle-class white women shoppers got whatever they wanted. I suppose that as a middle-class white woman myself, I should have felt empowered by this knowledge. Instead, I have come to understand this preferential treatment as a result of race and class privilege.

Most of the customers at both stores were women. At the Toy Warehouse we were told that women make 90 percent of the purchase decisions, so we were to treat women deferentially. Olive told me that the store abides by the "$19,800 rule." If a customer wanted to return merchandise and it was questionable whether we should take the return (because it had been broken or worn out by the customer, or because the customer had lost the receipt), we should err on the side of the customer. The company was willing to take a $200 loss because doing so might please the customer so much that she would return to the store and spend the rest of the $20,000 on each of her children.

But in my experience, only the white women got this kind of treatment. Not surprisingly, many developed a sense of entitlement and threw fits when they were not accommodated. . . .

Middle-class white women had a reputation at the store of being overly demanding and abusive. Susan, a thirty-five-year-old Latina, agreed with my observation that rich white women were the most demanding customers; she said they always demanded to see the manager and they always got mollified. In contrast, African American and Latina/o customers hardly ever complained. If they did complain, she said, they would not get any satisfaction.

Susan's remarks illustrate some of the elaborate stereotypes that service-desk workers used in the course of their daily transactions. Immediate assumptions were made about customers based on their race, gender, and apparent social class; workers responded to customers using these cues. Middle-class white women were the most privileged customers, so not surprisingly, many developed a sense of entitlement. One of the most eye-opening examples of white women's sense of entitlement that I witnessed in the Toy Warehouse was their refusal to check their bags at the counter. Stealing was a big problem in the store, so customers were required to leave all large bags and backpacks at the service desk. A large sign indicating this policy was posted on the store's entrance. The vast majority of customers carrying bags immediately approached the desk to comply with the rule. The exception was white women, who almost universally ignored the sign. When challenged, they would argue, and we would have to insist so as not to appear to be unfair to the other people. I guiltily recognized myself in their behavior. Since then, I always turn over my bag.

White women developed a sense of entitlement because in most instances they got what they wanted. Members of other groups who wanted to return used merchandise, or who needed special consideration, rarely were accommodated. . . .

It has been well documented that African Americans suffer discrimination in public places, including stores (Feagin and Sikes 1995). They report that they are followed by security personnel, treated harshly by attendants, and flatly refused service. The flip side of this discrimination is the privilege experienced by middle-class whites. This privilege is not recognized precisely because it is so customary. Whites expect first-rate service; when it is not forthcoming, some feel victimized, even discriminated against. This was especially apparent in the Toy Warehouse, where most of the sales people were black. I noticed that when white women customers were subjected to long waits in line or if they received what they perceived as uncaring attention, they would often sigh loudly, roll their eyes, and try to make eye contact with other whites, looking for a sign of recognition that the service they were receiving was inferior and unfair.

Just as white customers are treated with more respect, so are white service workers, especially by white customers. At the Toy Warehouse, where I was one of only four white women workers, I noticed that shoppers frequently assumed that I was in charge. . . .

In addition . . ., customers at both stores frequently assumed that I was an expert on childhood. This is not an altogether irrational assumption. I was working in a toy store, and I suppose that I looked like a mother with personal experience of children's toys. But I did not have children, and I knew virtually nothing about toys or children's popular culture before I took these jobs. And I was not alone in this. It is important to realize that workers being paid $7.50 an hour do not necessarily have any expertise regarding the merchandise they are selling. We received no training whatsoever. Any advice we gave we literally made up.

At the Toy Warehouse, most customers did not expect elaborate advice from the salesclerks. Anyone who has ever shopped in a big-box store has probably observed workers trying to avoid customers as if they were playing a game of hide-and-seek. Customers have to make a special effort to find a clerk if they need advice. Crossing the floor I would often look down to avoid eye contact with customers either because I was dealing with a previous request or I was trying to make it to the break room for my fifteen-minute rest. Any time we spent interacting with a customer was deducted from our break. . . .

In contrast, avoiding or ignoring customers was taboo at Diamond Toys. Although we complained about customers in the break room, we never expressed our disdain publicly. At Diamond Toys, our job was to cater to customers. It was not unusual to spend fifteen to twenty minutes assisting a single customer. . . .

The culture of the stores also reflected race and class dynamics. Diamond Toys embodied whiteness both physically and symbolically; the Toy Warehouse embodied a more diverse, creative, and flamboyant style. This was reflected in our uniforms. The dress code was strictly enforced at Diamond Toys, much to the chagrin of my younger coworkers, who especially hated the belted and tucked-in look. Some tried to subvert it by wearing their pants low on their hips, but this was a minor alteration. . . .

The dress code at Diamond Toys was not unlike the one that many area school districts had recently imposed on elementary and middle-school children, which probably explains my younger coworkers' disdain for them. But why do customers like them? Edward Morris (2005), who has written about school uniforms in minority schools, has argued that a "tucked in shirt" signifies whiteness, middle-class respectability, and a professional demeanor, especially for the middle-class teachers who enforce the dress code. (To the kids, the uniforms evoked prison garb comparisons.) This analysis matches my experience at Diamond Toys, where our uniforms seemed to reassure customers that we were professionals who knew what we were talking about.

At the Toy Warehouse we wore bright orange vests over matching company-issued camp shirts, giving us the look of warehouse attendants. The bright colors were intended, no doubt, to make us easy to spot on the floor. We were allowed to wear black jeans to work. Most of the young men wore fashionable low riders that hung below their underwear and dragged on the floor. The young women wore super skin-tight hip huggers. Because it was summer, we were also given the option to wear shorts. A coworker named Socorro told me that she was not planning to take advantage of that because people did not need to see the tattoos on her calves. Most of my other coworkers were only too eager to show off their art, as they called it. The younger ones had multiple piercings, including tongue studs. Careful attention was also paid to hairstyles—the more outrageous and intricate the better. Most men and women wore very elaborate and intricate hair designs incorporating dyeing, shaving, sculpting, braiding, and extensions. . . .

Realizing that white customers in particular treated them with disrespect and even disdain, my African American coworkers developed interactional skills to minimize their involvement with them. I noticed at the service desk that the black women who worked there did not smile or act concerned when customers came up for complaints or returns. They did their work well and efficiently, but they did not exude a sense that they really cared. Rather, they looked suspicious, or bored, or resigned, or even a little miffed. Over time I learned that this attitude of ennui or suspicion was cultivated as a way to garner respect for the work. It was saying, "This isn't my problem, it's your problem, but I will see what can be done to fix it." If workers were more enthusiastic and it turned out the problem could not be fixed, they would look incompetent, which was the assumption that too many white customers were willing to make of black women. So those workers made it appear that the problem was insurmountable and when they did resolve it (which was most of the time), they garnered a little bit of respect. But it was at the cost of appearing unfriendly, so the store received negative customer-service evaluations.

With experience, I developed my own set of facial gestures and attitudes to manage customers. At the cash register, I learned to look cheerful, unless there was a void and I had to wait for a manager to respond to a page, in which case I became expressionless and looked off to the distance, like a computer in shut-down mode. If I acted impatient, I learned, the customers would become impatient. At the service desk, where customers returned or exchanged merchandise, I learned to act like a student. To get a refund, customers had to explain what the problem was. I found that the best technique to do this work effectively was to bow my head a little, but raise my eyebrows and look into the eyes of the customer. No smiling and no frowning. This made me look a little skeptical, but also subservient. It also made me look stupid. I had to listen to the stories but not act as if I cared or was interested and then efficiently process the request. If they requested something that was against store policy, I just had to report that, without sounding apologetic or giving the impression that the rule was wrong. "That's just the rule, it's store policy, no exceptions." If they argued, I would call a manager. This kind of affectless performance kept customers under control and less likely to be insulting or to make a scene.

Manipulating customers through self-presentation constitutes an informal "feeling rule" (Hochschild 1983). These techniques for displaying affect were developed by workers to manage and minimize difficult customer interactions. I call them informal rules because management would have preferred that we always conveyed serious concern and solicitude, but workers at the Toy Warehouse knew that would only spell trouble. Moreover, the informal rules were sensitive to race and gender dynamics in a way that management rules could not be. The fact is that different groups had to use different means to assert themselves and their interests, and the stratification of the jobs at the store meant that we all had different levels of formal and informal power to resolve situations. White men had the most institutionalized power and authority in the stores. The store directors in both places where I worked were white men who could and did trump any decision made by managers or sales associates. Sales associates had severely limited options for resolving disputes, owing in large part to surveillance mechanisms intended to keep us from stealing. But maintaining control was also dependent on the race and gender of both workers and customers.

Interaction Breakdown: Social Control in the Toy Store

It may seem incongruous to talk about power and control in the context of toy shopping. But customers frequently misbehave in stores. In addition to seeing customers throwing fits at the service desk, every day I witnessed customers ripping open packages, hiding garbage, spilling soft drinks, and generally making a mess of the store.

As a middle-aged white woman, I could exercise some control over the extremes of this bad behavior. I could stand nearby, for example, and the customers might notice me and guiltily try to stuff the toy back into the box or replace the dozen toys they had pulled off the shelf. We were not allowed to confront customers, even if we suspected them of stealing or destroying the merchandise, but we were expected to develop subtle ways to control them. I could not do this as well as my male coworkers could, but I was definitely more respected (and feared) than my women coworkers who were African American, Asian American, and Latina. . . .

I did not have too much trouble controlling white women. The customers that I had the hardest time controlling were men. Men were outnumbered by women in both stores. At the Toy Warehouse, I saw them mostly on the weekends, which seemed to be the most popular time for fathers to come in with their children. At Diamond Toys, I observed men tourists shopping with their families, businessmen buying small gifts for their children back home, and during the Christmas season, men buying high-end toys for their wives. In general men seemed to be annoyed to be in the stores, and they sometimes acted annoyed with me, especially when unaccompanied by women. One white man at the Toy Warehouse tossed his shopping list at me when I was working at the service desk. He expected me to assemble the items for him or to get someone else to do it. Some men were just mean. On two occasions, men demanded to use my telephone, against which there were strict rules. I said they were not allowed to use it, and they just reached over the counter and did it anyway. I was terrified that my manager would walk by and yell at me, maybe even fire me. On another occasion at Diamond Toys, a business professor in town for a conference was upset because a Barney sippy cup he wanted to buy was missing its price tag and I could not find it listed in the store inventory. He made me call over the store director and subjected both of us to a critique of store operations, which he threatened to submit for publication to a business journal unless we sold him the sippy cup.

The sense of entitlement I observed in these men customers was different from that which I observed in white women. Perhaps the expectation that shopping was "women's work" made these men feel entitled to make me do their shopping for them or reorganize the store to make it more convenient for them. To assert masculinity while engaging in this otherwise feminine activity seemed to require them to disrupt the routinized clerk–customer relationship.

In an extreme manifestation of this shopping masculinity, on three occasions (all at the Toy Warehouse), men threw things in my direction. Once a male customer threw a toy that struck me on the head. The customer was a young African American, maybe thirty years old. . . . [He] was yelling at Jack [the store manager], using swear words. "Fuck this shit, I don't give a damn!" Jack was trying to calm him down, "Please do not use that language, sir, this is a toy store." The customer was so angry that he threw the toy on the counter, accidentally dislodging the phone, which came flying toward me, hitting me on the left side of my face and neck. I shrieked as I fell to the floor, and I thought I might cry. Jack said to Leticia, "Call the police *now*." The man started to walk toward the exit, but first he said loudly, "If I don't get a cash refund, my kids won't eat tonight," and he left the store (without his toy). . . .

Jack was not the only one who threatened to call the police when black men customers became angry in the store. I noticed that this particular strategy for control was also used by the African American women supervisors and manager at the Toy Warehouse.

African American shoppers sometimes resisted what they apparently perceived as discriminatory treatment, which is in keeping with the long tradition of black protest against racism in stores (Cohen 2003; Weems 1998). Some black customers were quick to speak out if they felt subjected to unfair or unequal treatment, including one who accused me of racism for not helping another black customer (I was not sure that she accepted my explanation). The rules of shopping are subject to constant negotiation and rewriting.

Conclusion

As a nation of consumers, we spend a great deal of our time in stores interacting with sales workers. In this [reading], I have tried to make a case for paying attention to these interactions as sites for the reproduction of social inequality.

In particular, I have argued that how we shop is shaped by and bolsters race, class, and gender inequalities. I have emphasized three dimensions of this process. First, corporations script the customer–server interaction in ways that are designed to appeal to a particular kind of customer. The fun, child-centered Toy Warehouse was designed to appeal to middle-class white women. The sophisticated and discriminating Diamond Toys was designed to appeal to an upper-class clientele. These rules influenced who entered the stores as customers and also shaped the hiring practices in the two stores. The Toy Warehouse was a dazzling mix of customers catered to by a staff of mostly African American workers, whereas Diamond Toys hired mainly whites to serve a mostly white, well-to-do clientele.

Second, actual interactions between clerks and customers stray from these ideal rituals in ways that take into account the social inequalities of race, class, and gender. Both clerks and customers drew on elaborate stereotypes in crafting their working and shopping practices. White customers received preferential treatment, and many developed a sense of entitlement because of this. Similarly, white workers were treated with more deference and respect, particularly by white shoppers. African American and Latina/o workers developed elaborate strategies to protect their self-respect in the face of this white privilege.

Third, when interactions break down, the ability to repair them depends on how the characteristics of the customer and the worker are interpreted. As a white woman I had a different repertoire of control strategies than my African American women coworkers. They had to reckon with racist as well as sexist assumptions from irate white customers, whereas most of my difficulties were due to customer sexism. White men had more power in the stores, but they seemed to have difficulty managing and controlling black customers, in particular, black men. Control is an achievement that must be negotiated anew with each service interaction.

Herbert Blumer (1969) wrote that people act toward things on the basis of the meanings that they give to them, and further, that those meanings arise in the course of interactions. The meanings of race, class, and gender are not given in the rituals handed down by management, nor are they brought into the store ready-made by the clerks and customers possessing these discrete demographic characteristics. Rather, they derive their meaning and significance through interactions that are the creative products of interpretive acts by individuals.

The theory of symbolic interactionism is useful for understanding race, class, and gender on the shopping floor. Moreover, in my view, this is a hopeful approach to analyzing the reproduction of inequalities: there is nothing inevitable about the ways that shopping interactions proceed on a daily basis. Because they are symbolically created, they can be recreated to lessen the social inequalities that they currently reproduce.

Author's Note: This article is drawn from a chapter in my book, *Inside Toyland: Working, Shopping, and Social Inequality* (University of California Press, 2006). Many thanks to Sherryl Kleinman for inviting me to deliver the Distinguished Lecture to the Society for the Study of Symbolic Interaction (SSSI). I am also grateful to Jessica Fields, and to the other members of SSSI who attended the talk and gave me valuable feedback. And thanks especially to editor Simon Gottschalk for his patience and support.

REFERENCES

Blumer, Herbert. 1969. *Symbolic Interactionism.* Berkeley: University of California Press.
Cohen, Lizabeth. 2003. *A Consumers' Republic: The Politics of Mass Consumption in Postwar America.* New York: Knopf.
Feagin, Joe and Melvin Sikes. 1995. *Living with Racism: The Black Middle Class Experience.* New York: Beacon.
Goffman, Erving. 1967. *Interaction Ritual: Essays on Face to Face Behavior.* Garden City, NY: Anchor.
———. 1977. "The Arrangement between the Sexes." *Theory and Society* 4:301–31.
Hochschild, Arlie. 1983. *The Managed Heart.* Berkeley: University of California Press.
Leidner, Robin. 1993. *Fast Food, Fast Talk: Service Work and the Routinization of Everyday Life.* Berkeley: University of California Press.
Michman, Ronald D. and Edward M. Mazze. 2001. *Specialty Retailers—Marketing Triumphs and Blunders.* Westport, CT: Quorum.
Morris, Edward. 2005. *An Unexpected Minority: White Kids in an Urban School.* New Brunswick, NJ: Rutgers University Press.
Weems, Robert E. 1998. *Desegregating the Dollar: African American Consumerism in the Twentieth Century.* New York: New York University Press.
West, Candace and Don Zimmerman. 1987. "Doing Gender." *Gender & Society* 1:125–51.

20

ANOREXIA NERVOSA AND BULIMIA
The Development of Deviant Identities

PENELOPE A. McLORG • DIANE E. TAUB

Sociologists have a long-standing interest in the study of social deviance, which is explored in the next three readings. *Deviance* is the recognized violation of social norms. As norms cover a wide range of human behavior, deviant acts are plentiful in any given society. Moreover, as illustrated in Reading 6 by David Rosenhan on the labeling of mental illness, whether a person is labeled deviant depends on how others perceive, define, and respond to that person's behavior. This reading by Penelope McLorg and Diane Taub further illustrates this process of deviance identification. In the reading, originally published in 1987, McLorg and Taub employ labeling theory to explain how eating disorders have become defined as deviant behaviors and how some young women acquire deviant identities by modifying their self-concepts to conform to the societal lebels of a person with an eating disorder. Penelope McLorg is director of the Gerontology Program and Diane Taub is a professor of sociology at Indiana University–Purdue University, Fort Wayne.

Introduction

Current appearance norms stipulate thinness for women and muscularity for men; these expectations, like any norms, entail rewards for compliance and negative sanctions for violations. Fear of being overweight—of being visually deviant—has led to a striving for thinness, especially among women. In the extreme, this avoidance of overweight engenders eating disorders, which themselves constitute deviance. Anorexia nervosa, or purposeful starvation, embodies visual as well as behavioral deviation; bulimia, binge-eating followed by vomiting and/or laxative abuse, is primarily behaviorally deviant.

Besides a fear of fatness, anorexics and bulimics exhibit distorted body images. In anorexia nervosa, a 20–25 percent loss of initial body weight occurs, resulting from self-starvation alone or in combination with excessive exercising, occasional binge-eating, vomiting and/or laxative abuse. Bulimia denotes cyclical (daily, weekly, for example) binge-eating followed by vomiting or laxative abuse; weight is normal or close to normal (Humphries, Wrobel, and Weigert 1982). Common physical manifestations of these eating disorders include menstrual cessation or irregularities and electrolyte imbalances; among behavioral traits are depression, obsessions/compulsions, and anxiety (Russell 1979; Thompson and Schwartz 1982).

Increasingly prevalent in the past two decades, anorexia nervosa and bulimia have emerged as major health and social problems. Termed an epidemic on college campuses (Brody, as quoted in Schur 1984:76), bulimia affects 13 percent of college students (Halmi, Falk, and Schwartz 1981). Less prevalent, anorexia nervosa was diagnosed in 0.6 percent of students utilizing a university health center (Stangler and Printz 1980). However, the overall mortality rate of anorexia nervosa is 6 percent (Schwartz and Thompson 1981) to 20 percent (Humphries et al. 1982); bulimia appears to be less life-threatening (Russell 1979).

Particularly affecting certain demographic groups, eating disorders are most prevalent among young, white, affluent (upper-middle to upper class) women in modern, industrialized countries (Crisp 1977; Willi and Grossman 1983). Combining all of these risk factors (female sex, youth, high socioeconomic status, and residence in an industrialized country), prevalence of anorexia nervosa in upper-class English girls' schools is reported at 1 in 100 (Crisp, Palmer, and Kalucy 1976). The age of onset for anorexia nervosa is bimodal at 14.5 and 18 years (Humphries et al. 1982); the most frequent age of onset for bulimia is 18 (Russell 1979).

Eating disorders have primarily been studied from psychological and medical perspectives.[1] Theories of etiology have generally fallen into three categories: the ego psychological (involving an impaired child–maternal environment); the family systems (implicating enmeshed, rigid families); and the endocrinological (involving a precipitating hormonal defect). Although relatively ignored in previous studies, the sociocultural components of anorexia nervosa and bulimia (the slimness norm and its agents of reinforcement, such as role models) have been postulated as accounting for the recent, dramatic increases in these disorders (Boskind-White 1985; Schwartz, Thompson, and Johnson 1982).[2]

Medical and psychological approaches to anorexia nervosa and bulimia obscure the social facets of the disorders and neglect the individuals' own definitions of their situations. Among the social processes involved in the development of an eating disorder is the sequence of conforming behavior, primary deviance, and secondary deviance. Societal reaction is the critical mediator affecting the movement through the deviant career (Becker 1973). Within a framework of labeling theory, this study focuses on the emergence of anorexic and bulimic identities, as well as on the consequences of being career deviants.

Methodology

Sampling and Procedures

Most research on eating disorders has utilized clinical subjects or nonclinical respondents completing questionnaires. Such studies can be criticized for simply counting and describing behaviors and/or neglecting the social construction of the disorders. Moreover, the work of clinicians is often limited by therapeutic orientation. Previous research may also have included individuals who were not in therapy on their own volition and who resisted admitting that they had an eating disorder.

Past studies thus disregard the intersubjective meanings respondents attach to their behavior and emphasize researchers' criteria for definition as anorexic or bulimic. In order to supplement these sampling and procedural designs, the present study utilizes participant observation of a group of self-defined anorexics and bulimics.[3] As the individuals had acknowledged their eating disorders, frank discussion and disclosure were facilitated.

Data are derived from a self-help group, BANISH, Bulimics/Anorexics in Self-Help, which met at a university in an urban center of the mid-South. Founded by one of the researchers (D.E.T.), BANISH was advertised in local newspapers as offering a group experience for individuals who were anorexic or bulimic. Despite the local advertisements, the campus location of the meeting may have selectively encouraged university students to attend. Nonetheless, in view of the modal age of onset and socioeconomic status of individuals with eating disorders, college students have been considered target populations (Crisp et al. 1976; Halmi et al. 1981).

The group's weekly two-hour meetings were observed for two years. During the course of this study, 30 individuals attended at least one of the meetings. Attendance at meetings was varied: Ten individuals came nearly every Sunday; five attended approximately twice a month; and the remaining 15 participated once a month or less frequently, often when their eating problems were "more severe" or "bizarre." The modal number of members at meetings was 12. The diversity in attendance was to be expected in self-help groups of anorexics and bulimics:

> Most people's involvement will not be forever or even a long time. Most people get the support they need and drop out. Some take the time to help others after they themselves have been helped but even they may withdraw after a time. It is a natural and in many cases *necessary* process (emphasis in original). (American Anorexia and Bulimia Association 1983)

Modeled after Alcoholics Anonymous, BANISH allowed participants to discuss their backgrounds and experiences with others who empathized. For many members, the group constituted their only source of help; these respondents were reluctant to contact health professionals because of shame, embarrassment, or financial difficulties.

In addition to field notes from group meetings, records of other encounters with all members were maintained. Participants visited the office of one of the researchers (D.E.T.), called both researchers by phone, and invited them to their homes or out for a cup of coffee. Such interaction facilitated genuine communication and mutual trust. Even among the 15 individuals who did not attend the meetings regularly, contact was maintained with 10 members on a monthly basis.

Supplementing field notes were informal interviews with 15 group members, lasting from two to four hours. Because they appeared to represent more extensive experience with eating disorders, these interviewees were chosen to amplify their comments about the labeling process, made during group meetings. Conducted near the end of the two-year observation period, the interviews focused on what the respondents thought antedated and maintained their eating disorders. In addition, participants described others' reactions to their behaviors as well as their own interpretations of these reactions. To protect the confidentiality of individuals quoted in the study, pseudonyms are employed.

Description of Members

The demographic composite of the sample typifies what has been found in other studies (Crisp 1977; Fox and James 1976; Herzog 1982; Schlesier-Stropp 1984). Group members' ages ranged from 19 to 36, with the modal age being 21. The respondents were white, and all but one were female. The sole male and three of the females were anorexic; the remaining females were bulimic.[4]

Primarily composed of college students, the group included four nonstudents, three of whom had college degrees. Nearly all members derived from upper-middle- or lower-upper-class households. Eighteen students and two nonstudents were never married and uninvolved in serious relationships; two nonstudents were married (one with two children); two students were divorced (one with two children); and six students were involved in serious relationships. The duration of eating disorders ranged from 3 to 15 years.

Conforming Behavior

In the backgrounds of most anorexics and bulimics, dieting figures prominently, beginning in the teen years (Crisp 1977; Johnson, Stuckey, Lewis, and Schwartz 1982; Lacey, Coker, and Birtchnell 1986). As dieters, these individuals are conformist in their adherence to the cultural norms emphasizing thinness (Garner, Garfinkel, Schwartz, and Thompson 1980; Schwartz, Thompson, and Johnson 1982). In our society, slim bodies are regarded as the most worthy and attractive; overweight is viewed as physically and morally unhealthy—"obscene," "lazy," "slothful," and "gluttonous" (DeJong 1980; Ritenbaugh 1982; Schwartz et al. 1982).

Among the agents of socialization promoting the slimness norm is advertising. Female models in newspaper, magazine, and television advertisements are uniformly slender. In addition, product names and slogans exploit the thin orientation; examples include "Ultra Slim Lipstick," "Miller Lite," and "Virginia Slims." While retaining pressures toward thinness, an Ayds commercial attempts a compromise for those wanting to savor food: "Ayds . . . so you can taste, chew, and enjoy, while you lose weight." Appealing particularly to women, a nationwide fast-food restaurant chain offers low-calorie selections, so individuals can have a "license to eat." In the latter two examples, the notion of enjoying food is combined with the message to be slim. Food and restaurant advertisements overall convey the pleasures of eating, whereas advertisements for other products, such as fashions and diet aids, reinforce the idea that fatness is undesirable.

Emphasis on being slim affects everyone in our culture, but it influences women especially because of society's traditional emphasis on women's appearance. The slimness norm and its concomitant narrow beauty standards exacerbate the objectification of women (Schur 1984). Women view themselves as visual entities and recognize that conforming to appearance expectations and "becoming attractive object[s] [are] role obligation[s]" (Laws, as quoted in Schur 1984:66). Demonstrating the beauty motivation behind dieting, a Nielson survey indicated that of the 56 percent of all women aged 24 to 54 who dieted during the previous year, 76 percent did so for cosmetic, rather than health, reasons (Schwartz et al. 1982). For most female group members, dieting was viewed as a means of gaining attractiveness and appeal to the opposite sex. The male respondent, as well, indicated that *when I was fat, girls didn't look at me, but when I got thinner, I was suddenly popular.*

In addition to responding to the specter of obesity, individuals who develop anorexia nervosa and bulimia are conformist in their strong commitment to other conventional norms and goals. They consistently excel at school and work (Bruch 1981; Humphries et al. 1982; Russell 1979), maintaining high aspirations in both areas (Lacey et al. 1986; Theander 1970). Group members generally completed college-preparatory courses in high school, aware from an early age that they would strive for a college degree. Also, in college as well as high school, respondents joined honor societies and academic clubs.

Moreover, pre-anorexics and -bulimics display notable conventionality as "model children" (Humphries et al. 1982:199), "the pride and joy" of their parents (Bruch 1981:215), accommodating themselves to the wishes of others. Parents of these individuals emphasize conformity and value achievement (Bruch 1981). Respondents felt that perfect or near-perfect grades were expected of them; however, good grades were not rewarded by parents, because "A's" were common for these children. In addition, their parents suppressed conflicts, to preserve the image of the "all-American family" (Humphries et al. 1982). Group members reported that they seldom, if ever, heard their parents argue or raise their voices.

Also conformist in their affective ties, individuals who develop anorexia nervosa and bulimia are strongly, even excessively, attached to their parents.

Respondents' families appeared close-knit, demonstrating palpable emotional ties. Several group members, for example, reported habitually calling home at prescribed times, whether or not they had any news. Such families have been termed "enmeshed" and "overprotective," displaying intense interaction and concern for members' welfare (Minuchin, Rosman, and Baker 1978; Selvini-Palazzoli 1978). These qualities could be viewed as marked conformity to the norm of familial closeness.[5]

Another element of notable conformity in the family milieu of pre-anorexics and -bulimics concerns eating, body weight and shape, and exercising (Humphries et al. 1982; Kalucy, Crisp, and Harding 1977). Respondents reported their fathers' preoccupation with exercising and their mothers' engrossment in food preparation. When group members dieted and lost weight, they received an extraordinary amount of approval. Among the family, body size became a matter of "friendly rivalry." One bulimic informant recalled that she, her mother, and her coed sister all strived to wear a size 5, regardless of their heights and body frames. Subsequent to this study, the researchers learned that both the mother and sister had become bulimic.

As pre-anorexics and -bulimics, group members thus exhibited marked conformity to cultural norms of thinness, achievement, compliance, and parental attachment. Their families reinforced their conformity by adherence to norms of family closeness and weight and body shape consciousness.

Primary Deviance

Even with familial encouragement, respondents, like nearly all dieters (Chernin 1981), failed to maintain their lowered weights. Many cited their lack of willpower to eat only restricted foods. For the emerging anorexics and bulimics, extremes such as purposeful starvation or binging accompanied by vomiting and/or laxative abuse appeared as "obvious solutions" to the problem of retaining weight loss. Associated with these behaviors was a regained feeling of control in lives that had been disrupted by a major crisis. Group members' extreme weight-loss efforts operated as coping mechanisms for entering college, leaving home, or feeling rejected by the opposite sex.

The primary inducement for both eating adaptations was the drive for slimness: With slimness came more self-respect and a feeling of superiority over "unsuccessful dieters." Brian, for example, experienced a "power trip" upon consistent weight loss through starvation. Binges allowed the purging respondents to cope with stress through eating while maintaining a slim appearance. As former strict dieters, Teresa and Jennifer used binging and purging as an alternative to the constant self-denial of starvation. Acknowledging their parents' desires for them to be slim, most respondents still felt it was a conscious choice on their part to continue extreme weight-loss efforts. Being thin became the "most important thing" in their lives—their "greatest ambition."

In explaining the development of an anorexic or bulimic identity, Lemert's (1951, 1967) concept of primary deviance is salient. Primary deviance refers to a transitory period of norm violations which do not affect an individual's self-concept or performance of social roles. Although respondents were exhibiting anorexic or bulimic behavior, they did not consider themselves to be anorexic or bulimic.

At first, anorexics' significant others complimented their weight loss, expounding on their new "sleekness" and "good looks." Branch and Eurman (1980) also found anorexics' families and friends describing them as "well groomed," "neat," "fashionable," and "victorious" (p. 631). Not until the respondents approached emaciation did some parents or friends become concerned and withdraw their praise. Significant others also became increasingly aware of the anorexics' compulsive exercising, preoccupation with food preparation (but not consumption), and ritualistic eating patterns (such as cutting food into minute pieces and eating only certain foods at prescribed times).

For bulimics, friends or family members began to question how the respondents could eat such large amounts of food (often in excess of 10,000 calories a day) and stay slim. Significant others also noticed calluses across the bulimics' hands, which were caused by repeated inducement of vomiting. Several bulimics were "caught in the act," bent over commodes. Generally, friends and family required substantial evidence before believing that the respondents' binging or purging was no longer sporadic.

Secondary Deviance

Heightened awareness of group members' eating behavior ultimately led others to label the respondents "anorexic" or "bulimic." Respondents differed in their histories of being labeled and accepting the labels. Generally first termed anorexic by friends, family, or medical personnel, the anorexics initially vigorously denied the label. They felt they were not "anorexic enough," not skinny enough; Robin did not regard herself as having the "skeletal" appearance she associated with anorexia nervosa. These group members found it difficult to differentiate between socially approved modes of weight loss—eating less and exercising more—and the extremes of those behaviors. In fact, many of their activities—cheerleading, modeling, gymnastics, aerobics—reinforced their pursuit of thinness. Like other anorexics, Chris felt she was being "ultra-healthy," with "total control" over her body.

For several respondents, admitting they were anorexic followed the realization that their lives were disrupted by their eating disorder. Anorexics' inflexible eating patterns unsettled family meals and holiday gatherings. Their regimented lifestyle of compulsively scheduled activities—exercising, school, and meals—precluded any spontaneous social interactions. Realization of their adverse behaviors preceded the anorexics' acknowledgment of their subnormal body weight and size.

Contrasting with anorexics, the binge/purgers, when confronted, more readily admitted that they were bulimic and that their means of weight loss was "abnormal." Teresa, for example, knew "very well" that her bulimic behavior was "wrong and unhealthy," although "worth the physical risks." While the bulimics initially maintained that their purging was only a temporary weight-loss method, they eventually realized that their disorder represented a "loss of control." Although these respondents regretted the self-indulgence, "shame," and "wasted time," they acknowledged their growing dependence on binging and purging for weight management and stress regulation.

The application of anorexic or bulimic labels precipitated secondary deviance, wherein group members internalized these identities. Secondary deviance refers to norm violations which are a response to society's labeling: "Secondary deviation . . . becomes a means of social defense, attack or adaptation to the overt and covert problems created by the societal reaction to primary deviance" (Lemert 1967:17). In contrast to primary deviance, secondary deviance is generally prolonged, alters the individual's self-concept, and affects the performance of his or her social roles.

As secondary deviants, respondents felt that their disorders "gave a purpose" to their lives. Nicole resisted attaining a normal weight because it was not "her"—she accepted her anorexic weight as her "true" weight. For Teresa, bulimia became a "companion"; and Julie felt "every aspect of her life," including time management and social activities, was affected by her bulimia. Group members' eating disorders became the salient element of their self-concepts so that they related to familiar people and new acquaintances as anorexics or bulimics. For example, respondents regularly compared their body shapes and sizes with those of others. They also became sensitized to comments about their appearance, whether or not the remarks were made by someone aware of their eating disorder.

With their behavior increasingly attuned to their eating disorders, group members exhibited role engulfment (Schur 1971). Through accepting anorexic or bulimic identities, individuals centered activities around their deviant role, downgrading other social roles. Their obligations as students, family members, and friends became subordinate to their eating and exercising rituals. Socializing, for example, was gradually curtailed because it interfered with compulsive exercising, binging, or purging.

Labeled anorexic or bulimic, respondents were ascribed a new status with a different set of role expectations. Regardless of other positions the individuals occupied, their deviant status, or master status (Becker 1973; Hughes 1958), was identified before all others. Among group members, Nicole, who was known as the "school's brain," became known as the "school's anorexic." No longer viewed as conforming model individuals, some respondents were termed "starving waifs" or "pigs."

Because of their identities as deviants, anorexics' and bulimics' interactions with others were altered. Group members' eating habits were scrutinized by friends and family and used as a "catchall" for everything negative that happened to them. Respondents felt self-conscious around individuals who knew of their disorders; for example, Robin imagined people "watching and whispering" behind her. In addition, group members believed others expected them to "act" anorexic or bulimic. Friends of some anorexic group members never offered them food or drink, assuming continued disinterest on the respondents' part. While being hospitalized, Denise felt she had to prove to others she was not still vomiting, by keeping her bathroom door open. Other bulimics, who lived in dormitories, were hesitant to use the restroom for normal purposes lest several friends be huddling at the door, listening for vomiting. In general, individuals interacted with the respondents largely on the basis of their eating disorder; in doing so, they reinforced anorexic and bulimic behaviors.

Bulimic respondents, whose weight-loss behavior was not generally detectable from their appearance, tried earnestly to hide their bulimia by binging and purging in secret. Their main purpose in concealment was to avoid the negative consequences of being known as a bulimic. For these individuals, bulimia connoted a "cop-out": Like "weak anorexics," bulimics pursued thinness but yielded to urges to eat. Respondents felt other people regarded bulimia as "gross" and had little sympathy for the sufferer. To avoid these stigmas or "spoiled identities," the bulimics shrouded their behaviors.

Distinguishing types of stigma, Goffman (1963) describes discredited (visible) stigmas and discreditable (invisible) stigmas. Bulimics, whose weight was approximately normal or even slightly elevated, harbored discreditable stigmas. Anorexics, on the other hand, suffered both discreditable and discredited stigmas—the latter due to their emaciated appearance. Certain anorexics were more reconciled than the bulimics to their stigmas: For Brian, the "stigma of anorexia was better than being fat." Common to the stigmatized individuals was an inability to interact spontaneously with others. Respondents were constantly on guard against topics of eating and body size.

Both anorexics and bulimics were held responsible by others for their behavior and presumed able to "get out of it if they tried." Many anorexics reported being told to "just eat more," while bulimics were enjoined to simply "stop eating so much." Such appeals were made without regard for the complexities of the problem. Ostracized by certain friends and family members, anorexics and bulimics felt increasingly isolated. For respondents, the self-help group presented a nonthreatening forum for discussing their disorders. Here, they found mutual understanding, empathy, and support. Many participants viewed BANISH as a haven from stigmatization by "others."

Group members, as secondary deviants, thus endured negative consequences, such as stigmatization, from being labeled. As they internalized the labels anorexic or bulimic, individuals' self-concepts were significantly influenced. When others interacted with the respondents on the basis of their eating disorders, anorexic or bulimic identities were encouraged. Moreover, group members' efforts to counteract the deviant labels were thwarted by their master status.

Discussion

Previous research on eating disorders has dwelt almost exclusively on medical and psychological facets. Although necessary for a comprehensive understanding of anorexia nervosa and bulimia, these approaches neglect the social processes involved. The phenomena of eating disorders transcend concrete disease entities and clinical diagnoses. Multifaceted and complex, anorexia nervosa and bulimia require a holistic research design, in which sociological insights must be included.

A limitation of medical and psychiatric studies, in particular, is researchers' use of a priori criteria in establishing salient variables. Rather than utilizing predetermined standards of inclusion, the present study allows respondents to construct their own reality. Concomitant to this innovative approach to eating disorders is the selection of a sample of self-admitted anorexics and bulimics. Individuals' perceptions of what it means to become anorexic or bulimic are explored. Although based on a small sample, findings can be used to guide researchers in other settings.

With only 5 to 10 percent of reported cases appearing in males (Crisp 1977; Stangler and Printz 1980), eating disorders are primarily a women's aberrance. The deviance of anorexia nervosa and bulimia is rooted in the visual objectification of women and attendant slimness norm. Indeed, purposeful starvation and binging and purging reinforce the notion that "a society gets the deviance it deserves" (Schur 1979:71). As noted (Schur 1984), the sociology of deviance has generally bypassed systematic studies of women's norm violations. Like male deviants, females endure label applications, internalizations, and fulfillments.

The social processes involved in developing anorexic or bulimic identities comprise the sequence of conforming behavior, primary deviance, and secondary deviance. With a background of exceptional adherence to conventional norms, especially the striving for thinness, respondents subsequently exhibit the primary deviance of starving or binging and purging. Societal reaction to these behaviors leads to secondary deviance, wherein respondents' self-concepts and master statuses become anorexic or bulimic. Within this framework of labeling theory, the persistence of eating disorders, as well as the effects of stigmatization, are elucidated.

Although during the course of this research some respondents alleviated their symptoms through psychiatric help or hospital treatment programs, no one was labeled "cured." An anorexic is considered recovered when weight is normal for two years; a bulimic is termed recovered after being symptom-free for one and one-half years (American Anorexia and Bulimia Association Newsletter 1985). Thus deviance disavowal (Schur 1971), or efforts after normalization to counteract deviant labels, remains a topic for future exploration.

ENDNOTES

[1]Although instructive, an integration of the medical, psychological, and sociocultural perspectives on eating disorders is beyond the scope of this paper.

[2]Exceptions to the neglect of sociocultural factors are discussions of sex-role socialization in the development of eating disorders. Anorexics' girlish appearance has been interpreted as a rejection of femininity and womanhood (Bruch 1981; Orbach 1979, 1985). In contrast, bulimics have been characterized as overconforming to traditional female sex roles (Boskind-Lodahl 1976).

[3]Although a group experience for self-defined bulimics has been reported (Boskind-Lodahl 1976), the researcher, from the outset, focused on Gestalt and behaviorist techniques within a feminist orientation.

[4]One explanation for fewer anorexics than bulimics in the sample is that, in the general population, anorexics are outnumbered by bulimics at 8 or 10 to 1 (Lawson, as reprinted in American Anorexia and Bulimia Association Newsletter 1985:1). The proportion of bulimics to anorexics in the sample is 6.5 to 1. In addition, compared to bulimics, anorexics may be less likely to attend a self-help group as they have a greater tendency to deny the existence of an eating problem (Humphries et al. 1982). However, the four anorexics in the present study were among the members who attended the meetings most often.

[5]Interactions in the families of anorexics and bulimics might seem deviant in being inordinately close. However, in the larger societal context, the family members epitomize the norms of family cohesiveness. Perhaps unusual in their occurrence, these families are still within the realm of conformity. Humphries and colleagues (1982) refer to the "highly enmeshed and protective" family as part of the "idealized family myth" (p. 202).

REFERENCES

American Anorexia/Bulimia Association. 1983, April. Correspondence.

American Anorexia/Bulimia Association Newsletter. 1985. 8(3).

Becker, Howard S. 1973. *Outsiders*. New York: Free Press.

Boskind-Lodahl, Marlene. 1976. "Cinderella's Stepsisters: A Feminist Perspective on Anorexia Nervosa and Bulimia." *Signs: Journal of Women in Culture and Society* 2:342–56.

Boskind-White, Marlene. 1985. "Bulimarexia: A Sociocultural Perspective." Pp. 113–26 in *Theory and Treatment of Anorexia Nervosa and Bulimia: Biomedical, Sociocultural and Psychological Perspectives*, edited by S. W. Emmett. New York: Brunner/Mazel.

Branch, C. H. Hardin and Linda J. Eurman. 1980. "Social Attitudes toward Patients with Anorexia Nervosa." *American Journal of Psychiatry* 137:631–32.

Bruch, Hilda. 1981. "Developmental Considerations of Anorexia Nervosa and Obesity." *Canadian Journal of Psychiatry* 26:212–16.

Chernin, Kim. 1981. *The Obsession: Reflections on the Tyranny of Slenderness*. New York: Harper & Row.

Crisp, A. H. 1977. "The Prevalence of Anorexia Nervosa and Some of Its Associations in the General Population." *Advances in Psychosomatic Medicine* 9:38–47.

Crisp, A. H., R. L. Palmer, and R. S. Kalucy. 1976. "How Common Is Anorexia Nervosa? A Prevalence Study." *British Journal of Psychiatry* 128:549–54.

DeJong, William. 1980. "The Stigma of Obesity: The Consequences of Naive Assumptions Concerning the Causes of Physical Deviance." *Journal of Health and Social Behavior* 21:75–87.

Fox, K. C. and N. McI. James. 1976. "Anorexia Nervosa: A Study of 44 Strictly Defined Cases." *New Zealand Medical Journal* 84:309–12.

Garner, David M., Paul E. Garfinkel, Donald Schwartz, and Michael Thompson. 1980. "Cultural Expectations of Thinness in Women." *Psychological Reports* 47:483–91.

Goffman, Erving. 1963. *Stigma*. Englewood Cliffs, NJ: Prentice-Hall.

Halmi, Katherine A., James R. Falk, and Estelle Schwartz. 1981. "Binge-Eating and Vomiting: A Survey of a College Population." *Psychological Medicine* 11:697–706.

Herzog, David B. 1982. "Bulimia: The Secretive Syndrome." *Psychosomatics* 23:481–83.

Hughes, Everett C. 1958. *Men and Their Work*. New York: Free Press.

Humphries, Laurie L., Sylvia Wrobel, and H. Thomas Wiegert. 1982. "Anorexia Nervosa." *American Family Physician* 26:199–204.

Johnson, Craig L., Marilyn K. Stuckey, Linda D. Lewis, and Donald M. Schwartz. 1982. "Bulimia: A Descriptive Survey of 316 Cases." *International Journal of Eating Disorders* 2(1):3–16.

Kalucy, R. S., A. H. Crisp, and Britta Harding. 1977. "A Study of 56 Families with Anorexia Nervosa." *British Journal of Medical Psychology* 50:381–95.

Lacey, Hubert J., Sian Coker, and S. A. Birtchnell. 1986. "Bulimia: Factors Associated with Its Etiology and Maintenance." *International Journal of Eating Disorders* 5:475–87.

Lemert, Edwin M. 1951. *Social Pathology*. New York: McGraw-Hill.

———. 1967. *Human Deviance, Social Problems and Social Control*. Englewood Cliffs, NJ: Prentice-Hall.

Minuchin, Salvador, Bernice L. Rosman, and Lester Baker. 1978. *Psychosomatic Families: Anorexia Nervosa in Context.* Cambridge, MA: Harvard University Press.

Orbach, Susie. 1979. *Fat Is a Feminist Issue.* New York: Berkeley.

———. 1985. "Visibility/Invisibility: Social Considerations in Anorexia Nervosa—a Feminist Perspective." Pp. 127–38 in *Theory and Treatment of Anorexia Nervosa and Bulimia: Biomedical, Sociocultural and Psychological Perspectives,* edited by S. W. Emmett. New York: Brunner/Mazel.

Ritenbaugh, Cheryl. 1982. "Obesity As a Culture-Bound Syndrome." *Culture, Medicine and Psychiatry* 6:347–61.

Russell, Gerald. 1979. "Bulimia Nervosa: An Ominous Variant of Anorexia Nervosa." *Psychological Medicine* 9:429–48.

Schlesier-Stropp, Barbara. 1984. "Bulimia: A Review of the Literature." *Psychological Bulletin* 95:247–57.

Schur, Edwin M. 1971. *Labeling Deviant Behavior.* New York: Harper & Row.

———. 1979. *Interpreting Deviance: A Sociological Introduction.* New York: Harper & Row.

———. 1984. *Labeling Women Deviant: Gender, Stigma, and Social Control.* New York: Random House.

Schwartz, Donald M. and Michael G. Thompson. 1981. "Do Anorectics Get Well? Current Research and Future Needs." *American Journal of Psychiatry* 138:319–23.

Schwartz, Donald M., Michael G. Thompson, and Craig L. Johnson. 1982. "Anorexia Nervosa and Bulimia: The Socio-Cultural Context." *International Journal of Eating Disorders* 1(3):20–36.

Selvini-Palazzoli, Mara. 1978. *Self-Starvation: From Individual to Family Therapy in the Treatment of Anorexia Nervosa.* New York: Jason Aronson.

Stangler, Ronnie S. and Adolph M. Printz. 1980. "DSM-III: Psychiatric Diagnosis in a University Population." *American Journal of Psychiatry* 137:937–40.

Theander, Sten. 1970. "Anorexia Nervosa." *Acta Psychiatrica Scandinavica Supplement* 214:24–31.

Thompson, Michael G. and Donald M. Schwartz. 1982. "Life Adjustment of Women with Anorexia Nervosa and Anorexic-like Behavior." *International Journal of Eating Disorders* 1(2):47–60.

Willi, Jurg and Samuel Grossman. 1983. "Epidemiology of Anorexia Nervosa in a Defined Region of Switzerland." *American Journal of Psychiatry* 140:564–67.

21

FRATERNITIES AND COLLEGIATE RAPE CULTURE
Why Are Some Fraternities More Dangerous Places for Women?

A. AYRES BOSWELL • JOAN Z. SPADE

Conflict theory suggests that, in our society, who and what the label "deviant" is placed on is based primarily on relative power. Those who have more authority and control define what is "normal" and what is deviant. Moreover, conflict theorists argue that social norms, including laws, generally reflect the interests of the rich and powerful. Thus, historically, we have property laws to protect against the theft of property of the landowning classes and domestic laws that protect the status of men, as patriarchs, within the family. This reading by A. Ayres Boswell and Joan Z. Spade, originally published in 1996, exemplifies this process, in which the privileged attempt to socially construct deviance and crime to their advantage. In particular, Boswell and Spade analyze the social contexts of and gendered relations in male fraternities that contribute to the high incidence of violence against women on many college campuses. Joan Z. Spade is a professor of sociology at the State University of New York, Buffalo.

D ate rape and acquaintance rape on college campuses are topics of concern to both researchers and college administrators. Some estimate that 60 to 80 percent of rapes are date or acquaintance rape (Koss, Dinero, Seibel, and Cox 1988). Further, 1 out of 4 college women say they were raped or experienced an attempted rape, and 1 out of 12 college men say they forced a woman to have sexual intercourse against her will (Koss, Gidycz, and Wisniewski 1985).

Although considerable attention focuses on the incidence of rape, we know relatively little about the context or the *rape culture* surrounding date and acquaintance rape. Rape culture is a set of values and beliefs that provide an environment conducive to rape (Buchwald, Fletcher, and Roth 1993; Herman 1984). The term applies to a generic culture surrounding and promoting rape, not the specific settings in which rape is likely to occur. We believe that the specific settings also are important in defining relationships between men and women.

Some have argued that fraternities are places where rape is likely to occur on college campuses (Martin and Hummer 1989; O'Sullivan 1993; Sanday 1990) and that the students most likely to accept rape myths and be more sexually aggressive are more likely to live in fraternities and sororities, consume higher doses of alcohol and drugs, and place a higher value on social life at college (Gwartney-Gibbs and Stockard 1989; Kalof and Cargill 1991). Others suggest that sexual aggression is learned in settings such as fraternities and is not part of predispositions or preexisting attitudes (Boeringer, Shehan, and Akers 1991). To prevent further incidences of rape on college campuses, we need to understand what it is about fraternities in particular and college life in general that may contribute to the maintenance of a rape culture on college campuses.

Our approach is to identify the social contexts that link fraternities to campus rape and promote a rape culture. Instead of assuming that all fraternities provide an environment conducive to rape, we compare the interactions of men and women at fraternities identified on campus as being especially *dangerous* places for women, where the likelihood of rape is high, to those seen as *safer* places, where the perceived probability of rape occurring is lower. Prior to collecting data for our study, we found that most women students identified some fraternities as having more sexually aggressive members and a higher probability of rape. These women also considered other fraternities as relatively safe houses, where a woman could go and get drunk if she wanted to and feel secure that the fraternity men would not take advantage of her.

We compared parties at houses identified as high-risk and low-risk houses as well as at two local bars frequented by college students. Our analysis provides an opportunity to examine situations and contexts that hinder or facilitate positive social relations between undergraduate men and women.

The abusive attitudes toward women that some fraternities perpetuate exist within a general culture where rape is intertwined in traditional gender scripts. Men are viewed as initiators of sex and women as either passive partners or active resisters, preventing men from touching their bodies (LaPlante, McCormick, and Brannigan 1980). Rape culture is based on the assumptions that men are aggressive and dominant whereas women are passive and acquiescent (Buchwald, Fletcher, and Roth 1993; Herman 1984). What occurs on college campuses is an extension of the portrayal of domination and aggression of men over women that exemplifies the double standard of sexual behavior in U.S. society (Barthel 1988; Kimmel 1993).

Sexually active men are positively reinforced by being referred to as "studs," whereas women who are sexually active or report enjoying sex are derogatorily labeled as "sluts" (Herman 1984; O'Sullivan 1993). These gender scripts are embodied in rape myths and stereotypes such as "She really wanted it; she just said no because she didn't want me to think she was a bad girl" (Burke, Stets, and Pirog-Good 1989; Jenkins and Dambrot 1987; Lisak and Roth 1988; Malamuth 1986; Muehlenhard and Linton 1987; Peterson and Franzese 1987). Because men's sexuality is seen as more natural, acceptable, and uncontrollable than women's sexuality, many men and women excuse acquaintance rape by affirming that men cannot control their natural urges (Miller and Marshall 1987).

Whereas some researchers explain these attitudes toward sexuality and rape using an individual or a psychological interpretation, we argue that rape has a social basis, one in which both men and women create and recreate masculine and feminine identities and relations. Based on the assumption that rape is part of the social construction of gender, we examine how men and women "do gender" on a college campus (West and Zimmerman 1987). We focus on fraternities because they have been identified as settings that encourage rape (Sanday 1990). By comparing fraternities that are viewed by women as places where there is a high risk of rape to those where women believe there is a low risk of rape as well as two local commercial bars, we seek to identify characteristics that make some social settings more likely places for the occurrence of rape.

Results

The Settings

Fraternity Parties   We observed several differences in the quality of the interaction of men and women at parties at high-risk fraternities compared to those at low-risk houses. A typical party at a low-risk house included an equal number of women and men. The social atmosphere was friendly, with considerable interaction between women and men. Men and women danced in groups and in couples, with many of the couples kissing and displaying affection toward each other. Brothers explained that, because many of the men in these houses had girlfriends, it was normal to see couples kissing on the dance floor. Coed groups engaged in conversations at many of these houses, with women and men engaging in friendly exchanges, giving the impression that they knew each other well. Almost no cursing and yelling was observed at parties in low-risk houses; when pushing occurred, the participants apologized. Respect for women extended to the women's bathrooms, which were clean and well supplied.

At high-risk houses, parties typically had skewed gender ratios, sometimes involving more men and other times involving more women. Gender segregation also was evident at these parties, with the men on one side of a room or in the bar drinking while women gathered in another area. Men treated women differently in the high-risk houses. The women's bathrooms in the high-risk houses were filthy, including clogged toilets and vomit in the sinks. When a brother was told of the mess in the bathroom at a high-risk house, he replied: *Good, maybe some of these beer wenches will leave so there will be more beer for us.*

Men attending parties at high-risk houses treated women less respectfully, engaging in jokes, conversations, and behaviors that degraded women. Men made a display of assessing women's bodies and rated them with thumbs up or thumbs down for the other men in the sight of the women. One man attending a party at a high-risk fraternity said to another: *Did you know that this week is Women's Awareness Week? I guess that means we get to abuse them more this week.* Men behaved more crudely at parties at high-risk houses. At one party, a brother dropped his pants, including his underwear, while dancing in front of several women. Another brother slid across the dance floor completely naked.

The atmosphere at parties in high-risk fraternities was less friendly overall. With the exception of greetings, men and women rarely smiled or laughed and spoke to each other less often than was the case at parties in low-risk houses. The few one-on-one conversations between women and men appeared to be strictly flirtatious (lots of eye contact, touching, and very close talking). It was rare to see a group of men and women together talking. Men were openly hostile, which made the high-risk parties seem almost threatening at times. For example, there was a lot of touching, pushing, profanity, and name calling, some done by women.

Students at parties at the high-risk houses seemed self-conscious and aware of the presence of members of the opposite sex, an awareness that was sexually charged. Dancing early in the evening was usually between women. Close to midnight, the sex ratio began to balance out with the arrival of more men or more women. Couples began to dance together but in a sexual way (close dancing with lots of pelvic thrusts). Men tried to pick up women using lines such as *Want to see my fish tank?* and *Let's go upstairs so that we can talk; I can't hear what you're saying in here.*

Although many of the same people who attended high-risk parties also attended low-risk parties, their behavior changed as they moved from setting to setting. Group norms differed across contexts as well. At a party that was held jointly at a low-risk house with a high-risk fraternity, the ambience was that of a party at a high-risk fraternity with heavier drinking, less dancing, and fewer conversations between women and men. The men from both high- and low-risk fraternities were very aggressive; a fight broke out, and there was pushing and shoving on the dance floor and in general.

As others have found, fraternity brothers at high-risk houses on this campus told about routinely discussing their sexual exploits at breakfast the morning after parties and sometimes at house meetings (cf. Martin and Hummer 1989; O'Sullivan 1993; Sanday 1990). During these sessions, the brothers we interviewed said that men bragged about what they did the night before with stories of sexual conquests often told by the same men, usually sophomores. The women involved in these exploits were women they did not know or knew but did not respect, or *faceless victims*. Men usually treated girlfriends with respect and did not talk about them in these storytelling sessions. Men from low-risk houses, however, did not describe similar sessions in their houses.

The Bar Scene　　The bar atmosphere and social context differed from those of fraternity parties. The music was not as loud, and both bars had places to sit and have conversations. At all fraternity parties, it was difficult to maintain conversations with loud music playing and no place to sit. The volume of music at parties at high-risk fraternities was even louder than it was at low-risk houses, making it virtually impossible to have conversations. In general, students in the local bars behaved in the same way that students did at parties in low-risk houses with conversations typical, most occurring between men and women.

The first bar, frequented by older students, had live entertainment every night of the week. Some nights were more crowded than others, and the atmosphere was friendly, relaxed, and conducive to conversation. People laughed and smiled and behaved politely toward each other. The ratio of men to women was fairly equal, with students congregating in mostly coed groups. Conversation flowed freely and people listened to each other.

Although the women and men at the first bar also were at parties at low- and high-risk fraternities, their behavior at the bar included none of the blatant sexual or intoxicated behaviors observed at some of these parties. As the evenings wore on, the number of one-on-one conversations between men and women increased and conversations shifted from small talk to topics such as war and AIDS. Conversations did not revolve around picking up another person, and most people left the bar with same-sex friends or in coed groups.

The second bar was less popular with older students. Younger students, often under the legal drinking age, went there to drink, sometimes after leaving campus parties. This bar was much smaller and usually not as crowded as the first bar. The atmosphere was more mellow and relaxed than it was at the fraternity parties. People went there to hang out and talk to each other.

On a couple of occasions, however, the atmosphere at the second bar became similar to that of a party at a high-risk fraternity. As the number of people in the bar increased, they removed chairs and tables, leaving no place to sit and talk. The music also was turned up louder, drowning out conversation. With no place to dance or sit, most people stood around but could not maintain conversations because of the noise and crowds. Interactions between women and men consisted mostly of flirting. Alcohol consumption also was greater than it was on the less crowded nights, and the number of visibly drunk people increased. The more people drank, the more conversation and socializing broke down. The only differences between this setting and that of a party at a high-risk house were that brothers no longer controlled the territory and bedrooms were not available upstairs.

Gender Relations

Relations between women and men are shaped by the contexts in which they meet and interact. As is the case on other college campuses, *hooking up* has replaced dating on this campus, and fraternities are places where many students hook up. Hooking up is a loosely applied term on college campuses that had different meanings for men and women on this campus.

Most men defined hooking up similarly. One man said it was something that happens

> *when you're really drunk and meet up with a woman you sort of know, or possibly don't know at all and don't care about. You go home with her with the intention of getting as much sexual, physical pleasure as she'll give you, which can range anywhere from kissing to intercourse, without any strings attached.*

The exception to this rule is when men hook up with women they admire. Men said they are less likely to press for sexual activity with someone they know and like because they want the relationship to continue and be based on respect.

Women's version of hooking up differed. Women said they hook up only with men they cared about and described hooking up as kissing and petting but not sexual intercourse. Many women said that hooking up was disappointing because they wanted longer-term relationships. First-year women students realized quickly that hook-ups were usually one-night stands with no strings attached, but many continued to hook up because they had few opportunities to develop relationships with men on campus. One first-year woman said: *70 percent of hook-ups never talk again and try to avoid one another; 26 percent may actually hear from them or talk to them again, and 4 percent may actually go on a date, which can lead to a relationship.* Another first-year woman said: *It was fun in the beginning. You get a lot of attention and kiss a lot of boys and think this is what college is about, but it gets tiresome fast.*

Whereas first-year women get tired of the hook-up scene early on, many men do not become bored with it until their junior or senior year. As one upperclassman said: *The whole game of hooking up became really meaningless and tiresome for me during my second semester of my sophomore year, but most of my friends didn't get bored with it until the following year.*

In contrast to hooking up, students also described monogamous relationships with steady partners. Some type of commitment was expected, but most people did not anticipate marriage. The term *seeing each other* was applied when people were sexually involved but free to date other people. This type of relationship involved less commitment than did one of boyfriend/girlfriend but was not considered to be a hook-up.

The general consensus of women and men interviewed on this campus was that the Greek system, called "the hill," set the scene for gender relations. The predominance of Greek membership and subsequent living arrangements segregated men and women. During the week, little interaction occurred between women and men after their first year in college because students in fraternities or sororities live and dine in separate quarters. In addition, many non-Greek upper-class students move off campus into apartments. Therefore, students see each other in classes or in the library, but there is no place where students can just hang out together.

Both men and women said that fraternities dominate campus social life, a situation that everyone felt limited opportunities for meaningful interactions. One senior Greek man said:

> *This environment is horrible and so unhealthy for good male and female relationships and interactions to occur. It is so segregated and male dominated. . . . It is our party, with our rules and our beer. We are allowing these women and other men to come to our party. Men can feel superior in their domain.*

Comments from a senior woman reinforced his views: *Men are dominant; they are the kings of the campus. It is their environment that they allow us to enter; therefore, we have to abide by their rules.* A junior woman described fraternity parties as

> *good for meeting acquaintances but almost impossible to really get to know anyone. The environment is so superficial, probably because there are so many social cliques due to the Greek system. Also, the music is too loud and the people are too drunk to attempt to have a real conversation, anyway.*

Some students claim that fraternities even control the dating relationships of their members. One senior woman said: *Guys dictate how dating occurs on this campus, whether it's cool, who it's with, how much time can be spent with the girlfriend and with the brothers.* Couples either left campus for an evening or hung out separately with their own same-gender friends at fraternity parties, finally getting together with each other at about 2 A.M. Couples rarely went together to fraternity parties. Some men felt that a girlfriend was just a replacement for a hook-up. According to one junior man: *Basically a girlfriend is someone you go to at 2 A.M. after you've hung out with the guys. She is the sexual outlet that the guys can't provide you with.*

Some fraternity brothers pressure each other to limit their time with and commitment to their girlfriends. One senior man said: *The hill [fraternities] and girlfriends don't mix.* A brother described a constant battle between girlfriends and brothers over who the guy is going out with for the night, with the brothers usually winning. Brothers teased men with girlfriends with remarks such as "whipped" or "where's the ball and chain?" A brother from a high-risk house said that few brothers at his house had girlfriends; some did, but it was uncommon. One man said that from the minute he was a pledge he knew he would probably never have a girlfriend on this campus because *it was just not the norm in my house. No one has girlfriends; the guys have too much fun with [each other].*

The pressure on men to limit their commitment to girlfriends, however, was not true of all fraternities or of all men on campus. Couples attended low-risk fraternity parties together, and men in the low-risk houses went out on dates more often. A man in one low-risk house said that about 70 percent of the members of his house were involved in relationships with women, including the pledges (who were sophomores).

Treatment of Women

Not all men held negative attitudes toward women that are typical of a rape culture, and not all social contexts promoted the negative treatment of women. When men were asked whether they treated the women on campus with respect, the most common response was "On an individual basis, yes, but when you have a group of men together, no." Men said that, when together in groups with other men, they sensed a pressure to be disrespectful toward women. A first-year man's perception of the treatment of women was that *they are treated with more respect to their faces, but behind closed doors, with a group of men present, respect for women is not an issue.* One senior man stated: *In general, college-aged men don't treat women their age with respect because 90 percent of them think of women as merely a means to sex.* Women reinforced this perception. A first-year woman stated: *Men here are more interested in hooking up and drinking beer than they are in getting to know women as real people.* Another woman said: *Men here use and abuse women.*

Characteristic of rape culture, a double standard of sexual behavior for men versus women was prevalent on this campus. As one Greek senior man stated: *Women who sleep around are sluts and get bad reputations; men who do are champions and get a pat on the back from their brothers.* Women also supported a double standard for sexual behavior by criticizing sexually active women. A first-year woman spoke out against women who are sexually active: *I think some girls here make it difficult for the men to respect women as a whole.*

One concrete example of demeaning sexually active women on this campus is the "walk of shame." Fraternity brothers come out on the porches of their houses the morning after parties and heckle women walking by. It is assumed that these women spent the night at fraternity houses and that the men they were with did not care enough about them to drive them home. Although sororities now reside in former fraternity houses, this practice continues and sometimes the victims of hecklings are sorority women on their way to study in the library.

A junior man in a high-risk fraternity described another ritual of disrespect toward women called "chatter." When an unknown woman sleeps over at the house, the brothers yell degrading remarks out the window at her as she leaves the next morning such as "Fuck that bitch" and "Who is that slut?" He said that sometimes brothers harass the brothers whose girlfriends stay over instead of heckling those women.

Fraternity men most often mistreated women they did not know personally. Men and women alike reported incidents in which brothers observed other brothers having sex with unknown women or women they knew only casually. A sophomore woman's experience exemplifies this anonymous state: *I don't mind if 10 guys were watching or it was videotaped. That's expected on this campus. It's the fact that he didn't apologize or even offer to drive me home that really upset me.* Descriptions of sexual encounters involved the satisfaction of men by nameless women. A brother in a high-risk fraternity described a similar occurrence:

> *A brother of mine was hooking up upstairs with an unattractive woman who had been pursuing him all night. He told some brothers to go outside the window and watch. Well, one thing led to another and they were almost completely naked when the woman noticed the brothers outside. She was then unwilling to go any further, so the brother went outside and yelled at the other brothers and then closed the shades. I don't know if he scored or not, because the woman was pretty upset. But he did win the award for hooking up with the ugliest chick that weekend.*

Attitudes toward Rape

The sexually charged environment of college campuses raises many questions about cultures that facilitate the rape of women. How women and men define their sexual behavior is important legally as well as interpersonally. We asked students how they defined rape and had them compare it to the following legal definition: the perpetration of an act of sexual intercourse with a female against her will and consent, whether her will is overcome by force or fear resulting from the threat of force, or by drugs or intoxicants; or when, because of mental deficiency, she is incapable of exercising rational judgment. (Brownmiller 1975:368)

When presented with this legal definition, most women interviewed recognized it as well as the complexities involved in applying it. A first-year woman said: *If a girl is drunk and the guy knows it and the girl says, "Yes, I want to have sex," and they do, that is still rape because the girl can't make a conscious, rational decision under the influence of alcohol.* Some women disagreed. Another first-year woman stated: *I don't think it is fair that the guy gets blamed when both people involved are drunk.*

The typical definition men gave for rape was "when a guy jumps out of the bushes and forces himself sexually onto a girl." When asked what date rape was, the most common answer was "when one person has sex with another person who did not consent." Many men said, however, that "date rape is when a woman wakes up the next morning and regrets having sex." Some men said that date rape was too gray an area to define. *Consent is a fine line,* said a Greek senior man student. For the most part, the men we spoke with argued that rape did not occur on this campus. One Greek sophomore man said: *I think it is ridiculous that someone here would rape someone.* A first-year man stated: *I have a problem with the word rape. It sounds so criminal, and we are not criminals; we are sane people.*

Whether aware of the legal definitions of rape, most men resisted the idea that a woman who is intoxicated is unable to consent to sex. A Greek junior man said: *Men should not be responsible for women's drunkenness.* One first-year man said: *If that is the legal definition of rape, then it happens all the time on this campus.* A senior man said: *I don't care whether alcohol is involved or not; that is not rape. Rapists are people that have something seriously wrong with them.* A first-year man even claimed that when women get drunk, they invite sex. He said: *Girls get so drunk here and then come on to us. What are we supposed to do? We are only human.*

Discussion and Conclusion

These findings describe the physical and normative aspects of one college campus as they relate to attitudes about and relations between men and women. Our findings suggest that an explanation emphasizing rape culture also must focus on those characteristics of the social setting that play a role in defining heterosexual relationships on college campuses (Kalof and Cargill 1991). The degradation of women as portrayed in rape culture was not found in all fraternities on this campus. Both group norms and individual behavior changed as students went from one place to another. Although individual men are the ones who rape, we found that some settings are more likely places for rape than are others. Our findings suggest that rape cannot be seen only as an isolated act and blamed on individual behavior and proclivities, whether it be alcohol consumption or attitudes. We also must consider characteristics of the settings that promote the behaviors that reinforce a rape culture.

Relations between women and men at parties in low-risk fraternities varied considerably from those in high-risk houses. Peer pressure and situational norms influenced women as well as men. Although many men in high- and low-risk houses shared similar views and attitudes about the Greek system, women on this campus, and date rape, their behaviors at fraternity parties were quite different.

Women who are at highest risk of rape are women whom fraternity brothers did not know. These women are faceless victims, nameless acquaintances— not friends. Men said their responsibility to such persons and the level of guilt they feel later if the hook-ups end in sexual intercourse are much lower if they hook up with women they do not know. In high-risk houses, brothers treated women as subordinates and kept them at a distance. Men in high-risk houses actively discouraged ongoing heterosexual relationships, routinely degraded women, and participated more fully in the hook-up scene; thus, the probability that women would become faceless victims was higher in these houses. The flirtatious nature of the parties indicated that women go to these parties looking for available men, but finding boyfriends or relationships was difficult at parties in high-risk houses. However, in the low-risk houses, where more men had long-term relationships, the women were not strangers and were less likely to become faceless victims.

The social scene on this campus, and on most others, offers women and men few other options to socialize. Although there may be no such thing as a completely safe fraternity party for women, parties at low-risk houses and commercial bars encouraged men and women to get to know each other better and decreased the probability that women would become faceless victims. Although both men and women found the social scene on this campus demeaning, neither demanded different settings for socializing, and attendance at fraternity parties is a common form of entertainment.

These findings suggest that a more conducive environment for conversation can promote more positive interactions between men and women. Simple changes would provide the opportunity for men and women to interact in meaningful ways such as adding places to sit and lowering the volume of music at fraternity parties or having parties in neutral locations, where men are not in control. The typical party room in fraternity houses includes a place to dance but not to sit and talk. The music often is loud, making it difficult, if not impossible, to carry on conversations; however, there were more conversations at the low-risk parties, where there also was more respect shown toward women. Although the number of brothers who had steady girlfriends in the low-risk houses as compared to those in the high-risk houses may explain the differences, we found that commercial bars also provided a context for interaction between men and women. At the bars, students sat and talked and conversations between men and women flowed freely, resulting in deep discussions and fewer hook-ups.

Alcohol consumption was a major focus of social events here and intensified attitudes and orientations of a rape culture. Although pressure to drink was evident at all fraternity parties and at both bars, drinking dominated high-risk fraternity parties, at which nonalcoholic beverages usually were not available and people chugged beers and became visibly drunk. A rape culture is strengthened by rules that permit alcohol only at fraternity parties. Under this system, men control the parties and dominate the men as well as the women who attend. As college administrators crack down on fraternities and alcohol on campus, however, the same behaviors and norms may transfer to other places such as parties in apartments or private homes where administrators have much less control. At commercial bars, interaction and socialization with others were as important as drinking, with the exception of the nights when the bar frequented by under-class students became crowded. Although one solution is to offer nonalcoholic social activities, such events receive little support on this campus. Either these alternative events lacked the prestige of the fraternity parties or the alcohol was seen as necessary to unwind, or both.

In many ways, the fraternities on this campus determined the settings in which men and women interacted. As others before us have found, pressures for conformity to the norms and values exist at both high-risk and low-risk houses (Kalof and Cargill 1991; Martin and Hummer 1989; Sanday 1990). The desire to be accepted is not unique to this campus or the Greek system (Holland and Eisenhart 1990; Horowitz 1988; Moffat 1989). The degree of conformity required by Greeks may be greater than that required in most social groups, with considerable pressure to adopt and maintain the image of their houses. The fraternity system intensifies the "groupthink syndrome" (Janis 1972) by solidifying the identity of the in-group and creating an us vs. them atmosphere. Within the fraternity culture, brothers are highly regarded and women are viewed as outsiders. For men in high-risk fraternities, women threatened their brotherhood; therefore, brothers discouraged relationships and harassed those who treated women as equals or with respect. The pressure to be one of the guys and hang out with the guys strengthens a rape culture on college campus by demeaning women and encouraging the segregation of men and women.

Students on this campus were aware of the contexts in which they operated and the choices available to them. They recognized that, in their interactions, they created differences between men and women that are not natural, essential, or biological (West and Zimmerman 1987). Not all men and women accepted the demeaning treatment of women, but they continued to participate in behaviors that supported aspects of a rape culture. Many women participated in the hook-up scene even after they had been humiliated and hurt because they had few other means of initiating contact with men on campus. Men and women alike played out this scene, recognizing its injustices in many cases but being unable to change the course of their behaviors.

Although this research provides some clues to gender relations on college campuses, it raises many questions. Why do men and women participate in activities that support a rape culture when they see its injustices? What would happen if alcohol were not controlled by groups of men who admit that they disrespect women when they get together? What can be done to give men and women on college campuses more opportunities to interact responsibly and get to know each other better? These questions should be studied on other campuses with a focus on the social settings in which the incidence of rape and the attitudes that support a rape culture exist. Fraternities are social contexts that may or may not foster a rape culture.

Our findings indicate that a rape culture exists in some fraternities, especially those we identified as high-risk houses. College administrators are responding to this situation by providing counseling and educational programs that increase awareness of date rape, including campaigns such as "No means no." These strategies are important in changing attitudes, values, and behaviors; however, changing individuals is not enough. The structure of campus life and the impact of that structure on gender relations on campus are highly determinative. To eliminate campus rape culture, student leaders and administrators must examine the situations in which women and men meet and restructure these settings to provide opportunities for respectful interaction. Change may not require abolishing fraternities; rather, it may require promoting settings that facilitate positive gender relations.

REFERENCES

Barthel, D. 1988. *Putting on Appearances: Gender and Advertising.* Philadelphia: Temple University Press.

Boeringer, S. B., C. L. Shehan, and R. L. Akers. 1991. "Social Contexts and Social Learning in Sexual Coercion and Aggression: Assessing the Contribution of Fraternity Membership." *Family Relations* 40:58–64.

Brownmiller, S. 1975. *Against Our Will: Men, Women and Rape.* New York: Simon & Schuster.

Buchwald, E., P. R. Fletcher, and M. Roth, eds. 1993. *Transforming a Rape Culture.* Minneapolis, MN: Milkweed Editions.

Burke, P., J. E. Stets, and M. A. Pirog-Good. 1989. "Gender Identity, Self-Esteem, Physical Abuse and Sexual Abuse in Dating Relationships." In *Violence in Dating Relationships: Emerging Social Issues,* edited by M. A. Pirog-Good and J. E. Stets. New York: Praeger.

Gwartney-Gibbs, P. and J. Stockard. 1989. "Courtship Aggression and Mixed-Sex Peer Groups." In *Violence in Dating Relationships: Emerging Social Issues,* edited by M. A. Pirog-Good and J. E. Stets. New York: Praeger.

Herman, D. 1984. "The Rape Culture." In *Women: A Feminist Perspective,* edited by J. Freeman. Mountain View, CA: Mayfield.

Holland, D. C. and M. A. Eisenhart. 1990. *Educated in Romance: Women, Achievement, and College Culture.* Chicago: University of Chicago Press.

Horowitz, H. I. 1988. *Campus Life: Undergraduate Cultures from the End of the 18th Century to the Present.* Chicago: University of Chicago Press.

Janis, I. L. 1972. *Victims of Groupthink.* Boston: Houghton Mifflin.

Jenkins, M. J. and F. H. Dambrot. 1987. "The Attribution of Date Rape: Observer's Attitudes and Sexual Experiences and the Dating Situation." *Journal of Applied Social Psychology* 17:875–95.

Kalof, I. and T. Cargill. 1991. "Fraternity and Sorority Membership and Gender Dominance Attitudes." *Sex Roles* 25:417–23.

Kimmel, M. S. 1993. "Clarence, William, Iron Mike, Tailhook, Senator Packwood, Spur Posse, Magic . . . and Us." In *Transforming a Rape Culture,* edited by E. Buchwald, P. R. Fletcher, and M. Roth. Minneapolis, MN: Milkweed Editions.

Koss, M. P., T. E. Dinero, C. A. Seibel, and S. L. Cox. 1988. "Stranger and Acquaintance Rape: Are There Differences in the Victim's Experience?" *Psychology of Women Quarterly* 12:1–24.

Koss, M. P., C. A. Gidycz, and N. Wisniewski. 1985. "The Scope of Rape: Incidence and Prevalence of Sexual Aggression and Victimization in a National Sample of Higher Education Students." *Journal of Consulting and Clinical Psychology* 55:162–70.

LaPlante, M. N., N. McCormick, and G. G. Brannigan. 1980. "Living the Sexual Script: College Students' Views of Influence in Sexual Encounters." *Journal of Sex Research* 16:338–55.

Lisak, D. and S. Roth. 1988. "Motivational Factors in Nonincarcerated Sexually Aggressive Men." *Journal of Personality and Social Psychology* 55:795–802.

Malamuth, N. 1986. "Predictors of Naturalistic Sexual Aggression." *Journal of Personality and Social Psychology* 50:953–62.

Martin, P. Y. and R. Hummer. 1989. "Fraternities and Rape on Campus." *Gender & Society* 3:457–73.

Miller, B. and J. C. Marshall. 1987. "Coercive Sex on the University Campus." *Journal of College Student Personnel* 28:38–47.

Moffat, M. 1989. *Coming of Age in New Jersey: College Life in American Culture.* New Brunswick, NJ: Rutgers University Press.

Muehlenhard, C. L. and M. A. Linton. 1987. "Date Rape and Sexual Aggression in Dating Situations: Incidence and Risk Factors." *Journal of Counseling Psychology* 34:186–96.

O'Sullivan, C. 1993. "Fraternities and the Rape Culture." In *Transforming a Rape Culture,* edited by E. Buchwald, P. R. Fletcher, and M. Roth. Minneapolis, MN: Milkweed Editions.

Peterson, S. A. and B. Franzese. 1987. "Correlates of College Men's Sexual Abuse of Women." *Journal of College Student Personnel* 28:223–28.

Sanday, P. R. 1990. *Fraternity Gang Rape: Sex, Brotherhood, and Privilege on Campus.* New York: New York University Press.

West, C. and D. Zimmerman. 1987. "Doing Gender." *Gender & Society* 1:125–51.

22

DESCENT INTO MADNESS
The New Mexico State Prison Riot

MARK COLVIN

One type of social deviance, according to sociologists, is crime. If *deviance* is the violation of a social norm, then a *crime* is the violation of social norms that have been made into laws. One type of social sanction that our society imposes on people found guilty of committing crimes is sentencing them to prison for various lengths of time. The United States has a high proportion of its population in prison compared to other countries, and many prisons are overcrowded and plagued with problems of violence and sexual assault. Sociologists have long studied the social structure and subcultures of prisons. This selection by Mark Colvin, professor and chair of Justice Studies at Kent State University, is written as the introduction to the 1997 book, *Descent into Madness: An Inmate's Experience of the New Mexico State Prison Riot* by Mike Rolland. Colvin was hired by the New Mexico attorney general's office to help with the investigation into the events and causes of the 1980 riot at the Penitentiary of New Mexico. In the excerpt that follows, Colvin provides important insights into the history and social structure of the prison and how the breakdown in that social structure enabled violence and disorganization to occur.

The riot at the Penitentiary of New Mexico (PNM) on February 2 and 3, 1980, is without parallel for its violence, destruction, and disorganization. During the 36 hours of the riot, 33 inmates were killed by other inmates; many of the victims were tortured and mutilated. (A 34th inmate died several months later from injuries he received during the riot.) As many as 200 inmates were severely injured from beatings, stabbings, and rapes. Many more suffered less serious injuries. In addition, scores of inmates were treated for overdoses of drugs taken from the prison's pharmacy during the riot. That more inmates did not die can be attributed to the dedicated work of medical personnel and emergency crews who treated the injured and transported them to local hospitals. In fact, many inmates were later surprised to learn of riot survivors whom they thought had certainly died during the event.

Seven of the 12 correctional officers who were taken hostage were beaten, stabbed, or sodomized. None of the hostages were killed. Some of the guard hostages were protected by small groups of inmates during the riot.

A few hostages were even assisted in leaving the prison during the riot by sympathetic inmates.

Correctional officers and many more inmates would have certainly died in the riot had it not been for heroic efforts of some prisoners who risked their lives to save others from harm. Indeed, this prison riot brought out not only the evil potential of human beings (upon which we tend to focus after such an event) but also the potential for virtue. We are quick to condemn the evil acts and use these as an excuse to label all prisoners as "animals." But to do so is to ignore the acts of kindness and courage displayed by many inmates; to ignore the fact that the overwhelming majority of inmates only wanted to escape the mayhem, the violence, and the fear; and to ignore the essential humanity of the great majority of the people we lock up in prisons. Focusing on the evil acts of those few prisoners who engaged in them also distracts us from the evil of a taxpayer-supported prison system that produces events like the New Mexico State Prison riot.

The riot caused $20 million in physical damage to the institution. Fires were started throughout the prison, and water flooded the prison water mains. More than $200 million in riot-related expenses were incurred by the state for medical, police, fire, and national guard response, lawsuits for injuries and wrongful death, transportation of inmates to federal and other state prison systems, prosecutions of crimes committed during the riot, and official investigations of the events and causes of the riot.

The official investigation of the riot was headed by then-Attorney General of New Mexico Jeff Bingaman. I was hired by the Attorney General as a principal researcher for the riot investigation. In that role, I, along with the riot investigation team, conducted more than 300 in-depth interviews with former and then-current prisoners, correctional officers, and corrections officials in an attempt to reconstruct the events of the riot and understand its long-term causes and effects. The riot investigation presented its findings and conclusions in a two-part report (Office of the Attorney General 1980a,b). More recently, I published a book that presents a detailed social and organizational history of the Penitentiary of New Mexico State Prison leading up to this riot (Colvin 1992). . . .

In this introduction, I hope to provide the reader with a context for understanding . . . the New Mexico State Prison riot. It is important to understand the history of this prison, since it was not always a violent and disorderly institution. It was only in the three to four years preceding the riot that the prison had moved toward becoming the type of violent and disorganized organization that could produce an event as brutal as the 1980 riot. . . .

Background of the Riot

The 1980 New Mexico State Prison riot stands in stark contrast to the 1971 Attica prison riot. At Attica, after a few hours of chaos and destruction in which three inmates were killed by other inmates, inmate leaders were able to take command of rioting inmates and turn the event into an organized protest about prison conditions; after that point, no other deaths occurred until state authorities violently retook the prison, killing 29 inmates and 10 guard hostages in the process (Wicker 1975). At New Mexico, inmate leaders, to the extent that there were any, were unable to organize inmates or stop the inmate-on-inmate violence. All inmates were killed by other inmates. No one was killed when state authorities retook the prison. The disorganization of the riot and the inmate-on-inmate killings, and the brutality of many of these killings, are what distinguish the New Mexico State Prison riot.

As stated, the Penitentiary of New Mexico (PNM) was not always a violent, disorganized prison. In fact, on July 14, 1976, inmates at this prison staged a well-organized, peaceful protest of prison conditions. In the previous six months, a new prison administration had begun dismantling prison programs and reducing inmate privileges. The curtailment of programs and special privileges soon led to an open confrontation between the new prison administration and inmates. Prisoners organized a massive sit-down strike in which nearly 800 of the prison's 912 inmates refused to leave their living quarters for work or meals. The level of participation in this 1976 strike demonstrated a high degree of solidarity and cooperation among inmates. There was no violence among inmates during this event. (In fact, no inmate had been killed by another inmate at this prison since before 1970.) The prison administration's response to this June 1976 inmate strike inaugurated a new era in staff and inmate relations and in relations among inmates. It was a new era characterized by coercion and violence.

The strike was broken by the staff with violence. Housing units were teargassed and many inmates were forced to run a gauntlet of prison staff members who were armed with ax handles (Office of the Attorney General 1980b; Colvin 1992). Leaders of the strike were identified and segregated or transferred out of state. The stable inmate leadership, which had been the impetus for inmate social cohesion, was thus systematically eliminated. The prison staff, after this point, began to rely increasingly on coercion to maintain control of the institution. The "hole," which had been closed since 1968, was reopened and used frequently; the number of inmates in disciplinary segregation grew substantially (from less than 5 percent of the inmate population before June 1976 to as much as 25 percent of the inmate population after June 1976).

As this crackdown on organized inmate activity continued at the prison, the corrections department was undergoing rapid and confusing organizational changes. Turnover in the state's top corrections post occurred repeatedly, with five different heads of the corrections department between 1975 and 1980. A similar turnover in the warden's position took place, with five penitentiary wardens between 1975 and 1980. This administrative confusion resulted in inconsistent policy directives from the top of the organization and in the emergence of a middle-level clique of administrators who were virtually unaccountable to anyone in authority. This clique of administrators, by the middle of 1978, had been left to run the prison in any fashion they saw fit.

Under this middle-level clique, there were growing inconsistencies in both security procedures and discipline of inmates. Some shift supervisors followed very closely the proper security procedures; others did not follow them at all. Lax security had long been a problem at PNM, but the tendency toward inconsistency in security operations worsened after 1978 when various shift supervisors ran the prison at their own discretion. Similar problems of inconsistency in discipline were also evident. Some shift captains would enforce rules, at times inappropriately placing inmates in the "hole" for minor violations, while other shift captains would fail to punish some major violations of rules. Consistency in operation and a set routine provides stability for an institution. At PNM, it was difficult for inmates to calculate which behaviors would be punished or when they would be punished. Inmates were thus kept off balance.

This inconsistency by the prison staff was often interpreted by inmates as blatant harassment. In some cases, correctional officers, including some lieutenants and captains, were caught up in a game of mutual harassment with inmates. The game proceeded through interactions in which an officer would verbally humiliate an inmate and the inmate would respond in kind. Often this led to confrontations in which the inmate was led off to disciplinary segregation. The minority of prison officers who engaged in these activities poisoned relations between the staff and inmates and created enormous hostility.

As the middle-level administrators gained dominance after 1978, a new coercive "snitch system" emerged. This system had its roots in the aftermath of the June 1976 inmate strike when staff members attempted to identify the strike leaders. Inmates were threatened with disciplinary lockup if they did not identify strike participants and leaders. By 1978, these tactics had become a key aspect of the institution's inmate control system. Since inmates were not forthcoming with voluntary information, many members of the correctional staff began soliciting information through threats and promises. Inmates were promised early parole consideration, protection, and transfer to minimum-security institutions. They were also threatened with being locked up in disciplinary segregation or, in other cases, were refused protective custody if they did not inform. Another coercive tactic was to intimidate an inmate by threatening to "hang a snitch jacket" on him. This tactic, which involved the threat of labeling an inmate a "snitch" (or informant) was used to solicit information, gain control over an inmate, and, in some instances, retaliate against an inmate.

This came to be known as the "snitch game." The "snitch game" had the effect of breaking apart any sense of inmate solidarity. . . .

Some inmates labeled as "snitches" may not have been informants at all. Correctional officers discussed with Attorney General investigators the labeling of inmates as "snitches" as a coercive tactic (quoted in Colvin 1992:154).

Correctional Officer: *If I was a guard and he was an inmate and I didn't like him, I'd punch him around and say, "Hey, man, let's put a snitch jacket on this guy." And another inmate come up behind me and I'd say, "Hey man, this*

*dude dropped a dime on this guy over here." They'll put a "jacket" on you and
life expectancy with a "jacket" on you isn't too long. . . .*

Interviewer: What was the purpose of doing this?

Correctional Officer: *To get even. . . . If I was to walk up to an inmate and
just started kicking the hell out of him, I would have a lawsuit on me, but what
goes on behind closed doors, only the inmates know.*

Whether an inmate had actually been an informant or not, the label of
"snitch" could have deadly consequences, a fact that was used to intimidate inmates and create friction among prisoners. After inmate solidarity
displayed during the June 1976 strike moved the prison administration to
smash inmate organization and leadership, the inmate society became
more fragmented and violent. From 1969 through July 1976 there were no
killings at PNM, no prison officers were attacked, and inmate fights and
sexual assaults were rare. From August 1976 to January 1980, six inmates
were killed by other inmates, several attacks on prison officers occurred,
and fighting among inmates became routine. And sexual assaults, by the
late 1970s, had become so routine that there was "at least one reported case
a day [and] 10 to 15 more nonreported cases daily" (*Albuquerque Journal,*
9/16/79:B1).

The administration's tactics for breaking up inmate solidarity led to a
series of changes within the inmate society that spawned violence and disorder. As inmate groups broke down into small, self-protective cliques,
forces within the inmate society that formerly were capable of holding back
disorder and violence among inmates diminished. The lack of inmate leaders in the late 1970s meant that new inmates entering PNM were no longer
under the restraints of an established order among inmates. Inmates could
no longer socialize new arrivals to the increasingly unstable environment.
Some of the new inmates directly challenged the power and control
exercised by older inmates who had not already been removed by the
administration.

While many observers relate the growing inmate violence to newly
arriving inmates, it does not appear that the violent behavior was being imported from outside. Rather, new inmates, as never before, were entering a
disorganized social situation with undefined roles and lack of leadership.
As they confronted, and were confronted by, this increasingly chaotic situation, many of the new inmates resorted to violence. . . .

Rather than importing the violence, inmates were becoming more violent
in reaction to a prison social structure that elicited such a response. With a
paucity of inmate leaders to guide and ease the transition to prison life for
younger inmates, these new inmates were left to their own devices to deal
with the fear of assault. By 1978, the fear of being assaulted, especially of being
sexually attacked, had become a prevalent feature of inmate life, especially for
younger inmates. These new inmates were faced with a deadly dilemma that
increasingly set the tone of inmate relations in the late 1970s. The fear created
by violent confrontations, or by the mere anticipation of them, produced

inmates who either submitted to the exploitation of other inmates (became "punks"), sought protection from officials (became "snitches"), or fought (to prove themselves as "good people" to other inmates by developing a reputation as violent). Most inmates agreed that the only rational choice when faced with the irrational confrontation of a sexual assault was to fight viciously and develop a reputation as someone who others "did not mess with." The other choices, submission or official protection, would lead to a prison experience of perpetual victimization.

In the late 1970s, confrontational situations among inmates sharply increased, forcing more inmates into the deadly dilemma of choosing a course of action against assaults. Some submitted and were marked as punks or homosexuals. This submission did not label them necessarily as sexual deviants but, more importantly, as "morally weak" individuals who would not stand up for themselves. Inmates who chose to seek protective custody, who in the inmates' vocabulary "pc'd up," were also seen as "weak" inmates who could not withstand the pressures of prison life. Added to being marked as weak was the stigma of being a snitch, since it was widely believed among inmates (though by no means always true) that protective custody was a payoff for informing. For "regular" inmates who were "on line" standing up for themselves in the daily battles with other inmates and the prison staff, an inmate who gives in to pressure from other inmates by not standing up for himself, and then gives in to pressure from the administration by informing, was truly a person of "weak moral character." A snitch label (whether deserved or not) thus implies the weakest of inmates who were so low as to sell out their fellow inmates because of fear and intimidation. These inmates were allowing both other inmates *and* the administration to humiliate them. Succumbing to other people's attempts at humiliation is the worst possible fate for a convict (Abbott 1981). Fear of humiliation drove much of the violence in the inmate society. Violent confrontations were events in which inmates' characters ("weak" or "strong") were being tested. They were also situations in which reputations for violence were being built.

Developing a reputation for violence became a full-time activity as a growing number of inmates were confronted by the prison's deadly dilemma. As inmates vied for violent reputations, the number of confrontational incidents between inmates increased. This competition for violent reputations accelerated the cycle of confrontations and produced a growing number of both violence-prone inmates and those who were perceived as weak. Under these circumstances, the struggle involved in relegating inmates to the roles of victims or victimizers became a monotonous, horrifying, daily occurrence.

The violence led to further fragmentation of the inmate society. Inmates increasingly formed into small cliques for self-protection. These cliques did not constitute the types of gang structures witnessed in other prisons (Irwin 1980; Jacobs 1977). For the most part, these cliques were very loosely organized groupings that provided inmates small, often temporary, "ecological niches" (Hagel-Seymour 1988) relatively free from the violence of the prison.

Some inmate groups began to emerge as influential in 1978. The ACLU lawsuit against PNM (*Duran v. Apodaca*) gave a few Chicano inmates a limited leadership role within some inmate factions. . . .

Other inmate cliques gained power by 1978 because of their violent reputations. In 1976 and 1977, Anglo convicts were very disorganized and were regularly attacked by Chicano inmates. Then, some strong Anglo cliques began to surface in 1977. One of the more notorious cliques was associated with three Anglo inmates who, on April 16, 1978, beat another Anglo inmate to death with a baseball bat for allegedly being a snitch. This clique emerged as an important power that struggled with other inmate cliques for dominance.

The inmates caught up in the competition for dominance and violent reputations composed PNM's hardcore cliques. While the total number of inmates involved in these hardcore cliques was about 150 of the more than 1,000 inmates in the prison, their behavior and disruptiveness set the tone for inmate social relations. In stark contrast to the early 1970s, when inmate leaders helped keep the lid on violence among inmates, inmate leadership, to the extent that it existed at all, fell by 1979 to these small, hardcore cliques of inmates who actively engaged in violence and disruption. These hardcore cliques, produced inadvertently by the administration's coercive tactics used to break up inmate solidarity, were leading the inmate society toward an implosion of violence. Inmate solidarity had indeed been eliminated by 1980. But the administration's control of the prison was now more precarious than ever. Their coercive tactics, including use of the "snitch game," produced a fragmented inmate society that promoted inmate-on-inmate violence. The riot that exploded at 1:40 A.M. on February 2, 1980, would reflect this fragmented inmate society and the coercive tactics of control that produced an inmate society.

Overview of the 1980 Riot at the Penitentiary of New Mexico

There were a number of forewarnings that a major disturbance was imminent, yet no decisive actions were taken. Forewarnings included a mix of rumors and intelligence, none of which could be confirmed. Officials had no way to distinguish reliable from unreliable information, a legacy of the coercive snitch system which often resulted in inmates telling officials anything (whether true or not) to escape punishment or receive protection. As it turned out, among the many rumors was one specific bit of information, concerning a possible hostage-taking, that was an accurate forewarning.

Shortly after midnight, on February 2, 1980, the evening and morning shifts completed a count of inmates in the institution, which held 1,157 inmates that night, including 34 in a modular unit outside the main penitentiary building. All inmates were accounted for at the time of the count. About 1 A.M., two groups composed of four correctional officers each began a routine check of all cellhouses and dormitories in the south wing of the prison.

At 1:40 A.M., one group, which included the shift captain, entered Dorm E-2, the upstairs dormitory in the E-wing.

Inmates in Dorm E-2 had been drinking "home brew" made of yeast and raisins smuggled in from the prison's kitchen. The inmates, sometime between 12:30 A.M. and 1:15 A.M., had hastily agreed upon a plan to jump the guards during their routine check of the dorm. It was not clear whether the plan included an attempt to exit the dormitory. Hostages would be taken in the dormitory; and if the entry door could be successfully jumped, additional hostages would be taken in the south wing of the prison. Beyond the plan to take some guards hostage, the inmates had no idea of what they would do next.

At 1:40 A.M., the dormitory door and the three officers who had just entered Dorm E-2 were jumped simultaneously. Inmates quickly overpowered the officer at the door and the other officers inside the dormitory. The guard at the door had the keys to other dormitories. Four hostages were then under the control of these inmates, who now had access to the main corridor.

At 1:45 A.M., inmates from Dorm E-2 jumped the officer outside Dorm F-2, seized the keys he held to other dormitories, and captured two other guards who were just entering Dorm F-2. A third guard, who had just entered the dorm, ran into the dayroom at the opposite end of the dorm; he was protected by some sympathetic Dorm F-2 inmates, who later helped him escape the prison. Total hostages were now eight, including the protected guard in the Dorm F-2 dayroom.

By 1:50 A.M., hundreds of inmates were milling around the main corridor in the south wing of the prison. At 1:57 A.M., two guards leaving the officers' mess hall, located in the central area of the institution, saw inmates beating and dragging a naked man (later identified as a hostage guard) up the south corridor toward the grill that separated the south wing from the central area of the prison. They also noticed that this corridor grill, contrary to prison policy, was open. Inmates were about to come through the opened grill. The two guards then raced north up the main corridor, passing the control center and entering the north wing of the prison, closing the corridor grill to the north wing behind them. Soon, scores of inmates were in front of the control center, which was separated from the rioters by what was supposed to be "shatterproof" glass. Inmates used a metal-canister fire extinguisher, pulled from the wall in the main corridor, to break the control center glass. The control center officers ran toward the front entrance of the prison and to the safety of the Tower 1 gatehouse. The inmates entered the control center through the smashed window and trashed its interior, sending keys flying in all directions from the key pegboards.

By 2:02 A.M., inmates had gained access to the north wing and to the administration wing, since the grills to these areas were opened electronically from the control center. It took the inmates time to find keys to specific cellblocks since keys were scattered by those inmates who first breached the control center, which indicates the unplanned nature of the takeover. But by 3 A.M., inmates had found the key to the disciplinary unit, Cellblock 3. Here they captured three more correctional officers, bringing the total to 11 hostages. (By this point, two guards had hidden themselves in the crawl space in the basement of Cellblock 5, where they remained undetected by rioters throughout the riot. And the hospital technician locked himself and seven inmate-patients into the upstairs floor of the Hospital Unit, where they also remained undetected until the riot was over.)

The first inmate killings during the riot occurred in Cellblock 3 at about 3:15 A.M. An inmate, shouting in Spanish, *No era yo. No lo hice.* (*It wasn't me. I didn't do it.*) was beaten, tortured, and mutilated. This inmate was assumed to have informed on other inmates who were also locked in the disciplinary unit. Another inmate, who was mentally disturbed and apparently had kept other Cellblock 3 inmates awake at night with his screams, was shot in the head at close range with a canister fired from a teargas launcher taken from the control center.

At about the same time, another group of inmates had found keys to the prison pharmacy, located on the first floor of the Hospital Unit. The pharmacy contained narcotics, barbiturates, and sedatives, which were ingested in massive doses by inmates throughout the riot.

Other inmates in the early morning hours of the first day of the riot found keys to the basement area of the prison, below the kitchen. Here they retrieved an acetylene blowtorch that was used at about 3:15 A.M. to open the far south corridor grill, leading to the Educational Unit and Dorm D-1, which contained the twelfth (and last) guard to be taken hostage. This blowtorch was later taken to the other end of the prison to open the far north corridor grill and Cellblock 5. Cellblock 5 was vacant due to renovation. But construction crews had left in the Cellhouse 2 additional acetylene torches. Later, these blowtorches would be used to open Cellblock 4, the Protective Custody unit.

The period between 3 A.M. and 7 A.M. was characterized by chaos, infighting, and violence. There was no leadership throughout the riot. Inmates' actions were completely uncoordinated. Some inmates were setting fires in the administrative offices, others in the Psychological Unit. At certain points, inmates manning walkie-talkies radioed for firefighting crews to come into the prison; when firefighters approached the prison they were driven back by other inmates who threw debris at them. Other inmates were fighting, forming into groups for self-protection, or hiding in fear.

While all these uncoordinated activities and fighting were going on during the early hours of the riot, a few inmates who had been released from Cellblock 3 and Cellhouse 6 discussed organizing the riot into a protest against the administration. These inmates included those involved in the ACLU lawsuit (*Duran v. Apodaca*). They managed in the early hours of the riot to get control of the three hostages captured in Cellblock 3. However, they were able to gain control of only one of the other nine hostages. The other hostages were being held by various groups in the south wing of the institution. A few were held by sympathetic inmates who protected them. The shift captain was moved frequently and may have been under the control of different groups throughout the riot, some of whom beat him mercilessly, others of whom tended to his wounds and protected him. Unlike the three hostages who were captured in Cellblock 3, who were treated relatively well for the remainder of the riot, many of the hostages held in the south wing of the prison were beaten, stabbed, and sodomized.

The Cellblock 3 and Cellhouse 6 inmates who were attempting to organize the riot into a protest had little influence on the behavior of the rioting inmates. One inmate, who identified himself as a leader in this attempt to turn the riot into a protest, said:

> *There were a few of us in here that were trying to freeze that [inmate-to-inmate violence] because it was wrong, it was dead wrong. Three hours after the riot started there was no stopping it. But there were a few of us that were saying, "Hey, if you want to burn it down, burn it down or tear it up or whatever you want, but quit killing people and don't turn this thing against ourselves. If you got to fight somebody now, fight the Man, fight the administration."* (Quoted in Colvin 1992:183–84)

But his and the other inmates' efforts to turn the riot into a protest were futile.

As fights began to break out in the south wing of the prison, injuries to inmates and killings began to increase. Many of the deaths that occurred in the south wing were the result of fights between small groups of inmates and between individuals. Fights over hostages held in the south wing occurred. Many inmates, perceived as weak or defenseless, were attacked and raped; those offering resistance were beaten severely, a few were killed. Some assaults in the south wing appeared to be random. Inmates suffered injuries when they were hacked with meat cleavers, stabbed, or hit with pipes for no reasons apparent to the victims. A few of the killings in the south wing also appear to have been random. Of the 33 killings during the riot, 17 occurred in the south wing, many in the early morning hours of the first day. Of the approximately 400 injuries and rapes, the vast majority also occurred in the south wing.

More inmates would have been killed had Dorm E-1 been entered by the rioters. This semi-protection unit's inmates successfully fought off attempts by rioters to enter this dorm. A sympathetic inmate, who had some friends in the unit, tossed a three-foot long wrench through a hole in the wire mesh above the dorm entrance. This inmate was immediately jumped by other inmates in the main corridor who had observed this action; he was beaten to death. But because he had tossed them this heavy wrench the Dorm E-1 inmates were able to knock bars out of a window at the rear of the dormitory and make it to the perimeter fence and surrender to authorities for safety. Up to 80 inmates housed in the semi-protection unit were saved by this inmate's action.

The most horrific killings of the riot occurred in the north wing of the penitentiary, specifically in Cellblock 4, the Protective Custody unit. By 7 A.M., small groups of inmates entered Cellblock 4 after burning through its entrance grills with blowtorches. As these inmates entered the cellblock, they began shouting the names of intended victims. As rioting inmates operated the control panels that gang locked and unlocked cell doors, many Cellblock 4 inmates were able to leave their cells, blend in with the rioters, and escape the carnage. Other Cellblock 4 inmates were not so fortunate. On tiers where inmates had jammed the locks to their cell grills, the gang locking and unlocking mechanisms would not operate. These inmates were trapped in their cells. Using blowtorches, rioting inmates cut through the bars of entrance grills to the individual cells containing inmates. As the intended victims suffered through the agonizing wait while their cells were entered, they were taunted and told in vivid detail exactly how they would be tortured and killed.

These protective custody inmates were apparently killed by four or five small groups, containing three to five inmates each. The groups appeared to have acted independently in choosing victims. Inmates were tortured, stabbed, mutilated, burned, bludgeoned, hanged, and thrown off upper-tier catwalks into the basement. One Cellblock 4 inmate, a 36-year-old African American, was killed and decapitated. Whether this occurred in the cellblock or elsewhere in the prison could not be established by investigators. His head was reportedly placed on a pole, paraded through the main corridor, and shown to the guards captured in Cellblock 3. This inmate's body was later deposited outside the prison's front entrance with the head stuffed between the legs. Another inmate, while reportedly still alive, had a steel rod hammered completely through his head. One inmate victim was drenched with glue and set on fire. Other atrocities were also reported to investigators. . . .

Most of the Cellblock 4 killings were apparently over by 10 A.M. on the first morning of the riot. More inmates would have undoubtedly died had they not been able to escape Cellblock 4. Besides those inmates who left their cells and escaped the protective custody unit when it was opened, other inmates living in this unit were rescued by sympathetic inmates. Some individual inmates entered Cellblock 4, found specific inmate friends, and sneaked them out of the unit. One contingent of about 20 African American inmates from Cellhouse 6 converged on Cellblock 4 about 7:30 A.M. to rescue one of their leaders, a Black Muslim minister, who had been locked in the protection unit. Upon his release, the Muslim minister told his followers to get as many protective custody inmates out of Cellblock 4 as possible. This group saved many of the intended victims (Anglo, Hispanic, and African American) from certain death. They brought these inmates to Cellhouse 6 where they combined forces for self-protection. At about noon, on the first day of the riot, they were able to fight their way to Dorm E-1 and leave the prison through the rear window that had been broken open earlier.

By noon on the first day, many inmates had managed to find routes from which to exit the prison and surrender to authorities who controlled the perimeter fence. By 5 P.M., more than 350 inmates had left the prison. They would continue to stream out of the prison for the rest of the riot. By 1 P.M. on the second (and final) day of the riot, only 100 of the prison's 1,157 inmates remained inside.

The final morning of the riot saw the setting of more fires, an increasingly larger stream of inmates leaving the prison to surrender to authorities, inmates being rushed to hospitals for injuries and pharmacy-drug overdoses, and bodies of inmates being deposited in the yard in front of the prison. Intermittent negotiations between state authorities and some prisoners continued and seemed to reach a climax by the final morning of the riot.

Throughout the riot, sporadic attempts at negotiating the release of hostages were made by state authorities. Negotiations were complicated by the fact that more than one group controlled hostages, and some of these groups had no interest in negotiating release. Three hostages were released at different times either in anticipation of or in response to talking to the news media. At one point, an NBC cameraman entered the prison's entrance lobby and recorded inmates' grievances. The lobby was filled with smoke as inmates presented their grievances about poor food, nepotism, harassment, overcrowding, idleness, inadequate recreation facilities, and arbitrary discipline practices by the administration. At another point, two inmates met with two news reporters just outside the entrance of the prison building. Beyond the release of these three hostages, however, negotiations with inmates had very little to do with the release of hostages or ending the riot.

Two hostages managed, with the help of sympathetic inmates, to leave the prison disguised as inmates. Other hostages were released by inmates because these inmates feared these hostages might die from injuries, which they thought would provoke an immediate retaking of the prison. One other hostage was released after an apparent agreement emerged from negotiations.

At about 8:30 A.M. on February 3, the second (and last) day of the riot, three Hispanic inmates (Lonnie Duran, Vincent Candelaria, and Kendrick Duran), who were among the few inmates attempting, unsuccessfully, to organize the riot into a protest over prison conditions, ironed out an agreement for ending the riot with prison authorities during a meeting in the gatehouse beneath Tower 1. The agreement had five points: (1) no retaliation against rioting inmates; (2) segregation policies be reviewed; (3) inmates be permitted to meet with the press; (4) no double-bunking of inmates in Cellblock 3; and (5) inmates be given water hoses to douse fires inside the prison. The Durans and Candelaria returned to the prison to seek approval from other inmates. They re-emerged from the prison shortly before noon for continued negotiations. By noon, only two hostages remained in the prison.

The final hour of negotiations leading up to the end of the riot was witnessed by reporter Peter Katel who later, with co-author Michael Serrill, gave the following account:

> The two Durans and Candelaria emerged from the prison and announced that they had approval from other inmates to sign the agreement negotiated [earlier that morning]. . . . Then negotiations became more

complicated. Other inmates joined the Durans and Candelaria at the negotiating table. They haggled over exactly how the agreement was to be implemented by prison officials. . . . Officials were particularly worried about the presence of three new inmates, William Jack Stephens, Michael Colby and Michael Price, at the negotiations. Colby and Stephens escaped on Dec. 9 and were recaptured. . . . In 1978, they, together with Price, beat another inmate to death with baseball bats. . . . Their commitment to a peaceful resolution of the riot was considered dubious. Later, they were identified as prime suspects in some of the [riot] killings. . . . At about 12:30 P.M., Colby, Stephens and other inmates rejoined the talks and started making new demands. . . . [Deputy Corrections Director Felix] Rodriguez says that at this point he began to worry that the Durans and Candelaria were losing control. He also began to wonder whether the majority of inmates inside were really aware of and had agreed to the five rather mild demands. (Serrill and Katel 1980:21)

Rodriguez, fearing that Colby and Stephens were gaining control of the situation, made a deal with them. He promised to transport them immediately to another prison out of state and told them to go back inside the prison to get their belongings. As soon as Colby and Stephens left, Rodriguez ordered Vincent Candelaria and Lonnie and Kendrick Duran (the inmates with whom he had been negotiating) to get the remaining two hostages, who were now seated blindfolded on the grass outside the main entrance. A few minutes later, at about 1:30 P.M., these last hostages were brought to Rodriguez. Immediately, police, National Guardsmen, and prison employees rushed the prison to retake it from the approximately 100 inmates still within. Authorities encountered no resistance from inmates during the retaking of the prison. No shots were fired. The riot was over.

Summary

The 1980 riot was a dramatic and explosive episode in a continuing pattern of disorder that had its roots several years earlier. Two things stand out as characteristics of the 1980 riot at PNM: the almost total lack of organization by inmates and the inmate-to-inmate violence that punctuated the event. The extreme violence was caused by a small number of inmates who belonged to some particularly violent inmate cliques. The emergence of these violent inmate cliques was largely an organizational phenomenon. They had their origin in the 1976 shift in tactics of inmate control, when measures, including the coercive snitch system, were used to undermine inmate solidarity. As inmate solidarity disintegrated, young prisoners began entering a social situation that elicited violence from a growing number of inmates. These social dynamics came together in the early morning hours of February 2, 1980, to produce the most horrific prison riot in history.

REFERENCES

Abbott, Jack Henry. 1981. *In the Belly of the Beast*. New York: Vintage.

Albuquerque Journal. 1979. "Prison Sexual Brutality Changes Inmate." September 16, sec. B, p. 1.

Colvin, Mark. 1992. *The Penitentiary in Crisis: From Accommodation to Riot in New Mexico*. Albany, NY: SUNY Press.

Hagel-Seymour, John. 1988. "Environmental Sanctuaries for Susceptible Prisoners." Pp. 267–84 in *The Pains of Imprisonment*, edited by Robert Johnson and Hans Toch. Prospect Hills, IL: Waveland Press.

Irwin, John. 1980. *Prisons in Turmoil*. Boston, MA: Little, Brown.

Jacobs, James B. 1977. *Stateville: The Penitentiary in Mass Society*. Chicago, IL: University of Chicago Press.

Office of the Attorney General. 1980a. *Report of the Attorney General on the February 2 and 3, 1980 Riot at the Penitentiary of New Mexico, Part I*. Santa Fe, NM: State of New Mexico.

———. 1980b. *Report of the Attorney General on the February 2 and 3 Riot at the Penitentiary of New Mexico, Part II*. Santa Fe, NM: State of New Mexico.

Serrill, Michael S. and Peter Katel. 1980. "New Mexico: The Anatomy of a Riot." *Corrections Magazine* 6 (April): 6–24.

Wicker, Tom. 1975. *A Time to Die*. New York: Ballantine.

SOCIAL CLASS

23

SOME PRINCIPLES OF STRATIFICATION

KINGSLEY DAVIS • WILBERT E. MOORE
WITH A RESPONSE BY MELVIN TUMIN

In the following four selections, we investigate social inequality that results from social class membership. *Social class* refers to categories of people who share common economic interests in a stratification system. The first selection is a classic piece excerpted from a 1945 article by sociologists Kingsley Davis and Wilbert E. Moore. Davis and Moore argue that not only are all societies stratified, but that stratification is a functional necessity. Davis and Moore also argue that stratification occurs because some social positions are more important to the social system than others, and as such, social positions are valued and rewarded differently. In 1953, sociologist Melvin Tumin published a response to Davis and Moore's classic article, which suggests that social stratification may be dysfunctional for society.

Starting from the proposition that no society is "classless," or unstratified, an effort is made to explain, in functional terms, the universal necessity which calls forth stratification in any social system. Next, an attempt is made to explain the roughly uniform distribution of prestige as between the major types of positions in every society. Since, however, there occur between one society and another great differences in the degree and kind of stratification, some attention is also given to the varieties of social inequality and the variable factors that give rise to them. . . .

Throughout, it will be necessary to keep in mind one thing—namely, that the discussion relates to the system of positions, not to the individuals occupying those positions. It is one thing to ask why different positions carry different degrees of prestige, and quite another to ask how certain individuals get into those positions. Although, as the argument will try to

Kingsley Davis and Wilbert E. Moore, "Some Principles of Stratification" from *American Sociological Review* 10, no. 2 (April 1945): 242–244.
Melvin Tumin, "Some Principles of Stratification: A Critical Analysis" from *American Sociological Review* 18, no. 4 (August 1953): 387–393.

show, both questions are related, it is essential to keep them separate in our thinking. Most of the literature on stratification has tried to answer the second question (particularly with regard to the ease or difficulty of mobility between strata) without tackling the first. The first question, however, is logically prior and, in the case of any particular individual or group, factually prior.

The Functional Necessity of Stratification

Curiously, however, the main functional necessity explaining the universal presence of stratification is precisely the requirement faced by any society of placing and motivating individuals in the social structure. As a functioning mechanism a society must somehow distribute its members in social positions and induce them to perform the duties of these positions. It must thus concern itself with motivation at two different levels: to instill in the proper individuals the desire to fill certain positions, and, once in these positions, the desire to perform the duties attached to them. Even though the social order may be relatively static in form, there is a continuous process of metabolism as new individuals are born into it, shift with age, and die off. Their absorption into the positional system must somehow be arranged and motivated. This is true whether the system is competitive or noncompetitive. A competitive system gives greater importance to the motivation to achieve positions, whereas a noncompetitive system gives perhaps greater importance to the motivation to perform the duties of the positions; but in any system both types of motivation are required.

If the duties associated with the various positions were all equally pleasant to the human organism, all equally important to societal survival, and all equally in need of the same ability or talent, it would make no difference who got into which positions, and the problem of social placement would be greatly reduced. But actually it does make a great deal of difference who gets into which positions, not only because some positions are inherently more agreeable than others, but also because some require special talents or training and some are functionally more important than others. Also, it is essential that the duties of the positions be performed with the diligence that their importance requires. Inevitably, then, a society must have, first, some kind of rewards that it can use as inducements, and, second, some way of distributing these rewards differentially according to positions. The rewards and their distribution become a part of the social order, and thus give rise to stratification.

One may ask what kind of rewards a society has at its disposal in distributing its personnel and securing essential services. It has, first of all, the things that contribute to sustenance and comfort. It has, second, the things that contribute to humor and diversion. And it has, finally, the things that contribute to self-respect and ego expansion. The last, because of the peculiarly social character of the self, is largely a function of the opinion of others, but it nonetheless ranks in importance with the first two. In any social system all three kinds of rewards must be dispensed differentially according to positions.

In a sense the rewards are "built into" the position. They consist in the "rights" associated with the position, plus what may be called its accompaniments or perquisites. Often the rights, and sometimes the accompaniments, are functionally related to the duties of the position. (Rights as viewed by the incumbent are usually duties as viewed by other members of the community.) However, there may be a host of subsidiary rights and perquisites that are not essential to the function of the position and have only an indirect and symbolic connection with its duties, but which still may be of considerable importance in inducing people to seek the positions and fulfill the essential duties.

If the rights and perquisites of different positions in a society must be unequal, then the society must be stratified, because that is precisely what stratification means. Social inequality is thus an unconsciously evolved device by which societies insure that the most important positions are conscientiously filled by the most qualified persons. Hence every society, no matter how simple or complex, must differentiate persons in terms of both prestige and esteem, and must therefore possess a certain amount of institutionalized inequality.

It does not follow that the amount or type of inequality need be the same in all societies. This is largely a function of factors that will be discussed presently.

The Two Determinants of Positional Rank

Granting the general function that inequality subserves, one can specify the two factors that determine the relative rank of different positions. In general those positions convey the best reward, and hence have the highest rank, which (a) have the greatest importance for the society and (b) require the greatest training or talent. The first factor concerns function and is a matter of relative significance; the second concerns means and is a matter of scarcity.

Differential Functional Importance

Actually a society does not need to reward positions in proportion to their functional importance. It merely needs to give sufficient reward to them to ensure that they will be filled competently. In other words, it must see that less essential positions do not compete successfully with more essential ones. If a position is easily filled, it need not be heavily rewarded, even though important. On the other hand, if it is important but hard to fill, the reward must be high enough to get it filled anyway. Functional importance is therefore a necessary but not a sufficient cause of high rank being assigned to a position.[1]

Differential Scarcity of Personnel

Practically all positions, no matter how acquired, require some form of skill or capacity for performance. This is implicit in the very notion of position, which implies that the incumbent must, by virtue of his incumbency, accomplish certain things.

There are, ultimately, only two ways in which a person's qualifications come about: through inherent capacity or through training. Obviously, in concrete activities both are always necessary, but from a practical standpoint the scarcity may lie primarily in one or the other, as well as in both. Some positions require innate talents of such high degree that the persons who fill them are bound to be rare. In many cases, however, talent is fairly abundant in the population but the training process is so long, costly, and elaborate that relatively few can qualify. Modern medicine, for example, is within the mental capacity of most individuals, but a medical education is so burdensome and expensive that virtually none would undertake it if the position of the M.D. did not carry a reward commensurate with the sacrifice.

If the talents required for a position are abundant and the training easy, the method of acquiring the position may have little to do with its duties. There may be, in fact, a virtually accidental relationship. But if the skills required are scarce by reason of the rarity of talent or the costliness of training, the position, if functionally important, must have an attractive power that will draw the necessary skills in competition with other positions. This means, in effect, that the position must be high in the social scale—must command great prestige, high salary, ample leisure, and the like.

How Variations Are to Be Understood

Insofar as there is a difference between one system of stratification and another, it is attributable to whatever factors affect the two determinants of differential reward—namely, functional importance and scarcity of personnel. Positions important in one society may not be important in another, because the conditions faced by the societies, or their degree of internal development, may be different. The same conditions, in turn, may affect the question of scarcity; for in some societies the stage of development, or the external situation, may wholly obviate the necessity of certain kinds of skill or talent. Any particular system of stratification, then, can be understood as a product of the special conditions affecting the two aforementioned grounds of differential reward.

Critical Response by Melvin Tumin

The fact of social inequality in human society is marked by its ubiquity and its antiquity. Every known society, past and present, distributes its scarce and demanded goods and services unequally. And there are attached to the positions which command unequal amounts of such goods and services certain highly morally toned evaluations of their importance for the society.

The ubiquity and the antiquity of such inequality have given rise to the assumption that there must be something both inevitable and positively functional about such social arrangements. . . . Clearly, the truth or falsity of such an assumption is a strategic question for any general theory of social organization. It is therefore most curious that the basic premises and implications of the assumption have only been most casually explored by American sociologists. . . .

Let us take [the Davis and Moore] propositions and examine them *seriatim.*

(1) *Certain positions in any society are more functionally important than others and require special skills for their performance.*

The key term here is "functionally important." The functionalist theory of social organization is by no means clear and explicit about this term. The minimum common referent is to something known as the "survival value" of a social structure. This concept immediately involves a number of perplexing questions. Among these are (a) the issue of minimum versus maximum survival, and the possible empirical referents which can be given to those terms; (b) whether such a proposition is a useless tautology since any *status quo* at any given moment is nothing more and nothing less than everything present in the *status quo.* In these terms, all acts and structures must be judged positively functional in that they constitute essential portions of the *status quo;* (c) what kind of calculus of functionality exists which will enable us, at this point in our development, to add and subtract long- and short-range consequences, with their mixed qualities, and arrive at some summative judgment regarding the rating an act or structure should receive on a scale of greater or lesser functionality? At best, we tend to make primarily intuitive judgments. Often enough, these judgments involve the use of value-laden criteria, or, at least, criteria which are chosen in preference to others not for any sociologically systematic reasons but by reason of certain implicit value preferences. . . .

A generalized theory of social stratification must recognize that the prevailing system of inducements and rewards is only one of many variants in the whole range of possible systems of motivation which, at least theoretically, are capable of working in human society. It is quite conceivable, of course, that a system of norms could be institutionalized in which the idea of threatened withdrawal of services, except under the most extreme circumstances, would be considered as absolute moral anathema. In such a case, the whole notion of relative functionality, as advanced by Davis and Moore, would have to be radically revised.

(2) *Only a limited number of individuals in any society have the talents which can be trained into the skills appropriate to these positions (i.e., the more functionally important positions).*

The truth of this proposition depends at least in part on the truth of proposition 1 above. It is, therefore, subject to all the limitations indicated above. But for the moment, let us assume the validity of the first proposition and concentrate on the question of the rarity of appropriate talent.

If all that is meant is that in every society there is a *range* of talent, and that some members of any society are by nature more talented than others, no sensible contradiction can be offered, but a question must be raised here regarding the amount of sound knowledge present in any society concerning the presence of talent in the population.

For, in every society there is some demonstrable ignorance regarding the amount of talent present in the population. *And the more rigidly stratified a society is, the less chance does that society have of discovering any new facts about the talents of its members.* Smoothly working and stable systems of stratification, wherever found, tend to build in obstacles to the further exploration of the range of available talent. This is especially true in those societies where the opportunity to discover talent in any one generation varies with the differential resources of the parent generation. Where, for instance, access to education depends upon the wealth of one's parents, and where wealth is differentially distributed, large segments of the population are likely to be deprived of the chance even to *discover* what are their talents.

Whether or not differential rewards and opportunities are functional in any one generation, it is clear that if those differentials are allowed to be socially inherited by the next generation, then the stratification system is specifically dysfunctional for the discovery of talents in the next generation. In this fashion, systems of social stratification tend to limit the chances available to maximize the efficiency of discovery, recruitment, and training of "functionally important talent."

. . . In this context, it may be asserted that there is some noticeable tendency for elites to restrict further access to their privileged positions, once they have sufficient power to enforce such restrictions. This is especially true in a culture where it is possible for an elite to contrive a high demand and a proportionately higher reward for its work by restricting the numbers of the elite available to do the work. The recruitment and training of doctors in modern United States is at least partly a case in point. . . .

(3) *The conversion of talents into skills involves a training period during which sacrifices of one kind or another are made by those undergoing the training.*

Davis and Moore introduce here a concept, "sacrifice," which comes closer than any of the rest of their vocabulary of analysis to being a direct reflection of the rationalizations, offered by the more fortunate members of a society, of the rightness of their occupancy of privileged positions. It is the least critically thought-out concept in the repertoire, and can also be shown to be least supported by the actual facts.

In our present society, for example, what are the sacrifices which talented persons undergo in the training period? The possibly serious losses involve the surrender of earning power and the cost of the training. The latter is generally borne by the parents of the talented youth undergoing training, and not by the trainees themselves. But this cost tends to be paid out of income which the parents were able to earn generally by virtue of *their* privileged positions in the hierarchy of stratification. That is to say, the parents' ability to pay for the training of their children is part of the differential *reward* they, the parents, received for their privileged positions in the society. And to charge this sum up against sacrifices made by the youth is falsely to perpetrate a bill or a debt already paid by the society to the parents. . . .

What tends to be completely overlooked, in addition, are the psychic and spiritual rewards which are available to the elite trainees by comparison with their age peers in the labor force. There is, first, the much higher prestige enjoyed by the college student and the professional-school student as compared with persons in shops and offices. There is, second, the extremely highly valued privilege of having greater opportunity for self-development. There is, third, all the psychic gain involved in being allowed to delay the assumption of adult responsibilities such as earning a living and supporting a family. There is, fourth, the access to leisure and freedom of a kind not likely to be experienced by the persons already at work.

If these are never taken into account as rewards of the training period it is not because they are not concretely present, but because the emphasis in American concepts of reward is almost exclusively placed on the material returns of positions. The emphases on enjoyment, entertainment, ego enhancement, prestige, and esteem are introduced only when the differentials in these which accrue to the skilled positions need to be justified. If these other rewards were taken into account, it would be much more difficult to demonstrate that the training period, as presently operative, is really sacrificial. Indeed, it might turn out to be the case that even at this point in their careers, the elite trainees were being differentially rewarded relative to their age peers in the labor force. . . .

(4) *In order to induce the talented persons to undergo these sacrifices and acquire the training, their future positions must carry an inducement value in the form of differential, i.e., privileged and disproportionate access to the scarce and desired rewards which the society has to offer.*

Let us assume, for the purposes of the discussion, that the training period is sacrificial and the talent is rare in every conceivable human society. There is still the basic problem as to whether the allocation of differential rewards in scarce and desired goods and services is the only or the most efficient way of recruiting the appropriate talent to these positions.

For there are a number of alternative motivational schemes whose efficiency and adequacy ought at least to be considered in this context. What can be said, for instance, on behalf of the motivation which De Man called "joy in work," Veblen termed "instinct for workmanship," and which we latterly have come to identify as "intrinsic work satisfaction"? Or, to what extent could the motivation of "social duty" be institutionalized in such a fashion that self-interest and social interest come closely to coincide? Or, how much prospective confidence can be placed in the possibilities of institutionalizing "social service" as a widespread motivation for seeking one's appropriate position and fulfilling it conscientiously?

Are not these types of motivations, we may ask, likely to prove most appropriate for precisely the "most functionally important positions"? Especially in a mass industrial society, where the vast majority of positions become standardized and routinized, it is the skilled jobs which are likely to retain most of the quality of "intrinsic job satisfaction" and be most readily identifiable as socially serviceable. Is it indeed impossible then to build these motivations into the socialization pattern to which we expose our talented youth? . . .

(5) *These scarce and desired goods consist of rights and perquisites attached to, or built into, the positions and can be classified into those things which contribute*

to (a) sustenance and comfort; (b) humor and diversion; (c) self-respect and ego expansion.

(6) *This differential access to the basic rewards of the society has as a consequence the differentiation of the prestige and esteem which various strata acquire. This may be said, along with the rights and perquisites, to constitute institutionalized social inequality, i.e., stratification.*

With the classification of the rewards offered by Davis and Moore there need be little argument. Some question must be raised, however, as to whether any reward system, built into a general stratification system, must allocate equal amounts of all three types of reward in order to function effectively, or whether one type of reward may be emphasized to the virtual neglect of others. This raises the further question regarding which type of emphasis is likely to prove most effective as a differential inducer. Nothing in the known facts about human motivation impels us to favor one type of reward over the other, or to insist that all three types of reward must be built into the positions in comparable amounts if the position is to have an inducement value.

It is well known, of course, that societies differ considerably in the kinds of rewards they emphasize in their efforts to maintain a reasonable balance between responsibility and reward. There are, for instance, numerous societies in which the conspicuous display of differential economic advantage is considered extremely bad taste. In short, our present knowledge commends to us the possibility of considerable plasticity in the way in which different types of rewards can be structured into a functioning society. This is to say, it cannot yet be demonstrated that it is *unavoidable* that differential prestige and esteem shall accrue to positions which command differential rewards in power and property.

What does seem to be unavoidable is that differential prestige shall be given to those in any society who conform to the normative order as against those who deviate from that order in a way judged immoral and detrimental. On the assumption that the continuity of a society depends on the continuity and stability of its normative order, some such distinction between conformists and deviants seems inescapable.

It also seems to be unavoidable that in any society, no matter how literate its tradition, the older, wiser, and more experienced individuals who are charged with the enculturation and socialization of the young must have more power than the young, on the assumption that the task of effective socialization demands such differential power.

But this differentiation in prestige between the conformist and the deviant is by no means the same distinction as that between strata of individuals each of which operates *within* the normative order, and is composed of adults. . . .

(7) *Therefore, social inequality among different strata in the amounts of scarce and desired goods, and the amounts of prestige and esteem which they receive, is both positively functional and inevitable in any society.*

If the objections which have heretofore been raised are taken as reasonable, then it may be stated that the only items which any society *must* distribute unequally are the power and property necessary for the performance of different tasks. If such differential power and property are viewed by all as commensurate with the differential responsibilities, and if they are culturally defined as *resources* and not as rewards, then no differentials in prestige and esteem need follow.

Historically, the evidence seems to be that every time power and property are distributed unequally, no matter what the cultural definition, prestige and esteem differentiations have tended to result as well. Historically, however, no systematic effort has ever been made, under propitious circumstances, to develop the tradition that each man is as socially worthy as all other men so long as he performs his appropriate tasks conscientiously. While such a tradition seems utterly utopian, no known facts in psychological or social science have yet demonstrated its impossibility or its dysfunctionality for the continuity of a society. The achievement of a full institutionalization of such a tradition seems far too remote to contemplate. Some successive approximations at such a tradition, however, are not out of the range of prospective social innovation.

What, then, of the "positive functionality" of social stratification? Are there other, negative, functions of institutionalized social inequality which can be identified, if only tentatively? Some such dysfunctions of stratification have already been suggested in the body of this [reading]. Along with others they may now be stated, in the form of provisional assertions, as follows:

1. Social stratification systems function to limit the possibility of discovery of the full range of talent available in a society. This results from the fact of unequal access to appropriate motivation, channels of recruitment, and centers of training.

2. In foreshortening the range of available talent, social stratification systems function to set limits upon the possibility of expanding the productive resources of the society, at least relative to what might be the case under conditions of greater equality of opportunity.

3. Social stratification systems function to provide the elite with the political power necessary to procure acceptance and dominance of an ideology which rationalizes the *status quo*, whatever it may be, as "logical," "natural," and "morally right." In this manner, social stratification systems function as essentially conservative influences in the societies in which they are found.

4. Social stratification systems function to distribute favorable self-images unequally throughout a population. To the extent that such favorable self-images are requisite to the development of the creative potential inherent in men, to that extent stratification systems function to limit the development of this creative potential.

5. To the extent that inequalities in social rewards cannot be made fully acceptable to the less privileged in a society, social stratification systems function to encourage hostility, suspicion, and distrust among the various segments of a society and thus to limit the possibilities of extensive social integration.

6. To the extent that the sense of significant membership in a society depends on one's place on the prestige ladder of the society, social stratification systems function to distribute unequally the sense of significant membership in the population.

7. To the extent that loyalty to a society depends on a sense of significant membership in the society, social stratification systems function to distribute loyalty unequally in the population.

8. To the extent that participation and apathy depend upon the sense of significant membership in the society, social stratification systems function to distribute the motivation to participate unequally in a population.

Each of the eight foregoing propositions contains implicit hypotheses regarding the consequences of unequal distribution of rewards in a society in accordance with some notion of the functional importance of various positions. These are empirical hypotheses, subject to test. They are offered here only as exemplary of the kinds of consequences of social stratification which are not often taken into account in dealing with the problem. They should also serve to reinforce the doubt that social inequality is a device which is uniformly functional for the role of guaranteeing that the most important tasks in a society will be performed conscientiously by the most competent persons.

The obviously mixed character of the functions of social inequality should come as no surprise to anyone. If sociology is sophisticated in any sense, it is certainly with regard to its awareness of the mixed nature of any social arrangement, when the observer takes into account long- as well as short-range consequences and latent as well as manifest dimensions.

ENDNOTE

[1]Unfortunately, functional importance is difficult to establish. To use the position's prestige to establish it, as is often unconsciously done, constitutes circular reasoning from our point of view. There are, however, two independent clues: (a) the degree to which a position is functionally unique, there being no other positions that can perform the same function satisfactorily; and (b) the degree to which other positions are dependent on the one in question. Both clues are best exemplified in organized systems of positions built around one major function. Thus in most complex societies the religious, political, economic, and educational functions are handled by distinct structures not easily interchangeable. In addition, each structure possesses many different positions, some clearly dependent on, if not subordinate to, others. In sum, when an institutional nucleus becomes differentiated around one main function, and at the same time organizes a large portion of the population into its relationships, *key* positions in it are of the highest functional importance. The absence of such specialization does not prove functional unimportance, for the whole society may be relatively unspecialized; but it is safe to assume that the more important functions receive the first and clearest structural differentiation.

24

WHO RULES AMERICA?
The Corporate Community and the Upper Class

G. WILLIAM DOMHOFF

Sociologists utilize various indicators to measure social class. For example, *socioeconomic status* (SES) is calculated using income, educational attainment, and occupational status. Sociologists also employ subjective indicators of social class, such as attitudes and values, class identification, and consumption patterns. This selection is by G. William Domhoff, a professor emeritus of psychology at the University of California, Santa Cruz, and it is taken from his 1998 book, *Who Rules America? Power and Politics in the Year 2000*. Using both objective and subjective indicators of social class status, Domhoff finds that in addition to wealth, the upper class shares a distinctive lifestyle through participation in various social institutions. Domhoff argues not only that there is a cohesive upper class in the United States, but also that the upper class has a disproportionate share of power through its control over economic and political decision making in this country.

Most Americans do not like the idea that there are social classes. Classes imply that people have relatively fixed stations in life. They fly in the face of beliefs about equality of opportunity and seem to ignore the evidence of upward social mobility. Even more, Americans tend to deny that social classes are based in wealth and occupational roles but then belie that denial through a fascination with rags-to-riches stories and the trappings of wealth. . . .

If there is an American upper class, it must exist not merely as a collection of families who feel comfortable with each other and tend to exclude outsiders from their social activities. It must exist as a set of interrelated social institutions. That is, there must be patterned ways of organizing the lives of its members from infancy to old age that create a relatively unique style of life, and there must be mechanisms for socializing both the younger generation and new adult members who have risen from lower social levels. If the class is a reality, the names and faces may change somewhat over the years, but the social institutions that underlie the upper class must persist with remarkably little change over several generations. This emphasis on the institutionalized nature of the upper class, which reflects a long-standing empirical tradition in studies of it, is compatible with the theoretical focus of the "new institutionalists" within sociology and political science.

Four different types of empirical studies establish the existence of an interrelated set of social institutions, organizations, and social activities. They are historical case studies, quantitative studies of biographical directories, open-ended surveys of knowledgeable observers, and interview studies with members of the upper-middle and upper classes. . . .

Prepping for Power

From infancy through young adulthood, members of the upper class receive a distinctive education. This education begins early in life in preschools that frequently are attached to a neighborhood church of high social status. Schooling continues during the elementary years at a local private school called a day school. During the adolescent years the student may remain at day school, but there is a strong chance that at least one or two years will be spent away from home at a boarding school in a quiet rural setting. Higher education will take place at one of a small number of heavily endowed private colleges and universities. Large and well-known Ivy League schools in the East and Stanford in the West head the list, followed by smaller Ivy League schools in the East and a handful of other small private schools in other parts of the country. Although some upper-class children may attend public high school if they live in a secluded suburban setting, or go to a state university if there is one of great esteem and tradition in their home state, the system of formal schooling is so insulated that many upper-class students never see the inside of a public school in all their years of education.

This separate educational system is important evidence for the distinctiveness of the mentality and lifestyle that exists within the upper class because schools play a large role in transmitting the class structure to their students. Surveying and summarizing a great many studies on schools in general, sociologist Randall Collins concludes: "Schools primarily teach vocabulary and inflection, styles of dress, aesthetic tastes, values and manners."[1] His statement takes on greater significance for studies of the upper class when it is added that only 1 percent of American teenagers attend independent private high schools of an upper-class nature.[2]

The training of upper-class children is not restricted to the formal school setting, however. Special classes, and even tutors, are a regular part of their extracurricular education. This informal education usually begins with dancing classes in the elementary years, which are seen as important for learning proper manners and the social graces. Tutoring in a foreign language may begin in the elementary years, and there are often lessons in horseback riding and music as well. The teen years find the children of the upper class in summer camps or on special travel tours, broadening their perspectives and polishing their social skills.

The linchpins in the upper-class educational system are the dozens of boarding schools founded in the last half of the nineteenth and the early part of the twentieth centuries. Baltzell concludes that these schools became "surrogate families" that played a major role "in creating an upper-class subculture on almost a national scale in America."[3] The role of boarding schools in providing connections to other upper-class social institutions is also important. As one informant explained to Ostrander in her interview study of upper-class women: *Where I went to boarding school, there were girls from all over the country, so I know people from all over. It's helpful when you move to a new city and want to get invited into the local social club.*[4]

It is within these few hundred schools that are consciously modeled after their older and more austere British counterparts that a distinctive style of life is inculcated through such traditions as the initiatory hazing of beginning students, the wearing of school blazers or ties, compulsory attendance at chapel services, and participation in esoteric sports such as squash and crew. Even a different terminology is adopted to distinguish these schools from public schools. The principal is a headmaster or rector, the teachers are sometimes called masters, and the students are in forms, not grades. Great emphasis is placed on the building of "character." The role of the school in preparing the future leaders of America is emphasized through the speeches of the headmaster and the frequent mention of successful alumni. Thus, boarding schools are in many ways the kind of highly effective socializing agent that sociologist Erving Goffman calls "total institutions," isolating their members from the outside world and providing them with a set of routines and traditions that encompass most of their waking hours.[5] The end result is a feeling of separateness and superiority that comes from having survived a rigorous education. As a retired business leader told one of my research assistants: *At school we were made to feel somewhat better* [than other people] *because of our class. That existed, and I've always disliked it intensely. Unfortunately, I'm afraid some of these things rub off on one.*[6]

Almost all graduates of private secondary schools go on to college, and almost all do so at prestigious universities. Graduates of the New England boarding schools, for example, historically found themselves at one of four large Ivy League universities: Harvard, Yale, Princeton, and Columbia. . . . Now many upper-class students attend a select handful of smaller private liberal arts colleges, most of which are in the East, but there are a few in the South and West as well.

Graduates of private schools outside of New England most frequently attend a prominent state university in their area, but a significant minority go to Eastern Ivy League and top private universities in other parts of the country. . . . A majority of private-school graduates pursue careers in business, finance, or corporate law. For example, a classification of the occupations of a sample of the graduates of four private schools—St. Mark's, Groton, Hotchkiss, and Andover—showed that the most frequent occupation for all but the Andover graduates was some facet of finance and banking. Others became presidents of medium-size businesses or were partners in large corporate law firms. A small handful went to work as executives for major national corporations.[7] . . .

Although finance, business, and law are the most typical occupations of upper-class males, there is no absence of physicians, architects, museum officials, and other professional occupations. This fact is demonstrated most systematically in Baltzell's study of Philadelphia: 39 percent of the Philadelphia architects and physicians listed in *Who's Who* for the early 1940s were also listed in the *Social Register,* as were 35 percent of the museum officials. These figures are close to the 51 percent for lawyers and the 42 percent for businessmen, although they are far below the 75 percent for bankers—clearly the most prestigious profession in Philadelphia at that time.[8] . . .

From kindergarten through college, then, schooling is very different for members of the upper class and it teaches them to be distinctive in many ways. In a country where education is highly valued and nearly everyone attends public schools, this private system benefits primarily members of the upper class and provides one of the foundations for the old-boy and old-girl networks that will be with them throughout their lives.

Social Clubs

Just as private schools are a pervasive feature in the lives of upper-class children, so, too, are private social clubs a major point of orientation in the lives of upper-class adults. These clubs also play a role in differentiating members of the upper class from other members of society. According to Baltzell, "the club serves to place the adult members of society and their families within the social hierarchy." He quotes with approval the suggestion by historian Crane Brinton that the club "may perhaps be regarded as taking the place of those extensions of the family, such as the clan and the brotherhood, which have disappeared from advanced societies."[9] Conclusions similar to Baltzell's resulted from an interview study in Kansas City: "Ultimately, say upper-class Kansas Citians, social standing in their world reduces to one issue: where does an individual or family rank on the scale of private club memberships and informal cliques?"[10]

The clubs of the upper class are many and varied, ranging from family-oriented country clubs and downtown men's and women's clubs to highly specialized clubs for yacht owners, gardening enthusiasts, and fox hunters. Many families have memberships in several different types of clubs, but the days when most of the men by themselves were in a half dozen or more clubs faded before World War II. Downtown men's clubs originally were places for having lunch and dinner, and occasionally for attending an evening performance or a weekend party. But as upper-class families deserted the city for large suburban estates, a new kind of club, the country club, gradually took over some of these functions. The downtown club became almost entirely a luncheon club, a site to hold meetings, or a place to relax on a free afternoon. The country club, by contrast, became a haven for all members of the family. It offered social and sporting activities ranging from dances, parties, and banquets to golf, swimming, and tennis. Special group dinners were often arranged for all members on Thursday night—the traditional maid's night off across the United States.

Sporting activities are the basis for most of the specialized clubs of the upper class. The most visible are the yachting and sailing clubs, followed by the clubs for lawn tennis or squash. The most exotic are the several dozen fox hunting clubs. They have their primary strongholds in rolling countrysides from southern Pennsylvania down into Virginia, but they exist in other parts of the country as well. Riding to hounds in scarlet jackets and black boots, members of the upper class sustain over 130 hunts under the banner of the Masters of Fox Hounds Association. The intricate rituals and grand feasts accompanying the event, including the Blessing of the Hounds by an Episcopal bishop in the Eastern hunts, go back to the eighteenth century in the United States.[11]

Initiation fees, annual dues, and expenses vary from a few thousand dollars in downtown clubs to tens of thousands of dollars in some country clubs, but money is not the primary barrier in gaining membership to a club. Each club has a very rigorous screening process before accepting new members. Most require nomination by one or more active members, letters of recommendation from three to six members, and interviews with at least some members of the membership committee. Names of prospective members are sometimes posted in the clubhouse, so all members have an opportunity to make their feelings known to the membership committee. Negative votes by two or three members of what is typically a ten- to twenty-person committee often are enough to deny admission to the candidate. The carefulness with which new members are selected extends to a guarding of club membership lists, which are usually available only to club members. Older membership lists are sometimes given to libraries by members or their surviving spouses, but for most clubs there are no membership lists in the public domain.

Not every club member is an enthusiastic participant in the life of the club. Some belong out of tradition or a feeling of social necessity. One woman told Ostrander the following about her country club: *We don't feel we should withdraw our support even though we don't go much.* Others mentioned a feeling of social pressure: *I've only been to [the club] once this year. I'm really a loner, but I feel I have to go and be pleasant even though I don't want to.* Another volunteered: *I think half the members go because they like it and half because they think it's a social necessity.*[12]

People of the upper class often belong to clubs in several cities, creating a nationwide pattern of overlapping memberships. These overlaps provide evidence for social cohesion within the upper class. An indication of the nature and extent of this overlapping is revealed by sociologist Philip Bonacich's study of membership lists for twenty clubs in several major cities across the country, including the Links in New York, the Century Association in New York, the Duquesne in Pittsburgh, the Chicago in Chicago, the Pacific Union in San Francisco, and the California in Los Angeles. Using his own original clustering technique based on Boolean algebra, his study revealed there was sufficient overlap among eighteen of the twenty clubs to form three regional groupings and a fourth group that provided a bridge between the two largest regional groups. The several dozen men who were in three or more of the clubs—most of them very wealthy people who also sat on several corporate boards—were especially important in creating the overall pattern. At the same time, the fact that these clubs often have from 1,000 to 2,000 members makes the percentage of overlap within this small number of clubs relatively small, ranging from as high as 20 to 30 percent between clubs in the same city to as low as 1 or 2 percent in clubs at opposite ends of the country.[13]

The overlap of this club network with corporate boards of directors provides evidence for the intertwining of the upper class and corporate community. In one study, the club memberships of the chairs and outside directors of the twenty largest industrial corporations were counted. The overlaps with upper-class clubs in general were ubiquitous, but the concentration of directors in a few clubs was especially notable. At least one director from twelve of the twenty corporations was a member of the Links Club, which Baltzell calls "the New York rendezvous of the national corporate establishment."[14] Seven of General Electric's directors were members, as were four from Chrysler, four from Westinghouse, three from IBM, and two from U.S. Steel. In addition to the Links, several other clubs had directors from four or more corporations. A study I did using membership lists from eleven prestigious clubs in different parts of the country confirmed and extended these findings. A majority of the top twenty-five corporations in every major sector of the economy had directors in at least one of these clubs, and several had many more. . . .

There seems to be a great deal of truth to the earlier-cited suggestion by Crane Brinton that clubs may function within the upper class the way that the clan or brotherhood does in tribal societies. With their restrictive membership policies, initiatory rituals, private ceremonials, and great emphasis on tradition, clubs carry on the heritage of primitive secret societies. They create among their members an attitude of prideful exclusiveness that contributes greatly to an in-group feeling and a sense of fraternity within the upper class.

In concluding this discussion of . . . [social clubs and] the intersection of the upper class and corporate community, it needs to be stressed that the [social club] is not a place of power. No conspiracies are hatched there, nor anywhere else. Instead, it is a place where powerful people relax, make new acquaintances, and enjoy themselves. It is primarily a place of social bonding. The main sociological function of . . . [social] clubs is stated by sociologist Thomas Powell, based on his own interview study of members in upper-class clubs:

> The clubs are a repository of the values held by the upper-level prestige groups in the community and are a means by which these values are transferred to the business environment. The clubs are places in which the beliefs, problems, and values of the industrial organization are discussed and related to the other elements in the larger community. Clubs, therefore, are not only effective vehicles of informal communication, but also valuable centers where views are presented, ideas are modified, and new ideas emerge. Those in the interview sample were appreciative of this asset; in addition, they considered the club as a valuable place to combine social and business contacts.[15]

The Female Half of the Upper Class

During the late nineteenth and early twentieth centuries, women of the upper class carved out their own distinct roles within the context of male domination in business, finance, and law. They went to separate private schools, founded their own social clubs, and belonged to their own volunteer associations. As young women and party goers, they set the fashions for society. As older women and activists, they took charge of the nonprofit social welfare and cultural institutions of the society, serving as fund-raisers, philanthropists, and directors in a manner parallel to what their male counterparts did in business and politics. To prepare themselves for their leadership roles, in 1901 they created the Junior League to provide internships, role models, mutual support, and training in the management of meetings.

Due to the general social changes of the 1960s—and in particular the revival of the feminist movement—the socialization of wealthy young women has changed somewhat in recent decades. Many private schools are now coeducational. Their women graduates are encouraged to go to major four-year colleges rather than finishing schools. Women of the upper class are more likely to have careers; there are already two or three examples of women who have risen to the top of their family's business. They are also more likely to serve on corporate boards. Still, due to its emphasis on tradition, there may be even less gender equality in the upper class than there is in the professional stratum; it is not clear how much more equality will be attained.

The female half of the upper class has been studied by several sociologists. Their work provides an important window into the upper class and class consciousness in general as well as a portrait of the socialization of well-born women. But before focusing on their work, it is worthwhile to examine one unique institution of the upper class that has not changed very much in its long history—the debutante party that announces a young woman's coming of age and eligibility for marriage. It contains general lessons on class consciousness and the difficulties of maintaining traditional socializing institutions in a time of social unrest.

The Debutante Season

The debutante season is a series of parties, teas, and dances that culminates in one or more grand balls. It announces the arrival of young women of the upper class into adult society with the utmost of formality and elegance. These highly expensive rituals—in which great attention is lavished on every detail of the food, decorations, and entertainment—have a long history in the upper class. They made their first appearance in Philadelphia in 1748 and Charleston, South Carolina, in 1762, and they vary only slightly from city to city across the country. They are a central focus of the Christmas social season just about everywhere, but in some cities debutante balls are held in the spring as well.

Dozens of people are involved in planning the private parties that most debutantes have before the grand ball. Parents, with the help of upper-class women who work as social secretaries and social consultants, spend many hours with dress designers, caterers, florists, decorators, bandleaders, and champagne importers, deciding on just the right motif for their daughter's coming out. Most parties probably cost between $25,000 and $75,000, but sometimes the occasion is so extraordinary that it draws newspaper attention. Henry Ford II spent $250,000 on a debutante party for one of his daughters, hiring a Paris designer to redo the Country Club of Detroit in an eighteenth-century chateau motif and flying in 2 million magnolia boughs from Mississippi to cover the walls of the corridor leading to the reception room. A Texas oil and real estate family chartered a commercial jet airliner for a party that began in Dallas and ended with an all-night visit to the clubs in the French Quarter of New Orleans.[16]

The debutante balls themselves are usually sponsored by local social clubs. Sometimes there is an organization whose primary purpose is the selection of debutantes and the staging of the ball, such as the Saint Cecelia Society in Charleston, South Carolina, or the Allegro Club in Houston, Texas. Adding to the solemnity of the occasion, the selection of the season's debutantes is often made by the most prominent upper-class males in the city, often through such secret societies as the Veiled Prophet in St. Louis or the Mardi Gras krewes in New Orleans.

Proceeds from the balls are usually given to a prominent local charity sponsored by members of the upper class. *Doing something for charity makes the participants feel better about spending,* explains Mrs. Stephen Van Rensselear Strong, a social press agent in New York and herself a member of the upper class.[17] It also makes at least part of the expense of the occasion tax deductible.

Evidence for the great traditional importance attached to the debut is to be found in the comments Ostrander received from women who thought the whole process unimportant but made their daughters go through it anyhow: *I think it's passé, and I don't care about it, but it's just something that's done,* explained one woman. Another commented: *Her father wanted her to do it. We do have a family image to maintain. It was important to the grandparents, and I felt it was an obligation to her family to do it.* When people begin to talk about doing something out of tradition or to uphold an image, Ostrander suggests, then the unspoken rules that dictate class-oriented behavior are being revealed through ritual behavior.[18]

Despite the great importance placed on the debut by upper-class parents, the debutante season came into considerable disfavor among young women as the social upheavals of the late 1960s and early 1970s reached their climax. This decline reveals that the reproduction of the upper class as a social class is an effort that must be made with each new generation. Although enough young women participated to keep the tradition alive, a significant minority refused to participate, which led to the cancellation of some balls and the curtailment of many others. Stories appeared on the women's pages across the country telling of debutantes who thought the whole process was "silly" or that the money should be given to a good cause. By 1973, however, the situation began to change again, and by the mid-1970s things were back to normal.[19]

The decline of the debutante season and its subsequent resurgence in times of domestic tranquility reveal very clearly that one of its latent functions is to help perpetuate the upper class from generation to generation. When the underlying values of the class were questioned by a few of its younger members, the institution went into decline. Attitudes toward such social institutions as the debutante ball are one indicator of whether adult members of the upper class have succeeded in insulating their children from the rest of society.

The Role of Volunteer

The most informative and intimate look at the adult lives of traditional upper-class women is provided in three different interview and observation studies, one on the East Coast, one in the Midwest, and one on the West Coast. They reveal the women to be both powerful and subservient, playing decision-making roles in numerous cultural and civic organizations but also accepting traditional roles at home vis-à-vis their husbands and children. By asking the women to describe a typical day and to explain which activities were most important to them, sociologists Arlene Daniels, Margot McLeod, and Susan Ostrander found that the role of community volunteer is a central preoccupation of upper-class women, having significance as a family tradition and as an opportunity to fulfill an obligation to the community. One elderly woman involved for several decades in both the arts and human services told Ostrander: *If you're privileged, you have a certain responsibility. This was part of my upbringing; it's a tradition, a pattern of life that my brothers and sisters do too.*[20]

This volunteer role is institutionalized in the training programs and activities of a variety of service organizations, especially the Junior League, which is meant for women between 20 and 40 years of age, including some upwardly mobile professional women. *Volunteerism is crucial and the Junior League is the quintessence of volunteer work,* said one woman. *Everything the League does improves the situation but doesn't rock the boat. It fits into existing institutions.*[21]

Quite unexpectedly, Ostrander found that many of the women serving as volunteers, fund-raisers, and board members for charitable and civic organizations viewed their work as a protection of the American way of life against the further encroachment of government into areas of social welfare. Some even saw themselves as bulwarks against socialism. *There must always be people to do volunteer work,* one said. *If you have a society where no one is willing, then you may as well have communism where it's all done by the government.* Another commented: *It would mean that the government would take over, and it would all be regimented. If there are no volunteers, we would live in a completely managed society which is quite the opposite to our history of freedom.* Another equated government support with socialism: *You'd have to go into government funds. That's socialism. The more we can keep independent and under private control, the better it is.*[22]

Despite this emphasis on volunteer work, the women placed high value on family life. They arranged their schedules to be home when children came home from school (thirty of the thirty-eight in Ostrander's study had three or more children), and they emphasized that their primary concern was to provide a good home for their husbands. Several wanted to have greater decision-making power over their inherited wealth, but almost all wanted to take on the traditional roles of wife and mother, at least until their children were grown.

In recent years, thanks to the pressures on corporations from the women's movement, upper-class women have expanded their roles to include corporate directorships. A study of women in the corporate community by former sociologist Beth Ghiloni, now a corporate executive, found that 26 percent of all women directors had upper-class backgrounds, a figure very similar to overall findings for samples of predominantly male directors. The figure was even higher, about 71 percent, for the one-fifth of directors who described themselves as volunteers before joining corporate boards. Many of these women told Ghiloni that their contacts with male corporate leaders on the boards of women's colleges and cultural organizations led to their selection as corporate directors.[23]

Women of the upper class are in a paradoxical position. They are subordinate to male members of their class, but they nonetheless exercise important class power in some institutional arenas. They may or may not be fully satisfied with their ambiguous power status, but they bring an upper-class, antigovernment perspective to their exercise of power. There is thus class solidarity between men and women toward the rest of society. Commenting on the complex role of upper-class women, feminist scholar Catherine Stimson draws the following stark picture: "First they must do to class what gender has done to their work—render it invisible. Next, they must maintain the same class structure they have struggled to veil."[24]

Marriage and Family Continuity

The institution of marriage is as important in the upper class as it is in any level of American society, and it does not differ greatly from other levels in its patterns and rituals. Only the exclusive site of the occasion and the lavishness of the reception distinguish upper-class marriages. The prevailing wisdom within the upper class is that children should marry someone of their own social class. The women interviewed by Ostrander, for example, felt that marriage was difficult enough without differences in "interests" and "background," which seemed to be the code words for class in discussions of marriage. Marriages outside the class were seen as likely to end in divorce.[25]

The original purpose of the debutante season was to introduce the highly sheltered young women of the upper class to eligible marriage partners. It was an attempt to corral what Baltzell calls "the democratic whims of romantic love," which "often play havoc with class solidarity."[26] But the day when the debut could play such a role was long past, even by the 1940s. The function of directing romantic love into acceptable channels was taken over by fraternities and sororities, singles-only clubs, and exclusive summer resorts.

However, in spite of parental concerns and institutionalized efforts to provide proper marriage partners, some upper-class people marry members of the upper-middle and middle classes. Although there are no completely satisfactory studies, and none that are very recent, what information is available suggests that members of the upper class are no more likely to marry within their class than people of other social levels. The most frequently cited evidence on upper-class marriage patterns appears as part of biographical studies of prominent families. Though these studies demonstrate that a great many marriages take place within the class—and often between scions of very large fortunes—they also show that some marriages are to sons and daughters of middle-class professionals and managers. No systematic conclusions can be drawn from these examples.

Wedding announcements that appear in major newspapers provide another source of evidence on this question. In a study covering prominent wedding stories on the society pages on Sundays in June for two different years one decade apart, it was found that 70 percent of the grooms and 84 percent of the brides had attended a private secondary school. Two-thirds of the weddings involved at least one participant who was listed in the *Social Register,* with both bride and groom listed in the *Social Register* in 24 percent of the cases.[27] However, those who marry far below their station may be less likely to have wedding announcements prominently displayed, so such studies must be interpreted with caution.

A study that used the *Social Register* as its starting point may be indicative of rates of intermarriage within the upper class, but it is very limited in its scope and therefore can only be considered suggestive. It began with a compilation of all the marriages listed in the Philadelphia *Social Register* for 1940 and 1960. Since the decision to list these announcements may be a voluntary one, a check of the marriage announcements in the *Philadelphia Bulletin* for those years was made to see if there were any marriages involving listees in the *Social Register* that had not been included, but none was found. One in every three marriages for 1940 and one in five for 1961 involved partners who were both listed in the *Social Register.* When private-school attendance and social club membership as well as the *Social Register* were used as evidence for upper-class standing, the rate of intermarriage averaged 50 percent for the two years. This figure is very similar to that for other social levels.[28]

The general picture for social class and marriage in the United States is suggested in a statistical study of neighborhoods and marriage patterns in the San Francisco area. Its results are very similar to those of the Philadelphia study using the *Social Register.* Of eighty grooms randomly selected from the highest-level neighborhoods, court records showed that 51 percent married brides of a comparable level. The rest married women from middle-level neighborhoods; only one or two married women from lower-level residential areas. Conversely, 63 percent of eighty-one grooms from the lowest-level neighborhoods married women from comparable areas, with under 3 percent having brides from even the lower end of the group of top neighborhoods. Completing the picture, most of the eighty-two men from middle-level areas married women from the same types of neighborhoods, but about 10 percent married into higher-level neighborhoods. Patterns of intermarriage, then, suggest both stability and some upward mobility through marriage into the upper class.[29]

Turning now to the continuity of the upper class, there is evidence that it is very great from generation to generation. This finding conflicts with the oft-repeated folk wisdom that there is a large turnover at the top of the American social ladder. Once in the upper class, families tend to stay there even as they are joined in each generation by new families and by middle-class brides and grooms who marry into their families. One study demonstrating this point began with a list of twelve families who were among the top wealthholders in Detroit for 1860, 1892, and 1902. After demonstrating their high social standing as well as their wealth, it traced their Detroit-based descendants to 1970. Nine of the twelve families still had members in the Detroit upper class; members from six of the families were directors of top corporations in the city. The study cast light on some of the reasons why the continuity is not even greater. One of the top wealthholders of 1860 had only one child, who in turn had no children. Another family dropped out of sight after the six children of the original 1860 wealthholder's only child went to court to divide the dwindling estate of $250,000 into six equal parts. A third family persisted into a fourth generation of four great-granddaughters, all of whom married outside of Detroit.[30] . . .

Tracing the families of the steel executives into the twentieth century, John Ingham determined that most were listed in the *Social Register,* were members of the most exclusive social clubs, lived in expensive neighborhoods, and sent their children to Ivy League universities. He concludes that "there has been more continuity than change among the business elites and upper classes in America," and he contrasts his results with the claims made by several generations of impressionistic historians that there has been a decline of aristocracy, the rise of a new plutocracy, or a passing of the old order.[31] . . .

It seems likely, then, that the American upper class is a mixture of old and new members. There is both continuity and social mobility, with the newer members being assimilated into the lifestyle of the class through participation in the schools, clubs, and other social institutions described [here]. There may be some tensions between those newly arrived and those of established status—as novelists and journalists love to point out—but what they have in common soon outweighs their differences.[32]

ENDNOTES

[1] Randall Collins, "Functional and Conflict Theories of Educational Stratification," *American Sociological Review* 36 (1971): 1010.

[2] "Private Schools Search for a New Role," *National Observer* (August 26, 1968), p. 5. For an excellent account of major boarding schools, see Peter Cookson and Caroline Hodges Persell, *Preparing for Power: America's Elite Boarding Schools* (New York: Basic Books, 1985).

[3] E. Digby Baltzell, *Philadelphia Gentlemen: The Making of a National Upper Class* (Glencoe, IL: Free Press, 1958), p. 339.

[4] Susan Ostrander, *Women of the Upper Class* (Philadelphia: Temple University Press, 1984), p. 85.

[5] Erving Goffman, *Asylums* (Chicago: Aldine, 1961).

[6] Interview conducted for G. William Domhoff by research assistant Deborah Samuels, February 1975; see also Gary Tamkins, "Being Special: A Study of the Upper Class" (Ph.D. Dissertation, Northwestern University, 1974).

[7] Steven Levine, "The Rise of the American Boarding Schools" (Senior Honors Thesis, Harvard University, 1975), pp. 128–30.

[8] Baltzell, *Philadelphia Gentlemen,* pp. 51–65.

[9] Baltzell, *Philadelphia Gentlemen,* p. 373.

[10] Richard P. Coleman and Lee Rainwater, *Social Standing in America* (New York: Basic Books, 1978), p. 144.

[11] Sophy Burnham, *The Landed Gentry* (New York: G. P. Putnam's Sons, 1978).

[12] Ostrander, *Women of the Upper Class,* p. 104.

[13] Philip Bonacich and G. William Domhoff, "Latent Classes and Group Membership," *Social Networks* 3 (1981).

[14] G. William Domhoff, *Who Rules America?* (Englewood Cliffs, NJ: Prentice-Hall, 1967), p. 26; E. Digby Baltzell, *The Protestant Establishment,* op. cit., p. 371.

[15] Thomas Powell, *Race, Religion, and the Promotion of the American Executive* (Columbus: Ohio State University Press, 1969), p. 50.

[16] Gay Pauley, "Coming-Out Party: It's Back in Style," *Los Angeles Times,* March 13, 1977, section 4, p. 22; "Debs Put Party on Jet," *San Francisco Chronicle,* December 18, 1965, p. 2.

[17] Pauley, "Coming-Out Party."

[18] Ostrander, "Upper-Class Women: Class Consciousness As Conduct and Meaning," *Women of the Upper Class,* pp. 93–94; Ostrander, *Women of the Upper Class,* pp. 89–90.

[19] "The Debut Tradition: A Subjective View of What It's All About," *New Orleans Times-Picayune,* August 29, 1976, section 4, p. 13; Tia Gidnick, "On Being 18 in '78: Deb Balls Back in Fashion," *Los Angeles Times,* November 24, 1978, part 4, p. 1; Virginia Lee Warren, "Many Young Socialites Want Simpler Debutante Party, or None," *New York Times,* July 2, 1972, p. 34; Mary Lou Loper, "The Society Ball: Tradition in an Era of Change," *Los Angeles Times,* October 28, 1973, part 4, p. 1.

[20] Ostrander, *Women of the Upper Class,* pp. 128–29. For three other fine accounts of the volunteer work of upper-class women, see Arlene Daniels, *Invisible Careers* (Chicago: University of Chicago Press, 1988); Margot MacLeod, "Influential Women Volunteers" (paper presented to the meetings of the American Sociological Association, San Antonio, August 1984); and Margot MacLeod, "Older Generation, Younger Generation: Transition in Women Volunteers' Lives" (unpublished manuscript, 1987). For women's involvement in philanthropy and on the boards of nonprofit organizations, see Teresa Odendahl, *Charity Begins at Home: Generosity and Self-Interest among the Philanthropic Elite* (New York: Basic Books, 1990), and Teresa Odendahl and Michael O'Neill, eds., *Women and Power in the Nonprofit Sector* (San Francisco: Jossey-Bass, 1994). For in-depth interviews of both women and men philanthropists, see Francie Ostrower, *Why the Wealthy Give: The Culture of Elite Philanthropy* (Princeton, NJ: Princeton University Press, 1995).

[21] Ostrander, *Women of the Upper Class,* pp. 113, 115.

[22] Ostrander, "Upper-Class Women," p. 84; Ostrander, *Women of the Upper Class,* pp. 132–37.

[23] Beth Ghiloni, "New Women of Power" (Ph.D. Dissertation, University of California, Santa Cruz, 1986), pp. 122, 159.

[24] Daniels, *Invisible Careers,* p. x.

[25] Ostrander, *Women of the Upper Class,* pp. 85–88.

[26] Baltzell, *Philadelphia Gentlemen,* p. 26.

[27] Paul M. Blumberg and P. W. Paul, "Continuities and Discontinuities in Upper-Class Marriages," *Journal of Marriage and the Family,* vol. 37, no. 1 (February 1975): 63–77; David L. Hatch and Mary A. Hatch, "Criteria of Social Status As Derived from Marriage Announcements in the *New York Times*," *American Sociological Review* 12 (August 1947): 396–403.

[28] Lawrence Rosen and Robert R. Bell, "Mate Selection in the Upper Class," *Sociological Quarterly* 7 (Spring 1966): 157–66. I supplemented the original study by adding the information on schools and clubs.

[29] Robert C. Tryon, "Identification of Social Areas by Cluster Analysis: A General Method with an Application to the San Francisco Bay Area," *University of California Publications in Psychology* 8 (1955); Robert C. Tryon, "Predicting Group Differences in Cluster Analysis: The Social Areas Problem," *Multivariate Behavioral Research* 2 (1967): 453–75.

[30] T. D. Schuby, "Class Power, Kinship, and Social Cohesion: A Case Study of a Local Elite," *Sociological Focus* 8, no. 3 (August 1975): 243–55; Donald Davis, "The Price of Conspicuous Production: The Detroit Elite and the Automobile Industry, 1900–1933," *Journal of Social History* 16 (1982): 21–46.

[31] John Ingham, *The Iron Barons* (Westport, CT: Greenwood Press, 1978), pp. 230–31. For the continuity of a more general sample of wealthy families, see Michael Allen, *The Founding Fortunes* (New York: Truman Talley Books, 1987).

[32] For further evidence of the assimilation of new members into the upper class, see the study of the social affiliations and attitudes of the successful Jewish business owners who become part of the upper class by Richard L. Zweigenhaft and G. William Domhoff, *Jews in the Protestant Establishment* (New York: Praeger, 1982).

25

RACE, HOMEOWNERSHIP, AND WEALTH

THOMAS M. SHAPIRO

As G. William Domhoff argues in the previous selection, social classes do exist in America, and social class distinctions can be observed through a variety of objective and subjective indicators. To understand social class relationships fully, however, sociologists must also examine racial-ethnic differences in the indicators of socioeconomic status. For example, data show persistent wealth discrepancies between whites and African Americans with similar achievements and credentials. Sociologist Thomas M. Shapiro has studied this racial inequality in wealth for two decades, resulting in several important books, including *The Hidden Cost of Being African American: How Wealth Perpetuates Inequality* (2004). The excerpt that follows is a research article based on that book published in the *Washington University Journal of Law and Policy* in 2006. Shapiro, the Pokross Professor of Law and Social Policy at Brandeis University, analyzes the racial-ethnic gap in assets and wealth.

Closing the racial wealth gap must be at the forefront of the civil rights agenda in the twenty-first century. This article examines homeownership as a main policy strategy to move toward this goal. The article opens by restating the crucial importance of closing the racial wealth gap, and offers an early assessment of this agenda. Next, the article argues that

Thomas M. Shapiro, "Race, Homeownership, and Wealth," *Washington University Journal of Law & Policy*, 20, 2006. Reprinted by permission of the *Washington University Journal of Law and Policy* and the author, Thomas M. Shapiro, Pokross Professor of Law and Social Policy, The Heller School for Social Policy and Management, Brandeis University.

homeownership is an appropriate strategy to attack the racial wealth gap. Finally, the article examines the various promises and many potential pitfalls and challenges facing minority homeownership.

I. Why Wealth Matters

Wealth, as distinguished from income, offers the key to understanding racial stratification in the United States, especially the persistence of racial inequality in a post-civil rights era in which minorities have made remarkable advances. A wealth perspective provides a fresh way to examine the "playing field." It provides a concrete way of analyzing how the past connects to the present, and thus provides a mechanism to refresh our historical memory of race. Further, a wealth perspective has significant implications for our thinking about affirmative action and our conceptualization of equality. First, however, I must outline this wealth perspective and explain why it is so important.

Wealth is the total value of a family's financial resources minus all debts. Income includes earnings from work or its substitutes, like pension, disability, unemployment insurance, or social assistance. Wealth is a special kind of money because it represents ownership and control of resources; income is essentially earnings or payments that replace earnings.

Most commentators and analysts are familiar and comfortable with the income comparisons that provide a window as to whether there is growing or declining racial economic inequality. However, the focus on wealth, "the net value of assets (e.g., ownership of stocks, money in the bank, real estate, business ownership, etc.) less debts," creates a different gestalt or perspective on racial inequality (Oliver & Shapiro 1995:30). This gestalt has two dimensions. The first is the conceptual distinction between income and assets. While income represents the flow of resources earned in a particular time period, such as a week, month or year, assets are a stock of resources that are saved or invested. Income is mainly used for day-to-day necessities, while assets are special monies—a "surplus resource available for improving life chances, providing further opportunities, securing prestige, passing status along to one's family" and securing economic security for present and future generations (Oliver & Shapiro 1995:32).

The second dimension is quantitative: to what extent is there asset parity between blacks and whites? Do blacks have access to resources that they can use to plan for their future, to enable their children to obtain a quality education, to provide for the next generation's head start, and to secure their place in the political community? For these reasons, we focus on the inequality of wealth as the *sine qua non* indicator of material well-being. Without sufficient assets, it is difficult to lay claim to economic security in American society.

Income and wealth are often confused both in the public mind and in the social science literature; indeed, the social science paradigm regarding family well-being and inequality has extended to a treatment of wealth only since the mid-1990s.[1] An assets perspective that examines family financial wealth facilitates an additional lens on how advantage and disadvantage is generated and passed along in America. Unlike education, jobs, or even income, wealth allows families to secure advantages and often is the vehicle for transferring inequality across generations. Wealth data for average American families was not collected systematically until the mid-1980s. While data availability provides the capacity for an asset perspective, difficult methodological and conceptual issues remain, such as how to value a home, how to conceptualize home appreciation, how to value a business, and how to treat retirement plans (Shapiro 2004).

The social sciences have neglected the wealth dimension when examining the status of American families in general, and racial inequality in particular. Instead of examining a foundation of property relations, our analyses have focused on occupation, education, and income inequality. This reliance on labor market and human capital indicators began to change, however, with the collection of wealth data for typical American families in the mid-1980s, and the social science and journalistic inequality discussion turned to wealth. Indeed, the increasing wealth concentration and the mounting racial wealth gap have become topics for public conversation and public policy issues, even if at this point they are not on the imminent political agenda (Wolff 2002).

The standard social science approach to examining racial inequality is to analyze how economic resources, opportunities, and power are distributed. With the focus being the economic dimension, most research has emphasized basic labor market components of jobs and wages. The work of William Julius Wilson (1996), for example, emphasizes the importance of African Americans' place in a changing occupational structure, shifts in wages, metropolitan economies, and a global economy. As a result, the effects of wealth disparity and family wealth on differing opportunities and well-being for families have been neglected both by the social sciences and by policy discussions. Further, among all the other racial gaps, whites and blacks are most persistently unequal along the wealth dimension (Shapiro 2004:33).

Wealth is different from income, and, most importantly, families use wealth in very different ways than they use income. Wealth is a storehouse of a family's financial resources and, when combined with income, frames the opportunity for families to secure the "good life," however they define it, typically by human capital development, business opportunities, home ownership, community location, health, travel, comfort, or security. Wealth, then, is a special kind of money utilized to launch social mobility, create opportunities and status, or pass along advantages to one's children. Two families with similar incomes but widely disparate wealth most likely do not share similar life trajectories, and we must consider this when thinking about inequality and public policy.

The importance of wealth was borne out in the stories of the nearly 200 families interviewed for the book, *The Hidden Cost of Being African American* (Shapiro 2004). Families discussed about how they think about assets, how they strategize to acquire wealth, how they plan to use assets, and how they actually use them. These families clearly view income and wealth very differently, so that wealth is seen as a special kind of money. We asked the families if they treated wealth differently than income. The pattern of answers was resoundingly affirmative, especially among those with ample assets. Wealth is seen first as a personal safety net, or an unspecified amount of money that is stored away to cushion against the unexpected health crisis, job termination, legal difficulty, or repair of the family car (Shapiro 2004:34–35).

Beyond serving as a personal safety net—all the more important as the social investment of the state withers—families also view financial wealth as "moving-ahead" money. One respondent succinctly summed it up by saying: *Income supplies life support, assets provide opportunities.* A middle-class Bostonian put it this way: *My income is limited. My assets I want to hang on to for future needs.* One Los Angeles mother captured the thinking of many we interviewed when she said that wealth *is definitely long term. We act as if it's not even there* (Shapiro 2004:34).

If income and wealth are highly correlated, such a distinction is interesting academically, but would be one without much of a difference. Sociologist Lisa Keister's *Wealth in America* reviews the correlation of income and wealth, and concludes that it is weak at best. According to Keister, this suggests that "studies that focus solely on income miss a large part of the story of advantage and disadvantage in America" (Keister 2000:10).

Having the capacity to represent inequality from the past, an examination of wealth not only gauges contemporary resources differences, but also suggests a future pattern of inequalities. I suggest a paradigm shift: Wealth changes our conception of racial inequality, its nature and magnitude, origins and transmission, and whether it is increasing or narrowing. Importantly, an examination of wealth allows an analytic window into the contemporary relevance of the historical legacy of African Americans; indeed, a wealth lens will broaden our understanding of the relationship between historical and contemporary considerations for class as well as for race.

Importantly, civil rights organizations already place the wealth gap on their agenda and have begun to build constituencies and public awareness for action.[2] While consensus is building on this agenda, how to move forward, and on which specific policies, is still a subject of debate. Thus, while homeownership is central to the discussion of closing the racial wealth gap, other mechanisms, ranging from Individual Development Accounts, to building community assets, to reparations, also offer important remedies. Framing racial inequality from a wealth perspective raises the issue of the deeply embedded racial structure of the United States.

II. The Homeownership Foundation

How do families accumulate wealth? This question goes directly to the heart of the American ethos and to my argument. The leading ideological and scholarly answer is that wealth emerges from hard work, disciplined consumption, savings and wise investments, with perhaps some luck thrown in. In this individual model, wealth builds slowly during one's lifetime and is life-cycle sensitive, with wealth building gradually in young families, accumulating mostly during the latter working years, and being utilized mostly during retirement.[3] This theory of wealth accumulation thus emphasizes the acquisition, accrual, and depletion of wealth within a lifetime, placing minimal weight on inheritance or on the consequences of state policies and institutional practices on subsequent wealth-accumulating opportunities.

Institutional theory and a sociology of wealth places greater value on inheritance, programs and practices. Homeownership and housing appreciation is the foundation of institutional accumulation. Indeed, for most Americans, home equity represents the largest reservoir of wealth: home wealth accounts for 60% of the total wealth among America's middle class. The empirically accurate American wealth narrative is not simply about individual hard work, discipline, and savings; notably it is also about structured homeownership opportunities, real estate markets, government programs encouraging homeownership, and residential segregation (Shapiro 2004:107–108).

America has a high homeownership rate, with 69% of Americans owning homes.[4] A series of federal policies that started in the 1930s made this high homeownership rate and subsequent middle-class wealth accumulation possible by creating a government-sponsored market. Federal policies helped, create a mortgage market where homes could be purchased with long-term, low-interest loans and relatively small down payments, most particularly through the Federal Housing Administration, the Veterans Administration, and the GI Bill. In conjunction with rising wages after World War II, these policies put the American dream of home ownership within the reach of millions of families (Jackson 1985). The beneficial tax treatment of home mortgages and capital gains on home sales makes home ownership more affordable. Transportation policies subsidized an infrastructure that prioritizes private automobiles and allows suburban development. While these federal policies and subsidies have been successful in anchoring America's middle class in home ownership, the same policies have traditionally reinforced residential segregation (Oliver & Shapiro 1995).

III. The Asset Poverty Line

This section examines the resource condition of typical American families by looking at wealth circumstances. The Asset Poverty Line (APL) is a tool that facilitates an examination of the wealth condition of American families. Using the conservative U.S. government policy as a standard, we asked how long can families survive at a poverty level in the absence of an income stream. In 1999, for example, the monthly poverty line for a family of four was $1392. Thus, to survive at the poverty line for three months, a family needed at least $4175 in financial assets (Shapiro 2004). Families with less than $4175 can thus be categorized as asset poor. It is worth noting the conservative assumptions require accepting the government poverty line, at least for purposes of this exercise. Adopting a three-month threshold, instead of, say, a six- or nine-month threshold, is another conservative assumption. The impact is that the actual number of families in asset poverty is underestimated. Nonetheless, the APL focuses attention on asset poverty.

Others, I hope, will push these boundaries. Nearly four households out of ten in the world's wealthiest nation do not own enough assets to live even a poverty lifestyle for three months.

> If poverty is something that affects not just one in every eight, nine, or ten families [as in the income definition of poverty] but four in ten, then we need to think about poverty very differently because it is much more characteristic of American families. Over half of black American families fell below the Asset Poverty Line in 1999. (Shapiro 2004:38)

Viewed in light of financial assets, America's families are far more fragile and precarious than previously thought. Moreover, both class and race features are clearly revealed.

IV. The Racial Wealth Gap

Sandra McCord lives in Los Angeles with her two daughters, Kalila and Myisha. Her neighborhood is poverty stricken and African American. Sandra has worked at various low-level, poverty wage jobs, but when I talked to her, she was in school working toward her degree. She has zero financial assets, owes money on some store charge cards, and manages to get by—barely—on less than poverty income. Hers is not an easy life. In the midst of her daily struggles, Sandra is more troubled about her daughters' futures. She believed that the local schools were horrible and unsafe, so she navigated the system to place her daughters in better ones. However, these schools are a one and a half hour public bus ride away, and Sandra must pay the bus fares. Bus fares do not cost much, unless, of course, you survive on a budget that is less than half of the poverty line. Each month this poses a cruel dilemma for Sandra: *Sometimes, to be honest, sometimes, sometimes, when I have to wait for my check . . . sometimes my kids will have to miss a couple of days of school* (Shapiro 2004:179–181). Choosing between school for your children or food on the table is not an excruciatingly tragic dilemma that most of us face at month's end. This is the price Sandra and her daughters pay for living in a poor neighborhood.

The McCords are one of nearly 200 families that I interviewed for *The Hidden Cost of Being African American*. While her story and choices may sound extreme, the lack of wealth among African Americans is a major explanation why racial inequality persists today. The typical African American family owns just $3000 in financial wealth (excluding homes) (Shapiro 2004:49).

The standard metric of racial inequality is to compare the incomes of average white and black families. This measure has ranged from approximately fifty-six cents on the dollar to sixty-two cents on the dollar from the mid-1960s until now. The range has been narrow, and not much movement has occurred toward more equality or toward closing the income gap.

Examining wealth dramatically changes this perspective. The net worth of typical white families is $81,000, compared to $8000 for black families (Shapiro 2004:47–49). A typical white family's wealth is more than $73,000 greater than the typical black family's, which is a marker of the racial wealth gap expressed in dollars. The baseline racial wealth gap also shows that black families own only a dime of wealth for every dollar owned by white families. One component of this paradigm shift is the magnitude of closing a fifty-nine cent on a dollar gap, to thinking about how to close a ten cent on a dollar gap.

The prevailing explanation for this robust racial wealth gap, of course, is rooted in inequalities in contemporary class-based achievements, such as occupation, education, and income.[5] Leveling these critical differences in school achievement, jobs, and paychecks, accordingly, will eradicate the racial wealth gap. Our analysis, and that of others (Keister 2000), demonstrates the shortcomings of this class-determinist perspective on racial inequality. In the best-case scenario, comparing equally achieving white and black middle class families illustrates the significance of the historical legacy of government policies and practices, and of race and continuing contemporary institutional discrimination.

When one defines the middle class by education (college degree), an income range, or occupational status (professional, white collar), the black middle class owns about twenty-five cents of wealth for every dollar of wealth owned by the white middle class (Shapiro 2004:90–91). Certainly, twenty-five cents on the dollar represents advancement over ten cents on the dollar, showing that achievement matters, but a huge racial wealth gap remains when one compares equally achieving whites and blacks. At least as important, one must ask why such a dramatic racial wealth gap remains. Although beyond the scope of this essay, I already have alluded to the enduring importance of how the past continues to play out in the present and the importance of contemporary institutional arrangements in promoting differential wealth accumulating opportunities with clear racial consequences.

Among the crucial issues facing families today is the effect of recent recession and jobless recovery on family economic security. My recent research argues that a widening wealth gap between minorities and whites is reversing the gains earned in schools and jobs, and is making inequality worse (Shapiro 2004:6–12). A report from the Pew Hispanic Center provides new data on family wealth and offers a sobering assessment of the precarious and fragile status of middle-class families—including white families, but most particularly Hispanic and African American families (Kochhar 2004).

In the years prior to the 2001 recession, white, Hispanic, and African American families generated wealth through savings, investment, and homeownership. More families acquired assets and family portfolios grew. In this context of wealth accumulation, however, the wealth gap between minority and white families was widened. The recession and its recovery brought wealth growth to an abrupt halt for millions of American families. During this period, Hispanic and African American families lost over one-quarter of their wealth, while the wealth of white families slowly grew.

In 2002, a typical Hispanic family owned eleven cents of wealth for every dollar owned by a typical white family, and African American families owned only seven cents.[6]

These net wealth losses illustrate how Hispanic and African American families, and low-to-middle income families in general, have shouldered the burden of tightening economic times and reduced social investment during the Bush administration. Over one in four (25%) Hispanic and African American families are asset-poor, having no liquid financial assets, compared to 13% of white families (Kochhar 2004:6). The research creates the inference that families with small or moderate amounts of wealth drew from their meager stockpile of savings to use as private safety nets. In addition to making tough choices, such as giving up health insurance or spacing out medical appointments and refilling prescriptions, this is the real story of how families adapt to recession, jobless recovery, stagnating wages, outsourcing, and a dwindling federal commitment to important safety nets like unemployment benefits and the minimum wage, which has not kept pace with inflation.

Interest-earning assets, such as savings bonds, IRA and Keogh accounts, 401(k) and thrift accounts, stocks and mutual funds, and business capital, declined precipitously among Hispanic families with assets (Kochhar 2004: 17–20). In African American families, stock and mutual fund investments plummeted by nearly two-thirds. Surely, this reflects investment losses, but it also represents the tapping of accounts to cover insecurities about employment and income losses. These families adapt by eating the acorns they stored for their future economic mobility and security. Families will not make up these setbacks easily or in a short time span.

While the income, educational achievement, and employment gaps among Hispanics, African Americans and whites remain steady or show some slight narrowing, the wealth gap increases. I made this argument in *The Hidden Cost of Being African American*. The report and current data from the Pew Hispanic Center further corroborate that a growing wealth gap reverses the gains earned in schools, on jobs, and in paychecks. An added compounding change is that the financial portfolios of Hispanics and African Americans have shrunk in the current economy.

More than any other economic attribute, wealth represents the sedimentation of historical inequalities in the American experience, in a sense the accumulation of advantages and disadvantages for different racial, class and ethnic groups (Oliver & Shapiro 1995:50–52). In this way, wealth provides a window to explore how our past influences the realities of today.

This is not simply a story about counting money; families think about using wealth first as a private safety net, and second as a vehicle to launch mobility into middle-class status, homeownership, business development, or a more secure retirement. The recent recession and recovery—along with current public policies—are a real step backward for the self-reliance and independence of Hispanics, African Americans, and other low-to-middle income families. These factors represent a double blow against equality and family well-being in America.

V. Homeownership and Institutional Discrimination

Homeownership is the largest component of the wealth portfolios of both white and black families. In 2002, housing wealth accounted for 63% of all wealth in African American families (Kochhar 2004:19, 36). In 2004, home-ownership reached historic highs, as 69% of American families lived in a home they owned. In 1995, 42.2% of African American families owned homes, increasing to a historic high of 49.5% in 2004. This 7.3% increase in African American homeownership is quite remarkable, and indicates striving, accomplishment, and success. The black-white homeownership gap stood at 28.5% in 1995 and narrowed to 26.2% in 2004 (Joint Center for Housing Studies 2005:36). Increasing black homeownership and rising home values are optimistic signs of closing the racial wealth gap. We might expect the homeownership gap to continue to close, as black homeownership starts from a considerably lower base while the higher white rate may be close to exhausting the potential of those who want to become homeowners.

However, the wealth accumulation and homeownership dynamics are marred by critical institutional factors. Nancy Denton's (2001) age-specific examination of homeownership rates for blacks and whites illustrates the importance of timing and of life course. The homeownership gap is widest for the younger age groups (twenty-five to twenty-nine years old), closes incrementally with age, and reaches its narrowest point for the elderly (seventy to seventy-four years old). Over the life course, the gap closes by almost half, which is very impressive. The simple conclusion is that whites can afford to buy homes earlier than can blacks. This underscores the importance of young couples needing significant parental financial support to afford homeownership (Shapiro 2004:60). In understanding this connection between homeownership and wealth accumulation, it is relevant that the earlier a family buys a home, the greater the likelihood that the home will appreciate in value and create more wealth.

As we think about closing the homeownership gap as a strategy for closing the racial wealth gap, we must attend to deeply rooted discriminatory institutional features. Three such features are apparent. First, financial institutions reject African Americans for home mortgages at considerably higher rates—about a 60% higher rejection rate—than whites, even when white and black families are equally creditworthy (Oliver & Shapiro 1995:141–47). As sanctioned community redlining diminishes under pressure from the civil rights movement, community organizations, the Community Reinvestment Act and other fair-lending and fair-housing laws,[7] it appears that financial institutions re-create similar results by constructing "objective" criteria of creditworthiness in such a way that individual minority families fall short far more often than white families, thereby redrawing redlines by family instead of by community.

Second, blacks approved for home mortgages often pay higher interest rates on home loans. Blacks pay interest rates of approximately one third of a percent higher than whites, or about $12,000 more for the average American home over a 30-year mortgage (Shapiro 2004:111–16). Part of this is due to the greater ability of white families to provide larger down payments and even to pay higher service fees for lowered interest rates. From interviews, discussions with bankers, and other data, it appears that many young white families can rely on significant family financial assistance with down payments and other costs. Nearly one-half of all white homeowners report that they received significant financial assistance from their families. In sharp contrast, seven out of eight African American homeowners purchased homes on their own. This inheritance results from the discriminatory housing markets of a previous era, marked by exclusion and residential segregation and backed by government support (Oliver & Shapiro 1995:16–18).

African Americans were frozen out of the greatest wealth building opportunities in American history. From the Homestead Act in the 1860s, to education and homeownership opportunities provided by the GI Bill and the Federal Housing Administration, to redlining through contemporary discrimination in housing markets, to the segregation tax on housing appreciation, major government-sponsored wealth building opportunities helped foster America's middle class and created much wealth (Shapiro 2004:189–91). Meanwhile, these same policies and practices left the African American community behind at the starting gate. Inheritance of our racial past thus becomes an integral part of the wealth narrative.

One indication that this history is alive today is the fact that most young couples can purchase homes only with significant financial assistance from their parents—especially to cover down payments. For example, Briggette and Joe Barry were having a tough time coming up with the down payment for their house (Shapiro 2004:73–74). They traded in the kids' saving bonds, worked two jobs each around the clock, and held garage sales, but they did not make much headway. Finally, Briggette's mom said, *Well this is stupid. We've got a lot of money here*, and provided significant funds to help with the down payment. This transformative asset moved the Barry family into a white, suburban, middle-class community that they otherwise could not have afforded. Our history denied this possible inheritance to African Americans, as they toiled in times and under conditions in which wealth accumulation was virtually foreclosed.

The third institutional dynamic of homeownership and home equity poses the most difficult challenges. Here, residential segregation meets housing appreciation. Homes have appreciated in value in most communities and in most areas of the country, except for in poor, minority, urban neighborhoods. On average, homes owned by whites appreciate in value approximately $28,000 more than those owned by blacks. Moreover, homes lose about 16% of their value when located in neighborhoods that are more than 10% black (Shapiro 2004:120–122). This gives a new (or old) meaning to the realtor's mantra: location, location, location. Just as home ownership creates wealth for both whites and blacks, it simultaneously widens the racial wealth gap under current conditions. . . .

Since homeownership results in wealth-building for most, we must consider ways to boost affordable homeownership. Similarly, we must pay more attention to protecting the assets that families already own, especially homes.

The documented trends in growing credit card debt,[8] rising predatory lending, and subprime loans endanger financial assets for low-income, elderly, and minority homeowners in particular.

Addressing inequities in home mortgage applications and attending to differences in mortgage rates is conceivable using existing laws, tools, and good will, but grappling with the supposedly objective, automated credit-scoring system for credit approvals will not be easy (Yinger 1995). More difficult and seemingly intractable barriers emerge when thinking through remedies for residential segregation. Because residential segregation is the lynchpin for race relations and the racial wealth gap, this must be part of the discussions (Massey & Denton 1993:110–14). . . .

Another caution against going overboard on homeownership is in order. Housing should be viewed as a continuum, with affordable housing—either homeownership, rental or transitional—the goal. Not all families at all phases of their life cycles are appropriate candidates for homeownership, and policy must take this into consideration. In addition, since housing appreciation depends upon location, prescriptions for homeownership must be tempered by a realistic assessment of property valuation and the types of public, social investments that improve neighborhoods.

My discussion here has focused mostly on the exchange value of homeownership. In the larger discussion of how families employ wealth to pass along advantages and opportunities to their children, it is important to note that homes also have use value. By this I mean that homeownership (or renting) locates a family in a set of community services, contexts, and relationships, and partially defines race and class identities. For example, most children attend school according to the geographic location of their housing. Because of this selection process and because most schools are funded by local taxes, housing affordability is a large determinant of school quality, resources, and peers (Shapiro 2004:167–82).

Finally, more attention is needed on protecting wealth accumulation and preservation, and on the political debate and the racialized state policies embedded in our tax code. Federal asset policies cost $335 billion in 2003, the vast majority of which are in tax expenditures or credits.[9] Most of these current asset policies subsidize homeownership through the mortgage interest deduction, create incentives for retirement savings, and subsidize saving and investment for those already well off. For example, one-third of these tax benefits accrue to the wealthiest one percent. Alternatively, representing the proverbial crumbs, 5 percent of the asset-related tax benefits go to the bottom 60 percent of the population. Reversing these priorities is a good starting part for inclusive asset building policies that promote equity.

ENDNOTES

[1] Included in this rapidly emerging literature are: Jennifer Jellison Holme, *Buying Homes, Buying Schools: School Choice and the Social Construction of School Quality*, 72 HARV. EDUC. REV. 177 (2002); Hyungsoo Kim & Jinkook Lee, *Unequal Effects of Elders' Health Problems on Wealth Depletion Across Race and Ethnicity*, 39 J. CONSUMER AFF. 148 (2005); Trina Williams Shanks, *The Impacts of Household Wealth on Child Development* (Ctr. for Soc. Dev., George Warren Brown Sch.

of Soc. Work, Wash. Univ., Working Paper No. 04-07, 2004), *available at* http://gwbweb.wustl.edu/csd/Publications/2004/WP04-07.pdf.

The work of Edward Wolff anchors much of the wealth inequality field. *See* EDWARD N. WOLFF, TOP HEAVY (2002). Many other scholars have made important contributions to understanding racial wealth inequality. These scholars include: Joseph G. Altonji et al., *Black/White Differences in Wealth*, 24 ECON. PERSP. 38 (2000); Kerwin Kofi Charles & Erik Hurst, *The Transition to Home Ownership and the Black-White Wealth Gap*, 84 REV. ECON. & STAT. 281 (2002); John Karl Scholz & Kara Levine, *U.S. Black-White Wealth Inequality*, in SOCIAL INEQUALITY 895 (Kathryn M. Neckerman ed., 2004).

[2] I refer to the work of many organizations, including the National Council of La Raza, the First Nations Development Institute, United for a Fair Economy, the Civil Rights Leadership Council, and others.

[3] *See* Franco Modigliani, *The Role of Intergenerational Transfers and Life Cycle Saving in the Accumulation of Wealth*, J. ECON. PERSP., Spring 1988, at 15, 16.

[4] JOINT CTR. FOR HOUS. STUDIES OF HARVARD UNIV., THE STATE OF THE NATION'S HOUSING: 2005, at 15–19 (2005).

[5] THE BLACK-WHITE TEST SCORE GAP (Christopher Jencks & Meredith Phillips eds., 1988); James P. Smith, *Race and Ethnicity in the Labor Market: Trends over the Short and Long Term*, in 2 AMERICA BECOMING 52, 52–97 (Neil J. Smelser et al. eds., 2001).

[6] RAKESH KUMAR KOCHHAR, THE WEALTH OF HISPANIC HOUSEHOLDS: 1996 to 2002 (2004). *Id.* at 5 (measuring the median net worth of white households as $88,651, that of Hispanic households as $7932, and that of Black households as $5988).

[7] JOINT CTR. FOR HOUS. STUDIES OF HARVARD UNIV., THE 25TH ANNIVERSARY OF THE COMMUNITY REINVESTMENT ACT: ACCESS TO CAPITAL IN AN EVOLVING FINANCIAL SERVICES SYSTEM (2002), *availabe at* http://www.jchs.harvard.edu/publications/governmentprograms/cra02–1.pdf.

[8] TAMARA DRAUT & JAVIER SILVA, BORROWING TO MAKE ENDS MEET: THE GROWTH OF CREDIT CARD DEBT IN THE 90s (2003), *available at* http://www.demos-USA.org/pubs/borrowing_to_make_ends_meet.pdf.

[9] CTR. FOR ENTER. DEV., HIDDEN IN PLAIN SIGHT: A LOOK AT THE $335-BILLION ASSET-BUILDING BUDGET 1 (2004).

REFERENCES

Denton, Nancy A. 2001. "Housing as a Means of Asset Accumulation: A Good Strategy for the Poor?" Pp. 232–244 in *Assets for the Poor: The Benefits of Spreading Asset Ownership*, edited by Thomas M. Shapiro and Edward N. Wolff. New York: Russell Sage Foundation.

Joint Center for Housing Studies. 2005. "The State of the Nation's Housing." Cambridge, MA: Harvard University.

Keister, Lisa A. 2000. *Wealth in America*. New York: Cambridge University Press.

Kochhar, Rakesh Kumar. 2004. *The Wealth of Hispanic Households: 1996–2002*. Washington, D.C.: Pew Hispanic Center.

Massey, Douglas S. and Nancy A. Denton. 1993. *American Apartheid: Segregation and the Making of the Underclass*. Cambridge, MA: Harvard University Press.

Oliver, Melvin L. and Thomas M. Shapiro. 1995. *Black Wealth/White Wealth: A New Perspective on Racial Inequality*. New York: Routledge Press.

Shapiro, Thomas M. 2004. *The Hidden Cost of Being African American: How Wealth Perpetuates Inequality*. New York: Oxford University Press.

Wilson, William Julius. 1996. *When Work Disappears: The World of the New Urban Poor*. New York: Vintage Books.

Wolff, Edward N. 2002. *Top Heavy*. New York: New Press.

Yinger, John. 1995. *Closed Doors, Opportunities Lost: The Continuing Costs of Housing Discrimination*. New York: Russell Sage Foundation.

26

NICKEL-AND-DIMED
On (Not) Getting By in America

BARBARA EHRENREICH

As the previous reading by Shapiro demonstrated, the American Dream and accumulation of wealth have been difficult to obtain for African Americans. They have also been impossible goals for the working poor. Instead, many working-class people struggle to meet the economic requirements of every-day survival. In the excerpt below, Barbara Ehrenreich describes what it is like to try to work and survive on the wages most unskilled workers receive in America. Ehrenreich began her field research in 1998 to find out whether welfare reform's back-to-work programs really have the ability to lift poor women out of poverty and provide them a future in the labor market. The results of Ehrenreich's research are published in her 2001 book, Nickel-and-Dimed: On (Not) Getting By in America.

At the beginning of June 1998 I leave behind everything that normally soothes the ego and sustains the body—home, career, companion, reputation, ATM card—for a plunge into the low-wage workforce. There, I become another, occupationally much diminished "Barbara Ehrenreich"—depicted on job-application forms as a divorced homemaker whose sole work experience consists of housekeeping in a few private homes. I am terrified, at the beginning, of being unmasked for what I am: a middle-class journalist setting out to explore the world that welfare mothers are entering, at the rate of approximately 50,000 a month, as welfare reform kicks in. Happily, though, my fears turn out to be entirely unwarranted: dur-ing a month of poverty and toil, my name goes unnoticed and for the most part unuttered. In this parallel universe where my father never got out of the mines and I never got through college, I am "baby," "honey," "blondie," and, most commonly, "girl."

My first task is to find a place to live. I figure that if I can earn $7 an hour—which, from the want ads, seems doable—I can afford to spend $500 on rent, or maybe, with severe economies, $600. In the Key West area, where I live, this pretty much confines me to flophouses and trailer homes—like the one, a pleasing fifteen-minute drive from town, that has no air-conditioning, no screens, no fans, no television, and, by way of diversion, only the challenge of evading the landlord's Doberman pinscher. The big problem with this place, though, is the rent, which at $675 a month is well beyond my reach. All right, Key West is expensive. But so is New York City, or the Bay Area, or Jackson Hole, or Telluride, or Boston, or any other place where tourists and the wealthy compete for living space with the people who clean their toilets and fry their hash browns.[1] Still, it is a shock to realize that "trailer trash" has become, for me, a demographic category to aspire to.

So I decide to make the common trade-off between affordability and convenience, and go for a $500-a-month efficiency thirty miles up a two-lane highway from the employment opportunities of Key West, meaning forty-five minutes if there's no road construction and I don't get caught behind some sun-dazed Canadian tourists. I hate the drive, along a roadside studded with white crosses commemorating the more effective head-on collisions, but it's a sweet little place—a cabin, more or less, set in the swampy back yard of the converted mobile home where my landlord, an affable TV repairman, lives with his bartender girlfriend. Anthropologically speaking, a bustling trailer park would be preferable, but here I have a gleaming white floor and a firm mattress, and the few resident bugs are easily vanquished.

Besides, I am not doing this for the anthropology. My aim is nothing so mistily subjective as to "experience poverty" or find out how it "really feels" to be a long-term low-wage worker. I've had enough unchosen encounters with poverty and the world of low-wage work to know it's not a place you want to visit for touristic purposes; it just smells too much like fear. And with all my real-life assets—bank account, IRA, health insurance, multiroom home—waiting indulgently in the background, I am, of course, thoroughly insulated from the terrors that afflict the genuinely poor.

No, this is a purely objective, scientific sort of mission. The humanitarian rationale for welfare reform—as opposed to the more punitive and stingy impulses that may actually have motivated it—is that work will lift poor women out of poverty while simultaneously inflating their self-esteem and hence their future value in the labor market. Thus, whatever the hassles involved in finding child care, transportation, etc., the transition from welfare to work will end happily, in greater prosperity for all. Now there are many problems with this comforting prediction, such as the fact that the economy will inevitably undergo a downturn, eliminating many jobs. Even without a downturn, the influx of a million former welfare recipients into the low-wage labor market could depress wages by as much as 11.9 percent, according to the Economic Policy Institute (EPI) in Washington, D.C.

But is it really possible to make a living on the kinds of jobs currently available to unskilled people? Mathematically, the answer is no, as can be shown by taking $6 to $7 an hour, perhaps subtracting a dollar or two an hour for child care, multiplying by 160 hours a month, and comparing the result to the prevailing rents. According to the National Coalition for the Homeless, for example, in 1998 it took, on average nationwide, an hourly wage of $8.89 to afford a one-bedroom apartment, and the Preamble Center for Public Policy estimates that the odds against a typical welfare recipient's landing a job at such a "living wage" are about 97 to 1. If these numbers are right, low-wage work is not a solution to poverty and possibly not even to homelessness.

It may seem excessive to put this proposition to an experimental test. As certain family members keep unhelpfully reminding me, the viability of low-wage work could be tested, after a fashion, without ever leaving my study. I could just pay myself $7 an hour for eight hours a day, charge myself for room and board, and total up the numbers after a month. Why leave the people and work that I love? But I am an experimental scientist by training. In that business, you don't just sit at a desk and theorize; you plunge into the everyday chaos of nature, where surprises lurk in the most mundane measurements. Maybe, when I got into it, I would discover some hidden economies in the world of the low-wage worker. After all, if 30 percent of the workforce toils for less than $8 an hour, according to the EPI, they may have found some tricks as yet unknown to me. Maybe— who knows?—I would even be able to detect in myself the bracing psychological effects of getting out of the house, as promised by the welfare wonks at places like the Heritage Foundation. Or, on the other hand, maybe there would be unexpected costs—physical, mental, or financial— to throw off all my calculations. Ideally, I should do this with two small children in tow, that being the welfare average, but mine are grown and no one is willing to lend me theirs for a month-long vacation in penury. So this is not the perfect experiment, just a test of the best possible case: an unencumbered woman, smart and even strong, attempting to live more or less off the land.

On the morning of my first full day of job searching, I take a red pen to the want ads, which are auspiciously numerous. Everyone in Key West's booming "hospitality industry" seems to be looking for someone like me— trainable, flexible, and with suitably humble expectations as to pay. . . .

Most of the big hotels run ads almost continually, just to build a supply of applicants to replace the current workers as they drift away or are fired, so finding a job is just a matter of being at the right place at the right time and flexible enough to take whatever is being offered that day. This finally happens to me at one of the big discount hotel chains, where I go, as usual, for housekeeping and am sent, instead, to try out as a waitress at the attached "family restaurant," a dismal spot with a counter and about thirty tables that looks out on a parking garage and features such tempting fare as "Polish [sic] sausage and BBQ sauce" on 95-degree days. Phillip, the dapper young West Indian who introduces himself as the manager, interviews me with about as much enthusiasm as if he were a clerk processing me for Medicare, the principal questions being what shifts can I work and when can I start. I mutter something about being woefully out of practice as a waitress, but he's already on to the uniform: I'm to show up tomorrow wearing black slacks and black shoes; he'll provide the rust-colored polo shirt with HEARTHSIDE embroidered on it, though I might want to wear my own shirt to get to work, ha ha. At the word "tomorrow," something between fear and indignation rises in my chest. I want to say, *Thank you for your time, sir, but this is just an experiment, you know, not my actual life.*

So begins my career at the Hearthside, I shall call it, one small profit center within a global discount hotel chain, where for two weeks I work from 2:00 till 10:00 P.M. for $2.43 an hour plus tips.[2] In some futile bid for gentility, the management has barred employees from using the front door, so my first day I enter through the kitchen, where a red-faced man with shoulder-length blond hair is throwing frozen steaks against the wall and yelling, *Fuck this shit! That's just Jack,* explains Gail, the wiry middle-aged waitress who is assigned to train me. *He's on the rag again*—a condition occasioned, in this instance, by the fact that the cook on the morning shift had forgotten to thaw out the steaks. For the next eight hours, I run after the agile Gail, absorbing bits of instruction along with fragments of personal tragedy. All food must be trayed, and the reason she's so tired today is that she woke up in a cold sweat thinking of her boyfriend, who killed himself recently in an upstate prison. No refills on lemonade. And the reason he was in prison is that a few DUIs caught up with him, that's all, could have happened to anyone. Carry the creamers to the table in a monkey bowl, never in your hand. And after he was gone she spent several months living in her truck, peeing in a plastic pee bottle and reading by candlelight at night, but you can't live in a truck in the summer, since you need to have the windows down, which means anything can get in, from mosquitoes on up.

At least Gail puts to rest any fears I had of appearing overqualified. From the first day on, I find that of all the things I have left behind, such as home and identity, what I miss the most is competence. Not that I have ever felt utterly competent in the writing business, in which one day's success augurs nothing at all for the next. But in my writing life, I at least have some notion of procedure: do the research, make the outline, rough out a draft, etc. As a server, though, I am beset by requests like bees: more iced tea here, ketchup over there, a to-go box for table fourteen, and where are the high chairs, anyway? Of the twenty-seven tables, up to six are usually mine at any time, though on slow afternoons or if Gail is off, I sometimes have the whole place to myself. There is the touch-screen computer-ordering system to master, which is, I suppose, meant to minimize server-cook contact, but in practice requires constant verbal fine-tuning: "That's gravy on the mashed, okay? None on the meatloaf," and so forth—while the cook scowls as if I were inventing these refinements just to torment him. Plus, something I had forgotten in the years since I was eighteen: about a third of a server's job is "side work" that's invisible to customers—sweeping, scrubbing, slicing, refilling, and restocking. If it isn't all done, every little bit of it, you're going to face the 6:00 P.M. dinner rush defenseless and probably go down in flames. I screw up dozens of times at the beginning, sustained in my shame entirely by Gail's support—*It's okay, baby, everyone does that sometime*—because, to my total surprise and despite the scientific detachment I am doing my best to maintain, I care. . . .

On my first Friday at the Hearthside there is a "mandatory meeting for all restaurant employees," which I attend, eager for insight into our overall marketing strategy and the niche (your basic Ohio cuisine with a tropical twist?) we aim to inhabit. But there is no "we" at this meeting. Phillip, our top manager except for an occasional "consultant" sent out by corporate headquarters, opens it with a sneer: "The break room—it's disgusting. Butts in the ashtrays, newspapers lying around, crumbs." This windowless little room, which also houses the time clock for the entire hotel, is where we stash our bags and civilian clothes and take our half-hour meal breaks. But a break room is not a right, he tells us. It can be taken away. We should also know that the lockers in the break room and whatever is in them can be searched at any time. Then comes gossip; there has been gossip; gossip (which seems to mean employees talking among themselves) must stop. Off-duty employees are henceforth barred from eating at the restaurant, because "other servers gather around them and gossip." When Phillip has exhausted his agenda of rebukes, Joan complains about the condition of the ladies' room and I throw in my two bits about the vacuum cleaner. But I don't see any backup coming from my fellow servers, each of whom has subsided into her own personal funk; Gail, my role model, stares sorrowfully at a point six inches from her nose. The meeting ends when Andy, one of the cooks, gets up, muttering about breaking up his day off for this almighty bullshit.

Just four days later we are suddenly summoned into the kitchen at 3:30 P.M., even though there are live tables on the floor. We all—about ten of us—stand around Phillip, who announces grimly that there has been a report of some "drug activity" on the night shift and that, as a result, we are now to be a "drug-free" workplace, meaning that all new hires will be tested, as will possibly current employees on a random basis. I am glad that this part of the kitchen is so dark, because I find myself blushing as hard as if I had been caught toking up in the ladies' room myself: I haven't been treated this way—lined up in the corridor, threatened with locker searches, peppered with carelessly aimed accusations—since junior high school. Back on the floor, Joan cracks, *Next they'll be telling us we can't have sex on the job.* When I ask Stu what happened to inspire the crackdown, he just mutters about "management decisions" and takes the opportunity to upbraid Gail and me for being too generous with the rolls. From now on there's to be only one per customer, and it goes out with the dinner, not with the salad. He's also been riding the cooks, prompting Andy to come out of the kitchen and observe— with the serenity of a man whose customary implement is a butcher knife— that *Stu has a death wish today.*

The other problem, in addition to the less-than-nurturing management style, is that this job shows no sign of being financially viable. You might imagine, from a comfortable distance, that people who live, year in and year out, on $6 to $10 an hour have discovered some survival stratagems unknown to the middle class. But no. It's not hard to get my co-workers to talk about their living situations, because housing, in almost every case, is the principal source of disruption in their lives, the first thing they fill you in on when they arrive for their shifts. After a week, I have compiled the following survey:

▾ Gail is sharing a room in a well-known downtown flophouse for which she and a roommate pay about $250 a week. Her roommate, a male friend, has begun hitting on her, driving her nuts, but the rent would be impossible alone.

▾ Claude, the Haitian cook, is desperate to get out of the two-room apartment he shares with his girlfriend and two other, unrelated, people. As far as I can determine, the other Haitian men (most of whom only speak Creole) live in similarly crowded situations.

▾ Annette, a twenty-year-old server who is six months pregnant and has been abandoned by her boyfriend, lives with her mother, a postal clerk.

▾ Marianne and her boyfriend are paying $170 a week for a one-person trailer.

▾ Jack, who is, at $10 an hour, the wealthiest of us, lives in the trailer he owns, paying only the $400-a-month lot fee.

▾ The other white cook, Andy, lives on his dry-docked boat, which, as far as I can tell from his loving descriptions, can't be more than twenty feet long. He offers to take me out on it, once it's repaired, but the offer comes with inquiries as to my marital status, so I do not follow up on it.

▾ Tina and her husband are paying $60 a night for a double room in a Days Inn. This is because they have no car and the Days Inn is within walking distance of the Hearthside. When Marianne, one of the breakfast servers, is tossed out of her trailer for subletting (which is against the trailer-park rules), she leaves her boyfriend and moves in with Tina and her husband.

▾ Joan, who had fooled me with her numerous and tasteful outfits (hostesses wear their own clothes), lives in a van she parks behind a shopping center at night and showers in Tina's motel room. The clothes are from thrift shops.[3]

It strikes me, in my middle-class solipsism, that there is gross improvidence in some of these arrangements. When Gail and I are wrapping silverware in napkins—the only task for which we are permitted to sit—she tells me she is thinking of escaping from her roommate by moving into the Days Inn herself. I am astounded: How can she even think of paying between $40 and $60 a day? But if I was afraid of sounding like a social worker, I come out just sounding like a fool. She squints at me in disbelief, *And where am I supposed to get a month's rent and a month's deposit for an apartment?* I'd been feeling pretty smug about my $500 efficiency, but of course it was made possible only by the $1,300 I had allotted myself for start-up costs when I began my low-wage life: $1,000 for the first month's rent and deposit, $100 for initial groceries and cash in my pocket, $200 stuffed away for emergencies. In poverty, as in certain propositions in physics, starting conditions are everything.

There are no secret economies that nourish the poor; on the contrary, there are a host of special costs. If you can't put up the two months' rent you need to secure an apartment, you end up paying through the nose for a room by the week. If you have only a room, with a hot plate at best, you can't save by cooking up huge lentil stews that can be frozen for the week ahead.

You eat fast food, or the hot dogs and styrofoam cups of soup that can be microwaved in a convenience store. If you have no money for health insurance—and the Hearthside's niggardly plan kicks in only after three months—you go without routine care or prescription drugs and end up paying the price. Gail, for example, was fine until she ran out of money for estrogen pills. She is supposed to be on the company plan by now, but they claim to have lost her application form and need to begin the paperwork all over again. So she spends $9 per migraine pill to control the headaches she wouldn't have, she insists, if her estrogen supplements were covered. Similarly, Marianne's boyfriend lost his job as a roofer because he missed so much time after getting a cut on his foot for which he couldn't afford the prescribed antibiotic.

My own situation, when I sit down to assess it after two weeks of work, would not be much better if this were my actual life. The seductive thing about waitressing is that you don't have to wait for payday to feel a few bills in your pocket, and my tips usually cover meals and gas, plus something left over to stuff into the kitchen drawer I use as a bank. But as the tourist business slows in the summer heat, I sometimes leave work with only $20 in tips (the gross is higher, but servers share about 15 percent of their tips with the busboys and bartenders). With wages included, this amounts to about the minimum wage of $5.15 an hour. Although the sum in the drawer is piling up, at the present rate of accumulation it will be more than a hundred dollars short of my rent when the end of the month comes around. Nor can I see any expenses to cut. True, I haven't gone the lentil-stew route yet, but that's because I don't have a large cooking pot, pot holders, or a ladle to stir with (which cost about $30 at Kmart, less at thrift stores), not to mention onions, carrots, and the indispensable bay leaf. I do make my lunch almost every day—usually some slow-burning, high-protein combo like frozen chicken patties with melted cheese on top and canned pinto beans on the side. Dinner is at the Hearthside, which offers its employees a choice of BLT, fish sandwich, or hamburger for only $2. The burger lasts longest, especially if it's heaped with gut-puckering jalapenos, but by midnight my stomach is growling again.

So unless I want to start using my car as a residence, I have to find a second, or alternative, job. I call all the hotels where I filled out housekeeping applications weeks ago—the Hyatt, Holiday Inn, Econo Lodge, Hojo's, Best Western, plus a half dozen or so locally run guesthouses. Nothing. Then I start making the rounds again, wasting whole mornings waiting for some assistant manager to show up, even dipping into places so creepy that the front-desk clerk greets you from behind bulletproof glass and sells pints of liquor over the counter. But either someone has exposed my real-life housekeeping habits—which are, shall we say, mellow—or I am at the wrong end of some infallible ethnic equation: most, but by no means all, of the working housekeepers I see on my job searches are African Americans, Spanish-speaking, or immigrants from the Central European post-Communist world, whereas servers are almost invariably white and monolingually English-speaking. When I finally get a positive response, I have been identified once again as server material. Jerry's, which is part of a well-known national family restaurant chain and physically attached here to another budget hotel chain, is ready to use me at once. The prospect is both exciting and terrifying, because, with about the same number of tables and counter seats, Jerry's attracts three or four times the volume of customers as the gloomy old Hearthside. . . .

I start out with the beautiful, heroic idea of handling the two jobs at once, and for two days I almost do it: the breakfast/lunch shift at Jerry's, which goes till 2:00, arriving at the Hearthside at 2:10, and attempting to hold out until 10:00. In the ten minutes between jobs, I pick up a spicy chicken sandwich at the Wendy's drive-through window, gobble it down in the car, and change from khaki slacks to black, from Hawaiian to rust polo. There is a problem, though. When during the 3:00 to 4:00 P.M. dead time I finally sit down to wrap silver, my flesh seems to bond to the seat. I try to refuel with a purloined cup of soup, as I've seen Gail and Joan do dozens of times, but a manager catches me and hisses *No eating!* though there's not a customer around to be offended by the sight of food making contact with a server's lips. So I tell Gail I'm going to quit, and she hugs me and says she might just follow me to Jerry's herself.

But the chances of this are minuscule. She has left the flophouse and her annoying roommate and is back to living in her beat-up old truck. But guess what? She reports to me excitedly later that evening: Phillip has given her permission to park overnight in the hotel parking lot, as long as she keeps out of sight, and the parking lot should be totally safe, since it's patrolled by a hotel security guard! With the Hearthside offering benefits like that, how could anyone think of leaving? . . .

Management at Jerry's is generally calmer and more "professional" than at the Hearthside, with two exceptions. One is Joy, a plump, blowsy woman in her early thirties, who once kindly devoted several minutes to instructing me in the correct one-handed method of carrying trays but whose moods change disconcertingly from shift to shift and even within one. Then there's B.J., a.k.a. B.J.-the-bitch, whose contribution is to stand by the kitchen counter and yell, *Nita, your order's up, move it!* or, *Barbara, didn't you see you've got another table out there? Come on, girl!* Among other things, she is hated for having replaced the whipped-cream squirt cans with big plastic whipped-cream-filled baggies that have to be squeezed with both hands—because, reportedly, she saw or thought she saw employees trying to inhale the propellant gas from the squirt cans, in the hope that it might be nitrous oxide. On my third night, she pulls me aside abruptly and brings her face so close that it looks as if she's planning to butt me with her forehead. But instead of saying, *You're fired,* she says, *You're doing fine.* The only trouble is I'm spending time chatting with customers: *That's how they're getting you.* Furthermore I am letting them "run me," which means harassment by sequential demands: you bring the ketchup and they decide they want extra Thousand Island; you bring that and they announce they now need a side of fries; and so on into distraction. Finally she tells me not to take her wrong. She tries to say things in a nice way, but you get into a mode, you know, because everything has to move so fast. . . .[4]

I make the decision to move closer to Key West. First, because of the drive. Second and third, also because of the drive: gas is eating up $4 to $5 a day, and although Jerry's is as high-volume as you can get, the tips average only 10 percent, and not just for a newbie like me. Between the base pay of $2.15 an hour and the obligation to share tips with the busboys and dishwashers, we're averaging only about $7.50 an hour. Then there is the $30 I had to spend on the regulation tan slacks worn by Jerry's servers—a setback it could take weeks to absorb. (I had combed the town's two downscale department stores hoping for something cheaper but decided in the end that these marked-down Dockers, originally $49, were more likely to survive a daily washing.) Of my fellow servers, everyone who lacks a working husband or boyfriend seems to have a second job: Nita does something at a computer eight hours a day; another welds. Without the forty-five-minute commute, I can picture myself working two jobs and having the time to shower between them.

So I take the $500 deposit I have coming from my landlord, the $400 I have earned toward the next month's rent, plus the $200 reserved for emergencies, and use the $1,100 to pay the rent and deposit on trailer number 46 in the Overseas Trailer Park, a mile from the cluster of budget hotels that constitute Key West's version of an industrial park. Number 46 is about eight feet in width and shaped like a barbell inside, with a narrow region—because of the sink and the stove—separating the bedroom from what might optimistically be called the "living" area, with its two-person table and half-sized couch. The bathroom is so small my knees rub against the shower stall when I sit on the toilet, and you can't just leap out of the bed; you have to climb down to the foot of it in order to find a patch of floor space to stand on. Outside, I am within a few yards of a liquor store, a bar that advertises "free beer tomorrow," a convenience store, and a Burger King—but no supermarket or, alas, laundromat. By reputation, the Overseas Park is a nest of crime and crack, and I am hoping at least for some vibrant, multicultural street life. But desolation rules night and day, except for a thin stream of pedestrian traffic heading for their jobs at the Sheraton or 7-Eleven. There are not exactly people here but what amounts to canned labor, being preserved from the heat between shifts.

In line with my reduced living conditions, a new form of ugliness arises at Jerry's. First we are confronted—via an announcement on the computers through which we input orders—with the new rule that the hotel bar is henceforth off-limits to restaurant employees. The culprit, I learn through the grapevine, is the ultra-efficient gal who trained me—another trailer-home dweller and a mother of three. Something had set her off one morning, so she slipped out for a nip and returned to the floor impaired. This mostly hurts Ellen, whose habit it is to free her hair from its rubber band and drop by the bar for a couple of Zins before heading home at the end of the shift, but all of us feel the chill. Then the next day, when I go for straws, for the first time I find the dry-storage room locked. Ted, the portly assistant manager who opens it for me, explains that he caught one of the dishwashers attempting to steal something, and, unfortunately, the miscreant will be with us until a replacement can be found—hence the locked door. I neglect to ask what he had been trying to steal, but Ted tells me who he is—the kid with the buzz cut and the earring. You know, he's back there right now.

I wish I could say I rushed back and confronted George to get his side of the story. I wish I could say I stood up to Ted and insisted that George be given a translator and allowed to defend himself, or announced that I'd find a lawyer who'd handle the case pro bono. The mystery to me is that there's not much worth stealing in the dry-storage room, at least not in any fence-able quantity: *Is Gyorgi here, and am having 200—maybe 250—ketchup packets. What do you say?* My guess is that he had taken—if he had taken anything at all—some Saltines or a can of cherry-pie mix, and that the motive for taking it was hunger.

So why didn't I intervene? Certainly not because I was held back by the kind of moral paralysis that can pass as journalistic objectivity. On the contrary, something new—something loathsome and servile—had infected me, along with the kitchen odors that I could still sniff on my bra when I finally undressed at night. In real life I am moderately brave, but plenty of brave people shed their courage in concentration camps, and maybe something similar goes on in the infinitely more congenial milieu of the low-wage American workplace. Maybe, in a month or two more at Jerry's, I might have regained my crusading spirit. Then again, in a month or two I might have turned into a different person altogether—say, the kind of person who would have turned George in.

But this is not something I am slated to find out. When my month-long plunge into poverty is almost over, I finally land my dream job— housekeeping. I do this by walking into the personnel office of the only place I figure I might have some credibility, the hotel attached to Jerry's, and confiding urgently that I have to have a second job if I am to pay my rent and, no, it couldn't be front-desk clerk. *All right,* the personnel lady fairly spits, *so it's housekeeping,* and she marches me back to meet Maria, the housekeeping manager, a tiny, frenetic Hispanic woman who greets me as "babe" and hands me a pamphlet emphasizing the need for a positive attitude. The hours are nine in the morning till whenever, the pay is $6.10 an hour, and there's one week of vacation a year. I don't have to ask about health insurance once I meet Carlotta, the middle-aged African American woman who will be training me. Carla, as she tells me to call her, is missing all of her top front teeth.

On that first day of housekeeping and last day of my entire project— although I don't yet know it's the last—Carla is in a foul mood. We have been given nineteen rooms to clean, most of them "checkouts," as opposed to "stay-overs," that require the whole enchilada of bed-stripping, vacuuming, and bathroom-scrubbing. When one of the rooms that had been listed as a stay-over turns out to be a checkout, Carla calls Maria to complain, but of course to no avail. *So make up the motherfucker,* Carla orders me, and I do the beds while she sloshes around the bathroom. For four hours without a break I strip and remake beds, taking about four and a half minutes per queen-sized bed, which I could get down to three if there were any reason to. We try to avoid vacuuming by picking up the larger specks by hand, but often there is nothing to do but drag the monstrous vacuum cleaner—it weighs about thirty pounds—off our cart and try to wrestle it around the floor. Sometimes Carla hands me the squirt bottle of "BAM" (an acronym for something that begins, ominously, with "butyric"; the rest has been worn off the label) and lets me do the bathrooms. No service ethic challenges me here to new heights of performance. I just concentrate on removing the pubic hairs from the bathtubs, or at least the dark ones that I can see. . . .

When I request permission to leave at about 3:30, another housekeeper warns me that no one has so far succeeded in combining housekeeping at the hotel with serving at Jerry's: *Some kid did it once for five days, and you're no kid.* With that helpful information in mind, I rush back to number 46, down four Advils (the name brand this time), shower, stooping to fit into the stall, and attempt to compose myself for the oncoming shift. So much for what Marx termed the "reproduction of labor power," meaning the things a worker has to do just so she'll be ready to work again. The only unforeseen obstacle to the smooth transition from job to job is that my tan Jerry's slacks, which had looked reasonably clean by 40-watt bulb last night when I hand-washed my Hawaiian shirt, prove by daylight to be mottled with ketchup and ranch-dressing stains. I spend most of my hour-long break between jobs attempting to remove the edible portions with a sponge and then drying the slacks over the hood of my car in the sun.

I can do this two-job thing, is my theory, if I can drink enough caffeine and avoid getting distracted by George's ever more obvious suffering.[5] The first few days after being caught he seemed not to understand the trouble he was in, and our chirpy little conversations had continued. But the last couple of shifts he's been listless and unshaven, and tonight he looks like the ghost we all know him to be, with dark half-moons hanging from his eyes. At one point, when I am briefly immobilized by the task of filling little paper cups with sour cream for baked potatoes, he comes over and looks as if he'd like to explore the limits of our shared vocabulary, but I am called to the floor for a table. I resolve to give him all my tips that night and to hell with the experiment in low-wage money management. At eight, Ellen and I grab a snack together standing at the mephitic end of the kitchen counter, but I can only manage two or three mozzarella sticks and lunch had been a mere handful of McNuggets. I am not tired at all, I assure myself, though it may be that there is simply no more "I" left to do the tiredness monitoring. What I would see, if I were more alert to the situation, is that the forces of destruction are already massing against me. There is only one cook on duty, a young man named Jesus ("Hay-Sue," that is) and he is new to the job. And there is Joy, who shows up to take over in the middle of the shift, wearing high heels and a long, clingy white dress and fuming as if she'd just been stood up in some cocktail bar.

Then it comes, the perfect storm. Four of my tables fill up at once. Four tables is nothing for me now, but only so long as they are obligingly staggered. As I bev table 27, tables 25, 28, and 24 are watching enviously. As I bev 25, 24 glowers because their bevs haven't even been ordered. Twenty-eight is four yuppyish types, meaning everything on the side and agonizing instructions as to the chicken Caesars. Twenty-five is a middle-aged black couple, who complain, with some justice, that the iced tea isn't fresh and the tabletop is sticky. But table 24 is the meteorological event of the century: ten British tourists who seem to have made the decision to absorb the American experience entirely by mouth. Here everyone has at least two drinks—iced tea and milk shake, Michelob and water (with lemon slice, please)—and a huge promiscuous orgy of breakfast specials, mozz sticks, chicken strips, quesadillas, burgers with cheese and without, sides of hash browns with cheddar, with onions, with gravy, seasoned fries, plain fries, banana splits. Poor Jesus! Poor me! Because when I arrive with their first tray of food—after three prior trips just to refill bevs—Princess Di refuses to eat her chicken strips with her pancake-and-sausage special, since, as she now reveals, the strips were meant to be an appetizer. Maybe the others would have accepted their meals, but Di, who is deep into her third Michelob, insists that everything else go back while they work on their "starters." Meanwhile, the yuppies are waving me down for more decaf and the black couple looks ready to summon the NAACP.

Much of what happened next is lost in the fog of war. Jesus starts going under. The little printer on the counter in front of him is spewing out orders faster than he can rip them off, much less produce the meals. Even the invincible Ellen is ashen from stress. I bring table 24 their reheated main courses, which they immediately reject as either too cold or fossilized by the microwave. When I return to the kitchen with their trays (three trays in three trips), Joy confronts me with arms akimbo: *What is this?* She means the food—the plates of rejected pancakes, hash browns in assorted flavors, toasts, burgers, sausages, eggs. *Uh, scrambled with cheddar,* I try, *and that's . . . NO,* she screams in my face. *Is it a traditional, a super-scramble, an eye-opener?* I pretend to study my check for a clue, but entropy has been up to its tricks, not only on the plates but in my head, and I have to admit that the original order is beyond reconstruction. *You don't know an eye-opener from a traditional?* she demands in outrage. All I know, in fact, is that my legs have lost interest in the current venture and have announced their intention to fold. I am saved by a yuppie (mercifully not one of mine) who chooses this moment to charge into the kitchen to bellow that his food is twenty-five minutes late. Joy screams at him to get the hell out of her kitchen, please, and then turns on Jesus in a fury, hurling an empty tray across the room for emphasis.

I leave. I don't walk out; I just leave. I don't finish my side work or pick up my credit-card tips, if any, at the cash register or, of course, ask Joy's permission to go. And the surprising thing is that you can walk out without permission, that the door opens, that the thick tropical night air parts to let me pass, that my car is still parked where I left it. There is no vindication in this exit, no fuck-you surge of relief, just an overwhelming, dank sense of failure pressing down on me and the entire parking lot. I had gone into this venture in the spirit of science, to test a mathematical proposition, but somewhere along the line, in the tunnel vision imposed by long shifts and relentless concentration, it became a test of myself, and clearly I have failed. Not only had I flamed out as a housekeeper/server, I had even forgotten to give George my tips, and, for reasons perhaps best known to hardworking, generous people like Gail and Ellen, this hurts. I don't cry, but I am in a position to realize, for the first time in many years, that the tear ducts are still there, and still capable of doing their job.

When I moved out of the trailer park, I gave the key to number 46 to Gail and arranged for my deposit to be transferred to her. She told me that Joan is still living in her van and that Stu had been fired from the Hearthside. I never found out what happened to George.

In one month, I had earned approximately $1,040 and spent $517 on food, gas, toiletries, laundry, phone, and utilities. If I had remained in my $500 efficiency, I would have been able to pay the rent and have $22 left over (which is $78 less than the cash I had in my pocket at the start of the month). During this time I bought no clothing except for the required slacks and no prescription drugs or medical care (I did finally buy some vitamin B to compensate for the lack of vegetables in my diet). Perhaps I could have saved a little on food if I had gotten to a supermarket more often, instead of convenience stores, but it should be noted that I lost almost four pounds in four weeks, on a diet weighted heavily toward burgers and fries.

How former welfare recipients and single mothers will (and do) survive in the low-wage workforce, I cannot imagine. Maybe they will figure out how to condense their lives—including child-raising, laundry, romance, and meals—into the couple of hours between full-time jobs. Maybe they will take up residence in their vehicles, if they have one. All I know is that I couldn't hold two jobs and I couldn't make enough money to live on with one. And I had advantages unthinkable to many of the long-term poor—health, stamina, a working car, and no children to care for and support. Certainly nothing in my experience contradicts the conclusion of Kathryn Edin and Laura Lein, in their [1997] book *Making Ends Meet: How Single Mothers Survive Welfare and Low-Wage Work,* that low-wage work actually involves more hardship and deprivation than life at the mercy of the welfare state. In the coming months and years, economic conditions for the working poor are bound to worsen, even without the almost inevitable recession. As mentioned earlier, the influx of former welfare recipients into the low-skilled workforce will have a depressing effect on both wages and the number of jobs available. A general economic downturn will only enhance these effects, and the working poor will of course be facing it without the slight, but nonetheless often saving, protection of welfare as a backup.

The thinking behind welfare reform was that even the humblest jobs are morally uplifting and psychologically buoying. In reality they are likely to be fraught with insult and stress. But I did discover one redeeming feature of the most abject low-wage work—the camaraderie of people who are, in almost all cases, far too smart and funny and caring for the work they do and the wages they're paid. The hope, of course, is that someday these people will come to know what they're worth, and take appropriate action.

ENDNOTES

[1] According to the Department of Housing and Urban Development, the "fair-market rent" for an efficiency is $551 here in Monroe County, Florida. A comparable rent in the five boroughs of New York City is $704; in San Francisco, $713; and in the heart of Silicon Valley, $808. The fair-market rent for an area is defined as the amount that would be needed to pay rent plus utilities for "privately owned, decent, safe, and sanitary rental housing of a modest (non-luxury) nature with suitable amenities."

[2] According to the Fair Labor Standards Act, employers are not required to pay "tipped employees," such as restaurant servers, more than $2.13 an hour in direct wages. However, if the sum of tips plus $2.13 an hour falls below the minimum wage, or $5.15 an hour, the employer is required to make up the difference. This fact was not mentioned by managers or otherwise publicized at either of the restaurants where I worked.

[3] I could find no statistics on the number of employed people living in cars or vans, but according to the National Coalition for the Homeless' 1997 report "Myths and Facts about Homelessness," nearly one in five homeless people (in twenty-nine cities across the nation) is employed in a full- or part-time job.

[4] In *Workers in a Lean World: Unions in the International Economy* (Verso, 1997), Kim Moody cites studies finding an increase in stress-related workplace injuries and illness between the mid-1980s and the early 1990s. He argues that rising stress levels reflect a new system of "management by stress," in which workers in a variety of industries are being squeezed to extract maximum productivity, to the detriment of their health.

[5] In 1996, the number of persons holding two or more jobs averaged 7.8 million, or 6.2 percent of the workforce. It was about the same rate for men and for women (6.1 versus 6.2), though the kinds of jobs differ by gender. About two-thirds of multiple jobholders work one job full-time and the other part-time. Only a heroic minority—4 percent of men and 2 percent of women—work two full-time jobs simultaneously. (From John F. Stinson Jr., "New Data on Multiple Jobholding Available from the CPS," in the *Monthly Labor Review,* March 1997.)

GENDER

27

GENDER AS STRUCTURE

BARBARA RISMAN

Gender stratification, examined in the next four selections, refers to those social systems in which socioeconomic resources and political power are distributed on the basis of one's sex and gender. In any social system, we can measure the gendered distribution of resources and rewards to see whether men or women have a higher social status. Objective indices of gender inequality include income, educational attainment, wealth, occupational status, mortality rates, and access to social institutions. In the selection that follows, Barbara Risman, a professor of sociology at the University of Illinois, Chicago, examines four theories that attempt to explain why gender stratification exists.

There are three distinct theoretical traditions that help us to understand sex and gender, and a fourth is now taking shape. The first tradition focuses on gendered selves, whether sex differences are biological or social in origin. The second tradition . . . focuses on how the social structure (as opposed to biology or individual learning) creates gendered behavior. The third tradition . . . emphasizes contextual issues and how doing gender re-creates inequality during interaction. The fourth, multilevel approach treats gender itself as built in to social life via socialization, interaction, and institutional organization. This new perspective integrates the previous ones; it is formed on the assumption that each viewpoint sheds different light on the same question. . . .

Gendered Selves

There are numerous theoretical perspectives within this tradition, but all share the assumption that maleness and femaleness are, or become, properties of individuals. . . . Research questions in this tradition focus on the development of sex differences and their relative importance for behavior. . . .

Sociobiologists have argued that such behaviors as male aggressiveness and female nurturance result from natural selection. Biosociologists stress the infant care skills in which females appear to excel. Their perspective has been criticized for its ethnocentrism and its selective use of biological species as evidence. . . .

More recent biosocial theories have posited complex interactions between environment and biological predispositions, with attention to explaining intrasex differences. This new version of biosociology may eventually help to identify the biological parameters that, in interaction with environmental stimuli, affect human behavior. . . .

Sex-role theory suggests that early childhood socialization is an influential determinant of later behavior, and research has focused on how societies create feminine women and masculine men. There is an impressive variety of sex-role explanations for gender-differentiated behavior in families. Perhaps the most commonly accepted explanation is reinforcement theory (e.g., Bandura and Walters 1963; Mischel 1966; and Weitzman 1979). Reinforcement theory suggests, for example, that girls develop nurturant personalities because they are given praise and attention for their interest in dolls and babies, and that boys develop competitive selves because they are positively reinforced for winning, whether at checkers or football. Although much literature suggests that the socialization experiences of boys and girls continue to differ dramatically, it is clearly the case that most girls raised in the 1990s have received ambiguous gender socialization: they have been taught to desire domesticity (dolls remain a popular toy for girls), as well as to pursue careers. For generations, African American girls have been socialized for both motherhood and paid work (Collins 1990).

Nancy Chodorow's (1978, 1989) feminist psychoanalytic analysis approach has also been influential, particularly in feminist scholarship. Chodorow develops an object-relations psychoanalytic perspective to explain how gendered personalities develop as a result of exclusively female mothering. . . . Chodorow notices . . . that mothers are responsible for young children almost universally. She argues that mothers relate to their boy and girl infants differently, fusing identities with their daughters while relating to their sons as separate and distinct. As a result, according to this feminist version of psychoanalysis, girls develop selves based on connectedness and relationships while boys develop selves based on independence and autonomy. In addition, boys must reject their first love-object (mother) in order to adopt masculinity, and they do this by rejecting and devaluing what is feminine in themselves and in society. Thus, we get nurturant women and independent men in a society dominated by men and which values independence. Many feminist studies have incorporated this psychoanalytic view of gender as an underlying assumption (Keller 1985; L. Rubin 1982; Williams 1989). . . .

Other feminist theorists, such as Ruddick (1989, 1992) and Aptheker (1989), build on the notion that the constant nature of mothering creates a certain kind of thinking, what Ruddick calls "maternal thinking." The logic of this argument does not depend on a psychoanalytic framework, but it implicitly uses one: through nurturing their children, women develop psychological frameworks that value peace and justice. Therefore, if women (or men who mothered children) were powerful political actors, governments would use more peaceful conflict resolution strategies and value social justice more highly.

All individualist theories, including sex-role socialization and psychoanalytic thought, posit that by adulthood most men and women have developed very different personalities. Women have become nurturant, person oriented, and child centered. Men have become competitive and work oriented. According to individualist theorists, there are limits to flexibility. Intensely held emotions, values, and inclinations developed during childhood coalesce into a person's self-identity. Although these theorists do not deny that social structures influence family patterns, nor that notions of gender meaning are always evolving . . . they focus on how culturally determined family patterns and sex-role socialization create gendered selves, which then provide the motivations for individuals to fill their socially appropriate roles.

Historically, sex-role theorists have assumed that men and women behave differently because gender resides primarily in personality. This approach has several serious conceptual weaknesses. . . . First, such theories usually presume behavioral continuity throughout the life course. In fact, women socialized for nurturance are capable of competitive and aggressive behavior, and men raised without any expectation of taking on primary responsibility can "mother" when they need to (Bielby and Bielby 1984; Gerson 1985, 1993; Risman 1987). Another weakness of these individualist-oriented theories is their oversocialized conception of human behavior—that once we know how an individual has been raised, the training is contained primarily inside his or her head (cf. Wrong 1961). Such theories might suggest, for example, that women do not revolt and are not necessarily unhappy with their subordinate status because they have been so well trained for femininity. . . .

This overdependence on internalization of culture and socialization leads to the most serious problem with sex-role theory: its depoliticization of gender inequality. Although sex-role socialization and revisionist psycho-analytic theorists often have explicitly feminist goals, their focus on sex dif-ferences has legitimated a dualistic conception of gender that relies on a reified male/female dichotomy. The very notion of comparing all men to all women without regard for diversity within groups presumes that gender is primarily about individual differences between biological males and biolog-ical females, downplaying the role of interactional expectations and the social structure.

The sex-role socialization theory is an application of a normative role theory for human behavior. It assumes that social stability is motivated pri-marily by beliefs and values acquired during socialization. Individuals are assumed to use whatever resources are available to realize these values and to maintain their identities. As Stokes and Hewitt (1976) have argued, social-ization cannot serve as the fundamental link between culture and action. In-deed, studies of intergenerational shifts in values suggest that economic and political conditions produce beliefs, attitudes, and preferences for action that overcome those acquired during childhood (Inglehart 1977, 1981; Lesthaeghe 1980). We cannot assume that internalization of norms—through psychoana-lytic processes or sex-role socialization—is the primary means by which society organizes human conduct. . . .

Structure vs. Personality

The overreliance on gendered selves as the primary explanation for sexual stratification led many feminist sociologists—myself included—to argue that what appear to be sex differences are really, in Epstein's terms, "decep-tive distinctions" (Epstein 1988; Kanter 1977; Risman and Schwartz 1989). Although empirically documented sex differences do occur, structuralists like me have argued that men and women behave differently because they fill different positions in institutional settings, work organizations, or fami-lies. That is, the previous structural perspectives on gender assume that work and family structures create empirically distinct male and female behavior. . . . Within this perspective, men and women in the same structural slots are expected to behave identically. Epstein's (1988) voluminous review of the multidisciplinary research on gender and sex differences is perhaps the strongest and most explicit support for a social-structural explanation of gendered behavior. She suggests that there are perhaps no empirically docu-mented differences that can be traced to the predispositions of males and females. Instead, the deceptive differences reflect women's lack of opportu-nity in a male-dominated society.

Gender relations in the labor force have received far more of this sort of structural analysis than have gender relations in intimate settings. Kanter's classic work *Men and Women of the Corporation* (1977) introduced this kind of structural perspective on gender in the workplace. Kanter showed that when women had access to powerful mentors, interactions with people like them-selves, and the possibility for upward mobility, they behaved like others—

regardless of sex—with similar advantages. These social network variables could explain success at work far better than could assumptions of masculine versus feminine work styles. Women were less often successful because they were more often blocked from network advantages, not because they feared success or had never developed competitive strategies. Men who lacked such opportunities did not advance, and they behaved with stereotypical feminine work styles. Kanter argued persuasively that structural system properties better explain sex differences in workplace behavior than does sex-role socialization. . . .

The application of a structural perspective to gender within personal relationships has been less frequent. . . . In a series of studies (Risman 1986, 1987, 1988), I tested whether apparent sex differences in parenting styles are better attributed to sex-role socialization or to the structural contingencies of adult life. The question I asked was "Can men mother?" The answer is yes, but only if they do not have women to do it for them. The lack of sex-role socialization for nurturance did not inhibit the development of male mothering when structural contingencies demanded it. This is an important part of the story, but not all of it. . . .

While applications of structural perspectives both to workplaces and to intimate relationships have furthered the sociological understanding of gender, there is a fundamental flaw in the logic of these arguments. . . .

Several studies (Williams 1992; Yoder 1991; Zimmer 1988) found that Kanter's hypotheses about the explanatory power of social structural variables such as relative numbers, access to mentors, and upward mobility are not, in fact, gender neutral. That is, Kanter's hypotheses are supported empirically only when societally devalued groups enter traditionally white male work environments. When white males enter traditionally female work environments, they do not hit the glass ceiling, they ride glass elevators. Reskin (1988) has suggested that we have so accepted these "structural" arguments that we sometimes forget that sexism itself stratifies our labor force. Evidence similarly points to continued existence of gendered behavior in family settings. Hertz reported that in her 1986 study of couples in which husbands and wives held equivalent, high-status corporate jobs and brought similar resources to their marriages, the wives continued to shoulder more responsibility for family work (even if that means hiring and supervising help). Despite the importance of structural variables in explaining behavior in families, the sex category itself remains a powerful predictor of who does what kind of family work (Brines 1994; South and Spitz 1994). Gender stratification remains even when other structural aspects of work or of family life are divorced from sex category. The interactionist theory discussed below helps us to understand why.

Doing Gender

This approach to gender was best articulated by West and Zimmerman in their 1987 article "Doing Gender." . . . West and Zimmerman suggest that once a person is labeled a member of a sex category, she or he is morally accountable for behaving as persons in that category do. That is, the person is expected to "do gender"; the ease of interaction depends on it. One of the groundbreaking aspects in this argument is that doing gender implies legitimating inequality. The authors suggest that, by definition, what is female in a patriarchal society is devalued. Within this theoretical framework, the very belief that biological males and females are essentially different (apart from their reproductive capabilities) exists to justify male dominance.

The tradition of doing gender has been well accepted in feminist sociology (West and Zimmerman's article was cited in journals more than one hundred times by 1995). West and Zimmerman articulated an insight whose time had come—that gender is not what we are but something that we do. Psychologists Deaux and Major (1990) . . . argue that interactional contexts take priority over individual traits and personality differences; others' expectations create the self-fulfilling prophecies that lead all of us to do gender. . . . They suggest that actual behavior depends on the interaction of participants' self-definitions, the expectations of others, and the cultural expectations attached to the context itself. I agree. The weakness in the doing-gender approach is that it undertheorizes the pervasiveness of gender inequality in organizations and gendered identities.

Although gender is always present in our interaction, it is not present only in interaction. We must have a theoretical link from material constraints to what we do now, to who we think we are. I suggest that the doing-gender perspective is incomplete because it slights the institutional level of analysis and the links among institutional gender stratification, situational expectations, and gendered selves.

West and Fenstermaker (1995) have extended the argument from doing gender to "doing difference." They suggest that just as we create inequality when we create gender during interaction, so we create race and class inequalities when we interact in daily life. Race does not generally hold the biologically based assumption of dichotomy (as sex category does), yet in American society we constantly use race categories to guide our interactional encounters. This extension of theoretical ideas from gender to the analysis of inequalities is perhaps the most important direction gender theorizing has taken in the past decade. . . .

Gender as Social Structure

The sex-differences literature, the doing-gender contextual analyses, and the structural perspectives are not necessarily incompatible, although I, as well as others, have portrayed them as alternatives (e.g., Epstein 1988; Ferree 1990; Kanter 1977; Risman 1987; Risman and Schwartz 1989). . . . My view of gender as a social structure incorporates each level of analysis. . . .

Lorber (1994) argues that gender is an entity in and of itself that establishes patterns of expectations for individuals, orders social processes of everyday life, and is built into all other major social organizations of society.

She goes further, however, to argue that gender difference is *primarily* a means to justify sexual stratification. Gender is so ubiquitous because unless we see difference, we cannot justify inequality. Lorber provides much cross-cultural, literary, and scientific evidence to show that gender difference is socially constructed and yet is universally used to justify stratification. She writes that "the continuing purpose of gender as a modern social institution is to construct women as a group to be subordinate to men as a group" (p. 33).

I build on this notion that gender is an entity in and of itself and has consequences at every level of analysis. And I share the concern that the very creation of difference is the foundation on which inequality rests. In my view, it is most useful to conceptualize gender as a structure that has consequences for every aspect of society. . . .

Gender itself must be considered a structural property of society. It is not manifested just in our personalities, our cultural rules, or other institutions. Gender is deeply embedded as a basis for stratification, differentiating opportunities and constraints. This differentiation has consequences on three levels: (1) at the individual level, for the development of gendered selves; (2) at the interactional level, for men and women face different expectations even when they fill the identical structural position; and (3) at the institutional level, for rarely will women and men be given identical positions. Differentiation at the institutional level is based on explicit regulations or laws regarding resource distribution, whether resources be defined as access to opportunities or actual material goods. (See Figure 27.1 for a schematic summary of the argument thus far.)

While the *gender structure* clearly affects selves, cultural rules, and institutions, far too much explanatory power is presumed to rest in the motivation of gendered selves. We live in a very individualistic society that teaches us to make our own choices and take responsibility for our own actions. What this has meant for theories about gender is that a tremendous amount of energy is spent on trying to understand why women and men "choose" to devote their life energies to such different enterprises. The distinctly sociological contribution to the explanation hasn't had enough attention: even

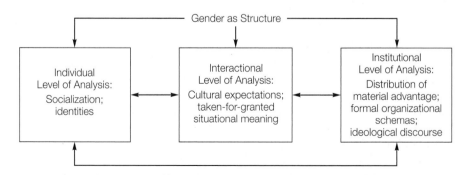

FIGURE 27.1   Gender as Structure.

when individual women and men do *not* desire to live gendered lives or to support male dominance, they often find themselves compelled to do so by the logic of gendered choices. That is, interactional pressures and institutional design create gender and the resultant inequality, even in the absence of individual desires. . . .

Choices often assumed to be based on personalities and individual preferences (e.g., consequences of the gender structure at the individual level) are better understood as social constructions based on institutionally constrained opportunities and the limited availability of nongendered cognitive images. . . .

Even if individuals are capable of change and wish to eradicate male dominance from their personal lives, the influence of gendered institutions and interactional contexts persists. These contexts are organized by gender stratification at the institutional level, which includes the distribution of material resources organized by gender, the ways by which formal organizations and institutions themselves are gendered, and gendered ideological discourse. For example, in a society in which girls are not taught to read, we could never find a young woman who would be considered a potential international leader. Nor would men denied access to jobs with "family wages" be seen by middle-class American women as good catches for husbands.

At this moment in American society, cultural rules and cognitive images that operate at the interactional level are particularly important in the persistence of gender stratification in families. It is not that sex-role socialization or early childhood experience is trivial; gender structure creates gendered selves. But, at this point in history, sex-role socialization itself is ambivalent. In addition, it is clear that even women with feminist worldviews and substantial incomes are constrained by gender structures.

In spite of the removal of some gender discrimination in both law and organizations, gender stratification remains. That is, formal access to opportunities may be gender neutral, yet equality of results may not ensue. Therefore, neither the individual-level explanations nor those based solely on institutional discrimination can explain continued gender stratification in families. Instead, the cognitive images to which we must respond during interaction are the engines that drive continued gender stratification when individuals desire egalitarian relationships and the law allows them (cf. Ridgeway 1997). . . .

The social structure clearly constrains gendered action even as it makes it possible. Wives, even those who have no motivation to provide domestic service to their husbands, are constrained to do so by social expectations. A husband who has a disheveled appearance reflects poorly on his wife's domestic abilities (in real life as well as in "ring around the collar" commercials). A wife will be sanctioned by friends and family for keeping a cluttered and dusty home; a husband will not be. Husbands' behaviors are constrained as well. A husband who is content with a relatively low-wage, low-stress occupation may be pressured (by his wife, among others) to provide more for his family. Few wives, however, are pressured into higher-stress, higher-wage occupations by their families. The expectations we face during ongoing interaction often push us to behave as others want us to (Heiss 1981).

Cultural images within marriage also make gendered action possible. Husbands are not free to work long hours in order to climb the career ladder or increase income unless they are superordinate partners in a system in which wives provide them the "leisure" (i.e., freedom from responsibility for self-care or family care) to do so. Some married women may leave jobs they dislike because the position of domestic wife is open to them. A husband and father unable to keep a job has few other options for gaining self-esteem and identity.

Individuals often act in a structurally patterned fashion, without much thought. Routine is taken for granted even when the action re-creates the inequitable social structure. A woman may choose to change her name upon marriage simply because it seems easier. (Some women may not even know they are making a choice, as name change is so routine in their social circle.) Yet by changing her name a woman implicitly supports and re-creates a reflective definition of wifehood. She does gender. Similarly, when a woman assents to her children carrying her husband's surname (even when she herself has retained her own), she is re-creating a patrilineal system by which family identity is traced primarily through the male line. In both these examples, a couple's intention may be to create a nuclear family identity and to avoid the awkwardness of hyphenated names for children. Whatever the intention, the structure has constrained the possible choices available to them. Their purposive actions may provide them with both the desired consequences (one family name) *and* the unintended consequence of re-creating a gender structure based on reflective female identity and patrilineal family names.

REFERENCES

Aptheker, Bettina. 1989. *Tapestries of Life: Women's Work, Women's Consciousness, and the Meaning of Daily Experience.* Amherst: University of Massachusetts Press.

Bandura, Albert and Richard H. Walters. 1963. *Social Learning and Personality.* New York: Holt, Rinehart and Winston.

Bielby, Denise D. and William T. Bielby. 1984. "Work Commitment and Sex-Role Attitudes." *American Sociological Review* 49:234–47.

Brines, Julie. 1994. "Economic Dependency and the Division of Labor." *American Journal of Sociology* 100(3):652–88.

Chodorow, Nancy. 1978. *The Reproduction of Mothering.* Berkeley: University of California Press.

———. 1989. *Feminism and Psychoanalytic Theory.* New Haven, CT: Yale University Press.

Collins, Patricia Hill. 1990. *Black Feminist Thought: Knowledge, Consciousness, and the Politics of Empowerment.* Boston: Unwin, Hyman.

Deaux, Kay and Brenda Major. 1990. "A Social–Psychological Model of Gender." In *Theoretical Perspectives on Sexual Difference,* edited by Deborah Rhode. New Haven, CT: Yale University Press.

Epstein, Cynthia Fuchs. 1988. *Deceptive Distinctions: Sex, Gender, and the Social Order.* New Haven, CT: Yale University Press.

Ferree, Myra Marx. 1990. "Beyond Separate Spheres: Feminism and Family Research." *Journal of Marriage and the Family* 53(4):866–84.

Gerson, Kathleen. 1985. *Hard Choices.* Berkeley: University of California Press.

———. 1993. *No Man's Land.* New York: Basic Books.

Heiss, Jerold. 1981. "Social Rules." In *Social Psychology: Sociological Perspectives,* edited by Morris Rosenberg and Ralph H. Turner. New York: Basic Books.

Hertz, Rosanna. 1986. *More Equal Than Others: Women and Men in Dual-Career Marriages.* Berkeley: University of California Press.

Inglehart, Ronald. 1977. *The Silent Revolution: Changing Values and Political Styles among Western Publics.* Princeton, NJ: Princeton University Press.

——. 1981. "Post-Materialism in an Environment of Insecurity." *American Political Science Review* 75:880–900.

Kanter, Rosabeth. 1977. *Men and Women of the Corporation.* New York: Harper and Row.

Keller, Evelyn Fox. 1985. *Reflections on Gender and Science.* New Haven, CT: Yale University Press.

Lesthaeghe, Ron. 1980. "On the Social Control of Human Reproduction." *Population and Development Review* 4:427–548.

Lorber, Judith. 1994. *Paradoxes of Gender.* New Haven, CT: Yale University Press.

Mischel, Walter. 1966. "A Social Learning View of Sex Differences in Behavior." Pp. 56–81 in *The Development of Sex Differences,* edited by Eleanor Maccoby. Stanford, CA: Stanford University Press.

Reskin, Barbara. 1988. "Bringing the Men Back In: Sex Differentiation and the Devaluation of Women's Work." *Gender & Society* 2:58–81.

Ridgeway, Cecilia. 1997. "Interaction and the Conservation of Gender Inequality: Considering Employment." *American Sociological Review* 62:218–35.

Risman, Barbara. 1986. "Can Men 'Mother'?: Life as a Single Father." *Family Relations* 35:95–102.

——. 1987. "Intimate Relationships from a Microstructural Perspective: Mothering Men." *Gender & Society* 1:6–32.

——. 1988. "Just the Two of Us: Parent–Child Relationships in Single Parent Homes." *Journal of Marriage and the Family* 50:1049–62.

Risman, Barbara and Pepper Schwartz. 1989. *Gender in Intimate Relationships.* Belmont, CA: Wadsworth.

Rubin, Lillian. 1982. *Intimate Strangers.* New York: Harper and Row.

Ruddick, Sara. 1989. *Maternal Thinking.* Boston: Beacon Press.

——. 1992. "Thinking About Fathers." In *Rethinking the Family: Some Feminist Questions,* edited by Barrie Thorne. Boston: Northeastern University Press.

South, Scott J. and Glenna Spitz. 1994. "Housework in Marital and Nonmarital Households." *American Sociological Review* 59:327–47.

Stokes, Randall and John Hewitt. 1976. "Aligning Actions." *American Sociological Review* 41:838–49.

Weitzman, Lenore Jacqueline. 1979. *Sex Role Socialization: A Focus on Women.* Palo Alto, CA: Mayfield.

West, Candace and Sarah Fenstermaker. 1995. "Doing Difference." *Gender & Society* 9:8–37.

West, Candace and Don H. Zimmerman. 1987. "Doing Gender." *Gender & Society* 1(2):125–51.

Williams, Christine. 1989. *Gender Differences at Work.* Berkeley: University of California Press.

——. 1992. "The Glass Escalator: Hidden Advantages for Men in the 'Female' Professions." *Social Problems* 39:253–67.

Wrong, Dennis H. 1961. "The Oversocialized Conception of Man in Modern Sociology." *American Sociological Review* 26:183–93.

Yoder, Janice. 1991. "Rethinking Tokenism: Looking Beyond Numbers." *Social Problems* 5:178–92.

Zimmer, Lynn. 1988. "Tokenism and Women in the Workplace: The Limits of Gender-Neutral Theory." *Social Problems* 35:64–77.

28

WHAT IT MEANS TO BE GENDERED ME
Life on the Boundaries of a
Dichotomous Gender System

BETSY LUCAL

Sociologists argue that individuals learn gender roles and gender stereotyping through socialization. Gender role socialization often reinforces gender inequality because men and women are expected to fulfill different and often opposite family and occupational roles. What are the implications of living in a gender system that recognizes "two and only two" genders? What about individuals whose gender displays are more ambiguous? In this excerpt, Betsy Lucal, a professor of sociology at Indiana University, South Bend, uses her biography to examine the social construction of gender and the implications of *gender bending* for gender identity and social interaction.

I understood the concept of "doing gender" (West and Zimmerman 1987) long before I became a sociologist. I have been living with the consequences of inappropriate "gender display" (Goffman 1976; West and Zimmerman 1987) for as long as I can remember.

My daily experiences are a testament to the rigidity of gender in our society, to the real implications of "two and only two" when it comes to sex and gender categories (Garfinkel 1967; Kessler and McKenna 1978). Each day, I experience the consequences that our gender system has for my identity and interactions. I am a woman who has been called "Sir" so many times that I no longer even hesitate to assume that it is being directed at me. I am a woman whose use of public restrooms regularly causes reactions ranging from confused stares to confrontations over what a man is doing in the women's room. I regularly enact a variety of practices either to minimize the need for others to know my gender or to deal with their misattributions.

I am the embodiment of Lorber's (1994) ostensibly paradoxical assertion that the "gender bending" I engage in actually might serve to preserve and perpetuate gender categories. As a feminist who sees gender rebellion as a significant part of her contribution to the dismantling of sexism, I find this possibility disheartening.

In this [reading], I examine how my experiences both support and contradict Lorber's (1994) argument using my own experiences to illustrate and reflect on the social construction of gender. My analysis offers a discussion of

Betsy Lucal, "What It Means to Be Gendered Me: Life on the Boundaries of a Dichotomous Gender System" from *Gender & Society* 13, No. 6 (December 1999): 781–797. Copyright © 1999 by Sociologists for Women in Society. Reprinted with the permission of Sage Publications, Inc.

the consequences of gender for people who do not follow the rules as well as an examination of the possible implications of the existence of people like me for the gender system itself. Ultimately, I show how life on the boundaries of gender affects me and how my life, and the lives of others who make similar decisions about their participation in the gender system, has the potential to subvert gender.

Because this [reading] analyzes my experiences as a woman who often is mistaken for a man, my focus is on the social construction of gender for women. My assumption is that, given the gendered nature of the gendering process itself, men's experiences of this phenomenon might well be different from women's.

The Social Construction of Gender

It is now widely accepted that gender is a social construction, that sex and gender are distinct, and that gender is something all of us "do." This conceptualization of gender can be traced to Garfinkel's (1967) ethnomethodological study of "Agnes."[1] In this analysis, Garfinkel examined the issues facing a male who wished to pass as, and eventually become, a woman. Unlike individuals who perform gender in culturally expected ways, Agnes could not take her gender for granted and always was in danger of failing to pass as a woman (Zimmerman 1992).

This approach was extended by Kessler and McKenna (1978) and codified in the classic "Doing Gender" by West and Zimmerman (1987). The social constructionist approach has been developed most notably by Lorber (1994, 1996). Similar theoretical strains have developed outside of sociology, such as work by Butler (1990) and Weston (1996). Taken as a whole, this work provides a number of insights into the social processes of gender, showing how gender(ing) is, in fact, a process.

We apply gender labels for a variety of reasons; for example, an individual's gender cues our interactions with her or him. Successful social relations require all participants to present, monitor, and interpret gender displays (Martin 1998; West and Zimmerman 1987). We have, according to Lorber, "no social place for a person who is neither woman nor man" (1994:96); that is, we do not know how to interact with such a person. There is, for example, no way of addressing such a person that does not rely on making an assumption about the person's gender ("Sir" or "Ma'am"). In this context, gender is "omnirelevant" (West and Zimmerman 1987). Also, given the sometimes fractious nature of interactions between men and women, it might be particularly important for women to know the gender of the strangers they encounter; do the women need to be wary, or can they relax (Devor 1989)?

According to Kessler and McKenna (1978), each time we encounter a new person, we make a gender attribution. In most cases, this is not difficult. We learn how to read people's genders by learning which traits culturally signify each gender and by learning rules that enable us to classify individuals with a wide range of gender presentations into two and only two gender categories.

As Weston observed, "Gendered traits are called attributes for a reason: People attribute traits to others. No one possesses them. Traits are the product of evaluation" (1996:21). The fact that most people use the same traits and rules in presenting genders makes it easier for us to attribute genders to them.

We also assume that we can place each individual into one of two mutually exclusive categories in this binary system. As Bem (1993) notes, we have a polarized view of gender; there are two groups that are seen as polar opposites. Although there is "no rule for deciding 'male' or 'female' that will always work" and no attributes "that always and without exception are true of only one gender" (Kessler and McKenna 1978:158, 1), we operate under the assumption that there are such rules and attributes. . . .

Patriarchal constructs of gender also devalue the marked category. Devor (1989) found that the women she calls "gender blenders" assumed that femininity was less desirable than masculinity; their gender blending sometimes was a product of their shame about being women. This assumption affects not only our perceptions of other people but also individuals' senses of their own gendered selves.

Not only do we rely on our social skills in attributing genders to others, but we also use our skills to present our own genders to them. The roots of this understanding of how gender operates lie in Goffman's (1959) analysis of the "presentation of self in everyday life," elaborated later in his work on "gender display" (Goffman 1976). From this perspective, gender is a performance, "a stylized repetition of acts" (Butler 1990:140, emphasis removed). Gender display refers to "conventionalized portrayals" of social correlates of gender (Goffman 1976). These displays are culturally established sets of behaviors, appearances, mannerisms, and other cues that we have learned to associate with members of a particular gender.

In determining the gender of each person we encounter and in presenting our genders to others, we rely extensively on these gender displays. Our bodies and their adornments provide us with "texts" for reading a person's gender (Bordo 1993). As Lorber noted, "Without the deliberate use of gendered clothing, hairstyles, jewelry, and cosmetics, women and men would look far more alike" (1994:18–19). Myhre summarized the markers of femininity as "having longish hair; wearing makeup, skirts, jewelry, and high heels; walking with a wiggle; having little or no observable body hair; and being in general soft, rounded (but not too rounded), and sweet-smelling" (1995:135). (Note that these descriptions comprise a Western conceptualization of gender.) Devor identified "mannerisms, language, facial expressions, dress, and a lack of feminine adornment" (1989:x) as factors that contribute to women being mistaken for men. . . .

But these processes also mean that a person who fails to establish a gendered appearance that corresponds to the person's gender faces challenges to her or his identity and status. First, the gender nonconformist must find a way in which to construct an identity in a society that denies her or him any legitimacy (Bem 1993). A person is likely to want to define herself or himself as "normal" in the face of cultural evidence to the contrary. Second, the individual also must deal with other people's challenges to identity and status—deciding how to respond, what such reactions to their appearance mean, and so forth.

Because our appearances, mannerisms, and so forth constantly are being read as part of our gender display, we do gender whether we intend to or not. For example, a woman athlete, particularly one participating in a nonfeminine sport such as basketball, might deliberately keep her hair long to show that, despite actions that suggest otherwise, she is a "real" (i.e., feminine) woman. But we also do gender in less conscious ways such as when a man takes up more space when sitting than a woman does. In fact, in a society so clearly organized around gender, as ours is, there is no way in which to not do gender (Lorber 1994).

Given our cultural rules for identifying gender (i.e., that there are only two and that masculinity is assumed in the absence of evidence to the contrary), a person who does not do gender appropriately is placed not into a third category but rather into the one with which her or his gender display seems most closely to fit; that is, if a man appears to be a woman, then he will be categorized as "woman," not as something else. Even if a person does not want to do gender or would like to do a gender other than the two recognized by our society, other people will, in effect, do gender for that person by placing her or him in one and only one of the two available categories. We cannot escape doing gender or, more specifically, doing one of two genders. (There are exceptions in limited contexts such as people doing "drag" [Butler 1990; Lorber 1994].)

People who follow the norms of gender can take their genders for granted. Kessler and McKenna asserted, "Few people besides transsexuals think of their gender as anything other than 'naturally' obvious"; they believe that the risks of not being taken for the gender intended "are minimal for nontranssexuals" (1978:126). However, such an assertion overlooks the experiences of people such as those women Devor (1989) calls "gender blenders" and those people Lorber (1994) refers to as "gender benders." As West and Zimmerman (1987) pointed out, we all are held accountable for, and might be called on to account for, our genders.

People who, for whatever reasons, do not adhere to the rules, risk gender misattribution and any interactional consequences that might result from this misidentification. What are the consequences of misattribution for social interaction? When must misattribution be minimized? What will one do to minimize such mistakes? In this [reading], I explore these and related questions using my biography.

For me, the social processes and structures of gender mean that, in the context of our culture, my appearance will be read as masculine. Given the common conflation of sex and gender, I will be assumed to be a male. Because of the two-and-only-two genders rule, I will be classified, perhaps more often than not, as a man—not as an atypical woman, not as a genderless person. I must be one gender or the other. I cannot be neither, nor can I be both. This norm has a variety of mundane and serious consequences for my everyday existence. Like Myhre (1995), I have found that the choice not to participate in femininity is not one made frivolously.

My experiences as a woman who does not do femininity illustrate a paradox of our two-and-only-two gender system. Lorber argued that "bending gender rules and passing between genders does not erode but rather preserves gender boundaries" (1994:21). Although people who engage in these behaviors and appearances do "demonstrate the social constructedness of sex, sexuality, and gender" (Lorber 1994:96), they do not actually disrupt gender. Devor made a similar point: "When gender blending females refused to mark themselves by publicly displaying sufficient femininity to be recognized as women, they were in no way challenging patriarchal gender assumptions" (1989:142). As the following discussion shows, I have found that my own experiences both support and challenge this argument. Before detailing these experiences, I explain my use of my self as data.

My Self As Data

This analysis is based on my experiences as a person whose appearance and gender/sex are not, in the eyes of many people, congruent. How did my experiences become my data? I began my research "unwittingly" (Krieger 1991). This [reading] is a product of "opportunistic research" in that I am using my "unique biography, life experiences, and/or situational familiarity to understand and explain social life" (Riemer 1988:121; see also Riemer 1977). It is an analysis of "unplanned personal experience," that is, experiences that were not part of a research project but instead are part of my daily encounters (Reinharz 1992). . . .

It also is useful, I think, to consider my analysis an application of Mills' (1959) "sociological imagination." Mills (1959) and Berger (1963) wrote about the importance of seeing the general in the particular. This means that general social patterns can be discerned in the behaviors of particular individuals. In this [reading], I am examining portions of my biography, situated in U.S. society during the 1990s, to understand the "personal troubles" my gender produces in the context of a two-and-only-two gender system. I am not attempting to generalize my experiences; rather, I am trying to use them to examine and reflect on the processes and structure of gender in our society.

Because my analysis is based on my memories and perceptions of events, it is limited by my ability to recall events and by my interpretation of those events. However, I am not claiming that my experiences provide the truth about gender and how it works. I am claiming that the biography of a person who lives on the margins of our gender system can provide theoretical insights into the processes and social structure of gender. Therefore, after describing my experiences, I examine how they illustrate and extend, as well as contradict, other work on the social construction of gender.

Gendered Me

Each day, I negotiate the boundaries of gender. Each day, I face the possibility that someone will attribute the "wrong" gender to me based on my physical appearance.

I am six feet tall and large-boned. I have had short hair for most of my life. For the past several years, I have worn a crew cut or flat top. I do not shave or otherwise remove hair from my body (e.g., no eyebrow plucking). I do not wear dresses, skirts, high heels, or makeup. My only jewelry is a class ring, a "men's" watch (my wrists are too large for a "women's" watch), two small earrings (gold hoops, both in my left ear), and (occasionally) a necklace. I wear jeans or shorts, T-shirts, sweaters, polo/golf shirts, button-down collar shirts, and tennis shoes or boots. The jeans are "women's" (I do have hips) but do not look particularly "feminine." The rest of the outer garments are from men's departments. I prefer baggy clothes, so the fact that I have "womanly" breasts often is not obvious (I do not wear a bra). Sometimes, I wear a baseball cap or some other type of hat. I also am white and relatively young (30 years old).[2]

My gender display—what others interpret as my presented identity—regularly leads to the misattribution of my gender. An incongruity exists between my gender self-identity and the gender that others perceive. In my encounters with people I do not know, I sometimes conclude, based on our interactions, that they think I am a man. This does not mean that other people do not think I am a man, just that I have no way of knowing what they think without interacting with them.

Living with It

I have no illusions or delusions about my appearance. I know that my appearance is likely to be read as "masculine" (and male) and that how I see myself is socially irrelevant. Given our two-and-only-two gender structure, I must live with the consequences of my appearance. These consequences fall into two categories: issues of identity and issues of interaction.

My most common experience is being called "Sir" or being referred to by some other masculine linguistic marker (e.g., "he," "man"). This has happened for years, for as long as I can remember, when having encounters with people I do not know.[3] Once, in fact, the same worker at a fast-food restaurant called me *Ma'am* when she took my order and *Sir* when she gave it to me.

Using my credit cards sometimes is a challenge. Some clerks subtly indicate their disbelief, looking from the card to me and back at the card and checking my signature carefully. Others challenge my use of the card, asking whose it is or demanding identification. One cashier asked to see my driver's license and then asked me whether I was the son of the cardholder. Another clerk told me that my signature on the receipt *had better match* the one on the card. Presumably, this was her way of letting me know that she was not convinced it was my credit card.

My identity as a woman also is called into question when I try to use women-only spaces. Encounters in public restrooms are an adventure. I have been told countless times that *This is the ladies' room*. Other women say nothing to me, but their stares and conversations with others let me know what they think. I will hear them say, for example, *There was a man in there*. I also get stares when I enter a locker room. However, it seems that women are less concerned about my presence there, perhaps because, given that it is a space for changing clothes, showering, and so forth, they will be able to make sure that I am really a woman. Dressing rooms in department stores also are problematic spaces. I remember shopping with my sister once and being offered a chair outside the room when I began to accompany her into the dressing room. . . .

Being perceived as a man has made me privy to male–male interactional styles of which most women are not aware. I found out, quite by accident, that many men greet, or acknowledge, people (mostly other men) who make eye contact with them with a single nod. For example, I found that when I walked down the halls of my brother's all-male dormitory making eye contact, men nodded their greetings at me. Oddly enough, these same men did not greet my brother; I had to tell him about making eye contact and nodding as a greeting ritual. Apparently, in this case I was doing masculinity better than he was!

I also believe that I am treated differently, for example, in auto parts stores (staffed almost exclusively by men in most cases) because of the assumption that I am a man. Workers there assume that I know what I need and that my questions are legitimate requests for information. I suspect that I am treated more fairly than a feminine-appearing woman would be. I have not been able to test this proposition. However, Devor's participants did report "being treated more respectfully" (1989:132) in such situations.

There is, however, a negative side to being assumed to be a man by other men. Once, a friend and I were driving in her car when a man failed to stop at an intersection and nearly crashed into us. As we drove away, I mouthed *stop sign* to him. When we both stopped our cars at the next intersection, he got out of his car and came up to the passenger side of the car, where I was sitting. He yelled obscenities at us and pounded and spit on the car window. Luckily, the windows were closed. I do not think he would have done that if he thought I was a woman. This was the first time I realized that one of the implications of being seen as a man was that I might be called on to defend myself from physical aggression from other men who felt challenged by me. This was a sobering and somewhat frightening thought.

Recently, I was verbally accosted by an older man who did not like where I had parked my car. As I walked down the street to work, he shouted that I should park at the university rather than on a side street nearby. I responded that it was a public street and that I could park there if I chose. He continued to yell, but the only thing I caught was the last part of what he said: *Your tires are going to get cut!* Based on my appearance that day—I was dressed casually and carrying a backpack, and I had my hat on backward—I believe he thought that I was a young male student rather than a female professor. I do not think he would have yelled at a person he thought to be a woman—and perhaps especially not a woman professor.

Given the presumption of heterosexuality that is part of our system of gender, my interactions with women who assume that I am a man also can be viewed from that perspective. For example, once my brother and I were shopping when we were "hit on" by two young women. The encounter ended before I realized what had happened. It was only when we walked away that I told him that I was pretty certain that they had thought both of us were men. A more common experience is realizing that when I am seen in public with one of my women friends, we are likely to be read as a heterosexual dyad. It is likely that if I were to walk through a shopping mall holding hands with a woman, no one would look twice, not because of their open-mindedness toward lesbian couples but rather because of their assumption that I was the male half of a straight couple. Recently, when walking through a mall with a friend and her infant, my observations of others' responses to us led me to believe that many of them assumed that we were a family on an outing, that is, that I was her partner and the father of the child.

Dealing with It

Although I now accept that being mistaken for a man will be a part of my life so long as I choose not to participate in femininity, there have been times when I consciously have tried to appear more feminine. I did this for a while when I was an undergraduate and again recently when I was on the academic job market. The first time, I let my hair grow nearly down to my shoulders and had it permed. I also grew long fingernails and wore nail polish. Much to my chagrin, even then one of my professors, who did not know my name, insistently referred to me in his kinship examples as "the son." Perhaps my first act on the way to my current stance was to point out to this man, politely and after class, that I was a woman.

More recently, I again let my hair grow out for several months, although I did not alter other aspects of my appearance. Once my hair was about two and a half inches long (from its original quarter inch), I realized, based on my encounters with strangers, that I had more or less passed back into the category of "woman." Then, when I returned to wearing a flat top, people again responded to me as if I were a man.

Because of my appearance, much of my negotiation of interactions with strangers involves attempts to anticipate their reactions to me. I need to assess whether they will be likely to assume that I am a man and whether that actually matters in the context of our encounters. Many times, my gender really is irrelevant, and it is just annoying to be misidentified. Other times, particularly when my appearance is coupled with something that identifies me by name (e.g., a check or credit card) without a photo, I might need to do something to ensure that my identity is not questioned. As a result of my experiences, I have developed some techniques to deal with gender misattribution.

In general, in unfamiliar public places, I avoid using the restroom because I know that it is a place where there is a high likelihood of misattribution and where misattribution is socially important. If I must use a public restroom, I try to make myself look as nonthreatening as possible. I do not wear a hat, and I try to rearrange my clothing to make my breasts more obvious. Here, I am trying to use my secondary sex characteristics to make my gender more obvious rather than the usual use of gender to make sex obvious. While in the restroom, I never make eye contact, and I get in and out as quickly as possible. Going in with a woman friend also is helpful; her presence legitimizes my own. People are less likely to think I am entering a space where I do not belong when I am with someone who looks like she does belong.[4]

To those women who verbally challenge my presence in the restroom, I reply, *I know,* usually in an annoyed tone. When they stare or talk about me to the women they are with, I simply get out as quickly as possible. In general, I do not wait for someone I am with because there is too much chance of an unpleasant encounter.

I stopped trying on clothes before purchasing them a few years ago because my presence in the changing areas was met with stares and whispers. Exceptions are stores where the dressing rooms are completely private, where there are individual stalls rather than a room with stalls separated by curtains, or where business is slow and no one else is trying on clothes. If I am trying on a garment clearly intended for a woman, then I usually can do so without hassle. I guess the attendants assume that I must be a woman if I have, for example, a women's bathing suit in my hand. But usually, I think it is easier for me to try the clothes on at home and return them, if necessary, rather than risk creating a scene. Similarly, when I am with another woman who is trying on clothes, I just wait outside.

My strategy with credit cards and checks is to anticipate wariness on a clerk's part. When I sense that there is some doubt or when they challenge me, I say, *It's my card.* I generally respond courteously to requests for photo ID, realizing that these might be routine checks because of concerns about increasingly widespread fraud. . . .

Another strategy I have been experimenting with is wearing nail polish in the dark bright colors currently fashionable. I try to do this when I travel by plane. Given more stringent travel regulations, one always must present a photo ID. But my experiences have shown that my driver's license is not necessarily convincing. Nail polish might be. I also flash my polished nails when I enter airport restrooms, hoping that they will provide a clue that I am indeed in the right place.

There are other cases in which the issues are less those of identity than of all the norms of interaction that, in our society, are gendered. My most common response to misattribution actually is to appear to ignore it, that is, to go on with the interaction as if nothing out of the ordinary has happened. Unless I feel that there is a good reason to establish my correct gender, I assume the identity others impose on me for the sake of smooth interaction. For example, if someone is selling me a movie ticket, then there is no reason to make sure that the person has accurately discerned my gender. Similarly, if it is clear that the person using "Sir" is talking to me, then I simply respond as appropriate. I accept the designation because it is irrelevant to the situation. It takes enough effort to be alert for misattributions and to decide which of them matter; responding to each one would take more energy than it is worth.

Sometimes, if our interaction involves conversation, my first verbal response is enough to let the other person know that I am actually a woman and not a man. My voice apparently is "feminine" enough to shift people's attributions to the other category. I know when this has happened by the apologies that usually accompany the mistake. I usually respond to the apologies by saying something like *No problem* and/or *It happens all the time.* Sometimes, a misattributor will offer an account for the mistake, for example, saying that it was my hair or that they were not being very observant.

These experiences with gender and misattribution provide some theoretical insights into contemporary Western understandings of gender and into the social structure of gender in contemporary society. Although there are a number of ways in which my experiences confirm the work of others, there also are some ways in which my experiences suggest other interpretations and conclusions.

What Does It Mean?

Gender is pervasive in our society. I cannot choose not to participate in it. Even if I try not to do gender, other people will do it for me. That is, given our two-and-only-two rule, they must attribute one of two genders to me. Still, although I cannot choose not to participate in gender, I can choose not to participate in femininity (as I have), at least with respect to physical appearance.

That is where the problems begin. Without the decorations of femininity, I do not look like a woman. That is, I do not look like what many people's commonsense understanding of gender tells them a woman looks like. How I see myself, even how I might wish others would see me, is socially irrelevant. It is the gender that I *appear* to be (my "perceived gender") that is most relevant to my social identity and interactions with others. The major consequence of this fact is that I must be continually aware of which gender I "give off" as well as which gender I "give" (Goffman 1959).

Because my gender self-identity is "not displayed obviously, immediately, and consistently" (Devor 1989:58), I am somewhat of a failure in social terms with respect to gender. Causing people to be uncertain or wrong about one's gender is a violation of taken-for-granted rules that leads to embarrassment and discomfort; it means that something has gone wrong with the interaction (Garfinkel 1967; Kessler and McKenna 1978). This means that my nonresponse to misattribution is the more socially appropriate response; I am allowing others to maintain face (Goffman 1959:1967). By not calling attention to their mistakes, I uphold their images of themselves as competent social actors. I also maintain my own image as competent by letting them assume that I am the gender I appear to them to be.

But I still have discreditable status; I carry a stigma (Goffman 1963). Because I have failed to participate appropriately in the creation of meaning with respect to gender (Devor 1989), I can be called on to account for my appearance. If discredited, I show myself to be an incompetent social actor. I am the one not following the rules, and I will pay the price for not providing people with the appropriate cues for placing me in the gender category to which I really belong.

I do think that it is, in many cases, safer to be read as a man than as some sort of deviant woman. "Man" is an acceptable category; it fits properly into people's gender worldview. Passing as a man often is the "path of least resistance" (Devor 1989; Johnson 1997). For example, in situations where gender does not matter, letting people take me as a man is easier than correcting them.

Conversely, as Butler noted, "We regularly punish those who fail to do their gender right" (1990:140). Feinberg maintained, "Masculine girls and women face terrible condemnation and brutality—including sexual violence—for crossing the boundary of what is 'acceptable' female expression" (1996:114). People are more likely to harass me when they perceive me to be a woman who looks like a man. For example, when a group of teenagers realized that I was not a man because one of their mothers identified me correctly, they began to make derogatory comments when I passed them. One asked, for example, "Does she have a penis?"

Because of the assumption that a "masculine" woman is a lesbian, there is the risk of homophobic reactions (Gardner 1995; Lucal 1997). Perhaps surprisingly, I find that I am much more likely to be taken for a man than for a lesbian, at least based on my interactions with people and their reactions to me. This might be because people are less likely to reveal that they have taken me for a lesbian because it is less relevant to an encounter or because they believe this would be unacceptable. But I think it is more likely a product of the strength of our two-and-only-two system. I give enough masculine cues that I am seen not as a deviant woman but rather as a man, at least in most cases. The problem seems not to be that people are uncertain about my gender, which might lead them to conclude that I was a lesbian once they realized I was a woman. Rather, I seem to fit easily into a gender category—just not the one with which I identify. . . .

Boundaries and margins are an important component of both my experiences of gender and our theoretical understanding of gendering processes. I am, in effect, both woman and not-woman. As a woman who often is a social man but who also is a woman living in a patriarchal society, I am in a unique position to see and act. I sometimes receive privileges usually limited to men, and I sometimes am oppressed by my status as a deviant woman. I am, in a sense, an outsider-within (Collins 1991). Positioned on the boundaries of gender categories, I have developed a consciousness that I hope will prove transformative (Anzaldua 1987).

In fact, one of the reasons why I decided to continue my nonparticipation in femininity was that my sociological training suggested that this could be one of my contributions to the eventual dismantling of patriarchal gender constructs. It would be my way of making the personal political. I accepted being taken for a man as the price I would pay to help subvert patriarchy. I believed that all of the inconveniences I was enduring meant that I actually was doing something to bring down the gender structures that entangled all of us.

Then, I read Lorber's (1994) *Paradoxes of Gender* and found out, much to my dismay, that I might not actually be challenging gender after all. Because of the way in which doing gender works in our two-and-only-two system, gender displays are simply read as evidence of one of the two categories. Therefore, gender bending, blending, and passing between the categories do not question the categories themselves. If one's social gender and personal (true) gender do not correspond, then this is irrelevant unless someone notices the lack of congruence.

This reality brings me to a paradox of my experiences. First, not only do others assume that I am one gender or the other, but I also insist that I *really am* a member of one of the two gender categories. That is, I am female; I self-identify as a woman. I do not claim to be some other gender or to have no gender at all. I simply place myself in the wrong category according to stereotypes and cultural standards; the gender I present, or that some people perceive me to be presenting, is inconsistent with the gender with which I identify myself as well as with the gender I could be "proven" to be. Socially, I display the wrong gender; personally, I identify as the proper gender.

Second, although I ultimately would like to see the destruction of our current gender structure, I am not to the point of personally abandoning gender. Right now, I do not want people to see me as genderless as much as I want them to see me as a woman. That is, I would like to expand the category of "woman" to include people like me. I, too, am deeply embedded in our gender system, even though I do not play by many of its rules. For me, as for most people in our society, gender is a substantial part of my personal identity (Howard and Hollander 1997). Socially, the problem is that I do not present a gender display that is consistently read as feminine. In fact, I consciously do not participate in the trappings of femininity. However, I do identify myself as a woman, not as a man or as someone outside of the two-and-only-two categories.

Yet, I do believe, as Lorber (1994) does, that the purpose of gender, as it currently is constructed, is to oppress women. Lorber analyzed gender as a "process of creating distinguishable social statuses for the assignment of rights and responsibilities" that ends up putting women in a devalued and oppressed position (1994:32). As Martin put it, "Bodies that clearly delineate gender status facilitate the maintenance of the gender hierarchy" (1998:495).

For society, gender means difference (Lorber 1994). The erosion of the boundaries would problematize that structure. Therefore, for gender to operate as it currently does, the category "woman" *cannot* be expanded to include people like me. The maintenance of the gender structure is dependent on the creation of a few categories that are mutually exclusive, the members of which are as different as possible (Lorber 1994). It is the clarity of the boundaries between the categories that allows gender to be used to assign rights and responsibilities as well as resources and rewards.

It is that part of gender—what it is used for—that is most problematic. Indeed, is it not *patriarchal*—or, even more specifically, *heteropatriarchal*—constructions of gender that are actually the problem? It is not the differences between men and women, or the categories themselves, so much as the meanings ascribed to the categories and, even more important, the hierarchical nature of gender under patriarchy that is the problem (Johnson 1997). Therefore, I am rebelling not against my femaleness or even my womanhood; instead, I am protesting contemporary constructions of femininity and, at least indirectly, masculinity under patriarchy. We do not, in fact, know what gender would look like if it were not constructed around heterosexuality in the context of patriarchy.

Although it is possible that the end of patriarchy would mean the end of gender, it is at least conceivable that something like what we now call gender could exist in a postpatriarchal future. The two-and-only-two categorization might well disappear, there being no hierarchy for it to justify. But I do not think that we should make the assumption that gender and patriarchy are synonymous. . . .

In a . . . book, *The Gender Knot,* Johnson (1997) argued that when it comes to gender and patriarchy, most of us follow the paths of least resistance; we "go along to get along," allowing our actions to be shaped by the gender system. Collectively, our actions help patriarchy maintain and perpetuate a system of oppression and privilege. Thus, by withdrawing our support from this system by choosing paths of greater resistance, we can start to chip away at it. Many people participate in gender because they cannot imagine any alternatives. In my classroom, and in my interactions and encounters with strangers, my presence can make it difficult for people not to see that there *are* other paths. In other words, following from West and Zimmerman (1987), I can subvert gender by doing it differently.

For example, I think it is true that my existence does not have an effect on strangers who assume that I am a man and never learn otherwise. For them, I do uphold the two-and-only-two system. But there are other cases in which my existence can have an effect. For example, when people initially take me for a man but then find out that I actually am a woman, at least for that moment, the naturalness of gender may be called into question. In these cases, my presence can provoke a "category crisis" (Garber 1992:16) because it challenges the sex/gender binary system.

The subversive potential of my gender might be strongest in my classrooms. When I teach about the sociology of gender, my students can see me as the embodiment of the social construction of gender. Not all of my students have transformative experiences as a result of taking a course with me; there is the chance that some of them see me as a "freak" or as an exception. Still, after listening to stories about my experiences with gender and reading literature on the subject, many students begin to see how and why gender is a social product. I can disentangle sex, gender, and sexuality in the contemporary United States for them. Students can begin to see the connection between biographical experiences and the structure of society. As one of my students noted, I clearly live the material I am teaching. If that helps me to get my point across, then perhaps I am subverting the binary gender system after all. Although my gendered presence and my way of doing gender might make others—and sometimes even me—uncomfortable, no one ever said that dismantling patriarchy was going to be easy.

ENDNOTES

Author's Note: I thank the journal's reviewers, my writing group (Linda Chen, Louise Collins, April Lidinsky, Margarete Myers, Monica Tetzlaff, and Becky Torstrick), Heather Bulan, and Linda Fritschner for their helpful comments on earlier versions of this article.

[1] Ethnomethodology has been described as "the study of commonsense practical reasoning" (Collins 1988:274). It examines how people make sense of their everyday experiences. Ethnomethodology is particularly useful in studying gender because it helps to uncover the assumptions on which our understandings of sex and gender are based.

[2] I obviously have left much out by not examining my gendered experiences in the context of race, age, class, sexuality, region, and so forth. Such a project clearly is more complex. As Weston pointed out, gender presentations are complicated by other statuses of their presenters: "What it takes to kick a person over into another gendered category can differ with race, class, religion, and time" (1996:168). Furthermore, I am well aware that my whiteness allows me to assume that my experiences are simply a product of gender (see, e.g., hooks 1981; Lucal 1996; Spelman 1988; West and Fenstermaker 1995). For now, suffice it to say that it is my privileged position on some of these axes and my more disadvantaged position on others that combine to delineate my overall experience.

[3] In fact, such experiences are not always limited to encounters with strangers. My grandmother, who does not see me often, twice has mistaken me for either my brother-in-law or some unknown man.

[4] I also have noticed that there are certain types of restrooms in which I will not be verbally challenged; the higher the social status of the place, the less likely I will be harassed. For example, when I go to the theater, I might get stared at, but my presence never has been challenged.

REFERENCES

Anzaldua, G. 1987. *Borderlands/La Frontera.* San Francisco: Aunt Lute Books.
Bem, S. L. 1993. *The Lenses of Gender.* New Haven, CT: Yale University Press.
Berger, P. 1963. *Invitation to Sociology.* New York: Anchor.
Bordo, S. 1993. *Unbearable Weight.* Berkeley: University of California Press.
Butler, J. 1990. *Gender Trouble.* New York: Routledge.
Collins, P. H. 1991. *Black Feminist Thought.* New York: Routledge.
Collins, R. 1988. *Theoretical Sociology.* San Diego: Harcourt Brace Jovanovich.
Devor, H. 1989. *Gender Blending: Confronting the Limits of Duality.* Bloomington: Indiana University Press.
Feinberg, L. 1996. *Transgender Warriors.* Boston: Beacon.
Garber, M. 1992. *Vested Interests: Cross-Dressing and Cultural Anxiety.* New York: HarperPerennial.
Gardner, C. B. 1995. *Passing By: Gender and Public Harassment.* Berkeley: University of California.
Garfinkel, H. 1967. *Studies in Ethnomethodology.* Englewood Cliffs, NJ: Prentice Hall.
Goffman, E. 1959. *The Presentation of Self in Everyday Life.* Garden City, NY: Doubleday.
———. 1963. *Stigma.* Englewood Cliffs, NJ: Prentice Hall.
———. 1976. "Gender Display." *Studies in the Anthropology of Visual Communication* 3:69–77.
hooks, b. 1981. *Ain't I a Woman: Black Women and Feminism.* Boston: South End Press.
Howard, J. A. and J. Hollander. 1997. *Gendered Situations, Gendered Selves.* Thousand Oaks, CA: Sage.
Johnson, A. G. 1997. *The Gender Knot: Unraveling Our Patriarchal Legacy.* Philadelphia: Temple University Press.
Kessler, S. J. and W. McKenna. 1978. *Gender: An Ethnomethodological Approach.* New York: John Wiley.
Krieger, S. 1991. *Social Science and the Self.* New Brunswick, NJ: Rutgers University Press.
Lorber, J. 1994. *Paradoxes of Gender.* New Haven, CT: Yale University Press.
———. 1996. "Beyond the Binaries: Depolarizing the Categories of Sex, Sexuality, and Gender." *Sociological Inquiry* 66:143–59.
Lucal, B. 1996. "Oppression and Privilege: Toward a Relational Conceptualization of Race." *Teaching Sociology* 24:245–55.
———. 1997. "'Hey, This Is the Ladies' Room!': Gender Misattribution and Public Harassment." *Perspectives on Social Problems* 9:43–57.
Martin, K. A. 1998. "Becoming a Gendered Body: Practices of Preschools." *American Sociological Review* 63:494–511.

Mills, C. W. 1959. *The Sociological Imagination.* London: Oxford University Press.

Myhre, J. R. M. 1995. "One Bad Hair Day Too Many, or the Hairstory of an Androgynous Young Feminist." In *Listen Up: Voices from the Next Feminist Generation,* edited by B. Findlen. Seattle, WA: Seal Press.

Reinharz, S. 1992. *Feminist Methods in Social Research.* New York: Oxford University Press.

Riemer, J. W. 1977. "Varieties of Opportunistic Research." *Urban Life* 5:467–77.

———. 1988. "Work and Self." In *Personal Sociology,* edited by P. C. Higgins and J. M. Johnson. New York: Praeger.

Spelman, E. V. 1988. *Inessential Woman: Problems of Exclusion in Feminist Thought.* Boston: Beacon.

West, C. and S. Fenstermaker. 1995. "Doing Difference." *Gender & Society* 9:8–37.

West, C. and D. H. Zimmerman. 1987. "Doing Gender." *Gender & Society* 1:125–51.

Weston, K. 1996. *Render Me, Gender Me.* New York: Columbia University Press.

Zimmerman, D. H. 1992. "They Were All Doing Gender, but They Weren't All Passing: Comment on Rogers." *Gender & Society* 6:192–98.

29

"DUDE, YOU'RE A FAG"
Adolescent Male Homophobia

C. J. PASCOE

Earlier readings (Readings 9, 13, and 28) examined how gender is constructed and socialized in the United States. Another interesting social institution to examine in terms of gender identity is the American high school. The high school experience reinforces gender distinctions and inequality in numerous ways, including through the curriculum, teaching styles, athletics, and the discourse among peers. The following reading by C. J. Pascoe, an assistant professor of sociology at Colorado College, examines adolescent male homophobia and how this discourse is less about sexuality and more about maintaining gender identity and the boundaries of masculinity.

The sun shone bright and clear over River High's annual Creative and Performing Arts Happening, or CAPA. During CAPA the school's various art programs displayed students' work in a fairlike atmosphere. The front quad sported student-generated computer programs. Colorful and ornate chalk art covered the cement sidewalks. Tables lined with student-crafted pottery were set up on the grass. Tall displays of students' paintings divided the rear quad. To the left of the paintings a television blared student-directed music videos. At the rear of the back quad, a square, roped-off area of cement served as a makeshift stage for drama, choir, and dance performances. Teachers released students from class to wander around the quads, watch performances, and look at the art. This freedom from class time lent the day an air of excitement because students were rarely allowed to roam the campus without a hall pass, an office summons, or a parent/faculty escort. In honor of CAPA, the school district bussed in elementary school students from the surrounding grammar schools to participate in the day's festivities.

Running through the rear quad, Brian, a senior, yelled to a group of boys visiting from the elementary schools, *There's a faggot over there! There's a faggot over there! Come look!* Following Brian, the ten-year-olds dashed down a hallway. At the end of the hallway Brian's friend Dan pursed his lips and began sashaying toward the little boys. As he minced, he swung his hips exaggeratedly and wildly waved his arms. To the boys Brian yelled, *Look at the faggot! Watch out! He'll get you!* In response, the ten-year-olds raced back down the hallway screaming in terror. Brian and Dan repeated this drama throughout the following half hour, each time with a new group of young boys.

Making jokes like these about faggots was central to social life at River High. Indeed, boys learned long before adolescence that faggots were simultaneously predatory and passive and that they were, at all costs, to be avoided. Older boys repeatedly impressed upon younger ones through these types of homophobic rituals that whatever they did, whatever they became, however they talked, they had to avoid becoming a faggot.

Feminist scholars of masculinity have documented the centrality of homophobic insults and attitudes to masculinity (Kimmel 2001; Lehne 1998), especially in school settings (Burn 2000; Kimmel 2003; Messner 2005; Plummer 2001; G. Smith 1998; Wood 1984). They argue that homophobic teasing often characterizes masculinity in adolescence and early adulthood and that antigay slurs tend to be directed primarily at gay boys. This reading both expands on and challenges these accounts of relationships between homophobia and masculinity. Homophobia is indeed a central mechanism in the making of contemporary American adolescent masculinity. A close analysis of the way boys at River High invoke the faggot as a disciplinary mechanism makes clear that something more than simple homophobia is at play in adolescent masculinity. The use of the word *fag* by boys at River High points to the limits of an argument that focuses centrally on homophobia. Fag is not only an identity linked to homosexual boys but an identity that can temporarily adhere to heterosexual boys as well. The fag trope is also a racialized disciplinary mechanism.

Homophobia is too facile a term with which to describe the deployment of *fag* as an epithet. By calling the use of the word *fag* homophobia—and letting the argument stop there—previous research has obscured the gendered nature of sexualized insults (Plummer 2001). Invoking homophobia to describe the ways boys aggressively tease each other overlooks the powerful relationship between masculinity and this sort of insult. Instead, it seems incidental, in this conventional line of argument, that girls do not harass each other and are not harassed in this same manner. This framing naturalizes the relationship between masculinity and homophobia, thus obscuring that such harassment is central to the formation of a gendered identity for boys in a way that it is not for girls.

Fag is not necessarily a static identity attached to a particular (homosexual) boy. Fag talk and fag imitations serve as a discourse with which boys discipline themselves and each other through joking relationships. Any boy can temporarily become a fag in a given social space or interaction. This does not mean that boys who identify as or are perceived to be homosexual aren't subject to intense harassment. Many are. But becoming a fag has as much to do with failing at the masculine tasks of competence, heterosexual prowess, and strength or in any way revealing weakness or femininity as it does with a sexual identity. This fluidity of the fag identity is what makes the specter of the fag such a powerful disciplinary mechanism. It is fluid enough that boys police their behaviors out of fear of having the fag identity permanently adhere and definitive enough so that boys recognize a fag behavior and strive to avoid it.

An analysis of the fag discourse also indicates ways in which gendered power works through racialized selves. The fag discourse is invoked differently by and in relation to white boys' bodies than it is by and in relation to African American boys' bodies. While certain behaviors put all boys at risk for becoming temporarily a fag, some behaviors can be enacted by African American boys without putting them at risk of receiving the label. The racialized meanings of the fag discourse suggest that something more than simple homophobia is involved in these sorts of interactions. It is not that gendered homophobia does not exist in African American communities. Indeed, making fun of "negro faggotry seems to be a rite of passage among contemporary black male rappers and filmmakers" (Riggs 1991:253). However, the fact that "white women and men, gay and straight, have more or less colonized cultural debates about sexual representation" (Julien and Mercer 1991:167) obscures varied systems of sexualized meanings among different racialized ethnic groups (Almaguer 1991). Thus far male homophobia has primarily been written about as a racially neutral phenomenon. However, as D. L. King's (2004) recent work on African American men and same-sex desire pointed out, homophobia is characterized by racial identities as well as sexual and gendered ones.

What Is a Fag? Gendered Meanings

Since you were little boys you've been told, "Hey, don't be a little faggot," explained Darnell, a football player of mixed African American and white heritage, as we sat on a bench next to the athletic field. Indeed, both the boys and girls I interviewed told me that *fag* was the worst epithet one guy could direct at another. Jeff, a slight white sophomore, explained to me that boys call each other fag because *gay people aren't really liked over here and stuff.* Jeremy, a Latino junior, told me that this insult literally reduced a boy to nothing. *To call someone gay or fag is like the lowest thing you can call someone. Because that's like saying that you're nothing.*

Most guys explained their or others' dislike of fags by claiming that homophobia was synonymous with being a guy. For instance, Keith, a white soccer-playing senior, explained, *I think guys are just homophobic.* However, boys were not equal-opportunity homophobes. Several students told me that these homophobic insults applied only to boys and not to girls. For example, while Jake, a handsome white senior, told me that he didn't like gay people, he quickly added, *Lesbians, okay, that's good.* Similarly Cathy, a popular white cheerleader, told me, *Being a lesbian is accepted because guys think, "Oh that's cool."* Darnell, after telling me that boys were warned about becoming faggots, said, *They [guys] are fine with girls. I think it's the guy part that they're like ewwww.* In this sense it was not strictly homophobia but a gendered homophobia that constituted adolescent masculinity in the culture of River High. It is clear, according to these comments, that lesbians were "good" because of their place in heterosexual male fantasy, not necessarily because of some enlightened approach to same-sex relationships. A popular trope in heterosexual pornography depicts two women engaging in sexual acts for the purpose of male titillation. The boys at River High are not unique in making this distinction; adolescent boys in general dislike gay men more than they dislike lesbians (Baker and Fishbein 1998). The fetishizing of sex acts between women indicates that using only the term *homophobia* to describe boys' repeated use of the word *fag* might be a bit simplistic and misleading.

Girls at River High rarely deployed the word *fag* and were never called fags. I recorded girls uttering *fag* only three times during my research. In one instance, Angela, a Latina cheerleader, teased Jeremy, a well-liked white senior involved in student government, for not ditching school with her: *You wouldn't 'cause you're a faggot.* However, girls did not use this word as part of their regular lexicon. The sort of gendered homophobia that constituted adolescent masculinity did not constitute adolescent femininity. Girls were not called dykes or lesbians in any sort of regular or systematic way. Students did tell me that *slut* was the worst thing a girl could be called. However, my field notes indicate that the word *slut* (or its synonym *ho*) appeared one time for every eight times the word *fag* appeared.

Highlighting the difference between the deployment of *gay* and *fag* as insults brings the gendered nature of this homophobia into focus. For boys and girls at River High *gay* was a fairly common synonym for "stupid." While this word shared the sexual origins of *fag,* it didn't *consistently* have the skew of gender-loaded meaning. Girls and boys often used *gay* as an adjective referring to inanimate objects and male or female people, whereas they used *fag* as a noun that denoted only unmasculine males. Students used *gay* to describe anything from someone's clothes to a new school rule that they didn't like. For instance, one day in auto shop, Arnie pulled out a large older version of a black laptop computer and placed it on his desk. Behind him Nick cried, *That's a gay laptop! It's five inches thick!* The rest of the boys in the class laughed at Arnie's outdated laptop. A laptop can be gay, a movie can be gay, or a group of people can be gay. Boys used *gay* and *fag* interchangeably when they referred to other boys, but *fag* didn't have the gender-neutral attributes that *gay* frequently invoked.

Surprisingly, some boys took pains to say that the term *fag* did not imply sexuality. Darnell told me, *It doesn't even have anything to do with being gay.* Similarly, J. L., a white sophomore at Hillside High (River High's cross-town rival), asserted, *Fag, seriously, it has nothing to do with sexual preference at all. You could just be calling somebody an idiot, you know?* I asked Ben, a quiet, white sophomore who wore heavy-metal T-shirts to auto shop each day, *What kind of things do guys get called a fag for?* Ben answered, *Anything . . . literally, anything. Like you were trying to turn a wrench the wrong way, "Dude, you're a fag." Even if a piece of meat drops out of your sandwich, "You fag!"* Each time Ben said, *You fag,* his voice deepened as if he were imitating a more masculine boy. While Ben might rightly *feel* that a guy could be called a fag for "anything . . . literally, anything," there were actually specific behaviors that, when enacted by most boys, could render them more vulnerable to a *fag* epithet. In this instance Ben's comment highlights the use of *fag* as a generic insult for incompetence, which in the world of River High, was central to a masculine identity. A boy could get called a fag for exhibiting any sort of behavior defined as unmasculine (although not necessarily behaviors aligned with femininity): being stupid or incompetent, dancing, caring too much about clothing, being too emotional, or expressing interest (sexual or platonic) in other guys. However, given the extent of its deployment and the laundry list of behaviors that could get a boy in trouble, it is no wonder that Ben felt a boy could be called fag for "anything." These nonsexual meanings didn't replace sexual meanings but rather existed alongside them.

One-third (thirteen) of the boys I interviewed told me that, while they might liberally insult each other with the term, they would not direct it at a homosexual peer. Jabes, a Filipino senior, told me, *I actually say it* [fag] *quite a lot, except for when I'm in the company of an actual homosexual person. Then I try not to say it at all. But when I'm just hanging out with my friends I'll be like, "Shut up, I don't want to hear you any more, you stupid fag."* Similarly J. L. compared homosexuality to a disability, saying there was *no way* he'd call an actually gay guy a fag because *there's people who are the retarded people who nobody wants to associate with. I'll be so nice to those guys, and I hate it when people make fun of them. It's like, "Bro do you realize that they can't help that?" And then there's gay people. They were born that way.* According to this group of boys, gay was a legitimate, or at least biological, identity.

There was a possibility, however slight, that a boy could be gay and masculine (Connell 1995). David, a handsome white senior dressed smartly in khaki pants and a white button-down shirt, told me, *Being gay is just a lifestyle. It's someone you choose to sleep with. You can still throw around a football and be gay.* It was as if David was justifying the use of the word *fag* by arguing that gay men could be men if they tried but that if they failed at it (i.e., if they couldn't throw a football) then they deserved to be called a fag. In other words, to be a fag was, by definition, the opposite of masculine, whether the word was deployed with sexualized or nonsexualized meanings. . . . While it was not necessarily acceptable to be gay, at least a man who was gay could do other things that would render him acceptably masculine. A fag, by the very definition of the word, could not be masculine. . . .

Becoming a Fag: Fag Fluidity

"The ubiquity of the word *faggot* speaks to the reach of its discrediting capacity" (Corbett 2001:4). It's almost as if boys cannot help shouting it out on a regular basis—in the hallway, in class, or across campus as a greeting. In my fieldwork I was amazed by the way the word seemed to pop uncontrollably out of boys' mouths in all kinds of situations. To quote just one of many instances from my field notes: two boys walked out of the PE locker room, and one yelled, *Fucking faggot!* at no one in particular. None of the other students paid them any mind, since this sort of thing happened so frequently. Similar spontaneous yelling of some variation of the word *fag*, seemingly apropos of nothing, happened repeatedly among boys throughout the school. This and repeated imitations of fags constitute what I refer to as a "fag discourse."

Fag discourse is central to boys' joking relationships. Joking cements relationships among boys (Kehily and Nayak 1997; Lyman 1998) and helps to manage anxiety and discomfort (Freud 1905). Boys both connect with one another and manage the anxiety around this sort of relationship through joking about fags. . . . They also lobbed the *fag* epithet at each other in a verbal game of hot potato, each careful to deflect the insult quickly by hurling it toward someone else. These games and imitations made up a fag discourse that highlighted the fag not as a static but rather as a fluid identity that boys constantly struggled to avoid.

In imitative performances the fag discourse functioned as a constant reiteration of the fag's existence, affirming that the fag was out there; boys reminded themselves and each other that at any moment they could become fags if they were not sufficiently masculine. At the same time these performances demonstrated that the boy who was invoking the fag was *not* a fag. Emir, a tall, thin African American boy, frequently imitated fags to draw laughs from other students in his introductory drama class. One day Mr. McNally, the drama teacher, disturbed by the noise outside the classroom, turned to the open door, saying, "We'll shut this unless anyone really wants to watch sweaty boys playing basketball." Emir lisped, "I wanna watch the boys play!" The rest of the class cracked up at his imitation. No one in the class actually thought Emir was gay, as he purposefully mocked both same-sex sexual desire (through pretending to admire the boys playing basketball) and an effeminate gender identity (through speaking with a lisp and in a high-pitched voice). Had he said this in all seriousness, the class most likely would have responded in stunned silence. Instead, Emir reminded them he was masculine by immediately dropping the fag act. After imitating a fag, boys assure others that they are not a fag by instantly becoming masculine again after the performance. They mock their own performed femininity and/or same-sex desire, assuring themselves and others that such an identity deserves derisive laughter.

Boys consistently tried to force others into the fag position by lobbing the *fag* epithet at each other. One day in auto shop, Jay was rummaging through a junk-filled car in the parking lot. He poked his head out of the trunk and asked, *Where are Craig and Brian?* Neil responded with *I think they're over there,* pointing, then thrusting his hips and pulling his arms back and forth to indicate that Craig and Brian might be having sex. The boys in auto shop laughed. This sort of joke temporarily labeled both Craig and Brian as faggots. Because the fag discourse was so familiar, the other boys immediately understood that Neil was indicating that Craig and Brian were having sex. However, these were not necessarily identities that stuck. Nobody actually thought Craig and Brian were homosexuals. Rather, the fag identity was fluid—certainly an identity that no boy wanted but that most boys could escape, usually by engaging in some sort of discursive contest to turn another boy into a fag.

In this way the fag became a hot potato that no boy wanted to be left holding. One of the best ways to move out of the fag position was to thrust another boy into that position. . . .

Given the pervasiveness of fag jokes and the fluidity of the fag identity, it is difficult for boys to consistently avoid the brand. As Ben stated, it almost seemed that a boy could get called a fag for "anything." But most readily acknowledged that there were spaces, behaviors, and bodily comportments that made one more likely to be subject to the fag discourse, such as bodily practices involving clothing and dancing. . . .

Racializing The Fag

While all groups of boys, with the exception of the Mormon boys, used the word *fag* or fag imagery in their interactions, the fag discourse was not deployed consistently or identically across social groups at River High. Differences between white boys' and African American boys' meaning making, particularly around appearance and dancing, reveal ways the specter of the fag was racialized. The specter of the fag, these invocations reveal, was consistently white. Additionally, African American boys simply did not deploy it with the same frequency as white boys. For both groups of boys, the *fag* insult entailed meanings of emasculation. However, African American boys were much more likely to tease one another for being white than for being a fag. Precisely because African American men are so hypersexualized in the United States, white men are, by default, feminized, so *white* was a stand-in for *fag* among many of the African American boys at River High. Two of the behaviors that put a white boy at risk for being labeled a fag didn't function in the same way for African American boys: clothing and dancing.

Perhaps because they are, by necessity, more invested in symbolic forms of power related to appearance (much like adolescent girls), a given African American boy's status is not lowered but enhanced by paying attention to clothing or dancing. Clean, oversized, carefully put together clothing is central to a hip-hop identity for African American boys who identify with hip-hop culture. . . .

The amount of attention and care given to clothing for white boys not identified with hip-hop culture (that is, most of the white boys at River High) would certainly cast them into an abject, fag position, as Ben indicated when he cried, jokingly, *I got my good panths all dirty!* White boys were not supposed to appear to care about their clothes or appearance because only fags cared about how they looked. However, African American boys involved in hip-hop culture talked frequently about whether their clothes, specifically their shoes, were dirty. . . .

Dancing was another arena that carried distinctly fag-associated meanings for white boys but masculine meanings for African American boys who participated in hip-hop culture. White boys often associated dancing with fags. However, dancing did not carry this sort of sexualized gender meaning for all boys at River High. For African American boys, dancing demonstrates membership in a cultural community (Best 2000). At River, African American boys frequently danced together in single-sex groups, teaching each other the latest dance moves, showing off a particularly difficult move, or making each other laugh with humorous dance moves. In fact, while in drama class, Liam and Jacob hit each other and joked through the entire dancing exercise, Darnell and Marc seemed very comfortable touching one another. They stood close to one another, heel to toe, as they were supposed to. Their bodies touched, and they gently and gracefully moved the other's arms and head in a way that was tender, not at all like the flailing of the two white boys. . . .

Reframing Homophobia

Homophobia is central to contemporary definitions of adolescent masculinity. Unpacking multilayered meanings that boys deploy through their uses of homophobic language and joking rituals makes clear that it is not just homophobia but a gendered and racialized homophobia. By attending to these meanings, I reframe the discussion as a fag discourse rather than simply labeling it as homophobia. The fag is an "abject" (Butler 1993) position, a position outside masculinity that actually constitutes masculinity. Thus masculinity, in part, becomes the daily interactional work of repudiating the threatening specter of the fag.

The fag extends beyond a static sexual identity attached to a gay boy. Few boys are permanently identified as fags; most move in and out of fag positions. Looking at fag as a discourse in addition to a static identity reveals that the term can be invested with different meanings in different social spaces. *Fag* may be used as a weapon with which to temporarily assert one's masculinity by denying it to others. Thus the fag becomes a symbol around which contests of masculinity take place. . . .

The *fag* epithet, when hurled at other boys, may or may not have explicit sexual meanings, but it always has gendered meanings. When a boy calls another boy a fag, it means he is not a man but not necessarily that he is a homosexual. The boys at River High knew that they were not supposed to call homosexual boys fags because that was mean. This, then, has been the limited success of the mainstream gay rights movement. The message absorbed by some of these teenage boys was that "gay men can be masculine, just like you." Instead of challenging gender inequality, this particular discourse of gay rights has reinscribed it. Thus we need to begin to think about how gay men may be in a unique position to challenge gendered as well as sexual norms. The boys in the drama performances show an alternative way to be teenage boys, which is about playing with gender, not just enforcing gender duality based on sexual meanings.

REFERENCES

Almaguer, Tomas. 1991. "Chicano Men: A Cartography of Homosexual Identity and Behavior." *Differences* 3(2):75–100.

Baker, Janet G. and Harold D. Fishbein. 1998. "The Development of Prejudice towards Gays and Lesbians by Adolescents." *Journal of Homosexuality* 36(1):89–100.

Burn, Shawn Megan. 2000. "Heterosexuals' Use of 'Fag' and 'Queer' to Deride One Another: A Contributor to Heterosexism and Stigma." *Journal of Homosexuality* 40(2):1–11.

Butler, Judith. 1993. *Bodies That Matter: On the Discursive Limits of "Sex."* New York: Routledge.

Connell, R. W. 1995. *Masculinities.* Berkeley, CA: University of California Press.

Corbett, Ken. 2001. "Faggot = Loser." *Studies in Gender and Sexuality* 2(1):3–28.

Freud, Sigmund. 1905. *The Basic Writings of Sigmund Freud.* Translated by A. A. Brill. New York: Modern Library.

Julien, Issac and Kobena Mercer. 1991. "True Confessions: A Discourse on Images of Black Male Sexuality." Pp. 167–73 in *Brother to Brother: New Writings by Black Gay Men,* edited by Essex Hemphill. Boston: Alyson Publications.

Kimmel, Michael. 2001. "Masculinity and Homophobia: Fear, Shame, and Silence in the Construction of Gender Identity." Pp. 266–87 in *The Masculinities Reader,* edited by Stephen Whitehead and Frank Barrett. Cambridge: Polity Press.

———. 2003. "Adolescent Masculinity, Homophobia, and Violence: Random School Shootings, 1982–2001." *American Behavioral Scientist* 46(10):439–58.

Kehily, Mary Jane and Anoop Nayak. 1997. "'Lads and Laughter': Humour and the Production of Heterosexual Masculinities." *Gender and Education* 9(1):69–87.

King, D. L. 2004. *On the Down Low: A Journey into the Lives of Straight Black Men Who Sleep with Men.* New York: Broadway Books.

Lehne, Gregory. 1998. "Homophobia among Men: Supporting and Defining the Male Role." Pp. 237–49 in *Men's Lives,* edited by Michael Kimmel and Michael Messner. Boston: Allyn and Bacon.

Lyman, Peter. 1998. "The Fraternal Bond as a Joking Relationship: A Case Study of the Role of Sexist Jokes in Male Group Bonding." Pp. 171–93 in *Men's Lives,* edited by Michael Kimmel and Michael Messner. Boston: Allyn and Bacon.

Messner, Michael. 2005. "Becoming 100% Straight." Pp. 227–32 in *Gender through the Prism of Difference,* edited by Maxine Baca Zinn, Pierrette Hondagneu-Sotelo, and Michael Messner. New York: Oxford University Press.

Plummer, David C. 2001. "The Quest for Modern Manhood: Masculine Stereotypes, Peer Culture and the Social Significance of Homophobia." *Journal of Adolescence* 24(1):15–23.

Riggs, Marlon. 1991. "Black Macho Revisited: Reflections of a Snap! Queen." Pp. 253–60 in *Brother to Brother: New Writings by Black Gay Men,* edited by Essex Hamphill. Boston: Alyson Publications.

Smith, George W. 1998. "The Ideology of 'Fag': The School Experience of Gay Students." *Sociological Quarterly* 39(2):309–35.

Wood, Julian. 1984. "Groping Towards Sexism: Boy's Sex Talk." Pp. 54–84 in *Gender and Generation,* edited by Angela McRobbie and Mica Nava. London: Macmillan.

30
_____

BECAUSE SHE LOOKS LIKE A CHILD

KEVIN BALES

The fourth and final reading in this section on gender examines a global form of gender inequality, female sexual slavery. In the readings on social class, we examined objective and subjective indicators of social class and social class inequality, including access to jobs, income, assets, and wealth. Another blatant indicator or form of inequality is the practice of violence against certain groups in the population. High rates of imprisonment, physical violence, and slavery are all methods of oppression used by some groups to dominate others. Kevin Bales, a professor of sociology at the University of Surrey, Roehampton, London, and director of Free the Slaves, the American sister organization of Anti-Slavery International, has studied contemporary forms of slavery for two decades. While this reading closely examines the lives of child prostitutes in Thailand, it shows how this exploitation is not unique to that country or to Asia. Women and children are exported to Japan, Germany, and the United States on a regular basis.

When Siri wakes it is about noon.[1] In the instant of waking she knows exactly who and what she has become. As she explained to me, the soreness in her genitals reminds her of the fifteen men she had sex with the night before. Siri is fifteen years old. Sold by her parents a year ago, she finds that her resistance and her desire to escape the brothel are breaking down and acceptance and resignation are taking their place.

In the provincial city of Ubon Ratchathani, in northeastern Thailand, Siri works and lives in a brothel. About ten brothels and bars, dilapidated and dusty buildings, line the side street just around the corner from a new Western-style shopping mall. Food and noodle vendors are scattered between the brothels. The woman behind the noodle stall outside the brothel where Siri works is also a spy, warder, watchdog, procurer, and dinner lady to Siri and the other twenty-four girls and women in the brothel.

The brothel is surrounded by a wall, with iron gates that meet the street. Within the wall is a dusty yard, a concrete picnic table, and the ubiquitous spirit house, a small shrine that stands outside all Thai buildings. A low door leads into a windowless concrete room that is thick with the smell of cigarettes, stale beer, vomit, and sweat. This is the "selection" room (*hong du*). On one side of the room are stained and collapsing tables and booths; on the other side is a narrow elevated platform with a bench that runs the length of the room. Spotlights pick out this bench, and at night the girls and women sit here under the glare while the men at the tables drink and choose the one they want.

Passing through another door, at the far end of the bench, the man follows the girl past a window, where a bookkeeper takes his money and records which girl he has selected. From there he is led to the girl's room. Behind its concrete front room, the brothel degenerates even further, into a haphazard shanty warren of tiny cubicles where the girls live and work. A makeshift ladder leads up to what may have once been a barn. The upper level is now lined with doors about five feet apart, which open into rooms of about five by seven feet that hold a bed and little else.

Scraps of wood and cardboard separate one room from the next, and Siri has plastered her walls with pictures of teenage pop stars cut from magazines. Over her bed, as in most rooms, there also hangs a framed portrait of the king of Thailand; a single bare lightbulb dangles from the ceiling. Next to the bed a large tin can holds water; there is a hook nearby for rags and towels. At the foot of the bed, next to the door, some clothes are folded on a ledge. The walls are very thin, and everything can be heard from the surrounding rooms; a shout from the bookkeeper echoes through all of them, whether their doors are open or closed.

After rising at midday, Siri washes herself in cold water from the single concrete trough that serves the brothel's twenty-five women. Then, dressed in a T-shirt and skirt, she goes to the noodle stand for the hot soup that is a Thai breakfast. Through the afternoon, if she does not have any clients, she chats with the other girls and women as they drink beer and play cards or make decorative handicrafts together. If the pimp is away the girls will joke around, but if not they must be constantly deferential and aware of his presence, for he can harm them or use them as he pleases. Few men visit in the afternoon, but those who do tend to have more money and can buy a girl for several hours if they like. Some will even make appointments a few days in advance.

At about five, Siri and the other girls are told to dress, put on their makeup, and prepare for the night's work. By seven the men will be coming in, purchasing drinks, and choosing girls; Siri will be chosen by the first of the ten to eighteen men who will buy her that night. Many men choose Siri because she looks much younger than her fifteen years. Slight and round faced, dressed to accentuate her youth, she could pass for eleven or twelve. Because she looks like a child, she can be sold as a "new" girl at a higher price, about $15, which is more than twice that charged for the other girls.

Siri is very frightened that she will get AIDS. Long before she understood prostitution she knew about HIV, as many girls from her village returned home to die from AIDS after being sold into the brothels. Every day she prays to Buddha, trying to earn the merit that will preserve her from the disease. She also tries to insist that her clients use condoms, and in most cases she is successful, because the pimp backs her up. But when policemen use her, or the pimp himself, they will do as they please; if she tries to insist, she will be beaten and raped. She also fears pregnancy, but like the other girls she receives injections of the contraceptive drug Depo-Provera. Once a month she has an HIV test. So far it has been negative. She knows that if she tests positive she will be thrown out to starve.

Though she is only fifteen, Siri is now resigned to being a prostitute. The work is not what she had thought it would be. Her first client hurt her, and at the first opportunity she ran away. She was quickly caught, dragged back, beaten, and raped. That night she was forced to take on a chain of clients until the early morning. The beatings and the work continued night after night, until her will was broken. Now she is sure that she is a very bad person to have deserved what has happened to her. When I comment on how pretty she looks in a photograph, how like a pop star, she replies, "I'm no star; I'm just a whore, that's all." She copes as best she can. She takes a dark pride in her higher price and the large number of men who choose her. It is the adjustment of the concentration camp, an effort to make sense of horror.

In Thailand prostitution is illegal, yet girls like Siri are sold into sex slavery by the thousands. The brothels that hold these girls are but a small part of a much wider sex industry. How can this wholesale trade in girls continue? What keeps it working? The answer is more complicated than we might think. Thailand's economic boom and its social acceptance of prostitution contribute to the pressures that enslave girls like Siri. . . .

One Girl Equals One Television

The small number of children sold into slavery in the past has become a flood today. This increase reflects the enormous changes in Thailand over the past fifty years as the country has gone through the great transformation of industrialization—the same process that tore Europe apart over a century ago. If we are to understand slavery in Thailand, we must understand these changes as well, for like so many other parts of the world, Thailand has always had slavery, but never before on this scale.

The economic boom of 1977 to 1997 had a dramatic impact on the northern villages. While the center of the country, around Bangkok, rapidly industrialized, the north was left behind. Prices of food, land, and tools all increased as the economy grew, but the returns for rice and other agriculture were stagnant, held down by government policies guaranteeing cheap food for factory workers in Bangkok. Yet visible everywhere in the north is a flood of consumer goods—refrigerators, televisions, cars and trucks, rice cookers, air conditioners—all of which are extremely tempting. Demand for these goods is high as families try to join the ranks of the prosperous. As it happens, the cost of participating in this consumer boom can be met from an old source that has become much more profitable: the sale of children.

In the past, daughters were sold in response to serious family financial crises. Under threat of losing its mortgaged rice fields and facing destitution, a family might sell a daughter to redeem its debt, but for the most part daughters were worth about as much at home as workers as they would realize when sold. Modernization and economic growth have changed all that. Now parents feel a great pressure to buy consumer goods that were unknown even twenty years ago; the sale of a daughter might easily finance a new television set. A recent survey in the northern provinces found that of the families who sold their daughters, two-thirds could afford not to do so but "instead preferred to buy color televisions and video equipment."[2] And from the perspective of parents who are willing to sell their children, there has never been a better market.

The brothels' demand for prostitutes is rapidly increasing. The same economic boom that feeds consumer demand in the northern villages lines the pockets of laborers and workers in the central plain. Poor economic migrants from the rice fields now work on building sites or in new factories, earning many times what they did on the land. Possibly for the first time in their lives, these laborers can do what more well-off Thai men have always done: go to a brothel. The purchasing power of this increasing number of brothel users strengthens the call for northern girls and supports a growing business in their procurement and trafficking.

Siri's story was typical. A broker, a woman herself from a northern village, approached the families in Siri's village with assurances of well-paid work for their daughters. Siri's parents probably understood that the work would be as a prostitute, since they knew that other girls from their village had gone south to brothels. After some negotiation they were paid 50,000 baht (US$2,000) for Siri, a very significant sum for this family of rice farmers.[3] This exchange began the process of debt bondage that is used to enslave the girls. The contractual arrangement between the broker and the parents requires that this money be paid by the daughter's labor before she is free to leave or is allowed to send money home. Sometimes the money is treated as a loan to the parents, the girls being both the collateral and the means of repayment. In such cases the exorbitant interest charged on the loan means there is little chance that a girl's sexual slavery will ever repay the debt.

Siri's debt of 50,000 baht rapidly escalated. Taken south by the broker, Siri was sold for 100,000 baht to the brothel where she now works. After her rape and beating Siri was informed that the debt she must repay to the brothel equaled 200,000 baht. In addition, Siri learned of the other payments she would be required to make, including rent for her room, at 30,000 baht per month, as well as charges for food and drink, fees for medicine, and fines if she did not work hard enough or displeased a customer.

The total debt is virtually impossible to repay, even at Siri's higher rate of 400 baht. About 100 baht from each client is supposed to be credited to Siri to reduce her debt and pay her rent and other expenses; 200 goes to the pimp and the remaining 100 to the brothel. By this reckoning, Siri must have sex with three hundred men a month just to pay her rent, and what is left over after other expenses barely reduces her original debt. For girls who can charge only 100 to 200 baht per client, the debt grows even faster. This debt bondage keeps the girls under complete control as long as the brothel owner and the pimp believe they are worth having. Violence reinforces the control, and any resistance earns a beating as well as an increase in the debt. Over time, if the girl becomes a good and cooperative prostitute, the pimp may tell her she has paid off the debt and allow her to send small sums home. This "paying off" of the debt usually has nothing to do with an actual accounting of earnings but is declared at the discretion of the pimp, as a means to extend the brothel's profits by making the girl more pliable. Together with rare visits home, money sent back to the family operates to keep her at her job.

Most girls are purchased from their parents, as Siri was, but for others the enslavement is much more direct. Throughout Thailand agents travel to villages, offering work in factories or as domestics. Sometimes they bribe local officials to vouch for them, or they befriend the monks at the local temple to gain introductions. Lured by the promise of good jobs and the money that the daughters will send back to the village, the deceived families dispatch their girls with the agent, often paying for the privilege. Once they arrive in a city, the girls are sold to a brothel, where they are raped, beaten, and locked in. Still other girls are simply kidnapped. This is especially true of women and children who have come to visit relatives in Thailand from Burma or Laos. At bus and train stations, gangs watch for women and children who can be snatched or drugged for shipment to brothels.

Direct enslavement by trickery or kidnapping is not really in the economic interest of the brothel owners. The steadily growing market for prostitutes, the loss of girls to HIV infection, and the especially strong demand for younger and younger girls make it necessary for brokers and brothel owners to cultivate village families so that they can buy more daughters as they come of age. In Siri's case this means letting her maintain ties with her family and ensuring that after a year or so she send a monthly postal order for 10,000 baht to her parents. The monthly payment is a good investment, since it encourages Siri's parents to place their other daughters in the brothel as well. Moreover, the young girls themselves become willing to go when their older sisters and relatives returning for holidays bring stories of the rich life to be lived in the cities of the central plain. Village girls lead a sheltered life, and the appearance of women only a little older than themselves with money and nice clothes is tremendously appealing. They admire the results of this thing called prostitution with only the vaguest notion of what it is. Recent research found that young girls knew that their sisters and neighbors had become prostitutes, but when asked what it means to be a prostitute their most common answer was *wearing Western clothes in a restaurant.*[4] Drawn by this glamorous life, they put up little opposition to being sent away with the brokers to swell an already booming sex industry.

By my own conservative estimate there are perhaps thirty-five thousand girls like Siri enslaved in Thailand. Remarkably, this is only a small proportion of the country's prostitutes. In the mid-1990s the government stated that there were 81,384 prostitutes in Thailand—but that official number is calculated from the number of registered (though still illegal) brothels, massage parlors, and sex establishments. One Thai researcher estimated the total number of prostitutes in 1997 to be around 200,000.[5] Every brothel, bar, and massage parlor we visited in Thailand was unregistered, and no one working with prostitutes believes the government figures. At the other end of the spectrum are the estimates put forward by activist organizations such as the Center for the Protection of Children's Rights. These groups assert that there are more than 2 million prostitutes. I suspect that this number is too high in a national population of 60 million. My own reckoning, based on information gathered by AIDS workers in different cities, is that there are between half a million and 1 million prostitutes.

Of this number, only about one in twenty is enslaved. Most become prostitutes voluntarily, though some start out in debt bondage. Sex is sold everywhere in Thailand: barbershops, massage parlors, coffee shops and cafés, bars and restaurants, nightclubs and karaoke bars, brothels, hotels, and even temples traffic in sex. Prostitutes range from the high-earning "professional" women who work with some autonomy, through the women working by choice as call girls or in massage parlors, to the enslaved rural girls like Siri. Many women work semi-independently in bars, restaurants, and nightclubs—paying a fee to the owner, working when they choose, and having the power to decide whom to take as a customer. Most bars and clubs cannot use an enslaved prostitute like Siri, as the women are often sent out on call and their clients expect a certain amount of cooperation and friendliness. Enslaved girls serve the lowest end of the market: the laborers, students, and workers who can afford only the 100 baht per half hour. It is low-cost sex in volume, and the demand is always there. For a Thai man, buying a woman is much like buying a round of drinks. But the reasons why such large numbers of Thai men use prostitutes are much more complicated and grow out of their culture, their history, and a rapidly changing economy.

"I Don't Want to Waste It, So I Take Her"

Until it was officially disbanded in 1910, the king of Thailand maintained a harem of hundreds of concubines, a few of whom might be elevated to the rank of "royal mother" or "minor wife." This form of polygamy was closely imitated by status-hungry nobles and emerging rich merchants of the nineteenth century. Virtually all men of any substance kept at least a mistress or a minor wife. For those with fewer resources, prostitution was a perfectly acceptable option, as renting took the place of out-and-out ownership.

Even today everyone in Thailand knows his or her place within a very elaborate and precise status system. Mistresses and minor wives continue to enhance any man's social standing, but the consumption of commercial sex has increased dramatically.[6] If an economic boom is a tide that raises all boats, then vast numbers of Thai men have now been raised to a financial position from which they can regularly buy sex. Nothing like the economic growth in Thailand was ever experienced in the West, but a few facts show its scale: in a country the size of Britain, one-tenth of the workforce moved from the land to industry in just the three years from 1993 to 1995; the number of factory workers doubled from less than 2 million to more than 4 million in the eight years from 1988 to 1995; and urban wages doubled from 1986 to 1996. Thailand is now the world's largest importer of motorcycles and the second-largest importer of pickup tricks, after the United States. Until the economic downturn of late 1997, money flooded Thailand, transforming poor rice farmers into wage laborers and fueling consumer demand.

With this newfound wealth, Thai men go to brothels in increasing numbers. Several recent studies show that between 80 and 87 percent of Thai men have had sex with a prostitute. Most report that their first sexual experience was with a prostitute. Somewhere between 10 and 40 percent of married men have paid for commercial sex within the past twelve months, as have up to 50 percent of single men. Though it is difficult to measure, these reports suggest something like 3 to 5 million regular customers for commercial sex. But it would be wrong to imagine millions of Thai men sneaking furtively on their own along dark streets lined with brothels; commercial sex is a social event, part of a good night out with friends. Ninety-five percent of men going to a brothel do so with their friends, usually at the end of a night spent drinking. Groups go out for recreation and entertainment, and especially to get drunk together. That is a strictly male pursuit, as Thai women usually abstain from alcohol. All-male groups out for a night on the town are considered normal in any Thai city, and whole neighborhoods are devoted to serving them. One man interviewed in a recent study explained, *When we arrive at the brothel, my friends take one and pay for me to take another. It costs them money; I don't want to waste it, so I take her.*[7] Having one's prostitute paid for also brings an informal obligation to repay in kind at a later date. Most Thais, men and women, feel that commercial sex is an acceptable part of an ordinary outing for single men, and about two-thirds of men and one-third of women feel the same about married men.[8] . . .

Millionaire Tiger and Billionaire Geese

Who are these modern slaveholders? The answer is anyone and everyone—anyone, that is, with a little capital to invest. The people who *appear* to own the enslaved prostitutes—the pimps, madams, and brothel keepers—are usually just employees. As hired muscle, pimps and their helpers provide the brutality that controls women and makes possible their commercial exploitation. Although they are just employees, the pimps do rather well for themselves. Often living in the brothel, they receive a salary and add to that income by a number of scams; for example, food and drinks are sold to customers at inflated prices, and the pimps pocket the difference. Much more lucrative is their control of the price of sex. While each woman has a basic price, the pimps size up each customer and pitch the fee accordingly. In this way a client may pay two or three times more than the normal rate, and all of the surplus goes to the pimp. In league with the bookkeeper, the pimp systematically cheats the prostitutes of the little that is supposed to be credited against their debt. If they manage the sex slaves well and play all of the angles, pimps can easily make ten times their basic wage—a great income for an ex-peasant whose main skills are violence and intimidation, but nothing compared to the riches to be made by the brokers and the real slaveholders.

The brokers and agents who buy girls in the villages and sell them to brothels are only short-term slaveholders. Their business is part recruiting agency, part shipping company, part public relations, and part kidnapping gang. They aim to buy low and sell high while maintaining a good flow of girls from the villages. Brokers are equally likely to be men or women, and they usually come from the regions in which they recruit. Some are local people dealing in girls in addition to their jobs as police officers, government bureaucrats, or even schoolteachers. Positions of public trust are excellent starting points for buying young girls. In spite of the character of their work, they are well respected. Seen as job providers and sources of large cash payments to parents, they are well known in their communities. Many of the women brokers were once sold themselves; some spent years as prostitutes and now, in their middle age, make their living by supplying girls to the brothels. These women are walking advertisements for sexual slavery. Their lifestyle and income, their Western clothes and glamorous, sophisticated ways promise a rosy economic future for the girls they buy. That they have physically survived their years in the brothel may be the exception—many more young women come back to the village to die of AIDS—but the parents tend to be optimistic.

Whether these dealers are local people or traveling agents, they combine the business of procuring with other economic pursuits. A returned prostitute may live with her family, look after her parents, own a rice field or two, and buy and sell girls on the side. Like the pimps, they are in a good business, doubling their money on each girl within two or three weeks; but also like the pimps, their profits are small compared to those of the long-term slaveholders.

The real slaveholders tend to be middle-aged businessmen. They fit seamlessly into the community, and they suffer no social discrimination for what they do. If anything, they are admired as successful, diversified capitalists. Brothel ownership is normally only one of many business interests for the slaveholder. To be sure, a brothel owner may have some ties to organized crime, but in Thailand organized crime includes the police and much of the government. Indeed, the work of the modern slaveholder is best seen not as aberrant criminality but as a perfect example of disinterested capitalism. Owning the brothel that holds young girls in bondage is simply a business matter. The investors would say that they are creating jobs and wealth. There is no hypocrisy in their actions, for they obey an important social norm: earning a lot of money is good enough reason for anything.

The slaveholder may in fact be a partnership, company, or corporation. In the 1980s, Japanese investment poured into Thailand, in an enormous migration of capital that was called "Flying Geese."[9] The strong yen led to buying and building across the country, and while electronics firms built television factories, other investors found that there was much, much more to be made in the sex industry. Following the Japanese came investment from the so-called Four Tigers (South Korea, Hong Kong, Taiwan, and Singapore), which also found marvelous opportunities in commercial sex. (All five of these countries further proved to be strong import markets for enslaved Thai girls, as discussed below.) The Geese and the Tigers had the resources to buy the local criminals, police, administrators, and property needed to set up commercial sex businesses. Indigenous Thais also invested in brothels as the sex industry boomed; with less capital, they were more likely to open poorer, working-class outlets.

Whether they are individual Thais, partnerships, or foreign investors, the slaveholders share many characteristics. There is little or no racial or ethnic difference between them and the slaves they own (with the exception of the Japanese investors). They feel no need to rationalize their slaveholding on racial grounds. Nor are they linked in any sort of hereditary ownership of slaves or of the children of their slaves. They are not really interested in their slaves at all, just in the bottom line on their investment.

To understand the business of slavery today we have to know something about the economy in which it operates. Thailand's economic boom included a sharp increase in sex tourism tacitly backed by the government. International tourist arrivals jumped from 2 million in 1981 to 4 million in 1988 to over 7 million in 1996.[10] Two-thirds of tourists were unaccompanied men; in other words, nearly 5 million unaccompanied men visited Thailand in 1996. A significant proportion of these were sex tourists.

The recent downturn in both tourism and the economy may have slowed, but not dramatically altered, sex tourism. In 1997 the annual illegal income generated by sex workers in Thailand was roughly $10 billion, which is more than drug trafficking is estimated to generate.[11] According to ECPAT, an organization working against child prostitution, the economic crisis in Southeast Asia may have increased the exploitation of young people in sex tourism:

> According to Professor Lae Dilokvidhayarat from Chulalongkorn University, there has been a 10 percent decrease in the school enrollment at primary school level in Thailand since 1996. Due to increased unemployment, children cannot find work in the formal sector, but instead are forced to "disappear" into the informal sector. This makes them especially vulnerable to sexual exploitation. Also, a great number of children are known to travel to tourist areas and to big cities hoping to find work.
>
> We cannot overlook the impact of the economic crisis on sex tourism, either. Even though travelling costs to Asian countries are approximately the same as before mid-1997, when the crisis began, the rates for sexual services in many places are lower due to increased competition in the business. Furthermore, since there are more children trying to earn money, there may also be more so-called situational child sex tourists, i.e., those who do not necessarily prefer children as sexual partners, but who may well choose a child if the situation occurs and the price is low.[12]

In spite of the economic boom, the average Thai's income is very low by Western standards. Within an industrializing country, millions still live in rural poverty. If a rural family owns its house and has a rice field, it might survive on as little as 500 baht ($20) per month. Such absolute poverty means a diet of rice supplemented with insects (crickets, grubs, and maggots are widely eaten), wild plants, and what fish the family can catch. If a family's standard of living drops below this level, which can be sustained only in the countryside, it faces hunger and the loss of its house or land. For most Thais, an income of 2,500 to 4,000 baht per month ($100 to $180) is normal. Government figures from December 1996 put two-thirds of the population at this level. There is no system of welfare or health care, and pinched budgets allow no space for saving. In these families, the 20,000 to 50,000 baht ($800 to $2,000) brought by selling a daughter provides a year's income. Such a vast sum is a powerful inducement that often blinds parents to the realities of sexual slavery. . . .

Burmese Prostitutes

The same economic boom that has increased the demand for prostitutes may, in time, bring an end to Thai sex slavery. Industrial growth has also led to an increase in jobs for women. Education and training are expanding rapidly across Thailand, and women and girls are very much taking part. The ignorance and deprivation on which the enslavement of girls depends are on the wane, and better-educated girls are much less likely to fall for the promises made by brokers. The traditional duties to family, including the debt of obligation to parents, are also becoming less compelling. As the front line of industrialization sweeps over northern Thailand, it is bringing fundamental changes. Programs on the television bought with the money from selling one daughter may carry warning messages to her younger sisters. As they learn more about new jobs, about HIV/AIDS, and about the fate of those sent to the brothels, northern Thai girls refuse to follow their sisters south. Slavery functions best when alternatives are few, and education and the media are opening the eyes of Thai girls to a world of choice.

For the slaveholders this presents a serious problem. They are faced with an increase in demand for prostitutes and a diminishing supply. Already the price of young Thai girls is spiraling upward. The slaveholders' only recourse is to look elsewhere, to areas where poverty and ignorance still hold sway. Nothing, in fact, could be easier: there remain large, oppressed, and isolated populations desperate enough to believe the promises of the brokers. From Burma to the west and Laos to the east come thousands of economic and political refugees searching for work; they are defenseless in a country where they are illegal aliens. The techniques that worked so well in bringing Thai girls to brothels are again deployed, but now across borders. . . .

Once in the brothels they are in an even worse situation than the enslaved Thai girls: because they do not speak Thai their isolation is increased, and as illegal aliens they are open to even more abuse. The pimps tell them repeatedly that if they set foot outside the brothel, they will be arrested. And when are arrested, Burmese and Lao girls and women are afforded no legal rights. They are often held for long periods at the mercy of the police, without charge or trial. A strong traditional antipathy between Thais and Burmese increases the chances that Burmese sex slaves will face discrimination and arbitrary treatment. Explaining why so many Burmese women were kept in brothels in Ranong, in southern Thailand, the regional police commander told a reporter for the *Nation*: "In my opinion it is disgraceful to let Burmese men [working in the local fishing industry] frequent Thai prostitutes. Therefore I have been flexible in allowing Burmese prostitutes to work here."[13]

A special horror awaits Burmese and Lao women once they reach the revolving door at the border. If they escape or are dumped by the brothel owners, they come quickly to the attention of the police, since they have no money for transport and cannot speak Thai. Once they are picked up, they are placed in detention, where they meet women who have been arrested in the periodic raids on brothels and taken into custody with only the clothes they are wearing. In local jails, the foreign women might be held without charge for as long as eight months while they suffer sexual and other abuse by the police. In time, they might be sent to the Immigrant Detention Center in Bangkok or to prison. In both places, abuse and extortion by the staff continue, and some girls are sold back to the brothels from there. No trial is necessary for deportation, but many women are tried and convicted of prostitution or illegal entry. The trials take place in Thai without interpreters, and fines are charged against those convicted. If they have no money to pay the fines, and most do not, they are sent to a factory-prison to earn it. There they make lightbulbs or plastic flowers for up to twelve hours a day; the prison officials decide when they have earned enough to pay their fine. After the factory-prison the women are sent back to police cells or the Immigrant Detention Center. Most are held until they can cover the cost of transportation (illegal aliens are required by law to pay for their own deportation); others are summarily deported. . . .

To Japan, Switzerland, Germany, the United States

Women and girls flow in both directions over Thailand's borders.[14] The export of enslaved prostitutes is a robust business, supplying brothels in Japan, Europe, and America. Thailand's Ministry of Foreign Affairs estimated in 1994 that as many as 50,000 Thai women were living illegally in Japan and working in prostitution. Their situation in these countries parallels that of Burmese women held in Thailand. The enticement of Thai women follows a familiar pattern. Promised work as cleaners, domestics, dishwashers, or cooks, Thai girls and women pay large fees to employment agents to secure jobs in rich, developed countries. When they arrive, they are brutalized and enslaved. Their debt bonds are significantly larger than those of enslaved prostitutes in Thailand, since they include airfares, bribes to immigration officials, the costs of false passports, and sometimes the fees paid to foreign men to marry them and ease their entry.

Variations on sex slavery occur in different countries. In Switzerland girls are brought in on "artist" visas as exotic dancers. There, in addition to being prostitutes, they must work as striptease dancers in order to meet the carefully checked terms of their employment. The brochures of the European companies that have leaped into the sex-tourism business leave the customer no doubt about what is being sold:

> Slim, sunburnt, and sweet, they love the white man in an erotic and devoted way. They are masters of the art of making love by nature, an art that we Europeans do not know. (Life Travel, Switzerland)

> [M]any girls from the sex world come from the poor north-eastern region of the country and from the slums of Bangkok. It has become a custom that one of the nice looking daughters goes into the business in order to earn money for the poor family . . . [Y]ou can get the feeling that taking a girl here is as easy as buying a package of cigarettes . . . little slaves who give real Thai warmth. (Kanita Kamha Travel, the Netherlands)[15]

In Germany they are usually bar girls, and they are sold to men by the bartender or bouncer. Some are simply placed in brothels or apartments controlled by pimps. After Japanese sex tours to Thailand began in the 1980s, Japan rapidly became the largest importer of Thai women. The fear of HIV in Japan has also increased the demand for virgins. Because of their large disposable incomes, Japanese men are able to pay considerable sums for young rural girls from Thailand. Japanese organized crime is involved throughout the importation process, sometimes shipping women via Malaysia or the Philippines. In the cities, the Japanese mob maintains bars and brothels that trade in Thai women. Bought and sold between brothels, these women are controlled with extreme violence. Resistance can bring murder. Because the girls are illegal aliens and often enter the country under false passports, Japanese gangs rarely hesitate to kill them if they have ceased to be profitable or if they have angered their slaveholders. Thai women deported from Japan also report that the gangs will addict girls to drugs in order to manage them more easily.

Criminal gangs, usually Chinese or Vietnamese, also control brothels in the United States that enslave Thai women. Police raids in New York, Seattle, San Diego, and Los Angeles have freed more than a hundred girls and women.[16] In New York, thirty Thai women were locked into the upper floors of a building used as a brothel. Iron bars sealed the windows and a series of buzzer-operated armored gates blocked exit to the street. During police raids, the women were herded into a secret basement room. At her trial, the brothel owner testified that she'd bought the women outright, paying between $6,000 and $15,000 for each. The women were charged $300 per week for room and board; they worked from 11:00 A.M until 4:00 A.M. and were sold by the hour to clients. Chinese and Vietnamese gangsters were also involved in the brothel, collecting protection money and hunting down escaped prostitutes. The gangs owned chains of brothels and massage parlors, through which they rotated the Thai women in order to defeat law enforcement efforts. After being freed from the New York brothel, some of the women disappeared—only to turn up weeks later in similar circumstances three thousand miles away, in Seattle. One of the rescued Thai women, who had been promised restaurant work and then enslaved, testified that the brothel owners "bought something and wanted to use it to the full extent, they didn't think those people were human beings."[17]

Official Indifference and a Growth Economy

In many ways, Thailand closely resembles another country, one that was going through rapid industrialization and economic boom one hundred years ago. Rapidly shifting its labor force off the farm, experiencing unprecedented economic growth, flooded with economic migrants, and run by corrupt politicians and a greedy and criminal police force, the United States then faced many of the problems confronting Thailand today. In the 1890s, political machines that brought together organized crime with politicians and police ran the prostitution and protection rackets, drug sales, and extortion in American cities. Opposing them were a weak and disorganized reform movement and a muckraking press. I make this comparison because it is important to explore why Thailand's government is so ineffective when faced with the enslavement of its own citizens, and also to remember that conditions *can* change over time. Discussions with Thais about the horrific nature of sex slavery often end with their assertion that "nothing will ever change this . . . the problem is just too big . . . and those with power will never allow change." Yet the social and economic underpinnings of slavery in Thailand are always changing, sometimes for the worse and sometimes for the better. No society can remain static, particularly one undergoing such upheavals as Thailand.

As the country takes on a new Western-style materialist morality, the ubiquitous sale of sex sends a clear message: women can be enslaved and exploited for profit. Sex tourism helped set the stage for the expansion of sexual slavery.

Sex tourism also generates some of the income that Thai men use to fund their own visits to brothels. No one knows how much money it pours into the Thai economy, but if we assume that just one-quarter of sex workers serve sex tourists and that their customers pay about the same as they would pay to use Siri, then 656 billion baht ($26.2 billion) a year would be about right. This is thirteen times more than the amount Thailand earns by building and exporting computers, one of the country's major industries, and it is money that floods into the country without any concomitant need to build factories or improve infrastructure. It is part of the boom raising the standard of living generally and allowing an even greater number of working-class men to purchase commercial sex.

Joining the world economy has done wonders for Thailand's income and terrible things to its society. According to Pasuk Phongpaichit and Chris Baker, economists who have analyzed Thailand's economic boom,

> Government has let the businessmen ransack the nation's human and natural resources to achieve growth. It has not forced them to put much back. In many respects, the last generation of economic growth has been a disaster. The forests have been obliterated. The urban environment has deteriorated. Little has been done to combat the growth in industrial pollution and hazardous wastes. For many people whose labour has created the boom, the conditions of work, health, and safety are grim.

Neither law nor conscience has been very effective in limiting the social costs of growth. Business has reveled in the atmosphere of free-for-all. The machinery for social protection has proved very pliable. The legal framework is defective. The judiciary is suspect. The police are unreliable. The authorities have consistently tried to block popular organizations to defend popular rights.[18]

The situation in Thailand today is similar to that of the United States in the 1850s; with a significant part of the economy dependent on slavery, religious and cultural leaders are ready to explain why this is all for the best. But there is also an important difference: this is the new slavery, and the impermanence of modern slavery and the dedication of human-rights workers offer some hope.

ENDNOTES

[1] Siri is, of course, a pseudonym; the names of all respondents have been changed for their protection. I spoke with them in December 1996.

[2] "Caught in Modern Slavery: Tourism and Child Prostitution in Thailand," Country Report Summary prepared by Sudarat Sereewat-Srisang for the Ecumenical Consultation held in Chiang Mai in May 1990.

[3] Foreign exchange rates are in constant flux. Unless otherwise noted, dollar equivalences for all currencies reflect the rate at the time of the research.

[4] From interviews done by Human Rights Watch with freed child prostitutes in shelters in Thailand, reported in Jasmine Caye, *Preliminary Survey on Regional Child Trafficking for Prostitution in Thailand* (Bangkok: Center for the Protection of Children's Rights, 1996), p. 25.

[5] Kulachada Chaipipat, "New Law Targets Human Trafficking," Bangkok *Nation*, November 30, 1997.

[6] Thais told me that it would be very surprising if a well-off man or a politician did not have at least one mistress. When I was last in Thailand there was much public mirth over the clash of wife and mistress outside the hospital room of a high government official who had suffered a heart attack, as each in turn barricaded the door.

[7] Quoted in Mark Van Landingham, Chanpen Saengtienchai, John Knodel, and Anthony Pramualratana, *Friends, Wives, and Extramarital Sex in Thailand* (Bangkok: Institute of Population Studies, Chulalongkorn University, 1995), p. 18.

[8] Van Landingham et al., 1995, pp. 9–25.

[9] Pasuk Phongpaichit and Chris Baker, *Thailand's Boom* (Chiang Mai: Silkworm Books, 1996), pp. 51–54.

[10] Center for the Protection of Children's Rights, *Case Study Report on Commercial Sexual Exploitation of Children in Thailand* (Bangkok, October 1996), p. 37.

[11] David Kyle and John Dale, "Smuggling the State Back In: Agents of Human Smuggling Reconsidered," in *Global Human Smuggling: Comparative Perspectives*, ed. David Kyle and Key Koslowski (Baltimore: Johns Hopkins University Press, 2001).

[12] "Impact of the Asian Economic Crisis on Child Prostitution," *ECPAT International Newsletter* 27 (May 1, 1999), found at http://www.ecpat.net/eng/Ecpat_inter/IRC/articles.asp?articleID=143&NewsID=21.

[13] "Ranong Brothel Raids Net 148 Burmese Girls," *Nation* (July 16 1993), p. 12.

[14] *International Report on Trafficking in Women (Asia-Pacific Region)* (Bangkok: Global Alliance Against Traffic in Women, 1996); Sudarat Sereewat, *Prostitution: Thai-European Connection* (Geneva: Comission on the Churches' Participation in Development, World Council of Churches, n.d.). Women's rights and antitrafficking organizations in Thailand have also published a number of personal accounts of women enslaved as prostitutes and sold overseas. These pamphlets are disseminated widely in the hope of making young women more aware

of the threat of enslavement. Good examples are Siriporn Skrobanek, *The Diary of Prang* (Bangkok: Foundation for Women, 1994); and White Ink (pseud.), *Our Lives, Our Stories* (Bangkok: Foundation for Women, 1995). They follow the lives of women "exported," the first to Germany and the second to Japan.

[15] The brochures are quoted in Truong, *Sex, Money, and Morality: Prostitution and Tourism in South-east Asia* (London: Zed Books, 1990), p. 178.

[16] Carey Goldberg, "Sex Slavery, Thailand to New York," *New York Times* (September 11, 1995), p. 81.

[17] Quoted in Goldberg.

[18] Phongpaichit and Baker, 1996, p. 237.

RACE AND ETHNICITY

31

WHAT IS RACIAL DOMINATION?

MATTHEW DESMOND • MUSTAFA EMIRBAYER

Race and ethnicity are the topics explored in the next four selections. *Race* is a creation of culture that reflects social distinctions and power. To say that race is a social construction, however, does not mean that race is not real. Many people believe in the existence of discrete biological racial categories. This first reading on the social construction of race is an excerpt from Matthew Desmond and Mustafa Emirbayer's 2009 article, "What Is Racial Domination?" Desmond is an assistant professor of sociology and social studies at Harvard, and Emirbayer is a professor of sociology at the University of Wisconsin at Madison. Together they have coauthored a number of books on racial issues in America. In this reading, Desmond and Emirbayer explain why race and racism are still a part of contemporary social life. They define both concepts and illustrate explanations for and misunderstandings about race and racism.

What Is Race?

You do not come into this world African or European or Asian; rather, this world comes into you. As literally hundreds of scientists have argued, you are not born with a race in the same way you are born with fingers, eyes, and hair. Fingers, eyes, and hair are natural creations, whereas race is a social fabrication (Duster 2003; Graves 2001). We define race as *a symbolic category,*

Matthew Desmond and Mustafa Emirbayer, "What Is Racial Domination?" *Du Bois Review*, 6:2 (2009), 335–355, Copyright © 2009 W.E.B. Du Bois Institute for African and African American Research, Reprinted by permission of Cambridge University Press and the authors.

based on phenotype or ancestry and constructed according to specific social and historical contexts, that is misrecognized as a natural category. This definition deserves to be unpacked.

Symbolic Category

A symbolic category belongs to the realm of ideas, meaning-making, and language. It is something actively created and recreated by human beings rather than pregiven, needing only to be labeled. Symbolic categories mark differences between grouped people or things. In doing so, they actually bring those people or things into existence (Bourdieu 2003). For example, the term "Native American" is a symbolic category that encompasses all peoples indigenous to the land that is known, today, as the United States. But the term "Native American" did not exist before non-Native Americans came to the Americas. Choctaws, Crows, Iroquois, Hopis, Dakotas, Yakimas, Utes, and dozens of other people belonging to indigenous tribes existed. The term "Native American" flattens under one homogenizing heading the immensely different histories, languages, traditional beliefs, and rich cultural practices of these various tribes. In naming different races, racial categories create different races.

Such insights into the importance of the symbolic have not always been appreciated. Consider, for example, Oliver Cromwell Cox's hypothesis "that racial exploitation and race prejudice developed among Europeans with the rise of capitalism and nationalism, and that because of the worldwide ramifications of capitalism, all racial antagonisms can be traced to the policies and attitudes of the leading capitalist people, the [W]hite people of Europe and North America" (1948:322). Though few scholars today would agree fully with Cox's reduction, many continue to advance structuralist claims, filtering racial conflict through the logic of class conflict (e.g., Reich 1981), regarding racial formation as a political strategy (e.g., Marx 1998), or concentrating on the legal construction of racial categories (e.g., Haney-López 1996). Helpful as they are, structuralist accounts often treat race as something given and accepted—that is, as a "real" label that attaches itself to people (Bonilla-Silva 1997) or as an imposed category that forms racial identity (Marx 1998)—and thereby overlook how actors create, reproduce, and resist systems of racial classification. . .

Phenotype or Ancestry

Race also is based on phenotype or ancestry. A person's phenotype is her or his physical appearance and constitution, including skeletal structure, height, hair texture, eye color, and skin tone. A person's ancestry is her or his family lineage, which often includes tribal, regional, or national affiliations. The symbolic category of race organizes people into bounded groupings based on their phenotype, ancestry, or both. It is difficult to say which matters more, phenotype or ancestry, in determining racial membership in the United States. In some settings, ancestry trumps phenotype; in others, the opposite is true.

Recent immigrants often are pigeonholed in one of the dominant racial categories because of their phenotype; however, many resist this classification because of their ancestry. For instance, upon arriving in the United States, many first generation West Indian immigrants, quite familiar with racism against African Americans, actively resist the label "Black." Despite their efforts, many are considered African American because of their dark skin (that is, they "look" Black to the American eye). The children of West African immigrants, many of whom are disconnected from their parents' ancestries, more readily accept the label "Black" (Waters 1999). And many individuals with mixed heritage often are treated as though they belonged only to one "race."

Some people, by contrast, rely on their phenotype to form a racial identity, though they are often grouped in another racial category based on their ancestry. Susie Guillory Phipps, a blond-haired blue-eyed woman who always considered herself "White," discovered, upon glancing at her birth certificate while applying for a passport, that her native state, Louisiana, considered her "Black." The reason was that Louisiana grouped people into racial categories according to the "one thirty-second rule," a rule that stated that anyone who was one thirty-second Black—regardless of what they looked like—was legally "Black." In 1982, Susie Guillory Phipps sued Louisiana for the right to be White. She lost. The state genealogist discovered that Phipps was the great-great-great-great-grandchild of a White Alabama plantation owner and his Black mistress and, therefore—although all of Phipps's other ancestors were White—she was to be considered "Black." (This outlandish law was finally erased from the books in 1983.) In this case, Phipps's ancestry (as identified by the state) was more important in determining her race than her phenotype (Davis 1991).

Social and Historical Contexts

Racial taxonomies are bound to their specific social and historical contexts. The racial categories that exist in America may not exist in other parts of the globe. In South Africa, racial groups are organized around three dominant categories: White, Black, and "Coloured." During apartheid, the Coloured category was designed to include all "mixed-race" people (Sparks 2006). More recently, the Black category has been expanded to include all groups oppressed under apartheid, not only those of African heritage but also those of Indian descent and (as of 2008) Chinese South Africans. In Brazil, five racial categories are employed in the official census: *Branca* (White), *Pardo* (Brown), *Preto* (Black), *Amarelo* (Asian), and *Indígena* (Indigenous). However, in everyday usage, many Brazilians identify themselves and one another through several other racial terms—including *moreno* (other type of brown), *moreno claro* (light brown), *negro* (another type of black), and *claro* (light)—which have much more to do with the tint of one's skin than with one's ancestry (Stephens 1999; Telles 2004). Before racial language was outlawed by the Communist regime, Chinese racial taxonomies were based first and foremost on blood purity, then on hair, then odor, then brain mass, then finally—and of least importance—skin color, which, according to the taxonomy, was divided into no less than ten shades (Dikötter 1992). And in Japan, a group called the Burakamin is considered to be unclean and is thought to constitute a separate race, although it is impossible to distinguish someone with Burakamin ancestry from the rest of the Japanese population (Eisenstadt 1998; Searle-Chatterjee and Sharma 1994).

Cross-national comparisons, then, reveal that systems of racial classification vary greatly from one country to the next. Racial categories, therefore, are *place-specific,* bound to certain geographic and social contexts. They also are *time-specific,* changing between different historical eras. As a historical product, race is quite new. Before the sixteenth century, race, as we know it today, did not exist. During the Middle Ages, prejudices were formed and wars waged against "other" people, but those "other" people were not categorized or understood as people of other races. Instead of the color line, the primary social division in those times was that between "civilized" and "uncivilized." The racial categories so familiar to us only began to calcify around the beginning of the nineteenth century, a mere two hundred years ago (Gossett 1965; Smedley 1999). In fact, the word, "race," has a very recent origin; it only obtained its modern meaning in the late eighteenth century (Hannaford 1996).

But racial domination survives by covering its tracks, by erasing its own history. It encourages us to think of the mystic boundaries separating, say, West from East, White from Black, Black from Asian, or Asian from Hispanic, as timeless separations, as divisions that have always been and will always be. We would be well served to remember, with Stuart Hall, that we must grapple with "the historical specificity of race in the modern world" (1980: 308) to gain an accurate understanding of racial phenomena. In the American context, the "Indian" was invented within the context of European colonization, as indigenous peoples of the Americas were lumped together under one rubric to be killed, uprooted, and exploited. Whiteness and Blackness were invented as antipodes within the context of English, and later American, slavery. More than any other institution, slavery would dictate the career of American racism: Blackness became associated with bondage, inferiority, and social death; Whiteness with freedom, superiority, and life. The Mexican American was invented within the context of the colonization of Mexico. At the end of the nineteenth century, the Asian American was invented as a response to immigration from the Far East. Whiteness expanded during the early years of the twentieth century as new immigrants from Southern, Central, and Eastern Europe transformed themselves from "lesser Whites" to, simply, "Whites." All the while, White supremacy was legitimated by racial discourses in philosophy, literature, and science. By the middle of the twentieth century, the racial categories so familiar to us today were firmly established. Although the second half of the twentieth century brought great changes in the realm of race—including the rise of the civil rights movement and the fall of Jim Crow—the racial categories that emerged in America over the previous 300 years remained, for the most part, unchallenged. Americans, White and non-White alike, understood themselves as raced, and, by and large, accepted the dominant racial classification even if they refused to accept the terms of racial inequality.

Misrecognized as Natural

The last part of the definition we have been unpacking has to do with a process of naturalization. This word signifies a metamorphosis of sorts, where something created by humans is mistaken as something dictated by nature. Racial categories are naturalized when these symbolic groupings—the products of specific historical contexts—are wrongly conceived as natural and unchangeable. We misrecognize race as natural when we begin to think that racial cleavages and inequalities can be explained by pointing to attributes somehow inherent in the race itself (as if they were biological) instead of understanding how social powers, economic forces, political institutions, and cultural practices have brought about these divisions.

Naturalized categories are powerful; they are the categories through which we understand the world around us. Such categories divide the world along otherwise arbitrary lines and make us believe that there is nothing at all arbitrary about such a division. What is more, when categories become naturalized, alternative ways of viewing the world begin to appear more and more impossible. Why, we might ask, should we only have five main racial groups? Why not ninety-five? Why should we divide people according to their skin color? Why not base racial divisions according to foot size, ear shape, teeth color, arm length, or height? Why is ancestry so important? Why not base our racial categories on regions—North, South, East, and West? One might find these suggestive questions silly, and, indeed, they are. But they are no sillier than the idea that people should be sorted into different racial groups according to skin color or blood composition. To twist Bourdieu's phrase, we might say, *when it comes to race, one never doubts enough* (1998 [1994]:36).

The system of racial classification at work in America today is not the only system imaginable, nor is it the only one that has existed in the young life of the United States. Race is far from fixed; rather, its forms, depending on the social, economic, political, and cultural pressures of the day, have shifted and fluctuated in whimsical and drastic ways over time (Duster 2001). Indeed, today's multiracial movement is challenging America's dominant racial categories (which remained relatively stable during the latter half of the twentieth century) as people of mixed heritage are refusing to accept as given the state's racial classification system (DaCosta 2007). Race is social through and through. Thus, we can regard race as a *well-founded fiction*. It is a fiction because it has no natural bearing, but it is nonetheless well founded since most people in society provide race with a real existence and divide the world through this lens.

Ethnicity and Nationality

The categories of ethnicity and nationality are intrinsically bound up with race. Ethnicity refers to a shared lifestyle informed by cultural, historical, religious, and/or national affiliations. Nationality is equated with citizenship, membership in a specific politically delineated territory controlled by a government (cf. Weber 1946). Race, ethnicity, and nationality are overlapping symbolic categories that influence how we see the world around us, how we view ourselves, and how we divide "us" from "them." The categories are mutually reinforcing insofar as each category educates, upholds, and is informed by the others. This is why these three categories cannot be understood in isolation from one another (Loveman 1999). For example, if someone identifies as ethnically Norwegian, which, for them, might include a shared lifestyle composed of Norwegian history and folklore, language, cultural rituals and festivals, and food, they may also reference a nationality, based in the state of Norway, as well as a racial group, White, since nearly all people of Norwegian descent would be classified as White by American standards. Here, ethnicity is informed by nationality (past or present) and signifies race.

Ethnicity often carves out distinctions and identities within racial groups. Ten people can be considered Asian American according to our modern racial taxonomy; however, those ten people might have parents or grandparents that immigrated to the United States from ten different countries, including Thailand, Vietnam, Cambodia, Singapore, China, South Korea, North Korea, Japan, Indonesia, and Laos. They might speak different languages, uphold different traditions, worship different deities, enjoy different kinds of food, and go through different experiences. What is more, many Asian countries have histories of conflict (such as China and Japan, North and South Korea). Accordingly, we cannot assume that a Chinese American and a Japanese American have similar lifestyles or see the world through a shared vision simply because they are both classified as "Asian" under American racial rubrics. Therefore, just as race, ethnicity, and nationality cannot be separated from one another, neither can all three categories be collapsed into one (cf. Brubaker et al., 2004).

Race and ethnicity (as well as nationality) are both marked and made. They are *marked* through America's racial taxonomy, as well as a global ethnic taxonomy, which seeks to divide the world into distinct categories. In this case, race and ethnicity impose themselves on you. They are *made* through a multiplicity of different practices—gestures, sayings, tastes, ways of walking, religious convictions, opinions, and so forth. In this case, you perform race or ethnicity. Ethnicity is a very fluid, layered, and situational construct. One might feel very American when voting, very Irish when celebrating St. Patrick's Day, very Catholic when attending Easter mass, very "New Yorker" when riding the subway, and very Northern when visiting a relative in South Carolina (Waters 1990). Race, too, can be performed to varying degrees. One might act "very Black" when celebrating Kwanza with relatives but may repress one's Blackness while in a business meeting with White colleagues.

Race as performance is "predicated on actions, on the things one does in the world, on how one behaves." As anthropologist John Jackson, Jr. notes, "You are not Black because you are (in essence) Black; you are Black . . . because of how you act—and not just in terms of one field of behavior (say, intellectual achievement in school) but because of how you juggle and combine many differently racialized and class(ed) actions (walking, talking, laughing, watching a movie, standing, emoting, partying) in an everyday matrix of performative possibilities" (2001:171, 188). Because racial domination attaches to skin color, a dark-skinned person can never completely escape its clutches simply by acting "not Black." But that person may choose one saying over another, one kind of clothing over another, one mode of interaction over another, because she believes such an action makes her more or less Black (cf. Johnson 2003). This is why we claim that race and ethnicity are ascribed and achieved, both marked and made. . . .

In some instances, non-Whites may perform ethnicity in order to resist certain racial classifications (as when African migrants teach their children to speak with an accent so they might avoid being identified as African Americans); in other instances, they might, in an opposite way, attempt to cleanse themselves of all ethnic markers (be they linguistic, religious, or cultural in nature) to avoid becoming victims of discrimination or stigmatization. Either way, their efforts may prove futile since those belonging to dominated racial groups have considerably less ethnic agency than those belonging to the dominant—and hence normalized—group.

One reason why race and ethnicity are relatively decoupled for White Americans but bound tightly together for non-White Americans is found in the history of the nation's immigration policies and practices. Until the late nineteenth century, immigration to America was deregulated and encouraged (with the exception of Chinese exclusion laws); however, at the turn of the century, native-born White Americans, who blamed immigrants for the rise of urban slums, crime, and class conflict, began calling for immigration restrictions. Popular and political support for restrictions swelled and resulted in the development of a strict immigration policy, culminating in the Johnson-Reed Act of 1924. America's new immigration law, complete with national quotas and racial restrictions on citizenship, would fundamentally realign the country's racial taxonomy. "The national origins system classified Europeans as nationalities and assigned quotas in a hierarchy of desirability," writes historian Mae Ngai in *Impossible Subjects: Illegal Aliens and the Making of Modern America*. "[B]ut at the same time the law deemed all Europeans to be part of a White race, distinct from those considered to be not [W]hite. Euro-American identities turned both on ethnicity—that is, a nationality-based cultural identity that is defined as capable of transformation and assimilation—and on a racial identity defined by [W]hiteness" (2004:7). Non-Whites, on the other hand, were either denied entry into the United States (as was the case for Asian migrants) or were associated with illegal immigration through harsh border control policies (as was the case for Mexicans). Indeed, the immigration laws of the 1920s applied the newly formed concept of "national origin" only to European nations; those classified as members of the "colored races" were conceived as bereft of a country of origin. The result, Ngai observes, was that "unlike Euro-Americans, whose ethnic and racial identities became uncoupled during the 1920s, Asians' and Mexicans' ethnic and racial identities remained conjoined" (2004:7–8).

The history of America's immigration policy underscores the intimate conception between race, ethnicity, citizenship, and national origin. Racial categories often are defined and changed by national lawmakers, as citizenship has been extended or retracted depending on one's racial ascription. The U.S. justice system has decided dozens of cases in ways that have solidified certain racial classifications in the law. During the nineteenth and twentieth centuries, legal cases handed down rulings that officially recognized Japanese, Chinese, Burmese, Filipinos, Koreans, Native Americans, and mixed-race individuals as "not White." In 1897, a Texas federal court ruled that Mexicans were legally "White." And Indian Americans, Syrians, and Arabians have been capriciously classified as both "White" and "not White" (Haney-López 1996). Briefly examining how the legal definitions of White and non-White have changed over the years demonstrates the incredibly unstable and fluid nature of racial categories. It also shows how our legal system helps to construct race. For instance, the "prerequisite cases" that determined peoples' race in order to determine their eligibility for U.S. citizenship resulted in poisonous symbolic consequences. Deemed worthy of citizenship, White people were understood to be upstanding, law-abiding, moral, and intelligent. Conversely, non-White people, from whom citizenship was withheld, were thought to be base, criminal, untrustworthy, and of lesser intelligence. For most of America's history, courts determined race, and race determined nationality; thus, nationality can only be understood within the context of U.S. racial and ethnic conflict (Loury 2001; Shklar 1991).

Five Fallacies about Racism

According to the Southern Poverty Law Center (2005), there are hundreds of active hate groups across the country. These groups are mostly found in the Southern states—Texas, Georgia, and South Carolina have over forty active groups per state—but California ranks highest in the nation, housing within its borders fifty-three groups. For some people, hate groups epitomize what the essence of racism amounts to: intentional acts of humiliation and hatred. While such acts undoubtedly are racist in nature, they are but the tip of the iceberg. To define racism only through extreme groups and their extreme acts is akin to defining weather only through hurricanes. Hurricanes are certainly a type of weather pattern—a harsh and brutal type—but so too are mild rainfalls, light breezes, and sunny days. Likewise, racism is much broader than violence and epithets. It also comes in much quieter, everyday-ordinary forms (cf. Essed 1991 [1984]).

Americans are deeply divided over the legacies and inner workings of racism, and a large part of this division is due to the fact that many Americans understand racism in limited or misguided ways (Alba et al.,

2005). We have identified five fallacies, recurrent in many public debates, fallacies one should avoid when thinking about racism.

(1) *Individualistic Fallacy.*—Here, racism is assumed to belong to the realm of ideas and prejudices. Racism is only the collection of nasty thoughts that a "racist individual" has about another group. Someone operating with this fallacy thinks of racism as one thinks of a crime and, therefore, divides the world into two types of people: those guilty of the crime of racism ("racists") and those innocent of the crime ("non-racists") (Wacquant 1997). Crucial to this misconceived notion of racism is intentionality. "Did I intentionally act racist? Did I cross the street because I was scared of the Hispanic man walking toward me, or did I cross for no apparent reason?" Upon answering "no" to the question of intentionality, one assumes one can classify one's own actions as "nonracist," despite the character of those actions, and go about his or her business as innocent.

This conception of racism simply will not do, for it fails to account for the racism that is woven into the very fabric of our schools, political institutions, labor markets, and neighborhoods. Conflating racism with prejudice, as Herbert Blumer (1958) pointed out fifty years ago, ignores the more systematic and structural forms of racism; it looks for racism within individuals and not institutions. Labeling someone a "racist" shifts our attention from the social surroundings that enforce racial inequalities and miseries to the individual with biases. It also lets the accuser off the hook—"He is a racist; I am not"—and treats racism as aberrant and strange, whereas American racism is rather normal. Furthermore, intentionality is in no way a prerequisite for racism. Racism is often habitual, unintentional, commonplace, polite, implicit, and well meaning (Brown et al., 2003). Thus, racism is located not only in our intentional thoughts and actions; it also thrives in our unintentional thoughts and habits, as well as in the social institutions in which we all are embedded (Bonilla-Silva 1997; Feagin et al., 2001).

(2) *Legalistic Fallacy.*—This fallacy conflates *de jure* legal progress with *de facto* racial progress. One who operates under the legalistic fallacy assumes that abolishing racist laws (racism in principle) automatically leads to the abolition of racism writ large (racism in practice). This fallacy will begin to crumble after a few moments of critical reflection. After all, we would not make the same mistake when it comes to other criminalized acts: Laws against theft do not mean that one's car will never be stolen. By way of tangible illustration, consider *Brown v. Board of Education*, the landmark case that abolished *de jure* segregation in schools. The ruling did not lead to the abolition of *de facto* segregation: fifty years later, schools are still drastically segregated and drastically unequal (Neckerman 2007; Oaks 2005). In fact, some social scientists have documented a nationwide movement of educational re-segregation, which has left today's schools even more segregated than those of 1954.

(3) *Tokenistic Fallacy.*—One guilty of the tokenistic fallacy assumes that the presence of people of color in influential positions is evidence of the eradication of racial obstacles. Although it is true that non-Whites have made

significant inroads to seats of political and economic power over the course of the last fifty years, a disproportionate number remain disadvantaged in these arenas (Alexander 2006). Exceptions do not prove the rule. We cannot, in good conscience, ignore the millions of African Americans living in poverty and, instead, point to Oprah Winfrey's millions as evidence for economic equality. Rather, we must explore how Winfrey's financial success can coexist with the economic deprivation of millions of Black women. We need to explore, in historian Thomas Holt's words, how the "simultaneous idealization of Colin Powell," or, for that matter, Barack Obama, "and demonization of blacks as a whole . . . is replicated in much of our everyday world" (2000:6) . . . .

(4) *Ahistorical Fallacy.*—This fallacy renders history impotent. Thinking hindered by the ahistorical fallacy makes a bold claim: Most U.S. history—namely, the period of time when this country did not extend basic rights to people of color (let alone classify them as fully human)—is inconsequential today. Legacies of slavery and colonialism, the eradication of millions of Native Americans, forced segregation, clandestine sterilizations and harmful science experiments, mass disenfranchisement, race-based exploitation, racist propaganda distributed by the state caricaturing Asians, Blacks, and Hispanics, racially motivated abuses of all kinds (sexual, murderous, and dehumanizing)—all of this, purport those operating under the ahistorical fallacy, are too far removed to matter to those living in the here-and-now. This idea is so erroneous it is difficult to take seriously. Today's society is directed, constructed, and molded by—indeed grafted onto—the past (Ngai 2004; Winant 2001). And race, as we have already seen, is a historical invention.

A "soft version" of the ahistorical fallacy might admit that events in the "recent past"—such as the time since the civil rights movement or the attacks on September 11—matter while things in the "distant past"—such as slavery or the colonization of Mexico—have little consequence. But this idea is no less fallacious than the "hard version," since many events in America's "distant past"—especially the enslavement and murder of millions of Africans—are the *most* consequential in shaping present-day society. In this vein, consider the question French historian Marc Bloch poses to us: "But who would dare to say that the understanding of the Protestant or Catholic Reformation, several centuries removed, is not far more important for a proper grasp of the world today than a great many other movements of thought or feeling, which are certainly more recent, yet more ephemeral" (1953:41)?

(5) *Fixed Fallacy.*—Those who assume that racism is fixed—that it is immutable, constant across time and space—partake in the fixed fallacy. Since they take racism to be something that does not develop at all, those who understand racism through the fixed fallacy are often led to ask questions such as: "Has racism increased or decreased in the past decade?" And because practitioners of the fixed fallacy usually take as their standard definition of racism only the most heinous forms—racial violence, for example—they confidently conclude that, indeed, things have gotten better.

It is important and useful to trace the career of American racism, analyzing, for example, how racial attitudes or measures of racial inclusion and exclusion have changed over time, and many social scientists have developed sophisticated techniques for doing so (e.g., Bobo 2001; Schuman et al., 1997). But the question, "Have things gotten better or worse?," is legitimate *only* after we account for the morphing attributes of racism. We cannot quantify racism like we can quantify, say, birthrates. The nature of "birthrate" does not fluctuate over time; thus, it makes sense to ask, "Are there more or less births now than there were fifty years ago?" without bothering to analyze if and how a birthrate is different today than it was in previous historical moments. American racism, on the other hand, assumes different forms in different historical moments. Although race relations today are informed by those of the past, we cannot hold to the belief that twenty-first-century racism takes on the exact same form as twentieth-century racism. And we certainly cannot conclude that there is "little or no racism" today because it does not resemble the racism of the 1950s. (Modern-day Christianity looks very different, in nearly every conceivable way, than the Christianity of the early church. But this does not mean that there is "little or no Christianity" today.) So, before we ask, "Have things gotten better or worse?," we should ponder the essence of racism today, noting how it differs from racism experienced by those living in our parents' or grandparents' generation. And we should ask, further, to quote Holt again, "What enables racism to reproduce itself after the historical conditions that initially gave it life have disappeared" (2000:20)?

Racial Domination

We have spent a significant amount of time talking about what racial domination is not but have yet to spell out what it is. We can delineate two specific manifestations of racial domination: institutional racism and interpersonal racism. *Institutional racism* is systemic White domination of people of color, embedded and operating in corporations, universities, legal systems, political bodies, cultural life, and other social collectives. The word "domination" reminds us that institutional racism is a type of power that encompasses the *symbolic power* to classify one group of people as "normal" and other groups of people as "abnormal"; the *political power* to withhold basic rights from people of color and marshal the full power of the state to enforce segregation and inequality; the *social power* to deny people of color full inclusion or membership in associational life; and the *economic power* that privileges Whites in terms of job placement, advancement, wealth, and property accumulation.

Informed by centuries of racial domination, institutional racism withholds from people of color opportunities, privileges, and rights that many Whites enjoy. Social scientists have amassed a significant amount of evidence documenting institutional racism, evidence that demonstrates how White people—strictly because of their Whiteness—reap considerable advantages when buying and selling a house, choosing a neighborhood in which to live, getting a job and moving up the corporate ladder, securing a first-class education, and seeking medical care (Massey 2007; Quillian 2006). That Whites accumulate more property and earn more income than members of minority populations, possess immeasurably more political power, and enjoy greater access to the country's cultural, social, medical, legal, and economic resources are well documented facts (e.g., Oliver and Shapiro 1997; Western 2006). While Whites have accumulated many opportunities due to racial domination, people of color have suffered from disaccumulation (Brown et al., 2003). Thus, if we talk about "Hispanic poverty," then we must also talk about White affluence; if we speak of "Black unemployment," then we must also keep in mind White employment; and if we ponder public policies for people of color, then we must also critically examine the public policies that directly benefit White people.

Below the level of institutions—yet directly informed by their workings—we find *interpersonal racism*. This is racial domination manifest in everyday interactions and practices. Interpersonal racism can be overt; however, most of the time, interpersonal racism is quite covert: it is found in the habitual, commonsensical, and ordinary practices of our lives. Our racist attitudes, as Lillian Smith remarked in *Killers of the Dream,* easily "slip from the conscious mind deep into the muscles" (1994 [1949]:96). Since we are disposed to a world structured by racial domination, we develop racialized dispositions—some conscious, many more unconscious and somatic—that guide our thoughts and behaviors. We may talk slowly to an Asian woman at the farmer's market, unconsciously assuming that she speaks poor English; we may inform a Hispanic man at a corporate party that someone has spilled their punch, unconsciously assuming that he is a janitor; we may ask to change seats if an Arab American man sits next to us on an airplane. Miniature actions such as these have little to do with one's intentional thoughts; they are orchestrated by one's practical sense, one's habitual knowhow, and informed by institutional racism. . . .

Intersecting Modes of Domination

Racial domination does not operate inside a vacuum, cordoned off from other modes of domination. On the contrary, it *intersects* with other forms of domination—those based on gender, class, sexuality, religion, nationhood, ability, and so forth. The notion that there is a monolithic "Arab American experience," "Asian American experience," or "White experience"—experiences somehow detached from other pieces of one's identity—is nothing but a chimera. Researchers have labeled such a notion "racial essentialism," for such a way of thinking boils down vastly different human experiences into a single "master category": race (Harris 2000). When we fail to account for these different experiences, we create silences in our narratives of the social world and fail to explain how overlapping systems of advantage and disadvantage affect individuals' opportunity structures, lifestyles, and social hardships. The idea of intersectionality implies that we cannot understand the lives of poor White single mothers or gay Black men by examining only one dimension of their lives—class, gender, race, or sexuality. Indeed, we must explore their lives in their full complexity, examining how these various dimensions come together and structure their existence. When we speak of racial domination, then, we must always bear in mind the ways in which it interacts with masculine domination (or sexism), heterosexual domination (or homophobia), class domination (poverty), religious persecution, disadvantages brought on by disabilities, and so forth (Collins 2000; Crenshaw 1990).

In addition, we should not assume that one kind of oppression is more important than another or that being advantaged in one dimension of life somehow cancels out other dimensions that often result in disadvantage. While it is true that poor Whites experience many of the same hardships as poor Blacks, it is not true that poverty somehow de-Whitens poor Whites. In other words, though they are in a similarly precarious economic position as poor Blacks, poor Whites still experience race-based privileges, while poor Blacks are oppressed not only by poverty but also by racism. In a similar vein, well-off people of color cannot "buy" their way out of racism. Despite their economic privilege, middle- and upper-class non-Whites experience institutional and interpersonal racism on a regular basis (Feagin 1991). But how, exactly, should we conceptualize these intersecting modes of domination? Many scholars have grappled with this question (e.g., Walby 2007; Yuval-Davis 2006), and we do so here, if only in the most provisional way.

The notion of intersectionality is perhaps as old as the social problems of racial, masculine, and class domination, but in recent memory it was popularized by activists who criticized the feminist and civil rights movements for ignoring the unique struggles of women of color. The term itself is credited to critical race scholar Kimberlé Crenshaw (1989), who imagined society as divided every which way by multiple forms of inequality. For Crenshaw, society resembled an intricate system of crisscrossing roads—each one representing a different social identity (e.g., race, gender, class, religion, age); one's unique social position (or structural location) could be identified by listing all the attributes of one's social identity and pinpointing the nexus (or intersection) at which all those attributes coalesced. This conception of intersectionality has been the dominant one for many years, leading scholars to understand overlapping modes of oppression as a kind of "matrix of domination" (Collins 2000). . . .

We believe a more analytically sophisticated and politically useful rendering of intertwined oppressions is Myra Marx Ferree's model of "interactive intersectionality" (cf. Prins 2006; Walby 2007). In this version, overlapping social identities are best understood, not as a collection of "points of intersection," but as a "figuration" (as Elias would have it) or "field" (as Bourdieu would) of shifting, deeply-dimensioned, and "mutually constituted *relationships*." This means "the 'intersection of gender and race' is not any number of specific *locations* occupied by individuals or groups (such as Black women) but a *process* through which 'race' takes on multiple 'gendered' meanings for particular women and men. . . . In such a complex system, gender is not a dimension limited to the organization of reproduction or family, class is not a dimension equated with the economy, and race is not a category reduced to the primacy of ethnicities, nations and borders, but all of the processes that systematically organize families, economies, and nations are co-constructed along with the meanings of gender, race, and class that are presented in and reinforced by these institutions separately and together" (Ferree 2009:85).

The best metaphor for intersecting modes of oppression, therefore, may not be that of crisscrossing roads but of a web or field of relations within which struggles over opportunities, power, and privileges take place (cf. Bourdieu 1996 [1992]; Emirbayer 1997). The implication of this new theoretical development is that if we focus strictly on race and ignore other sources of social inequality (such as class and gender), not only will we be deaf to the unique experiences of certain members of society—their voices drowned out by our violent and homogenizing categorization— but we will also (and always) fundamentally misunderstand our object of analysis: race itself. Intersectional analysis of the type that breaks with old modes of thinking (e.g., society as a "matrix of domination") and adopts a thoroughly relational perspective on multiple modes of oppression (e.g., "interactive intersectionality") is not an option but a *prerequisite* for fully understanding the nature of racial identity and racial domination.

REFERENCES

Alba, Richard, Rubén Rumbaut, and Karen Marotz. 2005. A Distorted Nation: Perceptions of Racial/Ethnic Group Sizes and Attitudes Toward Immigrants and Other Minorities. *Social Forces*, 84: 901–919.

Alexander, Jeffrey. 2006. *The Civil Sphere*. New York: Oxford University Press.

Bloch, Marc. 1953. *The Historian's Craft*. Translated by Peter Putnam. New York: Vintage.

Bloemraad, Irene. 2006. *Becoming a Citizen: Incorporating Immigrants and Refugees in the United States and Canada*. Berkeley, CA: University of California Press.

Blumer, Herbert. 1958. Race Prejudice as a Sense of Group Position. *The Pacific Sociological Review*, 1: 3–7.

Bobo, Lawrence. 2001. Racial Attitudes and Relations at the Close of the Twentieth Century. In Neil Smelser, William Julius Wilson, and Faith Mitchell (Eds.), *America Becoming: Racial Trends and their Consequences*, pp. 262–299. Washington, DC: National Academy Press.

Bonilla-Silva, Eduardo. 1997. Rethinking Racism: Toward a Structural Interpretation. *American Sociological Review*, 62: 465–480.

Bourdieu, Pierre. 2003. *Language and Symbolic Power*. Translated by Gino Raymond and Matthew Adamson. Cambridge, MA: Harvard University Press.

Bourdieu, Pierre. 1998 [1994]. Rethinking the State: Genesis and Structure of the Bureaucratic Field. Translated by Loïc Wacquant and Samar Farage. In Pierre Bourdieu (Ed.), *Practical Reason*, pp. 35–63. Stanford, CA: Stanford University Press.

Bourdieu, Pierre. 1996 [1992]. *The Rules of Art: Genesis and Structure of the Literary Field*. Translated by Susan Emanuel. Stanford, CA: Stanford University Press.

Bourdieu, Pierre, and Loïc Wacquant. 1992. *An Invitation to Reflexive Sociology*. Chicago, IL: University of Chicago Press.

Brown, Michael, Martin Carnoy, Elliott Currie, Troy Duster, David Oppenheimer, Marjorie Shultz, and David Wellman. 2003. *White-Washing Race: The Myth of a Color Blind Society*. Berkeley, CA: University of California Press.

Brubaker, Rogers, Mara Loverman, and Peter Stamatov. 2004. Ethnicity as Cognition. *Theory and Society*, 33: 31–64.

Collins, Patricia Hill. 2000. *Black Feminist Thought: Knowledge, Consciousness, and the Politics of Empowerment*, 2 ed. New York: Routledge.

Conley, Dalton. 2001. Universal Freckle, or How I Learned to Be White. In Birgit Brander Rasmussen, Eric Klinenberg, Irene Nexica, and Matt Wray (Eds.), *The Making and Unmaking of Whiteness*, pp. 25–42. Durham, NC: Duke University Press.

Cox, Oliver Cromwell. 1948. *Caste, Class, and Race: A Study in Social Dynamics.* Garden City, NY: Doubleday.

Crenshaw, Kimberlé. 1989. Demarginalizing the Intersection of Race and Sex: A Black Feminist Critique of Antidiscrimination Doctrine, Feminist Theory and Antiracist Politics. *University of Chicago Legal Forum*, 1989: 139–167.

Crenshaw, Kimberlé. 1990. Mapping the Margins: Intersectionality, Identity Politics, and Violence against Women of Color. *Stanford Law Review*, 42: 1241–1299.

DaCosta, Kimberly. 2007. *Making Multiracials: State, Family, and Market in the Redrawing of the Color Line.* Stanford, CA: Stanford University Press.

Davis, F. James. 1991. *Who Is Black? One Nation's Definition.* University Park, PA: Pennsylvania State University Press.

Dikötter, Frank. 1992. *The Discourse of Race in Modern China.* Stanford, CA: Stanford University Press.

Duster, Troy. 2003. Buried Alive: The Concept of Race in Science. In Alan Goodman, Deborah Heath, and Susan Lindee (Eds.), *Genetic Nature/Culture: Anthropology and Science beyond the Two-Culture Divide*, pp. 258–277. Berkeley, CA: University of California Press.

Duster, Troy. 2001. The "Morphing" Properties of Whiteness. In Birgit Brander Rasmussen, Eric Klinenberg, Irene Nexica, and Matt Wray (Eds.), *The Making and Unmaking of Whiteness*, pp. 113–137. Durham, NC: Duke University Press.

Eisenstadt, S.N. 1998. *Japanese Civilization: A Comparative View.* Chicago, IL: University of Chicago Press.

Emirbayer, Mustafa. 1997. Manifesto for Relational Sociology. *American Journal of Sociology*, 103: 281–317.

Essed, Philomena. 1991 [1984]. *Everyday Racism.* Claremont, CA: Hunter House.

Fanon, Frantz. 1967. *Black Skin, White Masks.* Translated by Charles Lam Markmann. New York: Grove Press.

Feagin, Joe. 1991. The Continuing Significance of Race: Antiblack Discrimination in Public Places. *American Sociological Review*, 56: 101–116.

Feagin, Joe, Hernan Vera, and Pinar Batur. 2001. *White Racism: The Basics*, Second Edition. New York: Routledge.

Ferree, Myra Marx. 2009. Inequality, Intersectionality and the Politics of Discourse: Framing Feminist Alliances. In Emanuela Lombardo, Petra Meier, and Mieke Verloo (Eds.), *The Discursive Politics of Gender Equality: Stretching, Bending, and Policy-Making*, pp. 84–101. New York: Routledge.

Gossett, Thomas. 1965. *Race: The History of an Idea in America.* New York: Schocken.

Graves, Joseph, Jr. 2001. *The Emperor's New Clothes: Biological Theories of Race at the Millennium.* New Brunswick, NJ: Rutgers University Press.

Hall, Stuart. 1980. Race Articulation and Societies Structured in Dominance. In UNESCO (Ed.), *Sociological Theories: Race and Colonialism*, pp. 305–345. Paris, FR: UNESCO.

Haney-López, Ian. 1996. *White by Law: The Legal Construction of Race.* New York: New York University Press.

Hannaford, Ivan. 1996. *Race: The History of an Idea in the West.* Baltimore, MD: The Johns Hopkins Press.

Harris, Angela. 2000. Race and Essentialism in Feminist Legal Theory. In Richard Delgado and Jean Stefancic (Eds.), *Critical Race Theory: The Cutting Edge*, Second Edition, pp. 261–274. Philadelphia, PA: Temple University Press.

Holt, Thomas. 2000. *The Problem of Race in the 21st Century.* Cambridge, MA: Harvard University Press.

Jackson, John, Jr. 2001. *Harlemworld: Doing Race and Class in Contemporary Black America.* Chicago, IL: University of Chicago Press.

Loury, Glenn. 2001. *The Anatomy of Racial Inequality.* Cambridge, MA: Harvard University Press.

Loveman, Mara. 1999. Is "Race" Essential? *American Sociological Review*, 64: 891–898.

Marx, Anthony. 1998. *Making Race and Nation: A Comparison of the United States, South Africa, and Brazil.* New York: Cambridge University Press.

Massey, Douglas. 2007. *Categorically Unequal: The American Stratification System.* New York: Russell Sage Foundation.

Neckerman, Kathryn. 2007. *Schools Betrayed: Roots of Failure in Inner-City Education.* Chicago, IL: University of Chicago Press.

Ngai, Mae. 2004. *Impossible Subjects: Illegal Aliens and the Making of Modern America.* Princeton, NJ: Princeton University Press.

Oaks, Jeannie. 2005. *Keeping Track: How Schools Structure Inequality,* Second Edition. New Haven, CT: Yale University Press.

Oliver, Melvin, and Thomas Shapiro. 1997. *Black Wealth/White Wealth.* New York: Routledge.

Prins, Baukje. 2006. Narrative Accounts of Origins: A Blind Spot in the Intersectional Approach? *European Journal of Women's Studies,* 13: 277–290.

Quillian, Lincoln. 2006. New Approaches to Understanding Racial Prejudice and Discrimination. *Annual Review of Sociology,* 32: 299–328.

Reich, Michael. 1981. *Racial Inequality: A Political-Economic Analysis* Princeton, NJ: Princeton University Press.

Schuman, Howard, Charlotte Steeh, Lawrence Bobo, and Maria Krysan. 1997. *Racial Attitudes in America: Trends and Interpretations,* revised edition. Cambridge, MA: Harvard University Press.

Searle-Chatterjee, Mary, and Ursula Sharma. 1994. *Contextualising Caste: Post-Dumontian Approaches.* Oxford, U.K.: Blackwell.

Shklar, Judith. 1991. *American Citizenship: The Quest for Inclusion.* Cambridge, MA: Harvard University Press.

Smedley, Audrey. 199). *Race in North America: Origin and Evolution of a Worldview,* Second Edition. Boulder, CO: Westview.

Smith, Lillian. 1994 [1949]. *Killers of the Dream,* 1994 edition. New York: Norton.

Southern Poverty Law Center Intelligence Project. 2005. *Active U.S. Hate Groups in 2005.* Montgomery, AL: Southern Poverty Law Center.

Sparks, Allister. 2006. *The Mind of South Africa: The Story of tbe Rise and Fall of Apartheid.* Johannesburg, ZA: Jonathan Ball.

Stephens, Thomas. 1999. *Dictionary of Latin American Racial and Ethnic Terminology.* Gainesville, FL: University of Florida Press.

Telles, Edward. 2004. *Race in Another America: The Significance of Skin Color in Brazil.* Princeton, NJ: Princeton University Press.

Wacquant, Loïc. 1997. For an Analytic of Racial Domination. *Political Power and Social Theory,* 11: 221–234.

Walby, Sylvia. 2007. Complexity Theory, Systems Theory, and Multiple Intersecting Social Inequalities. *Philosophy of the Social Sciences,* 37: 449–470.

Waters, Mary. 1990. *Ethnic Options: Choosing Identities in America.* Berkeley, CA: University of California Press.

Waters, Mary. 1999. *Black Identities: West Indian Immigrant Dreams and American Realities.* New York, Cambridge, MA: Russell Sage Foundation, Harvard University Press.

Weber, Max. 1946. Class, Status, Party. In H. H. Gerth and C. Wright Mills (Eds.), *From Max Weber: Essays in Sociology,* pp. 180–195. New York: Oxford University Press.

Western, Bruce. 2006. *Punishment and Inequality in America.* New York: Russell Sage Foundation.

Winant, Howard. 2001. *The World Is a Ghetto: Race and Democracy since World War II.* New York: Basic Books.

Yuval-Davis, Nira. 2006. Intersectionality and Feminist Politics. *European Journal of Women's Studies,* 13: 193–209.

32
_____

AT A SLAUGHTERHOUSE, SOME THINGS NEVER DIE

CHARLIE LeDUFF

Racism is any prejudice or discrimination against an individual or a group based on their race, ethnicity, or some other perceived difference. The following reading by Charlie LeDuff, a reporter for the *New York Times*, takes us inside one workplace site to examine the everyday reality of racial interactions among one group of employees. In the slaughterhouse in Tar Heel, North Carolina, racism occurs on many levels, including racial stereotyping, verbal harassment, and even the threat of physical violence and death. The employers also effectively use racist strategies, such as enforcing a racial hierarchy among workers and exploiting racial tensions among their workers, to maintain an economic advantage and social control over their employees.

Tar Heel, North Carolina

It must have been 1 o'clock. That's when the white man usually comes out of his glass office and stands on the scaffolding above the factory floor. He stood with his palms on the rails, his elbows out. He looked like a tower guard up there or a border patrol agent. He stood with his head cocked.

One o'clock means it is getting near the end of the workday. Quota has to be met and the workload doubles. The conveyor belt always overflows with meat around 1 o'clock. So the workers double their pace, hacking pork from shoulder bones with a driven single-mindedness. They stare blankly, like mules in wooden blinders, as the butchered slabs pass by.

It is called the picnic line: eighteen workers lined up on both sides of a belt, carving meat from bone. Up to 16 million shoulders a year come down that line here at the Smithfield Packing Company, the largest pork production plant in the world. That works out to about 32,000 a shift, sixty-three a minute, one every seventeen seconds for each worker for eight and a half hours a day. The first time you stare down at that belt you know your body is going to give in way before the machine ever will.

On this day the boss saw something he didn't like. He climbed down and approached the picnic line from behind. He leaned into the ear of a broad-shouldered black man. He had been riding him all day, and the day before. The boss bawled him out good this time, but no one heard what was said. The roar of the machinery was too ferocious for that. Still, everyone knew what was expected. They worked harder.

The white man stood and watched for the next two hours as the blacks worked in their groups and the Mexicans in theirs. He stood there with his head cocked.

At shift change the black man walked away, hosed himself down and turned in his knives. Then he let go. He threatened to murder the boss. He promised to quit. He said he was losing his mind, which made for good comedy since he was standing near a conveyor chain of severed hogs' heads, their mouths yoked open.

Who that cracker think he is? the black man wanted to know. There were enough hogs, he said, *not to worry about no fleck of meat being left on the bone. Keep treating me like a Mexican and I'll beat him.*

The boss walked by just then and the black man lowered his head.

Who Gets the Dirty Jobs

The first thing you learn in the hog plant is the value of a sharp knife. The second thing you learn is that you don't want to work with a knife. Finally you learn that not everyone has to work with a knife. Whites, blacks, American Indians, and Mexicans, they all have their separate stations.

The few whites on the payroll tend to be mechanics or supervisors. As for the Indians, a handful are supervisors; others tend to get clean menial jobs like warehouse work. With few exceptions, that leaves the blacks and Mexicans with the dirty jobs at the factory, one of the only places within a fifty-mile radius in this muddy corner of North Carolina where a person might make more than $8 an hour.

While Smithfield's profits nearly doubled in the past year, wages have remained flat. So a lot of Americans here have quit and a lot of Mexicans have been hired to take their places. But more than management, the workers see one another as the problem, and they see the competition in skin tones.

The locker rooms are self-segregated and so is the cafeteria. The enmity spills out into the towns. The races generally keep to themselves. Along Interstate 95 there are four tumbledown bars, one for each color: white, black, red, and brown.

Language is also a divider. There are English and Spanish lines at the Social Security office and in the waiting rooms of the county health clinics. This means different groups don't really understand one another and tend to be suspicious of what they do know.

You begin to understand these things the minute you apply for the job.

Blood and Burnout

Treat the meat like you going to eat it yourself, the hiring manager told the thirty applicants, most of them down on their luck and hungry for work. The Smithfield plant will take just about any man or woman with a pulse and a sparkling urine sample, with few questions asked. This reporter was hired using his own name and acknowledged that he was currently employed, but was not asked where and did not say.

Slaughtering swine is repetitive, brutish work, so grueling that three weeks on the factory floor leave no doubt in your mind about why the turnover is 100 percent. Five thousand quit and five thousand are hired every year. You hear people say, *They don't kill pigs in the plant, they kill people.* So desperate is the company for workers, its recruiters comb the streets of New York's immigrant communities, personnel staff members say, and word of mouth has reached Mexico and beyond.

The company even procures criminals. Several at the morning orientation were inmates on work release in green uniforms, bused in from the county prison.

The new workers were given a safety speech and tax papers, shown a promotional video and informed that there was enough methane, ammonia, and chlorine at the plant to kill every living thing here in Bladen County. Of the thirty new employees, the black women were assigned to the chitterlings room, where they would scrape feces and worms from intestines. The black men were sent to the butchering floor. Two free white men and the Indian were given jobs making boxes. This reporter declined a box job and ended up with most of the Mexicans, doing knife work, cutting sides of pork into smaller and smaller products.

Standing in the hiring hall that morning, two women chatted in Spanish about their pregnancies. A young black man had heard enough. His small town the next county over was crowded with Mexicans. They just started showing up three years ago—drawn to rural Robeson County by the plant—and never left. They stood in groups on the street corners, and the young black man never knew what they were saying. They took the jobs and did them for less. Some had houses in Mexico, while he lived in a trailer with his mother.

Now here he was, trying for the only job around, and he had to listen to Spanish, had to compete with peasants. The world was going to hell.

This is America and I want to start hearing some English, now! he screamed.

One of the women told him where to stick his head and listen for the echo. *Then you'll hear some English,* she said.

An old white man with a face as pinched and lined as a pot roast complained, *The tacos are worse than the niggers,* and the Indian leaned against the wall and laughed. In the doorway, the prisoners shifted from foot to foot, watching the spectacle unfold from behind a cloud of cigarette smoke.

The hiring manager came out of his office and broke it up just before things degenerated into a brawl. Then he handed out the employment stubs. *I don't want no problems,* he warned. He told them to report to the plant on Monday morning to collect their carving knives.

$7.70 an Hour, Pain All Day

Monday. The mist rose from the swamps and by 4:45 A.M. thousands of head-lamps snaked along the old country roads. Cars carried people from the back-woods, from the single and double-wide trailers, from the cinder-block houses and wooden shacks: whites from Lumberton and Elizabethtown; blacks from Fairmont and Fayetteville; Indians from Pembroke; the Mexicans from Red Springs and St. Pauls.

They converge at the Smithfield plant, a 973,000-square-foot leviathan of pipe and steel near the Cape Fear River. The factory towers over the tobacco and cotton fields, surrounded by pine trees and a few of the old whitewashed plantation houses. Built seven years ago, it is by far the biggest employer in this region, seventy-five miles west of the Atlantic and ninety miles south of the booming Research Triangle around Chapel Hill.

The workers filed in, their faces stiffened by sleep and the cold, like saucers of milk gone hard. They punched the clock at 5 A.M., waiting for the knives to be handed out, the chlorine freshly applied by the cleaning crew burning their eyes and throats. Nobody spoke.

The hallway was a river of brown-skinned Mexicans. The six prisoners who were starting that day looked confused.

What the hell's going on? the only white inmate, Billy Harwood, asked an older black worker named Wade Baker.

Oh, Baker said, seeing that the prisoner was talking about the Mexicans. *I see you been away for a while.*

Billy Harwood had been away—nearly seven years, for writing phony payroll checks from the family pizza business to buy crack. He was Rip Van Winkle standing there. Everywhere he looked there were Mexicans. What he didn't know was that one out of three newborns at the nearby Robeson County health clinic was a Latino; that the county's Roman Catholic church had a special Sunday Mass for Mexicans said by a Honduran priest; that the schools needed Spanish speakers to teach English.

With less than a month to go on his sentence, Harwood took the pork job to save a few dollars. The word in jail was that the job was a cakewalk for a white man.

But this wasn't looking like any cakewalk. He wasn't going to get a boxing job like a lot of other whites. Apparently inmates were on the bottom rung, just like Mexicans.

Billy Harwood and the other prisoners were put on the picnic line. Knife work pays $7.70 an hour to start. It is money unimaginable in Mexico, where the average wage is $4 a day. But the American money comes at a price. The work burns your muscles and dulls your mind. Staring down into the meat for hours strains your neck. After thousands of cuts a day your fingers no longer open freely. Standing in the damp 42-degree air causes your knees to lock, your nose to run, your teeth to throb.

The whistle blows at three, you get home by four, pour peroxide on your nicks by five. You take pills for your pains and stand in a hot shower trying to wash it all away. You hurt. And by eight o'clock you're in bed, exhausted, thinking of work.

The convict said he felt cheated. He wasn't supposed to be doing Mexican work. After his second day he was already talking of quitting. *Man, this can't be for real,* he said, rubbing his wrists as if they'd been in handcuffs. *This job's for an ass. They treat you like an animal.*

He just might have quit after the third day had it not been for Mercedes Fernández, a Mexican. He took a place next to her by the conveyor belt. She smiled at him, showed him how to make incisions. That was the extent of his on-the-job training. He was peep-eyed, missing a tooth and squat from the starchy prison food, but he acted as if this tiny woman had taken a fancy to him. In truth, she was more fascinated than infatuated, she later confided. In her year at the plant, he was the first white person she had ever worked with.

The other workers noticed her helping the white man, so unusual was it for a Mexican and a white to work shoulder to shoulder, to try to talk or even to make eye contact.

As for blacks, she avoided them. She was scared of them. *Blacks don't want to work,* Fernández said when the new batch of prisoners came to work on the line. *They're lazy.*

Everything about the factory cuts people off from one another. If it's not the language barrier, it's the noise—the hammering of compressors, the screeching of pulleys, the grinding of the lines. You can hardly make your voice heard. To get another's attention on the cut line, you bang the butt of your knife on the steel railings, or you lob a chunk of meat. Fernández would sometimes throw a piece of shoulder at a friend across the conveyor and wave good morning.

The Kill Floor

The kill floor sets the pace of the work, and for those jobs they pick strong men and pay a top wage, as high as $12 an hour. If the men fail to make quota, plenty of others are willing to try. It is mostly the blacks who work the kill floor, the stone-hearted jobs that pay more and appear out of bounds for all but a few Mexicans. Plant workers gave various reasons for this: the Mexicans are too small; they don't like blood; they don't like heavy lifting; or just plain *We built this country and we ain't going to hand them everything,* as one black man put it.

Kill-floor work is hot, quick, and bloody. The hog is herded in from the stockyard, then stunned with an electric gun. It is lifted onto a conveyor belt, dazed but not dead, and passed to a waiting group of men wearing blood-stained smocks and blank faces. They slit the neck, shackle the hind legs and watch a machine lift the carcass into the air, letting its life flow out in a purple gush, into a steaming collection trough.

The carcass is run through a scalding bath, trolleyed over the factory floor, and then dumped onto a table with all the force of a quarter-ton water balloon. In the misty-red room, men slit along its hind tendons and skewer the beast with hooks. It is again lifted and shot across the room on a pulley and bar, where it hangs with hundreds of others as if in some kind of horrific dry-cleaning shop. It is then pulled through a wall of flames and met on the other side by more black men who, stripped to the waist beneath their smocks, scrape away any straggling bristles.

The place reeks of sweat and scared animal, steam and blood. Nothing is wasted from these beasts, not the plasma, not the glands, not the bones. Everything is used, and the kill men, repeating slaughterhouse lore, say that even the squeal is sold.

The carcasses sit in the freezer overnight and are then rolled out to the cut floor. The cut floor is opposite to the kill floor in nearly every way. The workers are mostly brown—Mexicans—not black; the lighting yellow, not red. The vapor comes from cold breath, not hot water. It is here that the hog is quartered. The pieces are parceled out and sent along the disassembly lines to be cut into ribs, hams, bellies, loins, and chops.

People on the cut lines work with a mindless fury. There is tremendous pressure to keep the conveyor belts moving, to pack orders, to put bacon and ham and sausage on the public's breakfast table. There is no clock, no window, no fragment of the world outside. Everything is pork. If the line fails to keep pace, the kill men must slow down, backing up the slaughter. The boxing line will have little to do, costing the company payroll hours. The blacks who kill will become angry with the Mexicans who cut, who in turn will become angry with the white superintendents who push them.

10,000 Unwelcome Mexicans

The Mexicans never push back. They cannot. Some have legitimate work papers, but more, like Mercedes Fernández, do not.

Even worse, Fernández was several thousand dollars in debt to the smugglers who had sneaked her and her family into the United States and owed a thousand more for the authentic-looking birth certificate and Social Security card that are needed to get hired. She and her husband, Armando, expected to be in debt for years. They had mouths to feed back home.

The Mexicans are so frightened about being singled out that they do not even tell one another their real names. They have their given names, their work-paper names, and "Hey you," as their American supervisors call them. In the telling of their stories, Mercedes and Armando Fernández insisted that their real names be used, to protect their identities. It was their work names they did not want used, names bought in a back alley in Barstow, Texas.

Rarely are the newcomers welcomed with open arms. Long before the Mexicans arrived, Robeson County, one of the poorest in North Carolina, was an uneasy racial mix. In the 1990 census, of the 100,000 people living in Robeson, nearly 40 percent were Lumbee Indian, 35 percent white, and 25 percent black. Until a dozen years ago the county schools were de facto segregated, and no person of color held any meaningful county job from sheriff to court clerk to judge.

At one point in 1988, two armed Indian men occupied the local newspaper office, taking hostages and demanding that the sheriff's department be investigated for corruption and its treatment of minorities. A prominent Indian lawyer, Julian Pierce, was killed that same year, and the suspect turned up dead in a broom closet before he could be charged. The hierarchy of power was summed up on a plaque that hangs in the courthouse commemorating the dead of World War I. It lists the veterans by color: "white" on top, "Indian" in the middle, and "colored" on the bottom.

That hierarchy mirrors the pecking order at the hog plant. The Lumbees— who have fought their way up in the county apparatus and have built their own construction businesses—are fond of saying they are too smart to work in the factory. And the few who do work there seem to end up with the cleaner jobs.

But as reds and blacks began to make progress in the 1990s—for the first time an Indian sheriff was elected, and a black man is now the public defender—the Latinos began arriving. The United States Census Bureau estimated that one thousand Latinos were living in Robeson County in 1999. People only laugh at that number.

A thousand? Hell, there's more than that in the Wal-Mart on a Saturday afternoon, said Bill Smith, director of county health services. He and other officials guess that there are at least 10,000 Latinos in Robeson, most having arrived since 1997.

When they built that factory in Bladen, they promised a trickle-down effect, Smith said. *But the money ain't trickling down this way. Bladen got the money and Robeson got the social problems.*

In Robeson there is the strain on public resources. There is the substandard housing. There is the violence. In 1999 twenty-seven killings were committed in Robeson, mostly in the countryside, giving it a higher murder rate than Detroit or Newark. Three Mexicans were robbed and killed that fall. Latinos have also been the victims of highway stickups.

In the yellow-walled break room at the plant, Mexicans talked among themselves about their three slain men, about the midnight visitors with obscured faces and guns, men who knew that the illegal workers used mattresses rather than banks. Mercedes Fernández, like many Mexicans, would not venture out at night. *Blacks have a problem,* she said. *They live in the past. They are angry about slavery, so instead of working, they steal from us.*

She and her husband never lingered in the parking lot at shift change. That is when the anger of a long day comes seeping out. Cars get kicked and faces slapped over parking spots or fender benders. The traffic is a serpent. Cars jockey for a spot in line to make the quarter-mile crawl along the plant's one-lane exit road to the highway. Usually no one will let you in. A lot of the scuffling is between black and Mexican. . . .

Living It, Hating It

Billy Harwood had been working at the plant ten days when he was released from the Robeson County Correctional Facility. He stood at the prison gates in his work clothes with his belongings in a plastic bag, waiting. A friend dropped him at the Salvation Army shelter, but he decided it was too much like prison. Full of black people. No leaving after 10 P.M. No smoking indoors. *What you doing here, white boy?* they asked him.

He fumbled with a cigarette outside the shelter. He wanted to quit the plant. The work stinks, he said, *but at least I ain't a nigger. I'll find other work soon. I'm a white man.* He had hopes of landing a roofing job through a friend. The way he saw it, white society looks out for itself.

On the cut line he worked slowly and allowed Mercedes Fernández and the others to pick up his slack. He would cut only the left shoulders; it was easier on his hands. Sometimes it would be three minutes before a left shoulder came down the line. When he did cut, he didn't clean the bone; he left chunks of meat on it.

Fernández was disappointed by her first experience with a white person. After a week she tried to avoid standing by Billy Harwood. She decided it wasn't just the blacks who were lazy, she said.

Even so, the supervisor came by one morning, took a look at one of Harwood's badly cut shoulders and threw it at Fernández, blaming her. He said obscene things about her family. She didn't understand exactly what he said, but it scared her. She couldn't wipe the tears from her eyes because her gloves were covered with greasy shreds of swine. The other cutters kept their heads down, embarrassed.

Her life was falling apart. She and her husband both worked the cut floor. They never saw their daughter. They were twenty-six but rarely made love anymore. All they wanted was to save enough money to put plumbing in their house in Mexico and start a business there. They come from the town of Tehuacán, in a rural area about 150 miles southeast of Mexico City. His mother owns a bar there and a home but gives nothing to them. Mother must look out for her old age.

We came here to work so we have a chance to grow old in Mexico, Fernández said one evening while cooking pork and potatoes. Now they were into a smuggler for thousands. Her hands swelled into claws in the evenings and stung while she worked. She felt trapped. But she kept at it for the money, for the $9.60 an hour. The smuggler still had to be paid.

They explained their story this way: The coyote drove her and her family from Barstow a year ago and left them in Robeson. They knew no one. They did not even know they were in the state of North Carolina. They found shelter in a trailer park that had once been exclusively black but was rapidly filling with Mexicans. There was a lot of drug dealing there and a lot of tension. One evening, Armando Fernández said, he asked a black neighbor to move his business inside and the man pulled a pistol on him.

I hate the blacks, he said in Spanish, sitting in the break room not ten feet from Wade Baker and his black friends. Billy Harwood was sitting two tables away with the whites and Indians.

After the gun incident, Armando Fernández packed up his family and moved out into the country, to a prefabricated number sitting on a brick foundation off in the woods alone. Their only contact with people is through the satellite dish. Except for the coyote. The coyote knows where they live and comes for his money every other month.

Their five-year-old daughter has no playmates in the back country and few at school. That is the way her parents want it. *We don't want her to be American,* her mother said.

"We Need a Union"

The steel bars holding a row of hogs gave way as a woman stood below them. Hog after hog fell around her with a sickening thud, knocking her senseless, the connecting bars barely missing her face. As co-workers rushed to help the woman, the supervisor spun his hands in the air, a signal to keep working. Wade Baker saw this and shook his head in disgust. Nothing stops the disassembly lines.

We need a union, he said later in the break room. It was payday and he stared at his check: $288. He spoke softly to the black workers sitting near him. Everyone is convinced that talk of a union will get you fired. After two years at the factory, Baker makes slightly more than $9 an hour toting meat away from the cut line, slightly less than $20,000 a year, 45 cents an hour less than Mercedes Fernández.

I don't want to get racial about the Mexicans, he whispered to the black workers. *But they're dragging down the pay. It's pure economics. They say Americans don't want to do the job. That ain't exactly true. We don't want to do it for $8. Pay $15 and we'll do it.*

These men knew that in the late seventies, when the meat-packing industry was centered in northern cities like Chicago and Omaha, people had a union getting them $18 an hour. But by the mid-eighties, to cut costs, many of the packing houses had moved to small towns where they could pay a lower, nonunion wage.

The black men sitting around the table also felt sure that the Mexicans pay almost nothing in income tax, claiming eight, nine even ten exemptions. The men believed that the illegal workers should be rooted out of the factory. *It's all about money,* Baker said.

His co-workers shook their heads. *A plantation with a roof on it,* one said.

For their part, many of the Mexicans in Tar Heel fear that a union would place their illegal status under scrutiny and force them out. The United Food and Commercial Workers Union last tried organizing the plant in 1997, but the idea was voted down nearly two to one.

One reason Americans refused to vote for the union was because it refuses to take a stand on illegal laborers. Another reason was the intimidation. When workers arrived at the plant the morning of the vote, they were met by Bladen County deputy sheriffs in riot gear. "Nigger Lover" had been scrawled on the union trailer.

Five years ago the work force at the plant was 50 percent black, 20 percent white and Indian, and 30 percent Latino, according to union statistics. Company officials say those numbers are about the same today. But from inside the plant, the breakdown appears to be more like 60 percent Latino, 30 percent black, 10 percent white and red.

Sherri Buffkin, a white woman and the former director of purchasing who testified before the National Labor Relations Board in an unfair-labor-practice suit brought by the union in 1998, said in an interview that the company assigns workers by race. She also said that management had kept lists of union sympathizers during the '97 election, firing blacks and replacing them with Latinos. *I know because I fired at least fifteen of them myself,* she said.

The company denies those accusations. Michael H. Cole, a lawyer for Smithfield who would respond to questions about the company's labor practices only in writing, said that jobs at the Tar Heel plant were awarded through a bidding process and not assigned by race. The company also denies ever having kept lists of union sympathizers or singled out blacks to be fired.

The hog business is important to North Carolina. It is a multibillion-dollar-a-year industry in the state, with nearly two pigs for every one of its 7.5 million people. And Smithfield Foods, a publicly traded company based in Smithfield, Virginia, has become the No. 1 producer and processor of pork in the world. It slaughters more than 20 percent of the nation's swine, more than 19 million animals a year.

The company, which has acquired a network of factory farms and slaughterhouses, worries federal agriculture officials and legislators, who see it siphoning business from smaller farmers. And environmentalists contend that Smithfield's operations contaminate local water supplies. (The Environmental Protection Agency fined the company $12.6 million in 1996 after its processing plants in Virginia discharged pollutants into the Pagan River.) The chairman and chief executive, Joseph W. Luter III, declined to be interviewed.

Smithfield's employment practices have not been so closely scrutinized. And so every year, more Mexicans get hired. *An illegal alien isn't going to complain all that much,* said Ed Tomlinson, acting supervisor of the Immigration and Naturalization Service Bureau in Charlotte.

But the company says it does not knowingly hire illegal aliens. Smithfield's lawyer, Cole, said all new employees must present papers showing that they can legally work in the United States. *If any employee's documentation appears to be genuine and to belong to the person presenting it,* he said in his written response, *Smithfield is required by law to take it at face value.*

The naturalization service—which has only eighteen agents in North Carolina—has not investigated Smithfield because no one has filed a complaint, Ed Tomlinson said. *There are more jobs than people,* he said, *and a lot of Americans will do the dirty work for a while and then return to their couches and eat bonbons and watch Oprah.*

33

OUT OF SORTS
Adoption and (Un)Desirable Children

KATHERIN M. FLOWER KIM

In this reading, Katherin M. Flower Kim presents her findings of how race and racism influence the adoption decisions of white parents in the United States. Kim, an assistant professor of sociology at Austin Peay State University in Clarksville, Tennessee, interviewed 73 adoptive parents in central New York in the late 1990s. Kim investigates the ways parents in her study came to construct, sort, and talk about Asian children in general, and children from Korea in particular, as desirable for adoption and African American and Latino children as undesirable. This reading illustrates well several of the concepts related to race and racial inequality introduced in the Desmond and Emirbayer article, Reading 31.

Adoption has become an increasingly important and common path for forming a family with children, and it illustrates the importance adopters place on having a family that includes children. Yet adoption is not simply a case of adopting any child. Differential rates of adoption for different groups of children as well as categories of "waiting children" reflect the ways some children are considered more desirable than other children and helps explain why some children are more likely to be adopted, and adopted more quickly, than are other children. I draw on interview data collected during 1997–1999 from 43 mothers and 30 of their husbands in Central City, a pseudonym for a city in central New York, who adopted children from Korea in the 1980s and 1990s, to investigate the sorting, and in many instances ranking, of children throughout the adoption process. All but one of the participants identified themselves as white.[1] While their comments indicated that a range of factors contributed to parental perceptions and talk about (un)desirable children, this reading is principally concerned with exploring and analyzing the ways race shaped American parents' thinking and discourse about who was more or less desirable as a potential family member. More specifically, I use parents' descriptions of assembling their families to explore and highlight how they came to explain the desirability of children from Korea and the undesirability of African American children.

A key aspect of understanding constructions of desirable children and parental preferences for certain children is clarifying who the adopters are, particularly in terms of race. More specifically, the majority of parents who adopt through formal, legal channels[2] were, and continue to be, whites who experience fertility problems (May 1995; Roberts 1997). As Elaine Tyler May (1995:11) noted,

> "Barren" is a term laden with historical weight. It carries negative meanings: unproductive, sterile, bare, empty, stark, deficient, lacking, wanting, destitute, devoid. It is the opposite of fertile, lavish, abounding, productive. . . . Until the mid-nineteenth century, men were believed to be fertile if they were not impotent, so "barren" women carried the blame if a married couple did not have children. The term, like the condition, suggested moral and spiritual failure, and the words like "blame," "fault" and "guilt" have been attached to childlessness ever since.

From this perspective, the desire for white children was connected to the potential for parents, especially women, to avoid the social stigma of infertility.[3] Racial matching policies were, however, not only about avoiding the social stigma of infertility. Rather, preferences and policies regarding racial matching were also about supporting social norms related to race relations. More to the point, given the tension and polarization between U.S. whites and racial-ethnic minorities (especially those between whites and blacks), adopting white children and avoiding other children was not just about masking infertility; it was also a way of managing race relations and racism. Thus, the social location and characteristics of the majority of formal–legal adopters (i.e., whites), in conjunction with the sociohistorical context, offers a more complete explanation of why white infants were more desirable (and therefore adopted) and other infants and children were considered undesirable and subsequently not adopted.

Following World War II, a number of social changes occurred in the United States, which had important ramifications for adoption policies and practices, especially in relation to the availability of healthy, white infants. Factors, such as postwar affluence as well as changes in the age, education, and occupation of "birth" parents and adoption applicants, impacted adoption trends (Carp 2002). In addition, two of the most commonly cited shifts in sociocultural norms influencing adoption in the United States are the availability of contraception and abortion as well as an increased acceptance of out-of-wedlock births (Luker 1996; May 1995; Solinger 1992). These changes drastically decreased the number of healthy, white infants available for adoption, creating an atmosphere of scarcity for "desirable" children. The imbalance in formal legal adoption between the adopters (white middle/ upper class) and the desirable child (a healthy, white infant) was such that by the 1970s a "healthy white baby" was a request deemed unrealistic by social workers (Melosh 2002:162). In light of the "context of scarcity" some parents looked for alternatives to a healthy, white infant. One alternative was to reconstruct the desirable child to include non-white children as acceptable and pursue transracial adoption. Two options for transracial adoption were racial-ethnic minority children in the United States or children born outside the United States.

Healthy, but . . .

In my interviews, most parents pointed out that a notable and unique aspect of the adoption process was the opportunity to make specific choices about the children they would adopt. In various ways, they could sort potential family members as more or less desirable by indicating what types of children they were willing to adopt.[4] As such, notions of "choices" and "choosing" were central to parents' adoption narratives and practices,[5] and parents and adoption agencies expressed a range of feelings and practices regulating the choices parents could or could not make. Most adoptive parents initially indicated resistance, or at least ambivalence, to indicating preferences for certain characteristics of children. As if given a script, the majority of parents in my sample responded to the question "When thinking about adopting a child, what was important to you?" by noting they wanted only *a healthy* child. The consistency of the response was not entirely surprising given available cultural discourses and norms that emphasize the idea of wanting a healthy child.

Parents' responses indicated that when they expressed a desire for a healthy child, part of their wish did, in fact, translate into the literal physical health of the child. For instance, Paula, a mother of two adopted children, described taking the information provided by the adoption agency to the pediatrician to interpret the child's health. She noted:

> *Part of the issue was we certainly wanted and wished [for] a child who was in good health, and what do we know, we were sent these things that were both vague or unfamiliar to us, birth weights and heights and we had no sense of how to see if that meant anything, so I think one thing we did do was go to our pediatrician with the information we had. . . .*

Her response was typical of other adoptive parents' remarks as others noted seeking advice from a physician to evaluate the health status of the child.

Thus, parents' descriptions of their search for healthy children were remarkably similar. In general, they began their search for healthy children by exploring domestic adoptions. One mother, Erin, offered:

> *We looked at domestic . . . and we thought we'd talked with just about every-body in town and we were really discouraged because [my husband] was already thirty-nine and I was thirty-six and we thought [pause] you know if we have to wait ten years, that's too, we're too old. So we were really discouraged about it.*

Notably, although parents talked about pursuing "domestic adoption," they generally pursued only one specific type of domestic adoption. For most parents, "domestic" adoptions were understood and coded almost exclusively as the search for healthy, *white* infants. One clue to decoding parents' particular understanding of domestic adoption was the time frames they cited. More specifically, the waiting time this mother and others in my sample cited was, in fact, only reflective of the waiting time for healthy, white infants in the United States. Other children in the United

States were more readily available and did not have an extensive waiting time. For instance, in my interview with Amy, she described her experience with domestic adoption, and at one point in the interview, I attempted to clarify who was included in her domestic adoption search by asking her if she and her husband had investigated children other than healthy, white infants. She responded: . . . *but as far as other nationalities here [in the United States], I don't think that even occurred to us, come to think of it.* Amy's comments reinforced the idea that adoption was not about adopting *any* child and illustrated how some children were not included in domestic adoption searches. Importantly, rather than address the issue in terms of race, Amy took up the question of nonwhite children in terms of nationalities. While it is possible that she might not have understood my question, my strong sense is that answering it using the term "nationalities" may have allowed her to verbally maneuver through contested terrain. Furthermore, Amy does not make a distinction between the health status of children from other "nationalities" (likely coded as racial-ethnic minorities) here in the United States. Instead, the undesirability of children from "other nationalities here" was not necessarily linked to their health status. Rather, their "nationality" appeared to trump their health status, as well as their age. "Nationality" was used by parents as a primary factor for sorting children as undesirable.

Amy's report of not having children from "other nationalities" in the United States on her list of potentially adoptable children was not an isolated response. Although Amy was unique in invoking a language of "nationality," the claim that it did not occur to her to consider nonwhite children was shared by half of the participants. That it did not even occur to 50 percent of the participants to consider adopting children of color was a powerful statement about how race privilege operated, since one way privilege works is to socially buffer those in privileged positions from having to be aware of or consider minorities. In addition, it illustrated strong support for the contention that even when faced with the desire to have "healthy" children (and with the knowledge that there are children more readily available for adoption in the United States), some children were not considered desirable as potential family members because of their race-ethnicity or their nationality.[6]

On many occasions, getting informants to be specific and direct about their view on racial preference was difficult because rather than specifically articulating or addressing race, parents used language that was racially coded. As Amy's comments demonstrated, for example, one way to talk about race without specifying it was to substitute "nationalities," or as discussed earlier, parents frequently used "healthy child" and "domestic adoptions" to signal the search for healthy, white infants. The language choices were likely due to convention as well as more conscious efforts to avoid the appearance of racism. Regardless, parents traded on common assumptions about who were perceived as desirable children for adoption and with what characteristics.

In fact, all but two parents—of the 73 parents in my sample—talked about domestic adoptions almost exclusively in terms of white children, as evidenced by the extensive wait times they cited. Thus, by not specifying and articulating whiteness and still finding an interpretive community that understood what was meant without being explicit about the racialized dimensions, whiteness was, in a very real sense, so normative as to be taken for granted. While some may discount this point, I think it was precisely the subtlety of the racial codes and the ability of whiteness to remain hidden and taken for granted that was so powerful. For example, in the following excerpt, Donna talked about the advice she received from an adoption agency. Consider the way Donna and the adoption agency used the term "American." She said:

> We had gone to [the adoption agency] for an American adoption. . . . But I hate to say this, but it was true, [the agency], they said, don't even try for them because they're hard to get . . . the waiting list [was] as long as it would take for an American child.

In this case, both the agency and parents had a common understanding of "American child." Her description regarding difficulties of getting an "American child" and her focus on the waiting list indicated that the agency and the parents understood the search for an "American child" as the search for a healthy, white infant.

In another example that illustrated the narrow way "American" was used, Linda stated:

> Well, we were married for several years and um, unable to have children, and we finally decided that we would adopt. [Pause] So we started with um, like every other person, I guess, thinking about adopting an American baby. You know, so we started off with [the adoption agency], and um, . . . so we knew [this adoption agency] did adoption, so we went to a meeting, [pause] and um, to adopt an American baby, at that point it was like a 7-year wait, they just, I think, [were] not readily available. So we thought well, this is not going to do, because we were not terribly young at that point, um, [pause]. So we decided that we could go with a foreign adoption.

This mother considered it normative to start with an American baby. Yet, similar to other parents, as revealed by the extensive waiting period (7 years), it was normative for this mother to investigate only certain American children (i.e., whites), since other American children (i.e., racial-ethnic minorities) were, in fact, more readily available and did not necessarily have the extensive waiting period.

In contrast to those who were vague or used coded racial language, some parents were quite clear in verbalizing their unwillingness to consider adopting a child who was African American. In sharing her recollection of the adoption process, Marlene brought up her distress about the possibility of not being able to adopt a child.

> K: And so, . . . in pursuing avenues for adoption, how did you make that transition?

> M: Um, oh boy, all I remember is for me it was very traumatic because, I was afraid that we wouldn't be able to [adopt]. Um. . . . If we wanted a

> Black or Hispanic, if we wanted a Black or Hispanic child, [we could
> adopt] which we did not, so, we ruled that out.

Marlene was fairly definitive about not wanting a Black or Hispanic child.
She did not expand her explanation and specify that she would not accept a
Black or Hispanic child who was not healthy. Instead, race (for Hispanics
and Blacks) became a master status of children waiting to be adopted, and
they were, quite literally, sorted out of the adoption process by white parents.

In the following selection, Molly, a mother of one adopted boy and one
genetically-related daughter, clearly illustrated the desire for a healthy baby,
but not a healthy African American baby. Her account highlighted the way
some children were not able to shed the stigma associated with their racial
status. She stated:

> We wanted a healthy baby, we just wanted a healthy baby and um, . . . We had
> thought briefly about an African American baby . . . and I had some reservations
> about that also because I thought we would grow up right next to a culture that
> I don't always like very well. You know, and so that would be real strange if he
> felt like he had to act like, you know, one of the boys from the hood. That would
> be hard for us.

Molly's statement was important because it offered clues about why race
was a salient factor influencing the desirability of a child for some white parents. I read Molly's explanation for not wanting an African American baby as
a comment on the way race (understood as socially created) was frequently
used as a proxy for cultural practices. In this case, race had a specific
meaning for Molly. "African American" was understood as a set of distinct
(gendered) cultural practices, i.e., acting like a "boy from the hood." Thus, it
was not simply resistance to adopting an "African American" child as such,
but resistance to adopting what "African American" was presumed to mean
and signify culturally. From Molly's perspective, African American cultural
practices were oppositional to and incompatible with white cultural practices as indicated by her statement "That would be hard for us." Some parents, like Molly, seemed to believe that racial culture was so powerful that
their child would participate in it, regardless of how the family might socialize the child. Thus, the connection between race and presumed cultural practices was so strong that for some parents, it did not appear to make a difference whether the African American child was adopted as an *"infant."*
Parents' comments indicated that socialization could not erase the propen-
sity for oppositional racial and cultural practices.

There are different ways to think about and situate her comments. On the
one hand, it is possible that the resistance to adopting African American
children (including healthy infants) was because Molly and other parents
who shared similar perspectives, were aware of and sensitive to larger
structures of racism. For instance, although she did not cite the NABSW's
(National Association of Black Social Workers') position on transracial adoption (read as whites adopting Black children), she might have been aware of
their statement. It is also possible that she (and others) anticipated ways that

race would influence her child's behavior. That is, in the face of oppression and a society structured by and through racism, the family is only one agent of socialization and perhaps they felt truly unprepared and unequipped to deal with it.

Yet her statements also revealed a personal ambivalence—for Molly, adopting an African American meant engaging and confronting a culture that she "didn't always like very well." Her feelings concerning African Americans were focused on particular aspects of African American culture and reflected common stereotypes of "hood culture." Molly and other prospective parents relied on negative racial stereotypes (and therefore, incomplete and inaccurate information) throughout the decision-making process. From this framework, her sentiments were likely magnified when she considered that this child (read: bad boy from the hood) would be in the intimate and daily setting of her family.

In contrast to Molly and Marlene, who illustrated how race activated a wholesale rejection of some African American children, another respondent, Rachel, noted that an African American baby was not desirable unless the option was no baby. The following is an excerpt from the beginning of our conversation.

K: *Did you know where you wanted to adopt from?*

R: *Well, we probably didn't, you know, think that far ahead, you know, we were, um* [pause] *the way you mean it started for Korean?*

K: *Yes.*

R: *Well, okay, plain and simple in my mind, um* [pause] *if you waited for, . . . so, hey, you know, so I think anything, we probably didn't want to go* [pause] *I,* [pause] *I don't, I shouldn't say didn't, we wanted a baby, I was going to say didn't want an African American, but you know, we didn't really, we didn't really have to, ah, I mean versus no baby, I mean, I know we would have, but I'm just saying, because my son's godfather is African American, so we don't have anything against it, but, we're just saying, I'm white. . . .*

Both the format and content of Rachel's comments are instructive for a number of reasons. First, her explanation of how she came to adopt from Korea focused on her standpoint on adopting African American children. Rachel's feelings about adopting African American children were strong enough that even without direct probing (and even though we had just met and started the interview) she still shared information that is commonly considered taboo. In addition, her comments illustrated the ways hierarchies of racial desirability were constructed as well as how unstable these notions of desirability were. More specifically, the possibility of *not* having a child was able to transform Rachel's opinion about race. Although Rachel initially had reservations about adopting an African American child, an African American child would be desirable if it was the only way to have a family with children. As she described her feelings, Rachel indicated that they may not be popular or acceptable to say. I read her pauses and self interruptions (i.e., "um") as underscoring the difficulties of being honest about and articulating such sentiments, and thus raised larger issues about what the available and acceptable ways to talk about these feelings were. For instance, offering statements like "we don't have anything against it" is a common rhetorical strategy used in deflecting perceptions of racist attitudes. Noting that the godfather of one of their children is African American also may be perceived as a way to socially buffer against accusations of being a racist. These strategies perhaps serve as a method of contemporary racial etiquette (Collins 1998; Park 1950) thus making it seem more acceptable to have these feelings, or at least make it feel safer to express these feelings.

One of the two families who talked about being open to the possibility of adopting an African American child reported that it would present problems with their extended family. One mother, Becca, recalled phoning her mother after they received news that she and her husband were matched with a child and shared her experience of telling her mother. She stated:

> So [my husband and I] decided to tell our parents, so, we called up all excited that we were gonna be adopting, and [my mother] said after a dead silence, "Is the baby Black?" Interesting reaction. [Pause] And we said, "No," and [my mother] said, "That's fine."

In this mother's adoption experience, the issue of race dominated the interaction with her biological family. For the soon-to-be grandmother, race was framed as a binary: Black and not Black. Knowing the child was not Black appeared to be sufficient for accepting the child.

International: Why Korea?

> It was quick, it was easy, and they were Oriental, I mean that seemed like a nice thing. . . .

In deciding that "domestic" adoptions were not a viable option because of the lengthy waiting period for healthy, white infants coupled with resistance to adopting African American children whether or not they were healthy infants or other special needs children, parents shifted their attention to intercountry adoptions. Historically, Korea has been an important sending country of children for adoption, and during the 1980s, it was by far, the largest sending country. Yet, Korea has never been the sole country available to parents. Given the choices for intercountry adoption, why were children from Korea perceived and sorted as desirable?

A range of pragmatic factors influenced parental decisions to adopt from Korea. Since each sending country, as well as each adoption agency, constructed (un)desirable parents differently, participants said that Korea was an attractive country to adopt from because they met the eligibility requirements and were considered desirable parents. In addition, Korea met many of the other factors parents felt were important. Adopting a healthy infant was possible in a short period of time, it was generally convenient (e.g., parents were not required to travel to Korea), and parents felt that when adopting from Korea they were working with a well-established program.

Moreover, while all of these aspects were relevant to parents, as the quotation that opens this section states, unlike sentiments parents expressed about Black children, the racial status of a child from Korea was seen as a "nice thing." While some parents initially indicated ambivalence or trepidation about adopting a child from Korea, each of the parents came to view children from Korea as desirable. One way of explaining this change is that some contemporary stereotypes of Asians make Asian children seem more compatible with white, middle-class culture. For example, stereotypes of Asians as the model minority (Kibria 2002; Min 1995) or as "Honorary Whites" (Bonilla-Silva 2004; Tuan 1998) likely promote Asians, especially Asian females, as less oppositional and more compatible to whites than other racial-ethnic minorities.

In fact, most parents expressed fairly positive attitudes about the racial status and characteristics of children adopted from Korea. Kara, for example, did not recall investigating countries other than Korea. She shared:

> . . . *we never really looked at others, no, um, there, you know, there was something about the Asian culture, I don't know what it is, you know. I hate to sound hokey but um, there's something that, I don't know. [Pause] I remember one time [my husband] and I went out to dinner and we saw this family, mother, father and ah, a little Korean girl, she was only about 10 and we were just watching, and we just like couldn't take our eyes off her, you know? And we didn't want to stare but, you know, it's just, it just gave us a good feeling.*

Thus, Kara felt positively about Asian culture, and seeing another Korean child before she adopted gave her a good feeling about Korean features.

Molly also expressed enthusiasm regarding the physical characteristics of children adopted from Korea. After describing a meeting with a social worker who worked with Korean adoptions, Molly emphatically stated:

> *So you know, [my husband and I said], "Oh, the babies are beautiful!" We saw the babies and they had pictures of all these little toddlers, and they were so pretty.*

Amy echoed Molly's positive sentiments. At one point in our conversation, I asked her to expand on the process of adopting from Korea.

> K: *So how did you come up with Korea?*
>
> A: *Well, you know, that's a good question. My husband, I think [pause] thought of that idea because he thinks Asian people are beautiful, and they are beautiful . . . so he, I think he came up with that. He was kind of drawn to that.*

In Amy's and Molly's opinions, Asian babies were physically attractive, and thus, one nice thing about adopting children from Korea was the appeal of their physical characteristics.

In contrast to the examples above, Lois, a mother of an adopted son and daughter (both from Korea) noted that it was not necessarily anything about the racial status of Asians in particular that she was attracted to. Unlike Amy and Molly, Lois did not focus on the beauty of Asian babies. Rather, for her, there came a point where having a baby that physically resembled them in terms of race became secondary. She stated:

> [We] had contacted our attorney, actually, um, [pause] who had done a lot of adoptions and asked him, you know, what avenue, which avenues he thought would be best. And he sort of [pause] told us about a few different things, be-cause at this point we also were looking at a time frame where we didn't want to wait another 7 years, [pause] it wasn't important to us, to, to have [pause] um, [pause] a, you know, [pause] Caucasian baby that looks similar to us, or, or whatever, so [pause] so I contacted all these different agencies and asked them to send some information.

Lois' comments were instructive because they suggested that whiteness was pivotal to her decision-making process. Similar to other respondents, it was only in the face of a substantial wait time for healthy, white infants that the idea of having a baby that looks similar (i.e., racial matching) became less important for her.

While Lois' description indicated that it was "not important" to have a Caucasian baby, her description of the adoption process still points to an important tension. As previously discussed, there were children available in the United States who did not have an extended waiting period (i.e., Black and Latino infants). Yet, Black children and infants of color who were more readily available would not look like them, especially in terms of racial matching. Although I do not have specific evidence from this mother, one interpretation might be that even though it was not important to have a baby that looked similar, it was important that the child not look *too different*. More specifically, while Asian children might not provide an exact match, Asians might signal an acceptable amount of racial-ethnic difference. Additionally, the racial-ethnic differences may be perceived as compatible (and perhaps comple-mentary to) whiteness, especially within a framework of viewing Asians as "Honorary Whites." For instance, in an ironic twist, at different moments, some parents noted that they thought their adoptive kids looked like them. For example, Shelby described telling others about the physical features she felt were similar between her and her son. She stated: *What we used to say to people when [my son came], and we still do, "I think he has my straight hair and his father's brown eyes." So we tell him he looks like us too.* These cases may suggest that it is not just the racial status of Asians that is considered a "nice thing," but that parents needed to feel like they could make connections with their children about how similar they look. For instance, Holly pointed out that her daughters initiated comments about the physical similarities. She re-called her daughters saying: *Mommy, aren't we starting to look more like you?* Another mother, Ellen, commenting on her age and the fact that she was starting to color her hair and consequently every month it was a different color, noted how much she liked her daughter's hair. She stated: *I have always strived to have the same color as [my daughter]. I want to have the same color hair as her.* While talking about physical similarities between parents and children is not exclusive to families who adopt, such conversations do take on particular significance in adoption, especially in the context of race and racial dynamics. In light of racism, white parents adopting children from Korea might be understood as a way of avoiding direct engagement with racial dynamics that feel oppositional and, instead, engaging with parts that feel more comfortable. As illustrated by this mother's comments, in some cases, it may be more than merely comfort—it could be envy and admiration for certain characteristics like her daughter's hair.[7]

Discussion

This reading explored the ways adoptive parents used various characteristics to sort children as desirable or undesirable. While parents generally began their explanations by framing their responses such that having a healthy child was paramount, health was not necessarily the most important characteristic that shaped decisions about who parents would adopt. Instead, other factors, most notably, race, appeared to be significant, although at times it remained "unmarked" or racially coded. For Asians, specifically those from Korea, racial stereotypes appeared to act as a resource, which allowed them to be sorted as desirable potential family members in transracial adoptions. Conversely, for African Americans, race became their master status and, as signaled by the title of this piece, they were quite literally sorted out of the adoption process. As such, my data on adoption indicate support for Bonilla-Silva's (2004) contention that a system of tri-racialization is at work in the United States.

Studying adoption in general, and transracial, intercountry adoptions in particular, is sociologically relevant for a number of reasons. For one, written within constructions of racial desirability are constructions of undesirability. As such, racial-ethnic hierarchies (and at times binaries) are produced in which the desirable and the preferable child is understood and constructed in direct relation to the undesirable child (i.e., knowing who and what is desirable offers clues about what is undesirable and vice versa).

Additionally, interpretations and constructions of racial and gender desirability are, in large part, contingent upon and reflective of the preferences of the adopters. While parents' preferences for certain children might be framed as matters of individual choice and personal taste, focusing on their choices as merely individual preferences or private decisions leaves issues of larger social structures, such as racism and white privilege, unchallenged.[8] It is critical to realize that individual choices and preferences are inextricably linked and indeed embedded in broader social, cultural, and historical contexts—families and adoption do not occur outside of or independent from other sociohistorical forces. Thus, in terms of racial-ethnic preferences, parental decisions and inclinations for whites and Asians, and an avoidance of adopting Blacks and Latinos, can (and should) be understood within larger sociohistorical contexts and processes. In short, the issues, questions, and struggles adoptive parents described are significant not only because of the constructions of desirability themselves (i.e., which children are perceived as adoptable and which children are actually (not) adopted), but given historical and current social inequalities, these issues also contribute to our understanding of the ways privilege, especially parents' racial privilege, operates and, at certain moments, perpetuates social inequalities.

Finally, while one way of interpreting parents' accounts and standpoints is to view parents who would not adopt (or who showed hesitancy toward adopting) Black and Latino children as racist, those who were willing to adopt children of color as not racist, such a binary is weak and much too simplistic. Indeed, it is more complicated and complex than this statement. Certainly, those who (more openly) expressed hostility and ambivalence toward adopting Black children reflected and perpetuated racist ideologies. But those who were willing to adopt nonwhites also operated and were embedded in sociohistorical forces that were deeply implicated in racist ideologies and practices. Thus, openness to adopting a racial-ethnic minority, and a Black child in particular, does not mean adoptive parents have not absorbed and subscribed to other pieces of racism in the culture.

ENDNOTES

[1]The one exception to this was a father who identified himself as second-generation Chinese.

[2]I highlight the "formal legal" aspect of this process in an effort to address common assumptions and misperceptions that African Americans do not adopt or do not want to adopt. It is important to note that alternatives to the formal legal channels have been established and utilized by African Americans but have not been recognized as legitimate adoptions by the legal system. Often labeled "kinship adoptions" (Hill 1977; Stack 1974), these have been an important and integral part of African American family life, especially in light of persistent structural challenges (such as poverty) and oppression. In addition, current scholarship indicates that African Americans are just as likely to adopt as whites. One way to interpret the lack of parity in adoptions, then, is to revisit Joyce Ladner's (1977) assertion: "The fact that adoption agencies do not carry out a brisk business in placing children in black homes should not be used as documentation for the myth that blacks do not adopt. It is probably more reasonable to examine the effectiveness of agencies in locating and recruiting black adoptive parents" (p. 68). Part of a larger research project could indeed expand on this idea.

[3]Racial matching also allowed parents a degree of freedom in "hiding" the adoption from their child. In fact, until recently, concealing adoptions from children was not uncommon and was even advocated by some parents and professionals. For further discussion of secrecy and disclosure issues, see Grotevant and McRoy 1997; Carp 1998; and Baran, Reuben, and Sorosky 1997.

[4]In some cases, adoptive parents were required to choose or reject the actual children.

[5]The attention to the ways parents who adopt make "choices" often obscures and/or ignores the range of choices that parents who have genetically-related children make as well, e.g., who their partners or spouses are (their race-ethnicity, body type, etc.).

[6]Moreover, this highlights an important tension, since Amy's family, as well as that of others in this study, included children adopted from Korea. Her description revealed a common pattern—attention to other nationalities was directed toward Korea, not "other nationalities here," in the United States.

[7]Significantly, given cultural scripts, it is difficult to imagine substituting African American in this situation.

[8]As I write this conclusion, there is a small movement trying to bring awareness to the disparity in adoption fees for babies of different races. One U.S. ad campaign has a picture of three

infants, one white, one Black, and one who is a racial-ethnic minority with skin coloring in between the white and Black infants. Across each of the infants is their "value"—the white child has $35,000, the Black child has $4,000, and the child with the skin coloring in between the white and Black infants says $10,000.

REFERENCES

Baran, Annette, P. Reuben, and A. Sorosky. 1997. "Open Adoption." *Social Work* 21(2):97–100.

Bonilla-Silva, Eduardo. 2004. "From Bi-Racial to Tri-Racial: Towards a New System of Racial Stratification in the USA." *Ethnic and Racial Studies* 27(6):931–50.

Carp, Wayne E., ed. 1998. *Family Matters: Secrecy and Disclosure in the History of Adoption.* Cambridge: Harvard University Press.

———, ed. 2002. *Adoption in America: Historical Perspectives.* Ann Arbor: University of Michigan Press.

Collins, Patricia Hill. 1998. *Fighting Words: Black Women and the Search for Justice.* Minneapolis: University of Minnesota Press.

Grotevant, Harold and R. McRoy. 1997. "The Minnesota/Texas Adoption Research Project: Implications of Openness in Adoption for Development and Relationship." *Applied Developmental Science* 1(4):168–87.

Hill, Robert. 1977. *Informal Adoption among Black Families.* Washington, DC: National Urban League Research Department.

Kibria, Nazli. 2002. *Becoming Asian American: Second-Generation Chinese and Korean American Identities.* Baltimore: Johns Hopkins University Press.

Ladner, Joyce. 1977. *Mixed Families: Adopting across Racial Boundaries.* New York: Anchor Press/Doubleday.

Luker, Kristin. 1996. *Dubious Conceptions: The Politics of Teenage Pregnancy.* Cambridge: Harvard University Press.

May, Elaine Tyler. 1995. *Barren in the Promised Land: Childless Americans and the Pursuit of Happiness.* Boston: Harvard University Press.

Melosh, Barbara. 2002. *Strangers and Kin: The American Way of Adoption.* Cambridge: Harvard University Press.

Min, Pyong Gap. 1995. "Major Issues Relating to Asian American Experiences." In *Asian Americans: Contemporary Trends and Issues (1st ed.),* edited by Pyong Gap Min. Thousand Oaks: Sage.

Park, Robert. 1950. *Race and Culture.* Glencoe: Free Press.

Roberts, Dorothy. 1997. *Killing the Black Body: Race, Reproduction and the Meaning of Liberty.* New York: Pantheon.

Solinger, Rickie. 1992. "Race and 'Value': Black and White Illegitimate Babies, in the U.S., 1945–1965." In *Unequal Sisters: A Multicultural Reader in U.S. Women's History,* edited by Vicki L. Ruiz and Ellen Carol Dubois. New York: Routledge.

———. 1992. *Wake Up Little Susie: Single Pregnancy and Race before Roe v. Wade.* New York: Routledge.

Stack, Carol. 1974. *All Our Kin.* New York: Basic Books.

Tuan, Mia. 1998. *Forever Foreigners or Honorary Whites? The Asian Ethnic Experience Today.* New Brunswick, NJ: Rutgers University Press.

34
_____

YEARNING FOR LIGHTNESS
Transnational Circuits in the Marketing and Consumption of Skin Lighteners

EVELYN NAKANO GLENN

When sociologists study culture, we often distinguish between the material and nonmaterial aspects of culture. For example, *material aspects of culture* include religious artifacts, dress, dance and music forms, beauty styles, and other objects. *Nonmaterial aspects of culture* are things like belief systems, ideas, values, and social norms. One aspect of material culture that has received a lot of attention recently in the United States is the beauty culture. Much of this research focus has been on how women are harmed by the dominant beauty ideal in terms of eating disorders, cosmetic surgery, and expensive consumption of clothing and makeup. What scholarship currently demonstrates is that this gender inequality is also classed and raced: Women of different social classes and racial-ethnic groups are adversely impacted. In the selection excerpted below, Evelyn Nakano Glenn, a professor of women's studies and ethnic studies at the University of California at Berkeley, examines how the racial and gender stereotypes of the dominant U.S. culture influences global standards of beauty. Specifically, Glenn examines the skin lightening products that are marketed to women around the world who are trying to alter their appearance in order to look more Caucasian and conform to the racialized beauty norms of Western culture.

With the breakdown of traditional racial categories in many areas of the world, colorism, by which I mean the preference for and privileging of lighter skin and discrimination against those with darker skin, remains a persisting frontier of intergroup and intragroup relations in the twenty-first century. Sociologists and anthropologists have documented discrimination against darker-skinned persons and correlations between skin tone and socioeconomic status and achievement in Brazil and the United States (Hunter 2005; Sheriff 2001; Telles 2004). Other researchers have revealed that people's judgments about other people are literally colored by skin tone, so that darker-skinned individuals are viewed as less intelligent, trustworthy, and attractive than their lighter-skinned counterparts (Herring, Keith, and Horton 2003; Hunter 2005; Maddox 2004).

One way of conceptualizing skin color, then, is as a form of symbolic capital that affects, if not determines, one's life chances. The relation between skin color and judgments about attractiveness affect women most acutely, since women's worth is judged heavily on the basis of appearance. For example, men who have wealth, education, and other forms of human capital are considered "good catches," while women who are physically attractive may be considered desirable despite the lack of other capital. Although skin tone is usually seen as a form of fixed or unchangeable capital, in fact, men and women may attempt to acquire light-skinned privilege. Sometimes this search takes the form of seeking light-skinned marital partners to raise one's status and to achieve intergenerational mobility by increasing the likelihood of having light-skinned children. Often, especially for women, this search takes the form of using cosmetics or other treatments to change the appearance of one's skin to make it look lighter.

This article focuses on the practice of skin lightening, the marketing of skin lighteners in various societies around the world, and the multinational corporations that are involved in the global skin-lightening trade. An analysis of this complex topic calls for a multilevel approach. First, we need to place the production, marketing, and consumption of skin lighteners into a global political-economic context. I ask, How is skin lightening interwoven into the world economic system and its transnational circuits of products, capital, culture, and people? Second, we need to examine the mediating entities and processes by which skin lighteners reach specific national/ethnic/racial/class consumers. I ask, What are the media and messages, cultural themes and symbols, used to create the desire for skin-lightening products among particular groups? Finally, we need to examine the meaning and significance of skin color for consumers of skin lighteners. I ask, How do consumers learn about, test, and compare skin-lightening products, and what do they seek to achieve through their use?

The issue of skin lightening may seem trivial at first glance. However, it is my contention that a close examination of the global circuits of skin lightening provides a unique lens through which to view the workings of the Western-dominated global system as it simultaneously promulgates a "white is right" ideology while also promoting the desire for and consumption of Western culture and products.

Skin Lightening and Global Capital

Skin lightening has long been practiced in many parts of the world. Women concocted their own treatments or purchased products from self-styled beauty experts offering special creams, soaps, or lotions, which were either ineffective sham products or else effective but containing highly toxic materials such as mercury or lead. From the perspective of the supposedly enlightened present, skin lightening might be viewed as a form of vanity or a misguided and dangerous relic of the past.

However, at the beginning of the twenty-first century, the search for light skin, free of imperfections such as freckles and age spots, has actually accelerated, and the market for skin-lightening products has mushroomed in all parts of the world. The production and marketing of products that offer the prospect of lighter, brighter, whiter skin has become a multibillion-dollar global industry. Skin lightening has been incorporated into transnational flows of capital, goods, people, and culture. It is implicated in both the formal global economy and various informal economies. It is integrated into both legal and extralegal transnational circuits of goods. Certain large multinational corporations have become major players, spending vast sums on research and development and on advertising and marketing to reach both mass and specialized markets. Simultaneously, actors in informal or underground economies, including smugglers, transnational migrants, and petty traders, are finding unprecedented opportunities in producing, transporting, and selling unregulated lightening products.

One reason for this complex multifaceted structure is that the market for skin lighteners, although global in scope, is also highly decentralized and segmented along socioeconomic, age, national, ethnic, racial, and cultural lines. Whether the manufacturers are multibillion-dollar corporations or small entrepreneurs, they make separate product lines and use distinct marketing strategies to reach specific segments of consumers. Ethnic companies and entrepreneurs may be best positioned to draw on local cultural themes, but large multinationals can draw on local experts to tailor advertising images and messages to appeal to particular audiences.

The Internet has become a major tool/highway/engine for the globalized, segmented, lightening market. It is the site where all of the players in the global lightening market meet. Large multinationals, small local firms, individual entrepreneurs, skin doctors, direct sales merchants, and even eBay sellers use the Internet to disseminate the ideal of light skin and to advertise and sell their products. Consumers go on the Internet to do research on products and shop. Some also participate in Internet message boards and forums to seek advice and to discuss, debate, and rate skin lighteners. There are many such forums, often as part of transnational ethnic Web sites. For example, IndiaParenting.com and sukh-dukh.com, designed for South Asians in India and other parts of the world, have chat rooms on skin care and lightening, and Rexinteractive.com, a Filipino site, and Candymag.com, a site sponsored by a magazine for Filipina teens, have extensive forums on skin lightening. The discussions on these forums provide a window through which to view the meaning of skin color to consumers, their desires and anxieties, doubts and aspirations. The Internet is thus an important site from which one can gain a multilevel perspective on skin lightening.

Consumer Groups and Market Niches

Africa and African Diaspora

In Southern Africa, colorism is just one of the negative inheritances of European colonialism. The ideology of white supremacy that European colonists brought included the association of Blackness with primitiveness, lack of civilization, unrestrained sexuality, pollution, and dirt. The association of Blackness with dirt can be seen in a 1930 French advertising poster for Dirtoff. The poster shows a drawing of a dark African man washing his hands, which have become white, as he declares, "Le Savon Dirtoff me blanchit!" The soap was designed not for use by Africans but, as the poster notes, *pour mécaniciens, automobilistes, et ménagères*—French auto mechanics and housewives. Such images showing Black people "dramatically losing their pigmentation as a result of the cleansing process," were common in late nineteenth- and early twentieth-century soap advertisements, according to art historian Jean Michel Massing (1995:180).

Some historians and anthropologists have argued that precolonial African conceptions of female beauty favored women with light brown, yellow, or reddish tints. If so, the racial hierarchies established in areas colonized by Europeans cemented and generalized the privilege attached to light skin (Burke 1996; Ribane 2006:12). In both South Africa and Rhodesia/Zimbabwe, an intermediate category of those considered to be racially mixed was classified as "coloured" and subjected to fewer legislative restrictions than those classified as "native." Assignment to the coloured category was based on ill-defined criteria, and on arrival in urban areas, people found themselves classified as native or coloured on the basis of skin tone and other phenotypic characteristics. Indians arriving in Rhodesia from Goa, for example, were variously classified as "Portuguese Mulatto" or coloured. The multiplication of discriminatory laws targeting natives led to a growing number of Blacks claiming to be coloured in both societies (Muzondidya 2005:23–24).

The use of skin lighteners has a long history in Southern Africa, which is described by Lynn Thomas and which I will not recount here (in press). Rather, I will discuss the current picture, which shows both a rise in the consumption of skin-lightening products and concerted efforts to curtail the trade of such products. Despite bans on the importation of skin lighteners, the widespread use of these products currently constitutes a serious health issue in Southern Africa because the products often contain mercury, corticosteroids, or high doses of hydroquinone. Mercury of course is highly toxic, and sustained exposure can lead to neurological damage and kidney disease. Hydroquinone (originally an industrial chemical) is effective in suppressing melanin production, but exposure to the sun—hard to avoid in Africa—damages skin that has been treated. Furthermore, in dark-skinned people, long-term hydroquinone use can lead to ochronosis, a disfiguring condition involving gray and blue-black discoloration of the skin (Mahe, Ly, and Dangou 2003). The overuse of topical steroids can lead to contact eczema, bacterial and fungal infection, Cushing's syndrome, and skin atrophy (Margulies n.d.; Ntambwe 2004). . . .

As a result of the serious health effects, medical researchers have conducted interview studies to determine how prevalent the practice of skin lightening is among African women. They estimate that 25 percent of women in Bamaki, Mali; 35 percent in Pretoria, South Africa; and 52 percent in Dakar, Senegal, use skin lighteners, as do an astonishing 77 percent of women traders in Lagos, Nigeria (Adebajo 2002; del Guidice and Yves 2002; Mahe, Ly, and Dangou 2003; Malangu and Ogubanjo 2006).

There have been local and transnational campaigns to stop the manufacture of products containing mercury in the EU and efforts to inform African consumers of the dangers of their use and to foster the idea of Black pride. Governments in South Africa, Zimbabwe, Nigeria, and Kenya have banned the import and sale of mercury and hydroquinone products, but they continue to be smuggled in from other African nations (Dooley 2001; Thomas 2004).

Despite these efforts, the use of skin lighteners has been increasing among modernized and cosmopolitan African women. A South African newspaper reported that whereas in the 1970s, typical skin lightener users in South Africa were rural and poor, currently, it is upwardly mobile Black women, those with technical diplomas or university degrees and well-paid jobs, who are driving the market in skin lighteners. A recent study by Mictert Marketing Research found that 1 in 13 upwardly mobile Black women aged 25 to 35 used skin lighteners. It is possible that this is an underestimation, since there is some shame attached to admitting to using skin lighteners (Ntshingila 2005).

These upwardly mobile women turn to expensive imported products from India and Europe rather than cheaper, locally made products. They also go to doctors to get prescriptions for imported lighteners containing corticosteroids, which are intended for short-term use to treat blemishes. They continue using them for long periods beyond the prescribed duration, thus risking damage (Ntshingila 2005). This recent rise in the use of skin lighteners cannot be seen as simply a legacy of colonialism but rather is a consequence of the penetration of multinational capital and Western consumer culture. The practice therefore is likely to continue to increase as the influence of these forces grows.

African America

Color consciousness in the African American community has generally been viewed as a legacy of slavery, under which mulattos, the offspring of white men and slave women, were accorded better treatment than "pure" Africans. While slave owners considered dark-skinned Africans suited to fieldwork, lighter-skinned mulattos were thought to be more intelligent and better suited for indoor work as servants and artisans. Mulattos were also more likely to receive at least rudimentary education and to be manumitted. They went on to form the nucleus of many nineteenth-century free Black communities. After the Civil War, light-skinned mulattos tried to distance themselves from their darker-skinned brothers and sisters, forming exclusive civic and cultural organizations, fraternities, sororities, schools, and universities (Russell, Wilson, and Hall 1992:24–40). According to Audrey Elisa Kerr, common folklore in the African American community holds that elite African Americans used a "paper bag" test to screen guests at social events and to determine eligibility for membership in their organizations: anyone whose skin was darker than the color of the bag was excluded. Although perhaps apocryphal, the widespread acceptance of the story as historical fact is significant. It has been credible to African Americans because it was consonant with their observations of the skin tone of elite African American society (Kerr 2005).

The preference and desire for light skin can also be detected in the long-time practice of skin lightening. References to African American women using powders and skin bleaches appeared in the Black press as early as the 1850s, according to historian Kathy Peiss (1998). . . .

Currently, a plethora of brands is marketed especially to African Americans, including Black and White Cream, Nadolina (sans mercury), Ambi, Palmer's, DR Daggett and Remsdell (fade cream and facial brightening cream), Swiss Whitening Pills, Ultra Glow, Skin Success, Avre (which produces the Pallid Skin Lightening System and B-Lite Fade Cream), and Clear Essence (which targets women of color more generally). Some of these products contain hydroquinone, while others claim to use natural ingredients.

Discussions of skin lightening on African American Internet forums indicate that the participants seek not white skin but "light" skin like that of African American celebrities such as film actress Halle Berry and singer Beyonce Knowles. Most women say they want to be two or three shades lighter or to get rid of dark spots and freckles to even out their skin tones, something that many skin lighteners claim to do. Some of the writers believe that Halle Berry and other African American celebrities have achieved their luminescent appearance through skin bleaching, skillful use of cosmetics, and artful lighting. Thus, some skin-lightening products, such as the Pallid Skin Lightening System, purport to offer the "secret" of the stars. A Web site for Swiss Lightening Pills claims that "for many years Hollywood has been keeping the secret of whitening pills" and asks, rhetorically, "Have you wondered why early childhood photos of many top celebs show a much darker skin colour than they have now?"[1]

India and Indian Diaspora

As in the case of Africa, the origins of colorism in India are obscure, and the issue of whether there was a privileging of light skin in precolonial Indian societies is far from settled. Colonial-era and postcolonial Indian writings on the issue may themselves have been influenced by European notions of caste, culture, and race. Many of these writings expound on a racial distinction between lighter-skinned Aryans, who migrated into India from the North and darker-skinned "indigenous" Dravidians of the South. The wide range of skin color from North to South and the variation in skin tone within castes make it hard to correlate light skin with high caste. The most direct connection between skin color and social status could be found in the paler hue of those whose position and wealth enabled them to spend their lives sheltered indoors, compared to the darker hue of those who toiled outdoors in the sun (Khan 2008). . . .

Regardless of the origins of color consciousness in India, the preference for light skin seems almost universal today, and in terms of sheer numbers, India and Indian diasporic communities around the world constitute the largest market for skin lighteners. The major consumers of these products in South Asian communities are women between the ages of 16 and 35. On transnational South Asian blog sites, women describing themselves as "dark" or "wheatish" in color state a desire to be "fair." Somewhat older women seek to reclaim their youthful skin color, describing themselves as having gotten darker over time. Younger women tend to be concerned about looking light to make a good marital match or to appear lighter for large family events, including their own weddings. These women recognize the reality that light skin constitutes valuable symbolic capital in the marriage market (Views on Article n.d.). . . .

Many Indian women use traditional homemade preparations made of plant and fruit products. On various blog sites for Indians both in South Asia and diasporic communities in North America, the Caribbean, and the United Kingdom, women seek advice about "natural" preparations and trade recipes. Many commercial products are made by Indian companies and marketed to Indians around the globe under such names as "fairness cream," "herbal bleach cream," "whitening cream," and "fairness cold cream." Many of these products claim to be based on ayurvedic medicine and contain herbal and fruit extracts such as saffron, papaya, almonds, and lentils (Runkle 2004).

With economic liberalization in 1991, the number of products available on the Indian market, including cosmetics and skin care products, has mushroomed. Whereas prior to 1991, Indian consumers had the choice of two brands of cold cream and moisturizers, today, they have scores of products from which to select. With deregulation of imports, the rise of the Indian economy, and growth of the urban middle class, multinational companies see India as a prime target for expansion, especially in the area of personal care products. The multinationals, through regional subsidiaries, have developed many whitening product lines in various price ranges that target markets ranging from rural villagers to white-collar urban dwellers and affluent professionals and managers (Runkle 2005).

Southeast Asia: The Philippines

Because of its history as a colonial dependency first of Spain and then of the United States, the Philippines has been particularly affected by Western ideology and culture, both of which valorize whiteness. Moreover, frequent intermarriage among indigenous populations, Spanish colonists, and Chinese settlers has resulted in a substantially mestizo population that ranges widely on the skin color spectrum. The business and political elites have tended to be disproportionately light skinned with visible Hispanic and/or Chinese appearance. In the contemporary period, economic integration has led to the collapse of traditional means of livelihood, resulting in large-scale emigration by both working-class and middle-class Filipinos to seek better-paying jobs in the Middle East, Asia, Europe, and North America. An estimated 10 million Filipinos were working abroad as of 2004, with more than a million departing each year. Because of the demand for domestic workers, nannies, and care workers in the global North, women make up more than half of those working abroad (Tabbada 2006). . . .

Perhaps not surprising, interest in skin lightening seems to be huge and growing in the Philippines, especially among younger urban women. Synovate, a market research firm, reported that in 2004, 50 percent of respondents in the Philippines reported currently using skin lightener (Synovate 2004). Young Filipinas participate in several Internet sites seeking advice on lightening products. They seek not only to lighten their skin over-all but also to deal with dark underarms, elbows, and knees. Judging by their entries in Internet discussion sites, many teens are quite obsessed with finding "the secret" to lighter skin and have purchased and tried scores of different brands of creams and pills. They are disappointed to find that these products may have some temporary effects but do not lead to permanent change. They discuss products made in the Philippines but are most interested in products made by large European and American multinational cosmetic firms and Japanese and Korean companies. Clearly, these young Filipinas associate light skin with modernity and social mobility. Interesting to note, the young Filipinas do not refer to Americans or Europeans as having the most desir-able skin color. They are more apt to look to Japanese and Koreans or to Spanish- or Chinese-appearing (and light-skinned) Filipina celebrities, such Michelle Reis, Sharon Kuneta, or Claudine Baretto, as their ideals.[2]

The notion that Japanese and Korean women represent ideal Asian beauty has fostered a brisk market in skin lighteners that are formulated by Korean and Japanese companies. Asian White Skin and its sister company Yumei Misei, headquartered in Korea, sell Japanese and Korean skin care products in the Philippines both in retail outlets and online. Products include Asianwhiteskin Underarm Whitening Kit, Japanese Whitening Cream Enzyme Q-10, Japan Whitening Fruit Cream, Kang Tian Sheep Placenta Whitening Capsules, and Kyusoku Bhaku Lightening Pills (see http://yumeimise.com/store/index).

East Asia: Japan, China, and Korea

East Asian societies have historically idealized light or even white skin for women. Intage (2001), a market research firm in Japan, puts it, "Japan has long idolized ivory-like skin that is 'like a boiled egg'—soft, white and smooth on the surface." Indeed, prior to the Meiji Period (starting in the 1860s), men and women of the higher classes wore white-lead powder makeup (along with blackened teeth and shaved eyebrows). With modern-ization, according to Mikiko Ashikari, men completely abandoned makeup, but middle- and upper-class women continued to wear traditional white-lead powder when dressed in formal kimonos for ceremonial occasions, such as marriages, and adopted light-colored modern face powder to wear with Western clothes. Ashikari finds through observations of 777 women at sev-eral sites in Osaka during 1996–1997 that 97.4 percent of women in public wore what she calls "white face," that is, makeup that "makes their faces look whiter than they really are" (2003:3).

Intage (2001) reports that skin care products, moisturizers, face masks, and skin lighteners account for 66 percent of the cosmetics market in Japan. A perusal of displays of Japanese cosmetics and skin care products shows that most, even those not explicitly stated to be whitening products, carry names that contain the word "white," for example, facial masks labeled

"Clear Turn White" or "Pure White." In addition, numerous products are marketed specifically as whiteners. All of the leading Japanese firms in the cosmetics field, Shiseido, Kosa, Kanebo, and Pola, offer multiproduct skin-whitening lines, with names such as "White Lucent" and "Whitissimo." Fytokem, a Canadian company that produces ingredients used in skin-whitening products, reports that Japan's market in skin lighteners topped $5 billion in 1999 (Saskatchewan Business Unlimited 2005). With deregulation of imports, leading multinational firms, such as L'Oreal, have also made large inroads in the Japanese market. French products have a special cachet (Exhibitor Info 2006).

While the Japanese market has been the largest, its growth rate is much lower than those of Korea and China. Korea's cosmetic market has been growing at a 10 percent rate per year while that of China has been growing by 20 percent. Fytokem estimates that the market for skin whiteners in China was worth $1 billion in 2002 and was projected to grow tremendously. A 2007 Nielsen global survey found that 46 percent of Chinese, 47 percent of people in Hong Kong, 46 percent of Taiwanese, 29 percent of Koreans, and 24 percent of Japanese had used a skin lightener in the past year. As to regular users, 30 percent of Chinese, 20 percent of Taiwanese, 18 percent of Japanese and Hong Kongers, and 8 percent of Koreans used them weekly or daily. However, if money were no object, 52 percent of Koreans said they would spend more on skin lightening, compared to 26 percent of Chinese, 23 percent of Hong Kongers and Taiwanese, and 21 percent of Japanese (Nielsen 2007).

Latin America: Mexico and the Mexican Diaspora

Throughout Latin America, skin tone is a major marker of status and a form of symbolic capital, despite national ideologies of racial democracy. In some countries, such as Brazil, where there was African chattel slavery and extensive miscegenation, there is considerable color consciousness along with an elaborate vocabulary to refer to varying shades of skin. In other countries, such as Mexico, the main intermixture was between Spanish colonists and indigenous peoples, along with an unacknowledged admixture with African slaves. *Mestizaje* is the official national ideal. The Mexican concept of mestizaje meant that through racial and ethnic mixture, Mexico would gradually be peopled by a whiter "cosmic race" that surpassed its initial ingredients. Nonetheless, skin tone, along with other phenotypical traits, is a significant marker of social status, with lightness signifying purity and beauty and darkness signifying contamination and ugliness (Stepan 1991:135). The elite has remained overwhelmingly light skinned and European appearing while rural poor are predominantly dark skinned and Indigenous appearing.

Ethnographic studies of Mexican communities in Mexico City and Michoacan found residents to be highly color conscious, with darker-skinned family members likely to be ridiculed or teased. The first question that a relative often poses about a newborn is about his or her color

(Farr 2006, chap. 5; Guttman 1996:40; Martinez 2001). Thus, it should not be a surprise that individuals pursue various strategies to attain light-skinned identity and privileges. Migration from rural areas to the city or to the United States has been one route to transformation from an Indian to a mestizo identity or from a mestizo to a more cosmopolitan urban identity; another strategy has been lightening one's family line through marriage with a lighter-skinned partner. A third strategy has been to use lighteners to change the appearance of one's skin (Winders, Jones, and Higgins 2005:77–78).

In one of the few references to skin whitening in Mexico, Alan Knight claims that it was "an ancient practice . . . reinforced by film, television, and advertising stereotypes" (1990:100). As in Africa, consumers seeking low-cost lighteners can easily purchase mercury-laden creams that are still manufactured and used in parts of Latin America (e.g., Recetas de la Farmacia–Crema Blanqueadora, manufactured in the Dominican Republic, contains 6000 ppm of mercury) (NYC Health Dept. 2005). The use of these products has come to public attention because of their use by Latino immigrants in the United States. Outbreaks of mercury poisoning have been reported in Texas, New Mexico, Arizona, and California among immigrants who used Mexican–manufactured creams such as Crema de Belleza-Manning. The cream is manufactured in Mexico by Laboratories Vide Natural SA de CV., Tampico, Tamaulipas, and is distributed primarily in Mexico. However, it has been found for sale in shops and flea markets in the United States in areas located along the U.S.-Mexican border in Arizona, California, New Mexico, and Texas. The label lists the ingredient calomel, which is mercurous chloride (a salt of mercury). Product samples have been found to contain 6 to 10 percent mercury by weight (Centers for Disease Control 1996; U.S. Food and Drug Administration 1996).

For high-end products, hydroquinone is the chemical of choice. White Secret is one of the most visible products since it is advertised in a 30-minute, late-night television infomercial that is broadcast nationally almost nightly.[3] Jamie Winders and colleagues (2005), who analyze the commercial, note that the commercial continually stresses that White Secret is "una formula Americana." According to Winders, Jones, and Higgins, the American pedigree and English-language name endow White Secret with a cosmopolitan cachet and "a first worldliness." The infomercial follows the daily lives of several young urban women, one of whom narrates and explains how White Secret cream forms a barrier against the darkening rays of the sun while a sister product transforms the color of the skin itself. The infomercial conjures the power of science, showing cross sections of skin cells. By showing women applying White Secret in modern, well-lit bathrooms, relaxing in well-appointed apartments, and protected from damaging effects of the sun while walking around the city, the program connects skin lightening with cleanliness, modernity, and mobility (Winders, Jones, and Higgins 2005:80–84).

Large multinational firms are expanding the marketing of skin care products, including skin lighteners, in Mexico and other parts of Latin America. For example, Stiefel Laboratories, the world's largest privately held pharmaceutical company, which specializes in dermatology products, targets Latin America for skin-lightening products. Six of its 28 wholly owned subsidiaries are located in Latin America. It offers Clariderm, an over-the-counter hydroquinone cream and gel (2 percent), in Brazil, as well as Clasifel, a prescription-strength hydroquinone cream (4 percent), in Mexico, Peru, Bolivia, Venezuela, and other Latin American countries. It also sells Claripel, a 4 percent hydroquinone cream, in the United States.[4] . . .

Multinational Cosmetic and Pharmaceutical Firms and Their Targeting Strategies

Although there are many small local manufacturers and merchants involved in the skin-lightening game, I want to focus on the giant multinationals, which are fueling the desire for light skin through their advertisement and marketing strategies. The accounts of the skin-lightening markets have shown that the desire for lighter skin and the use of skin bleaches is accelerating in places where modernization and the influence of Western capitalism and culture are most prominent. Multinational biotechnology, cosmetic, and pharmaceutical corporations have coalesced through mergers and acquisitions to create and market personal care products that blur the lines between cosmetics and pharmaceuticals. They have jumped into the field of skin lighteners and correctors, developing many product lines to advertise and sell in Europe, North America, South Asia, East and Southeast Asia, and the Middle East (Wong 2004).

Three of the largest corporations involved in developing the skin-lightening market are L'Oreal, Shiseido, and Unilever. . . .

Unilever is known for promoting its brands by being active and visible in the locales where they are marketed. In India, Ponds sponsors the Femina Miss India pageant, in which aspiring contestants are urged to "be as beautiful as you can be." Judging by photos of past winners, being as beautiful as you can be means being as light as you can be. In 2003, partly in response to criticism by the All India Democratic Women's Association of "racist" advertisement of fairness products, Hindustani Lever launched the Fair and Lovely Foundation, whose mission is to "encourage economic empowerment of women across India" through educational and guidance programs, training courses, and scholarships.[5]

Unilever heavily promotes both Ponds and Fair & Lovely with television and print ads tailored to local cultures. In one commercial shown in India, a young, dark-skinned woman's father laments that he has no son to provide for him and his daughter's salary is not high enough. The suggestion is that she could neither get a better job nor marry because of her dark skin. The young woman then uses Fair & Lovely, becomes fairer, and lands a job as an airline hostess, making her father happy. A Malaysian television spot shows a college student who is dejected because she cannot get the attention of a classmate at the next desk. After using Pond's lightening moisturizer, she appears in class brightly lit and several shades lighter, and the boy says, "Why didn't I notice her before?" (BBC 2003).

Such advertisements can be seen as not simply responding to a preexisting need but actually creating a need by depicting having dark skin as a painful and depressing experience. Before "unveiling" their fairness, dark-skinned women are shown as unhappy, suffering from low self-esteem, ignored by young men, and denigrated by their parents. By using Fair & Lovely or Ponds, a woman undergoes a transformation of not only her complexion but also her personality and her fate. In short, dark skin becomes a burden and handicap that can be overcome only by using the product being advertised.

Conclusion

The yearning for lightness evident in the widespread and growing use of skin bleaching around the globe can rightfully be seen as a legacy of colonialism, a manifestation of "false consciousness," and the internalization of "white is right" values by people of color, especially women. Thus, one often-proposed solution to the problem is reeducation that stresses the diversity of types of beauty and desirability and that valorizes darker skin shades, so that lightness/whiteness is dislodged as the dominant standard.

While such efforts are needed, focusing only on individual consciousness and motives distracts attention from the very powerful economic forces that help to create the yearning for lightness and that offer to fulfill the yearning at a steep price. The manufacturing, advertising, and selling of skin lightening is no longer a marginal, underground economic activity. It has become a major growth market for giant multinational corporations with their sophisticated means of creating and manipulating needs.

The multinationals produce separate product lines that appeal to different target audiences. For some lines of products, the corporations harness the prestige of science by showing cross-sectional diagrams of skin cells and by displaying images of doctors in white coats. Dark skin or dark spots become a disease for which skin lighteners offer a cure. For other lines, designed to appeal to those who respond to appeals to naturalness, corporations call up nature by emphasizing the use of plant extracts and by displaying images of light-skinned women against a background of blue skies and fields of flowers. Dark skin becomes a veil that hides one's natural luminescence, which natural skin lighteners will uncover. For all products, dark skin is associated with pain, rejection, and limited options; achieving light skin is seen as necessary to being youthful, attractive, modern, and affluent—in short, to being "all that you can be."

ENDNOTES

[1] Discussions on Bright Skin Forum, Skin Lightening Board, are at http://excoboard.com/exco/forum.php?forumid=65288. Pallid Skin Lightening system information is at http://www. avreskincare.com/skin/pallid/index.html. Advertisement for Swiss Whitening Pills is at http://www.skinbleaching.net.

[2] Skin whitening forums are at http://www.candymag.com/teentalk/index.php/topic, 131753.0.html and http://www.rexinteractive.com/forum/topic.asp?TOPIC_ID=41.

[3] Discussion of the ingredients in White Secret is found at http://www.vsantivirus.com/hoax-white-secret.htm.

[4] I say that Stiefel targets Latin America because it markets other dermatology products, but not skin lighteners, in the competitive Asian, Middle Eastern, African, and European countries. Information about Stiefel products is at its corporate Web site, http://www.stiefel.com/why/about.aspx (accessed May 1, 2007).

[5] The Pond's Femina Miss World site is http://feminamissindia.indiatimes.com/articleshow/1375041.cms. The All India Democratic Women's Association objects to skin lightening and is at http://www.aidwa.org/content/issues_of_concern/women_and_media.php. Reference to Fair & Lovely campaign is at http://www.aidwa.org/content/issues_of_concern/women_and_media.php. "Fair & Lovely Launches Foundation to Promote Economic Empowerment of Women" (Press Release, March 11, 2003) is found at http://www.hll.com/mediacentre/release.asp?fl=2003/PR_HLL_031103.htm (all accessed December 2, 2006).

REFERENCES

Adebajo, S. B. 2002. An Epidemiological Survey of the Use of Cosmetic Skin Lightening Cosmetics among Traders in Lagos, Nigeria. *West African Journal of Medicine* 21 (1): 51–55.

Ashikari, Makiko. 2003. Urban Middle-Class Japanese Women and Their White Faces: Gender, Ideology, and Representation. *Ethos* 31 (1): 3, 3–4, 9–11.

BBC. 2003. India Debates "Racist" Skin Cream Ads. *BBC News World Edition*, July 24. http://news.bbc.co.uk/1/hi/world/south_asia/3089495.stm (accessed May 8, 2007).

Burke, Timothy. 1996. *Lifebuoy Men, Lux Women: Commodification, Consumption, and Cleanliness in Modern Zimbabwe*. Durham, NC: Duke University Press.

Centers for Disease Control and Prevention. 1996. *FDA Warns Consumers not to Use Crema De Belleza*. FDA Statement. Rockville, MD: U.S. Food and Drug Administration.

Del Guidice, P., and P. Yves. 2002. The Widespread Use of Skin Lightening Creams in Senegal: A Persistent Public Health Problem in West Africa. *International Journal of Dermatology* 41: 69–72.

Dooley, Erin. 2001. Sickening Soap Trade. *Environmental Health Perspectives*, October.

Exhibitor Info. 2006. http://www.beautyworldjapan.com/en/efirst.html (accessed May 8, 2007).

Farr, Marcia. 2006. *Rancheros in Chicagocan: Language and Identity in a Transnational Community*. Austin: University of Texas Press.

Guttman, Matthew C. 1996. *The Meanings of Macho: Being a Man in Mexico City*. Berkeley: University of California Press.

Herring, Cedric, Verna M. Keith, and Hayward Derrick Horton, eds. 2003. *Skin Deep: How Race and Complexion Matter in the "Color Blind" Era*. Chicago: Institute for Research on Race and Public Policy.

Hunter, Margaret. 2005. *Race, Gender, and the Politics of Skin Tone*. New York: Routledge.

Intage. 2001. Intelligence on the Cosmetic Market in Japan. http://www.intage.co.jp/expess/01_08/market/indexl.html (accessed November 2005).

Kerr, Audrey Elisa. 2005. The Paper Bag Principle: The Myth and the Motion of Colorism. *Journal of American Folklore* 118:271–89.

Khan, Aisha. 2008. "Caucasian," "Coolie," "Black," or "white"? Color and Race in the Indo-Caribbean Diaspora. Unpublished Paper.

Knight, Alan. 1990. Racism, Revolution, and Indigenismo: Mexico, 1910–1940. In *The Idea of Race in Latin America, 1870–1940*, Edited by Richard Graham. Austin: University of Texas Press.

Maddox, Keith B. 2004. Perspectives on Racial Phenotypicality Bias. *Personality and Social Psychology Review* 8:383–401.

Mahe, Antoine, Fatimata Ly, and Jean-Marie Dangou. 2003. Skin Diseases Associated with the Cosmetic Use of Bleaching Products in Women from Dakar, Senegal. *British Journal of Dermatology* 148 (3): 493–500.

Malangu, N., and G. A. Ogubanjo. 2006. Predictors of Tropical Steroid Misuse among Patrons of Pharmacies in Pretoria. *South African Family Practices* 48 (1): 14.

Margulies, Paul. n.d. Cushing's Syndrome: The Facts You need to Know. http://www.nadf.us/diseases/cushingsmedhelp.org/www/nadf4.htm (accessed May 1, 2007).

Martinez, Ruben. 2001. *Crossing Over: A Mexican Family on the Migrant Trail*. New York: Henry Holt.

Massing, Jean Michel. 1995. From Greek Proverb to Soap Advert: Washing the Ethiopian. *Journal of the Warburg and Courtauld Institutes* 58:180.

Muzondidya, James. 2005. *Walking a Tightrope, Towards a Social History of the Coloured Community of Zimbabwe*. Trenton, NJ: Africa World Press.

Nielsen. 2007. Prairie Plants Take Root. In *Health, Beauty & Personal Grooming: A Global Nielsen Consumer Report*, http://www.acnielsen.co.in/news/20070402.shtml (accessed May 3, 2007).

Ntambwe, Malangu. 2004. Mirror Mirror on the Wall, Who is the Fairest of them All? *Science in Africa, Africa's First On-Line Science Magazine*, March. http://www.scienceinafrica.co.za/2004/march/skinlightening.htm (accessed May 1, 2007).

Ntshingila, Futhi. 2005. Female Buppies Using Harmful Skin Lighteners. *Sunday Times, South Africa*, November 27. http://www.sundaytimes.co.za (accessed January 25, 2006).

NYC Health Dept. 2005. NYC Health Dept. Warns Against Use of "Skin Lightening" Creams Containing Mercury or Similar Products Which do not List Ingredients. http://www.nyc.gov/ html/doh/html/pr/pr008-05.shtml (accessed May 7, 2007).

Peiss, Kathy. 1998. *Hope in a Jar: The Making of America's Beauty Culture*. New York: Metropolitan Books.

Ribane, Nakedi. 2006. *Beauty: A Black Perspective*. Durban, South Africa: University of KwaZulu-Natal Press.

Runkle, Susan. 2004. Making "Miss India": Constructing Gender, Power and Nation. *South Asian Popular Culture* 2 (2): 145–59.

———. 2005. The Beauty Obsession. *Manushi* 145 (February). http://www.indiatogether.org/manushi/issue145/lovely.htm (accessed May 5, 2007).

Russell, Kathy, Midge Wilson, and Ronald Hall. 1992. *The Color Complex: The Politics of Skin Color among African Americans*. New York: Harcourt Brace Jankovich.

Saskatchewan Business Unlimited. 2005. Prairie Plants Take Root in Cosmetics Industry. *Saskatchewan Business Unlimited* 10 (1): 1–2.

Sheriff, Robin E. 2001. *Dreaming Equality: Color, Race and Racism in Urban Brazil*. New Brunswick, NJ: Rutgers University Press.

Stepan, Nancy Ley. 1991. *The Hour of Eugenics: Race, Gender, and Nation in Latin America*. Ithaca, NY: Cornell University Press.

Synovate. 2004. In:fact. http://www.synovate.com/knowledge/infact/issues/200406 (accessed March 21, 2007).

Telles, Edward E. 2004. *Race in Another America: The Significance of Skin Color in Brazil*. Princeton, NJ: Princeton University Press.

Thomas, Lynn M. (in press.) Skin lighteners in South Africa: Transnational entanglements and technologies of the Self. In *Shades of Difference: Why Skin Color Matters*, Edited by Evelyn Nakano Glenn. Stanford, CA: Stanford University Press.

Unilever. 2006. Annual Report, http://www.unilever.com/ourcompany/investorcentre/annual_reports/archives.asp (accessed May 6, 2007).

U.S. Food and Drug Administration. 1996. *FDA Warns Consumers not to Use Crema De Belleza*. FDA Statement, July 23. Rockville, MD: U.S. Food and Drug Administration.

Views on Article—Complextion. n.d. http://www.indiaparenting.com/beauty/beauty041book.shtml (accessed November 2005).

Winders, Jamie, John Paul Jones III, and Michael James Higgins. 2005. Making gueras: Selling White Identities on Late-Night Mexican Television. *Gender, Place and Culture* 12(1): 71–93.

Wong, Stephanie. 2004. Whitening Cream Sales Soar as Asia's Skin-Deep Beauties Shun Western Suntans. *Manila Bulletin*, http://www.mb.com.ph/issues/2004/08/24/SCTY2004082416969.html# (accessed March 24, 2007).

35

THE POWER ELITE

C. WRIGHT MILLS

Who really governs in the United States? In this selection, sociologist C. Wright Mills argues that the most important decisions in this country are made by a cohesive "power elite." This *power elite* consists of the top leaders in three areas: The corporate elite is made up of the executives from large companies; the military elite is the senior officers; and the small political elite includes the president and top officials in the executive and legislative branches. According to Mills' argument, these elite officials all know each other and act in unison when critical decisions must be made. This selection, originally published in 1956, is the first of three addressing power and politics.

The powers of ordinary men are circumscribed by the everyday worlds in which they live, yet even in these rounds of job, family, and neighborhood, they often seem driven by forces they can neither understand nor govern. "Great changes" are beyond their control, but affect their conduct and outlook nonetheless. The very framework of modern society confines them to projects not their own, but from every side, such changes now press upon the men and women of the mass society, who accordingly feel that they are without purpose in an epoch in which they are without power.

But not all men are in this sense ordinary. As the means of information and of power are centralized, some men come to occupy positions in American society from which they can look down upon, so to speak, and by their decisions mightily affect, the everyday worlds of ordinary men and women. They are not made by their jobs; they set up and break down jobs for thousands of others; they are not confined by simple family responsibilities; they can escape. They may live in many hotels and houses, but they are bound by no one community. They need not merely "meet the demands of the day and hour"; in some part, they create these demands and cause others to meet them. Whether or not they profess their power, their technical and political experience of it far transcends that of the underlying population. What Jacob Burckhardt [a German historian, 1818–1897] said of "great men," most Americans might well say of their elite: "They are all that we are not."

The power elite is composed of men whose positions enable them to transcend the ordinary environments of ordinary men and women; they are in positions to make decisions having major consequences. Whether they do or do not make such decisions is less important than the fact that they do occupy such pivotal positions: Their failure to act, their failure to make decisions, is itself an act that is often of greater consequence than the decisions they do make. For they are in command of the major hierarchies and organizations of modern society. They rule the big corporations. They run the machinery of the state and claim its prerogatives. They direct the military establishment. They occupy the strategic command posts of the social structure, in which are now centered the effective means of the power and the wealth and the celebrity which they enjoy.

The power elite are not solitary rulers. Advisers and consultants, spokesmen and opinion makers are often the captains of their higher thought and decision. Immediately below the elite are the professional politicians of the middle levels of power, in the Congress and in the pressure groups, as well as among the new and old upper classes of town and city and region. Mingling with them, in curious ways which we shall explore, are those professional celebrities who live by being continually displayed but are never, so long as they remain celebrities, displayed enough. If such celebrities are not at the head of any dominating hierarchy, they do often have the power to distract the attention of the public or afford sensations to the masses, or, more directly, to gain the ear of those who do occupy positions of direct power. More or less unattached, as critics of morality and technicians of power, as spokesmen of God and creators of mass sensibility, such celebrities and consultants are part of the immediate scene in which the drama of the elite is enacted. But that drama itself is centered in the command posts of the major institutional hierarchies.

The truth about the nature and the power of the elite is not some secret which men of affairs know but will not tell. Such men hold quite various theories about their own roles in the sequence of event and decision. Often they are uncertain about their roles, and even more often they allow their fears and their hopes to affect their assessment of their own power. No matter how great their actual power, they tend to be less acutely aware of it than of the resistances of others to its use. Moreover, most American men of affairs have learned well the rhetoric of public relations, in some cases even to the point of using it when they are alone, and thus coming to believe it. The personal awareness of the actors is only one of the several sources one must examine in order to understand the higher circles. Yet many who believe that there is no elite, or at any rate none of any consequence, rest their argument upon what men of affairs believe about themselves, or at least assert in public.

There is, however, another view: Those who feel, even if vaguely, that a compact and powerful elite of great importance does now prevail in America often base that feeling upon the historical trend of our time. They have felt, for example, the domination of the military event, and from this they infer that generals and admirals, as well as other men of decision influenced by them, must be enormously powerful. They hear that the Congress has again abdicated to a handful of men decisions clearly related to the issue of war or peace. They know that the bomb was dropped over Japan in the name of the United States of America, although they were at no time consulted about the matter. They feel that they live in a time of big decisions; they know that they are not making any. Accordingly, as they consider the present as history, they infer that at its center, making decisions or failing to make them, there must be an elite of power.

On the one hand, those who share this feeling about big historical events assume that there is an elite and that its power is great. On the other hand, those who listen carefully to the reports of men apparently involved in the great decisions often do not believe that there is an elite whose powers are of decisive consequence.

Both views must be taken into account, but neither is adequate. The way to understand the power of the American elite lies neither solely in recognizing the historic scale of events nor in accepting the personal awareness reported by men of apparent decision. Behind such men and behind the events of history, linking the two, are the major institutions of modern society. These hierarchies of state and corporation and army constitute the means of power; as such they are now of a consequence not before equaled in human history—and at their summits, there are now those command posts of modern society which offer us the sociological key to an understanding of the role of the higher circles in America.

Within American society, major national power now resides in the economic, the political, and the military domains. Other institutions seem off to the side of modern history, and, on occasion, duly subordinated to these. No family is as directly powerful in national affairs as any major corporation; no church is as directly powerful in the external biographies of young men in America today as the military establishment; no college is as powerful in the shaping of momentous events as the National Security Council. Religious, educational, and family institutions are not autonomous centers of national power; on the contrary, these decentralized areas are increasingly shaped by the big three, in which developments of decisive and immediate consequence now occur.

Families and churches and schools adapt to modern life; governments and armies and corporations shape it; and, as they do so, they turn these lesser institutions into means for their ends. Religious institutions provide chaplains to the armed forces where they are used as a means of increasing the effectiveness of its morale to kill. Schools select and train men for their jobs in corporations and their specialized tasks in the armed forces. The extended family has, of course, long been broken up by the industrial revolution, and now the son and the father are removed from the family, by compulsion if need be, whenever the army of the state sends out the call. And the symbols of all these lesser institutions are used to legitimate the power and the decisions of the big three.

The life-fate of the modern individual depends not only upon the family into which he was born or which he enters by marriage, but increasingly upon the corporation in which he spends the most alert hours of his best years; not only upon the school where he is educated as a child and adolescent, but also upon the state which touches him throughout his life; not only upon the church in which on occasion he hears the word of God, but also upon the army in which he is disciplined.

If the centralized state could not rely upon the inculcation of nationalist loyalties in public and private schools, its leaders would promptly seek to modify the decentralized educational system. If the bankruptcy rate among the top 500 corporations were as high as the general divorce rate among the 37 million married couples, there would be economic catastrophe on an international scale. If members of armies gave to them no more of their lives than do believers to the churches to which they belong, there would be a military crisis.

Within each of the big three, the typical institutional unit has become enlarged, has become administrative, and, in the power of its decisions, has become centralized. Behind these developments there is a fabulous technology, for as institutions, they have incorporated this technology and guide it, even as it shapes and paces their developments.

The economy—once a great scatter of small productive units in autonomous balance—has become dominated by two or three hundred giant corporations, administratively and politically interrelated, which together hold the keys to economic decisions.

The political order, once a decentralized set of several dozen states with a weak spinal cord, has become a centralized, executive establishment which has taken up into itself many powers previously scattered, and now enters into each and every cranny of the social structure.

The military order, once a slim establishment in a context of distrust fed by state militia, has become the largest and most expensive feature of government, and, although well-versed in smiling public relations, now has all the grim and clumsy efficiency of a sprawling bureaucratic domain.

In each of these institutional areas, the means of power at the disposal of decision makers have increased enormously; their central executive powers have been enhanced; within each of them modern administrative routines have been elaborated and tightened up.

As each of these domains becomes enlarged and centralized, the consequences of its activities become greater, and its traffic with the others increases. The decisions of a handful of corporations bear upon military and political as well as upon economic developments around the world. The decisions of the military establishment rest upon and grievously affect political life as well as the very level of economic activity. The decisions made within the political domain determine economic activities and military programs. There is no longer, on the one hand, an economy, and, on the other hand, a political order containing a military establishment unimportant to politics and to money making. There is a political economy linked, in a thousand ways, with military institutions and decisions. On each side of the world-split running through central Europe and around the Asiatic rimlands, there is an ever-increasing interlocking of economic, military, and political structures. If there is government intervention in the corporate economy, so is there corporate intervention in the governmental process. In the structural sense, this triangle of power is the source of the interlocking directorate that is most important for the historical structure of the present.

The fact of the interlocking is clearly revealed at each of the points of crisis of modern capitalist society—slump, war, and boom. In each, men of decision are led to an awareness of the interdependence of the major institutional orders. In the nineteenth century, when the scale of all institutions was smaller, their liberal integration was achieved in the automatic economy, by an autonomous play of market forces, and in the automatic political domain, by the bargain and the vote. It was then assumed that out of the imbalance and friction that followed the limited decisions then possible a new equilibrium would in due course emerge. That can no longer be assumed, and it is not assumed by the men at the top of each of the three dominant hierarchies.

For given the scope of their consequences, decisions—and indecisions— in any one of these ramify into the others, and hence top decisions tend either to become coordinated or to lead to a commanding indecision. It has not always been like this. When numerous small entrepreneurs made up the economy, for example, many of them could fail and the consequences still remain local; political and military authorities did not intervene. But now, given political expectations and military commitments, can they afford to allow key units of the private corporate economy to break down in slump? Increasingly, they do intervene in economic affairs, and as they do so, the controlling decisions in each order are inspected by agents of the other two, and economic, military, and political structures are interlocked.

At the pinnacle of each of the three enlarged and centralized domains, there have arisen those higher circles which make up the economic, the political, and the military elites. At the top of the economy, among the corporate rich, there are the chief executives; at the top of the political order, the members of the political directorate; at the top of the military establishment, the elite of soldier-statesmen clustered in and around the Joint Chiefs of Staff and the upper echelon. As each of these domains has coincided with the others, as decisions tend to become total in their consequence, the leading men in each of the three domains of power—the warlords, the corporation chieftains, the political directorate—tend to come together, to form the power elite of America.

The higher circles in and around these command posts are often thought of in terms of what their members possess: They have a greater share than other people of the things and experiences that are most highly valued. From this point of view, the elite are simply those who have the most of what there is to have, which is generally held to include money, power, and prestige—as well as all the ways of life to which these lead. But the elite are not simply those who have the most, for they could not "have the most" were it not for their positions in the great institutions. For such institutions are the necessary bases of power, of wealth, and of prestige, and at the same time, the chief means of exercising power, of acquiring and retaining wealth, and of cashing in the higher claims for prestige.

By the powerful we mean, of course, those who are able to realize their will, even if others resist it. No one, accordingly, can be truly powerful unless he has access to the command of major institutions, for it is over these institutional means of power that the truly powerful are, in the first instance, powerful. Higher politicians and key officials of government command such institutional power; so do admirals and generals, and so do the major owners and executives of the larger corporations. Not all power, it is true, is anchored in and exercised by means of such institutions, but only within and through them can power be more or less continuous and important.

Wealth also is acquired and held in and through institutions. The pyramid of wealth cannot be understood merely in terms of the very rich; for the great inheriting families, as we shall see, are now supplemented by the corporate institutions of modern society: Every one of the very rich families has been and is closely connected—always legally and frequently managerially as well—with one of the multimillion-dollar corporations.

The modern corporation is the prime source of wealth, but, in latter-day capitalism, the political apparatus also opens and closes many avenues to wealth. The amount as well as the source of income, the power over consumer's goods as well as over productive capital, are determined by position within the political economy. If our interest in the very rich goes beyond their lavish or their miserly consumption, we must examine their relations to modern forms of corporate property as well as to the state; for such relations now determine the chances of men to secure big property and to receive high income.

Great prestige increasingly follows the major institutional units of the social structure. It is obvious that prestige depends, often quite decisively, upon access to the publicity machines that are now a central and normal feature of all the big institutions of modern America. Moreover, one feature of these hierarchies of corporation, state, and military establishment is that their top positions are increasingly interchangeable. One result of this is the accumulative nature of prestige. Claims for prestige, for example, may be initially based on military roles, then expressed in and augmented by an educational institution run by corporate executives, and cashed in, finally, in the political order, where, for General Eisenhower and those he represents, power and prestige finally meet at the very peak. Like wealth and power, prestige tends to be cumulative: The more of it you have, the more you can get. These values also tend to be translatable into one another: The wealthy find it easier than the poor to gain power; those with status find it easier than those without it to control opportunities for wealth.

If we took the one hundred most powerful men in America, the one hundred wealthiest, and the one hundred most celebrated away from the institutional positions they now occupy, away from their resources of men and women and money, away from the media of mass communication that are now focused upon them—then they would be powerless and poor and uncelebrated. For power is not of a man. Wealth does not center in the person of the wealthy. Celebrity is not inherent in any personality. To be celebrated, to be wealthy, to have power requires access to major institutions, for the institutional positions men occupy determine in large part their chances to have and to hold these valued experiences.

The people of the higher circles may also be conceived as members of a top social stratum, as a set of groups whose members know one another, see one another socially and at business, and so, in making decisions, take one another into account. The elite, according to this conception, feel themselves to be, and are felt by others to be, the inner circle of "the upper social classes." They form a more or less compact social and psychological entity; they have become self-conscious members of a social class. People are either accepted into this class or they are not, and there is a qualitative split, rather than merely a numerical scale, separating them from those who are not elite. They are more or less aware of themselves as a social class, and they behave toward one another differently from the way they do toward members of other classes. They accept one another, understand one another, marry one another, tend to work and to think if not together at least alike.

Now, we do not want by our definition to prejudge whether the elite of the command posts are conscious members of such a socially recognized class, or whether considerable proportions of the elite derive from such a clear and distinct class. These are matters to be investigated. Yet in order to be able to recognize what we intend to investigate, we must note something that all biographies and memoirs of the wealthy and the powerful and the eminent make clear: No matter what else they may be, the people of these higher circles are involved in a set of overlapping "crowds" and intricately connected "cliques." There is a kind of mutual attraction among those who "sit on the same terrace"—although this often becomes clear to them, as well as to others, only at the point at which they feel the need to draw the line; only when, in their common defense, they come to understand what they have in common, and so close their ranks against outsiders.

The idea of such a ruling stratum implies that most of its members have similar social origins, that throughout their lives they maintain a network of informal connections, and that to some degree there is an interchangeability of position between the various hierarchies of money and power and celebrity. We must, of course, note at once that if such an elite stratum does exist, its social visibility and its form, for very solid historical reasons, are quite different from those of the noble cousinhoods that once ruled various European nations.

That American society has never passed through a feudal epoch is of decisive importance to the nature of the American elite, as well as to American society as a historic whole. For it means that no nobility or aristocracy, established before the capitalist era, has stood in tense opposition to the higher bourgeoisie. It means that this bourgeoisie has monopolized not only wealth but prestige and power as well. It means that no set of noble families has commanded the top positions and monopolized the values that are generally held in high esteem; and certainly that no set has done so explicitly by inherited right. It means that no high church dignitaries or court nobilities, no entrenched landlords with honorific accouterments, no monopolists of high army posts have opposed the enriched bourgeoisie and in the name of birth and prerogative successfully resisted its self-making.

But this does *not* mean that there are no upper strata in the United States. That they emerged from a "middle class" that had no recognized aristocratic superiors does not mean they remained middle class when enormous increases in wealth made their own superiority possible. Their origins and their newness may have made the upper strata less visible in America than elsewhere. But in America today there are in fact tiers and ranges of wealth and power of which people in the middle and lower ranks know very little and may not even dream. There are families who, in their well-being, are quite insulated from the economic jolts and lurches felt by the merely prosperous and those farther down the scale. There are also men of power who in quite small groups make decisions of enormous consequence for the underlying population.

36

THE IRONIES OF DIVERSITY

RICHARD L. ZWEIGENHAFT • G. WILLIAM DOMHOFF

Sociological research supports the thesis that a power elite still exists in this country, and that power is concentrated among a few social groups and institutions. Reading 24 by Domhoff and Reading 25 by Shapiro provide evidence toward the raced and classed mechanisms used to preserve social inequality and determine who has access to higher social classes. Two areas of debate inform this research: (1) what is the degree of interconnection among the three groups—the corporate, military, and political elite? And (2), what is the degree to which minorities have been able to gain access to the elite ranks of these three groups since C. Wright Mills wrote the original piece in 1956? The latter question is the focus of this reading by Richard L. Zweigenhaft, the Charles A. Dana Professor of Psychology at Guilford College, and G. William Domhoff, a research professor of psychology and sociology at the

University of California, Santa Cruz. In this excerpt from their 2006 book, *Diversity in the Power Elite: How It Happened, and Why It Matters,* Zweigenhaft and Domhoff examine how some minorities have gained access to the power elite, and why so many others are still excluded.

As the preceding [research has] shown in detail, the power elite and Congress are more diverse than they were before the civil rights movement and the social movements that followed in its tracks brought pressure to bear on corporations, politicians, and government. Although the power elite is still composed primarily of Christian, white men, there are now Jews, women, blacks, Latinos, and Asian Americans on the boards of the country's largest corporations; presidential cabinets are far more diverse than was the case fifty years ago; and the highest ranks of the military are no longer filled solely by white men. In the case of elected officials in Congress, the trend toward diversity is even greater for women and the other previously excluded groups that we have studied. At the same time, we have shown that the incorporation of members of the different groups has been uneven.

In this [reading], we look at the patterns that emerge from our specific findings to see if they help explain the gradual inclusion of some groups and the continuing exclusion of others. We also discuss the impact of diversity on the power elite and the rest of American society. We argue that most of the effects were unexpected and are ironic. The most important of these ironies relates to the ongoing tension between the American dream of individual advancement and fulfillment ("liberal individualism") and the class structure: We conclude that the racial, ethnic, and gender diversity celebrated by the power elite and the media actually reinforces the unchanging nature of the class structure and increases the tendency to ignore class inequalities.

Why Are Some Included?

The social movements and pressures for greater openness at the higher levels of American society have led to some representation for all previously excluded groups, but some have been more successful than others. Four main factors explain why some people come to be included: higher class origins, elite educations, a lighter skin color, and the ability to make oneself acceptable to established members of the power elite, which we call "identity management."

The Importance of Class

Those who have brought diversity to the power elite have tended to come from business and professional backgrounds, like the white, Christian males C. Wright Mills studied more than fifty years ago. Fully one-third of the women who have become corporate directors are from the upper class, and many others are from the middle and upper-middle classes. Most of the

Cuban Americans and Chinese Americans who have risen to the top have come from displaced ruling classes, a far cry from the conventional image of immigrants who start with nothing. The Jews and Japanese Americans in high positions have mostly been the products of two- and three-generational climbs up the social ladder. The first African American members of the corporate elite and the cabinet tended to come from the small black middle class that predated the civil rights movement. Although there is no systematic information on the social backgrounds of gay and lesbian leaders, who are treated in most studies as if they have no class origins, our anecdotal information suggests that many visible activists and professionals come from business and professional families as well.

A high-level social background, of course, makes it easier to acquire the values, attitudes, and styles that are necessary to hire, fire, and manage the work lives of employees with blue, white, and pink collars. This point can be extended to include even those from more modest circumstances, like Lauro Cavazos, whose father was a ranch foreman, or Katherine Ortega, Sue Ling Gin, and David Geffen, whose families owned small businesses, or David Mixner, whose father was in charge of minority farmhands on a farm he did not own. Most of those we studied, in other words, learned firsthand that a few people boss the majority or have independent professions based on academic credentials and that they were expected to be part of this managerial and professional stratum.

When we compare the newly arrived members of the power elite with their counterparts in Congress, however, two further generalizations emerge. First, members of the power elite tend to come from more privileged social backgrounds than elected officials. Second, the elected officials are more likely to be Democrats than Republicans. These two findings suggest that there are class and political dimensions to our findings on the differences between the power elite and Congress that cut across gender and ethnic lines. Now that the power elite is housed almost exclusively in the Republican Party and the liberal-labor coalition has become more important within the Democratic Party, the country's traditional regional, racial, and ethnic politics is being replaced by a more clear-cut class-and-race politics, with both the Republicans and Democrats now able to say that they are diverse in terms of leaders and candidates from all previously excluded groups. (Even the Republican Party can claim gay and lesbian members thanks to the Log Cabin Republicans, although many conservative Republicans would prefer not to.) And as everyone knows, the number of African Americans who are Republicans is very small, but they are important to the success of the party with centrist white voters because they "prove" that the party is trying to be inclusive of everyone.[1]

The Importance of Education

Class by no means explains all of our findings, however. Education also matters a great deal. The members of underrepresented groups who make it to the power elite are typically better educated than the white males who are already a part of it. This was seen with the European American women and African Americans on corporate boards and in presidential cabinets, as well as the successful Asian American immigrants. Education seems to have given them the edge needed to make their way into the power elite. In the case of many of the African Americans, new educational programs in elite private high schools, created in response to the disruptions of the 1960s, were more than an edge. They were essential. In effect, these scholarship programs in part compensated for the wealth they did not have.[2]

Moreover, it is not merely having academic degrees that matters but also where those degrees are from. Again and again, we saw that a significant number were from the same few schools that educate Christian, white, male leaders, such as Harvard, Yale, Princeton, and MIT on the East Coast, the University of Chicago in the Midwest, and Stanford on the West Coast. Whether it is Bill Clinton or George W. Bush in the White House, Hillary Clinton in the Senate from New York or Joseph Lieberman in the Senate from Connecticut, or Clarence Thomas on the Supreme Court, they all went to Yale in the 1960s.

These elite schools not only confer status on their graduates but also provide contacts with white male elites that are renewed throughout life at alumni gatherings and on other special occasions. School connections, in turn, lead to invitations to attend exclusive social events and join expensive social clubs, which extend the newcomers' social networks even further. With success in business or a profession comes invitations to serve on boards of trustees of elite foundations and universities, and the circle is completed.

In short, they have acquired the full complement of what is now called "social capital," the network of friends and contacts that provides access to jobs, financial capital, and marriage partners of high social standing. The newcomers thereby become part of the ongoing institutional framework that defines and shapes the power elite in the United States, even though only a few of them are likely to reach the very top. The individuals in the power elite may come and go, and they may diversify in gender, race, ethnicity, and sexual orientation, but there is stability and continuity in terms of the types of people who are fed into the set of institutions that define the power elite and dominate the American social structure.

As was true of social class origins, there is a difference in educational attainment between those in the power elite and those in Congress: the men and women elected to Congress are not as likely as those in the power elite to have attended elite colleges and universities or to have earned postgraduate degrees.

The Importance of Color

Just as class alone cannot explain all of our findings, neither can the combination of class and education: color also matters. African Americans and darker-skinned Latinos find it more difficult than others to use their educational credentials and social capital as passports to occupational success. This can be seen poignantly in our skin-color comparisons of successful blacks and Latinos. Even among those who had achieved some level of prominence (measured by inclusion in *Ebony*'s fiftieth anniversary issue or the *Hispanic Business* listing of "Hispanic influentials"), those who had made it into the power elite were lighter skinned than those who had not. On this score, our data simply reinforce earlier work by others. As the Glass Ceiling Commission reported, "Our society has developed an extremely sophisticated, and often denied, acceptability index based on gradations in skin color."[3]

Julia Alvarez, a writer whose novels have captured the difficulties of leaving one's Latin American home and coming, with far fewer material resources, to the United States to start anew, understands well the importance of one's class background in the old country and of light skin in the new country. In an essay about leaving the Dominican Republic and coming to the United States as a young girl, Alvarez acknowledges the advantages her family had over other immigrant families because they were well educated, had access to money, and (as she says, "most especially") were light skinned: "My family had not been among the waves of economic immigrants that left their island in the seventies, a generally darker-skinned, working-class group, who might have been the maids or workers in my mother's family house. We had come in 1960, political refugees, with no money but with 'prospects': Papi had a friend who was a doctor at the Waldorf Astoria and who helped him get a job; Mami's family had money in the Chase Manhattan Bank they could lend us. We had changed class in America—from Mami's elite family to middle-class Spics—but our background and education and most especially our pale skin had made mobility easier for us here."[4]

Alvarez's perceptive and honest assessment of the advantages she had (so different from the public relations stories put out by many corporate chieftains), coupled with the findings we have described on color discrimination, may help to explain why so few people of color have made it into the power elite. The failure of American society to accept darker-skinned citizens, especially African Americans, is the most difficult issue that needs to be understood by social scientists. We return to this issue in the next section, "Why Are Some Still Excluded?"

Identity Management

Finally, we have seen that the newcomers who join the power elite have found ways to demonstrate their loyalty to those who dominate American institutions—straight, white, Christian males. They know how to act and interact using the manners, style, and conversational repertoire of the already established elite, and they can hold their own in discussing the fine points of literature and the arts; that is, they have the "cultural capital" that comes from high-class origins or an elite education. When William T. Coleman recited great poetry with his fellow law clerk, Boston Brahmin Elliot Richardson, he was not only sharing a mutual love of poetry with a colleague and friend, he was demonstrating his elite educational background. Reading between the lines of traditional stereotypes, we can imagine Jewish and black executives being properly reserved, Asian American executives acting properly assertive, gay executives behaving in traditionally masculine ways, and lesbian executives acting in traditionally feminine ways. Within this context of identity management, we also can see why Cecily Cannan Selby decided to reduce tension at a dinner meeting with the previously all-male Avon Products board by lighting up a cigar and why Hazel O'Leary decided she had to learn to play golf if she wanted to advance in her corporate career. In all these ways, the newcomers are able to meet the challenge of moving into a "comfort zone" with those who decide who is and who is not acceptable for inclusion.

At the same time, . . . we drew on research on the sociology of organizations to stress that the demand for demonstrations of outward conformity by established leaders is not primarily a matter of personal prejudice or cultural heritage. It is, instead, the need for trust and smooth working relationships within complex organizations that leads to the marked preference for women and people of color who think and act like the straight, Christian males running those organizations. Such demonstrations may be especially important when there are suspicions that the newcomers might have lingering loyalties to those they have left behind. The social movements that arose in the 1960s were able to rock the boat enough to open up some space for non-traditional leaders, but not enough to change the way in which work is structured and institutions are managed. Unless, and until, changes are made in work structure and institutional cultures, underrepresented groups will be at a disadvantage in climbing the managerial hierarchy, even though they are now able to enter the competition.

In summary, class origins, an excellent education, and the proper appearance, especially in terms of lighter skin tone, are the building blocks for entry into the power elite, but identity management is the final step, the icing on the cake.

Why Are Some Still Excluded?

How is the continuing exclusion of African Americans and Latinos who are darker skinned to be explained? From the power-structure perspective that we favor, the answer is to be found in the economic and political domination of darker-skinned people that began when European settlers took North and South America from the Native Americans and imported an estimated ten to twelve million slaves from Africa in order to make the southern United States, the West Indies, and parts of Latin America even more profitable to them. This economically driven subjugation, which unfolded in brutal fashion shortly after 1492 in ways that are all too familiar, created the "racial hierarchy" that persists to this day based on a jumble of prejudices, cultural stereotypes, strategies of exclusion, and feelings of superiority on the part of those who are white.

The fact that both indigenous Indians and African slaves were conquered and subjugated in the United States is less visible today because there are so few Native Americans left. They are now often regarded positively as brave and heroic warriors, but until fairly recently, they were treated as less than human due to the first (and most successful, along with that in Australia) large-scale ethnic cleansing by a modern democracy. Their numbers dropped from an estimated 4 to 9 million in the pre-Columbian era in what is now the United States to 237,000 in 1900, when they were no longer a threat to the land hunger of the white settlers. Today, most of the approximately 1.5 million self-identified Native Americans not living on reservations are of mixed white and Indian heritage, and 59 percent of those who are married are married to whites.[5]

In the United States, then, and unlike many Latin American countries, where both Indians and former African slaves mostly occupy the bottom rungs of society or are complete outcasts, the brunt of the persistent sense of group superiority on the part of Euro Americans is on the significant percentage of the population—12 percent, as we noted earlier—who are descendants of slaves (and slave masters in some cases). In this country, being "black" means being stigmatized because the dishonored status of being a slave became identified with the racial features of "blackness."[6] In particular, skin color became the major means by which enslaved and conquered groups could be identified and stigmatized for purposes of keeping them subordinated. Hair texture and facial features were also part of the subordinating racial stereotyping, but "color" came to stand for the ensemble of identifying markers. (By contrast, the Slavic peoples enslaved by the Greeks and Romans, from whose language the word "slave" is derived, were able to blend in when their masters released them from bondage.)

In addition to carrying the legacy of slavery, which stripped people of any group or personal identity, rendered them subject to constant surveillance and violence, and regularly broke up roughly one-third of all nuclear families as a way to destroy feelings of kinship, African Americans also continued to endure subordination to white Americans in the postslavery era. In the South, that subordination began with the exploitative system called "tenant farming," which left African Americans with little more than their freedom, a mule, and a few farm implements.[7] In the North, African Americans were kept out of the best-paying construction jobs, often with the use of violence by white workers, despite their having the necessary skills. They also encountered cross burnings, race riots, and racial covenants in deeds of trust when they tried to live in white neighborhoods, which meant they were excluded from predominantly white public schools and forced to pay higher prices for housing that depreciated in value because whites would not live nearby.[8]

Under these circumstances, and until the 1960s, it was rare that any but a small number of African Americans could accumulate any wealth at all. Although the civil rights movement brought formal equality and voting power to African Americans, which in turn led to improved treatment in many social spheres and better jobs, especially with the government, the fact remains that it has been impossible for African Americans to close the socioeconomic gap with whites. According to detailed work on wealth accumulation by sociologist Thomas Shapiro, based on his own interviews in several cities, along with national surveys and government statistics, the typical

African American family has only one-tenth the wealth of the average white family (a net worth of $8,000 versus $81,000 for whites). This is because whites were able gradually to accumulate wealth throughout the twentieth century with the help of government-backed mortgages, large tax deductions on home mortgages, the GI Bill, and other programs that were available to very few, if any, African Americans at the time. Moreover, whites were able to pass down this wealth to their children through inheritance, not only at the time of death, but also in the form of what Shapiro calls "transformative assets," which include help with college tuition, down payments on new homes (which then appreciate in value), and gifts or loans to survive unexpected crises that cause a temporary drop in income.[9]

On the other hand, the historic legacy of income and wealth discrimination means that African Americans lack similar transformative assets. In addition, more black wealth goes to helping relatives and friends in need and to taking care of aging parents, so the little wealth African Americans do accumulate is less likely to be given to young adult children as transformative assets or eventually inherited by them. Even when blacks and whites are at the same level in terms of earnings, they are at different starting points in terms of wealth, making it impossible to close the gap through earnings. Both black and white families increased their financial wealth between 1988 and 1999, but there was nonetheless a $20,000 increase in the asset gap. Racial inequality is growing worse, not better, because of both the initial advantages enjoyed by whites and their greater capacity to pass on these advantages as transformative assets. As Shapiro concludes, "it is virtually impossible for people of color to earn their way to wealth through wages."[10]

This huge wealth differential is further compounded by continuing discrimination and exclusion on the part of whites, especially in the area of employment, where many whites wrongly think there is now color-blind fairness.[11] Although the official racist ideology of the past is now gone, or at least not verbalized in public, there is strong evidence that more covert forms of racism still persist that make many blacks feel uncomfortable or unwanted in white settings. In covert racism, which also has been called free-market and color-blind racism, traditional American values, especially those concerning the fairness of markets, including labor markets, are blended with antiblack attitudes in a way that allows whites to express antagonism toward blacks' demands ("Blacks are getting too demanding in their push for civil rights") or resentment over alleged special favors for blacks ("The government should not help blacks and other racial minorities—they should help themselves") without thinking of themselves as racists. White Americans say they simply want everyone to be treated the same, even though most of them know that African Americans are not treated equally.[12]

Then, too, more subtle forms of racial discrimination are uncovered in various kinds of social psychology experiments that have revealed "aversive racism," in which whites express egalitarian beliefs but also hold unacknowledged negative feelings about blacks. The resulting ambivalence means that they avoid blacks, especially when the norms are conflicting or ambiguous. The evidence for aversive and other subtle forms of racism is important because it reveals the persistence of cultural stereotypes about blacks and demonstrates that these stereotypes affect behavior, often at an unconscious level. These stereotypes, in turn, convey to African Americans that they continue to be seen as "different." They come to feel they are not respected, which naturally breeds resentment and hostility, which is then sensed by whites and said to be groundless in this day and age.[13]

This cycle of discrimination, exclusion, resentment, and mutual recrimination is very different from what happens to most of the groups who come to the United States as immigrants from Europe, Asia, or Latin America. They arrive with a sense of hope, often as families or in extended kin networks, and with an intact culture; these combine to enable them to endure the discrimination and exclusion they often face at the outset. As they persist in their efforts, the dominant majority grudgingly accepts some of them. The difference can be seen in the two most revealing indicators of acceptance by the dominant group, residential patterns and rates of intermarriage.

The most comprehensive study on residential patterns demonstrates that African Americans continue to live in predominantly black neighborhoods, but this is not the case for Latinos or Asian Americans. In *American Apartheid: Segregation and the Making of the Underclass,* sociologists Douglas Massey and Nancy Denton reveal just how persistent residential segregation has been in the United States. Using computerized data from the U.S. Censuses of 1970 and 1980, they looked at the thirty metropolitan areas with the largest black populations. Based on two different measures ("black-white segregation" and "spatial isolation"), they conclude that the 1970s showed virtually no increase in integration, "despite what whites said on opinion polls and despite the provisions of the Fair Housing Act."[14] Moreover, they did not find that degree of segregation for Hispanics and Asian Americans. "In fact," Massey and Denton conclude, "within most metropolitan areas, Hispanics and Asians are more likely to share a neighborhood with whites than with another member of their own group." In the final chapter of their book, Massey and Denton update their work to include 1990 Census data. They conclude that "there is little in recent data to suggest that processes of racial segregation have moderated much since 1980. . . . Racial segregation still constitutes a fundamental cleavage in American society."[15] This conclusion still holds based on data from the 2000 Census, which shows only a slight decline in residential segregation for African Americans, along with increasing segregation for everyone along class lines.[16]

There have been dozens of studies focusing on the recent marriage patterns of underrepresented groups. All of them point to increasing intermarriage occurring between the large white population and each previously excluded group except African Americans. The exact percentage of "outmarriage" varies with a number of factors, including country of birth, years of residency in the United States, region of residence, educational level, and income. For our emphasis on intermarriage as a sensitive indicator of integration and acceptance, research by sociologists Jerry Jacobs and Teresa Labov, using a 1 percent sample from the 1990 Census (539,279 marriages), provides an ideal test case. Table 36.1 summarizes the findings of their analysis

TABLE 36.1 Intermarriage by U.S.-Born Members of Ethnic and Racial Minorities

	Percentage Married to Non-Hispanic Whites	
Group	*Male (N)*	*Female (N)*
Filipino Americans	61 (106)	66 (103)
Native Americans	57 (1,212)	58 (1,234)
Cuban Americans	61 (92)	47 (137)
Chinese Americans	47 (140)	52 (152)
Japanese Americans	44 (216)	54 (266)
Puerto Rican Americans	42 (528)	35 (602)
Mexican Americans	31 (4,793)	28 (5,261)
African Americans	5 (9,804)	2 (9,581)

Source: Adapted from Jacobs and Labov, "Asian Brides, Anglo Grooms," 23, table 4.
Note: The table includes only individuals under age forty and excludes war brides and grooms.

of marriages to non-Hispanic white partners by American-born minorities under the age of forty.[17]

There are many dramatic findings in this table, including the very high percentage of native-born Asian Americans marrying non-Hispanic whites, but none is more germane to our point than the continuing low levels of intermarriage by African Americans to non-Hispanic whites. In a sample that focuses only on married couples, thereby excluding any distortion by the high percentage of unmarried males and females in the African American community, only 5 percent of married African American males and 2 percent of married African American females under age forty were married to non-Hispanic whites. This is less than one-sixth the percentage for the next-lowest group, Mexican Americans, and far below the 44 to 66 percent figures for various groups of Asian Americans. Even among African American college graduates, only 11 percent of the males and 3 percent of the females had married whites, whereas the percentages for all married Asian American college graduates as a group were 51 percent for males and 59 percent for females.[18]

As might be deduced from the higher percentage of Asian American college graduates marrying whites, there is a strong tendency for affluent immigrant minorities to marry affluent whites and for less affluent groups, like Mexican Americans and Puerto Ricans, to marry less affluent whites. The same pattern holds for marriages between African Americans and whites: the partners usually have similar education and occupation levels.[19]

To make matters more complex, most recent immigrant groups bring similar negative attitudes toward African Americans from their home countries, as in the case of nonblack Latinos, or soon adopt them once they are in the United States, as seen in the case of some Asian American groups. They often claim that African Americans do not see the "opportunities" that lie before them and do not work hard. Thus, most immigrants come to share the stereotypes and prejudices of the dominant white majority. . . .

Based on this analysis, we can see why the gains made by African Americans since the civil rights movement are in constant peril in a context where they have not been able to accumulate sufficient wealth to help their children or provide support in times of crisis. Given the ongoing discrimination and accumulated disadvantages, it may be that even the current rate of entry into the power elite will be difficult to maintain. Upwardly mobile black Americans could continue to be the exception rather than the rule without the strong support of affirmative action laws and programs at the federal level.[20] But such laws and programs have been trimmed back since the new conservative era began in the 1980s, making further progress problematic.

However, in a clear demonstration of the concerns members of the power elite have on this score, a small part of the decline in government support for equal opportunity has been offset by a set of corporate-sponsored programs for identifying and educating academically talented African American youngsters who can be groomed for elite universities and possible incorporation into the power elite. These programs begin in elementary school in some areas of the country, then carry through to private high schools, Ivy League universities, and corporate internships. They are financed by donations from the large charitable foundations that the corporate rich in turn influence through financial donations and directorship positions. Since we have written about these programs elsewhere, with a special emphasis on the first and largest of them, A Better Chance, founded in the early 1960s by a handful of New England boarding school headmasters with help from the Rockefeller Foundation, we will provide only three examples here.[21]

The Black Student Fund in Washington, D.C., places students in 42 private schools in Maryland, Virginia, and the District of Columbia with the help of foundation grants and personal gifts. Since its founding in 1964, it has served over two thousand students, 84 percent of whom have earned at least a BA. The Steppingstone Foundation in Boston and Philadelphia has a program for children in the fourth and fifth grades, who are prepared through two six-week summer sessions, Saturday classes, and after-school classes once a week for acceptance into both private and elite public schools that will see them through their high school years with the help of scholarship support. Between 1997 and 2005, 125 graduates of the Steppingstone program had enrolled in college. . . .

Prep for Prep in New York City may currently be the largest and most comprehensive of these programs. Created in 1978 as a pilot project under the auspices of Columbia University's Teachers College just as the full-scale attack on affirmative action was beginning, it takes in about 150 fifth graders and 60 seventh graders in New York City each year for a fourteen-month program to prepare them for placement in 36 private day schools and 10 boarding schools. . . .

As of 2003, Prep for Prep had worked with more than 2,500 students, and 951 had graduated from college. Fully 84 percent of those college graduates had attended schools characterized as "most selective" on the annual list published by *U.S. News & World Report,* and 40 percent had attended Ivy League schools.

Taken as a whole, this elementary to graduate school pipeline may produce several thousand potential members of the corporate community each year, if successful graduates of public high schools who receive business and law degrees are added to the prep school graduates. However, these programs are not large enough to provide opportunities for more than a tiny fraction of all African Americans without much more help from the government at the national, state, and local levels. They are primarily a way to provide a few highly educated Americans of African descent with the educational credentials to rise in the corporate community. For example, despite all these programs, the percentage of master's degrees awarded to blacks has been flat at about 6.5 percent since 1977, which demonstrates a significant underrepresentation. A shorter time series available from the government for master's degrees in business reveals a slight but steady increase between the 1994–1995 and 1999–2000 school years. During these six years, the percentages of black students receiving business degrees rose from 5.2 to 7.1 percent. We therefore believe that the potential pool of African Americans who can make their way into the power elite is growing at a much slower rate than for the other previously underrepresented groups. . . .

Do Members of Previously Excluded Groups Act Differently?

Perhaps it is not surprising that when we look at the business practices of the members of previously excluded groups who have risen to the top of the corporate world, we find that their perspectives and values do not differ markedly from those of their white male counterparts. When Linda Wachner, one of the first women to become CEO of a *Fortune*-level company, the Warnaco Group, concluded that one of Warnaco's many holdings, the Hathaway Shirt Company, was unprofitable, she decided to stop making Hathaway shirts and to sell or close down the factory. It did not matter to Wachner that Hathaway, which started making shirts in 1837, was one of the oldest companies in Maine, that almost all of the five hundred employees at the factory were working-class women, or even that the workers had given up a pay raise to hire consultants to teach them to work more effectively and, as a result, had doubled their productivity. The bottom-line issue was that the company was considered unprofitable, and the average wage of the Hathaway workers, $7.50 an hour, was thought to be too high. (In 1995, Wachner was paid $10 million in salary and stock, and Warnaco had a net income of $46.5 million.) *We did need to do the right thing for the company and the stockholders,* explained Wachner.[22]

Nor did ethnic background matter to Thomas Fuentes, a senior vice president at a consulting firm in Orange County, California, a director of Fleetwood Enterprises, and chairman of the Orange County Republican Party.

Fuentes targeted fellow Latinos who happened to be Democrats when he sent uniformed security guards to twenty polling places in 1988 "carrying signs in Spanish and English warning people not to vote if they were not U.S. citizens." The security firm ended up paying $60,000 in damages when it lost a lawsuit stemming from this intimidation.[23] We also can recall that the Fanjuls, the Cuban American sugar barons, have no problem ignoring labor laws in dealing with their migrant labor force, and that Sue Ling Gin, one of the Asian Americans on our list of corporate directors, explained to an interviewer that, at one point in her career, she had hired an all-female staff, not out of feminist principles but *because women would work for lower wages*. Linda Wachner, Thomas Fuentes, the Fanjuls, and Sue Ling Gin acted as employers, not as members of disadvantaged groups. That is, members of the power elite of both genders and of all ethnicities practice class politics.

Conclusion

The black and white liberals and progressives who challenged Christian, white, male homogeneity in the power structure starting in the 1950s and 1960s sought to do more than create civil rights and new job opportunities for men and women who had previously been mistreated and excluded, important though these goals were. They also hoped that new perspectives in the boardrooms and the halls of government would spread greater openness throughout the society. The idea was both to diversify the power elite and to shift some of its power to underrepresented groups and social classes. The social movements of the 1960s were strikingly successful in increasing the individual rights and freedoms available to all Americans, especially African Americans. As we have shown, they also created pressures that led to openings at the top for individuals from groups that had previously been ignored.

But as some individuals made it, and as the concerns of social movements, political leaders, and the courts gradually came to focus more and more on individual rights and individual advancement, the focus on "distributive justice," general racial exclusion, and social class was lost. The age-old American commitment to individualism, reinforced by tokenism and reassurances from members of the power elite, won out over the commitment to greater equality of income and wealth that had been one strand of New Deal liberalism and a major emphasis of left-wing activism in the 1960s.

We therefore conclude that the increased diversity in the power elite has not generated any changes in an underlying class system in which the top 1 percent of households (the upper class) own 33.4 percent of all marketable wealth, and the next 19 percent (the managerial, professional, and small business stratum) have 51 percent, which means that just 20 percent of the people own a remarkable 84 percent of the privately owned wealth in the United States, leaving a mere 16 percent of the wealth for the bottom 80 percent (wage and salary workers).[24] In fact, the wealth and income distributions became even more skewed starting in the 1970s as the majority of whites, especially in the South and Great Plains, switched their allegiance to the Republican Party and thereby paved the way for a conservative resurgence that is as antiunion, antitax, and antigovernment as it is determined to impose ultraconservative social values on all Americans.

The values of liberal individualism embedded in the Declaration of Independence, the Bill of Rights, and American civic culture were renewed by vigorous and courageous activists in the years between 1955 and 1975, but the class structure remains a major obstacle to individual fulfillment for the overwhelming majority of Americans. The conservative backlash that claims to speak for individual rights has strengthened this class structure, one that thwarts advancement for most individuals from families in the bottom 80 percent of the wealth distribution. This solidification of class divisions in the name of individualism is more than an irony. It is a dilemma.

Furthermore, this dilemma combines with the dilemma of race to obscure further the impact of class and to limit individual mobility, simply because the majority of middle-American whites cannot bring themselves to make common cause with African Americans in the name of greater individual opportunity and economic equality through a progressive income tax and the kind of government programs that lifted past generations out of poverty. These intertwined dilemmas of class and race lead to a nation that celebrates individualism, equal opportunity, and diversity but is, in reality, a bastion of class privilege, African American exclusion, and conservatism.

ENDNOTES

[1]On the continuing importance of class voting in the United States, contrary to recent claims based on weak methods, see Jeff Manza and Clem Brooks, *Social Cleavages and Political Change: Voter Alignments and U.S. Party Coalitions* (New York: Oxford University Press, 1999). On class voting by Latinos, see Barry Kosmin and Ariela Keysar, "Party Political Preferences of U.S. Hispanics: The Varying Impact of Religion, Social Class and Demographic Factors," *Ethnic and Racial Studies* 18, no. 2 (1995): 336–47. . . . On class voting by Chinese Americans, see Wendy Tam, "Asians—a Monolithic Voting Bloc?" *Political Behavior* 17, no. 2 (1995): 223–49.

[2]Richard L. Zweigenhaft and G. William Domhoff, *Blacks in the White Elite* (Lanham, MD: Rowman & Littlefield, 2003), 158–60.

[3]Glass Ceiling Commission, *Good for Business: Making Full Use of the Nation's Human Capital, a Fact-Finding Report of the Federal Glass Ceiling Commission* (Washington, D.C.: U.S. Government Printing Office, 1995), 95.

[4]Julia Alvarez, "A White Woman of Color," in *Half and Half: Writers on Growing Up Biracial and Bicultural,* ed. Claudine Chiawei O'Hearn, 139–49 (New York: Pantheon, 1998). . . .

[5]Michael Mann, *The Dark Side of Democracy: Explaining Ethnic Cleansing* (New York: Cambridge University Press, 2005); Karl Eschbach, "The Enduring and Vanishing American Indian: American Indian Population Growth and Intermarriage in 1990," *Ethnic and Racial Studies,* 18, no. 1 (1995): 89–108.

[6]Glenn Loury, *The Anatomy of Racial Inequality* (Cambridge: Harvard University Press, 2002), 69.

[7]Michael Schwartz, *Radical Protest and Social Structure: The Southern Farmers' Alliance and Cotton Tenancy, 1880–1890* (New York: Academic Press, 1976).

[8]Kevin Fox Gotham, *Race, Real Estate, and Uneven Development* (Albany: State University of New York Press, 2002); Michael K. Brown, Martin Carnoy, Elliott Currie, Troy Duster, David B. Oppenheimer, Marjorie M. Shultz, and David Wellman, *Whitewashing Race: The Myth of a Color-Blind Society* (Berkeley: University of California Press, 2003).

[9]Thomas M. Shapiro, *The Hidden Cost of Being African American: How Wealth Perpetuates Inequality* (New York: Oxford University Press, 2004).

[10]Shapiro, *Hidden Cost,* 2.

[11]Devah Pager and Bruce Western, "Discrimination in Low-Wage Labor Markets: Results from an Experimental Audit Study in New York City" (paper presented at the annual meeting of the American Sociological Association, Philadelphia, Pennsylvania, 2005); Deirdre A. Royster, *Race and the Invisible Hand: How White Networks Exclude Black Men from Blue-collar Jobs* (Berkeley: University of California Press, 2003).

[12]Lawrence Bobo and Ryan Smith, "From Jim Crow to Laissez-faire Racism: The Transformation of Racial Attitudes," in *Beyond Pluralism: The Conception of Groups and Group Identities in America*, ed. Wendy Katkin, Ned Landsman, and Andrea Tyree, 182–220 (Urbana: University of Illinois Press, 1998); Eduardo Bonilla-Silva, *Racism without Racists: Color-Blind Racism and the Persistence of Racial Inequality in the United States* (Lanham, MD: Rowman & Littlefield, 2003).

[13]James M. Jones, *Prejudice and Racism*, 2nd ed. (New York: McGraw-Hill, 1997); John F. Dovidio, "On the Nature of Contemporary Prejudice: The Third Wave," *Journal of Social Issues* 57, no. 4 (2001): 829–49.

[14]Douglas S. Massey and Nancy A. Denton, *American Apartheid: Segregation and the Making of the Underclass* (Cambridge: Harvard University Press, 1993), 61.

[15]Massey and Denton, *American Apartheid*, 67, 223.

[16]William Clark and Sarah Blue, "Race, Class, and Segregation Patterns in U.S. Immigrant Gateway Cities," *Urban Affairs Review* 39 (2004): 667–88; John Iceland, Cicely Sharpe, and Erika Steinmetz, "Class Differences in African American Residential Patterns in US Metropolitan Areas: 1990–2000," *Social Science Research* 34 (2005): 252–66.

[17]Jerry A. Jacobs and Teresa Labov, "Asian Brides, Anglo Grooms: Asian Exceptionalism in Intermarriage," Department of Sociology, University of Pennsylvania, October 1995; . . .

[18]Jacobs and Labov, "Sex Differences in Intermarriage," 11.

[19]Jerry A. Jacobs and Teresa Labov, "Gender Differentials in Intermarriage among Sixteen Race and Ethnic Groups," *Sociological Forum* 17 (2002): 621–46.

[20]See Sharon Collins, *Black Corporate Executives: The Making and Breaking of a Black Middle Class* (Philadelphia: Temple University Press, 1997). For a systematic empirical demonstration of the importance of such government policies using time series data, see Martin Carnoy, *Faded Dreams: The Politics and Economics of Race in America* (New York: Cambridge University Press, 1994).

[21]Zweigenhaft and Domhoff, *Blacks in the White Elite*, 2003.

[22]Sara Rimer, "Fall of a Shirtmaking Legend Shakes Its Maine Hometown," *New York Times*, May 15, 1996. See, also, Floyd Norris, "Market Place," *New York Times*, June 7, 1996; Stephanie Strom, "Double Trouble at Linda Wachner's Twin Companies," *New York Times*, August 4, 1996. Strom's article reveals that Hathaway Shirts "got a reprieve" when an investor group stepped in to save it.

[23]Claudia Luther and Steven Churm, "GOP Official Says He OK'd Observers at Polls," *Los Angeles Times*, November 12, 1988; Jeffrey Perlman, "Firm Will Pay $60,000 in Suit over Guards at Polls," *Los Angeles Times*, May 31, 1989.

[24]Edward N. Wolff, "Changes in Household Wealth in the 1980s and 1990s in the U.S." (working paper 407, Levy Economics Institute, Bard College, 2004), at www.levy.org.

37

THE RISE OF THE NEW GLOBAL ELITE

CHRYSTIA FREELAND

C. Wright Mills' notion of the power elite can be seen in many social contexts in the United States, including the recent political and economic maneuvering related to terrorism, homeland security, and the war in Iraq. We also see evidence of the power elite in the evolution of PACs (political action committees) to the new super PACs that get around campaign financing reforms and allow wealthy individuals and organizations to donate huge sums to political campaigns. The following reading by business journalist Chrystia Freeland is excerpted from a 2011 article in *The Atlantic*, where Freeland examines how the power elite is now a global phenomenon generated by the wealth created from transnational companies and the expansion of global capitalism. Freeland demonstrates well that this new global elite is increasingly separate from national governments and other social institutions that defined Mills' original view of the Iron Triangle in the United States: the U.S. government, the military, and American corporations.

If you happened to be watching NBC on the first Sunday morning in August last summer, you would have seen something curious. There, on the set of *Meet the Press*, the host, David Gregory, was interviewing a guest who made a forceful case that the U.S. economy had become "very distorted." In the wake of the recession, this guest explained, high-income individuals, large banks, and major corporations had experienced a "significant recovery"; the rest of the economy, by contrast—including small businesses and "a very significant amount of the labor force"—was stuck and still struggling. What we were seeing, he argued, was not a single economy at all, but rather "fundamentally two separate types of economy," increasingly distinct and divergent.

This diagnosis, though alarming, was hardly unique: drawing attention to the divide between the wealthy and everyone else has long been standard fare on the left. (The idea of "two Americas" was a central theme of John Edwards' 2004 and 2008 presidential runs.) What made the argument striking in this instance was that it was being offered by none other than the former five-term Federal Reserve chairman Alan Greenspan: iconic libertarian, preeminent defender of the free market, and (at least until recently) the nation's foremost devotee of Ayn Rand. When the high priest of capitalism himself is declaring the growth in economic inequality a national crisis, something has gone very, very wrong.

This widening gap between the rich and nonrich has been evident for years. In a 2005 report to investors, for instance, three analysts at Citigroup advised that "the World is dividing into two blocs—the Plutonomy and the rest":

> *In a plutonomy there is no such animal as "the U.S. consumer" or "the UK consumer," or indeed the "Russian consumer." There are rich consumers, few in number, but disproportionate in the gigantic slice of income and consumption they take. There are the rest, the "nonrich," the multitudinous many, but only accounting for surprisingly small bites of the national pie.*

Before the recession, it was relatively easy to ignore this concentration of wealth among an elite few. The wondrous inventions of the modern economy—Google, Amazon, the iPhone—broadly improved the lives of middle-class consumers, even as they made a tiny subset of entrepreneurs hugely wealthy. And the less-wondrous inventions—particularly the explosion of subprime credit—helped mask the rise of income inequality for many of those whose earnings were stagnant.

But the financial crisis and its long, dismal aftermath have changed all that. A multibillion-dollar bailout and Wall Street's swift, subsequent reinstatement of gargantuan bonuses have inspired a narrative of parasitic bankers and other elites rigging the game for their own benefit. And this, in turn, has led to wider—and not unreasonable—fears that we are living in not merely a plutonomy, but a plutocracy, in which the rich display outsize political influence, narrowly self-interested motives, and a casual indifference to anyone outside their own rarefied economic bubble.

Through my work as a business journalist, I've spent the better part of the past decade shadowing the new superrich: attending the same exclusive conferences in Europe; conducting interviews over cappuccinos on Martha's Vineyard or in Silicon Valley meeting rooms; observing high-powered dinner parties in Manhattan. Some of what I've learned is entirely predictable: the rich are, as F. Scott Fitzgerald famously noted, different from you and me.

What is more relevant to our times, though, is that the rich of today are also different from the rich of yesterday. Our light-speed, globally connected economy has led to the rise of a new superelite that consists, to a notable degree, of first- and second-generation wealth. Its members are hardworking, highly educated, jet-setting meritocrats who feel they are the deserving winners of a tough, worldwide economic competition—and many of them, as a result, have an ambivalent attitude toward those of us who didn't succeed so spectacularly. Perhaps most noteworthy, they are becoming a transglobal community of peers who have more in common with one another than with their countrymen back home. Whether they maintain primary residences in New York or Hong Kong, Moscow or Mumbai, today's superrich are increasingly a nation unto themselves.

The Winner-Take-Most Economy

The rise of the new plutocracy is inextricably connected to two phenomena: the revolution in information technology and the liberalization of global trade. Individual nations have offered their own contributions to income inequality—financial deregulation and upper-bracket tax cuts in the United States; insider privatization in Russia; rent-seeking in regulated industries in India and Mexico. But the shared narrative is that, thanks to globalization and technological innovation, people, money, and ideas travel more freely today than ever before.

Peter Lindert is an economist at the University of California at Davis and one of the leaders of the "deep history" school of economics, a movement devoted to thinking about the world economy over the long term—that is to say, in the context of the entire sweep of human civilization. Yet he argues that the economic changes we are witnessing today are unprecedented. *Britain's classic industrial revolution was far less impressive than what has been going on in the past 30 years*, he told me. The current productivity gains are larger, he explained, and the waves of disruptive innovation much, much faster.

From a global perspective, the impact of these developments has been overwhelmingly positive, particularly in the poorer parts of the world. Take India and China, for example: between 1820 and 1950, nearly a century and a half, per capita income in those two countries was basically flat. Between 1950 and 1973, it increased by 68 percent. Then, between 1973 and 2002, it grew by 245 percent, and continues to grow strongly despite the global financial crisis.

But within nations, the fruits of this global transformation have been shared unevenly. Though China's middle class has grown exponentially and tens of millions have been lifted out of poverty, the superelite in Shanghai and other east-coast cities have steadily pulled away. Income inequality has also increased in developing markets such as India and Russia, and across much of the industrialized West, from the relatively laissez-faire United States to the comfy social democracies of Canada and Scandinavia. Thomas Friedman is right that in many ways the world has become flatter; but in others it has grown spikier.

One reason for the spikes is that the global market and its associated technologies have enabled the creation of a class of international business megastars. As companies become bigger, the global environment more competitive, and the rate of disruptive technological innovation ever faster, the value to shareholders of attracting the best possible CEO increases correspondingly. Executive pay has skyrocketed for many reasons—including the prevalence of overly cozy boards and changing cultural norms about pay—but increasing scale, competition, and innovation have all played major roles.

Many corporations have profited from this economic upheaval. Expanded global access to labor (skilled and unskilled alike), customers, and capital has lowered traditional barriers to entry and increased the value of an ahead-of-the-curve insight or innovation. Facebook, whose founder, Mark Zuckerberg, dropped out of college just six years ago, is already challenging Google, itself hardly an old-school corporation. But the biggest winners have been individuals, not institutions. The hedge-fund manager John Paulson, for instance, single-handedly profited almost as much from the crisis of 2008 as Goldman Sachs did.

Meanwhile, the vast majority of U.S. workers, however devoted and skilled at their jobs, have missed out on the windfalls of this winner-take-most economy—or worse, found their savings, employers, or professions ravaged by the same forces that have enriched the plutocratic elite. The result of these divergent trends is a jaw-dropping surge in U.S. income inequality. According to the economists Emmanuel Saez of Berkeley and Thomas Piketty of the Paris School of Economics, between 2002 and 2007, 65 percent of all income growth in the United States went to the top 1 percent of the population. The financial crisis interrupted this trend temporarily, as incomes for the top 1 percent fell more than those of the rest of the population in 2008. But recent evidence suggests that, in the wake of the crisis, incomes at the summit are rebounding more quickly than those below. One example: after a down year in 2008, the top 25 hedge-fund managers were paid, on average, more than $1 billion each in 2009, quickly eclipsing the record they had set in prerecession 2007. . . .

The Road to Davos

To grasp the difference between today's plutocrats and the hereditary elite, who (to use John Stuart Mill's memorable phrase) "grow rich in their sleep," one need merely glance at the events that now fill high-end social calendars. The debutante balls and hunts and regattas of yesteryear may not be quite obsolete, but they are headed in that direction. The real community life of the 21st-century plutocracy occurs on the international conference circuit.

The best-known of these events is the World Economic Forum's annual meeting in Davos, Switzerland, invitation to which marks an aspiring plutocrat's arrival on the international scene. The Bilderberg Group, which meets annually at locations in Europe and North America, is more exclusive still—and more secretive—though it is more focused on geopolitics and less on global business and philanthropy. The Boao Forum for Asia, convened on China's Hainan Island each spring, offers evidence of that nation's growing economic importance and its understanding of the plutocratic culture. Bill Clinton is pushing hard to win his Clinton Global Initiative a regular place on the circuit. The TED conferences (the acronym stands for "Technology, Entertainment, Design") are an important stop for the digerati; Herb Allen's Sun Valley gathering, for the media moguls; and the Aspen Institute's Ideas Festival (co-sponsored by this magazine), for the more policy-minded.

Recognizing the value of such global conclaves, some corporations have begun hosting their own. Among these is Google's Zeitgeist conference, where I have moderated discussions for several years. One of the most recent gatherings was held last May at the Grove Hotel, a former provincial estate in the English countryside, whose 300-acre grounds have been transformed into a golf course and whose high-ceilinged rooms are now decorated with a mixture of antique and contemporary furniture. (Mock Louis XIV chairs—made, with a wink, from high-end plastic—are much in evidence.) Last year, Cirque du Soleil offered the 500 guests a private performance in an enormous tent erected on the grounds; in 2007, to celebrate its acquisition of YouTube, Google flew in overnight Internet sensations from around the world.

Yet for all its luxury, the mood of the Zeitgeist conference is hardly sybaritic. Rather, it has the intense, earnest atmosphere of a gathering of college summa cum laudes. This is not a group that plays hooky: the conference room is full from 9 a.m. to 6 p.m., and during coffee breaks the lawns are crowded with executives checking their BlackBerrys and iPads.

Last year's lineup of Zeitgeist speakers included such notables as Archbishop Desmond Tutu, London mayor Boris Johnson, and Starbucks CEO Howard Schultz (not to mention, of course, Google's own CEO, Eric Schmidt). But the most potent currency at this and comparable gatherings is neither fame nor money. Rather, it's what author Michael Lewis has dubbed "the new new thing"—the insight or algorithm or technology with the potential to change the world, however briefly. Hence the presence last year of three Nobel laureates, including Daniel Kahneman, a pioneer in behavioral economics. One of the business stars in attendance was the 36-year-old entrepreneur Tony Hsieh, who had sold his Zappos online shoe retailer to Amazon for more than $1 billion the previous summer. And the most popular session of all was the one in which Google showcased some of its new inventions, including the Nexus phone.

This geeky enthusiasm for innovation and ideas is evident at more intimate gatherings of the global elite as well. Take the elegant Manhattan dinner parties hosted by Marie-Josée Kravis, the economist wife of the private-equity billionaire Henry, in their elegant Upper East Side apartment. Though the china is Sèvres and the paintings are museum quality (Marie-Josée is, after all, president of the Museum of Modern Art's board), the dinner-table conversation would not be out of place in a graduate seminar. Mrs. Kravis takes pride in bringing together not only plutocrats such as her husband and Michael Bloomberg, but also thinkers and policy makers such as Richard Holbrooke, Robert Zoellick, and *Financial Times* columnist Martin Wolf, and leading them in discussion of matters ranging from global financial imbalances to the war in Afghanistan.

Indeed, in this age of elites who delight in such phrases as *outside the box* and *killer app,* arguably the most coveted status symbol isn't a yacht, a racehorse, or a knighthood; it's a philanthropic foundation—and, more than that, one actively managed in ways that show its sponsor has big ideas for reshaping the world. . . .

One of the most determined is the Ukrainian entrepreneur Victor Pinchuk, whose business empire ranges from pipe manufacturing to TV stations. With a net worth of $3 billion, Pinchuk is no longer content merely to acquire modern art: in 2009, he began a global competition for young artists, run by his art center in Kiev and conceived as a way of bringing Ukraine into the international cultural mainstream. Pinchuk hosts a regular lunch on the fringes of Davos and has launched his own annual "ideas forum," a gathering devoted to geopolitics that is held, with suitable modesty, in the same Crimean villa where Stalin, Roosevelt, and Churchill attended the Yalta Conference. Last September's meeting, where I served as a moderator, included Bill Clinton, International Monetary Fund head Dominique Strauss-Kahn, Polish president Bronislaw Komorowski, and Russian deputy prime minister Alexei Kudrin. . . .

As an entrée into the global superelite, Pinchuk's efforts seem to be working: on a visit to the U.S. last spring, the oligarch met with David Axelrod, President Obama's top political adviser, in Washington and schmoozed with Charlie Rose at a New York book party for *Time* magazine editor Rick Stengel. On a previous trip, he'd dined with Caroline Kennedy at the Upper East Side townhouse of HBO's Richard Plepler. Back home, he has entertained his fellow art enthusiast Eli Broad at his palatial estate (which features its own nine-hole golf course) outside Kiev, and has partnered with Soros to finance Ukrainian civil-society projects.

A Nation Apart

Pinchuk's growing international Rolodex illustrates another defining characteristic of today's plutocrats: they are forming a global community, and their ties to one another are increasingly closer than their ties to hoi polloi back home. As Glenn Hutchins, co-founder of the private-equity firm Silver Lake, puts it, *A person in Africa who runs a big African bank and went to Harvard might have more in common with me than he does with his neighbors, and I could well share more overlapping concerns and experiences with him than with my neighbors.* The circles we move in, Hutchins explains, are defined by "interests" and "activities" rather than "geography": *Beijing has a lot in common with New York, London, or Mumbai. You see the same people, you eat in the same restaurants, you stay in the same hotels. But most important, we are engaged as global citizens in crosscutting commercial, political, and social matters of common concern. We are much less place-based than we used to be.*

In a similar vein, the wife of one of America's most successful hedge-fund managers offered me the small but telling observation that her husband is better able to navigate the streets of Davos than those of his native Manhattan. When he's at home, she explained, he is ferried around town by a car and driver; the snowy Swiss hamlet, which is too small and awkward for limos, is the only place where he actually walks. An American media executive living in London put it more succinctly still: *We are the people who know airline flight attendants better than we know our own wives.*

America's business elite is something of a latecomer to this transnational community. In a study of British and American CEOs, for example, Elisabeth Marx, of the headhunting firm Heidrick & Struggles, found that almost a third of the former were foreign nationals, compared with just 10 percent of the latter. Similarly, more than two-thirds of the Brits had worked abroad for at least a year, whereas just a third of the Americans had done so.

But despite the slow start, American business is catching up: the younger generation of chief executives has significantly more international experience than the older generation, and the number of foreign and foreign-born CEOs, while still relatively small, is rising. The shift is particularly evident on Wall Street: in 2006, each of America's eight biggest banks was run by a native-born CEO; today, five of those banks remain, and two of the survivors—Citigroup and Morgan Stanley—are led by men who were born abroad.

Mohamed El-Erian, the CEO of Pimco, the world's largest bond manager, is typical of the internationalists gradually rising to the top echelons of U.S. business. The son of an Egyptian father and a French mother, El-Erian had a peripatetic childhood, shuttling between Egypt, France, the United States, the United Kingdom, and Switzerland. He was educated at Cambridge and Oxford and now leads a U.S.-based company that is owned by the German financial conglomerate Allianz SE.

Though El-Erian lives in Laguna Beach, California, near where Pimco is headquartered, he says that he can't name a single country as his own. *I have had the privilege of living in many countries,* El-Erian told me on a recent visit to New York. *One consequence is that I am a sort of global nomad, open to many perspectives.* As he talked, we walked through Midtown, which El-Erian remembered fondly from his childhood, when he'd take the crosstown bus each day to the United Nations International School. That evening, El-Erian was catching a flight to London. Later in the week, he was due in St. Petersburg.

Indeed, there is a growing sense that American businesses that don't internationalize aggressively risk being left behind. For all its global reach, Pimco is still based in the United States. But the flows of goods and capital upon which the superelite surf are bypassing America more often than they used to. Take, for example, Stephen Jennings, the 50-year-old New Zealander who co-founded the investment bank Renaissance Capital. Renaissance's roots are in Moscow, where Jennings maintains his primary residence, and his business strategy involves positioning the firm to capture the investment flows between the emerging markets, particularly Russia, Africa, and Asia. For his purposes, New York is increasingly irrelevant. In a 2009 speech in Wellington, New Zealand, he offered his vision of this post-unipolar business reality: *The largest metals group in the world is Indian. The largest aluminum group in the world is Russian. . . . The fastest-growing and largest banks in China, Russia, and Nigeria are all domestic.*

As it happens, a fellow tenant in Jennings' high-tech, high-rise Moscow office building recently put together a deal that exemplifies just this kind of intra-emerging-market trade. Last year, Digital Sky Technologies, Russia's largest technology investment firm, entered into a partnership with the South African media corporation Naspers and the Chinese technology company Tencent. All three are fast-growing firms with global vision—last fall, a DST spin-off called Mail.ru went public and immediately became Europe's most highly valued Internet company—yet none is primarily focused on the

United States. A similar harbinger of the intra-emerging-market economy was the acquisition by Bharti Enterprises, the Indian telecom giant, of the African properties of the Kuwait-based telecom firm Zain. A California technology executive explained to me that a company like Bharti has a competitive advantage in what he believes will be the exploding African market: *They know how to provide mobile phones so much more cheaply than we do. In a place like Africa, how can Western firms compete?*

The good news—and the bad news—for America is that the nation's own superelite is rapidly adjusting to this more global perspective. The U.S.-based CEO of one of the world's largest hedge funds told me that his firm's investment committee often discusses the question of who wins and who loses in today's economy. In a recent internal debate, he said, one of his senior colleagues had argued that the hollowing-out of the American middle class didn't really matter. *His point was that if the transformation of the world economy lifts four people in China and India out of poverty and into the middle class, and meanwhile means one American drops out of the middle class, that's not such a bad trade*, the CEO recalled.

I heard a similar sentiment from the Taiwanese-born, 30-something CFO of a U.S. Internet company. A gentle, unpretentious man who went from public school to Harvard, he's nonetheless not terribly sympathetic to the complaints of the American middle class. *We demand a higher paycheck than the rest of the world*, he told me. *So if you're going to demand 10 times the paycheck, you need to deliver 10 times the value. It sounds harsh, but maybe people in the middle class need to decide to take a pay cut.*

At last summer's Aspen Ideas Festival, Michael Splinter, CEO of the Silicon Valley green-tech firm Applied Materials, said that if he were starting from scratch, only 20 percent of his workforce would be domestic. *This year, almost 90 percent of our sales will be outside the U.S.*, he explained. *The pull to be close to the customers—most of them in Asia—is enormous.* Speaking at the same conference, Thomas Wilson, CEO of Allstate, also lamented this global reality: *I can get [workers] anywhere in the world. It is a problem for America, but it is not necessarily a problem for American business. . . . American businesses will adapt. . . .*

The Backlash

The cultural ties that bind the superrich to everyone else are fraying from both ends at once. Since World War II, the United States in particular has had an ethos of aspirational capitalism. As Soros told me, *It is easier to be rich in America than in Europe, because Europeans envy the billionaire, but Americans hope to emulate him.* But as the wealth gap has grown wider, and the rich have appeared to benefit disproportionately from government bailouts, that admiration has begun to sour.

One measure of the pricklier mood is how risky it has become for politicians to champion Big Business publicly. Defending Big Oil and railing against government interference used to be part of the job description of

Texas Republicans. But when Congressman Joe Barton tried to take the White House to task for its postspill "shakedown" of BP, he was immediately silenced by party elders. New York's Charles Schumer is sometimes described as "the senator from Wall Street." Yet when the financial-reform bill came to the Senate last spring—a political tussle in which each side furiously accused the other of carrying water for the banks—on Wall Street, Schumer was called the "invisible man" for his uncharacteristic silence on the issue.

In June, when I asked Larry Summers, then the president's chief economic adviser, about hedge funds' objections to the carried-interest tax reform, he was quick to disassociate himself from Wall Street's concerns. *If that's been the largest public-policy issue you've encountered*, he told me, *you've been traveling in different circles than I have been over the last several months.* I reminded him that he had in fact worked for a hedge fund, D. E. Shaw, as recently as 2008, and he emphasized his use of the qualifier *over the last several months.*

Critiques of the superelite are becoming more common even at gatherings of the superelite. At a *Wall Street Journal* conference in December 2009, Paul Volcker, the legendary former head of the Federal Reserve, argued that Wall Street's claims of wealth creation were without any real basis. *I wish someone*, he said, *would give me one shred of neutral evidence that financial innovation has led to economic growth—one shred of evidence.*

At Google's May Zeitgeist gathering, Desmond Tutu, the opening speaker, took direct aim at executive compensation. *I do have a very real concern about capitalism*, he lectured the gathered executives. *The Goldman Sachs thing. I read that one of the directors general—whatever they are called, CEO—took away one year as his salary $64 million. Sixty-four million dollars.* He sputtered to a stop, momentarily stunned by this sum (though, by the standards of Wall Street and Silicon Valley compensation, it's not actually that much money). In an op-ed in *The Wall Street Journal* last year, even the economist Klaus Schwab—founder of the World Economic Forum and its iconic Davos meeting—warned that "the entrepreneurial system is being perverted," and businesses that "fall back into old habits and excesses" could "undermin[e] social peace."

Bridging the Divide

Not all plutocrats, of course, are created equal. Apple's visionary Steve Jobs is neither the moral nor the economic equivalent of the Russian oligarchs who made their fortunes by brazenly seizing their country's natural resources. And while the benefits of the past decade's financial "innovations" are, as Volcker noted, very much in question, many plutocratic fortunes—especially in the technology sector—have been built on advances that have broadly benefited the nation and the world. That is why, even as the TARP-recipient bankers have become objects of widespread anger, figures such as Jobs, Bill Gates, and Warren Buffett remain heroes.

And, ultimately, that is the dilemma: America really does need many of its plutocrats. We benefit from the goods they produce and the jobs they create. And even if a growing portion of those jobs are overseas, it is better to be the home of these innovators—native and immigrant alike—than not. In today's hypercompetitive global environment, we need a creative, dynamic superelite more than ever.

There is also the simple fact that someone will have to pay for the improved public education and social safety net the American middle class will need in order to navigate the wrenching transformations of the global economy. (That's not to mention the small matter of the budget deficit.) Inevitably, a lot of that money will have to come from the wealthy—after all, as the bank robbers say, that's where the money is.

It is not much of a surprise that the plutocrats themselves oppose such analysis and consider themselves singled out, unfairly maligned, or even punished for their success. Self-interest, after all, is the mother of rationalization, and—as we have seen—many of the plutocracy's rationalizations have more than a bit of truth to them: as a class, they are generally more hardworking and meritocratic than their forebears; their philanthropic efforts are innovative and important; and the recent losses of the American middle class have in many cases entailed gains for the rest of the world.

But if the plutocrats' opposition to increases in their taxes and tighter regulation of their economic activities is understandable, it is also a mistake. The real threat facing the superelite, at home and abroad, isn't modestly higher taxes, but rather the possibility that inchoate public rage could cohere into a more concrete populist agenda—that, for instance, middle-class Americans could conclude that the world economy isn't working for them and decide that protectionism or truly punitive taxation is preferable to incremental measures such as the eventual repeal of the upper-bracket Bush tax cuts.

Mohamed El-Erian, the Pimco CEO, is a model member of the superelite. But he is also a man whose father grew up in rural Egypt, and he has studied nations where the gaps between the rich and the poor have had violent resolutions. *For successful people to say the challenges faced by the lower end of the income distribution aren't relevant to them is shortsighted*, he told me. Noting that *global labor and capital are doing better than their strictly national counterparts* in most Western industrialized nations, El-Erian added, *I think this will lead to increasingly inward-looking social and political conditions. I worry that we risk ending up with very insular policies that will not do well in a global world. One of the big surprises of 2010 is that the protectionist dog didn't bark. But that will come under pressure.*

The lesson of history is that, in the long run, superelites have two ways to survive: by suppressing dissent or by sharing their wealth. It is obvious which of these would be the better outcome for America, and the world. Let us hope the plutocrats aren't already too isolated to recognize this. Because, in the end, there can never be a place like Galt's Gulch.

38

CONVERGENCE
News Production in a Digital Age

ERIC KLINENBERG

This selection by Eric Klinenberg is the first of three readings to examine the institution of the media. Klinenberg, professor of sociology at New York University, argues that sociologists need to study the organizations of mass media to better understand their role in society. The mass media is a powerful institution not only because it is influential in molding public consciousness but because the ownership and control of the mass media are highly concentrated. Think of the AOL-Time Warner merger in recent years as one example of a media giant. In addition to owning networks, publishing houses, newspapers, and so on, AOL-Time Warner also owns the CNN news affiliate. This concentration of ownership ensures little diversity in the messages that the media promotes. Klinenberg's in-depth study of one news organization, below, illustrates how the constraints of time, space, and marketing pressure create a convergence in news media reporting. Journalists and editors are increasingly influenced by marketing research and new communication technologies to report the news in a certain way.

A paradox of contemporary sociology is that the discipline has largely abandoned the empirical study of journalistic organizations and news institutions at the moment when the media has gained visibility in political, economic, and cultural spheres; when other academic fields have embraced the study of media and society; and when leading sociological theorists—including Bourdieu (1998), Habermas (1989), Castells (1996), and Luhmann (2000)—have broken from the disciplinary cannon to argue that the media are key actors in modern life. Herbert Gans (1972) called attention to this "famine in media research" in a review article in the *American Journal of Sociology*. Yet—with the notable exceptions of a few landmark studies conducted in the 1970s (Tuchman 1978; Gans 1979; Fishman 1980)—in the past thirty years American sociologists have largely stayed out of newsrooms and ignored the conditions of journalistic production. Although a few studies are emerging of digital technologies in newsrooms, and of labor issues for journalists, the media scholar Timothy Cook (1998: x) noted that "it

Eric Klinenberg, "Convergence: News Production in a Digital Age." *Annals of the American Academy of Political and Social Sciences,* 597, January 2005. Copyright © 2005, American Academy of Political & Social Science. Reprinted by permission of Sage Publications, Inc.

is as if a virtual moratorium were placed on further studies" of newsrooms. The sociology of news organizations is all but dead.

Ironically, studies of media are flourishing elsewhere in the academy. Today, most major universities have developed schools, departments, and programs dedicated to media and communications. Political scientists consider the news organization a political institution (or "fourth estate"), and most government agencies employ public relations specialists to manage their representations in the public sphere. Economists attribute fluctuations in the market to reports and opinions broadcast in the specialized business media, and financial analysts pay close attention to the way media pundits cover various industries and companies. Anthropologists have discovered the centrality of media as a source of imagination, migration, and the articulation of identity, and they are observing sites of production, reception, and circulation in diverse settings (Appadurai 1996; Ginsburg, Abu-Lughod and Larkin 2002). . . .

If, indeed, there is consensus that media products are central to the operations of different fields of action, it is surprising that sociologists have stopped examining how organizations responsible for producing the news and information work. Research in other disciplines often emphasizes the importance of sociological studies of news institutions, only to cite work that is several decades old and no longer reliable to explain how newsrooms work. Lacking current research, critics are left to guess about the strategies, practices, and interests that shape major news corporations; determine the content of news products; and produce the "symbolic power" (Bourdieu 1994) of publicly defining, delimiting, and framing key issues and events. Communications scholars, for example, often rely on anecdotal evidence for their assessments of how changes in the media industry have affected conditions of news production. Within sociology, social problems scholars typically do careful work to *show that* journalists selectively frame public issues; yet they rarely follow up by going inside newsrooms and asking reporters and editors how they constructed their stories, instead *speculating about why* the coverage takes certain forms.[1]

There has been no shortage of activity and change within media institutions and the journalistic field since the 1970s. The past thirty years has been a revolutionary period in the news media, which have experienced

- ▾ the advent of cable television, the beginning of a twenty-four-hour news cycle, and the steady decline of newspaper readership levels (though not a decline in newspaper profitability);
- ▾ the introduction of advanced communications technologies, such as satellites, the Internet, desktop publishing, and, most important, computers, which were rarely used in the newsrooms of the 1970s;
- ▾ the demise of family-owned news organizations with special interests in supporting journalistic principles with lower revenues and the emergence of chain papers and multimedia production companies;
- ▾ the rise of conglomerate media giants that use synergistic production and distribution strategies (in which different branches of the company share and cross-promote each others' resources and services);

- ▾ the related destruction of legendary divisions between managerial and editorial operations, the mythical church and state of the journalistic field;
- ▾ the birth of new forms and formats, such as the television news magazine, dramatized news footage, and product-driven news sections;
- ▾ the deregulation of media markets, and specifically of restrictions on ownership of multiple media outlets in the same city; and
- ▾ a crisis of legitimacy for journalists, who often complain that new conditions of production undermine their capacity to meet their own standards, struggle with the emergence of a polarized labor force including a celebrity class of journalistic elites, and consistently rank at the bottom of opinion polls rating the popularity of various professions (Gans 2003).

These transformations are pervasive: in 1945, for example, roughly 80 percent of American daily papers were independently owned. By 2000, about 80 percent were owned and operated by publicly traded chains, and major media corporations were actively building lines of vertical and horizontal integration to link everything from news production to entertainment to advertising in-house (Dugger 2000). Yet in the United States, little ethnographic work penetrates these organizations to describe or explain how they work.

This article examines the point of journalistic production in one major news organization and shows how reporters and editors manage constraints of time, space, and market pressure under regimes of convergence news making. I describe how news organizations, like firms in other American industries during the recent phase of "flexible accumulation," have downsized their staffs while imposing new demands that workers become skilled at multitasking with new technologies. Digital systems for reporting, writing, file sharing, and printing facilitate this flexibility. I consider the implications of these conditions for the particular forms of intellectual and cultural labor that journalists produce, drawing connections between the political economy of the journalistic field, the organizational structure of multimedia firms, new communications technologies, and the qualities of content created by news workers.

This article grows out of a multiyear ethnographic project based on case studies of news organizations that began as print media but now use advanced technologies to produce and distribute content across platforms. Here, I draw upon field-work to show how changes in the journalistic field, particularly the rise of new technologies and the corporate integration of news companies, have led to a double fragmentation: first, for newsmakers, whose daily work has been interrupted and rearranged by additional responsibilities and new pressures of time and space; second, for news audiences, whom marketers have segmented into narrow units and who are encouraged to forge symbolic or imagined communities on the basis of market concerns. This article focuses on one particular but also particularly important case: Metro News, an emerging second-tier media corporation that is broadly considered an industry model organization for integrating different forms of media work.[2] Recently Metro News won *Fortune* magazine's survey for "most admired news company" several years in a row, the industry's leading publications routinely feature it as an exemplary case, and international firms visit often for tours of the facility. In the late 1990s I spent three weeks inside the Metro News newsroom, where I observed journalists and editors in action as they worked on stories, conducted formal editorial meetings, and searched for news. I also conducted and taped interviews with twenty-five reporters, editors, and managers. When I began the project, the news editor not only allowed me to sit in on meetings and interrupt his busy reporters. He also let me occupy an unused office in the corner of the main news floor, and I could bring reporters back into my private room and give them space to speak openly about their work.

Convergence and the New Media Market

Metro News has been a major player in the American politics and society since the mid-nineteenth century. For the first fifty years of its life, the Metro News company devoted its energy to local news and politics, and at the turn of the twentieth century, its editor gained attention by arguing that the mission of an urban paper is to acculturate and integrate new immigrants to local as well as American national culture. In the next decades, the company grew with the times, establishing a new paper in New York after World War I, a local radio station in the 1920s, and an affiliated television station in 1948. Still, the core of the company was its main paper, so when readership began to decline in the 1970s, Metro News, like most other newspaper companies, had to refashion its mission. Its new managers decided that a great newspaper could not survive unless it was embedded in a great news and entertainment network. This is the moment of rebirth for the Metro News and for other media organizations. Unfortunately, the classic sociological studies of news work were conducted just before this renaissance.

From 1975 until today, major media companies such as Metro News have evolved through four key development strategies: First, *taking companies out of private hands* (usually ending the control of wealthy families who held long ties to the news profession), *raising capital with public stock offerings* (Metro News, for example, went public in the early 1980s), and *reforming the corporate mission* to meet the bottom-line demands of stockholders. Second, and related, is *bringing in new corporate managers to streamline production systems in the newsroom* and to reduce labor costs. Third, *making massive investments in digital communications technologies* and remaking the corporate infrastructure. Fourth, *establishing lines of horizontal integration in the company*, which meant acquiring or merging with other content providers and distributors, such as television stations, Internet companies, and magazines, and linking the marketing as well as the news divisions across subsidiary firms. Metro News began aggressively purchasing new papers and local TV stations in the 1970s, and today its holdings include more than a dozen city newspapers, with major dailies in the largest urban markets. It owns a national television superstation, a share of another national network, and more than two dozen local TV stations. Finally, it operates a fleet of radio stations in leading markets, a book publisher, several television production companies, massive digital media investments, a professional sports franchise, and local cable television news stations that broadcast local news around the clock.

For the company, ownership of such diverse operations is the key to a *synergistic* mode of production (Auletta 1998), whereby each media outlet uses the products of the others to enhance its offerings and, to use the language of the industry, to *cross-promote its brands*. On the business side, synergy allows big news companies to integrate their advertising sales work and create special packages for clients; this gives them a major competitive advantage over smaller media companies and also increases the efficiency of their marketing projects. At the organizational level, the Metro News's acquisitions of newspapers in California, New York, and Florida allow the corporation to cut and streamline its slate of domestic and international bureaus. Local reporters in Los Angeles, Chicago, or New York City are both city and national correspondents because their work is used by different papers. Similarly, one foreign bureau can provide news and photography for several papers at once. And freelancers—who are increasingly popular with news companies—can broker deals with a corporate network rather than a single outlet. Digital communications infrastructures are crucial for this level of convergence since they allow for immediate circulation of content and distribute information in easily editable formats.

But this is only the beginning of synergy. Metro News also uses each branch of its operation to produce content for several media at once, and it has turned its company into a flexible producer. Within any single metropolitan news agency, the main newsroom is increasingly likely to contain a television studio, Internet production facilities, radio equipment, sophisticated graphics machines, and hundreds of computer terminals for print journalists. There are separate staffs for the different media, but workers in the various departments have frequent contact with each other, in part because they all produce material for many platforms.

Just what these cultural workers produce is the subject of major debate inside Metro News and the profession more broadly. Reporters and professional observers complain that the corporate management has classified their product as "content," a category that suits any story, image, or other form of intellectual property, rather than journalism (see Auletta 1998). According to journalists and editors, the craft distinctions between different genres of news work that historically organized the field are beginning to blur. Media managers argue that their staff should be able to tell stories across platforms, and many reporters are increasingly worried about bottom-line-driven assaults on their vocational techniques and professional values. Although the news media was born as a commercial medium and has always been deeply entangled with corporate, profit-driven interests, insiders fear that the logic of the market has penetrated to unprecedented depths of the modern newsroom (Underwood 1993; Downie and Kaiser 2001). In response, journalists are making use of the language of the professions, mobilizing the image of the professional journalist who is independent, specially trained, skeptical, and objective to defend their status from incursions by the market and new players in the field.

The New Newsroom

The organizational transformation of Metro News has produced major changes in the physical and social space of its offices. Reporters and editors can see powerful signs of their industry's transformation in their work spaces, which have been completely redesigned so that journalists can move freely between print, television, radio, and Internet outlets and meet the demands of the new media environment. The most striking difference in the newsroom is that in 1999 the company placed a television news studio at the physical and symbolic center of the office, directly in front of the editor's door, so that the editorial staff orbits around the studio. This is, of course, hardly an innocent move since journalists have fierce internal battles about the ways that television news culture—with its emphasis on video, sound bites, and soft features—threatens the integrity of other reporting practices.

For much of the newspaper staff, the emergence of television as the centerpiece of the organization signals the rise of a different journalistic mission, one determined by the production values of TV news. But then there is another, more seductive side of television: everyone, including print reporters, recognizes the power of TV to reach a massive audience, and for reporters, television represents a route to celebrity, wealth, and influence. In fact, one adviser to the company told me that the introduction of television into the newsroom had been *the biggest nonstory of the year. It turns out*, he explained, *that print reporters want to be on TV just as much as everyone else.*

Perhaps the deepest source of the journalists' frustration is their perception that the new environment has forced them to take on additional responsibilities in the same work period, which has particularly severe consequences for cultural production that requires serious, independent thinking. Of course, there is nothing new about either deadlines or news cycles. Modern journalists have always worked against the clock to meet their rigid production and distribution schedules, and news stories are necessarily written in haste. During the 1970s, national television news programs were broadcast once a day, in the early evening, which gave the production team a clear twenty-four-hour span to cover "breaking news." Most major newspapers were published in the early morning or afternoon, and with the contemporary printing technologies, reporters had to file their stories several hours in advance.

The time cycle for news making in the age of digital production is radically different: the regular news cycle has spun into an erratic and unending pattern that I characterize as a *news cyclone*. The advent of twenty-four-hour television news and the rapid emergence of instant Internet news sites have eliminated the temporal borders in the news day, creating an informational environment in which there is always breaking news to produce, consume, and—for reporters and their subjects—react against. In the new media world, a Metro News writer says, *There's a writing process that's just* constant, constant, constant . . . *in everything we're doing we're dealing with the clock.* Bang. Bang. Bang. Bang. Bang. *And that clock just goes on.*

Synergy and Digital Systems

So, just how has Metro News managed to meet the new time pressures and to increase the efficiency and productivity of its already busy staff? This is the deeper story of synergy, and it is also the place where digital technologies enter the picture. In the new media newsroom, journalists have to become *flexible laborers*, reskilled to meet demands from several media at once. And as companies break down the division of news labor, reporters experience a time compression that they make sense of through the language of stress and pressure. As one reporter explains,

> *Metro News is a multimedia company. . . . Increasingly, there are pressures to put reporters who are covering stories on television, and there are other demands that you have as a reporter for other ways of covering stories. Let me be specific. There have been pressures to participate in cyberspace . . . they put your stuff on cyberspace and they ask you to do other things, provide links, [create] other kinds of information. There's [also] an emphasis in journalism now, much more than ever, on graphics. So some of the time that you're writing the story has to be spent with the graphics team talking to them about what we're doing, so that their graphics can add to what we're doing and not simply repeat. But also you are providing some reporting information for graphics, which is a whole new layer. [All of this] requires conversations with other people in the newsroom, and that requires time taken away from just the story.* . . . [After describing other responsibilities involved in television and Internet she concludes:] *Very recently . . . one of the things that they decided to try was having reporters write conceptual headlines for their stories. . . . I think to some people it's like, just another thing to do. You know, we've already got graphics, we've already got ties to photo, sometimes we have to appear on TV and do cyberspace. And now we're going to have to make suggestions for headlines too?*

For Metro News, such coordinated news-making activities keep labor costs down and increase the output and efficiency of the production process. For reporters, though, the new regime creates real professional challenges: the more they work with different media, for example, the more they realize that content does not move easily from one medium to the next, and therefore they must develop techniques for translating work across platforms. It is no surprise, then, that the new journalism textbooks and curricular programs emphasize developing news skills that work in several media. Many veteran journalists worry that if television becomes the most valuable and important medium for major news companies, then being telegenic will become the most important journalistic skill and a criterion for entry-level reporting jobs. What is more immediately worrisome for journalists is that the new responsibilities also reduce the editorial staff's time to research, report, and even to think about their work. Time matters in special ways for cultural producers since incursions into the working schedule undermine one's ability to perform a craft (see Bourdieu 2000). The greatest fear among print journalists is that the production routines for daily television news will become normative in their medium as well. In a discussion with me, one reporter explained that

> some people are very concerned about the redesign of our newsroom and how our TV station is going to have a presence on the desk. Digital is going to be on the desk. And on the other hand, I think that it's all to the good and that the more we get integrated and familiar with these other areas, the more likely we will be in the future to be prepared for whatever happens in the future, rather than be isolated and out of print.

> **EK: Are you asked to take any other responsibilities?**

> So far I haven't been. I mean, I was asked one time to lead a chat room on ethnic issues by our digital folks. But there are a lot of other people who are constantly being asked to get on TV and talk about their stories. I just haven't really done that. I was on the television news for a project I did on National earlier this year on the elections . . . . So I haven't really been affected by that push. But I know of folks in Washington . . . I think they have pretty heavy TV duties in Washington, a lot of live stories on what they're covering. And that takes up a lot of their time. They have to write the scripts. OK, so they write their news stories and then they write their scripts and they don't get paid for that and it takes a lot of time. And I don't know if that's going to be coming for us as well.

> I guess my only concern is that right now we have for many years been the source for TV news. You know, they read us and then they go out and do their stories. So if having news television in here means that we'll get to do . . . I mean I would rather do my story for both mediums than have somebody scarf up my story and do it, and kind of steal it from me after I did all the work. So there's sort of two ways to look at it.

Editors have related concerns: they have to sustain a certain level of journalistic quality to maintain the company's reputation. Indeed, it is important to have Pulitzer Prize–winning investigations, and in the past several years, the Metro News has had many. But it achieves this system by introducing a new system of stratification inside the newsroom, with elite reporters given ample time to do large projects and a large staff of second-tier journalists responsible for much of the daily workload. This hierarchical arrangement is similar to those emerging in other cultural fields, including the academy.

In their most extreme forms, concerns about efficiency can push journalists to forgo traditional kinds of reporting and to rely, instead, on the most easily accessible information: news that is available online. In recent years, several leading professional news publications have run stories about the industry's most dangerous computer virus, whose symptoms include staying at the desk and using material from the Web for reporting that is faster and easier than work in the streets. There are several well-known cases in which journalists relying on Web-based information used faulty statistics as the basis for published stories. Reporters, particularly when they are working against the clock, are susceptible to Internet misinformation. Online reporting practices are unlikely to displace traditional reporting techniques, as some of the most concerned critics worry. But media organizations are learning that the same digital systems that improve journalists' ability to do research in the office can also have perverse effects.

The responsibility to produce content that can be used across platforms also places a different kind of pressure on editors and business managers. For them, directing a multimedia company requires ensuring that a sufficient level of content meets the needs of each medium, and this means that reporters assigned to key beats or stories have to produce even if they want more time to explore. According to one reporter, *Being productive means you're gathering information that is short order. . . . Everything, all the incentives, come down to producing for tomorrow.* One effect of this imperialism of the immediate is that Metro News, long renowned for serious and time-consuming investigative reports, has reduced the number of investigative stories. Between 1980 and 1995, the newspaper cut the number of investigative stories by 48 percent. One reporter explains his view of the change as follows: *The whole idea of giving reporters time and space to explore just doesn't seem like an efficient way to do business.* The core city reporting staff no longer has enough time to penetrate into the deep pockets of urban life and come up with surprising stories. Crime, local scandals, entertainment, all the events that are easy to cover have become more prominent in the city news. As one city editor told me,

> The best way to blanket the city, and the most efficient way to blanket the city, is to cover the [big] institutions [with beats]. So, it's hard to justify, from a resource standpoint, a more burdensome way of getting information, which is out on the streets. It's not efficient at all. There are no press releases, no spokespeople, and if there are, there is a bunch of spokespeople [saying different things]. And to sort through that and weave through that and get a clear picture is just time-consuming and it's harder to devote the resources to doing that.

Target Marketing and Media Segmentation

One of the most economically significant characteristics of digital news systems is that they have enabled media organizations to push the principles of target marketing to new levels, to make specialized information and entertainment products that appeal to narrow groups of consumers but that can be sold by one advertising staff (see Turow 1998). Competition within the American media market has fragmented the mass audience on which network television stations and major newspapers built their fortunes. According to one major media executive, *People want to know what their neighbors are up to. People want to know what's going on in their block. People want information that touches their lives* (quoted in Lieberman 1998). Today the strategy of most news companies is to locate and target affluent audiences. For many city papers, the major impact of new digital technologies (especially publishing technologies) is that they enable companies to target coverage to the suburban areas that contain most of the affluent readers whom advertisers want to reach. Using digital technologies, Metro News has expanded its system of zoned newspaper production and distribution so that it prints not only a special section for each of the zoned regions in the metropolitan area but occasionally different front pages, with special headlines, photos, and stories, as well. One reporter expressed her frustration with this system of target marketing:

> *Something might go on page one in the city and then something else will go in the suburbs in the suburban papers. . . . Oftentimes, we have stories that have been like page one in USA Today or the Wall Street Journal, but could only get read by people in one zone. So nobody saw the story if they lived in the suburbs, until they read it two weeks later on the front page of the USA Today, or until they saw it on TV because TV picked it up. So that's really frustrating from the point of view of the reporter who thinks they've got a nicely written story, to not get play because the editors think that won't be of interest to people in Dixon County. And then my argument to that is well these white people in Dixon County will be mighty interested when these Mexican people get pushed out and soon they'll be on their door-step. (Laughs,) And he said, well we can change the lead. "In a move that made white residents of Dixon County uneasy . . ."*

Yet there is an important exception to the rise of target-marketed news: it is not available to people who live in poor neighborhoods or suburbs and lack a strong base of desirable professionals for advertisers to target. As a former *Chicago Tribune* editor explains, "By reducing circulation efforts among low-income, minority readers, newspapers actually improve the overall demographic profile of their audiences, which they then use to justify raising advertising rates" (Squires 1993).

The Internet, rather than television or print, offers the most exciting possibilities for creating new forms of journalism with advanced technology and convergence production. The Internet is the ideal medium for deepening coverage with interactive links to video, text, and graphics, and the spatial constraints are relatively loose online. (In theory, of course, Internet reporting need not be bound by any spatial constraints. But many editors still try to sharpen their stories so that they conform to conventional narrative forms from print media.) Yet by 2003, few news organizations had developed a business model that generated profits for news Web sites, and particularly after the collapse of the dot-com industry, news companies were reluctant to invest significant resources in the most innovative kinds of online media production. A former editor who developed the new media offerings in one major Florida newspaper told me that

> *in most companies, the real convergence action involves putting print reporters on television, and that's just not the way to make convergence work. One thing is that it doesn't take advantage of the medium. There's nothing journalistically or technologically interesting about putting a print reporter on TV—it's just uses personnel in a more flexible way, getting more out of them. The real innovations in convergence journalism are going to come on the Web, or eventually on interactive television, where you can produce new kinds of content. Now the problem is that no one knows how to make a Web-based business model that works for journalism. So although the Internet is the best place to combine text, video, graphics, and interactivity—all the things that make multimedia production exciting—there's not much corporate interest in doing it because it's not really profitable, and it's not clear that it will be. And you can't get support for innovative news production if there's not a business model that works.*

Some participants in convergence projects argue that other, less visible journalistic benefits come from convergence production. Sharing resources and staff helps both television and newspaper companies expand the scope of their reporting, allowing them to cover stories that they would otherwise miss. A study by the Project for Excellence in Journalism found that convergence production systems can help improve the quality of television news since TV staffs are comparably small and print reporters bring depth to their offerings. But several newspaper reporters complain that the stories and sources from television tend to focus on crime and violence issues since those are major topics on local TV news.[3] Many print journalists believe that the greatest influence of television news practices on newspapers is to promote this visual information at the expense of textual depth, and they are anxious that the norms and forms of television will take over the paper.

Conclusion: Newsrooms in an Age of Digital Production

From the late nineteenth century, when American urban newspapers announced their project of integrating and acculturating new immigrants to local and national culture, journalists and social scientists have argued that news organizations "not only serve but create their communities" by providing raw materials for collective social and political life (Fuller 1996: 228). In recent years, cultural critics and sociologists have grown so interested in global circuits of information and the possibilities for cosmopolitan uses of news that they have scarcely recognized how media companies use the Internet and other advanced communication technologies to alter their local coverage. . . . According to Downie and Kaiser (2001), after September 11, the American news media exhibited an increased interest in foreign affairs and heightened international coverage. Yet one year later, in the new Afterword to the paperback edition of the same book (2002), they reported that soon after the disaster most news organizations returned to their pre–September 11 patterns of coverage. The optimism about the future of foreign reporting they expressed in the first edition seems unwarranted.

When news organizations do cover national and international events, editors and managers encourage journalists to "localize" the stories, that is, to illustrate why news far from home is relevant to the local community. One prominent media consultant told me that *if you want to write a story about the war in Kabul, you're better off tying it to the Kabul House restaurant in town.* In theory, news audiences can use advanced communications technologies to obtain enormous amounts of information about the world. In practice, as advertisers and news executives know, most people use the news to gain a world of information about their personal interests, their hometown, and themselves. Target marketing and convergence production techniques have helped to create informational islands of communities whose segregation in physical space is increasingly joined and reinforced by the differentiation of specialized news products. As Cass Sunstein (2001) argued, new media and digital technologies have played important roles in this segmenting process.

The consequences of the emergent journalistic and managerial practices described here are already visible. Convergence news companies expect their journalistic staff to be flexible and fast, and both editors and corporate managers are already revaluing their workers, considering multimedia skills in their story assignments as well as in hiring and retention decisions. Many journalists and media critics complain that the additional labor demands and the work speedup required for convergence have undermined the conditions of news production, mainly by reducing the time available to report, research, write, and reflect on stories. Convergence companies contest these claims, pointing to various awards won by staff in television, print, and the Internet as evidence that multimedia production enriches their offerings and improves their staff. Journalists respond by pointing to an emerging stratification of the labor force, in which major companies support a small elite corps of reporters who are able to conduct serious investigations and long-term projects, and the remaining majority who have more responsibilities than ever. Yet it is notoriously difficult to reliably appraise the overall quality of reporting across fields and themes. Instead of attempting a normative evaluation of whether the new conditions of production are good or bad for journalism, I conclude by explaining how convergence regimes and corporate managerial strategies affect various qualities of news content and features of news work.

The penetration of market principles and marketing projects into the editorial divisions of news organizations is one of the most dramatic changes in the journalistic field, and there is no question the mythical walls separating the editorial and advertising are mostly down. When Gans (1979) studied news organizations in the 1960s and 1970s, he found that editors would occasionally grant access to political officials and listen to their input for various stories and issues, but—as a matter of journalistic principle—not to advertisers or corporations. In the late 1990s, Times Mirror CEO and *Los Angeles Times* publisher Mark Willes generated professional outrage by announcing that advertisers should play a key role in shaping journalistic content. In the early 2000s, editorial meetings with advertisers and the internal marketing staff are routine, and the editors I met unabashedly reported that they worked hard to produce more marketable and profitable products. At the *Chicago Tribune,* architects integrated the famously separate elevator banks for management and journalists, symbolically eliminating the historical markers of journalism's sacred and profane sides. In 2003, managers at the *Dallas Morning News* even began handing out $100 bills to reporters who memorized the company's five business goals and could recite them on demand (Celeste 2003). . . .

The most notable examples of advertisers taking part in editorial decision making include the case of the *Los Angeles Times* sponsoring the Staples Center, sharing revenue on a 168-page magazine produced by the editorial staff and inserted into the Sunday paper in 1999; the new special sections determined by advertising and dedicated to mutual funds, communications and computer technologies, and home and gardening in most major newspapers; and the rise of service-oriented "news you can use," human interest, health, and entertainment reporting and of news beats such as "malls," "shopping," and "car culture" (Underwood 1993). Contemporary news organizations conduct extensive and expensive research to learn what kinds of content consumers want, too, and they have made important qualitative changes in their offerings to meet market demand. . . .

The most exciting innovations in journalistic forms, particularly those involving multimedia packages disseminated through the Internet, have received little support from news organizations because they are not profitable. Moreover, the celebrated genres of the American journalistic craft, particularly investigative reporting, long-term projects, and penetrating urban affairs work, have lost corporate support in all but the most elite publications because of their inefficiencies and the costs of production. One editor of a midsized newspaper told a *Columbia Journalism Review* editor, "If a story needs real investment of time and money, we don't do it anymore"; and a television newsman reports, "Instead of racing out of the newsroom with a camera crew when an important story breaks, we're more likely now to stay at our desks and work the phones, rewrite the wire copy, hire a local crew and a freelance producer to get pictures at the scene, then dig out some file footage, maps, or still photos for the anchor to talk in front of, or maybe buy some coverage from a video news service like Reuters, AP, or World Television News" (quoted in Hickey 1998).

Digital technologies have changed journalistic production in newsrooms, but not according to journalists' preferences. When conglomerates and publicly traded companies took over news organizations and entered the journalistic field, they imported corporate managerial techniques and developed new strategies to increase the productivity, efficiency, and profitability of news businesses (Squires 1993; Underwood 1993; Dugger 2000;

Downie and Kaiser 2001). Media executives and managerial-minded editors not only downsized their journalistic staffs, they also invented new regimes of convergence production to expand their offerings across media (Auletta 1998). They designed applications of digital technologies to facilitate the process of multimedia work and increase their capacity to repackage articles from one newspaper to another or one platform to another and invested lightly in innovations to basic journalistic forms, offering little support for multimedia offerings that take full advantage of the Internet's affordances. Digital systems in major news companies remain in embryonic stages of development, and it is difficult to predict how they will develop. But the political economy, cultural conventions, and regulatory restrictions governing the news industry will play powerful roles in determining how advanced communications technologies enter the matrix of journalistic production, just as they did before the digital age.

ENDNOTES

[1] A notable exception is Gilens (1999), who showed that major American news magazines vastly overrepresented African Americans in photographs of poor people, particularly the "undeserving" or unsympathetic poor. He then conducted interviews with photography editors to ask why they used these images and if they recognized their own patterns of representation.

[2] Metro News is a pseudonym.

[3] Downie and Kaiser (2001: 170) reported, "An exhaustive 1999 study of 590 local newscasts on fifty-nine stations in nineteen cities . . . found that nine of every ten local stories on those newscasts came 'from either the police scanner or scheduled events.' Fewer than one in ten stories came from the reporter's own initiatives."

REFERENCES

Appadurai, Arjun. 1996. *Modernity at Large: Cultural Dimensions of Globalization.* Minneapolis: University of Minnesota Press.

Auletta, Ken. 1998. Synergy City. *American Journalism Review,* May. http://www.ajr.org/article_printable.asp?id=2446/.

Bourdieu, Pierre. 1994. *Language and Symbolic Power.* Cambridge, MA: Harvard University Press.

————.1998. *On Television.* New York: New Press.

————.2000. *Pascalian Meditations.* Stanford, CA: Stanford University Press.

Castells, Manuel. 1996. *The Rise of the Network Society.* Oxford, UK: Blackwell.

Celeste, Eric. 2003. Snooze Alarm. *Dallas Observer,* February 13.

Cook, Timothy. 1998. *Governing with the News: The News Media as a Political Institution.* Chicago: University of Chicago Press.

Downie, Leonard, Jr., and Robert Kaiser. 2001. *The News About the News: American Journalism in Peril.* New York: Knopf.

Dugger, Ronnie. 2000. The Corporate Domination of Journalism. In *The Business of Journalism,* ed. William Serrin, 27–56. New York: New Press.

Fishman, Mark. 1980. *Manufacturing the News.* Austin: University of Texas Press.

Fuller, Jack. 1996. *News Values: Ideas for the Information Age.* Chicago: University of Chicago Press.

Gans, Herbert. 1972. The Famine in American Mass-communications Research: Comments on Hirsch, Tuchman, and Gecas. *American Journal of Sociology* 77:697–705.

————.1979. *Deciding What's News: A Study of CBS Evening News, NBC Nightly News, Newsweek, and Time.* New York: Pantheon.

Gilens, Martin. 1999. *Why Americans Hate Welfare: Race, Media, and the Politics of Antipoverty Policy.* Chicago: University of Chicago Press.

Ginsburg, Faye, Lila Abu-Lughod, and Brian Larkin, eds. 2002. *Media Worlds: Anthropology on New Terrain.* Berkeley: University of California Press.

Habermas, Jurgen. 1989. *The Structural Transformation of the Public Sphere.* Cambridge, MA: MIT Press.

Hickey, Neil. 1998. Money lust: How Pressure for Profit is Perverting Journalism. *Columbia Journalism Review,* July/August. http://archives.cjr.org/year/98/4/moneylust.asp/.

Lieberman, David. 1998. The Rise and Rise of 24-hour Local News. *Columbia Journalism Review,* November/December. http://archives.cjr.org/year/98/6/tvnews.asp/.

Luhmann, Niklas. 2000. *The Reality of the Mass Media.* Stanford, CA: Stanford University Press.

Squires, James. 1993. *Read All About It: The Corporate Takeover of America's Newspapers.* New York: Random House.

Sunstein, Cass. 2001. *Republic.com.* Princeton, NJ: Princeton University Press.

Tuchman, Gaye. 1978. *Making News: A Study in the Construction of Reality.* New York: Free Press.

Turow, Joseph. 1998. *Breaking Up America: Advertisers and the New Media World.* Chicago: University of Chicago Press.

Underwood, Doug. 1993. *When MBAs Rule the Newsroom.* New York: Columbia University Press.

39

GENDER IN TELEVISED SPORTS
News and Highlights Shows, 1989–2009

MICHAEL A. MESSNER • CHERYL COOKY

This second selection on the mass media is by Michael A. Messner, a professor of sociology and gender studies at the University of Southern California, and Cheryl Cooky, an assistant professor of women's studies, and health and kinesiology at Purdue University. This reading is an excerpt from the June 2010 report, "Gender in Televised Sports," which Messner has systematically investigated since 1989. This is the fifth wave of the longitudinal study (data collected in 1989, 1993, 1999, 2004, and 2009), which examines both the quantity and quality of the airtime news and highlights shows give to men's and women's sports. Many themes emerged from their research, including empirical evidence that shows gender inequality in news reporting. One mistaken assumption commonly made about gender equality is that changes in laws, such as the passing of Title IX, would eliminate disparities in men's and women's sports and create equal opportunities and respect between the sexes. While the laws have changed, other social structures in society have not, including the media.

Michael A. Messner and Cheryl Cooky, "Gender in Televised Sports: News and Highlights Shows, 1989–2009." June 2010, Center for Feminist Research, University of Southern California, Pp. 1–35. Reprinted by permission of the authors and the USC Center for Feminist Research. http://dornsife.usc.edu/cfr/gender-in-televised-sports

Introduction: *By Diana Nyad*[1]

For two decades, the *Gender in Televised Sports* report has tracked the progress—as well as the lack of progress—in the coverage of women's sports on television news and highlights shows. One of the positive outcomes derived from past editions of this valuable study has been a notable improvement in the often derogatory ways that sports commentators used to routinely speak of women athletes. The good news in this report is that there is far less insulting and overtly sexist treatment of women athletes than there was twenty or even ten years ago. The bad news, in these times of women's empowerment and success in most spheres of our society, is that the overall coverage of women's sports has declined to a level of outrageously small numbers.

Description of the Study

As with [earlier] studies, the central aim of the current study was to compare the quantity and quality of TV news and highlights shows' coverage of women's versus men's athletic events. So that we might comment on change and continuity over time, we replicated the previous iterations of the study. First, we analyzed three two-week segments (a total of six weeks) of televised sports news coverage on each of three local (Los Angeles) network affiliates. Second, we studied ESPN's *SportsCenter,* replicating our focus on this sports highlights show that we began in 1999 and continued in 2004.

Over the past decade, television news and highlights shows have introduced visual techniques (e.g., split screens and scrolling tickers) of conveying information that invite viewers to listen, view images, and read text that refer simultaneously to two or more stories. As in 2004, most of the 2009 sports news and highlights programs in our sample included a continual running "ticker" at the bottom of the television screen. The ticker uses written text to report game scores, headlines, and breaking sports news that may or may not be reported through the main conventional verbal reporting and visual images. We analyzed the quantity of ticker coverage devoted to women's and to men's sports.

Sample

Televised Sports News   We analyzed six weeks of television sports news (both the 6:00 P.M. segments and the 11:00 P.M. segments) on the three local network affiliates (KNBC, KCBS, and KABC). . . . in order to sample different time periods when different sports were being played, we analyzed three two-week periods: March 15–28; July 12–25; November 8–21. Amounts of airtime devoted to men's versus women's sports were measured. The scrolling ticker at the bottom of the screen (in cases where it was present) also was timed, to determine the proportion of ticker reports devoted to women's versus men's sports. In addition to the quantitative measures, we analyzed the quality of coverage in terms of visuals and verbal commentary.

ESPN SportsCenter   We analyzed three weeks of one-hour 11:00 P.M. ESPN's *SportsCenter.* These three weeks corresponded with the first week of each of the three network news segments: March 15–21, July 12–18, and November 8–14. We added *SportsCenter* to this study in 1999, so we can now compare our 2009 data with the 1999 and 2004 data. Amounts of airtime devoted to men's versus women's sports were measured. Following a practice begun in the 2004 study, the scrolling ticker at the bottom of the screen was timed, to determine the proportion of ticker reports devoted to women's versus men's sports. In addition to the quantitative measures, we analyzed the quality of coverage in terms of visuals and verbal commentary. . . .

Description of Findings

1. Sports News on Three Network Affiliates: Coverage of Women's Sports Plummets

Chasm between Coverage of Women's and Men's Sports Widens   In the 1989 and 1993 studies, we noted that female athletes rarely received coverage on the televised sports news. The 1999 study revealed an encouraging increase in the proportion of sports news devoted to coverage of women's sports, followed by a small decline in the 2004 study. . . . the 2009 proportion of airtime devoted to women's sports dropped precipitously to 1.6%, by far its lowest level in any year measured over the past two decades.

The Three Network Affiliates Share Similar Styles   In past studies, the three network affiliates showed very similar patterns of coverage, all devoting hugely disproportionate amounts of time to men's sports. These similarities continued with the 2009 study, but . . ., there were also differences. KNBC, which in the 2004 study showed the highest proportion of coverage of women's sports (8.9%), dropped off to 1.1% coverage of women's sports in the 2009 study. KABC and KCBS both hovered closer to the 2% level, also representing a regression in coverage of women's sports from previous studies.

As in past studies, there was little difference between the evening and late-night editions of the three news shows, in terms of coverage of women's sports. Also consistent with past years of the study, the November period of the sample contained the least amount of coverage of women's sports (almost none). There was marginally more coverage of women's sports during the March and July periods.

2. ESPN SportsCenter: Declining Coverage of Women's Sports

In 1999 (when we added *SportsCenter* to the study) and again in 2004, the proportion of the popular highlights show's coverage devoted to women's

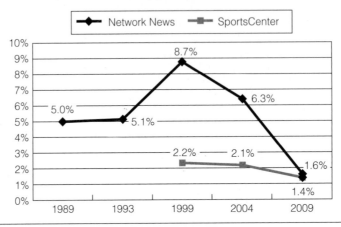

FIGURE 39.1 **News and SportsCenter Airtime Devoted to Women's Sports, 1989–2009.**

sports was significantly lower than proportions devoted by TV news shows. As Figure 39.1 illustrates, *SportsCenter's* coverage of women's sports declined in 2009 to 1.4%, just a hair lower than the combined coverage of the three network news shows.

3. Ticker Time: Women's Sports on the Margins

ESPN's *SportsCenter* and two of the network affiliate news shows (KNBC and KCBS) continually ran a scrolling ticker text bar at the bottom of the screen, reporting scores and other sports news. The proportion of "ticker time" devoted to women's sports on KNBC and KCBS was 4.6%, more than triple the proportion of the thin airtime they devoted to women's sports in their main broadcasts. In 2009, *SportsCenter* devoted 2.7% of its ticker time to women's sports. While this is almost double the 1.4% main coverage that *SportsCenter* devoted to women's sports, it represents a decline from 2004, when the highlights show devoted 8.5% of its ticker time to women's sports.

4. Men's "Big Three" Sports Are the Central Focus

Men Always Lead   Every sports news or highlights broadcast begins with a lead story that sets the tone of the broadcast. Lead stories, especially those on *SportsCenter,* tend also to be the longest stories of the broadcast, containing the highest production values (often including multiple interviews, game footage, musical montage, graphic statistics, ancillary on-site reporters, etc.). In our sample, 100% of the *SportsCenter* programs and 100% of the sports news shows began with a men's sports topic as the lead story.

Not All Men's Sports Are in the Spotlight   As Figure 39.2 illustrates, both ESPN's *SportsCenter* and the network affiliates' news shows devoted the vast majority of their attention to three men's sports. When combining all main coverage and ticker time, the three men's sports of football, basketball, and

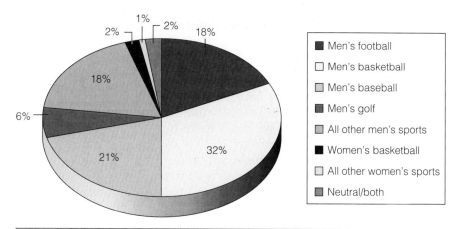

FIGURE 39.2 **Sports Covered in Combined (Main plus Ticker) Coverage on TV News and *SportsCenter*, 2009.**

baseball received a combined 71.7% of all coverage. Men's golf was a distant fourth, receiving 5.6% of the coverage. Nineteen other men's sports shared 18% of the total coverage. Meanwhile, basketball was the only women's sport to receive anything close to substantial attention, garnering 1.5% of the overall coverage. Four other women's sports (golf, soccer, tennis and softball) shared less than 1% of the total combined coverage. In previous iterations of the study, tennis was usually the most commonly covered women's sport (43% of all women's sports stories in the 2004 study were tennis stories). This was not the case in 2009.

Even When Not in Season, the "Big Three" Are Given Center Stage   Reporters continually delivered stories on men's sports that were out of season, including especially stories on professional (and occasionally college) football in March and July, pro baseball in November, and pro basketball in July, as Table 39.1 shows.

TABLE 39.1 Main Coverage of "Big Three" Men's Sports While out of Season (Number of Stories; Minutes: Seconds)

	KABC, KNBC & KCBS	ESPN *SportsCenter*
November men's baseball stories	32 stories 17:01	8 stories 5:52
March & July men's football stories	26 stories 14:11	42 stories 46:18
July men's basketball stories	60 stories 35:31	21 stories 14:44

5. Unequal Coverage of Women's and Men's Pro and College Basketball

Figure 39.2 and Table 39.1 showed that coverage of the "Big Three" men's sports, even when out of season, far exceeded the coverage of all women's sports, whether in-season or not. However, overall comparisons of men's and women's sports might be seen as misleading—like comparing apples and oranges—since there are still some men's sports (men's pro football and baseball in particular) for which there are no fully developed women's equivalents. Thus, it is instructive to compare a sport for which there are equivalent men's and women's teams and leagues. For this purpose, we compared the coverage of professional and college women's and men's basketball.

The NBA Is Where Coverage Happens   Table 39.2 shows a comparison of coverage of the WNBA (the Women's National Basketball Association) and coverage of the NBA (the men's National Basketball Association). Breaking down in-season and out-of-season coverage of the men's and women's professional leagues sheds light on the depth of the gender asymmetries in news and highlights shows.

TABLE 39.2 Coverage of WNBA and NBA, in Season and out of Season (Number of Stories; Minutes: Seconds)

	March	*July*
WNBA on KABC, KNBC & KCBS	(out of season) 0 stories; 0:00	(in season) 3 stories; 2:51
WNBA on ESPN *SportsCenter*	(out of season) 0 stories; 0:00	(in season) 5 stories; 2:40
NBA on KABC, KNBC & KCBS	(in season) 51 stories; 43:25	(out of season) 60 stories; 35:31
NBA on ESPN *SportsCenter*	(in season) 21 stories; 22:26	(out of season) 21 stories; 14:44

The WNBA received scant coverage in the main reports of both the network news and *SportsCenter* broadcasts—even when in season. But . . . the WNBA did receive significant in-season coverage in the rolling ticker at the bottom of the screen.

When in season (July) the vast majority (70 of 78) of WNBA stories that appeared on the combined news and highlights shows were literally marginalized to the scrolling ticker. Only eight WNBA stories were given airtime in the main broadcast. When out of season (March), WNBA coverage was entirely absent from the both the main reports and the ticker. Meanwhile,

NBA stories continued to be given generous main story and ticker coverage, whether in-season or out-of-season. Figure 39.3 compares the ticker and main coverage of WNBA and NBA, combining the total number of in-season and out-of-season stories on the news and highlights shows during the March and July samples.

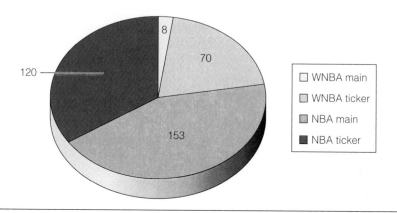

FIGURE 39.3   Number of Pro Basketball Stories, Combined News and Highlights Shows

March Madness: Mainly for Men   Coverage of women's and men's college basketball during the month of March offers perhaps an even better contrast, since these sports are being played during the same time frame. . . . news shows ignored entirely women's college basketball games while ESPN gave them token attention. Meanwhile, both the news and highlights shows were lavishing major attention on men's college basketball.

This comparison of women's and men's NCAA basketball reveals the highly asymmetrical coverage of the same women's and men's event during the same temporal frame. Akin to the coverage of the WNBA, the very scant attention given to women's NCAA basketball (all of it appearing on ESPN) was mostly relegated to the margins of the screen on the scrolling ticker.

It's not that the generous coverage of the men's tournament left no time for covering the women's tournament. Producers decided to cover other things instead. On March 20, for instance, KABC spent all of its 3:33-long sports report on the men's NCAA tournament, closing with a lengthy humorous story about Shaquille O'Neill going "mano a mano" with a 93-year-old grandmother in a contest to pick NCAA men's tournament winners. As viewers see the old woman, dressed in a suit and dress shoes and awkwardly trying to dribble a basketball, commentator Curt Sandoval quips that the woman "knows absolutely nothing about basketball and is picking games on instinct." On March 23, KNBC devoted generous coverage to the men's tournament and none to the women's, but spent thirty seconds covering a gag feature about a burger with 5000 calories and 300 grams of fat that fans can now purchase at a minor league baseball park in Michigan. And the next day, KNBC gave women's sports a nod with a story that featured shots of tennis star Serena Williams wearing a short dress, climbing out of a sun roof of a car onto its roof to play tennis, lobbing a ball back and forth against male player Andy Murray who stood atop another car. This stunt was intended to promote the start of the Ericsson Open tournament. Commentator Mario Solis quipped, "Tennis anyone? . . . I hope nobody decides to use a drop shot!" This was the only mention of women's sports during this broadcast. Also on March 24, during the heart of the women's tournament, KABC ran a 1-minute, 31-second feature on the 70th anniversary of Little League Baseball, and during its 11:00 broadcast a 29-second feature on 2 ½-year-old "pool prodigy" Keith O'Dell.

Shifting Portrayals of Women

In past studies, we pointed to commentators' common practice of using sarcastic humor in portraying women athletes (and sometimes women spectators) as objects of ridicule, as participants in laughable "gag sports" (e.g., a woman's nude bungee jump in 1999 and a "weightlifting granny" in 2004), and/or as sexual objects. In 2004, we noted a decline in disrespectful or insulting treatment of women, compared with previous years. In 2009, we saw even less of this sort of sexist treatment of women, though this may in part reflect that women in any form were absent from the broadcasts. We outline below four themes that emerged in the rare occasions when women were afforded some airtime.

Rare Moments of Respectful Coverage   In 2009, we found a few instances where resources and time were devoted to delivering high-quality and respectful reports on a women's sporting event. For instance, on November 14, *SportsCenter* presented a 20-second-long story highlighting an upcoming Baylor vs. Tennessee women's college basketball game. The story was respectful in tone and included compelling game footage. A notable chunk of *SportsCenter's* meager coverage of women's sports during our March sample was devoted to a series of features entitled "Celebrating Women's History Month: Her Triumph, Her Story." One of these thirty-second-long stories would run during the hour-long broadcast, each focusing on an individual woman athlete, such as Rachel Fico, one of "the nation's finest in high school softball," and college skier Kelly Brush, who had been paralyzed in an accident but still participates in downhill skiing. Each "Her Story" feature was cordoned off from regular *SportsCenter* highlights, presented as something distinct and separate (appearing at the end of a commercial break, before the resumption of *SportsCenter's* regular sports highlights report, which contained little or no coverage of that day's women's sports events). The "Her Story" features had high technical quality and were delivered in a respectful tone.

Sexualized Gag Stories   The news broadcasts included a small number of sexualized gag stories about women that seemed like throwbacks to 1990s broadcasts. For instance, on November 11, 2009, KNBC's Fred Roggin delivered a gag story on a new Japanese product:

> "How 'bout this: With the holiday season quickly approaching, here's a perfect stocking stuffer for that woman who loves to play golf. A Japanese

designer has created a bra that unfolds into a putting green. The 'Make-The-Putt Bra' turns into a self-contained, five-foot-long mat that comes complete with a tee and golf balls. [Viewers see footage of a Japanese woman wearing a short, pleated white skirt, modeling the bra, putting a golf ball into the hole within the breast cup portion of the bra.] If that's not enough, the bra also comes with a motivational tape that blares the traditional Japanese words of encouragement, 'Nice in!' Yes, it is truly a gift that keeps on giving."

The "Japanese Putting Bra" was a twenty-four-second-long story embedded in a broadcast consisting otherwise of stories on four men's pro sports (football, baseball, soccer, and ice hockey), and within a two-week stretch of time when KNBC had almost no coverage of women's sports.

On July 18, in a report that focused entirely on men's sports, KABC's Curt Sandoval closed with a 28-second-long story on the Laker Girls Tryouts. In taped footage of the tryouts, viewers saw young dancing women wearing sports bra tops and bikini bottoms, as cameras positioned below them panned up from their legs to their abdomens, their breasts, and finally their faces, during which Sandoval reported:

"Finally, with Trevor Ariza in Houston and Lamar Odom's contract off the table, Laker fans needed something to smile about. We bring you the Laker Girl tryouts. Good to see life is actually well in El Segundo for Laker fans today. Several dozens putting on their best show to try to win that coveted—highly coveted— spot on the Laker Girl roster. Just ask Paula Abdul if it can help your career. We wish all the ladies well tonight." A female co-anchor responds, "You just made Danny's evening" (referring to KABC weatherman Danny Romero). Off-screen, laughter erupts, to which Sandoval responds, "We aim to please."

Fights, Assault, and Scandals   Women's sports were apparently deemed newsworthy when the news angle involved physical violence, egregious rule-breaking, or economic problems within the sport itself. For instance, on November 11, KNBC's Fred Roggin devoted 39 seconds (of a broadcast of 2:40 that otherwise covered only men's sports) to a graphic discussion of alarm over soccer player Elizabeth Lambert's on-field hair-pulling assault on another player. *SportsCenter* used a clip of Lambert's hair-pulling incident as one of its November 8 "Ultimate Highlights Clips." And on November 9, KABC did a short story on a fight that broke out in the stands at a high school girls' soccer game. On July 13, KABC's Curt Sandoval reported that LPGA commissioner Caroline Bivens had been ousted as a result of "a major revolt on the women's tour." Noting the devastating impact that the declining economy has recently had on women's golf, Sandoval concluded that "It's a great game of golf they play. It's just that the golf fans want to see the big hitters like Tiger, so we wish them well to get that resolved."

Women as Girlfriends, Wives, and Mothers   When women do nudge into the frame of news and highlights shows, they are commonly presented in conventional heterosexual roles, including as wives or girlfriends of prominent male athletes. On July 12, KABC's Curt Sandoval reported on auto-racing star Dario Franchitti, showing a clip of him during a moment of victory, kissing his celebrity wife: "Another fabulous outing for Dario Franchitti. Like life's not good enough: He's married to Ashley Judd." A July 14 story on KABC focused on USC quarterback Matt Cassel's newly signed $63 million NFL contract. Commentator Rob Fukuzaki joked that it "definitely pays . . . dating a quarterback at USC," to which his male co-anchor laughed and said, *I'm not touchin' that one!* And on November 16, KABC reported that NFL running back LaDainian Tomlinson had been motivated to have a standout game after his wife left a surprise gift in his locker: a positive pregnancy test.

A common way to portray successful women athletes was to foreground their status as wives or mothers. For instance, a July 18 KABC story on beach volleyball champion Kerri Walsh mentioned her husband's volleyball win that day and noted her own announcement that she is ready to return to play only two months after giving birth. Similarly, on July 12, *SportsCenter* delivered a short WNBA promotion for the next day's WNBA game to be broadcast on ESPN, saying "the new mom Candace Parker leads the Los Angeles Sparks to Connecticut to take on the Sun."

SportsCenter's "Her Story" segment on March 20 delivered high-quality production and respectful commentary on a woman athlete, while presenting her within the familiar frame of woman-as-partner to a high-profile male athlete. The story of Olympics track and field champion Sanya Richards was narrated by her fiancé, pro football player Aaron Ross. "Hello," Ross began, "My name is Aaron Ross, of the New York Giants. And I want to tell to you today about my fiancé, Sanya Richards." As viewers saw still photos of Richards competing, Ross' voice-over continued, "Her work ethic is second to none. I train with her and still to this day have not been able to make it through a workout." Viewers saw taped clips of Ross and Richards working out together, as Ross explained that the night before the finals in the Olympics in Beijing, Richards said, "I'm going to go out there and give it my all." "And she sure did. She came home with a gold."

Negative Depictions of Men?   Sprinkled throughout the 2009 study were a few stories that made fun of men athletes, sexualized them, or focused on their transgressions. For instance, on July 23, KNBC's Fred Roggin mocked soccer star David Beckham's declining athletic skills and his ascending status as an international sex symbol: "David Beckham was—was—a great player. But now he's the Anna Kournikova of soccer. Women love to look at him. And, let's be honest, some men do as well. But with that said, there's plenty of people out there that simply don't like him now." In addition, there were several stories during July on all of the news shows that focused on NFL quarterback Ben Roethlisberger having been accused of raping a woman in Lake Tahoe. There was also the occasional standalone story, such as the KNBC report in July on Logan Campbell, an athlete from New Zealand who, in order to raise money for his training for the Olympic Games, had opened a brothel. The main difference in how these negative or derogatory stories about men athletes were presented, as compared with those on women, was that they were embedded within a seemingly unending flow of respectful and celebratory stories about men's sports and male athletes. By contrast, a negative story on a woman athlete usually stood alone as the only women's sports story in a particular broadcast. . . .

V. Analysis and Interpretation of Findings:
A Deepening Silence

The first *Gender in Televised Sports* report was issued in 1990, nearly two decades after Title IX fueled an explosion of girls' and women's athletic participation in the United States. The 1990 report heralded the recent surge of girls' participation in youth sports, the dramatic upswing of girls' and women's high school and college sports opportunities and participation, and the stirrings of growth in women's professional sports. The study concluded that since women's sports received only 5% of TV news coverage, people who get all or most of their information from television news would have little idea how dramatically sports had changed. One common response to the 1990 study was an optimistic view: members of the public and many students with whom we discussed our findings assumed that TV coverage was simply lagging behind the surging popularity of women's sports; they predicted that media coverage would gradually catch up to the growing participation rates of girls and women in sport.

Twenty years later, this optimistic prediction of an evolutionary rise in TV news coverage of women's sports has proven to be wrong. During the ensuing two decades, girls' participation in youth sports has continued to rise (Sabo & Veliz 2008; Staurowsky et al., 2009). In 1971, only 294,000 U.S. high school girls played interscholastic sports, compared with 3.7 million boys. In 1989, the first year of our sports media study, high school boy athletes still outnumbered girls, 3.4 million to 1.8 million. By 2009, the high school sports participation gap had closed further, with 4.4 million boys and 3.1 million girls playing (National Federation of State High School Associations 2009). This trend is echoed in college sports. In 1972, the year Title IX was enacted there were only a little over 2 women's athletics teams per college. By 2010, the number had risen to 8.64 teams per NCAA school (Carpenter & Acosta 2010). Women's professional sports, including the WNBA (which began play in 1997), has developed a somewhat stronger foothold in the larger pro sports marketplace. However, during this two decades of growth in women's sports, the gap between TV news and highlights shows' coverage of women's and men's sports has not narrowed, it has widened. Women's sports in 2009 received a paltry 1.6% of the coverage on TV news, and an anemic 1.4% on ESPN's *SportsCenter*.

Why the Silence?

This deepening silence about women's sports in mainstream televised news and highlights shows is nothing short of stunning, especially when considered alongside the fact that the world of sports is no longer a "male preserve," in which boys and men enjoy privileged and exclusive access to sport participation opportunities. To be sure, there is an expanding array of media sources of sports information, including Internet Web sites, which fans of women's sports can tap for news about their favorite athletes or teams. Though it is nowhere near the level of the seemingly 24/7 live broadcasts of men's sports across the TV dial, the number of live broadcasts of women's sports has also expanded over the past twenty years (including far more women's NCAA basketball tournament games shown live today than in 1989). But television news and highlights shows remain two extremely important sources of sports information. Their continued tendency to ignore or marginalize women's sports helps to maintain the myth that sports are exclusively by, about, and for men.

How can we explain the growing chasm between coverage of women's and men's sports in our six-week sample? We are cautious in interpreting why coverage of women's sports has nearly evaporated, based entirely on our content analysis of the programming. To answer this "why" question would require a study that also focuses on the production end of news and highlights shows. What assumptions and values guide the decisions of producers, editors, and TV sports commentators on what sports stories are important to cover, and how to cover them? When asked, producers, commentators, and editors will usually explain their lack of attention to women's sports by arguing that they are constrained by a combination of market forces, and by their desire to give viewers "what they want to see." We understand programmers' desire to respond to market realities and viewer preferences; however, our discussion below points to ways in which the focus on men's sports is driven by a broad range of factors.

Tighter Budgets, Narrowed Focus?

The expansion of new media has been accompanied by shrinking revenues for traditional mass media, leading to tighter budgets and staff cuts for traditional news outlets. In a March 2010 editorial blog, *Los Angeles Times* sports editor Mike James responded to reader complaints about the newspaper's lack of coverage of college women's basketball and other smaller-market sports:

> True, we haven't been covering a lot of women's basketball this season, aside from a couple of features, largely because women's basketball hasn't been a major draw in L.A. . . . Consequently, we have to make the difficult decisions every day on what events and sports we do cover and those that we can't. Our decision has been to try to make sure we reach the greatest number of readers we can with resources available, and regrettably, that means that some areas don't get much regular coverage. (Edgar 2010)

James' lament about the impact of recent staff cuts at the *LA Times* would surely be echoed by hundreds of newspaper editors across the nation. As reporters and other sports news staff are cut, newspapers play it safe and assign their remaining staff to big-market sports teams that, they assume, "the greatest number of readers" want to read about. However, it is unlikely that the well-documented financial decline of print journalism can explain the increasingly paltry coverage of women's sports in television news. And it certainly cannot explain the scant coverage on ESPN's *SportsCenter*. In its 2010 media guide published for potential advertisers, ESPN claims that it is the "Most viewed ad supported cable channel," and crows that the 2009 broadcast year was ESPN's "highest rated ever" (ESPN 2010:5). Clearly, ESPN has no shortage of viewers, or presumably of advertising revenue. The network's decision to ignore women's sports must be due to other factors.

Pitching Sports News and Highlights to Men?

ESPN tells potential advertisers that in 2009 it was the top cable network viewed consistently by men aged 18–54, and that it has been "Men's favorite TV network since 1998" (ESPN 2010:5). Clearly, the ways in which ESPN targets its programming to male viewers is reflective of a larger trend, wherein TV producers carve out market niches that situate male viewers in the electronic equivalent of locker rooms characterized by male banter and ironic humor (Farred 2000; Messner & Montez de Oca 2005; Nylund 2007).

A foundational assumption of those who create programming for men on programs like *SportsCenter* seems to be that men want to think of women as sexual objects of desire, or perhaps as mothers, but not as powerful, competitive athletes. This is a questionable assumption, especially when we consider the dramatic growth of men's support for their daughters' athletic participation in recent decades (Messner 2009; Sabo & Veliz 2008). But even if this sexist assumption accurately captures the desires and values of a large swath of the U.S. male demographic that watches ESPN, it is probably inaccurate to operate from the same assumptions concerning viewers of evening TV news. After all, a sports report on the evening and late-night news is a short (two to five minute) segment embedded within a larger news report that is being viewed by a diverse audience. Presumably a large proportion of TV news viewers are women, many of whom are unlikely to find the male-centric views of the locker room or its ironic, sexist banter to be very inviting. We wonder how many women—and indeed, how many men—simply tune out when the sports segment of the evening news begins.

Packaging Women Athletes for Presumed Male Viewers?

In past iterations of this study, we pointed to the ways that sexist humor in sports commentary made fun of women and trivialized women athletes (and often women spectators at sporting events). We argued that this trivialization and sexualization of women in the broadcasts served to marginalize women's sports, while also creating a viewing experience for male viewers that meshed neatly with the feeling of a locker room culture that affirms the centrality of men (Messner, Duncan & Cooky 2003; Kane & Maxwell, in press). In 2004, we noted a lessening of this sort of trivialization and sexualization of women in the broadcasts. Our 2009 study revealed that these practices nearly disappeared.

It is a positive development that sports news and highlights viewers are less often seeing disparaging and sexist portrayals of women (Berstein 2002; Daniels 2009; Daniels & LaVoi, in press). However, this decline in negative portrayals of women has not been accompanied by an increase in routine coverage of women's sports. Instead, when the news and highlights shows ceased to portray women athletes in trivial and sexualized ways, they nearly ceased portraying them at all.

Viewing the woman athlete through the male gaze of sexualized humor is apparently (and thankfully) now discredited; instead, now women athletes are being repackaged to be seen through another male gaze—as family members. The "women's sports history" segments during the March segment of *SportsCenter* offer an intriguing glimpse into programmers' assumptions about how to present women's sports to male viewers who are used to being fed a steady diet of men's sports. While these special segments had high technical quality and were produced in ways that were respectful of the accomplishments of the women athletes, two elements were notable. First, these features were placed in a netherland between regular *SportsCenter* stories and ESPN commercial breaks. Clearly, they were meant to be viewed as something different, separate and apart from the regular sports highlight shows (which on these nights continued their normal coverage of mostly the "Big Three" men's sports). Second, one of them was narrated by the voice-over of the male fiancé of the woman athlete being featured. We interpret this as a strategy to make a woman athlete recognizable and palatable to a presumably male audience: in (mostly) rejecting the past practices of making a woman athlete familiar and "consumable" to a male audience by sexualizing her, producers in 2009 were more likely to package the woman athlete instead as a family member, in a familiar role as mother, girlfriend, or wife.

This repackaging of women athletes meshes with the larger commercial project of packaging women athletes as heterosexual mothers/wives. This practice has been criticized both for the ways in which it renders lesbian and other women athletes marginal or invisible, and also for the ways in which it maintains the public view of women athletes from the vantage point of men's continued positions of centrality in social life (Pfister 2010).

Connected with the silencing of women athletes is the fact that the voices of women commentators are still entirely absent from TV sports news, and very rare on *SportsCenter.* Unlike TV news anchor, reporter, and weather announcer positions, the occupation of TV sports commentator is still very sex-segregated (Etling & Young 2007; Sheffer & Shultz 2007). Women have had a very difficult time breaking in to sports broadcasting, remaining relegated at best to marginal roles such as "sideline reporter" during an NBA or men's college basketball game. Viewers of sports news and highlights shows are treated to a constant barrage of words and images about men's sports, narrated by a cacophony of men's voices.

Audiences and Audience-Building

In the absence of audience research, we must be cautious in drawing conclusions about the meanings that TV viewers make of sports news and highlights shows. However, we can speculate on these questions, based on our analysis of the trends over the past twenty years and the dominant meanings that are conveyed in the patterns of gendered coverage of sports stories.

It has been known for many years that sports news and highlights shows do not simply "give viewers what they want," in some passive response to demand. Instead, there is a dynamic reciprocal relationship between commercial sports and the sports media. Media scholar Sut Jhally called this self-reinforcing monetary and promotional loop the "sports-media complex" (Jhally 1984). When we add fans into this loop, we can see how information and pleasure-enhancement are part of a circuit that promotes and actively builds audiences for men's sports, while simultaneously providing profits for men's sports organizations, commercial sponsors, and the sports media. Sports fans seek out news wraps and highlights of games—even of games they have already watched in their entirety— not simply for information, but because viewing these reports enhances and amplifies the feelings—the tension, suspense, and exhilaration—they may have enjoyed a few hours earlier.

TV news and highlights shows do not simply "reflect" fan interest in certain sports, as sports commentators and editors often argue. They also help to generate and sustain enthusiasm for the sports they cover, thus becoming a key link in fans' emotional connection to the agony and ecstasy of spectator sports. Fans of men's sports—especially the Big Three of football, basketball, and baseball—are used to having this fix routinely delivered free of charge to their living rooms. This emotional enhancement is but one element of the larger role of TV sports news in building audiences for men's sports. Meanwhile their silence helps to ensure smaller audiences for women's sports, while keeping fans of women's sports on emotional life-support.

We have noted in past studies how a comparison of coverage of women's and men's NCAA basketball offers an especially valuable window into TV news' audience-building functions (Messner, Duncan & Wachs 1996). Our 2009 data enhance our understanding of how audience-building works. As we noted above, far less time was devoted to reporting on the women's NCAA tournament than on the men's. What was most striking in the 2009 study was the amount of time all of the news and highlight shows spent on (and the enthusiastic, even excited tone within which they couched) reports about upcoming men's NCAA tournament seedings and match-ups. Little or no such anticipatory reports on the women's games appeared on the broadcasts. Even after the tournament games started, reports on the women's games were, at best, usually relegated to the ticker. Meanwhile, the men's tournament was receiving large chunks of coverage in every broadcast.

Audience-building for men's sports permeates the mass media in a seemingly organic manner. As such, these promotional efforts are more easily taken for granted and, ironically, may be less visible *as* promotion. News and highlights shows are two important links in a huge apparatus of audience-building for men's sports. But they rarely operate this way for women's sports.

How Can Change Occur?

Can these stubborn patterns of inequitable coverage of women's sports be broken or changed? Clearly, the longitudinal data from our study shows that there is no reason to expect an evolutionary growth in media coverage of women's sports. To the contrary, our research shows that the proportion of coverage devoted to women's sports on televised news over the past twenty years has actually declined, and there is no reason to believe that this trend will reverse itself in the next twenty years unless producers decide that it is in their interests to do so. For this to happen in a substantial way, power relations and perceptions of gender will have to continue to change within sport organizations, with commercial sponsors who promote and advertise sports, and within the mass media. These shifts in perception will not come about by themselves, but will involve changes and pressures from a number of directions.

One important source of such change within the mass media would involve an affirmative move toward developing and supporting more women sports reporters and commentators. While we should be cautious in assuming that women reporters will necessarily cover sports differently from the ways that men do, there is some evidence to suggest that women sports reporters are less likely to cover women athletes in disrespectful ways and more likely to advocate expanding the coverage of women's sports (Hardin & Whiteside 2008; Kian & Hardin 2009; LaVoi et al., 2007).

Sports organizations too can contribute to change by providing the sports media with more and better information about women athletes. Indeed, a longitudinal study shows that university sports information departments have vastly improved their presentation of women's sports in their annual media guides (Kane & Buysse 2005). Sports fans can also be an active part of this loop to promote change: audience members can complain directly to the producers of sports programs—to tell them that they do not appreciate sexist treatment of women in sports news and highlights shows, and to tell them that they want to see more and better coverage of actual women's sports. That's why, perhaps, they call it "demand."

Overall, we find the results of this study to be discouraging. Clearly, change has happened, but not in the direction of increased coverage of women's sports. In recent years, sports news and highlights shows have evidenced a retrenchment, expressed through a narrowed focus on a few commercially central men's sports.

ENDNOTE

[1]Diana Nyad is formerly a commentator with Fox Sports News and ABC Sports, and currently contributes a weekly column for National Public Radio.

REFERENCES

Bernstein, A. 2002. "Is It Time for a Victory Lap? Changes in the Media Coverage of Women in Sport," *International Review for the Sociology of Sport* 37: 415–428.

Carpenter, L. J. & V. Acosta 2010. *Women in Intercollegiate Sport: A Longitudinal, National Study, Thirty-Three Year Update. http://www.acostacarpenter.org/*

Daniels, E. A. 2009. "Sex Objects, Athletes and Sexy Athletes: How Media Representations of Women Athletes Can Impact Adolescent Girls and College Women," *Journal of Adolescent Research* 24: 399–423.

Daniels, E., & N. M. LaVoi, in Press. "Athletics as Solution and Problem: Sports Participation for Girls and the Sexualization of Female Athletes," In T. A. Roberts and E. L. Zubriggen (Eds.) *The Sexualization of Girls and Girlhood.* New York: Oxford University Press.

Edgar, D. 2010. "Which Sports to Cover? It's a Tough Call," *Los Angeles Times* Editorial Blog, March 12. http://latimesblogs.latimes.com/readers/2010/03/which-sports-to-cover-its-a-tough-call.html

ESPN 2010. *2010 Pocket Guide.* ESPN Marketing and Sales. http://www.espncms.com/

Etling, L., & R. Young 2007. "Sexism and Authoritativeness of Female Sportscasters," *Communication Research Reports,* 121–130.

Farred, G. 2000. "Cool as the Other Side of the Pillow: How ESPN's *SportsCenter* has Changed Television Sports Talk," *Journal of Sport and Social Issues* 24: 96–117.

Hardin, M. & E. Whiteside 2008. "Maybe Its Not a 'Generational Thing': Values and Beliefs of Aspiring Sport Journalists about Race and Gender," *Media Report to Women* 36: 8–16.

Jhally, S. 1984. "The Spectacle of Accumulation: Material and Cultural Factors in the Evolution of the Sports/Media Complex," *Insurgent Sociologist* 12.

Kane, M. J., & H. D. Maxwell (in press). "Expanding the Boundaries of Sport Media Research: Using Critical Theory to Explore Consumer Responses to Representations of Women's Sports," *Journal of Sport Management.*

Kian, E. M. & Hardin, M. 2009. Framing of Sports Coverage Based on the Sex of Sports Writers: Female Journalists Counter Traditional Gendering of Media Coverage. *International Journal of Sport Communication,* 2, 185–204.

LaVoi, N. M., Buysse, J., Maxwell, H. D., & Kane, M. J. 2007. "The Influence of Occupational Status and Sex of Decision Maker on Media Representations in Intercollegiate Athletics," *Women in Sport & Physical Activity Journal,* 15: 32–43.

Messner, M. A. 2009. *It's All for the Kids: Gender, Families and Youth Sports.* Berkeley: University of California Press.

Messner, M. A., M. Carlisle Duncan & C. Cooky 2003. "Silence, Sports Bras, and Wrestling Porn: The Treatment of Women in Televised Sports News and Highlights," *Journal of Sport and Social Issues* 27: 38–51.

Messner, M. A., M. Carlisle Duncan & F. L. Wachs 1996. "The Gender of Audience-Building: Televised Coverage of Men's and Women's NCAA Basketball," *Sociological Inquiry* 66: 422–439.

Messner, M. A. & Montez de Oca, J. 2005. "The Male Consumer as Loser: Beer and Liquor Ads in Mega Sports Media Events." *Signs: Journal of Women in Culture and Society* 30: 1879–1909.

National Federation of State High School Associations 2009. *2008–09 High school Athletics Parcipation Survey.* http://www.nfhs.orq

Nylund, D. 2007 *Beer, Babes and Balls: Masculinity and Sports Talk Radio.* State University of New York Press.

Pfister, G. 2010. Women in Sport: Gender Relations and Future Perspectives. *Sport in Society,* 13, 234–248.

Sabo, D. F. & P. Veliz 2008. *Youth Sport in America.* East Meadow, NY: Women's Sports Foundation.

Sheffer, M. L. & Brad Schultz 2007. "Double Standard: Why Women Have Trouble Getting Jobs in Local Television Sports," *Journal of Sports Media,* 2, 77–101.

Staurowsky, E. J., DeSousa, M. J., Ducher, G., Gentner, N., Miller, K. E., Shakib, S., Theberge, N., & Williams, N. 2009. *Her Life Depends on It II: Sport, Physical Activity, and the Health and Well-being of American Girls and Women.* East Meadow, NY: Women's Sports Foundation.

40

CONTROLLING THE MEDIA IN IRAQ

ANDREW M. LINDNER

Andrew M. Lindner, an assistant professor of sociology at Concordia College in Moorhead, Minnesota, studies the intersection of media, politics, and society. One fascinating aspect of the mass media is an investigation into

Andrew M. Lindner, "Controlling the Media in Iraq." *Contexts,* Vol. 7, No. 2, pp. 32–38, May, 2008. Copyright © 2008 American Sociological Association. Reprinted by permission of Sage Publications, Inc.

how other social institutions affect it. Some scholars believe that the mass media is the fourth power institution that should be added to C. Wright Mills' definition of the power elite (the three institutions of the military, the economy, and the government; see Reading 35). Others argue that the mass media is ultimately controlled by the other institutions in terms of advertising messages, political campaign ads, sports coverage, and even the reporting of news (see Klinenberg's research in Reading 38). In the excerpt below, Lindner examines how the institution of the military controls the media reporting of war through a technique called *embedded journalism.*

In 2003, nearly 600 journalists working for news agencies from around the world traveled alongside U.S. and coalition forces as they invaded Iraq. The Pentagon's embedded journalists program allowed reporters for the first time to attach themselves to military units. While Bush Administration officials hailed it for its intimate access to soldiers' lives, media watchdogs criticized its often restrictive nature and publicly worried reporters would do little more than serve up rosy stories about soldiers' courage and homesickness.

Critics also argued the embedding program was essential to the administration's attempt to build popular support for the war in Iraq. Several influential members of the Pentagon leadership and the administration believed the media contributed to defeat in the Vietnam War by demoralizing the American public with coverage of atrocities and seemingly futile guerilla warfare. They hoped to avoid a similar result in Iraq by limiting journalists' coverage of darker stories on combat, the deaths of Iraqi civilians, and property damage. As media commentator Marvin Kalb noted, the embedding program was *part of the massive, White House-run strategy to sell . . . the American mission in this war.*

While anecdotal examples of the worst excesses of embedded reporters abound, only a few studies have systematically considered news coverage by embedded reporters. Those studies show the program provided reporters with an insider's view of the military experience, but also essentially blocked them from providing much coverage of the Iraqi experience of the war.

By examining the content of articles rather than the tone, and comparing embedded and nonembedded journalists' articles, it becomes clear that the physical, and perhaps psychological, constraints of the embedding program dramatically inhibited a journalist's ability to cover civilians' war experiences. While most embedded reporters didn't shy away from describing the horrors of war, the structural conditions of the embedded program kept them focused on the horrors facing the troops, rather than upon the thousands of Iraqis who died.

By comparison, independent reporters who were free to roam successfully interviewed coalition soldiers and Iraqi civilians alike, covering both the major events of the war and the human-interest stories of civilians.

But given the far greater frequency and prominence of published articles penned by embedded journalists, ultimately the embedding program proved a victory for the armed services in the historical tug-of-war between the press and military over journalistic freedom during wartime.

War Reporting in Perspective

From the Pentagon's perspective, the embedding program represented a potential compromise in a long-standing conflict between the press and the military over journalistic freedoms in a war zone. In the past 150 years, with the growth of both contemporary warfare and the modern media apparatus, the armed forces and the press have often been at odds in a battle to control information dissemination.

While accounts of warfare go back as far as cave paintings, most war historians mark William Howard Russell, an Irish special correspondent for the *London Times,* as the first modern war reporter. In 1853, Russell was dispatched to Malta to cover English support for Russian troops in the Crimean War. His first-hand reports from the front lines, often criticizing British military leadership, were unique at the time and stirred up much controversy back in England, both rallying support from some quarters and scandalizing military leaders and the royal family. Bending under political pressure, the *Times* agreed to a degree of self-censorship, but a precedent had been set and news consumers would continue to expect the same caliber of war coverage in the future.

Since Russell's time, the relationship between the media and military has undergone many transformations. During World War II, American military and political leaders carefully noted the morally reprehensible yet highly effective propaganda of the Nazi party, most notably Leni Riefenstahl's *Triumph of the Will.* They responded with their own propaganda series, *Why We Fight,* created through the combined talents of director Frank Capra and Disney's animation staff.

In terms of frontline coverage, the United States military exercised limited censorship with a largely cooperative and nationalistic press, yielding what military scholar Brendan McLane called, "from the military perspective . . . a golden age of war reporting." Even independently minded reporter Edward R. Murrow, later a hero to many journalists for his bold castigation of the McCarthy hearings, provided assurances of the moral righteousness of the American military campaign alongside vivid descriptions of Allied bombing raids.

By contrast, the low levels of censorship, convenient transportation, and the significant technological advancement of television made coverage of the conflict in Vietnam the ideal of war coverage for much of the press. Lyndon B. Johnson's administration policy of "minimum candor" with the press as well as the military's efforts to push only those stories that emphasized progress led to the widespread belief in a "credibility gap" between what government officials claimed and the reality of the situation.

However, even if military and political leaders were successful in obstructing journalists in the White House press room, the very nature of a guerilla conflict with an ever-shifting frontline gave journalists in Vietnam excellent access to soldiers and civilians alike. In addition, with the advent of television and advancements in the portability of TV cameras, reporters were able to transmit powerful images of the conflict into living rooms, censored only by editors' sense of propriety and Federal Communications Commission (FCC) regulations.

While collective memory of the journalism during the Vietnam War today tends to be of the courageous release of the Pentagon Papers by *New York Times* reporters or the image of the free-roaming photo-journalist played by Dennis Hopper in *Apocalypse Now,* it's worth noting that, for more than 10 years until the late 1960s, the majority of the press corps complacently accepted the official story. Nonetheless, the important distinction between the modes of war reporting in World War II and Vietnam is that war correspondents in Vietnam— David Halberstam, Stanley Karnow, and Peter Arnett among them—always had the opportunity to roam and report on the story they chose.

More than three decades later, it has become axiomatic that most military leaders and many among the political right believe a liberal-leaning press corps "lost" the Vietnam War by demoralizing the public with horrific images and accounts of atrocities. And, indeed, this simmering resentment has made military-media relations since Vietnam incredibly tense. During the first Gulf War, the media furiously complained about the infamous "press pools" that forced journalists into parroting official press releases from military headquarters in Kuwait. On occasion, selected journalists were allowed to ride with military minders on a tour of the battlefield after the struggle had ended and the bodies were removed. In the mid-1990s, the military was left similarly fuming as journalists arrived in Somalia before the troops.

Pentagon leadership, well aware that an ongoing feud with the press was not in its best interests, formed two workgroups to study the issue of how better to manage the press in wartime. In 1984, under the leadership of Brigadier General Winant Sidle, a military panel was charged to examine how to conduct military operations while protecting military lives and the security of the operation but also keeping the American public informed through the media. In the wake of complaints about the Desert Storm press pools, military and media leaders met for the Pentagon-Media Conference in 1992 and agreed on several principles of news coverage in a combat zone.

In the intervening years prior to the embedding program, technological changes once again altered the nature of war reporting. As satellite phones became more portable journalists became more self-sufficient, able to coordinate with newsrooms and feed reports, images, and video instantaneously. The newfound capacity of journalists to transmit information on the spot presented a new set of threats to operational security. Without the traditional lag-time of war reporting, even well-intentioned journalists might accidentally reveal information of strategic significance, such as locations or troop levels. Based on the recommendations of the various workgroups and the practical consequences of technological innovation, Pentagon officials began to develop training programs and other provisions for embedding in the next major conflict.

Into the Fray

In 2002, as the specter of conflict with Iraq began to loom larger, Pentagon officials announced a week-long "Embed Boot Camp" for journalists hoping to participate in the program. Reporters were outfitted with Kevlar helmets and military garb, slept in barracks bunks, and ate military grub in the mess hall aboard the USS *Iwo Jima*. Marines trained them in military jargon, tactical marches, direct fire, nuclear-biological-chemical attacks, and combat first aid.

Perhaps more significantly, embedded reporters were forced to sign a contract and agree to the "ground rules"—allow their reports to be reviewed by military officials prior to release, to be escorted at all times by military personnel, and to allow the government to dismiss them at any time for any reason.

Before a single word was printed, many speculated that embedded reporters would fall victim to Stockholm Syndrome, the condition, named after a notorious 1973 incident in the Swedish city, in which hostages begin to identify with their captors. Media commentators like Andrew Jacobs at *The New York Times*, Richard Leiby at *The Washington Post*, and Carol Brightman at *The Nation* argued that as embedded journalists became socialized into military culture, they would develop relationships with the soldiers and start reporting from the military point of view.

While labeling this condition Stockholm Syndrome is perhaps slightly inflammatory, much sociological research suggests socialization is one of the military's greatest strengths. In his classic collection of essays, *Asylums*, Erving Goffman noted the military is a total institution that not only controls all an individual's activities, but also informs the construction of identity and relationships. In total institutions, such as the military, prison, or mental institutions, Goffman argued, the individual must go through a process of mortification that undercuts the individual's civilian identity and constructs a new identity as a member of the institution. In such a communal culture, individuality is constantly repressed in the name of the institution's larger values and goals.

In the case of embedded journalists, it's easy to imagine how they might have come to identify with the military mission or, at the very least, the other members of their units. In addition to wearing military-issue camouflage uniforms, embedded journalists had to share living and sleeping space as well as food and water with their units. If embedded reporters ended up telling the story of the war from the soldiers' point of view, as so many critics charged, it would simply be the natural and expected result of a process of re-socialization.

However, a different, and arguably more compelling, explanation exists for why embedded reporters might depict the war in a military-centric manner: they didn't have the freedom to roam. George C. Wilson, for example, embedded for *National Journal*, compared it to being the second dog on a dogsled team, writing, "You see and hear a lot of the dog directly in front of you, and you see what is passing by on the left and right, but you cannot get out of the traces to explore intriguing sights you pass, without losing your spot on the moving team."

Many sociological studies have observed that journalists, whether reporting from a newsroom in New York or a bunker in Baghdad, encounter what Mark Fishman has called a "bureaucratically constructed universe." The constraints of journalists' "universes" lead them to make certain assumptions, engage in specific practices, and only pursue particular types of stories. For example, a typical beat reporter is constrained by technical requirements such as word counts, the publication's ideological commitments, and professional ideas about what is and isn't newsworthy.

Several commentators, notably Michael Massing in the *New York Review of Books,* argued that in addition to these common limitations, the embedding program made covering soldiers' experiences easy, while covering the experiences of Iraqi civilians was difficult, if not impossible. From the Pentagon's perspective, the ease of access to soldiers was the essential strength of the embedding program. As Deputy Assistant Secretary of Defense for Public Affairs Bryan Whitman told *The Nation,* "you get extremely deep, rich coverage of what's going on in a particular unit."

Alternatives to Embedding

Although the embedding program was the dominant form of reporting during the early days of Operation Iraqi Freedom, two alternatives did exist. Though slightly more expensive than embedding, some news organizations opted to station a reporter in Baghdad. These journalists bunkered down at the Sheraton Ishtar or the Palestine Hotel in central Baghdad and watched as the American "shock and awe" bombing raid wrought death and destruction on the city.

During the first few weeks of the war, many Baghdad-stationed journalists attended briefing sessions led by Iraqi government officials and were escorted on tours of the city by official Iraqi minders. As Saddam Hussein's government collapsed, Baghdad-stationed reporters took to the streets to cover the conflict and its consequences, either alone or with hired bodyguards.

The second alternative—funding an independent reporter with the freedom to roam—was far more costly and largely the province of elite news sources, particularly *The New York Times* and other national newspapers and wire services. In the weeks and months before the conflict began, many of these independent reporters traveled through Iran or Turkey into Iraqi Kurdistan and followed the slow advance of Kurdish forces and U.S. Special Forces toward Kirkuk and Mosul. Other independent reporters, after hiring a four-wheel-drive vehicle and private security team, fanned out across the country, often buckling down in potential battlegrounds like Fallujah and Basrah. While ground commanders interacted positively with independent reporters, on several occasions Pentagon officials criticized what they called "four-wheel-drive" and "cowboy" journalists for operating outside of the embedding program.

Like the embedded reporters, the other two arrangements for reporting from Iraq—being stationed in Baghdad or independent—represent distinct journalistic social locations (often defined in sociology as sets of rules, expectations, and relations based on status) that channeled journalists toward producing certain types of content and limited access to other types.

While embedded reporters had nearly unlimited access to coalition soldiers, Baghdad-stationed reporters would seem to have the most extensive access to Iraqi civilians. Although media accounts have suggested both embedded and Baghdad-stationed reporters presented a narrow view of the war, we would expect independent reporters, with the freedom and resources to roam at will were the least constrained of the three types of journalists, and, therefore, most likely to produce articles that balanced the Iraqi and the military experiences of the war.

Nonetheless, given that embedded reporting was the dominant form of reporting from Iraq (both in sheer numbers and in prominence), if the claims regarding embedding are true, then the vast majority of the news coming out of Iraq may have emphasized military successes and the heroics of soldiers, rather than the consequences of the invasion for the Iraqi people.

The Embedding Effect

Much of the existing systematic research on the embedding program has focused on the issue of rhetorical tone. Adopting an approach similar to the Stockholm Syndrome explanation, these researchers have argued that embedded reporters tend to sympathize with the soldiers they cover and adopt a more supportive tone when describing the mission in Iraq.

For example, a 2005 cross-cultural study of various network and cable television news programs found 9 percent of embedded reporters adopted a supportive tone as opposed to only 5.6 percent of "unilateral" reporters. Another 2006 study of 452 articles from American national daily newspapers found that compared to nonembedded reporters, embedded reporters produced coverage significantly more positive about the military and "implied a greater trust toward military personnel." Research by the same group of scholars found similar results in broadcast news. These studies clearly suggest the embedding program encourages journalists to adopt a positive outlook on both the soldiers with whom they live and the military mission as a whole.

While these findings tell us much about the social psychological consequences of embedding, without considering the actual content of news reports it's difficult to answer the more sociological question of how the various journalistic social locations inhibited or enabled journalists' access to various types of stories. The only research to address the substantive content of embedded reporting is a 2004 Project for Excellence in Journalism (PEJ) study that examined 108 embedded reports from 10 different television programs. Among the results, PEJ found 61 percent of reports were live and unedited, 21.3 percent showed weapons fired, and combat was the most commonly discussed topic, covered in 41 percent of stories. Unfortunately, the PEJ study didn't incorporate a comparison group of nonembedded journalists. Without such a group, we can't compare the effects of various journalistic contexts on cultural production.

A study of the substantive content produced by embedded reporters and both types of nonembedded reporters would allow us to consider two questions of considerable sociological interest. First, we can better understand how institutional contexts in a war zone can shape the ability of journalists to report on various types of stories (or speak to varying types of people). By contrast, while a study of tone can tell us about how context shapes affective dispositions and/or ideological commitments, it does little to answer more concerning questions of limitations of access. Second, by focusing on content rather than tone, we learn more about what kind of information news consumers received. The capacity of governments to influence the types of information citizens have access to is an enduring theme of sociology, harking back to preeminent social thinkers from Karl Marx to C. Wright Mills.

A Soldier's Eye View

To consider how the context of the embedding program may have limited journalists' access and, thus, information about the war to the wider public, two research assistants and I studied five articles by each of the English-language print reporters in Iraq during the first six weeks of the war. We coded 742 articles by 156 journalists for five types of news coverage representing the soldier's experience of the war and five types representing the Iraqi civilians' experience. By comparing the differences in news coverage among embedded, independent, and Baghdad-stationed journalists, we are better able to understand how these different journalistic social locations may have limited reporters' ability to present a balanced portrayal of the war.

To capture the extent to which journalists depicted the soldier's experience in Iraq, we recorded the frequency of news coverage of combat, military movement, soldier fatalities, the use of a soldier as a source, and the inclusion of a soldier human interest story Figure 40.1. As the results dramatically demonstrate, embedded reporters provided the most extensive coverage in

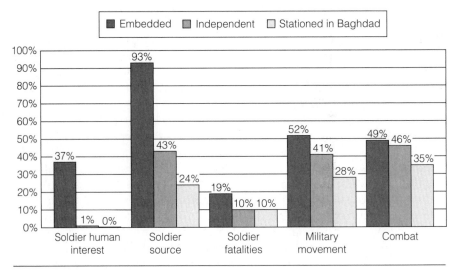

FIGURE 40.1   **News Coverage Representing the Soldier's Experience**

all five categories representing the soldier's experience of the war. Such thorough coverage of military happenings is perhaps unsurprising, considering embedded journalists used a soldier as a source in 93 percent of all articles, more than twice as frequently as independent journalists.

More remarkable in light of much of the criticism of the embedding program is the fact that embedded reporters wrote about technical and often gritty subjects like combat and military movement in about half the articles. Clearly the common claim that embedded reporters wrote only "fluff pieces" about homesick soldiers is patently false (although soldier human interest stories were fairly common, appearing in 37 percent of all articles by embedded reporters).

Nonetheless, it's worth noting that Baghdad-stationed reporters, and in particular independent reporters, were fairly effective at portraying the military perspective of the war. Though both types of nonembedded reporters rarely covered soldier human interest stories, they both used soldiers as sources and covered combat and military movement in a quarter or more of the articles. In fact, independent reporters covered the "hard facts" of the war (like combat and military movement) nearly as frequently as embedded reporters.

To document the extent of news coverage of the Iraqi civilian experience of the war, we noted the frequency of coverage of bombings, property damage, civilian fatalities, the use of an Iraqi civilian as a source, and the inclusion of an Iraqi human interest story Figure 40.2. The results show embedded reporters put forward a highly military-focused vision of the war, covering bombing and civilian fatalities and using Iraqis as a source far less frequently than either independents or reporters stationed in Baghdad.

Baghdad-stationed reporters provided the most extensive coverage of the consequences of the invasion, reporting on bombing, property damage,

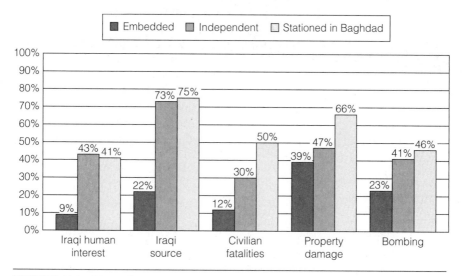

FIGURE 40.2   News Coverage Representing the Iraqi Civilian Experience

and/or civilian fatalities in half the articles. While independent reporters didn't conduct all types of coverage as well as Baghdad-stationed reporters, they used an Iraqi source in nearly three quarters of the articles and covered Iraqi human interest stories in 43 percent of their articles.

Most troubling of all the disparities among embedded, Baghdad-stationed, and independent journalists is in their respective coverage of civilian fatalities. While estimates of Iraqi civilian fatalities during this period of the war vary widely, at least 2,100 civilians died during the first six weeks of the invasion. Though civilian deaths were acknowledged in half the articles by Baghdad-stationed reporters and 30 percent of articles by independent reporters, only 12 percent of articles by embedded reporters noted the human toll of the war on the Iraqi people.

These findings strongly suggest the Pentagon's embedding program—the dominant journalistic arrangement during the Iraq War—channeled reporters toward producing war coverage from the soldier's point of view. While Baghdad-stationed reporters were similarly narrow in covering the Iraqi civilian experience of the war, independent reporters, who had freedom to roam and chose their sources and topics, produced the greatest balance between depicting the military and the Iraqi experience of the war.

Although the embedding program didn't print only good news, it did tend to emphasize military successes while downplaying the war's consequences. With upwards of 90 percent of articles by embeds using soldiers as a source, as long as the soldiers stayed positive, the story stayed positive. And thus, an administration that hoped to build support for the war by depicting it as a successful mission with limited costs was able to do so through the embed program and without some of the more heavy-handed propaganda efforts of Operation Desert Storm.

It's important to remember the embedding program was the only officially sanctioned mode of reporting, so we can't say the three arrangements for journalists painted a complete portrait of the war. A full 64 percent of print journalists in Iraq were embedded (the figure is even higher among TV journalists). In terms of visibility, the imbalance toward embedded coverage is even more striking—of the 186 articles in the sample that ultimately appeared on the front page of a newspaper, 71 percent were written by embedded reporters. Based on the content of articles by embedded journalists and the overwhelming dominance of the embedding program, it seems clear that, in the aggregate, the majority of the news coverage of the war was skewed toward the soldier's experience and failed to fully recognize the extent of the human and material costs.

Embedding, Then and Now

Shortly after President George W. Bush declared an end to "major combat" in Iraq in 2003, most embedding terms came to an end. For a time, Iraq was considered safe enough by most western media outlets that journalists rented houses in Baghdad or freely traveled throughout the country. By

September 2006 only 11 journalists were embedded with units in Iraq. However, as insurgent resistance grew many were forced to retreat to the safety of hotels protected by blast walls, occasionally taking excursions in armored cars with Iraqi bodyguards.

Today, a variation on the original embedding program exists, with journalists "embedding" with units on a particular mission or for shorter periods of time. Even journalists committed to depicting the Iraqi experience of the ongoing conflict, such as Jon Lee Anderson of *The New Yorker,* have traveled on brief stints with Army units because it's one of the least dangerous ways to cover the insurgency.

At the same time, the rules of the embedding contract have become more restrictive. In June 2007, *The New York Times* reported that embedded reporters would now be required to obtain signatures of consent before mentioning the names of soldiers used in moving or still images as well as in audio recordings. Some journalists have contended the new rules further enhance the military's ability to limit the release of undesirable news.

In the case of a future large-scale invasion (in Iran or Somalia, for example), both Pentagon officials and media industry leaders have indicated an interest in reviving the full embedding program. Should this happen, both sides must reconsider the nature of the embedding program, given its well-documented pattern of leading journalists to produce reports that present the military in a more positive and less objective light.

RECOMMENDED RESOURCES

Jon Lee Anderson. *The Fall of Baghdad* (Penguin Press, 2004). A beautifully written and vivid portrait of the first six weeks of the war by a Baghdad-stationed reporter.

Department of Defense. "Pentagon Embedding Agreement" February 23, 2003. The contract journalists must sign before embedding with a military unit.

Department of Defense. "CJCS Media-Military Relations Panel (Sidle Panel)" August 23, 1984. The report of the findings of the Sidle Panel, which led to the development of the embedding program.

Mark Fishman. *Manufacturing the News* (University of Texas Press, 1980). An excellent sociological account of the journalistic process.

Andrew Jacobs. "My Week at Embed Boot Camp," *The New York Times Magazine* February 3, 2003. A fascinating description of the activities at embed boot camp and the enthusiasm of military officials and journalists alike about the program.

41

OVER THE COUNTER
McDonald's

ROBIN LEIDNER

The economy and work are the focus of the next three readings. The first reading is Robin Leidner's 1993 case study, "Over the Counter: McDonald's,"
which takes us inside one employment organization and reveals what it is
like to work there. Leidner, a professor of sociology at the University of Pennsylvania, shows how McDonald's employees are intensively socialized.
Thus, this reading illustrates well the concept of *adult socialization*, as discussed by both Granfield in his research on students in law school (Reading 15) and Dyer's piece on socialization in the military (Reading 16). Leidner
also illustrates how the work itself is reduced to simple steps, and therefore
routinized, so that managers and owners can maintain the most control over
their product and over their employees. This process of increased routinization in the workplace has a long history in industrialization, especially within
factory work. Many social analysts, including Karl Marx (1818–1883), have
argued that the routinization of work leads to workers' feeling alienated from
their products and from their sense of self.

Organizations have many ways of obtaining the cooperation of participants, ranging from persuasion and enticement to force and curtailment of options. All organizations "hope to make people want to do
what the organization needs done" (Biggart 1989:128), but when they cannot
count on success in manipulating people's desires they can do their best to
compel people to act in the organization's interests.

Organizations choose strategies that rely on socialization and social control
in varying mixtures that are determined by the aims of the organization, the
constraints set by the organizational environment and the nature of the work,
and the interests and resources of the parties involved. In service-providing organizations, upper-level management must concern itself with the wishes and
behavior of service recipients and various groups of workers.[1] For each group,
service organizations try to find the most effective and least costly ways to get
people to act in the organizations' interests, proffering various carrots and
sticks, making efforts to win hearts and minds, closing off choices.

Organizations that routinize work exert control primarily by closing off choices. There is much room for variation, however, in what aspects of the work organizations will choose to routinize, how they go about it, and how much freedom of decision making remains. Moreover, even when routines radically constrain choice, organizations still must socialize participants and set up systems of incentives and disincentives to ensure the compliance of workers and customers.

. . . McDonald's . . . take[s] routinization to extremes . . . includ[ing] pre-determination of action and transformation of character. . . . McDonald's stresses minute specification of procedures, eliminating most decision making for most workers, although it does make some efforts to standardize operations by transforming the characters of its store-level managers. . . .

This . . . [selection] show[s] how the compan[y's] approaches to routinizing the work of those who interact with customers depend largely on the predictability of service recipients' behavior, which in turn depends on the kinds of resources the organizations have available to channel consumer behavior. . . . At McDonald's . . . the routines sharply limit the workers' autonomy without giving them much leverage over customers.

McDonald's

No one ever walks into a McDonald's and asks, *So, what's good today?* except satirically. The heart of McDonald's success is its uniformity and predictability. Not only is the food supposed to taste the same every day everywhere in the world, but McDonald's promises that every meal will be served quickly, courteously, and with a smile. Delivering on that promise over 20 million times a day in 54 countries is the company's colossal challenge (*McDonald's Annual Report* 1990:2). Its strategy for meeting that challenge draws on scientific management's most basic tenets: Find the One Best Way to do every task and see that the work is conducted accordingly.[2]

To ensure that all McDonald's restaurants serve products of uniform quality, the company uses centralized planning, centrally designed training programs, centrally approved and supervised suppliers, automated machinery and other specially designed equipment, meticulous specifications, and systematic inspections. To provide its customers with a uniformly pleasant "McDonald's experience," the company also tries to mass produce friendliness, deference, diligence, and good cheer through a variety of socialization and social control techniques. Despite sneers from those who equate uniformity with mediocrity, the success of McDonald's has been spectacular.

McFacts

By far the world's largest fast-food company, McDonald's has over 11,800 stores worldwide (*McDonald's Annual Report* 1990:1), and its 1990 international sales surpassed those of its three largest competitors combined (Berg 1991 sec. 3:6).[3] In the United States, consumer familiarity with McDonald's is virtually universal: The company estimates that 95 percent of U.S. consumers eat at a McDonald's at least once a year (Koepp 1987:58). McDonald's 1990 profits were $802.3 million, the third highest profits of any retailing company in the world (*Fortune* 1991:179). At a time when the ability of many U.S. businesses to compete on the world market is in question, McDonald's continues to expand around the globe—most recently to Morocco—everywhere remaking consumer demand in its own image.

As politicians, union leaders, and others concerned with the effects of the shift to a service economy are quick to point out, McDonald's is a major employer. McDonald's restaurants in the United States employ about half a million people (Bertagnoli 1989:33), including one out of 15 first-time job seekers (Wildavsky 1989:30). The company claims that 7 percent of all current U.S. workers have worked for McDonald's at some time (Koepp 1987:59). Not only has McDonald's directly influenced the lives of millions of workers, but its impact has also been extended by the efforts of many kinds of organizations, especially in the service sector, to imitate the organizational features they see as central to McDonald's success. . . .

The relentless standardization and infinite replication that inspire both horror and admiration are the legacy of Ray Kroc, a salesman who got into the hamburger business in 1954, when he was 52 years old, and created a worldwide phenomenon.[4] His inspiration was a phenomenally successful hamburger stand owned by the McDonald brothers of San Bernardino, California. He believed that their success could be reproduced consistently through carefully controlled franchises, and his hamburger business succeeded on an unprecedented scale. The basic idea was to serve a very few items of strictly uniform quality at low prices. Over the years, the menu has expanded somewhat and prices have risen, but the emphasis on strict, detailed standardization has never varied. . . .

Enforcement of McDonald's standards has been made easier over the years by the introduction of highly specialized equipment. Every company-owned store in the United States now has an "in-store processor," a computer system that calculates yields and food costs, keeps track of inventory and cash, schedules labor, and breaks down sales by time of day, product, and worker (*McDonald's Annual Report* 1989:29). In today's McDonald's, lights and buzzers tell workers exactly when to turn burgers or take fries out of the fat, and technologically advanced cash registers, linked to the computer system, do much of the thinking for window workers. Specially designed ketchup dispensers squirt exactly the right amount of ketchup on each burger in the approved flower pattern. The french-fry scoops let workers fill a bag and set it down in one continuous motion and help them gauge the proper serving size.

The extreme standardization of McDonald's products, and its workers, is closely tied to its marketing. The company advertises on a massive scale—in 1989, McDonald's spent $1.1 billion systemwide on advertising and promotions (*McDonald's Annual Report* 1989:32). In fact, McDonald's is the single most advertised brand in the world (*Advertising Age* 1990:6).[5] The national advertising assures the public that it will find high standards of quality, service, and cleanliness at every McDonald's store. The intent of the strict quality-control standards applied to every aspect of running a McDonald's outlet, from proper cleaning of the bathrooms to making sure the hamburgers are served hot, is to help franchise owners keep the promises made in the company's advertising.[6]

The image of McDonald's outlets promoted in the company's advertising is one of fun, wholesomeness, and family orientation. Kroc was particularly concerned that his stores not become teenage hangouts, since that would discourage families' patronage. To minimize their attractiveness to teenage loiterers, McDonald's stores do not have jukeboxes, video games, or even telephones. Kroc initially decided not to hire young women to work behind McDonald's counters for the same reason: "They attracted the wrong kind of boys" (Boas and Chain 1976:19).

You Deserve a Break Today: Conditions of Employment

Although McDonald's does not want teenagers to hang out on its premises, it certainly does want them to work in the stores. Almost half of its U.S. employees are under 20 years old (Wildavsky 1989:30). In recent years, as the McDonald's chain has grown faster than the supply of teenagers, the company has also tried to attract senior citizens and housewives as workers. What people in these groups have in common is a preference or need for part-time work, and therefore a dearth of alternative employment options. Because of this lack of good alternatives, and because they may have other means of support for themselves and their dependents, many people in these groups are willing to accept jobs that provide less than subsistence wages.

Traditionally, McDonald's has paid most of its employees the minimum wage, although labor shortages have now forced wages up in some parts of the country, raising the average hourly pay of crew people to $4.60 by 1989 (Gibson and Johnson 1989:B1). Benefits such as health insurance and sick days are entirely lacking for crew people at most franchises. In fact, when the topic of employee benefits was introduced in a class lecture at McDonald's management training center, it turned out to refer to crew meetings, individual work-evaluation sessions, and similar programs to make McDonald's management seem accessible and fair.

The lack of more tangible benefits is linked to the organization of employment at McDonald's as part-time work. According to the manager of the franchise I studied, all McDonald's hourly employees are officially part-time workers, in that no one is guaranteed a full work week. The company's labor practices are designed to make workers bear the costs of uncertainty based on fluctuation in demand. McDonald's places great emphasis on having no more crew people at work at any time than are required by customer flow at that period, as measured in half-hour increments. Most workers therefore have fluctuating schedules, and they are expected to be flexible about working late or leaving early depending on the volume of business.

Not surprisingly, McDonald's employee-turnover rates are extremely high. Turnover averaged 153 percent in 1984, and 205 percent in 1985 (training center lecture). These high rates are partly attributable to the large percentage of teenage workers, many of whom took the job with the intention of working for only a short time. However, the limited job rewards, both financial and personal, of working at McDonald's are certainly crucial contributing factors.

Some argue that the conditions of employment at McDonald's are unproblematic to the workers who take them. If we assume that most McDonald's workers are teenagers who are in school and are not responsible for supporting themselves or others, then many of the features of McDonald's work do not seem so bad. Fringe benefits and employment security are relatively unimportant to them, and the limited and irregular hours of work may actually be attractive (see Greenberger and Steinberg 1986). These arguments are less persuasive when applied to other McDonald's employees, such as mothers of young children, and retirees, although those workers might similarly appreciate the part-time hours, and access to other forms of income and benefits could make McDonald's employment conditions acceptable, if not desirable. Employment security would not be important to the many people who choose to work at McDonald's as a stopgap or for a limited period.[7] Many of the workers at the franchise I studied had taken their jobs with the intention of holding them only temporarily, and many were being supported by their parents. However, other workers there were trying to support themselves and their dependents on earnings from McDonald's, sometimes in combination with other low-paying jobs. . . .

McDonald's wants both managers and workers to dedicate themselves to the values summed up in its three-letter corporate credo, "QSC." Quality, service, and cleanliness are the ends that the company's thousands of rules and specifications are intended to achieve. Kroc promised his customers QSC,[8] and he believed firmly that if, at every level of the organization, McDonald's workers were committed to providing higher-quality food, speedier service, and cleaner surroundings than the competition, the success of the enterprise was assured. McDonald's extraordinarily elaborate training programs are designed both to teach McDonald's procedures and standards and to instill and enforce corporate values.

Kroc approached his business with a zeal and dedication that even he regarded as religious: "I've often said that *I believe in God, family, and McDonald's—and in the office that order is reversed*" (Kroc with Anderson 1977:124 [emphasis in original]). Throughout the organization, Kroc is still frequently quoted and held up as a model, and nowhere is his ongoing influence more apparent than at Hamburger University.

Taking Hamburgers Seriously: Training Managers

McDonald's main management training facility is located on 80 beautifully landscaped acres in Oak Brook, Illinois, a suburb of Chicago. Its name, Hamburger University, captures the thoroughness and intensity with which McDonald's approaches management training, and it also suggests the comic possibilities of immersion in McDonald's corporate world.[9] The company tries to produce managers "with ketchup in their veins," a common McDonald's phrase for people who love their work, take pride in it, and are extraordinarily hardworking, competitive, and loyal to McDonald's. A line I heard frequently at Hamburger U. was "We take hamburgers very seriously here." Nothing I saw called this fixity of purpose into doubt.

Ensuring uniformity of service and products in its far-flung empire is a major challenge for McDonald's. In each McDonald's store, in regional training centers, and at Hamburger University, crew people, managers, and franchisees learn that there is a McDonald's way to handle virtually every detail of the business and that doing things differently means doing things wrong. Training begins in the stores, where crew people are instructed using materials provided by the corporation and where managers prepare for more advanced training. Management trainees and managers seeking promotion work with their store managers to learn materials in manuals and workbooks provided by the corporation. When they have completed the manual for the appropriate level, they are eligible for courses taught in regional training centers and at Hamburger University: the Basic Operations Course, the Intermediate Operations Course, the Applied Equipment Course, and, finally, the Advanced Operations Course, taught only at Hamburger University. Altogether, the full training program requires approximately six hundred to one thousand hours of work. It is required of everyone who wishes to own a McDonald's store, and it is strongly recommended for all store managers. By the time trainees get to Hamburger University for the Advanced Operations Course, they have already put in considerable time working in a McDonald's store—two to three and a half years, on average—and have acquired much detailed knowledge about McDonald's workings.

Hamburger University sometimes offers special programs and seminars in addition to the regular training courses. For example, a group of McDonald's office workers attended Hamburger University during my visit; a training manager told me that they had been brought in to get *a* "little shot of ketchup and mustard."[10]

The zeal and competence of franchisees and managers are of special concern to McDonald's, since they are the people responsible for daily enforcement of corporate standards. Their training therefore focuses as much on building commitment and motivation as on extending knowledge of company procedures. In teaching management skills, McDonald's also works on the personalities of its managers, encouraging both rigid adherence to routines and, somewhat paradoxically, personal flexibility. Flexibility is presented as a virtue both because the company wants to minimize resistance to adopting McDonald's ways of doing things and to frequent revision of procedures, and because managers must provide whatever responsiveness to special circumstances the system has, since crew people are allowed virtually no discretion. Hamburger University therefore provides a large dose of personal-growth cheerleading along with more prosaic skills training. . . .

The curriculum of the Advanced Operating Course includes inculcation with pride in McDonald's. Sessions are devoted to McDonald's history and

McDonald's dedication to ever-improving QSC. Lectures are sprinkled with statistics attesting to McDonald's phenomenal success. Students hear the story of Ray Kroc's rise to wealth and prominence, based on his strength of character and willingness to work hard, and are assigned his autobiography, *Grinding It Out* (Kroc with Anderson 1977). Kroc is quoted frequently in lectures, and students are encouraged to model themselves on him. They are told repeatedly that they have all proven themselves "winners" by getting as far as they have at McDonald's. The theme throughout is "We're the best in the world, we know exactly what we're doing, but our success depends on the best efforts of every one of you."[11]

About 3,500 students from all over the world attend classes at Hamburger University each year, most of them taking the Advanced Operations Course (Rosenthal 1989). Those who complete the course receive diplomas proclaiming them Doctors of Hamburgerology. As late as 1978 or 1979, a training manager told me, most classes included only one or two women, but women now comprise 40–60 percent of the students, and women and minorities now make up 54 percent of McDonald's franchisees (Bertagnoli 1989:33). In my homeroom, however, the proportion of women was much smaller, and there was just a handful of minority students.

The course lasts two weeks and is extremely rigorous. Class time is about evenly divided between work in the labs and lectures on store operations and personnel management. In the labs, trainees learn the mechanics of ensuring that McDonald's food is of consistent quality and its stores in good working order. They learn to check the equipment and maintain it properly so that fries cook at precisely the right temperature, shakes are mixed to just the right consistency, and ice cubes are uniform. "Taste of Quality" labs reinforce McDonald's standards for food quality. For instance, in a Condiments Lab, trainees are taught exactly how to store vegetables and sauces, what the shelf lives of these products are, and how they should look and taste. Samples of "McDonald's quality" Big Mac Special Sauce are contrasted with samples that have been left too long unrefrigerated and should be discarded. The importance of serving only food that meets McDonald's standards is constantly emphasized and, a trainer pointed out, "McDonald's has standards for everything, down to the width of the pickle slices. . . ."

The training at Hamburger University combines a sense of fun with dead seriousness about keeping McDonald's on top in the hamburger business through relentless quality control and effective management of workers and customers. It is up to the owners and managers of individual McDonald's stores to make that happen. . . .

Learning the Job

As a manager at Hamburger University explained to me, the crew training process is how McDonald's standardization is maintained, how the company ensures that Big Macs are the same everywhere in the world. The McDonald's central administration supplies franchisees with videotapes and other materials for use in training workers to meet the company's exacting specifications. The company produces a separate videotape for each job in the store, and it encourages franchisees to keep their tape libraries up-to-date as product specifications change. The Hamburger University professor who taught the Advanced Operating Course session on training said that, to keep current, franchisees should be buying 10 or 12 tapes a year. For each work station in the store, McDonald's also has a "Station Operation Checklist" (SOC), a short but highly detailed job description that lays out exactly how the job should be done: how much ketchup and mustard go on each kind of hamburger, in what sequence the products customers order are to be gathered, what arm motion is to be used in salting a batch of fries, and so on. . . .

The Routine

McDonald's had routinized the work of its crews so thoroughly that decision making had practically been eliminated from the jobs. As one window worker told me, *They've tried to break it down so that it's almost idiot-proof.* Most of the workers agreed that there was little call for them to use their own judgment on the job, since there were rules about everything. If an unusual problem arose, the workers were supposed to turn it over to a manager.

Many of the noninteractive parts of the window workers' job had been made idiot-proof through automation.[12] The soda machines, for example, automatically dispensed the proper amount of beverage for regular, medium, and large cups. Computerized cash registers performed a variety of functions handled elsewhere by human waitresses, waiters, and cashiers, making some kinds of skill and knowledge unnecessary. As a customer gave an order, the window worker simply pressed the cash register button labeled with the name of the selected product. There was no need to write the orders down, because the buttons lit up to indicate which products had been selected. Nor was there any need to remember prices, because the prices were programmed into the machines. Like most new cash registers, these added the tax automatically and told workers how much change customers were owed, so the window crew did not need to know how to do those calculations. The cash registers also helped regulate some of the crew's interactive work by reminding them to try to increase the size of each sale. For example, when a customer ordered a Big Mac, large fries, and a regular Coke, the cash register buttons for cookies, hot apple pies, ice cream cones, and ice cream sundaes would light up, prompting the worker to suggest dessert. It took some skill to operate the relatively complicated cash register, as my difficulties during my first work shift made clear, but this organizationally specific skill could soon be acquired on the job.

In addition to doing much of the workers' thinking for them, the computerized cash registers made it possible for managers to monitor the crew members' work and the store's inventory very closely.[13] For example, if the number of Quarter Pounder with Cheese boxes gone did not match the number of Quarter Pounders with Cheese sold or accounted for as waste, managers might suspect that workers were giving away or taking food. Managers could easily tell which workers had brought in the most money during a given interval and who was doing the best job of persuading customers to buy a particular item. The computerized system could also complicate what would otherwise have been simple customer requests, however. For example, when a man who had not realized the benefit of ordering his son's food as a Happy Meal came back to the counter to ask whether his little boy could have one of the plastic beach pails the Happy Meals were served in, I had to ask a manager what to do, since fulfilling the request would produce a discrepancy between the inventory and the receipts.[14] Sometimes the extreme systematization can induce rather than prevent idiocy, as when a window worker says she cannot serve a cup of coffee that is half decaffeinated and half regular because she would not know how to ring up the sale.[15]

The interactive part of window work is routinized through the Six Steps of Window Service and also through rules aimed at standardizing attitudes and demeanors as well as words and actions. The window workers were taught that they represented McDonald's to the public and that their attitudes were therefore an important component of service quality. Crew people could be reprimanded for not smiling, and often were. The window workers were supposed to be cheerful and polite at all times, but they were also told to be themselves while on the job. McDonald's does not want its workers to seem like robots, so part of the emotion work asked of the window crew is that they act naturally. "Being yourself" in this situation meant behaving in a way that did not seem stilted. Although workers had some latitude to go beyond the script, the short, highly schematic routine obviously did not allow much room for genuine self-expression.

Workers were not the only ones constrained by McDonald's routines, of course. The cooperation of service recipients was crucial to the smooth functioning of the operation. In many kinds of interactive service work . . . constructing the compliance of service recipients is an important part of the service worker's job. The routines such workers use may be designed to maximize the control each worker has over customers. McDonald's window workers' routines were not intended to give them much leverage over customers' behavior, however. The window workers interacted only with people who had already decided to do business with McDonald's and who therefore did not need to be persuaded to take part in the service interaction. Furthermore, almost all customers were familiar enough with McDonald's routines to know how they were expected to behave. For instance, I never saw a customer who did not know that she or he was supposed to come up to the counter rather than sit down and wait to be served. This customer training was accomplished through advertising, spatial design, customer experience, and the example of other customers, making it unnecessary for the window crew to put much effort into getting customers to fit into their work routines.[16]

McDonald's ubiquitous advertising trains consumers at the same time that it tries to attract them to McDonald's. Television commercials demonstrate how the service system is supposed to work and familiarize customers with new products. Additional cues about expected customer behavior are provided by the design of the restaurants. For example, the entrances usually lead to the service counter, not to the dining area, making it unlikely that customers will fail to realize that they should get in line, and the placement of waste cans makes clear that customers are expected to throw out their own trash. Most important, the majority of customers have had years of experience with McDonald's, as well as with other fast-food restaurants that have similar arrangements. The company estimates that the average customer visits a McDonald's 20 times a year (Koepp 1987:58), and it is not uncommon for a customer to come in several times per week. For many customers, then, ordering at McDonald's is as routine an interaction as it is for the window worker. Indeed, because employee turnover is so high, steady customers may be more familiar with the work routines than the workers serving them are. Customers who are new to McDonald's can take their cue from more experienced customers.[17]

Not surprisingly, then, most customers at the McDonald's I studied knew what was expected of them and tried to play their part well. They sorted themselves into lines and gazed up at the menu boards while waiting to be served. They usually gave their orders in the conventional sequence: burgers or other entrees, french fries or other side orders, drinks, and desserts. Hurried customers with savvy might order an item "only if it's in the bin," that is, ready to be served. Many customers prepared carefully so that they could give their orders promptly when they got to the counter. This preparation sometimes became apparent when a worker interrupted to ask, *What kind of dressing?* or *Cream and sugar?*, flustering customers who could not deliver their orders as planned.

McDonald's routines, like those of other interactive service businesses, depend on the predictability of customers, but these businesses must not grind to a halt if customers are not completely cooperative. Some types of deviations from standard customer behavior are so common that they become routine themselves, and these can be handled through subroutines (Stinchcombe 1990:39). McDonald's routines work most efficiently when all customers accept their products exactly as they are usually prepared; indeed, the whole business is based on this premise. Since, however, some people give special instructions for customized products, such as "no onions," the routine allows for these exceptions.[18] At the franchise I studied, workers could key the special requests into their cash registers, which automatically printed out "grill slips" with the instructions for the grill workers to follow. Under this system, the customer making the special order had to wait for it to be prepared, but the smooth flow of service for other customers was not interrupted. Another type of routine difficulty was customer dissatisfaction with food quality. Whenever a customer had a complaint about the food— cold fries, dried-out burger—window workers were authorized to supply a new product immediately without consulting a supervisor.[19]

These two kinds of difficulties—special orders and complaints about food—were the only irregularities window workers were authorized to handle. The subroutines increased the flexibility of the service system, but they did not increase the workers' discretion, since procedures were in place for dealing with both situations. All other kinds of demands fell outside the window crew's purview. If they were faced with a dispute about money, an extraordinary request, or a furious customer, workers were instructed to call a manager; the crew had no authority to handle such problems.

Given the almost complete regimentation of tasks and preemption of decision making, does McDonald's need the flexibility and thoughtfulness of human workers? As the declining supply of teenagers and legislated increases in the minimum wage drive up labor costs, it is not surprising that McDonald's is experimenting with electronic replacements. So far, the only robot in use handles behind-the-scenes work rather than customer interactions. ARCH (Automated Restaurant Crew Helper) works in a Minnesota McDonald's where it does all the frying and lets workers know when to prepare sandwich buns, when supplies are running low, and when fries are no longer fresh enough to sell. Other McDonald's stores (along with Arby's and Burger King units) are experimenting with a touch-screen computer system that lets customers order their meals themselves, further curtailing the role of the window worker. Although it requires increased customer socialization and cooperation, early reports are that the system cuts service time by 30 seconds and increases sales per window worker 10–20 percent (Chaudhry 1989:F61).

Overview

McDonald's pioneered the routinization of interactive service work and remains an exemplar of extreme standardization. Innovation is not discouraged at McDonald's; the company favors experimentation, at least among managers and franchisees. Ironically, though, "the object is to look for new, innovative ways to create an experience that is exactly the same no matter what McDonald's you walk into, no matter where it is in the world" (Rosenthal 1989:12). Thus, when someone in the field comes up with a good idea—and such McDonald's success stories as the Egg McMuffin and the Big Mac were store-level inspirations (Koepp 1987:60)—the corporation experiments, tests, and refines the idea and finally implements it in a uniform way systemwide. One distinctive feature of McDonald's-style routinization is that there, to a great extent, uniformity is a goal in itself. . . .

McDonald's . . . does promise uniform products and consistent service, and to provide them the company has broken down virtually every task required to run a store into detailed routines with clear instructions and standards. For those routines to run smoothly, conditions must be relatively predictable, so McDonald's tries to control as many contingencies as possible, including the attitudes and behavior of workers, managers, and customers. The company uses a wide array of socialization and control techniques to ensure that these people are familiar with McDonald's procedures and willing to comply with them.

Most McDonald's work is organized as low-paying, low-status, part-time jobs that give workers little autonomy. Almost every decision about how to do crew people's tasks has been made in advance by the corporation, and many of the decisions have been built into the stores' technology. Why use human workers at all, if not to take advantage of the human capacity to respond to circumstances flexibly? McDonald's does want to provide at least a simulacrum of the human attributes of warmth, friendliness, and recognition. For that reason, not only workers' movements but also their words, demeanor, and attitudes are subject to managerial control.

Although predictability is McDonald's hallmark, not all factors can be controlled by management. One of the most serious irregularities that store management must deal with is fluctuation in the flow of customers, both expected and unexpected. Since personnel costs are the most manipulable variable affecting a store's profitability, managers want to match labor power to consumer demand as exactly as possible. They do so by paying all crew people by the hour, giving them highly irregular hours based on expected sales—sometimes including split shifts—and sending workers home early or keeping them late as conditions require. In other words, the costs of uneven demand are shifted to workers whenever possible. Since most McDonald's crew people cannot count on working a particular number of hours at precisely scheduled times, it is hard for them to make plans based on how much money they will earn or exactly what times they will be free. Workers are pressured to be flexible in order to maximize the organization's own flexibility in staffing levels. In contrast, of course, flexibility in the work process itself is minimized.

Routinization has not made the crew people's work easy. Their jobs, although highly structured and repetitive, are often demanding and stressful. Under these working conditions, the organization's limited commitment to workers, as reflected in job security, wages, and benefits, makes the task of maintaining worker motivation and discipline even more challenging. A variety of factors, many orchestrated by the corporation, keeps McDonald's crew people hard at work despite the limited rewards. Socialization into McDonald's norms, extremely close supervision (both human and electronic), individual and group incentives, peer pressure, and pressure from customers all play their part in getting workers to do things the McDonald's way.

Because franchisees and store-level managers are responsible for enforcing standardization throughout the McDonald's system, their socialization includes a more intensive focus on building commitment to and pride in the organization than does crew training. In fact, it is the corporate attempt at transforming these higher-level McDonald's people by making them more loyal, confident, flexible, and sensitive to others, as well as more knowledgeable about company procedures, that makes the extreme rigidity of the crew training workable. The crew people do not have to be trusted with decision-making authority, because all unusual problems are referred to managers. Their more extensive training gives them the knowledge and attitudes to make the kinds of decisions the corporation would approve. . . . In addition to thorough socialization, McDonald's managers and franchisees are subjected to close corporate oversight. Every aspect of their stores' operations is rated by corporate staff, and they are sanctioned accordingly.

Despite elaborate socialization and social controls, McDonald's stores do not, of course, carry out every corporate directive exactly as recommended. In the store I studied, managers did not always provide their workers with the mandated support and encouragement, crew trainers did not always follow the four-step training system, and window workers did not always carry out the Six Steps of Window Service with the required eye contact and smile. There were many kinds of pressures to deviate from corporate standards. Nonetheless, the benefits of standardization should not be underestimated. As every Durkheimian knows, clear rules and shared standards provide support and coherence as well as constraint. Although some aspects of the routines did strike the participants as overly constraining, undignified, or silly, the approved routines largely worked. In all of these examples of deviation, the routines would have produced more efficient and pleasant service, and those that apply to management and training would have benefited workers as well as customers.

Obtaining the cooperation of workers and managers is not enough to ensure the smooth functioning of McDonald's relatively inflexible routines. Customers must be routinized as well. Not only do customers have to understand the service routine and accept the limited range of choices the company offers, they also must be willing to do some kinds of work that are done for them in conventional restaurants, including carrying food to the table and throwing out their trash. Experience, advertising, the example set by other customers, and clear environmental cues familiarize customers with McDonald's routines, and most want to cooperate in order to speed service. For these reasons, McDonald's interactive service workers do not have to direct most customers, and window workers' routines are therefore not designed to give them power over customers.

ENDNOTES

[1] Suppliers, competitors, and other parties outside of the organization are also relevant actors, but organizational efforts to control their behavior will not be considered here (see Prus 1989).

[2] The 1990s may bring unprecedented changes to McDonald's. Although its overseas business continues to thrive, domestic sales have been declining. To overcome the challenges to profitability presented by the economic recession, lower-priced competitors, and changes in consumer tastes, CEO Michael Quinlan has instituted experimental changes in the menu, in pricing strategy, and even in the degree of flexibility granted to franchisees (see *Advertising Age* 1991; Berg 1991; *McDonald's Annual Report* 1990; Therrien 1991).

[3] McDonald's restaurants are generally referred to as "stores" by McDonald's staff. The company's share of the domestic fast-food market has declined from 18.7 percent in 1985 to 16.6 percent in 1990 (Therrien 1991).

[4] Information about McDonald's history comes primarily from Boas and Chain 1976; Kroc with Anderson 1977; Love 1986; Luxenberg 1985; and McDonald's training materials. Reiter's (1991) description of Burger King reveals numerous parallels in the operation of the two companies, although Burger King, unlike McDonald's, is a subsidiary of a multinational conglomerate.

[5] In addition to paid advertising, McDonald's bolsters its public image with promotional and philanthropic activities such as an All-American High School Basketball Game, essay contests and scholarship programs for black and Hispanic students, and Ronald McDonald Houses where outpatient children and their families and the parents of hospitalized children can stay at minimal cost.

[6] Conversely, details of the routines are designed with marketing in mind. The bags that hold the regular-size portions of french fries are shorter than the french fries are, so that when workers fill them with their regulation french-fry scoops, the servings seem generous, overflowing the packaging. The names of the serving sizes also are intended to give customers the impression that they are getting a lot for their money: French fries come in regular and large sizes, sodas in regular, medium, and large cups. I was quickly corrected during a work shift when I inadvertently referred to an order for a "small" drink.

[7] Some commentators fall into the trap of assuming that workers' preferences are determinative of working conditions, a mistake they do not make when discussing higher-status workers such as faculty who must rely on a string of temporary appointments.

[8] Actually, Kroc usually spoke of QSCV—quality, service, cleanliness, and value (see Kroc with Anderson 1977)—but QSC was the term used in most McDonald's training and motivational materials at the time of my research. The company cannot enforce "value" because antitrust restrictions prevent McDonald's from dictating prices to its franchisees (Love 1986:145). Nevertheless, recent materials return to the original four-part pledge of QSC & V (see, e.g., *McDonald's Annual Report* 1989:i).

[9] Branches of Hamburger University now operate in London, Munich, and Tokyo (*McDonald's Annual Report* 1989:28). Burger King University is similar in many respects (Reiter 1991).

[10] The effort to involve corporate employees in the central mission of the organization extends beyond such special programs. McDonald's prides itself on keeping its corporate focus firmly on store-level operations, and it wants all its employees to have a clear idea of what it takes to make a McDonald's restaurant work. Therefore, all McDonald's employees, from attorneys to data-entry clerks, spend time working in a McDonald's restaurant.

[11] Biggart (1989:143–47) shows that both adulation of a charismatic founder and repeated characterization of participants as winners are common in direct-sales organizations. Like McDonald's, such organizations face the problem of motivating people who are widely dispersed geographically and who are not corporate employees.

[12] The in-store processors similarly affected managers' work. A disaffected McDonald's manager told Garson, "There is no such thing as a McDonald's manager. The computer manages the store" (Garson 1988:39).

[13] Garson (1988) provides an extended discussion of this point.

[14] The manager gave him the pail but had to ring it up on the machine as if he had given away a whole Happy Meal.

[15] Thanks to Charles Bosk for this story.

[16] Mills (1986) elaborates on "customer socialization." Environmental design as a factor in service provision is discussed by Wener (1985) and Normann (1984).

[17] The importance of customer socialization becomes apparent when people with very different consumer experiences are introduced to a service system. When the first McDonald's opened in the Soviet Union in 1990, Moscow's citizens did not find the system immediately comprehensible. They had to be persuaded to get on the shortest lines at the counter, since they had learned from experience that desirable goods were available only where there are long lines (Goldman 1990).

[18] Burger King's "Have it your way" campaign virtually forced McDonald's to allow such customized service.

[19] The defective food or its container was put into a special waste bin. Each shift, one worker or manager had the unenviable task of counting the items in the waste bin so that the inventory could be reconciled with the cash intake.

REFERENCES

Advertising Age. 1990. "Adman of the Decade: McDonald's Fred Turner: Making All the Right Moves," January 1, p. 6.

———. 1991. "100 Leading National Advertisers: McDonald's," September 25, pp. 49–50.

Berg, Eric N. 1991. "An American Icon Wrestles with a Troubled Future." *New York Times,* May 12, sec. 3, pp. 1, 6.

Bertagnoli, Lisa. 1989. "McDonald's: Company of the Quarter Century." *Restaurants and Institutions,* July 10, pp. 32–60.

Biggart, Nicole Woolsey. 1989. *Charismatic Capitalism: Direct Selling Organizations in America.* Chicago: University of Chicago Press. Pp. 128, 143–47.

Boas, Max and Steve Chain. 1976. *Big Mac: The Unauthorized Story of McDonald's.* New York: New American Library. P. 19.

Chaudhry, Rajan. 1989. "Burger Giants Singed by Battle." *Nation's Restaurant News,* August 7, p. F61.

"Fortune Global Service 500: The 50 Largest Retailing Companies." 1991. *Fortune,* August 26, p. 179.

Garson, Barbara. 1988. *The Electronic Sweatshop: How Computers Are Transforming the Office of the Future into the Factory of the Past.* New York: Simon and Schuster. P. 39.

Gibson, Richard and Robert Johnson. 1989. "Big Mac Plots Strategy to Regain Sizzle." *Wall Street Journal,* September 29, p. B1.

Goldman, Marshall. 1990. Presentation at colloquium on Reforming the Soviet Economy, University of Pennsylvania, May 17.

Greenberger, Ellen and Laurence Steinberg. 1986. *When Teenagers Work: The Psychological and Social Costs of Adolescent Employment.* New York: Basic Books.

Koepp, Stephen. 1987. "Big Mac Strikes Back." *Time,* April 13, p. 60.

Kroc, Ray with Robert Anderson. 1977. *Grinding It Out: The Making of McDonald's.* Chicago: Contemporary Books. P. 124.

Love, John F. 1986. *McDonald's: Behind the Arches.* New York: Bantam Books. P. 145.

Luxenberg, Stan. 1985. *Roadside Empires: How the Chains Franchised America.* New York: Viking.

McDonald's Annual Report. 1989. Oak Brook, Illinois. Pp. i, 28, 29, 32.

———. 1990. Oak Brook, Illinois. Pp. 1–2.

Mills, Peter K. 1986. *Managing Service Industries: Organizational Practices in a Post-Industrial Economy.* Cambridge, MA: Ballinger.

Normann, Richard. 1984. *Service Management: Strategy and Leadership in Service Businesses.* Chichester, England: Wiley.

Prus, Robert. 1989. *Pursuing Customers: An Ethnography of Marketing Activities.* Newbury Park, CA: Sage.

Reiter, Ester. 1991. *Making Fast Food: From the Frying Pan into the Fryer.* Montreal: McGill-Queen's University Press.

Rosenthal, Herman M. 1989. "Inside Big Mac's World." *Newsday,* June 4, p. 12.

Stinchcombe, Arthur L. 1990. *Information and Organizations.* Berkeley: University of California Press. P. 39.

Therrien, Lois. 1991. "McRisky." *Business Week,* October 21, pp. 114–22.

Wener, Richard E. 1985. "The Environmental Psychology of Service Encounters." Pp. 101–12 in *The Service Encounter: Managing Employee/Customer Interaction in Service Businesses,* edited by John A. Czepiel, Michael R. Solomon, and Carol F. Surprenant. Lexington, MA: Lexington Books.

Wildavsky, Ben. 1989. "McJobs: Inside America's Largest Youth Training Program." *Policy Review* 49:30–37.

42

RACIALIZING THE GLASS ESCALATOR
Reconsidering Men's Experiences
with Women's Work

ADIA HARVEY WINGFIELD

Sociologists argue that individuals learn gender roles and gender stereotyping through socialization. Gender role socialization often reinforces gender inequality because men and women are expected to fulfill different family and occupation roles. For example, recall the waitresses in Meika Loe's research (Reading 9), who were expected to fulfill certain stereotyped gender roles as part of their employment. Thus, in U.S. society, women traditionally are assigned the roles of waitress, nurse, teacher, and secretary, which typically have less social status and lower salaries than male occupational roles. In 1992, Christine L. Williams did a study of what happens when men enter traditionally defined "female" occupations and theorized a new concept of gendered work upward mobility called *the glass escalator*. The study excerpted here by Adia Harvey Wingfield, a professor of sociology at Georgia State University, utilizes Williams' concept of the glass escalator to study how black men in nursing experience gendered advantages and disadvantages in a female-dominated occupation.

Sociologists who study work have long noted that jobs are sex segregated and that this segregation creates different occupational experiences for men and women (Charles and Grusky 2004). Jobs predominantly filled by women often require "feminine" traits such as nurturing, caring, and empathy, a fact that means men confront perceptions that they are unsuited for the requirements of these jobs. Rather than having an adverse effect on their occupational experiences, however, these assumptions facilitate men's entry into better paying, higher status positions, creating what Williams (1995) labels a "glass escalator" effect.

The glass escalator model has been an influential paradigm in understanding the experiences of men who do women's work. Researchers have identified this process among men nurses, social workers, paralegals, and librarians and have cited its pervasiveness as evidence of men's consistent advantage in the workplace, such that even in jobs where men are numerical minorities they are likely to enjoy higher wages and faster promotions (Floge

Adia Harvey Wingfield, "Racializing the Glass Escalator; Reconsidering Men's Experiences with Women's Work." *Gender & Society*, Vol. 23, No. 1, February 2009, pp. 5–26. Copyright © 2006 Sociologists for Women in Society. Reprinted by permission of Sage Publications, Inc.

and Merrill 1986; Heikes 1991; Williams 1989, 1995). Most of these studies implicitly assume a racial homogenization of men workers in women's professions, but this supposition is problematic for several reasons. For one, minority men are not only present but are actually overrepresented in certain areas of reproductive work that have historically been dominated by white women (Duffy 2007). Thus, research that focuses primarily on white men in women's professions ignores a key segment of men who perform this type of labor. Second, and perhaps more important, conclusions based on the experiences of white men tend to overlook the ways that intersections of race and gender create different experiences for different men. While extensive work has documented the fact that white men in women's professions encounter a glass escalator effect that aids their occupational mobility . . . , few studies, if any, have considered how this effect is a function not only of gendered advantage but of racial privilege as well.

In this [reading], I examine the implications of race–gender intersections for minority men employed in a female-dominated, feminized occupation, specifically focusing on Black men in nursing. Their experiences doing "women's work" demonstrate that the glass escalator is a racialized as well as gendered concept.

Theoretical Framework

In her classic study *Men and Women of the Corporation*, Kanter (1977) offers a groundbreaking analysis of group interactions. Focusing on high-ranking women executives who work mostly with men, Kanter argues that those in the extreme numerical minority are tokens who are socially isolated, highly visible, and adversely stereotyped. Tokens have difficulty forming relationships with colleagues and often are excluded from social networks that provide mobility. Because of their low numbers, they are also highly visible as people who are different from the majority, even though they often feel invisible when they are ignored or overlooked in social settings. Tokens are also stereotyped by those in the majority group and frequently face pressure to behave in ways that challenge and undermine these stereotypes. Ultimately, Kanter argues that it is harder for them to blend into the organization and to work effectively and productively, and that they face serious barriers to upward mobility. . . .

In her groundbreaking study of men employed in various women's professions, Williams (1995) further develops this analysis of how power relationships shape the ways men tokens experience work in women's professions. Specifically, she introduces the concept of the glass escalator to explain men's experiences as tokens in these areas. Like Floge and Merrill (1986) and Heikes (1991), Williams finds that men tokens do not experience the isolation, visibility, blocked access to social networks, and stereotypes in the same ways that women tokens do. In contrast, Williams argues that even though they are in the minority, processes are in place that actually facilitate their opportunity and advancement. Even in culturally feminized occupations, then, men's advantage is built into the very structure and everyday interactions of these jobs so that men find themselves actually struggling to remain in place. For these men, "despite their intentions, they face invisible pressures to move up in their professions. Like being on a moving escalator, they have to work to stay in place" (Williams 1995: 87).

The glass escalator term thus refers to the "subtle mechanisms in place that enhance [men's] positions in [women's] professions" (Williams 1995: 108). These mechanisms include certain behaviors, attitudes, and beliefs men bring to these professions as well as the types of interactions that often occur between these men and their colleagues, supervisors, and customers. Consequently, even in occupations composed mostly of women, gendered perceptions about men's roles, abilities, and skills privilege them and facilitate their advancement. The glass escalator serves as a conduit that channels men in women's professions into the uppermost levels of the occupational hierarchy. Ultimately, the glass escalator effect suggests that men retain consistent occupational advantages over women, even when women are numerically in the majority (Budig 2002; Williams 1995).

Though this process has now been fairly well established in the literature, there are reasons to question its generalizability to all men. In an early critique of the supposed general neutrality of the token, Zimmer (1988) notes that much research on race comes to precisely the opposite of Kanter's conclusions, finding that as the numbers of minority group members increase (e.g., as they become less likely to be "tokens"), so too do tensions between the majority and minority groups. . . . Reinforcing, while at the same time tempering, the findings of research on men in female-dominated occupations, Zimmer (1988: 71) argues that relationships between tokens and the majority depend on understanding the underlying power relationships between these groups and "the status and power differentials between them." Hence, just as men who are tokens fare better than women, it also follows that the experiences of Blacks and whites as tokens should differ in ways that reflect their positions in hierarchies of status and power.

The concept of the glass escalator provides an important and useful framework for addressing men's experiences in women's occupations, but so far research in this vein has neglected to examine whether the glass escalator is experienced among all men in an identical manner. Are the processes that facilitate a ride on the glass escalator available to minority men? Or does race intersect with gender to affect the extent to which the glass escalator offers men opportunities in women's professions? In the next section, I examine whether and how the mechanisms that facilitate a ride on the glass escalator might be unavailable to Black men in nursing.[1]

Relationships with Colleagues and Supervisors

One key aspect of riding the glass escalator involves the warm, collegial welcome men workers often receive from their women colleagues. Often, this reaction is a response to the fact that professions dominated by women are frequently low in salary and status and that greater numbers of men help improve prestige and pay (Heikes 1991). Though some women workers resent the apparent ease with which men enter and advance in women's professions, the generally warm welcome men receive stands in stark contrast to the cold reception, difficulties with mentorship, and blocked access to social networks that women often encounter when they do men's work (Roth 2006; Williams 1992). In addition, unlike women in men's professions, men who do women's work frequently have supervisors of the same sex. Men workers can thus enjoy a gendered bond with their supervisor in the context of a collegial work environment. These factors often converge, facilitating men's access to higher-status positions and producing the glass escalator effect. . . .

For Black men in nursing, however, gendered racism may limit the extent to which they establish bonds with their colleagues and supervisors. The concept of gendered racism suggests that racial stereotypes, images, and beliefs are grounded in gendered ideals (Collins 1990, 2004; Harvey Wingfield 2007). Gendered racist stereotypes of Black men in particular emphasize the dangerous, threatening attributes associated with Black men and Black masculinity, framing Black men as threats to white women, prone to criminal behavior, and especially violent. Collins (2004) argues that these stereotypes serve to legitimize Black men's treatment in the criminal justice system through methods such as racial profiling and incarceration, but they may also hinder Black men's attempts to enter and advance in various occupational fields.

For Black men nurses, gendered racist images may have particular consequences for their relationships with women colleagues, who may view Black men nurses through the lens of controlling images and gendered racist stereotypes that emphasize the danger they pose to women. This may take on a heightened significance for white women nurses, given stereotypes that suggest that Black men are especially predisposed to raping white women. Rather than experiencing the congenial bonds with colleagues that white men nurses describe, Black men nurses may find themselves facing a much cooler reception from their women coworkers. . . .

Suitability for Nursing and Higher-Status Work

The perception that men are not really suited to do women's work also contributes to the glass escalator effect. In encounters with patients, doctors, and other staff, men nurses frequently confront others who do not expect to see them doing "a woman's job." Sometimes this perception means that patients mistake men nurses for doctors; ultimately, the sense that men do not really belong in nursing contributes to a push *"out* of the most feminine-identified areas and *up* to those regarded as more legitimate for men" (Williams 1995: 104). The sense that men are better suited for more masculine jobs means that men workers are often assumed to be more able and skilled than their women counterparts. As Williams writes (1995: 106), "Masculinity is often associated with competence and mastery," and this implicit definition stays with men even when they work in feminized fields. Thus, part of the perception that men do not belong in these jobs is rooted in the sense that, as men, they are more capable and accomplished than women and thus belong in jobs that reflect this. Consequently, men nurses are mistaken for doctors and are granted more authority and responsibility than their women counterparts, reflecting the idea that, as men, they are inherently more competent (Heikes 1991; Williams 1995).

Black men nurses, however, may not face the presumptions of expertise or the resulting assumption that they belong in higher-status jobs. Black professionals, both men and women, are often assumed to be less capable and less qualified than their white counterparts. In some cases, these negative stereotypes hold even when Black workers outperform white colleagues (Feagin and Sikes 1994). The belief that Blacks are inherently less competent than whites means that, despite advanced education, training, and skill, Black professionals often confront the lingering perception that they are better suited for lower-level service work (Feagin and Sikes 1994). Black men in fact often fare better than white women in blue-collar jobs such as policing and corrections work (Britton 1995), and this may be, in part, because they are viewed as more appropriately suited for these types of positions. . . .

Establishing Distance from Femininity

An additional mechanism of the glass escalator involves establishing distance from women and the femininity associated with their occupations. Because men nurses are employed in a culturally feminized occupation, they develop strategies to disassociate themselves from the femininity associated with their work and retain some of the privilege associated with masculinity. Thus, when men nurses gravitate toward hospital emergency wards rather than obstetrics or pediatrics, or emphasize that they are only in nursing to get into hospital administration, they distance themselves from the femininity of their profession and thereby preserve their status as men despite the fact that they do "women's work." Perhaps more important, these strategies also place men in a prime position to experience the glass escalator effect, as they situate themselves to move upward into higher-status areas in the field. . . .

For Black men, the desire to reject femininity may be compounded by racial inequality. Theorists have argued that as institutional racism blocks access to traditional markers of masculinity such as occupational status and economic stability, Black men may repudiate femininity as a way of accessing the masculinity—and its attendant status—that is denied through other routes (hooks 2004; Neal 2005). Rejecting femininity is a key strategy men use to assert masculinity, and it remains available to Black men even when other means of achieving masculinity are unattainable. Black men nurses may be more likely to distance themselves from their women colleagues and to reject the femininity associated with nursing, particularly if they feel that they experience racial discrimination that renders occupational advancement inaccessible. Yet if they encounter strained relationships with women colleagues and men supervisors because of gendered racism or racialized stereotypes, the efforts to distance themselves from femininity still may not result in the glass escalator effect.

On the other hand, some theorists suggest that minority men may challenge racism by rejecting hegemonic masculine ideals. . . . The results of these studies suggest that Black men nurses may embrace the femininity associated with nursing if it offers a way to combat racism. In these cases, Black men nurses may turn to pediatrics as a way of demonstrating sensitivity and therefore combating stereotypes of Black masculinity, or they may proudly identify as nurses to challenge perceptions that Black men are unsuited for professional, white-collar positions.

Taken together, all of this research suggests that Black men may not enjoy the advantages experienced by their white men colleagues, who ride a glass escalator to success. In this article, I focus on the experiences of Black men nurses to argue that the glass escalator is a racialized as well as a gendered concept that does not offer Black men the same privileges as their white men counterparts.

Data Collection and Method

I collected data through semistructured interviews with 17 men nurses who identified as Black or African American. Nurses ranged in age from 30 to 51 and lived in the southeastern United States. Six worked in suburban hospitals adjacent to major cities, six were located in major metropolitan urban care centers, and the remaining five worked in rural hospitals or clinics. All were registered nurses or licensed practical nurses.

Six identified their specialty as oncology, four were bedside nurses, two were in intensive care, one managed an acute dialysis program, one was an orthopedic nurse, one was in ambulatory care, one was in emergency, and one was in surgery. The least experienced nurse had worked in the field for five years; the most experienced had been a nurse for 26 years. I initially recruited participants by soliciting attendees at the 2007 National Black Nurses Association annual meetings and then used a snowball sample to create the remainder of the data set. All names and identifying details have been changed to ensure confidentiality.

I conducted interviews during the fall of 2007. They generally took place in either my campus office or a coffee shop located near the respondent's home or workplace. The average interview lasted about an hour. Interviews were tape-recorded and transcribed. Interview questions primarily focused on how race and gender shaped the men's experiences as nurses. Questions addressed respondents' work history and current experiences in the field, how race and gender shaped their experiences as nurses, and their future career goals. The men discussed their reasons for going into nursing, the reactions from others on entering this field, and the particular challenges, difficulties, and obstacles Black men nurses faced. Respondents also described their work history in nursing, their current jobs, and their future plans. Finally, they talked about stereotypes of nurses in general and of Black men nurses in particular and their thoughts about and responses to these stereotypes. I coded the data according to key themes that emerged: relationships with white patients versus minority patients, personal bonds with colleagues versus lack of bonds, opportunities for advancement versus obstacles to advancement. . . .

Findings

The results of this study indicate that not all men experience the glass escalator in the same ways. For Black men nurses, intersections of race and gender create a different experience with the mechanisms that facilitate white men's advancement in women's professions. Awkward or unfriendly interactions with colleagues, poor relationships with supervisors, perceptions that they are not suited for nursing, and an unwillingness to disassociate from "feminized" aspects of nursing constitute what I term *glass barriers* to riding the glass escalator.

Reception from Colleagues and Supervisors

When women welcome men into "their" professions, they often push men into leadership roles that ease their advancement into upper-level positions. Thus, a positive reaction from colleagues is critical to riding the glass escalator. Unlike white men nurses, however, Black men do not describe encountering a warm reception from women colleagues (Heikes 1991). Instead, the men I interviewed find that they often have unpleasant interactions with women coworkers who treat them rather coldly and attempt to keep them at bay. Chris is a 51-year-old oncology nurse who describes one white nurse's attempt to isolate him from other white women nurses as he attempted to get his instructions for that day's shift:

> She turned and ushered me to the door, and said for me to wait out here, a nurse will come out and give you your report. I stared at her hand on my arm, and then at her, and said, "Why? Where do you go to get your reports?" She said, "I get them in there." I said, "Right. Unhand me." I went right back in there, sat down, and started writing down my reports.

Kenny, a 47-year-old nurse with 23 years of nursing experience, describes a similarly and particularly painful experience he had in a previous job where he was the only Black person on staff:

> [The staff] had nothing to do with me, and they didn't even want me to sit at the same area where they were charting in to take a break. They wanted me to sit somewhere else. . . . They wouldn't even sit at a table with me! When I came and sat down, everybody got up and left.

These experiences with colleagues are starkly different from those described by white men in professions dominated by women (see Pierce 1995; Williams 1989). Though the men in these studies sometimes chose to segregate themselves, women never systematically excluded them. Though I have no way of knowing why the women nurses in Chris's and Kenny's workplaces physically segregated themselves, the pervasiveness of gendered racist images that emphasize white women's vulnerability to dangerous Black men may play an important role. For these nurses, their masculinity is not a guarantee that they will be welcomed, much less pushed into leadership roles. As Ryan, a 37-year-old intensive care nurse says, *[Black men] have to go further to prove ourselves. This involves proving our capabilities,* proving to colleagues that you can lead, *be on the forefront* (emphasis added). The warm welcome and subsequent opportunities for leadership cannot be taken for granted. In contrast, these men describe great challenges in forming congenial relationships with coworkers who, they believe, do not truly want them there.

In addition, these men often describe tense, if not blatantly discriminatory, relationships with supervisors. While Williams (1995) suggests that men supervisors can be allies for men in women's professions by facilitating promotions and upward mobility, Black men nurses describe incidents of being overlooked by supervisors when it comes time for promotions. Ryan, who has worked at his current job for 11 years, believes that these barriers block upward mobility within the profession:

> *The hardest part is dealing with people who don't understand minority nurses. People with their biases, who don't identify you as ripe for promotion. I know the policy and procedure, I'm familiar with past history. So you can't tell me I can't move forward if others did.* [How did you deal with this?] *By knowing the chain of command, who my supervisors were. Things were subtle. I just had to be better. I got this mostly from other nurses and supervisors. I was paid to deal with patients, so I could deal with* [racism] *from them. I'm not paid to deal with this from colleagues.*

Kenny offers a similar example. Employed as an orthopedic nurse in a predominantly white environment, he describes great difficulty getting promoted, which he primarily attributes to racial biases:

> *It's almost like you have to, um, take your ideas and give them to somebody else and then let them present them for you and you get no credit for it. I've applied for several promotions there and, you know, I didn't get them. . . . When you look around to the, um, the percentage of African Americans who are actually in executive leadership is almost zero percent. Because it's less than one percent of the total population of people that are in leadership, and it's almost like they'll go outside of the system just to try to find a Caucasian to fill a position. Not that I'm not qualified, because I've been master's prepared for 12 years and I'm working on my doctorate.*

According to Ryan and Kenny, supervisors' racial biases mean limited opportunities for promotion and upward mobility. This interpretation is consistent with research that suggests that even with stellar performance and solid work histories, Black workers may receive mediocre evaluations from white supervisors that limit their advancement (Feagin 2006; Feagin and Sikes 1994). For Black men nurses, their race may signal to supervisors that they are unworthy of promotion and thus create a different experience with the glass escalator. . . .

Perceptions of Suitability

Like their white counterparts, Black men nurses also experience challenges from clients who are unaccustomed to seeing men in fields typically dominated by women. As with white men nurses, Black men encounter this in surprised or quizzical reactions from patients who seem to expect to be treated by white women nurses. Ray, a 36-year-old oncology nurse with 10 years of experience, states,

> *Nursing, historically, has been a white female's job [so] being a Black male it's a weird position to be in. . . . I've, several times, gone into a room and a male patient, a white male patient has, you know, they'll say, "Where's the pretty nurse? Where's the pretty nurse? Where's the blonde nurse?" . . . "You don't have one. I'm the nurse."*

Yet while patients rarely expect to be treated by men nurses of any race, white men encounter statements and behaviors that suggest patients expect them to be doctors, supervisors, or other higher-status, more masculine positions (Williams 1989, 1995). In part, this expectation accelerates their ride on the glass escalator, helping to push them into the positions for which they are seen as more appropriately suited.

(White) men, by virtue of their masculinity, are assumed to be more competent and capable and thus better situated in (nonfeminized) jobs that are perceived to require greater skill and proficiency. Black men, in contrast, rarely encounter patients (or colleagues and supervisors) who immediately expect that they are doctors or administrators. Instead, many respondents find that even after displaying their credentials, sharing their nursing experience, and, in one case, dispensing care, they are still mistaken for janitors or service workers. Ray's experience is typical:

> *I've even given patients their medicines, explained their care to them, and then they'll say to me, "Well, can you send the nurse in?"*

Chris describes a somewhat similar encounter of being misidentified by a white woman patient:

> *I come [to work] in my white uniform, that's what I wear—being a Black man, I know they won't look at me the same, so I dress the part—I said good evening, my name's Chris, and I'm going to be your nurse. She says to me, "Are you from housekeeping?" . . . I've had other cases. I've walked in and had a lady look at me and ask if I'm the janitor.*

Chris recognizes that this patient is evoking racial stereotypes that Blacks are there to perform menial service work. He attempts to circumvent this very perception through careful self-presentation, wearing the white uniform to indicate his position as a nurse. His efforts, however, are nonetheless met with a racial stereotype that as a Black man he should be there to clean up rather than to provide medical care. . . .

These negative stereotypes can affect Black men nurses' efforts to treat patients as well. The men I interviewed find that masculinity does not automatically endow them with an aura of competency. In fact, they often describe interactions with white women patients that suggest that their race minimizes whatever assumptions of capability might accompany being men. They describe several cases in which white women patients completely refused treatment. Ray says,

> *With older white women, it's tricky sometimes because they will come right out and tell you they don't want you to treat them, or can they see someone else.*

Ray frames this as an issue specifically with older white women, though other nurses in the sample described similar issues with white women of all ages. Cyril, a 40-year-old nurse with 17 years of nursing experience, describes a slightly different twist on this story:

> *I had a white lady that I had to give a shot, and she was fine with it and I was fine with it. But her husband, when she told him, he said to me, I don't have any problem with you as a Black man, but I don't want you giving her a shot.*

This dynamic, described primarily among white women patients and their families, presents a picture of how Black men's interactions with clients are shaped in specifically raced and gendered ways that suggest they are less rather than more capable. These interactions do not send the message that Black men, because they are men, are too competent for nursing and really belong in higher-status jobs. Instead, these men face patients who mistake them for lower-status service workers and encounter white women patients (and their husbands) who simply refuse treatment or are visibly uncomfortable with the prospect. These interactions do not situate Black men nurses in a prime position for upward mobility. Rather, they suggest that the experience of Black men nurses with this particular mechanism of the glass escalator is the manifestation of the expectation that they should be in lower-status positions more appropriate to their race and gender.

Refusal to Reject Femininity

Finally, Black men nurses have a different experience with establishing distance from women and the feminized aspects of their work. Most research shows that as men nurses employ strategies that distance them from femininity (e.g., by emphasizing nursing as a route to higher-status, more masculine jobs), they place themselves in a position for upward mobility and the glass escalator effect (Williams 1992). For Black men nurses, however, this process looks different. Instead of distancing themselves from the femininity associated with nursing, Black men actually embrace some of the more feminized attributes linked to nursing. In particular, they emphasize how much they value and enjoy the way their jobs allow them to be caring and nurturing. Rather than conceptualizing caring as anathema or feminine (and therefore undesirable), Black men nurses speak openly of caring as something positive and enjoyable.

This is consistent with the context of nursing that defines caring as integral to the profession. As nurses, Black men in this line of work experience professional socialization that emphasizes and values caring, and this is reflected in their statements about their work. Significantly, however, rather than repudiating this feminized component of their jobs, they embrace it. Tobias, a 44-year-old oncology nurse with 25 years of experience, asserts,

> *The best part about nursing is helping other people, the flexibility of work hours, and the commitment to vulnerable populations, people who are ill. . . .*

For many of these nurses, willingness to embrace caring is also shaped by issues of race and racism. In their position as nurses, concern for others is connected to fighting the effects of racial inequality. Specifically, caring motivates them to use their role as nurses to address racial health disparities, especially those that disproportionately affect Black men. Chris describes his efforts to minimize health issues among Black men:

> *With Black male patients, I have their history, and if they're 50 or over I ask about the prostate exam and a colonoscopy. Prostate and colorectal death is so high that that's my personal crusade.*

Ryan also speaks to the importance of using his position to address racial imbalances:

> *I really take advantage of the opportunities to give back to communities, especially to change the disparities in the African American community. I'm more than just a nurse. As a faculty member at a major university, I have to do community hours, services. Doing health fairs, in-services on research, this makes an impact in some disparities in the African American community. [People in the community] may not have the opportunity to do this otherwise.*

As Lamont (2000) indicates in her discussion of the "caring self," concern for others helps Chris and Ryan to use their knowledge and position as nurses to combat racial inequalities in health. Though caring is generally considered a "feminine" attribute, in this context it is connected to challenging racial health disparities. Unlike their white men colleagues, these nurses accept and even embrace certain aspects of femininity rather than rejecting them. They thus reveal yet another aspect of the glass escalator process that differs for Black men. As Black men nurses embrace this "feminine" trait and the avenues it provides for challenging racial inequalities, they may become more comfortable in nursing and embrace the opportunities it offers.

Conclusions

Existing research on the glass escalator cannot explain these men's experiences. As men who do women's work, they should be channeled into positions as charge nurses or nursing administrators and should find themselves virtually pushed into the upper ranks of the nursing profession. But without exception, this is not the experience these Black men nurses describe. Instead of benefiting from the basic mechanisms of the glass escalator, they face tense relationships with colleagues, supervisors' biases in achieving promotion, patient stereotypes that inhibit caregiving, and a sense of comfort with some of the feminized aspects of their jobs. These "glass barriers" suggest that the glass escalator is a racialized concept as well as a gendered one. The main contribution of this study is the finding that race and gender intersect to determine which men will ride the glass escalator. The proposition that men who do women's work encounter undue opportunities and advantages appears to be unequivocally true only if the men in question are white. . . .

It is also especially interesting to consider how men describe the role of women in facilitating—or denying—access to the glass escalator. Research on white men nurses includes accounts of ways white women welcome them and facilitate their advancement by pushing them toward leadership positions (Floge and Merrill 1986; Heikes 1991; Williams 1992, 1995). In contrast, Black men nurses in this study discuss white women who do not seem eager to work with them, much less aid their upward mobility. These different responses indicate that shared racial status is important in determining who rides the glass escalator. If that is the case, then future research should consider whether Black men nurses who work in predominantly Black settings are more likely to encounter the glass escalator effect. In these settings, Black men nurses' experiences might more closely resemble those of white men nurses.

Finally, it is important to consider how these men's experiences have implications for the ways the glass escalator phenomenon reproduces racial and gendered advantages. Williams (1995) argues that men's desire to differentiate themselves from women and disassociate from the femininity of their work is a key process that facilitates their ride on the glass escalator. She ultimately suggests that if men reconstruct masculinity to include traits such as caring, the distinctions between masculinity and femininity could blur and men "would not have to define masculinity as the negation of femininity" (Williams 1995: 188). This in turn could create a more equitable balance between men and women in women's professions. However, the experiences of Black men in nursing, especially their embrace of caring, suggest that accepting the feminine aspects of work is not enough to dismantle the glass escalator and produce more gender equality in women's professions. The fact that Black men nurses accept and even enjoy caring does not minimize the processes that enable *white* men to ride the glass escalator. This suggests that undoing the glass escalator requires not only blurring the lines between masculinity and femininity but also challenging the processes of racial inequality that marginalize minority men.

ENDNOTE

[1] I could not locate any data that indicate the percentage of Black men in nursing. According to 2006 census data, African Americans compose 11 percent of nurses, and men are 8 percent of nurses (http://www.census.gov/compendia/statab/tables/08s0598.pdf). These data do not show the breakdown of nurses by race and sex.

REFERENCES

Britton, Dana. 1995. *At Work in the Iron Cage*. New York: New York University Press.

Budig, Michelle. 2002. Male Advantage and the Gender Composition of Jobs: Who Rides the Glass Escalator? *Social Forces* 49 (2): 258–77.

Charles, Maria, and David Grusky. 2004. *Occupational Ghettos: The Worldwide Segregation of Women and Men*. Palo Alto, CA: Stanford University Press.

Collins, Patricia Hill. 1990. *Black Feminist Thought*. New York: Routledge.

_____. 2004. *Black Sexual Politics*. New York: Routledge.

Duffy, Mignon. 2007. Doing the Dirty Work: Gender, Race, and Reproductive Labor in Historical Perspective. *Gender & Society* 21:313–36.

Feagin, Joe. 2006. *Systemic Racism*. New York: Routledge.

Feagin, Joe, and Melvin Sikes. 1994. *Living With Racism*. Boston: Beacon Hill Press.

Floge, Liliane, and Deborah M. Merrill. 1986. Tokenism Reconsidered: Male Nurses and Female Physicians in a Hospital Setting. *Social Forces* 64:925–47.

Harvey Wingfield, Adia. 2007. The Modern Mammy and the Angry Black Man: African American Professionals' Experiences with Gendered Racism in the Workplace. *Race, Gender, and Class* 14 (2): 196–212.

Heikes, E. Joel. 1991. When Men Are the Minority: The Case of Men in Nursing. *Sociological Quarterly* 32:389–401.

hooks, bell. 2004. *We Real Cool*. New York: Routledge.

Kanter, Rosabeth Moss. 1977. *Men and Women of the Corporation*. New York: Basic Books.

Lamont, Michelle. 2000. *The Dignity of Working Men*. New York: Russell Sage.

Neal, Mark Anthony. 2005. *New Black Man*. New York: Routledge.

Roth, Louise. 2006. *Selling Women Short: Gender and Money on Wall Street*. Princeton, NJ: Princeton University Press.

Williams, Christine. 1992. The Glass Escalator: Hidden Advantages for Men in the "Female" Professions. *Social Problems* 39 (3): 253–67.

_____. 1995. *Still a Man's World: Men Who Do Women's Work*. Berkeley: University of California Press.

Zimmer, Lynn. 1988. Tokenism and Women in the Workplace: The Limits of Gender Neutral Theory. *Social Problems* 35 (1): 64–77.

43

THE TIME BIND
When Work Becomes
Home and Home Becomes Work

ARLIE RUSSELL HOCHSCHILD

What are the relationships between work life and family life? How do individuals negotiate the role demands of both social institutions? Arlie Russell Hochschild, a professor of sociology at the University of California at Berkeley, investigates these questions in her three-year study of a large corporation, which she calls "Amerco." Hochschild interviewed 130 employees,

Arlie Russell Hochschild, excerpt from *The Time Bind: When Work Becomes Home and Home Becomes Work*. Copyright © 1997 by Arlie Russell Hochschild. Reprinted by arrangement with Henry Holt and Company, LLC.

including middle and upper management, clerks, and factory workers, most of whom were working parents. Hochschild also talked with human resource specialists, psychologists, child-care workers, and homemakers who were married to Amerco employees. In this selection, adapted from her book *The Time Bind: When Work Becomes Home and Home Becomes Work* (1997), Hochschild discusses her findings about the changing relationship between work life and home life for many working parents.

It's 7:40 A.M. when Cassie Bell, 4, arrives at the Spotted Deer Child-Care Center, her hair half-combed, a blanket in one hand, a fudge bar in the other. *I'm late,* her mother, Gwen, a sturdy young woman whose short-cropped hair frames a pleasant face, explains to the child-care worker in charge. *Cassie wanted the fudge bar so bad, I gave it to her,* she adds apologetically.

Pleeese, *can't you take me with you?* Cassie pleads.

You know I can't take you to work, Gwen replies in a tone that suggests that she has been expecting this request. Cassie's shoulders droop. But she has struck a hard bargain—the morning fudge bar—aware of her mother's anxiety about the long day that lies ahead at the center. As Gwen explains later, she continually feels that she owes Cassie more time than she gives her—she has a "time debt."

Arriving at her office just before 8, Gwen finds on her desk a cup of coffee in her personal mug, milk no sugar (exactly as she likes it), prepared by a co-worker who managed to get in ahead of her. As the assistant to the head of public relations at a company I will call Amerco, Gwen has to handle responses to any reports that may appear about the company in the press—a challenging job, but one that gives her satisfaction. As she prepares for her first meeting of the day, she misses her daughter, but she also feels relief; there's a lot to get done at Amerco.

Gwen used to work a straight eight-hour day. But over the last three years, her workday has gradually stretched to eight and a half or nine hours, not counting the e-mail messages and faxes she answers from home. She complains about her hours to her co-workers and listens to their complaints—but she loves her job. Gwen picks up Cassie at 5:45 and gives her a long, affectionate hug.

At home, Gwen's husband, John, a computer programmer, plays with their daughter while Gwen prepares dinner. To protect the dinner "hour"— 8:00–8:30—Gwen checks that the phone machine is on, hears the phone ring during dinner but resists the urge to answer. After Cassie's bath, Gwen and Cassie have "quality time," or "Q.T.," as John affectionately calls it. Half an hour later, at 9:30, Gwen tucks Cassie into bed.

There are, in a sense, two Bell households: the rushed family they actually are and the relaxed family they imagine they might be if only they had time. Gwen and John complain that they are in a time bind. What they say they want seems so modest—time to throw a ball, to read to Cassie, to witness the small dramas of her development, not to speak of having a little fun and romance themselves. Yet even these modest wishes seem strangely out of reach. Before going to bed, Gwen has to e-mail messages to her colleagues in preparation for the next day's meeting; John goes to bed early, exhausted—he's out the door by 7 every morning.

Nationwide, many working parents are in the same boat. More mothers of small children than ever now work outside the home. In 1993, 56 percent of women with children between 6 and 17 worked outside the home full time year-round; 43 percent of women with children 6 and under did the same. Meanwhile, fathers of small children are not cutting back hours of work to help out at home. If anything, they have increased their hours at work. According to a 1993 national survey conducted by the Families and Work Institute in New York, American men average 48.8 hours of work a week, and women 41.7 hours, including overtime and commuting. All in all, more women are on the economic train, and for many—men and women alike— that train is going faster.

But Amerco has "family-friendly" policies. If your division head and supervisor agree, you can work part time, share a job with another worker, work some hours at home, take parental leave or use "flex time." But hardly anyone uses these policies. In seven years, only two Amerco fathers have taken formal parental leave. Fewer than 1 percent have taken advantage of the opportunity to work part time. Of all such policies, only flex time—which rearranges but does not shorten work time—has had a significant number of takers (perhaps a third of working parents at Amerco).

Forgoing family-friendly policies is not exclusive to Amerco workers. A 1991 study of 188 companies conducted by the Families and Work Institute found that while a majority offered part-time shifts, fewer than 5 percent of employees made use of them. Thirty-five percent offered "flex place"—work from home—and fewer than 3 percent of their employees took advantage of it. And an earlier Bureau of Labor Statistics survey asked workers whether they preferred a shorter workweek, a longer one or their present schedule. About 62 percent preferred their present schedule; 28 percent would have preferred longer hours. Fewer than 10 percent said they wanted a cut in hours.

Still, I found it hard to believe that people didn't protest their long hours at work. So I contacted Bright Horizons, a company that runs 136 company-based child-care centers associated with corporations, hospitals and federal agencies in 25 states. Bright Horizons allowed me to add questions to a questionnaire they sent out to 3,000 parents whose children attended the centers. The respondents, mainly middle-class parents in their early 30s, largely confirmed the picture I'd found at Amerco. A third of fathers and a fifth of mothers described themselves as "workaholic," and 1 out of 3 said their partners were.

To be sure, some parents have tried to shorten their hours. Twenty-one percent of the nation's women voluntarily work part time, as do 7 percent of men. A number of others make under-the-table arrangements that don't show up on surveys. But while working parents say they need more time at home, the main story of their lives does not center on a struggle to get it. Why? Given the hours parents are working these days, why aren't they taking advantage of an opportunity to reduce their time at work?

The most widely held explanation is that working parents cannot afford to work shorter hours. Certainly this is true for many. But if money is the whole explanation, why would it be that at places like Amerco, the best-paid employees—upper-level managers and professionals—were the least interested in part-time work or job sharing, while clerical workers who earned less were more interested?

Similarly, if money were the answer, we would expect poorer new mothers to return to work more quickly after giving birth than rich mothers. But among working women nationwide, well-to-do new mothers are not much more likely to stay home after 13 weeks with a new baby than low-income new mothers. When asked what they look for in a job, only a third of respondents in a recent study said salary came first. Money is important, but by itself, money does not explain why many people don't want to cut back hours at work.

A second explanation goes that workers don't dare ask for time off because they are afraid it would make them vulnerable to layoffs. With recent downsizings at many large corporations, and with well-paying, secure jobs being replaced by lower-paying, insecure ones, it occurred to me that perhaps employees are "working scared." But when I asked Amerco employees whether they worked long hours for fear of getting on a layoff list, virtually everyone said no. Even among a particularly vulnerable group—factory workers who were laid off in the downturn of the early 1980s and were later rehired—most did not cite fear for their jobs as the only, or main, reason they worked overtime. For unionized workers, layoffs are assigned by seniority, and for nonunionized workers, layoffs are usually related to the profitability of the division a person works in, not to an individual work schedule.

Were workers uninformed about the company's family-friendly policies? No. Some even mentioned that they were proud to work for a company that offered such enlightened policies. Were rigid middle managers standing in the way of workers using these policies? Sometimes. But when I compared Amerco employees who worked for flexible managers with those who worked for rigid managers, I found that the flexible managers reported only a few more applicants than the rigid ones. The evidence, however counterintuitive, pointed to a paradox: workers at the company I studied weren't protesting the time bind. They were accommodating to it.

Why? I did not anticipate the conclusion I found myself coming to: namely, that work has become a form of "home" and home has become "work." The worlds of home and work have not begun to blur, as the conventional wisdom goes, but to reverse places. We are used to thinking that home is where most people feel the most appreciated, the most truly "themselves," the most secure, the most relaxed. We are used to thinking that work is where most people feel like "just a number" or "a cog in a machine." It is where they have to be "on," have to "act," where they are least secure and most harried.

But new management techniques so pervasive in corporate life have helped transform the workplace into a more appreciative, personal sort of social world. Meanwhile, at home the divorce rate has risen, and the emotional demands have become more baffling and complex. In addition to teething, tantrums and the normal developments of growing children, the needs of elderly parents are creating more tasks for the modern family—as are the blending, unblending, re-blending of new stepparents, stepchildren, exes and former in-laws.

This idea began to dawn on me during one of my first interviews with an Amerco worker. Linda Avery, a friendly, 38-year-old mother, is a shift supervisor at an Amerco plant. When I meet her in the factory's coffee-break room over a couple of Cokes, she is wearing blue jeans and a pink jersey, her hair pulled back in a long, blond ponytail. Linda's husband, Bill, is a technician in the same plant. By working different shifts, they manage to share the care of their 2-year-old son and Linda's 16-year-old daughter from a previous marriage. *Bill works the 7 A.M. to 3 P.M. shift while I watch the baby,* she explains. *Then I work the 3 P.M. to 11 P.M. shift and he watches the baby. My daughter works at Walgreen's after school.*

Linda is working overtime, and so I begin by asking whether Amerco required the overtime or whether she volunteered for it. *Oh, I put in for it,* she replies. I ask her whether, if finances and company policy permitted, she'd be interested in cutting back on the overtime. She takes off her safety glasses, rubs her face and, without answering my question, explains:

> *I get home, and the minute I turn the key, my daughter is right there. Granted, she needs somebody to talk to about her day. . . . The baby is still up. He should have been in bed two hours ago, and that upsets me. The dishes are piled in the sink. My daughter comes right up to the door and complains about anything her stepfather said or did, and she wants to talk about her job. My husband is in the other room hollering to my daughter, "Tracy, I don't ever get any time to talk to your mother, because you're always monopolizing her time before I even get a chance!" They all come at me at once.*

Linda's description of the urgency of demands and the unarbitrated quarrels that await her homecoming contrast with her account of arriving at her job as a shift supervisor:

> *I usually come to work early, just to get away from the house. When I arrive, people are there waiting. We sit, we talk, we joke. I let them know what's going on, who has to be where, what changes I've made for the shift that day. We sit and chitchat for 5 or 10 minutes. There's laughing, joking, fun.*

For Linda, home has come to feel like work and work has come to feel a bit like home. Indeed, she feels she can get relief from the "work" of being at home only by going to the "home" of work. Why has her life at home come to seem like this? Linda explains it this way:

> *My husband's a great help watching our baby. But as far as doing housework or even taking the baby when I'm at home, no. He figures he works five days a week; he's not going to come home and clean. But he doesn't stop to think that I work seven days a week. Why should I have to come home and do the housework without help from anybody else? My husband and I have been through this over and over again. Even if he would just pick up from the kitchen table and stack the dishes for me, that would make a big difference. He does nothing. On his weekends off, he goes fishing. If I want any time off, I have to get a sitter. He'll help out if I'm not here, but the minute I am, all the work at home is mine.*

With a light laugh, she continues: *So I take a lot of overtime. The more I get out of the house, the better I am. It's a terrible thing to say, but that's the way I feel.*

When Bill feels the need for time off, to relax, to have fun, to feel free, he climbs in his truck and takes his free time without his family. Largely in response, Linda grabs what she also calls "free time"—at work. Neither Linda nor Bill Avery wants more time together at home, not as things are arranged now.

How do Linda and Bill Avery fit into the broader picture of American family and work life? Current research suggests that however hectic their lives, women who do paid work feel less depressed, think better of themselves and are more satisfied than women who stay at home. One study reported that women who work outside the home feel more valued at home than housewives do. Meanwhile, work is where many women feel like "good mothers." As Linda reflects:

> *I'm a good mom at home, but I'm a better mom at work. At home, I get into fights with Tracy. I want her to apply to a junior college, but she's not interested. At work, I think I'm better at seeing the other person's point of view.*

Many workers feel more confident they could "get the job done" at work than at home. One study found that only 59 percent of workers feel their "performance" in the family is "good or unusually good," while 86 percent rank their performance on the job this way.

Forces at work and at home are simultaneously reinforcing this "reversal." This lure of work has been enhanced in recent years by the rise of company cultural engineering—in particular, the shift from Frederick Taylor's principles of scientific management to the Total Quality principles originally set out by W. Edwards Deming. Under the influence of a Taylorist world view, the manager's job was to coerce the worker's mind and body, not to appeal to the worker's heart. The Taylorized worker was deskilled, replaceable and cheap, and as a consequence felt bored, demeaned and unappreciated.

Using modern participative management techniques, many companies now train workers to make their own work decisions, and then set before their newly "empowered" employees moral as well as financial incentives. At Amerco, the Total Quality worker is invited to feel recognized for job accomplishments. Amerco regularly strengthens the familylike ties of co-workers by holding "recognition ceremonies" honoring particular workers or self-managed production teams. Amerco employees speak of "belonging to the Amerco family," and proudly wear their "Total Quality" pins or "High Performance Team" T-shirts, symbols of their loyalty to the company and of its loyalty to them.

The company occasionally decorates a section of the factory and serves refreshments. The production teams, too, have regular get-togethers. In a New Age recasting of an old business slogan—"The Customer Is Always Right"—Amerco proposes that its workers "Value the Internal Customer." This means: Be as polite and considerate to co-workers inside the company as you would be to customers outside it. How many recognition ceremonies for competent performance are being offered at home? Who is valuing the internal customer there?

Amerco also tries to take on the role of a helpful relative with regard to employee problems at work and at home. The education-and-training division offers employees free courses (on company time) in "Dealing with Anger," "How to Give and Accept Criticism," "How to Cope with Difficult People."

At home, of course, people seldom receive anything like this much help on issues basic to family life. There, no courses are being offered on "Dealing with Your Child's Disappointment in You" or "How to Treat Your Spouse Like an Internal Customer."

If Total Quality calls for "reskilling" the worker in an "enriched" job environment, technological developments have long been deskilling parents at home. Over the centuries, store-bought goods have replaced homespun cloth, homemade soap and home-baked foods. Day care for children, retirement homes for the elderly, even psychotherapy are, in a way, commercial substitutes for jobs that a mother once did at home. Even family-generated entertainment has, to some extent, been replaced by television, video games and the VCR. I sometimes watched Amerco families sitting together after their dinners, mute but cozy, watching sitcoms in which television mothers, fathers and children related in an animated way to one another while the viewing family engaged in relational loafing.

The one "skill" still required of family members is the hardest one of all—the emotional work of forging, deepening or repairing family relationships. It takes time to develop this skill, and even then things can go awry. Family ties are complicated. People get hurt. Yet as broken homes become more common—and as the sense of belonging to a geographical community grows less and less secure in an age of mobility—the corporate world has created a sense of "neighborhood," of "feminine culture," of family at work. Life at work can be insecure; the company can fire workers. But workers aren't so secure at home, either. Many employees have been working for Amerco for 20 years but are on their second or third marriages or relationships. The shifting balance between these two "divorce rates" may be the most powerful reason why tired parents flee a world of unresolved quarrels and unwashed laundry for the orderliness, harmony and managed cheer of work. People are getting their "pink slips" at home.

Amerco workers have not only turned their offices into "home" and their homes into workplaces; many have also begun to "Taylorize" time at home, where families are succumbing to a cult of efficiency previously associated mainly with the office and factory. Meanwhile, work time, with its ever longer hours, has become more hospitable to sociability—periods of talking with friends on e-mail, patching up quarrels, gossiping. Within the long workday of many Amerco employees are great hidden pockets of inefficiency while, in the far smaller number of waking weekday hours at home, they are, despite themselves, forced to act increasingly time-conscious and efficient.

The Averys respond to their time bind at home by trying to value and protect "quality time." A concept unknown to their parents and grandparents, "quality time" has become a powerful symbol of the struggle against the growing pressures at home. It reflects the extent to which modern parents feel the flow of time to be running against them. The premise behind "quality time" is that the time we devote to relationships can somehow be separated from ordinary time. Relationships go on during quantity time, of course, but then we are only passively, not actively, wholeheartedly, specializing in our emotional ties. We aren't "on." Quality time at home becomes like an office appointment. You don't want to be caught "goofing off around the water cooler" when you are "at work."

Quality time holds out the hope that scheduling intense periods of togetherness can compensate for an overall loss of time in such a way that a relationship will suffer no loss of quality. But this is just another way of transferring the cult of efficiency from office to home. We must now get our relationships in good repair in less time. Instead of nine hours a day with a child, we declare ourselves capable of getting "the same result" with one intensely focused hour.

Parents now more commonly speak of time as if it is a threatened form of personal capital they have no choice but to manage and invest. What's new here is the spread into the home of a financial manager's attitude toward time. Working parents at Amerco owe what they think of as time debts at home. This is because they are, in a sense, inadvertently "Taylorizing" the house—speeding up the pace of home life as Taylor once tried to "scientifically" speed up the pace of factory life.

Advertisers of products aimed at women have recognized that this new reality provides an opportunity to sell products, and have turned the very pressure that threatens to explode the home into a positive attribute. Take, for example, an ad promoting Instant Quaker Oatmeal: it shows a smiling mother ready for the office in her square-shouldered suit, hugging her happy son. A caption reads: "Nicky is a very picky eater. With Instant Quaker Oatmeal, I can give him a terrific hot breakfast in just 90 seconds. And I don't have to spend any time coaxing him to eat it!" Here, the modern mother seems to have absorbed the lessons of Frederick Taylor as she presses for efficiency at home because she is in a hurry to get to work.

Part of modern parenthood seems to include coping with the resistance of real children who are not so eager to get their cereal so fast. Some parents try desperately not to appease their children with special gifts or smooth-talking promises about the future. But when time is scarce, even the best parents find themselves passing a system-wide familial speed-up along to the most vulnerable workers on the line. Parents are then obliged to try to control the damage done by a reversal of worlds. They monitor mealtime, homework time, bedtime, trying to cut out "wasted" time.

In response, children often protest the pace, the deadlines, the grand irrationality of "efficient" family life. Children dawdle. They refuse to leave places when it's time to leave. They insist on leaving places when it's not time to leave. Surely, this is part of the usual stop-and-go of childhood itself, but perhaps, too, it is the plea of children for more family time and more control over what time there is. This only adds to the feeling that life at home has become hard work.

Instead of trying to arrange shorter or more flexible work schedules, Amerco parents often avoid confronting the reality of the time bind. Some minimize their ideas about how much care a child, a partner, or they themselves "really need." They make do with less time, less attention, less understanding, and less support at home than they once imagined possible. They *emotionally downsize* life. In essence, they deny the needs of family members, and they themselves become emotional ascetics. If they once "needed" time with each other, they are now increasingly "fine" without it.

Another way that working parents try to evade the time bind is to buy themselves out of it—an approach that puts women in particular at the heart of a contradiction. Like men, women absorb the work-family speed-up far more than they resist it; but unlike men, they still shoulder most of the workload at home. And women still represent in people's minds the heart and soul of family life. They're the ones—especially women of the urban middle and upper-middle classes—who feel most acutely the need to save time, who are the most tempted by the new "time saving" goods and services—and who wind up feeling the most guilty about it. For example, Playgroup Connections, a Washington-area business started by a former executive recruiter, matches playmates to one another. One mother hired the service to find her child a French-speaking playmate.

In several cities, children home alone can call a number for "Grandma, Please!" and reach an adult who has the time to talk with them, sing to them or help them with their homework. An ad for Kindercare Learning Centers, a for-profit child-care chain, pitches its appeal this way: "You want your child to be active, tolerant, smart, loved, emotionally stable, self-aware, artistic and get a two-hour nap. Anything else?" It goes on to note that Kindercare accepts children 6 weeks to 12 years old and provides a number to call for the Kindercare nearest you. Another typical service organizes children's birthday parties, making out invitations ("sure hope you can come") and providing party favors, entertainment, a decorated cake and balloons. Creative Memories is a service that puts ancestral photos into family albums for you.

An overwhelming majority of the working mothers I spoke with recoiled from the idea of buying themselves out of parental duties. A bought birthday party was "too impersonal," a 90-second breakfast "too fast." Yet a surprising amount of lunchtime conversation between female friends at Amerco was devoted to expressing complex, conflicting feelings about the lure of trading time for one service or another. The temptation to order flash-frozen dinners or to call a local number for a homework helper did not come up because such services had not yet appeared at Spotted Deer Child-Care Center. But many women dwelled on the question of how to decide where a mother's job began and ended, especially with regard to babysitters and television. One mother said to another in the breakroom of an Amerco plant:

> *Damon doesn't settle down until 10 at night, so he hates me to wake him up in the morning and I hate to do it. He's cranky. He pulls the covers up. I put on cartoons. That way, I can dress him and he doesn't object. I don't like to use TV that way. It's like a drug. But I do it.*

The other mother countered:

Well, Todd is up before we are, so that's not a problem. It's after dinner, when I feel like watching a little television, that I feel guilty, because he gets too much TV at the sitter's.

As task after task falls into the realm of time-saving goods and services, questions arise about the moral meanings attached to doing or not doing such tasks. Is it being a good mother to bake a child's birthday cake (alone or together with one's partner)? Or can we gratefully save time by ordering it, and be good mothers by planning the party? Can we save more time by hiring a planning service, and be good mothers simply by watching our children have a good time? *Wouldn't that be nice!* one Amerco mother exclaimed. As the idea of the "good mother" retreats before the pressures of work and the expansion of motherly services, mothers are in fact continually reinventing themselves.

The final way working parents tried to evade the time bind was to develop what I call "potential selves." The potential selves that I discovered in my Amerco interviews were fantasy creations of time-poor parents who dreamed of living as time millionaires.

One man, a gifted 55-year-old engineer in research and development at Amerco, told how he had dreamed of taking his daughters on a camping trip in the Sierra Mountains:

I bought all the gear three years ago when they were 5 and 7, the tent, the sleeping bags, the air mattresses, the backpacks, the ponchos. I got a map of the area. I even got the freeze-dried food. Since then the kids and I have talked about it a lot, and gone over what we're going to do. They've been on me to do it for a long time. I feel bad about it. I keep putting it off, but we'll do it, I just don't know when.

Banished to garages and attics of many Amerco workers were expensive electric saws, cameras, skis, and musical instruments, all bought with wages it took time to earn. These items were to their owners what Cassie's fudge bar was to her—a substitute for time, a talisman, a reminder of the potential self.

Obviously, not everyone, not even a majority of Americans, is making a home out of work and a workplace out of home. But in the working world, it is a growing reality, and one we need to face. Increasing numbers of women are discovering a great male secret—that work can be an escape from the pressures of home, pressures that the changing nature of work itself are only intensifying. Neither men nor women are going to take up "family-friendly" policies, whether corporate or governmental, as long as the current realities of work and home remain as they are. For a substantial number of time-bound parents, the stripped-down home and the neighborhood devoid of community are simply losing out to the pull of the workplace.

There are several broader, historical causes of this reversal of realms. The last 30 years have witnessed the rapid rise of women in the workplace. At the same time, job mobility has taken families farther from relatives who might lend a hand, and made it harder to make close friends of neighbors who could help out. Moreover, as women have acquired more education and have joined men at work, they have absorbed the views of an older, male-oriented work world, its views of a "real career," far more than men have taken up their share of the work at home. One reason women have changed more than men is that the world of "male" work seems more honorable and valuable than the "female" world of home and children.

So where do we go from here? There is surely no going back to the mythical 1950s family that confined women to the home. Most women don't wish to return to a full-time role at home—and couldn't afford it even if they did. But equally troubling is a workaholic culture that strands both men and women outside the home.

For a while now, scholars on work-family issues have pointed to Sweden, Norway, and Denmark as better models of work-family balance. Today, for example, almost all Swedish fathers take two paid weeks off from work at the birth of their children, and about half of fathers and most mothers take additional "parental leave" during the child's first or second year. Research shows that men who take family leave when their children are very young are more likely to be involved with their children as they grow older. When I mentioned this Swedish record of paternity leave to a focus group of American male managers, one of them replied, *Right, we've already heard about Sweden.* To this executive, paternity leave was a good idea not for the U.S. today, but for some "potential society" in another place and time.

Meanwhile, children are paying the price. In her book *When the Bough Breaks: The Cost of Neglecting Our Children,* the economist Sylvia Hewlett claims that "compared with the previous generation, young people today are more likely to underperform at school; commit suicide; need psychiatric help; suffer a severe eating disorder; bear a child out of wedlock; take drugs; be the victim of a violent crime." But we needn't dwell on sledgehammer problems like heroin or suicide to realize that children like those at Spotted Deer need more of our time. If other advanced nations with two-job families can give children the time they need, why can't we?

Author's Note: Over three years, I interviewed 130 respondents for a book. They spoke freely and allowed me to follow them through "typical" days, on the understanding that I would protect their anonymity. I have changed the names of the company and of those I interviewed, and altered certain identifying details. Their words appear here as they were spoken.—A.R.H.

44

THE PROTESTANT ETHIC
AND THE SPIRIT OF CAPITALISM

MAX WEBER

The institution of religion is the topic of the following three selections. Sociologists have long studied how religion affects the social structure and the personal experience of individuals in society. Max Weber (1864–1920), for example, often placed the institution of religion at the center of his social analyses. Weber was particularly concerned with how changes in the institution of religion influenced changes in other social institutions, especially the economy. The selection excerpted here is from Weber's definitive and most famous study, *The Protestant Ethic and the Spirit of Capitalism* (1905). In his analysis of capitalism, Weber argues that the early Protestant worldviews of Calvinism and Puritanism were the primary factors in influencing the development of a capitalist economic system. Without the Protestant Reformation and a change in societal values toward rationality, capitalism would not have evolved as we know it today.

A product of modern European civilization, studying any problem of universal history, is bound to ask himself to what combination of circumstances the fact should be attributed that in Western civilization, and in Western civilization only, cultural phenomena have appeared which (as we like to think) lie in a line of development having *universal* significance and value. . . . All over the world there have been merchants, wholesale and retail, local and engaged in foreign trade. . . .

But in modern times the Occident has developed, in addition to this, a very different form of capitalism which has appeared nowhere else: the rational capitalistic organization of (formally) free labour. Only suggestions of it are found elsewhere. Even the organization of unfree labour reached a considerable degree of rationality only on plantations and to a very limited extent in the *Ergasteria* of antiquity. In the manors, manorial workshops, and domestic industries on estates with serf labour it was probably somewhat less developed. Even real domestic industries with free labour have definitely been proved to have existed in only a few isolated cases outside the Occident. . . .

Rational industrial organization, attuned to a regular market, and neither to political nor irrationally speculative opportunities for profit, is not, however, the only peculiarity of Western capitalism. The modern rational organization of the capitalistic enterprise would not have been possible without two other important factors in its development: the separation of business from the household, which completely dominates modern economic life, and closely connected with it, rational bookkeeping. . . .

Hence in a universal history of culture the central problem for us is not, in the last analysis, even from a purely economic viewpoint, the development of capitalistic activity as such, differing in different cultures only in form: the adventurer type, or capitalism in trade, war, politics, or administration as sources of gain. It is rather the origin of this sober bourgeois capitalism with its rational organization of free labour. Or in terms of cultural history, the problem is that of the origin of the Western bourgeois class and of its peculiarities, a problem which is certainly closely connected with that of the origin of the capitalistic organization of labour, but is not quite the same thing. For the bourgeois as a class existed prior to the development of the peculiar modern form of capitalism, though, it is true, only in the Western hemisphere.

Now the peculiar modern Western form of capitalism has been, at first sight, strongly influenced by the development of technical possibilities. Its rationality is today essentially dependent on the calculability of the most important technical factors. But this means fundamentally that it is dependent on the peculiarities of modern science, especially the natural sciences based on mathematics and exact and rational experiment. On the other hand, the development of these sciences and of the technique resting upon them now receives important stimulation from these capitalistic interests in its practical economic application. It is true that the origin of Western science cannot be attributed to such interests. Calculation, even with decimals, and algebra have been carried on in India, where the decimal system was invented. But it was only made use of by developing capitalism in the West, while in India it led to no modern arithmetic or book-keeping. Neither was the origin of mathematics and mechanics determined by capitalistic interests. But the *technical* utilization of scientific knowledge, so important for the living conditions of the mass of people, was certainly encouraged by economic considerations, which were extremely favourable to it in the Occident. But this encouragement was derived from the peculiarities of the social structure of the Occident. We must hence ask, from *what* parts of that structure was it derived, since not all of them have been of equal importance?

Among those of undoubted importance are the rational structures of law and of administration. For modern rational capitalism has need, not only of the technical means of production, but of a calculable legal system and of administration in terms of formal rules. Without it adventurous and speculative trading capitalism and all sorts of politically determined capitalisms are possible, but no rational enterprise under individual initiative, with fixed capital and certainty of calculations. Such a legal system and such administration have been available for economic activity in a comparative state of legal and formalistic perfection only in the Occident. We must hence inquire where that law came from. Among other circumstances, capitalistic interest have in turn undoubtedly also helped, but by no means alone nor even principally, to prepare the way for the predominance in law and administration of a class of jurists specially trained in rational law. But these interests did not themselves create that law. Quite different forces were at work in this development. And why did not the capitalistic interests do the same in China or India? Why did not the scientific, the artistic, the political, or the economic development there enter upon that path of rationalization which is peculiar to the Occident?

For in all the above cases it is a question of the specific and peculiar rationalism of Western culture. . . . It is hence our first concern to work out and to explain genetically the special peculiarity of Occidental rationalism, and within this field that of the modern Occidental form. Every such attempt at explanation must, recognizing the fundamental importance of the economic factor, above all take account of the economic conditions. But at the same time the opposite correlation must not be left out of consideration. For though the development of economic rationalism is partly dependent on rational technique and law, it is at the same time determined by the ability and disposition of men to adopt certain types of practical rational conduct. When these types have been obstructed by spiritual obstacles, the development of rational economic conduct has also met serious inner resistance. The magical and religious forces, and the ethical ideas of duty based upon them, have in the past always been among the most important formative influences on conduct. In the studies collected here we shall be concerned with these forces.

Two older essays have been placed at the beginning which attempt, at one important point, to approach the side of the problem which is generally most difficult to grasp: the influence of certain religious ideas on the development of an economic spirit, or the *ethos* of an economic system. In this case we are dealing with the connection of the spirit of modern economic life with the rational ethics of ascetic Protestantism. Thus we treat here only one side of the causal chain. . . .

. . . [T]hat side of English Puritanism which was derived from Calvinism gives the most consistent religious basis for the idea of the calling. . . . For the saints' everlasting rest is in the next world; on earth man must, to be certain of his state of grace, "do the works of him who sent him, as long as it is yet day." Not leisure and enjoyment, but only activity serves to increase the glory of God according to the definite manifestations of His will.

Waste of time is thus the first and in principle the deadliest of sins. The span of human life is infinitely short and precious to make sure of one's own election. Loss of time through sociability, idle talk, luxury, even more sleep than is necessary for health, six to at most eight hours, is worthy of absolute moral condemnation. It does not yet hold, with Franklin, that time is money, but the proposition is true in a certain spiritual sense. It is infinitely valuable because every hour lost is lost to labour for the glory of God. Thus inactive contemplation is also valueless, or even directly reprehensible if it is at the expense of one's daily work. . . .

[T]he same prescription is given for all sexual temptation as is used against religious doubts and a sense of moral unworthiness: "Work hard in your calling." But the most important thing was that even beyond that labour came to be considered in itself the end of life, ordained as such by God. St. Paul's "He who will not work shall not eat" holds unconditionally for everyone. Unwillingness to work is symptomatic of the lack of grace.

Here the difference from the mediæval viewpoint becomes quite evident. Thomas Aquinas also gave an interpretation of that statement of St. Paul. But for him labour is only necessary *naturali ratione* for the maintenance of individual and community. Where this end is achieved, the precept ceases to have any meaning. Moreover, it holds only for the race, not for every individual. It does not apply to anyone who can live without labour on his possessions, and of course contemplation, as a spiritual form of action in the Kingdom of God, takes precedence over the commandment in its literal sense. Moreover, for the popular theology of the time, the highest form of monastic productivity lay in the increase of the *Thesaurus ecclesliæ* through prayer and chant.

. . . For everyone without exception God's Providence has prepared a calling, which he should profess and in which he should labour. And this calling is not, as it was for the Lutheran, a fate to which he must submit and which he must make the best of, but God's commandment to the individual to work for the divine glory. This seemingly subtle difference had far-reaching psychological consequences, and became connected with a further development of the providential interpretation of the economic order which had begun in scholasticism.

It is true that the usefulness of a calling, and thus its favour in the sight of God, is measured primarily in moral terms, and thus in terms of the importance of the goods produced in it for the community. But a further, and, above all, in practice the most important, criterion is found in private profitableness. For if that God, whose hand the Puritan sees in all the occurrences of life, shows one of His elect a chance of profit, he must do it with a purpose. Hence the faithful Christian must follow the call by taking advantage of the opportunity. "If God show you a way in which you may lawfully get more than in another way (without wrong to your soul or to any other), if you refuse this, and choose the less gainful way, you cross one of the ends of your calling, and you refuse to be God's steward, and to accept His gifts and use them for Him when He requireth it: you may labour to be rich for God, though not for the flesh and sin.". . .

The superior indulgence of the *seigneur* and the parvenu ostentation of the *nouveau riche* are equally detestable to asceticism. But, on the other hand, it has the highest ethical appreciation of the sober, middle-class, self-made man. "God blesseth His trade" is a stock remark about those good men who had successfully followed the divine hints. The whole power of the God of the Old Testament, who rewards His people for their obedience in this life, necessarily exercised a similar influence on the Puritan who . . . compared his own state of grace with that of the heroes of the Bible. . . .

Although we cannot here enter upon a discussion of the influence of Puritanism in all . . . directions, we should call attention to the fact that the toleration of pleasure in cultural goods, which contributed to purely aesthetic or athletic enjoyment, certainly always ran up against one characteristic limitation: They must not cost anything. Man is only a trustee of the goods which have come to him through God's grace. He must, like the servant in the parable, give an account of every penny entrusted to him, and it is at least hazardous to spend any of it for a purpose which does not serve the glory of God but only one's own enjoyment. What person, who keeps his eyes open, has not met representatives of this viewpoint even in the present? The idea of a man's duty to his possessions, to which he subordinates himself as an obedient steward, or even as an acquisitive machine, bears with chilling weight on his life. The greater the possessions the heavier, if the ascetic attitude toward life stands the test, the feeling of responsibility for them, for holding them undiminished for the glory of God and increasing them by restless effort. The origin of this type of life also extends in certain roots, like so many aspects of the spirit of capitalism, back into the Middle Ages. But it was in the ethic of ascetic Protestantism that it first found a consistent ethical foundation. Its significance for the development of capitalism is obvious.

This worldly Protestant asceticism, as we may recapitulate up to this point, acted powerfully against the spontaneous enjoyment of possessions; it restricted consumption, especially of luxuries. On the other hand, it had the psychological effect of freeing the acquisition of goods from the inhibitions of traditionalistic ethics. It broke the bonds of the impulse of acquisition in that it not only legalized it, but (in the sense discussed) looked upon it as directly willed by God. . . .

As far as the influence of the Puritan outlook extended, under all circumstances—and this is, of course, much more important than the mere encouragement of capital accumulation—it favoured the development of a rational bourgeois economic life; it was the most important, and above all the only consistent influence in the development of that life. It stood at the cradle of the modern economic man.

To be sure, these Puritanical ideals tended to give way under excessive pressure from the temptations of wealth, as the Puritans themselves knew very well. With great regularity we find the most genuine adherents of Puritanism among the classes which were rising from a lowly status, the small bourgeois and farmers while the *beati possidentes*, even among Quakers, are often found tending to repudiate the old ideals. It was the same fate which again and again befell the predecessor of this worldly asceticism, the monastic asceticism of the Middle Ages. In the latter case, when rational economic activity had worked out its full effects by strict regulation of conduct and limitation of consumption, the wealth accumulated either succumbed directly to the nobility, as in the time before the Reformation, or monastic discipline threatened to break down, and one of the numerous reformations became necessary.

In fact the whole history of monasticism is in a certain sense the history of a continual struggle with the problem of the secularizing influence of wealth.

The same is true on a grand scale of the worldly asceticism of Puritanism. The great revival of Methodism, which preceded the expansion of English industry toward the end of the eighteenth century, may well be compared with such a monastic reform. We may hence quote here a passage from John Wesley himself which might well serve as a motto for everything which has been said above. For it shows that the leaders of these ascetic movements understood the seemingly paradoxical relationships which we have here analysed perfectly well, and in the same sense that we have given them. He wrote:

> I fear, wherever riches have increased, the essence of religion has decreased in the same proportion. Therefore I do not see how it is possible, in the nature of things, for any revival of true religion to continue long. For religion must necessarily produce both industry and frugality, and these cannot but produce riches. But as riches increase, so will pride, anger, and love of the world in all its branches. How then is it possible that Methodism, that is, a religion of the heart, though it flourishes now as a green bay tree, should continue in this state? For the Methodists in every place grow diligent and frugal; consequently they increase in goods. Hence they proportionately increase in pride, in anger, in the desire of the flesh, the desire of the eyes, and the pride of life. So, although the form of religion remains, the spirit is swiftly vanishing away. Is there no way to prevent this—this continual decay of pure religion? We ought not to prevent people from being diligent and frugal; *we must exhort all Christians to gain all they can, and to save all they can; that is, in effect, to grow rich.*

As Wesley here says, the full economic effect of those great religious movements, whose significance for economic development lay above all in their ascetic educative influence, generally came only after the peak of the purely religious enthusiasm was past. Then the intensity of the search for the Kingdom of God commenced gradually to pass over into sober economic virtue; the religious roots died out slowly, giving way to utilitarian worldliness. Then, as Dowden puts it, as in *Robinson Crusoe,* the isolated economic man who carries on missionary activities on the side takes the place of the lonely spiritual search for the Kingdom of Heaven of Bunyan's pilgrim, hurrying through the marketplace of Vanity. . . .

A specifically bourgeois economic ethic had grown up. With the consciousness of standing in the fullness of God's grace and being visibly blessed by Him, the bourgeois business man, as long as he remained within the bounds of formal correctness, as long as his moral conduct was spotless and the use to which he put his wealth was not objectionable, could follow his pecuniary interests as he would and feel that he was fulfilling a duty in doing so. The power of religious asceticism provided him in addition with sober, conscientious, and unusually industrious workmen, who clung to their work as to a life purpose willed by God.

Finally, it gave him the comforting assurance that the unequal distribution of the goods of this world was a special dispensation of Divine Providence, which in these differences, as in particular grace, pursued secret ends unknown to men. . . .

One of the fundamental elements of the spirit of modern capitalism, and not only of that but of all modern culture: Rational conduct on the basis of the idea of the calling, was born—that is what this discussion has sought to demonstrate—from the spirit of Christian asceticism. One has only to reread the passage from Franklin, quoted at the beginning of this essay, in order to see that the essential elements of the attitude which was there called the spirit of capitalism are the same as what we have just shown to be the content of the Puritan worldly asceticism, only without the religious basis, which by Franklin's time had died away. . . .

Since asceticism undertook to remodel the world and to work out its ideals in the world, material goods have gained an increasing and finally an inexorable power over the lives of men as at no previous period in history. Today the spirit of religious asceticism—whether finally, who knows?—has escaped from the cage. But victorious capitalism, since it rests on mechanical foundations, needs its support no longer. The rosy blush of its laughing heir, the Enlightenment, seems also to be irretrievably fading, and the idea of duty in one's calling prowls about in our lives like the ghost of dead religious beliefs. Where the fulfilment of the calling cannot directly be related to the highest spiritual and cultural values, or when, on the other hand, it need not be felt simply as economic compulsion, the individual generally abandons the attempt to justify it at all. In the field of its highest development, in the United States, the pursuit of wealth, stripped of its religious and ethical meaning, tends to become associated with purely mundane passions, which often actually give it the character of sport.

No one knows who will live in this cage in the future, or whether at the end of this tremendous development entirely new prophets will arise, or there will be a great rebirth of old ideas and ideals, or, if neither, mechanized petrification, embellished with a sort of convulsive self-importance. For of the last stage of this cultural development, it might well be truly said: "Specialists without spirit, sensualists without heart; this nullity imagines that it has attained a level of civilization never before achieved."

But this brings us to the world of judgments of value and of faith, with which this purely historical discussion need not be burdened. . . .

Here we have only attempted to trace the fact and the direction of its influence to their motives in one, though a very important point. But it would also further be necessary to investigate how Protestant Asceticism was in turn influenced in its development and its character by the totality of social conditions, especially economic. The modern man is in general, even with the best will, unable to give religious ideas a significance for culture and national character which they deserve. But it is, of course, not my aim to substitute for a one-sided materialistic an equally one-sided spiritualistic causal interpretation of culture and of history. Each is equally possible, but each, if it does not serve as the preparation, but as the conclusion of an investigation, accomplishes equally little in the interest of historical truth.

45

RELIGION AND SOCIETY
Of Gods and Demons

STEVEN P. DANDANEAU

Many early sociologists, including Max Weber, Emile Durkheim, and Karl Marx, studied the institution of religion. One current area of inquiry is how could these early social thinkers study this influential social institution, but remain themselves, nonreligious? Steven P. Dandaneau, Associate Provost and associate professor of sociology at the University of Tennessee, raises this question in the selection below. In addition to providing the reader with an overview of early sociological thinking about religion, Dandaneau also illustrates many of the concepts that concern contemporary sociologists who study this institution. In the tradition of C. Wright Mills, Dandaneau grounds our perception of religion using the sociological imagination. This piece demonstrates the significance of both history and biography in understanding the import of religion in society today.

He [Mills] was always fond of saying that there were two types of Americans worth talking to: clergymen and students.

—IRVING LOUIS HOROWITZ[1]

W hat if a sociologist were to stumble across a crowded parking lot in Clearwater, Florida, where hundreds had gathered to see the image of the Madonna (*the* Madonna, not the recording artist) as it appeared in the window of Suncoast Savings Bank at the corner of State Route 13 and Blah Street? Imagine hundreds of candles lit, hundreds of dreadfully serious looking people, television satellite trucks, flowers, crowds of people crying or standing back and just staring at the image, brisk sales of T-shirts at a nearby oil-change business depicting the apparition, people in wheelchairs, people holding rosaries and praying, and police officers dutifully controlling the traffic and watching over this unusual scene. Would a sociologist, even a sociologist who was a Catholic believer, think that the Virgin Mary had made an appearance in the windowpanes of Suncoast Savings Bank? Probably not.

Or imagine a sociologist plunked down at a contest between the Dallas Cowboys and the Miami Dolphins, facing off in the National Football League's Super Bowl. There are plenty of rituals to observe; a man dressed like a stereotypical cowboy roams the sideline (he is a "mascot"); females dance and dress so as to display much of their body (they are "cheerleaders"); contestants, all males, gesture and dance after certain successful moments in the competition (they act out their "signature celebration"); and spectators wave objects or are adorned to indicate their allegiance to either the team named for a species of aquatic mammal (reputedly a relatively smart animal) or to the team named for a type of occupation involving all facets of care for a particular type of domesticated livestock (mythologized as the epitome of rugged American individualism). And then there is an interlude that is produced as a spectacle meant to instill awe, and there is the sense, widely shared and promoted, that this gathering is the most important place to be in the world at this moment. Would a sociologist see religion in this coliseum? Probably.

Or imagine weeks later in the same arena that a former football coach stands before tens of thousands of men who call themselves "Promise Keepers." Mainly Protestant Christian men, they have gathered to pledge all allegiance to a specific creed, one that lists responsibilities along with privileges due to them *as men* of a particular faith. Or imagine the arena is again a football field and the "Honor Guard" is entering, carrying a cloth dyed in blue, red, and white that features stars and stripes and is hung on an ornate stick with the golden figure of a large bird perched on top. The crowd stands and on cue they collectively vocalize an organized sound. They sing this national anthem, in other words, and so pledge their allegiance to this flag, which is to say, to the sacred idea of a particular nation-state. They are displaying their nationalism, and they tend to do so even if they are not particularly nationalistic. A person carrying the flag of Timbuktu runs across the field and knocks over a young U.S. Marine, identifiable by his uniform, carrying the Stars and Stripes. The man with the sacred flag of Timbuktu stomps on the sacred flag of the United States of America. What would happen? How would a sociologist analyze this situation?

These descriptions mix real and imagined scenarios that, taken together, highlight the question of whether religion stands apart from social institutions. Is religion, any religion, truly transcendent? The examples could be multiplied endlessly and in a less ethnocentric fashion. We could imagine the conclusion to the holy month of Ramadan, as the Islamic faithful gather in Mecca and prepare to feast for three days, or we could ponder the popularity of the Dalai Lama and his Tibetan Buddhism, which in the United States has the actors Harrison Ford and Richard Gere as prominent spokespersons. Or we could examine less popular manifestations of religion, such as cults like the Branch Davidians of Waco, Texas (C. Wright Mills' place of birth) or the Church of Scientology, which counts actor John Travolta among its spokespeople but which is banned in Germany. Most sociologists would see all of these phenomena as begging for sociological explanation, that is, for explanations that use the same concepts that apply to other social practices and institutions.

In this reading, we shall examine the nature of religion as a social institution and as a point of significant conflict between classical sociological thinking and other types of thinking common today. The aim here is not to denigrate religion but, rather, to display the workings of the sociological imagination vis-à-vis religion, understood as a universal cultural phenomenon and as a powerful, widespread, and diverse set of institutionalized social practices. Furthermore, the aim is to reflect on the meaning of this classic analysis for the structure and development of the sociological imagination itself. Why were the classic sociologists, and Mills, for the most part, nonreligious? What was their view of the future of religion? How did their view of religion affect their view of modern society and its fate?. . .

In answering these questions, we shall stress the significance of what sociologists call *structural analysis,* that is, systematic thinking about how patterns of life and belief are reproduced across time and space such that social institutions—composed of roles, positions, groups, norms, values, and rituals—are created and maintained, thereby building and rebuilding society. . . .

The Classical View of Religion

There is a fair amount of agreement between how most people think about religion and how most sociologists think about religion. This is perhaps to be expected since most sociologists, at least in the United States, are themselves members of a religious community. For example, most people think of religion as something that is special or sacred. By this people usually mean that religion is something that stands apart or *should* stand apart from the merely everyday aspects of life, the profane or grittily human; something that, in contrast to everyday life, commands our respect and whose symbols evoke awe and make us feel and feel deeply. This commonsense understanding is also essentially the position on religion taken by the famous French sociologist Emile Durkheim (1858–1917).

Like Max Weber and Karl Marx, Durkheim is generally regarded as one of the foremost founding sociologists. Indeed, he is often regarded as the first true sociologist since his would-be competitors for this title never identified themselves as sociologists per se nor worked to define and establish an academic discipline called "sociology." But Durkheim did, and did so, at least in France, with considerable success.

In his last and perhaps most complex book *The Elementary Forms of Religious Life* (1912), Durkheim used his secondhand knowledge of so-called primitive tribal religious practices, which he acquired by reading anthropological description, to develop an explanation or theory of *all* religions, including modern religions.[2] The heart of Durkheim's theory is this: religion is not merely a social institution; it is the "eminently social" social institution.[3]

This idea cuts in two directions. In Durkheim's view, religions stand apart in that they lay claim to a sacred realm that transcends all things social; but religious forces are human forces or, what for Durkheim is the same thing, moral forces. Indeed, for Durkheim, "the idea of society is the soul of religion," which is to say, it is really society (and not some god) that is the true object of our awe and respect and that makes us feel and feel deeply.[4] It is society, not some god or spirit, that is sacred. It is society, experienced as a totality, that brings us to our knees. Durkheim wrote:

> The concept of totality is only the abstract form of the concept of society: it is the whole which includes all things, the supreme class which embraces all classes.
>
> At bottom, the concept of totality, that of society and that of divinity are very probably only different aspects of the same notion.[5]

For Durkheim, all religions are thus at base the same; "they respond to the same needs, they play the same role, they depend on the same causes." It also follows that so-called primitive religions are thus "no less respectable" than so-called advanced or modern religions and also that religion itself, as the face of society, is indeed a very special, sacred thing.[6]

Despite this special status of religion, even aspects of social life that are not in and of themselves religious contain elements of ritual and attention to the sacred and so borrow the form of religion for purposes that are not religious. The Super Bowl is not a religious event, nor is the singing of the national anthem. But these ritual aspects of American popular culture and nationalism borrow the sacred aura of religion.

In short, although they respect the sacred nature of religion, most sociologists (not all) understand religious institutions as social institutions, and most sociologists, like Durkheim, think that the religion of the Australian aboriginals and the religion of France have essentially the same social characteristics, the same basic social purposes, and the same origin in human social development. Furthermore, most sociologists understand social institutions as collective social enterprises requiring rituals to maintain their cohesiveness. . . .

Observable Patterns

Before we further analyze religious social institutions, it is helpful to clarify some basic empirical matters. There are roughly, as we have noted, 6 billion human beings in the world today. About 2 billion of these humans identify themselves as Christians. About 1 billion people are Muslims or adherents to the Islamic faith, followers of the God Allah and his prophet Mohammad. In other words, about one-half of the people in the world today are either Christian or Muslim. There are another roughly 1 billion people who are nonreligious. This is a diverse grouping, which includes but is not limited to atheists, free thinkers, and agnostics. Thus, two-thirds of the people in the world today are either Christian, Muslim, or nonbelievers. The remaining one-third, or 2 billion people, are primarily composed of Hindus, Buddhists, and adherents of various Chinese folk religions such as Taoism and Confucianism. There are, of course, many other very small religious groups. Sikhs, for example, account for roughly 0.4 and Jews 0.3 percent of the world population. Various tribal religions account for roughly two percent of the world's total.[7]

In the United States, the distribution of religious affiliation is quite different. Roughly eighty-six percent of Americans identify themselves as members of various Christian groups. Thus, whereas Christians make up only thirty-five percent of the world total, they are easily the dominant religious grouping in the United States. However, internal subdivisions are important in the U.S. Christian majority just as they are worldwide. Roughly fifty-nine percent of all Americans are Protestants, whereas only twenty-seven percent are Catholics. The remaining fourteen percent of Americans who are neither Protestant Christians nor Catholic Christians are composed of Jews, who represent roughly two percent of the U.S. total and other relatively small groups representing all the various religions of the world and people who do not view themselves as members of a religion.[8] . . .

Religious Institutions as Social Institutions

In examining religion, sociologists observe patterns such as those just described. Religious affiliation, participation, and the varying intensity of religious feeling—"religiosity"—are not randomly distributed across human populations. The United States is a predominantly Christian society, whereas Saudi Arabia is a predominantly Islamic society. The United States is a predominantly Protestant society, whereas Mexico is a predominantly Catholic society. American religiosity is greater than western European religiosity. What causes these patterns? To answer this question, sociologists step back from the worldview of any particular religion to grasp the whole of religious life in terms of the total history of human beings.

The vast majority of human existence, of course, transpired without any of today's religions being present. During the roughly ninety-nine percent of the time that humans have walked the earth as a distinct animal species, they have done so in gathering and hunting societies. These were small bands of people, probably numbering 20 to 50 members, who, among other things, spurned permanent settlement and practiced forms of what we would today call animistic religion. "Animism" is a concept that groups together diverse belief systems that share the idea that the world is inhabited and affected by supernatural spirits (e.g., tree spirits, bird spirits, buffalo spirits, rock spirits, ocean spirits, air spirits, the Great Spirit). But hunting and gathering societies and their animism are virtually extinct today. Most people today, especially the inhabitants of modern societies, do not swat a fly and feel as though they have killed a spiritual being. Most people do not see in rock and water anything other than inanimate objects there for human use and manipulation. Most people today do not, or at least do not seriously, practice magic, nor do they engage in ritual animal sacrifice. Nor do they worship totems, even if their favorite sports team is symbolized by one. This abandonment of animism is an important measure of the secularization—or disenchantment, despiritualization—of the world.

The largest of today's religious institutions, then, have a relatively short history. Roughly speaking, Judaism is 3,000 years old, the main Chinese folk religions are 2,500 years old, Christianity is 2,000 years old, and Islam is a mere 1,300 years old. More specific, the period from roughly 500 B.C. to roughly 300 A.D. is often described as "the axial age" of modern religious life because in this period there arose a tremendous revolution in human consciousness.[9] It was defined by a rapid movement away from animism and toward the idea of human-like gods (*pantheism*) and eventually to the idea of a single human-like god (*monotheism*). Today's dominant monotheistic religions, particularly Christianity, arose during or, in the case of Islam, shortly after this time. Why?

The American sociologist, Rodney Stark, provides one explanation for this development. In his book, *The Rise of Christianity* (1996), Stark poses the following question: "How did a tiny and obscure messianic movement from the edge of the Roman Empire dislodge classical paganism and become the dominant faith of Western civilization?"[10] In general, this was a time of relatively rapid human population increase, early urbanization, and the expansion of philosophically minded political empires, namely, the ancient Greeks and Romans. Stark argues, in particular, that Roman cities were characterized by widespread disease, poverty, and ethnic conflict.[11] Their inhabitants were suffering great hardships. Better than the established paganism and philosophies of the day, Christianity offered spiritual solace and encouraged material comfort for an expanding and suffering urban population. "It grew," wrote Stark, "because Christians constituted an intense community" that was "able to generate an 'invincible obstinacy'" to its would-be competitors and oppressors.[12] Stark estimates that the total number of Christians grew rapidly in the first 300 years of the first Christian millennium, from 0 to more than 30 million by the time that the Roman emperor, Constantine, made Christianity the official religion of the Roman Empire in 316 A.D.[13]

Christianity's subsequent status as the state religion of the Roman Empire also contributed mightily to its continuing success. Once ensconced in Western culture as the dominant religion, Christianity would wait another 1,500 years before the rise of modern European society would disperse its teachings the world over. Of course, Christianity also had to endure many internal conflicts, including the separation of Eastern and Western varieties and, at the dawn of the modern age, the *Protest*-ant Re-*formation*. Still, its worldwide prospects were rosy due to its being deeply embedded in a powerful type of society. Latin America is today predominantly Catholic because of its mainly Spanish colonizers, whereas the United States is, historically speaking, predominantly Protestant due to the hard-won political domination of Protestant English colonizers over their mainly French Catholic and Spanish Catholic rivals. The religion of the indigenous peoples in America, of course, was as ill-fated as was their entire way of life.

Once established and backed by overwhelming force, Christianity could reproduce itself through inculcation of new members born into affiliated families and through its close association with dominant political and cultural institutions. But Christianity also appeals to those who continue to suffer, as seen in its form as Latin America's "liberation theology." Likewise, Islam, Chinese folk religions, Judaism, and other modern religions share histories that are intimately bound up with the mundane facts of human social development. The sociologist who examines religious institutions worldwide sees similar developments in all human societies.

The success of religions at reproducing themselves today depends on maintaining their mass appeal while fitting themselves into the framework of modern political and cultural realities. Thus, in the United States, for example, roughly eighty percent of Roman Catholics believe that the use of contraceptives should be allowed within the Catholic Church, and as many as fifty percent reject the doctrine of papal infallibility.[14] A church that did not tolerate their deviation from official teachings would risk self-annihilation. Among members of the Jewish faith in the United States, more than a third choose to marry people who are not Jewish.[15] This, in its own way, threatens the reproduction of Judaism in this society, but it also bespeaks a modern cosmopolitanism. U.S. Protestants, in particular, have shown themselves adept at transcending the pulpit by using television to reinvigorate and expand their constituencies, filling the airwaves with broadcasts pitched to a postmodern audience. Whether the issue is dogma versus individual freedom, ethnocentrism versus cosmopolitanism, or old versus new technology, each of these religious groups demonstrates its adaptation to modern society.

Many religions have come and gone; their failure to produce cohesion among a founding group of followers and thereafter reproduce themselves more widely owed less to their intrinsic character than to their social and cultural environment. Religion may claim to stand apart from the workings of society and culture, but in its unavoidable form as a social institution composed of social groups participating in one or another culture or subculture, it clearly does not.

Consider the following self-reflection by one well-known American Protestant minister:

> *It is quite easy for me to think of a God of love mainly because I grew up in a family where love was central and where lovely relationships were ever present. It is quite easy for me to think of the universe as basically friendly mainly because of my uplifting hereditary and environmental circumstances. It is quite easy for me to lean more toward optimism than pessimism about human nature mainly because of my childhood experiences. It is impossible to get at the roots of one's religious attitudes without taking in account the psychological and historical factors that play upon the individual.*

In this statement, the author, who is most certainly a believer, concedes that one's socialization—that is, the learning process through which one acquires a distinctive selfhood through interaction with others and one's social environment as a whole—bears considerably on one's eventual religious make-up. In fact, the author wrote that his religious attitudes are mainly the result of his socialization. Social experience is, therefore, posited as a critical variable in religious self-development. This would mean that some societies or some groups encourage one type of religious development while others encourage something else. Therefore, the author of the statement is recognizing the sociocultural variability of religious attitudes.

Even if they are otherwise skeptical of the fruits of Western social science, sophisticated religious thinkers understand the importance of socialization for religious self-development. This is true even if they remain convinced that religion is not fully reducible to its social incarnation. Indeed, as we have noted, many sociologists are personally religious. Such is not as uncommon as one might expect. The reverse is also true: many religious thinkers are sociologically oriented. The author of the above autobiographical reflection is Dr. Martin Luther King, Jr., who, with these words, displayed less his notable belief in God and more his appreciation for an altogether secular sociological thinking. . . .

The Borderland between Faith and Reason

At this point, let us shift focus a bit and try to answer the questions posed at the outset of this chapter. It is one thing to empirically describe worldwide religious affiliations or to sketch historical change in religious practices and note a few ways that religion has been used to catalyze change or to conclude that religion is a social institution embedded in ongoing human cultures. These statements are really the stuff of ordinary, empirically oriented sociology. It is quite another thing, however, to return to the realm of the sacred and query religion's status and meaning for today's world. This is a subject that requires the sociological imagination because the sociological imagination is located at the crossroads of social structure, history, and biography— a point that is never fixed in any cognitive map alive to the always changing world—and thus transcends strictly empirical questions and observations. One can and should study facts about religion but that would always be an insufficient basis on which to erect any serious understanding of religion. Indeed, one can study *any* and *all* empirical trends and never develop even the rudiments of a truly sociological imagination.

Thus it is, perhaps, no surprise then that the main founders of sociology each viewed religion as extremely important. For Durkheim, all religions contain truth, the truth of society's importance over and above individuals; therefore, in his view, "there are no religions which are false."[17] For Marx religion is "the sentiment of a heartless world, and the soul of soulless conditions."[18] Marx meant that humans have projected their highest ideals and most humane values in the religious sphere of life. These ideals and values are, for Marx, rightly regarded as sacred and should be acted on with utter seriousness. In Weber's most widely read work, *The Protestant Ethic and the Spirit of Capitalism* (1904–05), he argues that the Protestant Reformation, a primarily religious affair, was critical for the birth of modern, Western society which is, ironically, an unprecedentedly secular form of society.[19]

The overarching irony is that neither Marx, Weber, nor Durkheim were themselves among the faithful. Instead, each viewed the claims that each and every particular religion makes for itself as essentially illusionary. For Marx, religion was "the sentiment of a heartless world" but also "the opium of the people," which is to say, a drug distributed by elites to the masses that promises them a false salvation and distracts people from the real possibilities for realizing in the here and now, as it were, the salvation of a heaven on earth. Weber spoke of the many and various clashes between the world's "gods and demons" and sarcastically remarked, "He who yearns for seeing should go to the cinema. . . ."[20] In *The Elementary Forms of Religious Life,* Durkheim wrote simply that "the old gods are growing old or already dead, and others are not yet born."[21]

But why were these classical sociologists (and many other intellectuals of their day) themselves nonbelievers? Perhaps a sociological answer is fitting. The nineteenth and early twentieth centuries, when these three men lived, was a time of rapid social change. This was a time when human beings were explicitly and systematically analyzing the power of society over the individual, realizing the interconnectedness of all living things (including natural forces but also far-flung human populations), and for the first time witnessing the explanatory power of natural and social science, which were revolutionizing the way humans would see the world, the "heavens," and the invisible forces that shaped and determined visible events in the world, natural or otherwise. Never before had humans been able to study all religions, for example, and never before had they the scientific sensibilities or means to discern the workings of natural and social forces. Another way of putting this is that never before had the totality been so revealed, the totality of nature and the totality of society within nature. This was the age of Charles Darwin, after all, and of Sigmund Freud. From natural evolution to the analysis of dreams, modern people were on the cusp of realizing, or so it seemed, the truth of all things.

Thus, while Durkheim was a child in a family that boasted a long line of rabbis, Weber had a mother who was a fervent Protestant, and Marx grew up in a family that was Jewish but whose father had converted to Protestantism for political reasons, none of these early socialization experiences could withstand the force of their learning as adults. For these three, at any rate, the power of religion to reproduce itself in the young was vanquished by the sobering effects of the new sciences of nature and of society. Thus they came to see sociology and religion as inherently opposed to one another. To them, religion represented the illusions of an irretrievable past and sociology represented the promise of enlightenment for an open and undefined future. . . . In this moment, not believing in a religion must have felt just as natural as believing once did for people of times past.

This nonbelieving was a significant contributor to the early development of the sociological imagination. To have ready-made answers to questions discourages the search for new answers. Why try to explain, for example, the causes of war if war and all manner of human "inhumanity" are already explained by the existence of "evil"? The ready availability and plausibility of nonscientific, transhuman answers thwarts the pursuit of empirical evidence in support of *social* theories or explanations. Furthermore, why try to promote the sociological imagination if history making is always and already under the control of a trans-social being, a god or a force, with a predetermined plan for human history? Why pursue the self-knowledge that the sociological imagination promises if the truly important relationship between the self and other exists in a sacred spiritual relationship with some great other who is not human and cannot be known in simple human terms? It would seem that, for the believer, social science in general and the sociological imagination in particular would have at the very least a curtailed significance. It certainly would lose any ultimate significance because it would be trumped by a form of knowing that purports to transcend what can be known by means of simple, human knowing. . . .

ENDNOTES

[1] Irving Louis Horowitz, ed., *Power, Politics & People: The Collected Essays of C. Wright Mills* (Oxford, U.K.: Oxford University Press, 1963), 6.

[2] Emile Durkheim, *The Elementary Forms of Religious Life,* trans. Joseph Ward Swain (1912; reprint, New York: Free Press, 1965).

[3] Ibid., 22.

[4] Ibid., 466.

[5] Ibid., 490.

[6] Ibid., 15.

[7] *The World Almanac and Book of Facts 2000* (Mahwah, N.J.: Primedia Reference, 2000), 659.

[8] U.S. Census Bureau, *Statistical Abstract of the United States, 1999* (Washington, D.C., 1999), 71, table 89.

[9] See Stephen K. Sanderson, *Macrosociology: An Introduction to Human Societies,* 4th ed. (New York: Longman, 1999), especially pp. 370–3.

[10] Rodney Stark, *The Rise of Christianity: A Sociologist Reconsiders History* (Princeton, N.J.: Princeton University Press, 1996), 3.

[11] Ibid., especially pp. 156–8.

[12] Ibid., 208.

[13] Ibid., 7.

[14] Giddens and Duneier, *Introduction to Sociology,* 422–3.

[15] Ibid., 423.

[16] Martin Luther King, Jr. from "Autobiography of Religious Development" (Crozer Theological Seminar, 1949). Available at www.triadntr.net/rdavis/mlkqts.htm

[17] Durkheim, *The Elementary Forms of Religious Life,* 15.

[18] Marx wrote: "*Religious* suffering is at the same time an *expression* of real suffering and a *protest* against real suffering. Religion is the sigh of the oppressed creature, the sentiment of a heartless world, and the soul of soulless conditions. It is the *opium* of the people." See Marx, "Contribution to the Critique of Hegel's *Philosophy of Right:* Introduction," in *The Marx-Engels Reader,* ed. Robert C. Tucker, 2d ed. (New York: Norton, 1972), 54, emphases in original.

[19] Max Weber, *The Protestant Ethic and the Spirit of Capitalism* (1904 and 1905; reprint, New York: Charles Scribner's Sons, 1958).

[20] Ibid., 29.

[21] Durkheim, *The Elementary Forms of Religious Life,* 475.

46

MUSLIMS IN AMERICA

JEN'NAN GHAZAL READ

Americans have many misperceptions about the Islamic religion and about Muslims living in America. Muslim Americans are not a monolithic group, nor are they necessarily uniformly religious and devout. This selection is by Jen'nan Ghazal Read, a professor in the Sociology Department and Global Health Institute at Duke University. Read also is a Carnegie Scholar studying the political, cultural, and economic integration of Muslim Americans and Arab Americans in the United States. This reading provides a demographic overview of the 2 to 8 million Muslims living in America. While two-thirds of Muslim Americans are immigrants, an increasing number are converts among the native-born population. In addition, Read argues that, while Muslim Americans tend to be highly educated, fluent in English, and politically conscious, they are very diverse in terms of their social and political views.

Seven years after the terrorist attacks on U.S. soil catapulted Muslims into the American spotlight, concerns and fears over their presence and assimilation remain at an all-time high.

Recent national polls find that four in 10 Americans have an unfavorable view of Islam, five in 10 believe Islam is more likely than other religions to encourage violence, and six in 10 believe Islam is very different from their own religion. All this despite the fact that seven in 10 admit they know very little about Islam. And yet Americans rank Muslims second only to atheists as a group that doesn't share their vision of American society.

These fears have had consequences. In 2001, the U.S. Department of Justice recorded a 1,600 percent increase in anti-Muslim hate crimes from the prior year, and these numbers rose 10 percent between 2005 and 2006. The Council on American-Islamic Relations processed 2,647 civil rights complaints in 2006, a 25 percent increase from the prior year and a 600 percent increase since 2000. The largest category involved complaints against U.S. government agencies (37 percent).

Clearly, many Americans are convinced Muslim Americans pose some kind of threat to American society.

Two widespread assumptions fuel these fears. First, that there's only one kind of Islam and one kind of Muslim, both characterized by violence and antidemocratic tendencies. Second, that being a Muslim is the most salient identity for Muslim Americans when it comes to their political attitudes and

Jen'nan Ghazal Read, "Muslims in America," *Contexts*, Vol. 7, No. 4, pp. 39–43. November, 2008.

behaviors, that it trumps their social class position, national origin, racial/ethnic group membership, or gender—or worse, that it trumps their commitment to a secular democracy.

Research on Muslim Americans themselves supports neither of these assumptions. Interviews with 3,627 Muslim Americans in 2001 and 2004 by the Georgetown University Muslims in the American Public Square (MAPS) project and 1,050 Muslim Americans in 2007 by the Pew Research Center show that Muslim Americans are diverse, well integrated, and largely mainstream in their attitudes, values, and behaviors.

The data also show that being a Muslim is less important for politics than how Muslim you are, how much money you make, whether you're an African American Muslim or an Arab American Muslim, and whether you're a man or a woman.

The notion that Muslims privilege their Muslim identity over their other interests and affiliations has been projected onto the group rather than emerged from the beliefs and practices of the group itself. It's what sociologists call a social construction, and it's one that has implications for how these Americans are included in the national dialog.

Some Basic Demographics

Let's start with who Muslim Americans really are. While size estimates of the population range anywhere from 2 million to 8 million, there is general agreement on the social and demographic characteristics of the community.

Muslim Americans are the most ethnically diverse Muslim population in the world, originating from more than 80 countries on four continents. Contrary to popular belief, most are not Arab. Nearly one-third are South Asian, one-third are Arab, one-fifth are U.S.-born black Muslims (mainly converts), and a small but growing number are U.S.-born Anglo and Hispanic converts. Roughly two-thirds are immigrants to the United States, but an increasing segment is second- and third-generation, U.S.-born Americans. The vast majority of immigrants have lived in the United States for 10 or more years.

Muslim Americans also tend to be highly educated, politically conscious, and fluent in English, all of which reflects the restrictive immigration policies that limit who gains admission into the United States. On average, in fact, Muslim Americans share similar socioeconomic characteristics with the general U.S. population: one-fourth has a bachelor's degree or higher, one-fourth lives in households with incomes of $75,000 per year or more, and the majority are employed. However, some Muslims do live in poverty and have poor English language skills and few resources to improve their situations.

One of the most important and overlooked facts about Muslim Americans is that they are not uniformly religious and devout. Some are religiously devout, some are religiously moderate, and some are nonpracticing and secular, basically Muslim in name only, similar to a good proportion of U.S. Christians and Jews. Some attend a mosque on a weekly basis and pray every day, and others don't engage in either practice. Even among the more

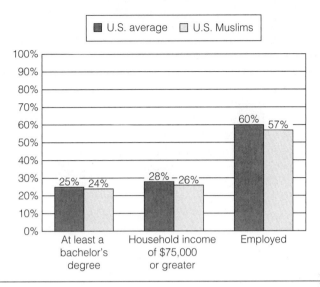

FIGURE 46.1   Socioeconomic Characteristics of American Muslims

religiously devout, there is a sharp distinction between being a good Muslim and being an Islamic extremist.

None of this should be surprising. Many Muslim Americans emigrated from countries in the Middle East (now targeted in the war on terror) in order to practice—or not practice—their religion and politics more freely in the United States. And their religion is diverse. There is no monolithic Islam that all Muslims adhere to. Just as Christianity has many different theologies, denominations, and sects, so does Islam. And just like Christianity, these theologies, denominations, and sects are often in conflict and disagreement over how to interpret and practice the faith tradition. This diversity mimics other ethnic and immigrant groups in the United States.

Evidence from the MAPS project, Pew Research Center, and General Social Survey demonstrates that Muslim Americans are much more politically integrated than the common stereotypes imply. Consider some common

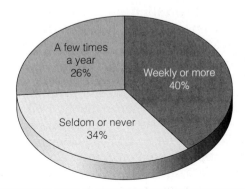

FIGURE 46.2   American Muslim Mosque Attendance

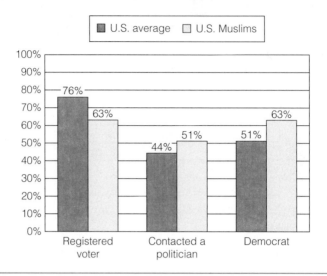

FIGURE 46.3   Political Involvement of American Muslims

indicators of political involvement, such as party affiliation, voter registration, and contact with politicians. Compared to the general public, Muslim Americans are slightly less likely to be registered to vote, reflecting the immigrant composition and voter eligibility of this group (63 percent compared to 76 percent of the general population), slightly more likely to have contacted a politician (51 percent compared to 44 percent of the general population), and slightly more likely to affiliate with the Democratic Party, which falls in line with other racial and ethnic minorities (63 percent compared to 51 percent of the general population).

All these data demonstrate that, contrary to fears that Muslim Americans comprise a monolithic minority ill-suited to participation in American democracy, Muslim Americans are actually highly diverse and already politically integrated. They are also in step with the rest of the American public on today's most divisive political issues.

Attitudes, Values, and Variation

The majority of both Muslim Americans (69 percent) and the general public (76 percent) oppose gay marriage, favor increased federal government spending to help the needy (73 percent and 63 percent, respectively), and disapprove of President George W. Bush's job performance (67 percent and 59 percent). Muslim Americans are slightly more conservative than the general public when it comes to abortion (56 percent oppose it, compared to 46 percent) as well as the federal government doing more to protect morality in society (59 percent compared to 37 percent).

The one area in which American Muslims are not entirely in step with the general public is foreign policy, especially having to do with the Middle East. In 2007, for example, the general public was nearly four times as likely

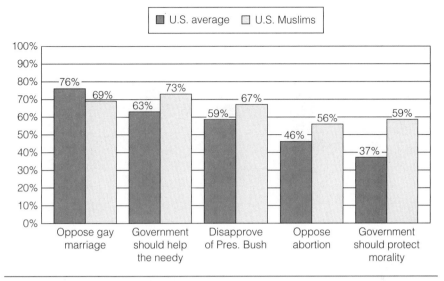

FIGURE 46.4   Views on Social and Domestic Issues

to say the war in Iraq was the "right decision" and twice as likely to provide the same response to the war in Afghanistan (61 percent compared to 35 percent of Muslim Americans).

In short, these numbers tell us that Muslim Americans lean to the right on social issues (like most Americans), but to the left on foreign policy. But these generalizations don't tell the whole story—in particular, these averages don't demonstrate the diversity that exists within the Muslim population by racial and ethnic group membership, national origin, socioeconomic status, degree of religiosity, or nativity and citizenship status.

Consider, for example, Muslim Americans' levels of satisfaction and feelings of inclusion (or exclusion) in American society—major building blocks of a liberal democracy. In examining how these perceptions vary by racial and ethnic group membership within the group, we see that African American Muslims express more dissatisfaction and feel more excluded from American society than Arab or South Asian Muslims. They're more likely to feel the United States is fighting a war against Islam, to believe Americans are intolerant of Islam and Muslims, and to have experienced discrimination in the past year (whether racial, religious, or both is unclear). South Asians feel the least marginalized, and Arab Muslims fall in between. These racial and ethnic differences reflect a host of factors, including the immigrant composition and higher socioeconomic status of the South Asian and Arab populations and the long-standing racialized and marginalized position of African Americans. Indeed, many (though not all) African Americans converted to Islam seeking a form of religious inclusion they felt lacking in the largely white Judeo-Christian traditions.

(Incidentally, most African American Muslims adhere to mainstream Islam [Sunni or Shi'a], similar to South Asian and Arab Muslim populations. They should not be confused with the Nation of Islam, a group that became popular during the civil rights era by providing a cultural identity that

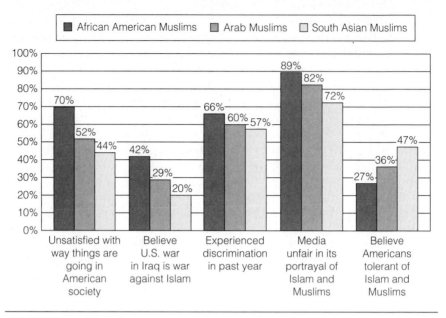

FIGURE 46.5   Diversity among American Muslims

separated black Americans from mainstream Christianity. Indigenous Muslims have historically distanced themselves from the Nation of Islam in order to establish organizations that focus more on cultural and religious [rather than racial] oppression.)

Before we can determine whether religion is the driving force behind all Muslims' political opinions and behaviors—whether Islam, as is popularly assumed, trumps Muslim Americans' other commitments and relationships to nationality, ethnicity, race, and even democracy—let's step back and place Muslim Americans in a broader historical context of religion and American politics.

When Religion Matters, and Doesn't

Muslim Americans aren't the first religious or ethnic group considered a threat to American's religious and cultural unity. At the turn of the 20th century, Jewish and Italian immigrants were vilified in the mainstream as racially inferior to other Americans. Of course today those same fears have been projected onto Hispanic, Asian, and Middle Eastern immigrants. The Muslim American case shares with these other immigrant experiences the fact that with a religion different from the mainstream comes the fear that it will dilute, possibly even sabotage, America's thriving religious landscape.

Yes, thriving. By all accounts, the United States is considerably more religious than any of its economically developed Western counterparts. In 2000, 93 percent of Americans said they believed in God or a universal spirit, 86 percent claimed affiliation with a specific religious denomination, and 67 percent reported membership in a church or synagogue. The vast majority of American adults identify themselves as Christian (56 percent Protestant and 25 percent Catholic), with Judaism claiming the second largest group of adherents (2 percent), giving America a decidedly Judeo-Christian face. There are an infinite number of denominations within these broad categories, ranging from the ultra-conservative to the ultra-liberal. And there is extensive diversity among individuals in their levels of religiosity within any given denomination, again ranging from those who are devout, practicing believers to those who are secular and nonpracticing.

This diversity has sparked extensive debates among academics, policymakers, and pundits over whether American politics is characterized by "culture wars," best summarized as the belief that Americans are polarized into two camps, one conservative and one liberal, on moral and ethical issues such as abortion and gay rights. Nowhere has the debate played out more vividly than the arena of religion and politics, where religiously based mobilization efforts by the Christian right helped defeat liberal-leaning candidates and secure President Bush's reelection in 2004. Electoral victories, however, haven't usually translated into policy victories, as evidenced by the continued legality of abortion and increasing protection of gay rights. So when does religion matter for politics and when doesn't it?

Here we come back to the Muslim American case. Like Muslim Americans, Americans generally have multiple, competing identities that shape their political attitudes and behaviors—93 percent of Americans may believe in God or a universal spirit but 93 percent of Americans don't base their politics on that belief alone. In other words, just because most Americans are religiously affiliated doesn't mean most Americans base their politics on religion. To put it somewhat differently, the same factors that influence other Americans' attitudes and behaviors influence Muslim Americans' attitudes and behaviors. Those who are more educated, have higher incomes, higher levels of group consciousness, and who feel more marginalized from mainstream society are more politically active than those without these characteristics. Similar to other Americans, these are individuals who feel they have more at stake in political outcomes, and thus are more motivated to try to influence such outcomes.

Muslims, on average, look like other Americans on social and domestic policies because, on average, they share the same social standing as other Americans, and on average, they are about as religious as other Americans. Consider two common indicators of religiosity, frequency of prayer and frequency of church attendance, and compare Muslim Americans to Christian Americans. Both groups are quite religious, with the majority praying everyday (70 percent of Christians compared to 61 percent of Muslims) and a sizeable proportion attending services once a week or more (45 percent compared to 40 percent). And they look similar with respect to attitudes on gay rights and abortion, in part because Christian and Muslim theology take similar stances on procreation and gender roles.

Again, these numbers tell only part of the story. What's missing is that religion's relationship to politics is multidimensional. In more complex analyses it has become clear that the more personal dimensions of religious identity—or being a devout Muslim who prays every day—have little influence on political attitudes or behaviors, which runs counter to stereotypes that link Islamic devotion to political fanaticism.

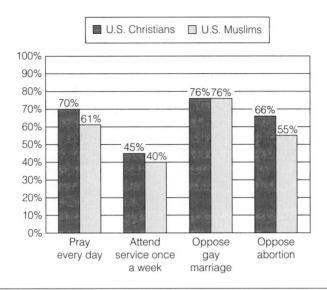

FIGURE 46.6 American Muslims Compared to Christians

In contrast, the more organized dimensions of Muslim identity, namely frequent mosque attendance, provide a collective identity that stimulates political activity. This is similar to what we know about the role of the church and synagogue for U.S. Christians and Jews. Congregations provide a collective environment that heightens group consciousness and awareness of issues that need to be addressed through political mobilization. Thus, it is somewhat ironic that one of the staunchest defenders of the war on terror—the Christian right—may be overlooking a potential ally in the culture wars—devout Muslim Americans.

An Exceptional Experience

In many ways these findings track closely with what we know about the religion-politics connection among other U.S. ethnic and religious groups, be they Evangelical Christians or African Americans. They also suggest that the Muslim experience may be less distinct than popular beliefs imply. In fact, Muslim Americans share much in common with earlier immigrant groups who were considered inassimilable even though they held mainstream American values (think Italian, Irish, and Polish immigrants).

At the same time, though, we can't deny that the Muslim American experience, particularly since 9/11, has been "exceptional" in a country marked by a declining salience of religious boundaries and increasing acceptance of religious difference. Muslim Americans have largely been excluded from this ecumenical trend. If we're going to face our nation's challenges in a truly democratic way, we need to move past the fear that Muslim Americans are un-American so we can bring them into the national dialogue.

RECOMMENDED RESOURCES

Anny Bakalian and Mehdi Bozorgmehr. *Backlash 9/11: Middle Eastern and Muslim Americans Respond* (University of California Press, 2009). One of the comprehensive assessments of the experiences of Middle Eastern Americans in the aftermath of 9/11.

Clem Brooks and Jeff Manza. "Social Cleavages and Political Alignments: U.S. Presidential Elections, 1960 to 1992," *American Sociological Review* (1997) 62: 934–946. A sociological framework for understanding how social group memberships, such as gender and race, impact Americans in presidential elections.

Nancy Foner. *In a New Land: A Comparative View of Immigration* (New York University Press, 2005). A thorough historical, comparative account of immigration in the United States.

Gary Gerstle and John Mollenkopf, eds. *E Pluribus Unum? Contemporary and Historical Perspectives on Immigrant Political Incorporation* (Russell Sage Foundation, 2001). This edited volume places contemporary immigration politics in historical and comparative context.

Ted J. Jelen. "Religion and Politics in the United States: Persistence, Limitations, and the Prophetic Voice," *Social Compass* (2006) 53: 329–343. A useful overview of the U.S. religion-politics connection situated in comparison to other Western, industrialized nations.

HEALTH AND MEDICINE

47

INSTITUTIONS, INTEREST GROUPS, AND IDEOLOGY
An Agenda for the Sociology of Health Care Reform

JILL QUADAGNO

Medical sociology is one of the largest and fastest growing sub-specialties within the discipline of sociology. Medical sociologists are concerned with all aspects of the social institution of medicine, including the socialization of doctors, the social construction of health and illness, and the social structure of hospitals and the health care system. Given current evidence from a variety of sources, there is no doubt that the United States has a health care system in crisis. The following three readings illustrate different sociological perspectives about health and illness in the United States. The first reading is by Jill Quadagno, a professor of sociology in the Pepper Institute on Aging and Public Policy at Florida State University. In this excerpt, taken from a 2010 research article in the *Journal of Health and Social Behavior*, Quadagno examines how social institutions and ideologies in society affect the organization of health care and, ultimately, will determine whether the United States can successfully change its health care system.

Jill Quadagno, "Institutions, Interest Groups, and Ideology: An Agenda for the Sociology of Health Care Reform." *Journal of Health and Social Behavior,* S1(2): 125–136. Copyright © 2010 American Sociological Association. Reprinted by permission of Sage Publications, Inc.

All Western, industrialized nations are facing similar challenges associated with population aging, changing family structure, increasing labor force participation of women, and expanding public budgets. These trends have important consequences for health care systems. Population aging creates massive numbers of frail, older people who need long-term care and help managing activities of daily living, while declining fertility and more dual-earner households reduce the number of family members who can provide this help. As expenditures for health care rise, governments are forced to make unpopular choices about how to allocate resources between competing needs for medical care, education, and other social goods.

In the United States, health care currently consumes one-eighth of national resources and is the largest item in many state budgets. It is also the largest single business expense for many employers, with average family premiums rising by 131 percent between 1999 and 2009. Some firms responded by dropping health benefits to employees. In 1999, 66 percent of all firms offered health benefits, compared to just 60 percent ten years later. Among small firms the decline in coverage has been more severe, with 62 percent offering health benefits in 1999 but only 46 percent by 2009 (Kaiser Family Foundation 2009). Other companies have continued to offer benefits but have shifted more of the cost burden to employees. Even firms that offer generous health insurance to regular employees increasingly use contract workers hired through "temp" agencies to perform specific tasks. Since these workers are not technically employees, they are not entitled to fringe benefits.

Problems in the health care system have a ripple effect throughout the economy. The burden of paying for medical care is a gnawing source of economic insecurity for families. Nearly half of people who file for bankruptcy do so because of illness or injury and loss of resultant wages (Thorne and Warren 2008). The recession that began in 2008 has exacerbated the problem, as millions of people lost their jobs and their health benefits. Some hospitals have been forced to close due to tighter credit, higher borrowing costs, investment losses, and an increase in destitute patients.

In the 2008 election Barack Obama promised to reform the health care system, despite many other pressing national needs: wars in Iraq and Afghanistan, the largest budget deficit in history, historic levels of unemployment, and billions lost in pension savings and housing wealth. To some critics this promise seemed like folly. Yet poor economic conditions and wars have not deterred other presidents from embarking on ambitious social initiatives. The crowning achievement of Franklin Roosevelt's New Deal, the Social Security Act of 1935, was enacted in the midst of a deep economic crisis. In the 1960s Lyndon Johnson waged a War on Poverty and committed the federal government to a program of health insurance for the aged despite a budgetary crisis and an escalating war in Vietnam. What the current period has in common with these earlier eras is an acceptance of the role of government as a major actor, a strong emphasis on planning, and a president elected with a wide popular mandate and a commitment to social reform (Lipset 1996).

In March of 2010 President Obama kept the promise he had made during his 2008 presidential campaign. Initially it seemed that he would be defeated, after Senate Democrats lost a seat in a special election held in Massachusetts to fill a vacancy created by the death of Senator Ted Kennedy, who ironically was a lifelong champion of universal coverage. Then, like a phoenix rising from the ashes, the House Democrats passed the bill, which the president signed into law on March 23, achieving a feat that had stymied other presidents since the 1930s. What was left in its wake was a fertile source of data for sociologists. Sociologists are uniquely qualified to analyze policy outcomes, because sociological theory recognizes that health care systems are shaped by historical precedents and embedded in larger institutions and specific cultural contexts (Light 2004). Sociologists also understand that although health care systems are bound by policy legacies, embedded constituencies, and path-dependent processes, they are not rigid, static, and impervious to change. A key question, then, is how existing health care systems respond to new needs. In addition, an important related question concerns the strategies that allow health care systems to transcend their institutional and ideological limits. In this article, I consider the ways institutions, interest groups, and ideology have affected the organization of the health care system in the United States as well as in other nations. I then discuss opportunities for sociological analysis that this era of restructuring will bring.

Institutions

Health care systems consist of organizations that both deliver care and medical services (hospitals, physicians' practices, clinics) and that arrange for the financing of care (governments, agencies, states, local communities, and private insurance companies). These organizations are embedded within welfare states, which are based on particular institutional logics and distributional principles that restructure class relations in specific ways (Esping-Andersen 1999). For example, welfare states vary in the extent to which they target benefits to the poor rather than grant universal benefits to all as a right of citizenship. They also vary in scope, with some nations having a wide array of programs and others lacking core benefits, such as with the case of national health insurance in the United States (Korpi and Palme 1998). Such variation has intrigued social scientists, who have sought to devise typologies for classifying nations based on their welfare strategies.

Welfare State Regimes

The most frequently cited welfare state typology was developed by Esping-Andersen (1990) who identified three distinct regime types in western nations; each has a different effect on the class structure. "Social democratic" regimes provide extensive welfare benefits granted to all as a right of citizenship, with private benefits having only a marginal place. The primary exemplars of this strategy are the Scandinavian countries of Sweden, Norway, and Finland. "Conservative" regimes are found in Catholic countries and are more concerned with supporting the traditional family and maintaining hereditary status relationships. Countries in this category include France,

Germany, Italy, and Austria. Finally, "liberal" welfare states are characterized by extensive reliance on means-testing, a preference for the market over the state, and government subsidies to encourage private welfare. The United Kingdom, Canada, Australia, and the United States are typically considered liberal welfare states. Although other social scientists have modified these categories somewhat, or added additional types that include non-Western nations, the basic typology has endured (Arts and Gelissen 2002). . . .

The American Welfare State

In all typologies based on pension characteristics, the United States is the archetype of the liberal welfare state. Its income security programs include universal benefits for workers granted as an earned right, notably Social Security and Disability Insurance, but also poverty-based benefits where eligibility is determined by a means-test, Temporary Assistance for Needy Families (TANF) being the primary example. Most distinctive about the American welfare state is the heavy emphasis on private with employer-based pensions, which are partially publicly funded through tax subsidies (Howard 2007).

The U.S. health care system has several distinctive features, including the lack of universal coverage but also relatively generous benefits for people 65 and older, means-tested benefits for the poor, and employment-based benefits for working-age adults. In many respects, this organizational structure replicates the income security system. Like Social Security, Medicare is a universal benefit funded by a payroll tax on workers and employers with eligibility determined by previous work history. Consistent with a liberal welfare state, however, Medicare does not cover all health-related expenses; rather, it leaves a lucrative "medigap" market for private insurers. Also unlike Social Security, where the federal government makes direct cash payments to beneficiaries, in Medicare, private insurance companies make payments to providers. A consequence of this structure is that it creates numerous constituencies with a vested interest in preventing benefit cuts and advocating for additional services.

Medicaid, the federal state program of health insurance for the very poor and the permanently disabled, typifies the poverty-based focus of a liberal welfare state. Yet Medicaid also covers the medically indigent, people who are not totally destitute but whose medical expenses exceed their income (Grogan and Patashnik 2003). Further, since Medicaid was enacted, it has expanded well beyond a poverty-based structure through waivers that allow states to experiment without meeting strict federal rules and regulations (Kail, Quadagno, and Dixon 2009). States have used Medicaid waivers to achieve broad program changes outside of the legislative process. Among the measures adopted are higher income levels, more generous asset tests, and the incorporation of groups that are not categorically eligible (Schneider 1997; Ku and Garrett 2000).

Programmatic Medicaid expansions have also occurred through the State Children's Health Insurance Program (SCHIP), enacted in 1997. The SCHIP increased federal funds to the states to cover low-income children (Cunningham 2003), and it also allowed states to use SCHIP funds to cover uninsured parents (Kaiser Commission on Medicaid and the Uninsured

2005). The incentive of a larger federal match encouraged some states to create generous SCHIP programs for both children and low-income adults. In 2008, New Jersey's SCHIP program covered children in families with income up to 350 percent of the poverty level; Connecticut, Missouri, and Vermont covered children up to 300 percent. Thus, Medicaid is not only a means-tested benefit for the poor and near-poor; it also funds health care for a substantial number of children and adults who are not poor (Kail et al. 2009).

The U.S. health care system also includes private health insurance that is subsidized by the tax system. Employers are allowed to write off contributions for employee health insurance premiums as a tax-deductible business expense and employees are relieved from having to pay taxes on health benefits received (Howard 1997). The private insurance system is also divided between large, self-insured firms and smaller businesses and individuals that purchase health benefits from commercial insurance companies. These forms of coverage differ in how they are regulated and how benefits are taxed, and the constituents they support frequently differ on policy preferences (Quadagno 2005). Thus, although the U.S. health care system is consistent with a liberal welfare state regime in some respects, the fit is imperfect and more complex than implied by that simple model. . . .

Interest Groups and Social Movements

The institutions that make up the health care system in the United States, as well as in other nations, have been produced through political struggles between opposing interests. In some instances, the objective has been to correct a perceived injustice. In the 1910s, for example, Progressive activists and labor leaders condemned insurance companies and demanded greater government regulation of private insurance (Hoffman forthcoming). In the 1960s civil rights groups supported the drive for Medicare and then fought for racial equality in access to hospitals (Smith 1999). In the 1990s the AIDS activist movement ACT UP organized to fight insurers' discrimination against people with AIDS, then expanded its agenda to demand the inclusion of women, children, and AIDS victims in government-funded research (Epstein 2007).

In other instances, the goal has been to protect existing advantages. For example, when President Jimmy Carter introduced a plan for an across-the-board cap on hospital charges in 1979, the Federation of American Hospitals (FAH), the organization of for-profit hospitals, formed a coalition to defeat him. The FAH created a national steering committee to coordinate activities in the states, mailed thousands of letters to every hospital administrator in the country, and devised an alternative "voluntary" cost containment plan. The Carter plan never made it out of the Senate Finance Committee (Quadagno 2005).

Although privileged groups have often led health care campaigns to protect their various market positions, they have found it advantageous in some instances to form coalitions with the less privileged. A prime example is the managed care movement, which took off in the early 1980s when large companies such as General Motors hired managed care firms to rein in health care costs. As these firms instituted cost containment measures, they angered physicians, who resented the threat to their cultural authority, and frustrated patients, who felt they received callous treatment or were unjustly denied services (Mechanic 2004). In the mid-1990s physicians joined with patient groups to wage war against managed care. They lobbied state legislatures to regulate HMOs, filed class action suits against managed care firms, and demanded patients' rights. In response, states enacted a flurry of measures prohibiting HMOs from denying claims for emergency room use, requiring hospitals to allow patients at least minimal stays following childbirth, and giving patients the right to sue when denial of treatment resulted in injury or death (Mechanic 2004; Quadagno 2005). Thus, what appeared superficially to be a spontaneous citizen movement actually reflected the mobilization of advocacy organizations, especially those involving physicians. . . .

Social movements have also mobilized in health care debates to defend core principles and beliefs. President Bill Clinton's plan for universal health care would have required all health plans to cover abortion, effectively nullifying the laws of 37 states that restricted state funding of abortion. In response, a coalition of religious groups launched a massive campaign against it, lobbying legislators, distributing postcards and letters through churches, and developing a national media campaign. The U.S. Conference of Catholic Bishops initiated a letter-writing campaign opposing that feature of the bill. Other conservative Christian groups, including the Southern Baptist Convention, the Christian Coalition, and Concerned Women for America vehemently opposed the entire plan but roused their constituents around abortion (Quadagno and Rohlinger 2009). Some scholars attribute the defeat of Clinton's health care plan to the opposition of the health insurance industry and small business organizations, which hired thousands of lobbyists and public relations firms and spent more than $140 million in the effort to defeat it (Quadagno 2004, 2005). Others emphasize the institutional characteristics of the American state with its numerous veto points (Hacker 2002). However, the grassroots opposition stirred up by religious conservatives was also an important factor.

Ideology

Health care systems are not only organized around social structures and political institutions; they also incorporate values and ideologies from the larger culture. While these ideologies provide core principles under which health care systems operate, they exist "within a specific framework of politics, organization, power, and money" (Stevens 2007:223). As a result, health care systems devoted to similar principles still vary considerably in how they are funded and administered and in how medical services are distributed. Alternatively, health care systems based on different value systems may, nonetheless, adopt similar characteristics due to the similar organizational and environmental challenges they face (Mechanic and Rochefort 1996). These include the development of science and new technologies, limits on resources, the diffusion of cultural patterns, and the increase in consumer knowledge about medical care options.

The Principle of Social Solidarity: Health Care as a Right

In many European countries health care systems are devoted to the principle of social solidarity. Social solidarity refers to an ideological framework with both moral and operational dimensions. As a moral concept, solidarity is based on an understanding that individuals and groups share common risks and that citizens of a community are obligated to care for each other in times of hardship (Keen, Light, and Mays 2001). In operation, solidarity has three dimensions: risk solidarity, income solidarity, and scope solidarity. Risk solidarity means that premiums should be unrelated to health risk, that each member of the group should have access to health insurance, and that the cost of disease and medical care should be distributed across all members of the group. Income solidarity emphasizes that premiums (or contributions) should be related to ability to pay and should thus vary with income. Finally, scope means that members are entitled to receive a comprehensive package of benefits (Maarse and Paulus 2003).

Although the solidarity principle reflects specific ideals, it takes many different forms. In Sweden the central government uses tax revenues to fund health services supplemented by state grants and user co-payments. The government also sets the regulatory framework. However, regional political units called county councils administer the system and are responsible for operating the hospitals and for providing care to all citizens at subsidized costs. In Germany coverage is financed through contributions by employers and employees and obtained through the labor market. The only criterion for eligibility is employment, with nonworking spouses and children covered through their partner or parent. Germany has no state-run health insurance program or government-run national health system. However, participation in sickness funds is mandatory, risk-rating is prohibited, and insurance plans are heavily regulated. Premiums are based on wages or income, not on health risk, and everyone is covered (Amelung, Glied, and Topan 2003).

The Market Principle: Health Care as a Commodity

An alternative vision, prominent in the United States, is that health care is not a right. Busch (2008–2009) articulates the most common rationale for this arrangement:

> Modern liberalism has staked much on the notion that health care is a right. . . . Clearly, however, health care is not a natural right as the founders or John Locke would have understood it. . . . There is no evidence that they considered provision of health care necessary for realizing natural rights. . . . The great danger of health-care-as-a-right is that it threatens to supplant the American republic's key political principles. Accepting a positive government obligation to fund social services claimed as a matter of right would lead inexorably to government without limits. (p. 15)

Similarly, columnist Jonah Goldberg (2009) claims that, "Health care cannot be a right because rights cannot come from government" (p. 10A).

Those who oppose the idea that medical care is a right argue instead that it is a commodity, to be bought and sold like any other market good. This concept, health care as commodity, is reflected in both private and public health benefits. It is most evident in health insurance plans sold to individuals and small groups where the profit motive dominates. In these plans the insurer establishes premiums based on the health risk represented by each policyholder or group. Until the 2010 health care reform was enacted, insurers could refuse to cover some diseases and exclude preexisting conditions entirely (Light 1992). The market principle is also reflected in the hospital sector where the objective of for-profit hospitals is to maximize revenues and avoid uninsured patients (Relman 2009).

Public health insurance programs also contain elements of the market principle. As noted above, for-profit private insurance companies are allowed to sell profitable supplemental "medigap" policies for services not included in Medicare. More recently, the Medicare Modernization Act of 2003 provided incentives for beneficiaries to switch from traditional Medicare to private, for-profit managed care plans (Hacker 2006).

On the other hand, the solidarity principle is also present in both public and private health benefits. Medicare is based on the understanding that old age is a shared risk for families and individuals across the life course. It is funded by people of working age who willingly pay because they recognize that they, too, will grow old one day (Cook and Barrett 1992). The solidarity principle is also present in the community-rated plans offered by large firms. Community rating distributes costs widely, sets premiums unrelated to health risk, and provides all group members access to health care (Glied 2005).

Further, the American public responds positively to messages emphasizing social solidarity. For example, during the 2008 election, focus group research conducted for the Obama campaign found that the public responded most positively to messages that emphasized social solidarity, and that they rejected the idea that health care was a commodity:

> We need a guarantee of quality, affordable health care for all of us. We need to set and enforce the rules so insurance companies put our health care before their profits. (Lake 2008)

However, the same study also revealed that people feared the threat of socialism and supported consumer choice:

> His [Obama's] plan . . . will be just another big government bureaucracy, like the IRS, operating inefficiently and costing taxpayers hundreds and billions of dollars. . . . Instead of a big government program to bring socialized medicine to America, we need to give consumers more of their own money back and more options to choose the health insurance plan that's right for them. (Lake 2008)

These examples make it clear that the U.S. health care system includes a mix of principles and does not reside within a single ideological framework.

In some cases, solidarity predominates; in others, the market rules. This ambivalence provides ammunition for critics of greater government involvement but it also provides a rationale for universal coverage.

Health Care Systems in Transformation

The debate over health care reform that has recently taken place, not only in the United States but in all Western nations, is fundamentally a question of how to balance private needs with public budgets. Many nations have also begun restructuring the way medical care is funded and delivered (Hacker 2006). On the one hand, any nation's options are limited by its existing structure, which suggests continuing diversity. On the other hand, similar environmental conditions may narrow available options, resulting in convergence (Mechanic and Rochefort 1996). At issue is how organizational contexts influence opportunities for restructuring. Some of the issues involved have already been addressed in the restructuring of pension programs. What is uncertain is whether health care reforms are following the same principles driving pension reform. . . .

Health Care Reform in the United States

The health care system in the United States is facing the same problems that European nations have already begun to address. The challenge was how to enact reform within the context of the existing network of public and private benefits while satisfying the numerous constituencies surrounding them. The health care reform debate of 2009–2010 highlighted the relevance of institutions, interest groups, and ideology in understanding the dynamics of policymaking in the United States.

One of the most controversial issues was the public option, which would offer an alternative to private insurance in a competitive market. This was the proposal most vehemently opposed by private insurance companies, who feared that a new public program could out-compete private insurance on price and quality (Harwood 2009).

The industry launched a campaign on Capitol Hill against it, grounded in a study published by the Lewin Group, a health policy consulting firm that is owned by one of the largest insurers, UnitedHealthGroup. The lobbyists contended that a government-run plan, which would have favorable tax and regulatory treatment, would undermine the private insurance industry. Leading insurers, including UnitedHealth, urged their employees around the country to speak out. Company "advocacy hot line" operations and sample letters and statements were made available to an army of industry employees in nearly every congressional district. At town hall meetings held by members of Congress home for the August recess, boisterous critics mobilized attacks on the as-yet-unspecified plan, reinforced by conservative radio talk show hosts like Glenn Beck and Sean Hannity. Some insurers supplemented the effort with local advertising, often designed to put pressure on specific members of Congress. Late in the spring, Blue Cross and Blue Shield of North Carolina prepared advertisements attacking the public option (Hamburger and Geiger 2009). The final bill included no public option.

Another debate concerned the future of the employment-based system. In the United States the system of private health benefits for working age adults was constructed at a time when a Fordist model of the life course predominated. Fordism represented an image of continuous work with a single employer and a guarantee of income and health security. It was incorporated into the trade unions' collective bargaining agreements in rigid seniority systems, and it guaranteed automatic cost-of-living increases and a package of benefits protecting workers against the hazards of unemployment, old age, and illness. Although the Fordist promise was always an ideal type and never available to all workers, especially women and minorities, it became the standard for unionized manufacturing workers, public sector employees, and some service jobs, especially at upper management levels (Quadagno, Hardy, and Hazelrigg 2003).

As the concept of lifetime employment began to erode in the 1970s, it has become normative for most people to work for multiple employers over the life course. The problem is that health benefits remain tied to the employment contract, even as employers' commitment to providing them has waned. Yet employment-based benefits are difficult to restructure because they have generated a constituency of trade unions and employer associations that monitor all efforts to modify the tax structure that sustains them. However, there are also opponents, notably commercial insurers, who would like to weaken the tax subsidy and expand the individual insurance market (Quadagno and McKelvey 2008). They lobbied for policies to eliminate the preferential tax status of employer-based plans and adopt health savings accounts coupled with a basic policy to cover catastrophic medical expenses. The result would "level the playing field" between the self-insured firms and the commercial insurance companies that provide coverage for individuals and small groups (Jost 2007; Quadagno and McKelvey 2008).

To demonstrate their willingness to compromise, the organizations representing commercial insurers were willing to accept guaranteed issue without preexisting condition exclusions and no lifetime caps on coverage if these regulations were accompanied by an individual mandate. An individual mandate would expand the market by bringing young, healthy people into the system to help pay the costs of older, sicker people. Under these conditions, insurers will do quite well. They would have a very stable pool of customers, they would have people receiving government subsidies to help them purchase coverage, and they would be paid the full costs of the benefits that they provide plus their administrative costs (Hamburger and Geiger 2009). The final bill included stringent regulations on insurers coupled with the bonus of the individual mandate.

A third controversy arose in the 2009 health care reform debate over whether federal funds would be used to pay for abortions, either directly or through subsidies to insurance companies. When the House of Representatives was debating its bill, Catholic bishops worked behind the scenes to lobby for abortion restrictions. To win the support of pro-life Democrats, the president promised to sign an Executive Order banning the use of federal funds to pay for elective abortion. Thus, institutions, interests groups, and ideology all shaped the outcome of reform.

Conclusion

The restructuring of health care systems is occurring all over the world, creating a rich source of data for sociologists and other health policy scholars. There is, first, the landscape of institutional structures, which will invariably be altered by the massive health care reform bill of 2010. At the most macro level, the issues concern whether the concept of welfare state regime is useful in understanding health care reform and to what extent institutional legacies lock in particular policy options. Within the United States analyses of the health care reform debate should focus on how existing institutional structures influenced the course of the debate. For example, any expansion of Medicaid has important implications for the state agencies that administer the program, on state budgetary priorities and on the stance of governors. Given the contentious discussions over regulations of the insurance industry, what role did the insurance industry play in the final measure? Sociologists are inherently interested in determining whose interests might be furthered by any legislation and why some groups fail while others succeed in achieving their objectives. Of particular relevance for sociological theory is what activities, strategies, and tactics lead to a favorable outcome for a particular group. There is also the issue of how the reform debate was affected by the power structure within the insurance industry between the self-insured firms and the commercial insurers that operate in the small group market. Another topic of interest is how the media portrayed interest group activities.

Finally, there is the question of how ideology was employed in the debate surrounding health care reform. As we have seen, the U.S. health care system was not created around a single ideology, such as social solidarity, or even a core principle that health care is a right. Rather, an alternative ideology asserts that health care is a commodity, that patients are consumers, and that government benefits represent socialism. Both these views exist in public opinion and within the structure of both public and private benefits. The only certainty is that the analysis of health care reform and its consequences provides a fruitful agenda that involves this entire institutional and ideological legacy.

ACKNOWLEDGMENTS

I thank David Mechanic and an anonymous reviewer for helpful comments on an earlier draft of this article.

REFERENCES

Amelung, Volker, Sherry Glied, and Angelina Topan. 2003. "Health Care and the Labor Market: Learning from the German Experience." *Journal of Health Politics, Policy and Law* 28 (4):693–714.

Arts, Wilhelmus and John Gelissen. 2002. "Three Worlds of Welfare Capitalism or More? A State-of-the-Art Report." *Journal of European Social Policy* 12(2):137–58.

Busch, Andrew E. 2008–2009. "Is Health Care a Right?" *Claremont Review of Books* (Winter): 14–17. Retrieved November 4, 2009. (http://www.claremont.org/publications/crb/).

Cook, Fay Lomax and Edith Barrett. 1992. *Support for the American Welfare State.* New York: Columbia University Press.

Cunningham, P. J. 2003. "SCHIP Making Progress: Increased Take-Up Contributes to Coverage Gains." *Health Affairs* 22(4): 163–72.

Epstein, Steven, 2007. *Inclusion: The Politics of Difference in Medical Research.* Chicago, IL: University of Chicago Press.

Esping-Andersen, Gosta. 1990. *The Three Worlds of Welfare Capitalism.* Cambridge, England: Polity Press.

———. 1999. *Social Foundations of Postindustrial Economies.* New York: Oxford University Press.

Glied, Sherry. 2005. "The Employer-Based Health Insurance System: Mistake or Cornerstone?" Pp. 37–52 in *Policy Challenges in Modern Health Care,* edited by D. Mechanic, L. Rogut, D. Colby, and J. Knickman. New Brunswick, NJ: Rutgers University Press.

Goldberg, Jonah. 2009. "Obamacare Is a Simple Bait-and-Switch." *Tallahassee Democrat,* July 27, p. A10.

Grogan, Colleen and Eric Patashnik. 2003. "Between Welfare Medicine and Mainstream Entitlement: Medicaid at the Political Crossroads." *Journal of Health Politics, Policy and Law* 28(5):821–58.

Hacker, Jacob. 2002. *The Divided Welfare State.* Cambridge, England: Cambridge University Press.

———. 2006. *The Great Risk Shift.* New York: Oxford University Press.

Hamburger, Tom and Kim Geiger. 2009. "Healthcare Insurers Get Upper Hand." *Los Angeles Times,* October 24, p. A1.

Harwood, John. 2009. "The Lobbying Web." *New York Times,* August 2, Opinion WK 1, 4.

Hoffman, Beatrix. Forthcoming. "The Challenge of Universal Health Care: Social Movements, Presidential Leadership, and Private Power." In *Social Movements and the Transformation of American Health,* edited by M. Zald, S. R. Levitsky, and J. Banaszak-Holl. New York: Oxford University Press.

Howard, Christopher. 2007. *The Welfare State Nobody Knows.* Princeton, NJ: Princeton University Press.

Jost, Timothy. 2007. *Health Care at Risk: A Critique of the Consumer-Driven Movement.* Durham, NC: Duke University Press.

Kail, Ben Lennox, Jill Quadagno, and Marc Dixon. 2009. "Can States Lead the Way to Universal Coverage? The Effect of Health Care Reform on the Uninsured." *Social Science Quarterly* 90(5): 1–20.

Kaiser Commission on Medicaid and the Uninsured. 2005. *Medicaid Section 1115 Waivers: Current Issues: Key Facts, January 2005.* Washington, DC: The Kaiser Family Foundation.

Kaiser Family Foundation. 2009. "Employer Health Benefits: 2009 Summary of Findings." Retrieved September 23, 2009 (http://ehbs.kff.org/pdf/2009/7937).

Keen, Justin, Donald Light, and Nicholas Mays. 2001. *Public-Private Relations in Health Care.* London: King's Fund.

Korpi, Walter and Joakim Palme. 1998. "The Paradox of Redistribution and Strategies of Equality: Welfare State Institutions, Inequality and Poverty in the Western Countries." *American Sociological Review* 63:661–87.

Ku, L. and B. Garrett. 2000. "How Welfare Reform and Economic Factors Affected Medicaid Participation: 1984–1996." Urban Institute Discussion Paper No. 16, The Urban Institute, Washington, DC.

Lake, Celinda. 2008. "Health Care in the 2008 Election." Presented at the National Congress on Health Care Reform, September 24, Washington, DC.

Light, Donald. 1992. "The Practice and Ethics of Risk-Rated Insurance." *Journal of the American Medical Association* 267:2503–2508.

———. 2004. "Ironies of Success: A New History of the American Health Care System." *Journal of Health and Social Behavior* 45(Extra Issue): 1–24.

Lipset, Seymour Martin. 1996. *American Exceptionalism.* New York: W.W. Norton.

Mechanic, David. 2004. "The Rise and Fall of Managed Care." *Journal of Health and Social Behavior* 45(Extra Issue):76–86.

Mechanic, David and David Rochefort. 1996. "Comparative Medical Systems." *Annual Review of Sociology* 22:239–70.

Quadagno, Jill. 2004. "Why the United States Has No National Health Insurance: Stakeholder Mobilization Against the Welfare State, 1945–1996." *Journal of Health and Social Behavior* 45(Extra Issue) :25–44.

———. 2005. *One Nation, Uninsured: Why the U.S. Has No National Health Insurance*. New York: Oxford University Press.

Quadagno, Jill, Melissa Hardy, and Lawrence Hazelrigg. 2003. "Labour Market Transitions and the Erosion of the Fordist Lifecycle: Discarding Older Workers in the Automobile Manufacturing and Banking Industries in the United States." *Geneva Papers on Risk and Insurance* 28(4): 640–51.

Quadagno, Jill and Brandon McKelvey. 2008. "The Transformation of American Health Insurance." Pp. 10–31 in *Health Care at Risk: Expert Perspectives on America's Ailing Health System—and How to Heal It*, edited by J. Hacker. New York: Columbia University Press.

Quadagno, Jill and Deana Rohlinger. 2009. "Religious Conservatives in U.S. Welfare State Politics." Pp. 236–66 in *The Western Welfare State and Its Religious Roots*, edited by K. van Kersbergen and P. Manow. New York: Cambridge University Press.

Relman, Arnold. 2008. "The Health Care Industry: Where Is It Taking Us?" Pp. 280–86 in *The Sociology of Health and Illness*, edited by P. Conrad. New York: Worth Publishers.

Schneider, S. K. 1997. "Medicaid Section 1115 Waivers: Shifting Health Care Reform to the States." *Publius* 27(2):89–109.

Smith, David B. 1999. *Health Care Divided: Race and Healing a Nation*. Ann Arbor: University of Michigan Press.

Stevens, Rosemary. 2007. *The Public-Private Health Care State*. New Brunswick, NJ: Transaction.

Thorne, Deborah and Elizabeth Warren. 2008. "Get Sick, Go Broke." Pp. 66–87 in *Health At Risk: America's Ailing Health System—And How to Heal It*, edited by J. Hacker. New York: Columbia University Press.

48

SAND CASTLES AND SNAKE PITS

LILLIAN B. RUBIN

How should society treat the mentally ill? For decades, sociologists have researched this question, resulting in such classic studies as Erving Goffman's *Asylums* (1961) and David L. Rosenhan's "On Being Sane in Insane Places" (Reading 6). Today, the deinstitutionalization movement has meant that fewer mentally ill people are hospitalized; instead, they are more likely to be treated with psychotropic drugs on an outpatient basis. In this selection, Lillian B. Rubin, an internationally known sociologist and writer, examines the unintended consequences of public policies, which have led to an increase in the homeless population generally, and to an increase of mentally ill people among the homeless.

The walk from my home on top of San Francisco's Nob Hill down to my studio at its bottom is a lesson in class and status in America. As each few blocks take me down another rung on the socioeconomic ladder, I move from the clean, well-tended streets at the summit through increasingly littered, ill-kept neighborhoods where property values decrease as the numbers of potholes and homeless people increase. At the bottom of the hill sits the notorious "Tenderloin," a district that houses what the Victorians called "the lower orders," where the desperate and the dangerous hang on every street corner waiting for the local food kitchen to open its doors.

Three blocks later, I'm downtown looking at the visible signs of gentrification—an upscale shopping mall featuring the recently opened Bloomingdale's West Coast flagship store and an Intercontinental Hotel under construction next door. From there I pass into the more industrial parts of the city, where my studio sits in an old warehouse building, an entrance to the freeway on one corner and St. Vincent de Paul's homeless shelter—the biggest in the city—on the other.

How did this, the richest nation in the world, give birth to an enormous population of people who live on the streets or in shelters—men, women, and children, impoverished, desperate, and very often mentally ill? Three-quarters of a million Americans in 2005, [a] recent national estimate, without a place to call home—a reckoning that most experts agree is far too low because it includes only those they could find to count. How did homelessness become so pervasive that a college student in the class on poverty in America I taught a few years ago couldn't conceive of a world without "the homeless"?

Are you saying there didn't used to be homeless? he asked, bewildered. *They've always been there, all my life,* he continued, as other students nodded assent. How is it that even those of us who remember a time when homelessness was something that happened in India, not here in these United States, have become so inured to the sight of people living on the street that we walk past and around them without really seeing them?

Maybe it takes a few years of working next door to people without homes to see them, not as an undifferentiated mass—"the homeless"—but as men and women (mostly men) with whom I share a greeting when I arrive in the morning, people with names and faces and hard-luck stories. They're unclean, unkempt, and with a bone-deep weariness that seems to seep out of their pores, yet someone offers help when he sees me struggling to manage more than I can comfortably carry up the stairs. And once, when I tripped and fell, another picked me up off the sidewalk, wiped the blood off my face (never mind that he pulled a filthy rag of a handkerchief out of his pocket to do the job), and despite my protests, refused to leave until he saw me safely to my destination.

Homelessness in America isn't new, but it had a distinctly different flavor and meaning in earlier times. Then, homelessness was a transient phenomenon, generally tied to a sudden seismic event or the cycles of the economy. The Great Depression, for example, spawned a "hobo" population, mostly men from rural and urban communities who wandered from one part of the country to another in a fruitless search for work that didn't exist. But when the depression lifted and the economy brightened, they found jobs and homes. American cities, too, have always had pockets of homelessness, the skid row "bums" in neighborhoods like the Bowery in New York, "West Madison" in Chicago, the Tenderloin in San Francisco where the poor, the transient, the sick sought escape, and where alcoholics, still clutching the bottle, could be seen sleeping on the streets. But modern homelessness isn't just about "bums" or "hobos," nor is it confined to some small out-of-sight corner of the city. Instead, it's on our streets and in our face and, for those of us who live in any major city in the country, it's an inescapable fact of life.

They're black and brown and less often white; they're usually single and mostly men. For some being without a home is episodic, the result of an illness, an injury, a layoff, or for some of the women, domestic violence. The problem clears, and they're back on their feet—at least until the next time. But for hundreds of thousands of Americans, homelessness is a near-permanent, chronic condition from which there is currently no real escape.

The large structural forces that have changed the face of homelessness are no mystery: an increasingly stratified society with little opportunity for the unschooled and unskilled, a minimum wage that doesn't approach a living wage, unemployment and underemployment, cuts in public assistance, and urban rents that continue to rise well beyond what an unskilled worker can afford. But all of these together would not have created the scale of the problem we now face without the aid of two major public policy initiatives: the Housing Act, passed by Congress in 1949, and the Community Mental Health Centers Act, signed into law by President John F. Kennedy in 1963— good ideas with lofty goals, whose unintended consequences we see in the legions of homeless on the streets of our cities today.

In the landmark Housing Act of 1949, Congress declared that every American deserves a "decent home and a suitable living environment" and instituted a complex set of provisions to achieve that goal. For the growing post–World War II middle class, the increased authorization for the Federal Housing Administration (FHA) mortgage insurance (known as Title II) was a bonanza that helped millions realize the dream of home-ownership. But for the poor, Title I, which called for an urban redevelopment program, became a disaster when its stated intent—to provide federal funds to upgrade decaying inner cities—fell victim to greedy local governments and the developers in their employ. Urban renewal, as it was known, soon became little more than an excuse for "poor removal" as bulldozers and wrecking balls demolished entire neighborhoods, some of them home to poor but vital communities, others featuring the shabby tenements, boardinghouses, and dilapidated hotels that offered single-room occupancy (SRO) housing to the poor, the lonely, the debilitated, the ill, and the drug addicts. And despite a provision (Title III) that committed the federal government to building 810,000 new public housing units—another policy that experience has shown created at least as many problems as it solved—local, state, and federal governments looked the other way as urban renewal, with its promise of increased land values, quickly came to replace concerns for housing, and far more living units were destroyed than were built.

This isn't to say that urban renewal was a failure for everyone. Not by a long shot. Parts of many inner cities did, indeed, become more attractive, as blighted neighborhoods were cleared for such amenities as hotels, shops, cultural centers, and even small patches of green. But in the game of winners and losers, it's no surprise that only the poor lost. The developers lined their pockets. Local governments reaped the reward of increased land values as the new steel, concrete, and glass towers attracted business that brought jobs and revenue to the city. The glossy high-rise condominium buildings that rose in place of rundown homes, tenements, and SROs brought the affluent, who had fled to the suburbs decades earlier, back to the city where they could now live in style and comfort while enjoying the convenience of having Macy's, Neiman Marcus, a bank branch, and the city's cultural offerings at their doorstep. Only the poor and the sick were left with no place to go, except into the streets or the public housing projects that now look and are more like prisons for the poor than the "decent home and suitable living environment" Congress declared as every American's right.

Lest anyone think urban renewal is a thing of the past, I'll be happy to take them on a tour of the projects under way in my hometown of San Francisco or, if that's too far to go, to direct them to a *New York Times* article of June 16, 2007, whose opening words tell the story: "For nearly three decades, Charlotte Johnson witnessed the drug dealing and violence on the streets in front of her modest row house in East Baltimore. She rode it out only to face a new challenge today—the community's transformation under the largest planned urban renewal in the country, which could soon drive her out of the neighborhood."

Step back to the past again, to 1963 and the Community Mental Health Centers Act, a historic piece of legislation whose good intentions would set the stage for yet another social debacle. The American mental health reform movement has a long and not very successful history. In 1868, after Elizabeth Packard was released from an asylum to which her husband had committed her some years earlier, she founded the Anti-Insane Asylum Society and published a series of pamphlets describing her experiences. Shocking as her tale was, her entreaties for public attention fell on deaf ears, because most people then still believed that madness was the result of demonic possession.

Forty years later, Clifford W. Beers's *A Mind That Found Itself* was somewhat more successful in stimulating public interest, but it would be several more decades before *The Snake Pit*, a film starring Olivia de Havilland, opened in 1948 to a stunned American audience. Everyone knew, of course, that there were insane asylums, places where crazy people were locked up so the rest of us could sleep easily at night. But it is testimony to the power of film that the visual images woke the American conscience in ways that hundreds of thousands of written words had not. Suddenly, the "insane" were not just some undifferentiated mass, they were women and men hidden from view in human warehouses, held in the care of sadistic guards, shackled to walls in dungeonlike cells, and subjected to torturous "treatments"— immersed in tanks of ice water, spun in chairs for hours, secluded naked in isolation rooms, restrained in straitjackets or cuffed hand and foot to a bed in spread-eagled position, force-fed medications, shocked with high volts of electricity to the brain, and lobotomized—all by psychiatrists who knew little about the cause or relief of their symptoms.

Still, the mental health reform movements didn't gain any real traction until the mid-1950s, when the development of psychotropic medications gave promise of symptom relief, if not a cure, for some of the worst of the mental ailments. Although the new drugs were not without significant, and often dangerous, side effects, thousands of patients were taking them and, by the end of the decade, people who would once have been committed to asylums for life were managing to live outside them and tell their stories.

The hope the new medications brought, coupled with the various rights movements that were roiling society in the 1960s, set the stage for the emergence of a vigorous patients' rights movement, led largely by former hospital patients and their families. They offered a stinging critique of institutional psychiatry that was instrumental in discrediting the practices and treatments that had turned hospitals into snake pits, called for an end to involuntary commitment, and demanded that patients have a voice in their treatment.

The presidency of John F. Kennedy gave the reform movement a big lift when his family made their private pain public with the announcement that a family member had been mentally ill and institutionalized for years. With increasing pressure from the reformers and the backing of a sympathetic president, Congress passed the Community Mental Health Centers Act in 1963, which sought to create an alternative to institutionalization in state mental hospitals by developing a system of mental health centers that would focus on preventive, community-based outpatient care.

What happened? It's always easier for the federal government to spell out good ideas than it is to put up the hard cash necessary to make them work. So perhaps the simplest explanation is that the road to hell is paved with unfunded and underfunded government programs. Still, there's rarely a single cause to explain either the success or failure of a policy initiative.

As the social and political background changed in the decades following the passage of the Community Mental Health Centers Act, the good intentions that brought it into being faded away. The Vietnam War was a continuing drain on the public purse. Tax revolts and antigovernment ideologies of both the right and the left blossomed in the 1970s, which, together with the recession of the early 1980s, further weakened both the government's coffers and its resolve. Ronald Reagan's election to the presidency in 1980 turned a budding conservative movement into a full-scale revolution that changed the American social and political landscape for decades to come. All these played a part in restricting federal funding for social programs, including mental health, so that by the mid-1980s the regional funding model the 1963 law promised—never enough even at the beginning—was scaled back, and mental health services shifted once again to state and local levels until now, when federal funds support only about 2 percent of total state mental health budgets.

But long before federal funds dried up, the states played their part in turning a good idea into a fiasco. Until the new law, mental health care was the province and the burden of the states. When the federal government entered the picture with a plan for community care and the promise of funds to support it, it was a gift that offered states relief from the enormous financial costs of supporting a large hospitalized patient population. Not surprisingly, therefore, state and local officials spoke the language of mental health advocacy and community care, but they acted on their concern for fiscal policy. Without waiting for the promise of the law to become a reality, they jumped on the deinstitutionalization bandwagon and transferred tens of thousands of mentally ill women and men, many who had spent years in confinement, to communities that had no way to support their care.

Before long, the few Community Mental Health Centers (CMHCs) that existed were overwhelmed by demands they simply couldn't meet. It was a devastating experience for both the patients and the professionals. *We had no choice but to turn people out into the street,* one veteran of the time recalls. *The state hospital, the place of last resort, was gone; there were no halfway homes, no treatment programs, nothing.* Yet deinstitutionalization continued, ultimately closing nearly half the hospitals in the country and dramatically reducing bed capacity in those that are left, leaving uncounted tens of thousands of people to fend for themselves.

Although thousands of deinstitutionalized patients made a more or less successful transition to life outside the hospital, living with families or in adult group homes where they existed, many others fell through the cracks—and are still falling. For serious mental illnesses such as schizophrenia and bipolar disorder are not a one-time problem that can be cured with a pill. Even patients who seem to be doing well need regular monitoring and counseling if they're not to slip and fall. Moreover, welcome as each new generation of psychotropic drugs has been, they are no free lunch for the men and women who must live on them to maintain their sanity. For along with the gift of gaining some control over the delusions of schizophrenia or the excessive mood swings of bipolar disorder, come side effects that can range from such discomfiting problems as weight gain and blurred vision, to serious and sometimes irreversible neuromotor difficulties with Parkinsonian symptoms that can disfigure a life.

In addition to physical side effects that can be almost as disabling as the disease itself, drugs that alter the mind also alter consciousness in ways that challenge a person's experience of self. Patients often complain that they "feel different," that, as one person said to me some years ago, *I feel like a stranger to myself*—feelings that drive a very large proportion of the mentally ill to stop taking the drugs, which inevitably throws them into crisis.

Ask any family with a schizophrenic or bipolar member, and you'll hear stories about the weird and sometimes dangerous behavior that suddenly appears when the patient secretly stops taking medication. Listen to them speak of the difficulty of finding their way through the chaotic maze of uncoordinated public agencies that is now our mental health system, only to fail because there are no beds or community services available. Hear their agony as they describe what it's like to find a loved one living on the street and be helpless to do anything about it.

In the recent uproar about the Virginia Tech shootings, the executive director of the Virginia Commission on Mental Health Reform was asked why a young man who had been diagnosed as "mentally ill and in need of hospitalization" wasn't either hospitalized or closely monitored in an outpatient setting before he walked onto the campus and killed thirty-two people. His reply? *The system doesn't work very well.* An understatement of breathtaking proportions.

Whether homelessness or crazed killing sprees, they don't happen because "the system doesn't work very well," but because it's broken, not just in Virginia but throughout the land. The Virginia Tech shooter wasn't closely monitored by mental health professionals because, whatever the services his community may say it offers, there simply are never enough resources or staff to provide them. Homelessness isn't an accident or an artifact of some strange modern urban disease, but a product of failed social policy. It got its first big push when urban renewal destroyed poor neighborhoods without offering adequate housing alternatives. Deinstitutionalization shoved it even harder when the plan to provide community-based mental health services turned out to be an empty promise, starved of funds even before the first patients were sent off to find their unsteady way into communities that had no services or facilities for them. And while all this was happening, the patients' rights movement won victories in the legislatures and the courts (including the United States Supreme Court in 1999 in *Olmstead v. L.C.*) that make it virtually impossible to hold someone with serious and sometimes dangerous mental problems involuntarily for more than a few days without proof, certified by a court, that the person is an immediate threat to society and/or to self—a test that isn't easy to meet absent violence or proof of intent to commit it.

You think it's a problem, just try living with it, sighed the director of a clinic with whom I spoke recently about the mental health problems of the homeless.

> *We try, but we don't have the staff or the resources. And even if I could find a bed for some of the worst of them—which, frankly, I usually can't—if they don't want to go, the law won't let me hold them for more than seventy-two hours no matter how crazy they are. So what's the point? You knock yourself out to find a place where maybe, just maybe, they can get help, and a couple of days later, they're back out on the street.*

True, but even for those who are amenable to treatment, the best any mentally ill homeless person is likely to get these days is a bed to rest in just long enough for the doctors to find the right drug regimen to stabilize a crisis. After that he or she is back out into the community with no services, no follow-up, and no place to live—a revolving door that never stops turning.

The result? About 500,000 of the 750,000 homeless Americans, men and women who are sick, desperate, and without hope, presently live in shelters or on the streets because of some form of mental illness. Yes, there are other social and economic forces that have contributed to the rise of homelessness. But the virtual epidemic we know today wouldn't exist without the fallout from two historic public policy initiatives: the Housing Act of 1949 that set urban renewal in motion and the Community Mental Health Centers Act of 1963 that sought to reform the mental health system—both well-intentioned, if flawed, good ideas that fell victim to the law of unintended consequences.

Do we conclude then that good intentions don't matter, that, as conservatives would have it, it's the nature of government to make a mess of even the best ideas, and that, therefore, we need less and less government intervention, no matter what the intent? I don't think so. True, government is not always as efficient as we'd like it to be. It's too cumbersome, too often unprepared for the unforeseen consequences of its actions, too slow to correct its mistakes, and our legislators are too often more beholden to special interests than to the common good. But even in a pluralist democracy like ours, where legislation is the product of compromise and negotiation that can subvert the framers' good intentions, it doesn't always happen that way, as the Social Security and Medicare programs aptly demonstrate. Not that they're perfect, not that the compromises made to ensure their passage haven't left their mark. But compare the successes of the original single-payer Medicare program to the recent Medicare Prescription Drug Benefit—a complicated bureaucratic nightmare that relies on the private sector to provide insurance. Despite the fact that our costs exceed anything government-insured programs spend in countries that offer better, cheaper, and more complete drug coverage, Medicare Part D, as the drug benefit is known here, has brought far more benefit to the insurance companies and their pharmaceutical allies than to the old and the sick.

How, then, do we avoid the unintended consequences that can cause the kind of social dislocation and personal pain I've described here? Perhaps we can't; perhaps it's in the nature of the system—any system—that we can't always foresee the pitfalls until we tumble into them. But the problems of legislation such as the Medicare Prescription Drug Benefit should remind us that it isn't government's attempts at reform that need to be curbed but the influence of corporate America on the legislative process. Indeed, recent experience—the turn to the private sector for what earlier had been part of the public trust, the many revelations of corporate malfeasance, greed, and incompetence—suggests that only the willfully blind can continue to insist that the government has no place in reform and that the private sector will always do it better and cheaper.

49

A SLOW, TOXIC DECLINE
Dialysis Patients, Technological Failure, and the Unfulfilled Promise of Health in America

KEITH WAILOO

One important aspect of medical sociology is the study of social inequalities caused by the distribution and treatment of certain illnesses. That is to say, how do *morbidity* (rates of sickness) and *mortality* (rates of death) vary among people of different races, genders, and social class backgrounds? In the United States, social inequality is particularly evident in the distribution of renal failure and dialysis patients among poor and minority populations and the availability of resources for treatment. Nowhere was this inequity more evident than in New Orleans after Hurricane Katrina displaced thousands of people and created a massive health crisis for hospitals, nursing homes, and outpatient clinics, which lost electrical power and access to dialysis machines after the storm. In the selection below, Keith Wailoo, a medical historian, who is a professor at Princeton University jointly appointed in the Department of History and the Woodrow Wilson School of Public and International Affairs, describes the horrific consequences of the social inequities he saw concerning this health crisis after Hurricane Katrina. This excerpt, taken from the 2010 book, *Katrina's Imprint: Race and Vulnerability in America,* examines how U.S. government and medical officials responded to the critical needs of dialysis patients before, during, and after the massive storm and power outage caused by Hurricane Katrina.

Hurricane Katrina made private illness experiences and health vulnerabilities shockingly public, and nothing more graphically captures this fact than the drama surrounding dialysis patients in the days after the storm. Their commonplace and everyday problems were thrown open to deeper scrutiny, framed as a metaphor for the tragic moment and, as I shall argue, a metaphor for the nation's unfulfilled political and economic commitments. Many commentators rightly connected the story of these patients to the uneven and endemic health vulnerabilities that long predated the storm. "How many of the dead will turn out to be dialysis patients?" asked one expert. One July 2007 study answered that "the best guess is that of over 5,800 Gulf Coast dialysis patients affected by Katrina, 2.5 percent died in the month after the storm—although given the high mortality rate among dialysis patients, it is difficult to determine how many deaths were storm-related."[1] Commentaries placed dialysis squarely in the center of political analysis. In one ironic letter in the *San Diego Union Tribune,* the writer voiced deep disdain for the delayed and incompetent federal response: "And across the ocean in his supposed cave, I can picture Osama bin Laden, who can manage to get dialysis while, on Thursday, Charity Hospital in New Orleans had only fruit punch to offer its patients."[2] In this telling, the story epitomized government's broken promise to its most needy citizens.

This [reading] examines what the appearance of dialysis patients in the story of Katrina reveals about race, health, region, and the nation's commitments. In the hours and days following the storm, diabetics and patients whose kidneys had failed and who depended on dialysis technology figured prominently in news coverage. They were unable to move themselves out of harm's way for want of transportation and further immobilized because of their health challenges. "Thousands of victims of Hurricane Katrina face homelessness and devastation," announced the National Kidney Foundation, "but kidney patients without access to dialysis treatment face life-threatening danger."[3] They needed what had become over the previous two decades a standard medical treatment to cleanse their blood, but the instrument itself depended on clean water, running electricity, and medical staff and facilities. Many of these patients were diabetics whose kidneys had failed. Requiring regular dialysis treatments, such people found themselves stranded in airports, in homes, in the Superdome—tethered to a city without electricity and lacking medical services—suffering from a slow, toxic demise as impurities built up in their bodies. This small subset of victims symbolized a peculiarly American kind of vulnerability arising from poor access in a technology-rich environment. Among the most vulnerable of the vulnerable, they became—along with the elderly in nursing homes, the residents of Charity Hospital, the cancer patients, and other infirm citizens of the region—a graphic symbol of Katrina's toll. One Washington, D.C.–based kidney specialist predicted in the *Washington Post* on September 13, 2005, "It's going to take months, if not years, to actually find out what proportion of the dead were actually dialysis patients."[4]

As one physician in the Tulane University Department of Nephrology later stated, the dialysis machines were part of a more extensive technological system that failed: "I had a group of about seven or eight patients that we needed to take care of, then we got ten additional patients from the Superdome brought by the police, and a few people walked into the ER needing dialysis," . . . [but in the immediate wake of the storm] "we didn't have enough water pressure." At first, only two machines could be run, but then "about six or seven hours later we lost the pressure completely."[5] The other problem for such patients was that, even if the pressure returned, the water was not potable. And clean water was also essential for running these machines that do the essential work of the kidneys—removing toxins from the blood that build up slowly in the course of normal life. As another New Orleans specialist later noted, "People didn't understand the extent to which they were a special needs population."[6] In these stranded patients, even those who were evacuated "were very worse off for the trip they had to make under the conditions. . . . People were lined up [for example] waiting for machines up in Baton Rogue."[7]

These people's predicaments were powerful reminders of health promises unfulfilled in America. They were a subset of Louisiana's many health problems, which included low immunization rates; high rates of stroke, diabetes, and heart disease; and deteriorating public health infrastructure.[8] All of these problems had social origins. Susceptibility to kidney failure, for example, had grown over the decades, making the population more and more dependent on dialysis. And since the early 1970s, the federal government had sanctioned a special relationship between patients and dialysis through a law granting universal access to the technology. It was, then, a technology with a unique place in the health care system—a federally mandated entitlement for citizens if their kidneys failed. Thus the dialysis story in Katrina was not merely a local crisis; it was in some sense a national one. But the federal guarantee of dialysis meant little if water, electricity, equipment, and cooperation in the social delivery of care did not exist.

Dialysis patients turned up as a recurring leitmotif in the media's efforts to convey the gravity of the Katrina story.[9] The failure of dialysis technology—like failed levees, canals, and pumps—revealed the weakness inherent in a technologically reliant society. And just as proximity to the levees and residence in low-lying homes had a distinctly racial cast, so too did the story of dialysis.

The Stroke Belt, the Diabetes Burden, and Dependence on Dialysis

New Orleans and Louisiana are part of the so-called stroke belt—a stretch of states across the American Southeast associated with high rates of stroke and an array of hypertension-related disorders.[10] Since the 1940s, experts have pondered the reasons, speculating that high-fat diets and obesity, smoking, genetic predisposition, or other unknown factors are responsible for these elevated rates.[11] The "belt" remains an enigma, but many experts believe that diet and higher rates of hypertension among African Americans put them at increased risk of stroke. The high rate of hypertension was also linked to other aliments. "In the Southeast," noted one researcher in 1994, "hypertension is the most common cause of ESRD [kidney failure], followed by diabetes mellitus, occurring most frequently in older minority patients, particularly blacks." Kidney failure—the endpoint in a cascade of other ailments—was, he concluded, "a Southern epidemic."[12]

The correlation between end-stage renal disease (ESRD), diabetes, and being black cut in many directions—and these links were also associated with income. Diabetes is believed to be caused by "a complex interplay of genetic, cultural, social and environmental influences, as well as health care inequities."[13] In Louisiana as elsewhere, the correlation between poverty and diabetes is also well established. Some 11 percent of black people in the state and 7.2 percent of white people were diabetic in the years before Katrina, among the highest occurrences in the nation. These rates rise in the population as incomes falls, and as a 2004 report noted, nearly 16 percent of people in Louisiana with incomes under $15,000 per year were diabetic. Conversely, the income correlation with diabetes showed that for people with incomes over $50,000 per year, the percentage dropped to 4.8 percent. Only a few months before Katrina, in March 2005, one physician cautioned that given this complex array of factors—from diet to obesity to poverty and diabetes—the vulnerability of black Americans in the region to kidney failure was disturbingly high.[14]

By 2005, Louisiana was second only to Washington, D.C., in the per capita rate of kidney failure, much of which resulted from diabetes. New Orleans was not exactly "ground zero" for American diabetes, but it was a close second—a major player in a national epidemic of kidney disease.[15] But, as one commentator noted a week before Katrina struck, these ailments were not high-profile disorders like AIDS, breast cancer, and prostate cancer—and the regional health challenges, although known to health experts, did not receive sustained or widespread public attention. "Where," he wondered, "are the lapel ribbons and the walkathons [for diabetes]?"[16]

Kidney failure is a less glamorous form of debility—a less prominent force in the identity-based struggles of patients' advocates for public attention and resources. It was this often-concealed, private reality that came starkly into view in the days after Katrina struck, propelling dialysis patients into the public eye as they battled for health services. Media coverage of Katrina—by spotlighting dialysis—made momentarily visible a form of debility, dependence, and death that is widespread and intimately linked to the region's culture and geography. But the sudden appearance of dialysis also draws our attention to a deeper story of a region and the nation: the story of kidney failure and dialysis intersects, as we shall see, with other stories about how technology-based dependence came about in the first place and feeds vulnerability, and how the promise of government and the federal entitlement to health services had brought these sufferers to a new political crossroads.

Who Lives and Who Dies: Vulnerability and Technological Dependence in Historical Perspective

To look more deeply into the story of diabetics and dialysis is to uncover a complex historical relationship between human beings, disease, technology, and the role of government in health care—a history that illuminates the irony of technology in the making of vulnerability. Indeed, this was not the first time dialysis made national headlines. Several decades before Katrina struck, dialysis patients had figured as an important touchstone in the national debate about vulnerability, government, and citizenship.

As the historian Steven Peitzman notes, a profound racial disparity exists in cities across the nation in the rate of kidney failure, which is three or four times higher for blacks than whites.[17] The disproportion, "apparent to all by the 1980s," he writes, has numerous origins, but principal among them is diabetes and less access to early kidney care, leading to organ failure in end-stage renal disease (ESRD). "Whatever the reasons for so much ESRD among blacks in the United States and elsewhere," Peitzman observes, a convergence has emerged between the dialysis experience and the broader African American experience: "'[G]oing on dialysis' is nearly as familiar a part of African American life in the cities as is going to church."[18]

But there is also a deeper backstory, for type 2 diabetes—in which the body does not produce enough insulin or becomes resistant to insulin—is often linked to diet and obesity. Thus, the economic geography of the region and the history of the southern diet, particularly New Orleans cuisine, also have become implicated in the question of dialysis reliance. The Big Easy, after all, has long been associated with good eating—carrying one set of meanings for tourists and another for residents. So, many people dependent on dialysis in New Orleans were brought to this fateful juncture with Hurricane Katrina through particular historical and social processes; yet their stories cannot be separated from additional social factors that are important in explaining how, and why, peoples' kidneys can fail—from urinary tract infection (severe, untreated) to lead poisoning and HIV. Thus were race, diet, and a host of urban factors, along with poverty, implicated in higher rates of diabetes.

Dialysis in this country—a technology to allay the effects of slow, toxic death—has always been intimately tied to the logic of American government and to the debate over government's relationship to vulnerable citizens. The ability to artificially cleanse the blood of harmful waste products via hemodialysis emerged as a technical possibility after World War II, but access to the life saving technology became an entitlement through federal law in the early 1970s—at a crucial moment in U.S. history. With passage of Public Law 92–603 in October 1972, a "dialysis entitlement" within a Social Security amendment committed the nation to paying the cost of dialysis for all patients (wealthy or poor) whose kidneys had failed. These people with end-stage renal disease were beneficiaries of a liberal era of still-expanding government services.[19] The driving force behind the ESRD legislation was the glaring inequalities of the era—with the shocking role played by income and economic privilege in private access to dialysis, thus determining who lived and who died. "In the earliest years of chronic dialysis," observes Steven Peitzman, "the number of people who might benefit from the procedure exceeded its availability."[20] In the 1960s, hospitals with the still-scarce dialysis machines found that it was necessary to choose worthy recipients from among the many who sought to benefit. In a few well-known cases, hospitals with few dialysis facilities formed panels (criticized as "God committees") to decide on the criteria for distributing access to this rare, life-extending commodity. Precisely because the vagaries of class played such a powerful and unfortunate role in who did and did not get dialysis, pressure for equity grew. ESRD legislation thus sought to remedy these flaws, while building on the unprecedented passage only a few years earlier of Medicare, which ensured federal health coverage for the elderly. The argument for covering ESRD at the time was compelling: American technological prowess was well demonstrated. We could, after all, send men to the moon; surely, the nation could ensure access to lifesaving kidney dialysis. But as one of the Senate staffers involved in the legislation later recalled, "ironically, rather than serving as a demonstration or pilot, the ESRD legislation proved to be the last train out of the station for national health insurance. No other group has had a chance to get on board."[21]

For more than the past three decades, then, the story of dialysis and the government's commitment to extending life has been a political one—tied closely to the growth of the national health care system and its underlying political and economic commitments. But the growth of dialysis has also spawned a large and growing sector of private, commercial dialysis centers, many of them in the South (where diabetes is more prevalent). And as the incidence of ESRD has increased year by year—"growing about 3 percent a year, fueled by the rise of diabetes"—and the number of dialysis patients has expanded, the cost and profit associated with this unique entitlement has grown too, along with the debate over whether the U.S. as a nation could afford to live up to its commitment to care for these patients.[22]

The story of dialysis and diabetes in Katrina is, in some ways, one of the latest chapters in this unfolding political debate over government's priorities, its citizens, and how the state responds to those in need. The disease and its treatment are also part of the story of growing dependence on a technology that is tied to the ideals of a liberal society. Thus, the emergence of dialysis patients into the national spotlight during Katrina was not dramatically new. Long before the storm struck New Orleans, they had been identified as a particularly vulnerable group, warranting special protection and safeguards. Only a year earlier, New Orleans' mayor Ray Nagin had acknowledged as much. Looking out into the Gulf at the looming threat of Hurricane Ivan, he observed that the city's *priorities are first to secure the ongoing treatment of seriously ill patients in hospitals and for people on dialysis machines.*[23] From the era of the "God committees" into the age of ESRD and Katrina, the history of dialysis showed how society wavers in its commitment to these citizens.[24] Against this political backdrop, it should not surprise us that the plight of dialysis/diabetes patients was one prominent story within the broader Katrina narrative and that it carried powerful technological and historical resonance. These resonances hung in the air as one Florida medic commented when the waters remained high, *people have been without medicine and in some cases without dialysis for coming up on a week,* and he reminded listeners about the deadly consequences of the buildup of toxins in the blood if these conditions were to continue.[25]

Dialysis patients were not the only ones made vulnerable by disability, of course; the health effects were widespread, yet technologically dependent dialysis patients often epitomized the crisis. The chairman of the Touro Infirmary Hospital, Stephen Kupperman, observed on September 3 that *the government was totally unprepared for something of this size. . . . We could not get any assistance . . . at first.* The hospital ultimately turned to private buses and private air ambulances, with a little assistance from government helicopters, to evacuate patients and staff.[26] Many hospitalized patients could not be moved at all, notes one subsequent study, because "for patients who were disoriented or on respirators on in traction, for example, evacuation posed enormous logistical challenges."[27] But in the news coverage, the diabetics and dialysis patients often stood out. As one New Orleans citizen wrote at the time, "On Tuesday evening, my skeletal neighbor Kip, a kidney-transplant patient, waded home alone by flashlight from the convention center, where there were neither dialysis machines nor buses to get him to one. His last treatment had been four days earlier, and he was bloating. We had to get him out."[28] Another article early in the aftermath reported that a nurse at the United Medical Rehab Hospital in the city worried that "several diabetic patients had been without dialysis for nearly a week and after the fruit cocktail and peanut butter ran out, the staff broke into the candy and drink machines for sugary items to keep patients from going into shock."[29] Her voice cracking, she complained, "these are people who are not going to make it." Reports on September 5 from a hospital in Atlanta found that of those who fled, "many survivors are shell-shocked, unable to eat or sleep. Some need intravenous hydration; others suffer from not receiving regular dialysis treatment."[30] And nine days later, the *Wall Street Journal* bemoaned that "health officials are searching for hundreds of dialysis patients—about half of the 3,000 or 3,500 patients whose dialysis centers were destroyed were unaccounted for.[31] And a year later, dialysis continued to frame the storm's effects. One reassessment of life and death at the Houston Astrodome (where many New Orleans residents had been taken) commented that "doctors, administrators and staff from the Harris County Hospital District created a 'virtual hospital without beds' at the Astrodome. Among the seventeen thousand cases handled at the clinic were kidney patients in desperate need of dialysis and diabetics suffering from lack of insulin."[32]

Coverage of the human drama of patients dying while waiting for dialysis inevitably blurred the more complex issues of region, class, race, technology, history, disease, and government that had created this crisis. The story of dialysis provoked some to see New Orleans as a city outside the narrative of American technological progress, a city left behind. For some observers, dialysis became a vehicle for talking about profound failures to progress. In the midst of the wreckage, one observer described a "frail fellow, a diabetic whose limbs are too swollen to walk . . . unable to obtain dialysis treatment for a week, being pushed along in a wheelchair by an elderly friend."[33] Seeing the sad picture, one disgusted resident spat out, "We are a third world city in a first world country."[34] Frequently using the word "primitive," CNN's Sanjay Gupta reported from the airport that "the utter lack of coordination" combined with the devastating impact of the water throughout the city meant that "it was more primitive than what we saw in Iraq. In some ways, it was more primitive than what we saw in Sri Lanka during the tsunami as well."[35] And reflecting on the story of dialysis patients, another Tulane-based nephrologist recalled, "conditions were pretty primitive for the period of time from Monday when the storm hit until Friday when the complete evacuation went on."[36]

Understanding diabetes and dialysis (with its unique national history and regional profile) considerably expands our understanding of the failure that was Katrina. The notion that a privileged society with its complex systems of technological care had so obviously failed its most defenseless citizens provoked outrage at the time. But as we now approach the fifth anniversary of the 2005 storm, the story of dialysis and Katrina has largely subsided from the headlines, reemerging from time to time in subtle ways. It is now mostly left to specialists in health and nephrology to ask crucial questions. Where have the dialysis patients of New Orleans gone? How many have died? Will the survivors return? Will the dialysis centers of the city be rebuilt? These questions are, even now, unanswerable because of the massive dispersion of population. Nearly a year after the story, one physician at Tulane noted, "Prior to Hurricane Katrina there were about eight thousand [dialysis] patients in the state of Louisiana. About four thousand of those . . . resided in the New Orleans metropolitan area. . . . And since the storm I think it's only half the level."[37] Another Tulane physician noted that two of the three university dialysis units were not functioning: "Both of those flooded; neither is open right now. One . . . received such structural damage that it will have to be rebuilt." Would it be rebuilt? "You can't open a dialysis unit in a way unless you have patients, and the patients can't come back unless there is a dialysis unit. . . . You can't do one without the other."[38] And a study done two years after Katrina found that "before the 2005 hurricane season, there were 2,011 and 362 dialysis patients residing in the [two] parishes (the Louisiana equivalent to counties) most affected by hurricanes Katrina and Rita, respectively. Each of these parishes had experienced increases in dialysis patient populations over the past 5 years. However, following the storms, there were 1,014 and 316 dialysis patients residing in the affected parishes."[39] Where those patients went remains something of a public health mystery.

The questions embedded in the story of dialysis are microcosms of a large question about the nation's commitment to its people most at risk. In the storm itself, health policy researchers Bradford Gray and Kathy Hebert noted, "the situation was particularly urgent for hospitals that lost power, communications, and water/sewer service, and that couldn't resupply such essentials as drugs, blood, linen, and food."[40] Many dialysis centers and diabetes care clinics, hard hit that month, disappeared in the months after the storm.[41] "According to figures assembled by the Louisiana Hospital Association (LHA) during the storm," Gray and Hebert continued, "1,749 patients occupied the 11 hospitals surrounded by the floodwaters."[42] In this context, what happened to dialysis patients became a microcosm of the broader social drama. Their dispersion from New Orleans still raises fundamental questions about what kind of new city will emerge in the wake of the storm and whether its medical infrastructure will ever be the same. In the end, the story of the dialysis patients reveals particular faces in the human geography of vulnerability and suffering. But in its broadest features, the story remains a tale about the limits of American technological capacity; the intersecting economic, cultural, and historical dynamics of disease; the changing nature of the government's fragile promises to its vulnerable citizens; and the nation's inability to maintain a steady spotlight on, let alone care for, its people in need.

ENDNOTES

[1] "Kidney Specialists Review Plans for Disaster Response," *Science Daily*, June 22, 2007, http://www.sciencedaily.com/releases/2007/06/ 070620121247.htm. The report summarizes a new finding published in the *Clinical Journal of the American Society of Nephropology*.

[2] Lynn Macey, "Letters to the Editor: Hurricane Katrina," *San Diego Union Tribune*, September 7, 2005, B9.

[3] "National Kidney Foundation Offers Information, Resources to Kidney Patients Affected by Hurricane Katrina," *PR Newswire*, September 2, 2005, http://www.highbeam.com/doc/ 1P2-13202169.htm.

[4] January W. Payne, "At Risk before the Storm Struck: Prior Health Disparities Due to Race, Poverty Multiply Death, Disease," *Washington Post*, September 13, 2005.

[5] Vecihi Batuman (Department of Nephrology, Tulane University Medical Center), interviewed by Richard Mizelle Jr. (graduate assistant, Rutgers University), July 20, 2006.

[6] Paul Muntner (Department of Epidemiology, Tulane University Medical Center), interviewed by Richard Mizelle Jr. (graduate assistant, Rutgers University), July 20, 2006.

[7] Ibid.

[8] National Center for Health Statistics (NCHS), *Health, United States, 2004—with Chartbook on the Trends in Health of Americans* (Hyattsville, Md.: NCHS, 2004), http://www.ncbi.nlm.gov/ books/bookres.fcgi/healthus04/healthus04.pdf. Cited in Bailus Walker and Rueben Warren, "Katrina Perspectives," *Journal of Health Care for the Poor and Underserved* 18 (2007): 233–240.

[9] An earlier book of mine, *Dying in the City of the Blues* (Chapel Hill: University of North Carolina Press, 2001), provided the starting point for my analysis. In the story of one disease—sickle cell anemia—one can see the intersection of disease, race, and politics in the South, and the ways that we can use the study of particular maladies, pains, and health experiences offers a lens on a broader discourse of race, health, and American society.

[10] David Warnock et al., "Prevalence of Chronic Kidney Disease and Anemia among Participants in the Reasons for Geographic and Racial Differences in Stroke (REGARDS) Cohort Study: Baseline Results," *Kidney International* 68 (2005): 1427–1431.

[11] Douglas J. Lanska and Lewis H. Kuller, "The Geography of Stroke Mortality in the United States and the Concept of a Stroke Belt," *Stroke* 26 (1995): 1145–1149; Daniel T. Lackland and Michael A. Moore, "Hypertension-Related Mortality and Morbidity in the Southeast," *Southern Medical Journal* 90 (February 1997): 191–198.

[12] Michael A. Moore, "End-Stage Renal Disease: A Southern Epidemic," *Southern Medical Journal* 87 (October 1994): 1013–1017.

[13] Janice P. Lea and Susanne B. Nicholas, "Diabetes Mellitus and Hypertension: Key Risk Factors for Kidney Disease," *Journal of the American Medical Association* 94 (suppl.) (August 2002): 7S–15S, quote on 7S.

[14] Moore, "End-Stage Renal Disease."

[15] There are more than four hundred thousand people on dialysis nationwide. A disproportionate percentage of dialysis centers and patients are in the South.

[16] Ranit Mishori, "A Dubious Distinction: The District Is at the Front of a National Surge in Kidney Disease," *Washington Post*, August 23, 2005, F1.

[17] Steven J. Peitzman, *Dropsy, Dialysis, Transplant: A Short History of Failing Kidneys* (Baltimore: Johns Hopkins University Press, 2007), 128.

[18] Ibid., 129.

[19] Richard Rettig, "Origins of the Medicare Kidney Disease Entitlement: The Social Security Amendments of 1972," in *Biomedical Politics*, ed. Kathi E. Hanna (Washington, D.C.: Institute of Medicine and National Academy Press, 1982).

[20] Peitzman, *Dropsy, Dialysis, Transplant*. 112.

[21] James Mongan quoted in Charles Plante, "Reflections on the Passage of the End-Stage Renal Disease Medicare Program," *American Journal of Kidney Disease* 35 (2000): 48. For a broader discussion of Medicare politics and the place of kidney dialysis within it, see Jonathan Oberlander, *The Political Life of Medicare* (Chicago: University of Chicago Press, 2003).

[22] Andrew Pollack, "The Dialysis Business: Fair Treatment?" *New York Times*, September 16, 2007, 1.

[23] Nagin quoted in "New Orleans Battens Down Hatches for Hurricane Ivan," *Irish Times*, September 15, 2004: 15.

[24]David Sanders and Jesse Durkheimer, "Medical Advance and Legal Lag: Hemodialysis and Kidney Transplantation," *UCLA Law Review* 15 (1968): 357–413; see also Committee on Chronic Kidney Disease, *Report of the Committee on Chronic Kidney Dialysis* (Washington, D.C.: U.S. Bureau of the Budget, 1967); and Rettig, "Origins of the Medicare Kidney Disease Entitlement."

[25]M.A.J. McKenna, "Katrina Aftermath: Medical: CDC Flies in to Deal with Health Crisis," *Atlanta Journal-Constitution,* September 4, 2005, 5A.

[26]Quoted in Felicity Barringer and Donald McNeil Jr, "Grim Triage for Ailing and Dying at a Makeshift Airport Hospital," *New York Times,* September 3, 2005, A4.

[27]Bradford Gray and Kathy Hebert, "Hospitals in Hurricane Katrina: Challenges Facing Custodial Institutions in a Disaster," *Journal of Health Care for the Poor and Underserved* 18 (2007): 283, 298, quote on 286.

[28]Quoted in James Nolan, "Our Hell in High Water," *Washington Post,* September 4, 2005: B1.

[29]Quoted in Allen G. Breed, "Katrina Survivors Face Tragedy, Triumph," Associated Press Online, August 31, 2005, http://www.ewoss.com/articles/D8CBE5182.aspx.

[30]Patricia Guthrie, "Metro Facilities Face Long-Term Health Burden," *Atlanta Journal-Constitution,* September 5, 2005, 1A.

[31]Michael J. McCarthy, "The Katrina Cleanup: Health Officials Seek Missing Dialysis Patients," *Wall Street Journal,* September 14, 2005, A10; "Hurricane: Health Officials Search for Missing Dialysis Patients," *American Health Line,* September 14, 2005.

[32]Allan Turner, "Katrina: One Year Later," *Houston Chronicle,* August 28, 2006, A1.

[33]Rosie DiManno, "Tales of Woe Shame a Nation," *Toronto Star,* September 2, 2005, A1.

[34]Quoted in ibid.

[35]Tom Foreman, Adora Udoji, Sanjay Gupta, Jamie McIntyre, Jeff Koinange, Barbara Starr, Miles O'Brien, and Soledad O'Brien, "Hurricane Katrina's Aftermath," *American Morning: CNN* (transcript), September 3, 2005.

[36]Lee Hamm (nephrologist, chair of the Department of Medical Education, Tulane University), interviewed by Richard Mizelle Jr. (graduate assistant, Rutgers University), July 20, 2006.

[37]Myra Kleinpeter (Department of Medicine, Tulane University), interviewed by Richard Mizelle Jr. (graduate assistant, Rutgers University), July 20, 2006.

[38]Hamm, interview.

[39]M[yra] A. Kleinpeter, "Shifts in Dialysis Patients from Natural Disasters in 2005," *Hemodialysis International* 11, suppl. 3 (October 2007): 33. As another study by a Baton Rouge nephrologist notes, "No matter how quickly a dialysis unit may reopen after some local or regional disaster, there exists the real possibility that the facility may experience economic consequences that may threaten the very survival of the unit." These challenges include loss of patients and staff, problems in obtaining property or flood insurance, replacement of destroyed dialysis machines, and difficulties in receiving government assistance such as Small Business Administration loans. Robert J. Kenney, "Emergency Preparedness Concepts for Dialysis Facilities: Reawakening after Hurricane Katrina," *Clinical Journal of the American Society of Nephrology* 2 (2007): 812–813.

[40]Gray and Hebert, "Hospitals in Hurricane Katrina."

[41]Adrienne Allen, Wayne Harris, and Kathleen Kennedy, "A Diabetes Pharmaceutical Care Clinic in an Underserved Community," *Journal of Health Care for the Poor and Underserved* 18 (2007): 255–261.

[42]Gray and Hebert, "Hospitals in Hurricane Katrina," 284.

50

CIVILIZE THEM WITH A STICK

MARY CROW DOG • RICHARD ERDOES

Few students are aware of our nation's policies toward Native Americans, which included the separation of Indian children from their families and cultures so that these children could be "civilized" into the dominant society. Consequently, beginning in 1879, thousands of Native American children were forced to leave the reservation to attend boarding schools, day schools, or schools in converted army posts. These total institutions used tactics similar to those used by the military to resocialize the young Native Americans. The peak period for Native American boarding schools was 1879–1930, but they continue, in some places, today. In the following selection, taken from *Lakota Woman* (1990), Mary Crow Dog and Richard Erdoes reveal how the institution of education can be an agent of social control whose purpose is to assimilate racial-ethnic populations, such as Native Americans, into the dominant culture. Crow Dog is a Native American activist and Erdoes is the ghostwriter of her autobiography.

. . . Gathered from the cabin, the wickiup, and the tepee,
partly by cajolery and partly by threats;
partly by bribery and partly by force,
they are induced to leave their kindred
to enter these schools and take upon themselves
the outward appearance of civilized life.

—ANNUAL REPORT OF THE DEPARTMENT OF INTERIOR, 1901

It is almost impossible to explain to a sympathetic white person what a typical old Indian boarding school was like; how it affected the Indian child suddenly dumped into it like a small creature from another world, helpless, defenseless, bewildered, trying desperately and instinctively to survive and sometimes not surviving at all. I think such children were like the victims of Nazi concentration camps trying to tell average, middle-class Americans what their experience had been like. Even now, when these schools are much improved, when the buildings are new, all gleaming steel and glass, the food tolerable, the teachers well trained and well intentioned, even trained in child psychology—unfortunately the psychology of white children, which is different from ours—the shock to the child upon arrival is still tremendous. Some just seem to shrivel up, don't speak for days on end, and have an empty look in their eyes. I know of an 11-year-old on another reservation who hanged herself, and in our school, while I was there, a girl jumped out of the window, trying to kill herself to escape an unbearable situation. That first shock is always there.

Although the old tiyospaye has been destroyed, in the traditional Sioux families, especially in those where there is no drinking, the child is never left alone. It is always surrounded by relatives, carried around, enveloped in warmth. It is treated with the respect due to any human being, even a small one. It is seldom forced to do anything against its will, seldom screamed at, and never beaten. That much, at least, is left of the old family group among full-bloods. And then suddenly a bus or car arrives, full of strangers, usually white strangers, who yank the child out of the arms of those who love it, taking it screaming to the boarding school. The only word I can think of for what is done to these children is kidnapping.

Even now, in a good school, there is impersonality instead of close human contact; a sterile, cold atmosphere, an unfamiliar routine, language problems, and above all the maza-skan-skan, that damn clock—white man's time as opposed to Indian time, which is natural time. Like eating when you are hungry and sleeping when you are tired, not when that damn clock says you must. But I was not taken to one of the better, modern schools. I was taken to the old-fashioned mission school at St. Francis, run by the nuns and Catholic fathers, built sometime around the turn of the century and not improved a bit when I arrived, not improved as far as the buildings, the food, the teachers, or their methods were concerned.

In the old days, nature was our people's only school and they needed no other. Girls had their toy tipis and dolls, boys their toy bows and arrows. Both rode and swam and played the rough Indian games together. Kids watched their peers and elders and naturally grew from children into adults. Life in the tipi circle was harmonious—until the whiskey peddlers arrived with their wagons and barrels of "Injun whiskey." I often wished I could have grown up in the old, before-whiskey days.

Oddly enough, we owed our unspeakable boarding schools to the do-gooders, the white Indian-lovers. The schools were intended as an alternative to the outright extermination seriously advocated by generals Sherman and Sheridan, as well as by most settlers and prospectors overrunning our land. "You don't have to kill those poor benighted heathen," the do-gooders said, "in order to solve the Indian Problem. Just give us a chance to turn them into useful farmhands, laborers, and chambermaids who will break their backs for you at low wages." In that way the boarding schools were born. The kids were taken away from their villages and pueblos, in their blankets and moccasins, kept completely isolated from their families—sometimes for as long as ten years—suddenly coming back, their short hair slick with pomade, their necks raw from stiff, high collars, their thick jackets always short in the sleeves and pinching under the arms, their tight patent leather shoes giving them corns, the girls in starched white blouses and clumsy, high-buttoned boots—caricatures of white people. When they found out— and they found out quickly—that they were neither wanted by whites nor by Indians, they got good and drunk, many of them staying drunk for the rest of their lives. I still have a poster I found among my grandfather's stuff, given to him by the missionaries to tack up on his wall. It reads:

1. Let Jesus save you.
2. Come out of your blanket, cut your hair, and dress like a white man.
3. Have a Christian family with one wife for life only.
4. Live in a house like your white brother. Work hard and wash often.
5. Learn the value of a hard-earned dollar. Do not waste your money on giveaways. Be punctual.
6. Believe that property and wealth are signs of divine approval.
7. Keep away from saloons and strong spirits.
8. Speak the language of your white brother. Send your children to school to do likewise.
9. Go to church often and regularly.
10. Do not go to Indian dances or to the medicine men.

The people who were stuck upon "solving the Indian Problem" by making us into whites retreated from this position only step by step in the wake of Indian protests.

The mission school at St. Francis was a curse for our family for generations. My grandmother went there, then my mother, then my sisters and I. At one time or other, every one of us tried to run away. Grandma told me once about the bad times she had experienced at St. Francis. In those days they let students go home only for one week every year. Two days were used up for transportation, which meant spending just five days out of 365 with her family. And that was an improvement. Before grandma's time, on many reservations they did not let the students go home at all until they had finished school. Anybody who disobeyed the nuns was severely punished. The building in which my grandmother stayed had three floors, for girls only. Way up in the attic were little cells, about five by five by ten feet. One time she was in church and instead of praying she was playing jacks. As punishment they took her to one of those little cubicles where she stayed in darkness because the windows had been boarded up. They left her there for a whole week with only bread and water for nourishment. After she came out she promptly ran away, together with three other girls. They were found and brought back. The nuns stripped them naked and whipped them. They used a horse buggy whip on my grandmother. Then she was put back into the attic—for two weeks.

My mother had much the same experiences but never wanted to talk about them, and then there I was, in the same place. The school is now run by the BIA—the Bureau of Indian Affairs—but only since about 15 years ago. When I was there, during the 1960s, it was still run by the Church. The Jesuit fathers ran the boys' wing and the Sisters of the Sacred Heart ran us—with the help of the strap. Nothing had changed since my grandmother's days. I have been told recently that even in the '70s they were still beating children at that school. All I got out of school was being taught how to pray. I learned quickly that I would be beaten if I failed in my devotions or, God forbid, prayed the wrong way, especially prayed in Indian to Wakan Tanka, the Indian Creator.

The girls' wing was built like an F and was run like a penal institution. Every morning at five o'clock the sisters would come into our large dormitory to wake us up, and immediately we had to kneel down at the sides of our beds and recite the prayers. At six o'clock we were herded into the church for more of the same. I did not take kindly to the discipline and to marching by the clock, left-right, left-right. I was never one to like being forced to do something. I do something because I feel like doing it. I felt this way always, as far as I can remember, and my sister Barbara felt the same way. An old medicine man once told me:

> Us Lakotas are not like dogs who can be trained, who can be beaten and keep on wagging their tails, licking the hand that whipped them. We are like cats, little cats, big cats, wildcats, bobcats, mountain lions. It doesn't matter what kind, but cats who can't be tamed, who scratch if you step on their tails.

But I was only a kitten and my claws were still small.

Barbara was still in the school when I arrived and during my first year or two she could still protect me a little bit. When Barb was a seventh grader she ran away together with five other girls, early in the morning before sunrise. They brought them back in the evening. The girls had to wait for two hours in front of the mother superior's office. They were hungry and cold, frozen through. It was wintertime and they had been running the whole day without food, trying to make good their escape. The mother superior asked each girl, "Would you do this again?" She told them that as punishment they would not be allowed to visit home for a month and that she'd keep them busy on work details until the skin on their knees and elbows had worn off. At the end of her speech she told each girl, "Get up from this chair and lean over it." She then lifted the girls' skirts and pulled down their underpants. Not little girls either, but teenagers. She had a leather strap about a foot long and four inches wide fastened to a stick, and beat the girls, one after another, until they cried. Barb did not give her that satisfaction but just clenched her teeth. There was one girl, Barb told me, the nun kept on beating and beating until her arm got tired.

I did not escape my share of the strap. Once, when I was 13 years old, I refused to go to Mass. I did not want to go to church because I did not feel well. A nun grabbed me by the hair, dragged me upstairs, made me stoop over, pulled my dress up (we were not allowed at the time to wear jeans), pulled my panties down, and gave me what they called "swats"—25 swats with a board around which Scotch tape had been wound. She hurt me badly.

My classroom was right next to the principal's office and almost every day I could hear him swatting the boys. Beating was the common punishment for not doing one's homework, or for being late to school. It had such a bad effect upon me that I hated and mistrusted every white person on sight, because I met only one kind. It was not until much later that I met sincere white people I could relate to and be friends with. Racism breeds racism in reverse.

The routine at St. Francis was dreary. Six A.M., kneeling in church for an hour or so; seven o'clock, breakfast; eight o'clock, scrub the floor, peel spuds, make classes. We had to mop the dining room twice every day and scrub the tables. If you were caught taking a rest, doodling on the bench with a fingernail or knife, or just rapping, the nun would come up with a dish towel and just slap it across your face, saying, "You're not supposed to be talking, you're supposed to be working!" Monday mornings we had cornmeal mush, Tuesday oatmeal, Wednesday rice and raisins, Thursday cornflakes, and Friday all the leftovers mixed together or sometimes fish. Frequently the food had bugs or rocks in it. We were eating hot dogs that were weeks old, while the nuns were dining on ham, whipped potatoes, sweet peas, and cranberry sauce. In winter our dorm was icy cold while the nuns' rooms were always warm.

I have seen little girls arrive at the school, first graders, just fresh from home and totally unprepared for what awaited them, little girls with pretty braids, and the first thing the nuns did was chop their hair off and tie up what was left behind their ears. Next they would dump the children into tubs of alcohol, a sort of rubbing alcohol, "to get the germs off." Many of the nuns were German immigrants, some from Bavaria, so that we sometimes speculated whether Bavaria was some sort of Dracula country inhabited by monsters. For the sake of objectivity I ought to mention that two of the German fathers were great linguists and that the only Lakota-English dictionaries and grammars which are worth anything were put together by them.

At night some of the girls would huddle in bed together for comfort and reassurance. Then the nun in charge of the dorm would come in and say, "What are the two of you doing in bed together? I smell evil in this room. You girls are evil incarnate. You are sinning. You are going to hell and burn forever. You can act that way in the devil's frying pan." She would get them out of bed in the middle of the night, making them kneel and pray until morning. We had not the slightest idea what it was all about. At home we slept two and three in a bed for animal warmth and a feeling of security.

The nuns and the girls in the two top grades were constantly battling it out physically with fists, nails, and hair-pulling. I myself was growing from a kitten into an undersized cat. My claws were getting bigger and were itching for action. About 1969 or 1970 a strange young white girl appeared on the reservation. She looked about 18 or 20 years old. She was pretty and had long, blond hair down to her waist, patched jeans, boots, and a backpack. She was different from any other white person we had met before. I think her name was Wise. I do not know how she managed to overcome our reluctance and distrust, getting us into a corner, making us listen to her, asking us how we were treated. She told us that she was from New York. She was the first real hippie or Yippie we had come across. She told us of people called the Black Panthers, Young Lords, and Weathermen. She said, "Black people are getting it on. Indians are getting it on in St. Paul and California. How about you?" She also said, "Why don't you put out an underground paper, mimeograph it. It's easy. Tell it like it is. Let it all hang out." She spoke a strange lingo but we caught on fast.

Charlene Left Hand Bull and Gina One Star were two full-blood girls I used to hang out with. We did everything together. They were willing to join me in a Sioux uprising. We put together a newspaper which we called the *Red Panther*. In it we wrote how bad the school was, what kind of slop we had to eat—slimy, rotten, blackened potatoes for two weeks—the way we were beaten. I think I was the one who wrote the worst article about our principal of the moment, Father Keeler. I put all my anger and venom into it. I called him a goddam wasičun son of a bitch. I wrote that he knew nothing about Indians and should go back to where he came from, teaching white children whom he could relate to. I wrote that we knew which priests slept with which nuns and that all they ever could think about was filling their bellies and buying a new car. It was the kind of writing which foamed at the mouth, but which also lifted a great deal of weight from one's soul.

On Saint Patrick's Day, when everybody was at the big powwow, we distributed our newspapers. We put them on windshields and bulletin boards, in desks and pews, in dorms and toilets. But someone saw us and snitched on us. The shit hit the fan. The three of us were taken before a board meeting. Our parents, in my case my mother, had to come. They were told that ours was a most serious matter, the worst thing that had ever happened in the school's long history. One of the nuns told my mother, "Your daughter really needs to be talked to." "What's wrong with my daughter?" my mother asked. She was given one of our *Red Panther* newspapers. The nun pointed out its name to her and then my piece, waiting for mom's reaction. After a while she asked, "Well, what have you got to say to this? What do you think?"

My mother said,

> Well, when I went to school here, some years back, I was treated a lot worse than these kids are. I really can't see how they can have any complaints, because we was treated a lot stricter. We could not even wear skirts halfway up our knees. These girls have it made. But you should forgive them because they are young. And it's supposed to be a free country, free speech and all that. I don't believe what they done is wrong.

So all I got out of it was scrubbing six flights of stairs on my hands and knees, every day. And no boy-side privileges.

The boys and girls were still pretty much separated. The only time one could meet a member of the opposite sex was during free time, between 4 and 5:30, in the study hall or on benches or the volleyball court outside, and that was strictly supervised. One day Charlene and I went over to the boys' side. We were on the ball team and they had to let us practice. We played three extra minutes, only three minutes more than we were supposed to. Here was the nuns' opportunity for revenge. We got 25 swats. I told Charlene, "We are getting too old to have our bare asses whipped that way. We are old enough to have babies. Enough of this shit. Next time we fight back. Charlene only said, Hoka-hay! . . ."

In a school like this there is always a lot of favoritism. At St. Francis it was strongly tinged with racism. Girls who were near-white, who came from what the nuns called "nice families," got preferential treatment. They waited on the faculty and got to eat ham or eggs and bacon in the morning. They got the easy jobs while the skins, who did not have the right kind of background—myself among them—always wound up in the laundry room sorting out 10-bushel baskets of dirty boys' socks every day. Or we wound up scrubbing the floors and doing all the dishes. The school therefore fostered fights and antagonism between whites and breeds, and between breeds and skins. At one time Charlene and I had to iron all the robes and vestments the priests wore when saying Mass. We had to fold them up and put them into a chest in the back of the church. In a corner, looking over our shoulders, was a statue of the crucified Savior, all bloody and beaten up. Charlene looked up and said, "Look at that poor Indian. The pigs sure worked him over." That was the closest I ever came to seeing Jesus.

I was held up as a bad example and didn't mind. I was old enough to have a boyfriend and promptly got one. At the school we had an hour and a half for ourselves. Between the boys' and the girls' wings were some benches where one could sit. My boyfriend and I used to go there just to hold hands and talk. The nuns were very uptight about any boy-girl stuff. They had an exaggerated fear of anything having even the faintest connection with sex. One day in religion class, an all-girl class, Sister Bernard singled me out for some remarks, pointing me out as a bad example, an example that should be shown. She said that I was too free with my body. That I was holding hands which meant that I was not a good example to follow. She also said that I wore unchaste dresses, skirts which were too short, too suggestive, shorter than regulations permitted, and for that I would be punished. She dressed me down before the whole class, carrying on and on about my unchastity. . . .

We got a new priest in English. During one of his first classes he asked one of the boys a certain question. The boy was shy. He spoke poor English, but he had the right answer. The priest told him, "You did not say it right. Correct yourself. Say it over again." The boy got flustered and stammered. He could hardly get out a word. But the priest kept after him: "Didn't you hear? I told you to do the whole thing over. Get it right this time." He kept on and on.

I stood up and said, "Father, don't be doing that. If you go into an Indian's home and try to talk Indian, they might laugh at you and say," "Do it over correctly. Get it right this time!"

He shouted at me, "Mary, you stay after class. Sit down right now!"

I stayed after class, until after the bell. He told me, "Get over here!" He grabbed me by the arm, pushing me against the blackboard, shouting, "Why are you always mocking us? You have no reason to do this."

I said, "Sure I do. You were making fun of him. You embarrassed him. He needs strengthening, not weakening. You hurt him. I did not hurt you."

He twisted my arm and pushed real hard. I turned around and hit him in the face, giving him a bloody nose. After that I ran out of the room, slamming the door behind me. He and I went to Sister Bernard's office. I told her, "Today I quit school. I'm not taking any more of this, none of this shit anymore. None of this treatment. Better give me my diploma. I can't waste any more time on you people."

Sister Bernard looked at me for a long, long time. She said, "All right, Mary Ellen, go home today. Come back in a few days and get your diploma." And that was that. Oddly enough, that priest turned out okay. He taught a class in grammar, orthography, composition, things like that. I think he wanted more respect in class. He was still young and unsure of himself. But I was in there too long. I didn't feel like hearing it. Later he became a good friend of the Indians, a personal friend of myself and my husband. He stood up for us during Wounded Knee and after. He stood up to his superiors, stuck his neck way out, became a real people's priest. He even learned our language. He died prematurely of cancer. It is not only the good Indians who die young, but the good whites, too. It is the timid ones who know how to take care of themselves who grow old. I am still grateful to that priest for what he did for us later and for the quarrel he picked with me—or did I pick it with him?—because it ended a situation which had become unendurable for me. The day of my fight with him was my last day in school.

51

A SCHOOL IN A GARDEN

MITCHELL L. STEVENS

The next reading in this section on education also examines social inequality in schools. Instead of examining federal boarding schools for Native Americans, Mitchell L. Stevens, a professor of sociology at Stanford University, studies how elite colleges reinforce the social class structure in society. Stevens reviews a number of potential theories related to education and social class inequality, including *social reproduction theory*, the *transformation thesis*, and *credentialism*. His data are from 18 months of fieldwork during 2000–2001, when Stevens lived on campus at an elite college and studied the college admissions and financial aid process. Stevens was particularly interested in what factors influenced college choice among students, and what factors influenced a college's decision to admit a student. The excerpt below is from Stevens' 2007 book *Creating a Class: College Admissions and the Education of Elites.*

Set at a high elevation overlooking farmland, sleepy towns, and hardwood forests, the College enjoys a geographical prominence commensurate with its stunning campus. Lovely old buildings from the early campaigns resemble pieces of a giant chess set, carefully positioned around shady quadrangles. Slate roofs and mullioned windows convey a sense of history. A few of the facades are illuminated in the evenings, making them visible for miles into the surrounding valleys. The most impressive route of arrival carries drivers through a sweeping lawn dotted with perennial beds and specimen trees. Lovingly tended, the trees are a special point of pride. Many employees can name a favorite. Each trunk gets an annual skirting of fresh mulch. The sycamores near the chapel receive special medications.

The campus is an important constant in the College's history. Like many private schools throughout the northeastern United States, this one was built by Protestant churchmen at what was once a cutting edge of American frontier. Hilltops were school builders' preferred sites for hygienic as well as symbolic reasons. Higher elevations were presumed to enjoy cleaner air, a notable advantage in a coal-burning industrial society, and also encouraged flattering allusions to Athens and Zion. The virtues of this particular hill have long been touted by College boosters. An information pamphlet for prospective students published in 1917 promises tidy walks crisscrossing under "fine old trees, which form the backdrop for the brown-grey buildings." "In a situation so beautiful and naturally healthful," explains another passage, "the College is further safeguarded by a modern sanitation system and its own water supply from spring fed reservoirs." Later literature describes the physical plant in other terms but continues to praise its beauty. A 1973 viewbook quotes a student's enthusiastic description: "This is a beautiful campus. In the fall especially, it's the most gorgeous place I ever hope to see. The air is clean and you are just totally removed from all the things that are making it so hard to live in cities these days."[1] Technological advances in color photography and the luminous capacities of computer screens would give subsequent advocates ever more vivid tools for disseminating their news. Surveys of admitted students throughout the College's history would confirm the campus as a prominent factor in many matriculation decisions.

Schools like this one—private, lush, residential, and with selective undergraduate admissions—constitute only a tiny fraction of the colleges and universities in the United States, yet they enjoy historical and cultural influence in great disproportion to their number. They are among the nation's most enduring and most emulated organizations. Early Americans built schools to train religious leaders of many different faiths, to gain an edge over neighboring towns and denominations, and to put particular towns and cities on the map. A school on a hill could be a light in the darkness, a glimmer of intellectual sophistication, a sign that a community was going places, making progress, looking up. As the frontier moved westward, the older institutions became models for school founders in every corner of the country. Colleges in the northeastern United States became benchmarks of excellence in virtually all things: curriculum, faculty, athletics, admissions, aesthetics. Even today, with the thousands of U.S. colleges and universities, degrees conferred by a relative handful of private, highly selective, affluent colleges and universities "back East" bear a subtle but unmistakable cachet.[2]

For eighteen months in 2000 and 2001, I lived and worked at one of these schools as a researcher. I resided in an apartment on its campus, ate often in its cafeterias, borrowed books from its library, and took my exercise on its wooded trails. I spent most of my working hours in the College's Office of Admissions and Financial Aid, where I tried to get as close as I could to the people who made decisions.

I was not alone in my interest. Selective admissions policies have been the object of increasing public fascination and debate in recent years. Courts, legislatures, and college presidents argue over the appropriate criteria selective schools should use when figuring out who they will admit. Magazines rank "the best" institutions by how many applicants they turn away. Growing numbers of private consultants make their livings off of the anxieties of people facing the elite college search.[3]

Despite all of the attention being paid to selective admissions, however, we know remarkably little about how admissions officers go about making decisions about real applicants in real time. I wanted to know how the decisions got made, and with what consequence for those who hoped to someday attend schools like the College. There are many excellent historical studies, and quite a few workplace memoirs by admissions officers themselves, but almost no reports based on critical scholarly observation.[4] Also remarkable is that, despite all the hype about selective college access, apparently no scholar in any field has taken a stab at explaining the hype itself. Many parents, especially those of the affluent upper middle class, worry ever more and ever earlier about their children's fate in the selective college admissions game, but it is not clear why. Why, in a society where a decent college education has become almost as accessible as a good cup of coffee, when virtually every state in the union underwrites at least one good research university, has admission to a handful of very expensive, often geographically remote private schools grown ever more competitive in recent years? What, if anything, has changed that makes attendance at particular institutions, and not just any college, seem so important to so many? I suggest an answer to these questions by looking out on the landscape of contemporary America through the front door of a highly selective private college.

I went to this place with a long-standing interest in two features of our national culture that are as influential as they are contradictory. On the one hand, Americans place very high value on the appraisal of people as individuals. Whether in schools, workplaces, or department stores, we believe that individualized consideration is better than standardized care. We like personalized attention, first names, and custom made. On the other hand, we put great faith in the fairness of universal standards. In our schools, workplaces, and courts of law, we tend to believe that everyone should be evaluated on the same terms. We tend to be suspicious when institutions make exceptions to their officially universal rules, using terms like *special preferences* and *discrimination* to call foul on the deviations. We might in theory settle the contradiction between universalism and individualism by making a clear choice between them when we build our institutions, creating systems for the management of human beings in which either the rules apply to absolutely everyone, or in which there are no hard-and-fast rules at all. But we don't choose. Instead, and despite the contradictions, we tend to create institutions that mix the two ideals together.

Nowhere is the commingling of individualism and universalism more apparent than in schools. On the one hand, we tend to view personalized instruction as the sine qua non of educational excellence. We sing the praises of small classrooms and "individualized education programs." We are understanding when people demand choices about where their children will go to school. Many parents and teachers alike cry to the heavens when school officials ask that standard curricula be taught in standardized ways. On the other hand, Americans are zealous educational universalists. On the political left, progressive reformers have long and quite successfully championed a dream of universal schooling—initially to the point of literacy, next to the completion of high school and, in recent years, to college degrees. The 1954 *Brown v. Board of Education* U.S. Supreme Court decision, considered by many to be a sacred event in our national history, preaches a gospel of educational universalism, making explicit the notion that public schooling should be apportioned equally to all citizens. On the political right, reformers have recently, and also quite successfully, pressed for universal measures of students' academic accomplishment and school performance. The centerpiece of the Bush administration's No Child Left Behind Act, for example, is the obligation that schools receiving federal funding demonstrate the progress of their students through standardized tests. It is difficult to imagine a more universal measure of individual performance than machine-graded, multiple-choice exams backed by the authority of the national government. Rather than making a choice between individualism and universalism in our schools, then, we pursue the virtues of both ideals at the same time.

Highly selective liberal arts schools like the College also embody the commingling of individualism and universalism. On the one hand, their signature organizational characteristics are their intimate size and their mission of service to students as whole persons. On the other hand, the competition for admission means that these schools also are beholden to powerful cultural expectations that they evaluate every applicant according to universal standards of merit. At their admissions front doors, elite liberal arts schools are expected to be individualistic and universalistic simultaneously. This is why it seemed to me that an admissions office would be a good site for examining what happens when these two ideals are brought together routinely, with what advantages and costs to applicants and schools.

An additional thing that had long intrigued me about liberal arts colleges is that they are quintessentially American institutions. The liberal arts organizational ideal—of a small, residential campus, geared primarily, if not exclusively, to highly individualized undergraduate instruction—was invented and nurtured in the United States, and in stark contrast to our model of research universities, it has not traveled beyond national borders. One looks almost in vain for schools built on the liberal arts model anywhere else in the world. I began my inquiry suspecting that the national peculiarity of the liberal arts form might hold some larger lessons about culture, schooling, and social class in America. This [study] is my effort to work out those lessons. . . .

College and Class

College educations are now crucial components of our national class structure. Most people presume that a college degree is a prerequisite for a financially comfortable adulthood, and a large corpus of sociological research on the relationship between educational attainment and life chances largely confirms the conventional wisdom.[5] Attainment of the relatively secure, well-compensated jobs held by the affluent upper middle class virtually requires a college education. Those without college degrees increasingly are relegated to less lucrative and less stable work. But even though there is wide agreement about the economic importance of college, there has been enduring controversy on the question of why educational attainment has come to play its now-pivotal role in the American class system.

One answer, often called the *reproduction* thesis, holds that variation in educational attainment essentially is a coating for preexisting class inequalities. The reproduction thesis was built from Karl Marx's insights about how powerful groups inevitably create social and cultural systems that legitimate their own class advantage. From this perspective college degrees, and the classroom time and schoolwork they represent, provide palatable justification for the tendency of privileged families to hand privilege down to their children. Adherents of the reproduction thesis support their argument by pointing out the obdurate correlation between parents' socioeconomic status and their offspring's school completion in general.[6] And of the Horatio Algers who do not fit this general pattern—the high academic achievers who graduate from prestigious colleges and go on to positions of wealth and influence, despite the odds—reproduction theorists explain that the exceptions are important in giving the education system its veneer of class neutrality. It is important for public acceptance of the whole enterprise that at least some of the less advantaged can make schooling work for them.

A second answer, which we might call the *transformation* thesis, makes different sense of the very same correlation between family privilege and educational attainment. This thesis argues that the replacement of traditional social hierarchies with educational ones is a definitive chapter in every society's progress toward modernity. German sociologist Max Weber, the first proponent of the transformation thesis, famously argued that as societies modernized, inequalities of family, caste, and tribe gradually give way to hierarchies predicated on individual achievement. In modern times individuals accumulate status and power as they move through the elaborate bureaucracies that characterize all industrial societies: large corporations, centralized governments, highly bureaucratized religious organizations, and schools. These forms of organization tend to distribute rewards on the basis of demonstrated individual accomplishment, not inherited privilege.[7] The transformation thesis would have us see that the ultimate value of college degrees lies in their capacity to confer advantages independently of their recipients' social backgrounds. If the correlation between parents' privilege and children's educational attainment were exact—if accomplishment in school neatly paralleled class origins—then schooling would not be so coveted by people from humble backgrounds. As it is, education is broadly perceived by people from all social classes as an effective mechanism of social mobility, because it *is* capable of moving people up, and down, the class hierarchy.

During the 1960s and 1970s, social scientists became adept at assessing these ideas empirically, using statistical techniques to model the relationships between family background, educational attainment, and individual prosperity over the life course. Exploiting a growing cache of numerical data sets and ongoing advances in computer technology, researchers such as Peter Blau, Otis Dudley Duncan, and Christopher Jencks developed a rich tradition of empirical scholarship about the role of schooling in mediating social inequality. Although work in this tradition is vast and diverse, two of its findings have been remarkably consistent: formal schooling does indeed have independent effects on individual life chances, and, at the same time, parents tend to use formal education as a primary means of handing privilege down to their children. Educational transformation and educational reproduction, in other words, go hand in hand.[8]

In a series of influential writings in the 1970s, sociologist Randall Collins deftly integrated the two theses, creating a term so pithy and evocative that it has shaped public and scholarly conversations about college ever since. Collins argued that the reproduction theorists were correct: the terms of social privilege are deeply contested in every modern society, and the haves perennially seek to translate their advantages into forms that render them legitimate in the eyes of have-nots. But he added that the transformation thesis also is true: privileged groups create educational institutions that have considerable independence from the people who pay for them. Schools function as quasi-autonomous third parties between haves who support them and have-nots. The academically accomplished kids who attend Harvard or Stanford on full scholarships, and the tuition-paying rich kids who flunk out of the same schools, are living embodiments of this institutional autonomy. Collins described this system of educational legitimation as *credentialism*, and the educationally stratified world it engendered *the credential society*.[9]

During the same decades that social scientists were developing this line of inquiry, the U.S. federal and state governments were actively building the largest higher education infrastructure in world history. Part of the justification for this expansion had to do with the more optimistic of social scientists' findings on education and individual life outcomes. If people's employment and earnings prospects were measurably improved through postsecondary schooling, the policy reasoning went, then a virtuous government would be right to expand opportunities for college attendance. In the decades following World War II, the U.S. state and federal governments did precisely that. Between 1945 and 1980 they dramatically grew the size and mission of public research universities, provided many millions of dollars in student grant and loan programs, and elaborately subsidized a whole tier of institutions—community colleges—to provide truly mass higher education opportunity.[10]

The United States was so successful at increasing the ranks of college graduates that as early as the mid-1970s social scientists were talking about "credential inflation"—the diminution of the value of college degrees in a labor market that was being flooded with them. As with credentialing before it, the credential inflation idea caught on quickly with the general public. It helped people articulate their sense that a mere college degree might not be sufficient for the attainment of upper-middle-class comforts. Many came to presume that the optimal educational choices were to earn additional credentials in graduate school or to seek especially prestigious and supposedly more valuable undergraduate degrees.[11] This is the most prominent explanation for the recent growth of demand for seats at colleges with nationally recognized names.

Worries about credential inflation notwithstanding, policy makers and the general public have conceived of college so optimistically for so long that pointing out the very limited extent to which expanded college access has changed the distribution of privilege in this country remains an unpopular thing to do. Nevertheless it is true: higher education has not been the great American equalizer. To be sure, there are proportionally more college graduates in this country than in any previous era, but, with only a few exceptions, the overall distribution of educational attainment remains stubbornly correlated with socioeconomic background.[12]

This does not mean, however, that the expansion of higher education has been without consequence for the character of the national class system. My research suggests that one profound result of higher education's expansion has been the entrenchment of a complicated, publicly palatable, and elaborately costly machinery through which wealthy parents hand privilege down to their children. My intention in this [study] is to reveal this machinery and explain how it organizes American society more generally.

The pursuit of college credentials is the widest and most dependable path to the good life that American society currently provides, and the terms of college admission have become the instructions families use when figuring out how to ensure their own children's future prosperity. The rise of the credential society has been accompanied by a value system in which the terms of college admission are also the goals of ideal child rearing and the standards of youthful accomplishment in American popular culture. These goals and standards are most explicitly depicted in the attributes elite colleges say they are looking for in applicants: measurable academic and athletic ability, demonstrated artistic accomplishment, and formally recognized philanthropic service.

Affluent families have a big advantage in meeting these goals and standards because they have relatively more resources to invest in doing so. Keenly aware of the terms of elite college admission, privileged parents do everything in their power to make their children into ideal applicants. They pay for academically excellent high schools. They shower their children with books and field trips and lots of adult attention. They nurture athletic talent through myriad youth sports programs. They encourage and fund early glimmers of artistic interest. They channel kids with empathic hearts toward exotic and traceable forms of humanitarian service. In the process of doing all of this, affluent families fashion an entire way of life organized around the production of measurable virtue in children.

On this line of thinking, the ever more frenzied activity surrounding selective admissions in the nation's most comfortable neighborhoods and school districts is essentially ceremonial. By the time upper-middle-class seventeen-year-olds sit down to write their applications, most of the race to top colleges has already been run and they already enjoy comfortable leads. For these kids the big question is not whether they will be admitted to an elite institution, but which particular schools will offer them spots. Nevertheless the intense final lap of the admissions race has profound importance as a ritual of just deserts. The simple fact that precise outcomes remain uncertain for everyone up to the very end serves to assure us that admission prizes are never won without persistence, steady wits, and hard work.

Status Counts and Status Rivals

How do all of the families with children in this race know just which colleges carry the most prestige? This is the puzzle to which much of my own inquiry attends, in large measure because the scholarly literature is virtually bereft of solutions. Rather than try to figure out what makes some schools more prestigious than others, social scientists typically rely on demand as prestige's proxy: the more people who apply to go there despite very low odds of admission, the more elite a school must be.[13] But remarkably, just where extraordinary desirability comes from is almost never directly considered.[14] Instead social scientists have relied on a tautology: the more people want to be admitted to a place, the more elite its diploma.

I will show that there is wisdom in this tautology, as long as we perceive of admissions statistics not as proxies of status but as status itself. In the absence of any definitive authority to decree which colleges and universities in America were to be the best, educators themselves worked out, over the course of the twentieth century, two systems of calibrating their status relative to one another. One system is admissions statistics. The measure of an institution's prestige has come to de defined, in part, by the proportion of each year's applicants it turns away. . . . Perhaps because status by numbers seemed too coldly calculative, perhaps because Americans have always been a little skeptical about academics and their ivory towers, educators also worked out a second system to mark institutional status: intercollegiate athletics. This system works much like the pecking orders that develop in school lunchrooms and playgrounds, in which children's popularity is marked by the company they keep. . . . in U.S. higher education the prestige of any one school is determined in part by the prestige of the other schools it meets on its playing fields.

The importance of undergraduate admissions selectivity and intercollegiate athletics to institutional status goes far in explaining why colleges and universities care so much about these aspects of organizational life. Admissions and sports are not mere adjuncts to the main business of U.S. higher education. They are integral parts of the whole enterprise.

Physical Education

One of the many revealing documents in the College's archive is a survey report from the late 1930s titled "A Study of the Reasons Given by 145 Members of the Freshman Class for Their Coming to the College." It is impossible to know the degree of rigor with which this survey was carried out, but its figures tell an evocative story. The survey appears to have given respondents a choice of some sixty factors that may have influenced their decision to attend the school. The list ranges widely, from "Academic reputation" to "Fraternity connections" and "Infirmary care." The single most frequently cited reason for attending is an item under the category "Physical Aspects": *Attraction of the campus* garners 67 mentions, a virtual tie with *General advantages of small college* and *Academic reputation*. Little wonder, then, that a document titled "Tentative Publicity Program," filed alongside the survey results, includes *Beauty of the campus* high on its list of recommended emphases.

This beauty is an asset that the College carefully maintains and actively promotes. Many of the facilities put up in recent years pay homage to the structures surrounding the oldest central quadrangles. As if in defiance of cost, stone facades and slate roofs adorn even some of the newest and largest buildings. Tidy footpaths, immunized to mud by an intricate terra cotta drainage system, lace through terraced gardens so beguiling that they are favored sites for wedding photographers. Otherwise quiet summer afternoons rumble with the din of motorized maintenance as physical plant workers aerate, mow, and fertilize many acres of lawns. In a custom shared by many of its similarly spectacular peer institutions, the College annually produces a full-color calendar of the most favored campus views and distributes it free to the institution's many alumni and friends.

Yet despite the great care and pride with which colleges attend to their physical appearance, sociologists of education have almost entirely ignored campus aesthetics. It is as if we have presumed that the job of conferring credentials is the most, or even the only, important work elite schools do. This blindness to aesthetics is part of a larger myopia in the sociology of education, and in the scholarly literature on stratification more broadly, about the sensual aspects of class. While we have become ever more sophisticated in our appreciation of how educational credentialing works, we have given ever less attention to the myriad ways in which schools produce a whole range of social values: intellectual, physical, aesthetic, and emotional.

Insights of the French sociologist Pierre Bourdieu provide a useful corrective to American sociologists' narrow focus on credentials as the primary produce of schools. Bourdieu argued that social class is about much more than where people fall in a society's distribution of wealth. It also entails particular patterns of aesthetic production, consumption, and sensual experience. What a society calls beautiful, for example, and what it makes beautiful in turn, are every bit as important to marking class distinctions as wealth and credentials are. On this line of thinking, it is no accident that in the schools to which they send their children, as much as in the neighborhoods they live in and the museums they patronize, the upper classes in every society go to great lengths to define what is beautiful and then surround themselves with the material embodiments of those definitions.[15]

On this line of thinking about class distinction, the physical appearance of human bodies matters as much as that of the physical worlds those bodies inhabit. Aspects of our corporeal bodies—how we carry them through space and attend to their shape, adornment, and longevity—also are important ways through which we mark class differences. Because bodies are such visible and consequential embodiments of class, parents go to great lengths to maintain and improve their children's physical health and appearance: through clothing, diet, and personal hygiene, and, significantly for purposes here, through sport and exercise. This, I . . . argue, is how the institutional status interests supporting college athletics and the class interests of families come together. The rigors of team athletics serve to maintain interorganizational status clubs and, at the same time, to develop physically impressive men and women.

Hard Choices

Because social scientists have so long been interested in the role of schooling in social stratification, they have developed a large body of knowledge about those factors that, in the aggregate, predict admission to and graduation from elite schools. We know that admission to elite schools is highly correlated with parents' socioeconomic standing—in large measure because affluent parents translate their privilege into educational opportunities, which in turn produce the academic achievement rewarded by selective colleges. We know also that wealthy parents invest heavily in the extracurricular enrichments through which extraordinary athletic and artistic talents are developed. Considerable evidence makes it clear that athletic talent, especially, is systematically rewarded by selective college admissions offices. We know that elite schools systematically favor applicants who are children of their own alumni—presumably because these so-called "legacy" admissions will curry favor with alumni and make them more generous donors to their alma mater. And we know that since the 1970s, selective colleges have given systematic preference to members of certain minority groups—presumably in response to public demands for the racial integration of elite higher education in the wake of the civil rights movement.[16] Yet for all of the quantitative evidence social scientists have amassed about who in general is admitted to elite schools, we know very little about how admissions officers go about the business of making decisions.[17] Even though we know that selective colleges favor the academically and athletically accomplished, the children of alumni, and members of particular racial groups, we have relied almost entirely on inference to explain how *particular* decisions are made. To wit: we have not looked carefully at how admissions officers know what they do about applicants, how they organize and make sense of that information and assess its validity, and how they adjudicate between what might be regarded as competing attributes of applications. We know almost nothing about how officers balance incentives to reward high academic accomplishment, athletic skill, legacy or minority status, and the ability to pay full tuition. We have not looked carefully at the many exigencies faced by real admissions officers in their day-to-day work, or at the strategies officers have devised to manage these exigencies.

Sociologists have learned a lot about how decisions are made in complex organizations generally, however. We know that for any consequential choice, evaluative authority tends to be dispersed among multiple parties. We know about the difficulties inherent in getting all of the relevant parties to a decision onto the same page or even into the same room at the same time. We know that the amount and kind of information available to decision makers is crucial to what decisions ultimately get made.[18] I here put these insights into the service of understanding elite college access in particular, and the organization of elite schooling in America more broadly.

Oft-repeated wisdom in admissions circles is that officers do not evaluate applicants; they evaluate applications. The distinction is important. Officers may never meet the people represented in the files. Instead they assess what they call the "admissibility" of applicants on the basis of the information at their disposal: test scores and grade point averages; the academic profile of the sending high school; the content and detail of recommendation letters; assessments of athletic talent logged by college coaches; standardized assessments of financial need. Assembling a strong application file is a crucial step in any bid for admission to an elite college, because decisions often are made exclusively on the basis of the information inside the file.

However, . . . the ability to assemble a strong application is not evenly distributed across the population. Those without an inkling of how decisions are made by admissions officers are at a distinct disadvantage. Those who do have such inklings develop them at various points in their or their children's academic careers. If one gets wise to the system only when the student in question is a junior in high school, it is too late to remake choices that could have been made to better advantage years before. Even if parents are wise to the system the day their children are born, their knowledge is of little consequence if it is not matched by the resources required to put it into practice: the means to live in a community with excellent schools, expert college guidance, and a student culture with a forward orientation toward college; the time and cash to invest in after-school sports leagues, summer music camps, private tutors, and horizon-expanding travel.

The fact that elite colleges make admissions decisions primarily on the basis of applicants' documented accomplishments is a triumph of meritocracy. The days when old-school connections were enough to get through the doors of top schools, and when dark skin or a Jewish surname were enough to be excluded, are over. In their place has arisen an information-based evaluative regime that nevertheless systematically favors the wealthy, well educated, and well connected. The mechanisms of preference have changed. Measurable accomplishment is the baseline criterion selective colleges now use to sort applications. But in general, only the relatively wealthy are able to afford the infrastructure necessary to produce that accomplishment in their children. Upper-middle-class Americans have responded to the triumph of educational meritocracy by creating a whole new way of life organized around the production of measurably talented children and the delivery of news about kids to the right places at the right times. This system is expensive and time-consuming. Consequently, the distribution of elite college acceptance letters is as skewed by class as it has always been.

That admissions statistics and athletic competitions are primary mechanisms of status differentiation in our national higher education system; that elite colleges are sensual and emotional organizations as much as academic ones; and that the machinery producing the talent and information now demanded by elite colleges is elemental to the class structure of American society—all are rather large arguments . . . about a small school. My goal in making them is to suggest new solutions to enduring puzzles about schooling and inequality in the United States. The importance of those puzzles makes them worth a reach.

ENDNOTES

[1] Americans' ambivalence about the relationship between urbanity and intellect is deep and enduring. See Morton G. White and Lucia White, *The Intellectual versus the City, from Thomas Jefferson to Frank Lloyd Wright* (Cambridge, Mass.: Harvard University Press, 1962).

[2] Excellent histories of early higher education in the United States include: John R. Thelin, *A History of American Higher Education* (Baltimore: Johns Hopkins University Press, 2004); Christopher J. Lucas, *American Higher Education: A History* (New York: St. Martin's Press, 1994); Laurence R. Veysey, *The Emergence of the American University* (Chicago: University of Chicago Press, 1965); Frederick Rudolph, *The American College and University: A History* (Athens: University of Georgia Press, 1990 [1962]); and the collected papers in Roger L. Geiger, ed., *The American College in the Nineteenth Century* (Nashville, Tenn.: Vanderbilt University Press, 2000).

[3] For recent critical commentary on the growing competitiveness of selective college admissions, see the essays in Lloyd Thacker, ed., *College Unranked: Ending the College Admissions Frenzy* (Cambridge, Mass.: Harvard University Press, 2005).

[4] Journalistic and "insider" accounts of selective college admissions include Jacques Steinberg, *The Gatekeepers: Inside the Admissions Process of Premier College* (New York: Viking, 2002); Rachel Toor, *Admissions Confidential: An Insider's Account of the Elite College Selection Process* (New York: St. Martin's Press, 2001); Jean H. Fetter, *Questions and Admissions: Reflections on 100,000 Admissions Decisions at Stanford* (Stanford: Stanford University Press, 1995); Michelle A. Hernandez, *A Is for Admission: The Insider's Guide to Getting into the Ivy League and Other Top Colleges* (New York: Warner Books, 1997).

[5] For cross-national analyses of the relationship between higher education and social stratification in modern societies, see Richard Breen and Jan O. Jonnson, "Inequality of Opportunity in Comparative Perspective: Recent Research on Educational Attainment and Social Mobility," *Annual Review of Sociology* 31 (2005): 223–243; also the essays in Yossi Shavit, Richard Arum, and Adam Gamoran, eds., *Expansion, Differentiation, and Inequality of Access in Higher Education: A Comparative Study* (Stanford: Stanford University Press, 2007).

[6] The paradigmatic text on the reproduction approach to educational inequality in U.S. social science is Samuel Bowles and Herbert Gintis, *Schooling in Capitalist America: Educational Reform and the Contradictions of Economic Life* (New York: Basic Books, 1976). Bowles and Gintis reprise their argument in light of subsequent scholarship in Bowles and Gintis, "Schooling in Capitalist America Revisited," *Sociology of Education* 75 (2002): 1–18.

[7] Max Weber, "The 'Rationalization' of Education and Training," in H. H. Gerth and C. Wright Mills, eds., *From Max Weber: Essays in Sociology* (New York: Oxford University Press, 1946), 240–244.

[8] Classic works in this tradition include Peter Blau and Otis Dudley Duncan, *The American Occupational Structure* (New York: Wiley, 1967); Christopher Jencks, *Inequality* (New York: Basic Books, 1972); Robert D. Mare, "Change and Stability in Educational Stratification," *American Sociological Review* 46 (1981): 72–87. For recent reviews, see Breen and Jonnson, "Inequality of Opportunity"; Grace Kao and Jennifer S. Thompson, "Racial and Ethnic Stratification in Educational Achievement and Attainment," *Annual Review of Sociology* 29 (2003): 417–442.

[9] Randall Collins, "Functional and Conflict Theories of Educational Stratification," *American Sociological Review* 36 (1971): 1002–1019; Randall Collins, *The Credential Society: An Historical Sociology of Education and Stratification* (New York: Academic Press, 1979). Also David K. Brown, *Degrees of Control: A Sociology of Educational Expansion and Occupational Credentialism* (New York: Teachers College Press, 1995). Years before Collins crystallized the notion, Christopher Jencks and David Riesman laid important groundwork for the credentialing idea in *The Academic Revolution* (Garden City, N.Y.: Doubleday, 1968). For an excellent critical review of scholarship in this tradition from Weber's early work onward, see David K. Brown, "The Social Sources of Educational Credentialism: Status Cultures, Labor Markets, and Organizations," in "Current of Thought: Sociology of Education at the Dawn of the 21st Century," special issue, *Sociology of Education* 74 (2001): 19–34.

[10] See Thelin, *American Higher Education*, 260–316; Jencks and Riesman, *Academic Revolution*; Clark Kerr, *The Uses of the University* (Cambridge, Mass.: Harvard University Press, 2001 [1963]). On community colleges, see Kevin J. Dougherty, *The Contradictory College: The Conflicting Origins, Impacts, and Futures of the Community College* (Albany: State University of New York Press, 1994); also Steven Brint and Jerome Karabel, *The Diverted Dream: Community Colleges and the Promise of Educational Opportunity in America, 1900–1985* (New York: Oxford University Press, 1989).

[11] Richard B. Freeman, *The Overeducated American* (New York: Academic Press, 1976). See also Randall Collins, "Credential Inflation and the Future of Universities," in Steven Brint, ed., *The Future of the City of Intellect: The Changing American University* (Stanford: Stanford University Press, 2002), 23–46.

[12] For a critical summary of the effects of this expansion on social stratification in the United States, see Josipa Roksa, Eric Grodsky, Richard Arum, and Adam Gamoran, "United States: Changes in Higher Education and Social Stratification," in Shavit, Arum, and Gamoran, *Expansion, Differentiation, and Inequality,* 165–191.

[13] See, for example, Christopher Avery, Andrew Fairbanks, and Richard Zeckhauser, *The Early Admissions Game: Joining the Elite* (Cambridge, Mass.: Harvard University Press, 2003); and the collected essays in Caroline M. Hoxby, ed., *College Choices: The Economics of Where to Go, When to Go, and How to Pay for It* (Chicago: University of Chicago Press/National Bureau of Economic Research, 2004).

[14] I here cite two exceptions. Roger L. Geiger clearly describes the current status system predicated on admissions selectivity in "The Competition for High-Ability Students: Universities in a Key Marketplace," in Brint, *Future of the City of Intellect*, 82–106. However, Geiger has no complete explanation for just why admissions selectivity became such a prominent index of prestige. Second, Arthur L. Stinchcombe, in his *Information and Organizations* (Berkeley: University of California Press, 1990), provides an elegant analysis of the relationship between the scholarly productivity of faculty and the relative prestige of the schools that employ them. Stinchcombe's arguments are not incompatible with my own.

[15] See, for example, Pierre Bourdieu, "Cultural Reproduction and Social Reproduction," Jerome Karabel and A. H. Halsey, eds., *Power and Ideology in Education* (New York: Oxford University Press, 1977), 487–511; Bourdieu, *Reproduction in Education, Society, Culture* (Beverly Hills, Calif.: Sage, 1977); Bourdieu, "The Forms of Capital," in John G. Richardson, ed., *Handbook of Theory and Research for the Sociology of Education* (New York: Greenwood Press, 1986), 241–258; Bourdieu, "Sport and Social Class," in Chandra Mukerji and Michael Schudson, eds., *Rethinking Popular Culture* (Berkeley: University of Califonia Press, 1991), 357–373. For an influential study that uses college completion as a marker of cultural distinctions between the middle and uppermiddle classes, see Michèle Lamont, *Money, Morals, and Manners: The Culture of the French and American Upper-Middle Class* (Chicago: University of Chicago Press, 1992). For examples of scholarly work applying Bourdieu's insights to a range of cultural distinction projects, see Michèle Lamont and Marcel Fournier, eds., *Cultivating Differences: Symbolic Boundaries and the Making of Inequality* (Chicago: University of Chicago Press, 1992). My thinking on these matters has been much shaped by two articles by Paul Dimaggio: "Cultural Entrepreneurship in Nineteenth-Century Boston: The Creation of an Organizational Base for High Culture in America," *Media, Culture and Society* 4 (1982): 33–50; and "Cultural Entrepreneurship in Nineteenth Century Boston, Part II: The Classification and Framing of American Art," *Media, Culture and Society* 4 (1982): 303–322. A recent critical review of Bourdieu's influence on the sociology of education in the United States is Annette Lareau and Elliot B. Weininger, "Cultural Capital in Educational Research: A Critical Assessment," *Theory and Society* 32 (2003): 567–606. On the inscription of identity onto physical landscapes and the ubiquity of the garden as metaphor and catalyst for this fascinating process, see Maria Kefalas, *Working-Class Heroes: Protecting Home, Community, and Nation in a Chicago Neighborhood* (Berkeley: University of Chicago Press, 2003); and Chandra Mukerji, *Territorial Ambitions and the Gardens of Versailles* (Cambridge, Mass.: Cambridge University Press, 1997).

[16] On parental investment in children's academic and extracurricular capacities generally, see Annette Lareau, *Unequal Childhoods: Class, Race, and Family Life* (Berkeley: University of California Press, 2003). On patterned preferences for various categories of applicants, see, for example, Thomas J. Espenshade, Chang Y. Chung, and Joan L. Walling, "Admission Preferences for Minority Students, Athletes, and Legacies at Elite Universities," *Social Science Quarterly* 85 (2004): 1422–46. A recent journalistic account of admissions preferences for the children of wealthy and alumni parents is Daniel Golden, *The Price of Admission: How America's Ruling Class Buys Its Way into College—and Who Gets Left Outside the Gates* (New York: Crown, 2006).

[17] The important exception here is David Karen's empirical observations in the admissions office at Harvard College in the 1980s. See his "Toward a Political-Organizational Model of Gatekeeping: The Case of Elite Colleges," *Sociology of Education* 63 (1990): 227–240; also David Karen, "'Achievement' and 'Ascription' in Admission to an Elite College: A Political-Organizational Analysis," *Sociological Forum* 6 (1991): 349–380. Karen's work confirms patterned preferences for athletes, legacies, and members of certain minority groups. However, it provides only schematic analysis of how admissions officers manage these preferences and make tradeoffs among them.

[18] The sociological literature on decision making in complex organizations is large and diffuse. My thinking has been informed most strongly by James G. March and Johan P. Olsen, *Ambiguity and Choice in Organizations* (Bergen, Norway: Universitetsforlaget, 1976); James G. March and Herbert A. Simon, *Organizations* (New York: Wiley, 1958); Walter W. Powell, *Getting into Print: The Decision Making Process in Scholarly Publishing* (Chicago: University of Chicago Press, 1985); and Stinchcombe, *Information and Organizations*.

52

BAD BOYS
Public Schools in the Making
of Black Masculinity

ANN ARNETT FERGUSON

The previous selection illustrates how schools socially produce and reproduce social class distinctions in the United States. In so doing, schools are an
important agent of *social reproduction*—they socially reproduce social inequalities that maintain social stratification. Schools also produce and reproduce
race and gender distinctions found in society. The selection that follows examines the social reproduction of race and gender in American public schools.
In particular, this excerpt, from Ann Arnett Ferguson's 2000 book, *Bad Boys:
Public Schools in the Making of Black Masculinity,* examines the effects gender
and racial stereotyping have on African American school boys. Ferguson, an
associate professor emeritus of African American studies at Smith College,
explores why African American boys are more often labeled as troublemakers
than are other gender or racial-ethnic groups of children.

S oon after I began fieldwork at Rosa Parks Elementary School, one of the
adults, an African American man, pointed to a black boy who walked by
us in the hallway.[1] *That one has a jail-cell with his name on it*, he told me. We
were looking at a ten-year-old, barely four feet tall, whose frail body was
shrouded in baggy pants and a hooded sweatshirt. The boy, Lamar, passed
with the careful tread of someone who was in no hurry to get where he was
going. He was on his way to the Punishing Room of the school. As he glanced
quickly toward and then away from us, the image of the figure of Tupac
Shakur on the poster advertising the movie *Juice* flashed into my mind. I suppose it was the combination of the hooded sweatshirt, the guarded expression
in his eyes, and what my companion had just said that reminded me of the face
on the film poster that stared at me from billboards and sidings all over town.

I was shocked that judgment and sentence had been passed on this child
so matter-of-factly by a member of the school staff. But by the end of the
school year, I had begun to suspect that a prison cell might indeed have a
place in Lamar's future. What I observed at Rosa Parks during more than
three years of fieldwork in the school, heard from the boy himself, from his
teachers, from his mother, made it clear that just as children were tracked
into futures as doctors, scientists, engineers, word processors, and fast-food
workers, there were also tracks for some children, predominantly African

American and male, that led to prison. This [reading] tells the story of the making of these bad boys, not by members of the criminal justice system, on street corners, or in shopping malls, or video arcades, but in and by school, through punishment. It is an account of the power of institutions to create, shape, and regulate social identities.

Unfortunately, Lamar's journey is not an isolated event, but traces a disturbing pattern of African American male footsteps out of classrooms, down hallways, and into disciplinary spaces throughout the school day in contemporary America. Though African American boys made up only one-quarter of the student body at Rosa Parks, they accounted for nearly half the number of students sent to the Punishing Room for major and minor misdeeds in 1991–92. Three-quarters of those suspended that year were boys, and, of those, four-fifths were African American.[2] In the course of my study it became clear that school labeling practices and the exercise of rules operated as part of a hidden curriculum to marginalize and isolate black male youth in disciplinary spaces and brand them as criminally inclined.

But trouble is not only a site of regulation and stigmatization. Under certain conditions it can also be a powerful occasion for identification and recognition. This study investigates this aspect of punishment through an exploration of the meaning of school rules and the interpretation of trouble from the youth's perspective. What does it mean to hear adults say that you are bound for jail and to understand that the future predicted for you is "doing time" inside prison walls? What does school trouble mean under such deleterious circumstances? How does a ten-year-old black boy fashion a sense of self within this context? Children like Lamar are not just innocent victims of arbitrary acts; like other kids, he probably talks out of turn, argues with teachers, uses profanities, brings contraband to school. However, I will argue, the meaning and consequences of these acts for young black males like himself are different, highly charged with racial and gender significance with scarring effects on adult life chances.

The pattern of punishment that emerges from the Rosa Parks data is not unique. Recent studies in Michigan, Minnesota, California, and Ohio reveal a similar pattern.[3] In the public schools of Oakland, California, for example, suspensions disproportionately involved African American males, while in Michigan schools, where corporal punishment is still permitted, blacks were more than five times more likely to be hit by school adults than were whites. In the Cincinnati schools, black students were twice as likely to end up in the inhouse suspension room—popularly known as the "dungeon"—and an overwhelming proportion of them were male.[4] In an ominous parallel to Cincinnati's dungeon, disciplinary space at Rosa Parks is designated the "Jailhouse." . . .

Dreams

This [reading] began with an anecdote about the school's vice principal identifying a small boy as someone who had a jail-cell with his name on it. I started with this story to illustrate how school personnel made predictive decisions about a child's future based on a whole ensemble of negative assumptions about African American males and their life-chances. The kids, however, imagined their future in a more positive light. They neither saw themselves as being "on the fast track to prison," as predicted by school personnel, nor did they see themselves as working at low-level service jobs as adults. The boys, in fact, had a decidedly optimistic view about their future.

This scenario, at such variance with that of the administrator's, became clear to me in my final semester at Rosa Parks, when the sixth-graders wrote an essay on the jobs they would like to have as adults. As I scanned these written accounts of students' dreams, I became conscious of a striking pattern. The overwhelming majority of the boys aspired to be professional athletes—playing basketball, baseball, or football—when they grew up. The reasons they gave for this choice were remarkably similar: the sport was something they were good at; it was work they would enjoy doing; and they would make a lot of money.[5] They acknowledged it would be extremely difficult to have such a career, but, they argued, if you worked hard and had the talent, you could make it.

These youthful essays confirmed what the boys had told me in interviews about the adult occupations they imagined for themselves. While a few had mentioned other options such as becoming a stand-up comedian, a Supreme Court justice, or a rap musician, almost all expressed the desire to play on an NBA or NFL team. This was not just an empty fantasy. Most of the boys with whom I had contact in my research were actively and diligently involved in after-school sports, not just as play, but in the serious business of preparing themselves for adult careers. This dream was supported in tangible ways by parents who boasted about their sons' prowess, found time to take them to practice, and cheered their teams on at games. I had assumed initially that these after-school sports activities were primarily a way of parents keeping kids busy to guard against their getting into drugs and sex. However, after talking to parents and kids I realized that what I observed was not just about keeping boys out of trouble but was preparation for future careers.

The occupational dreams of these boys are not at all unique. A survey by Northeastern University's Center for the Study of Sport in Society found that two-thirds of African American males between the ages of thirteen and eighteen believe they can earn a living playing professional sports.[6] Nor is this national pattern for black youth really surprising. For African American males, disengagement from the school's agenda for approval and success is a psychic survival mechanism; so imagining a future occupation for which schooling seems irrelevant is eminently rational. A career as a professional athlete represents the possibility of attaining success in terms of the dominant society via a path that makes schooling seem immaterial, while at the same time affirming central aspects of identification.

I have argued that the boys distance themselves from the school's agenda to avoid capitulating to its strategies for fashioning a self for upward mobility—strategies requiring black youth to distance themselves from family and neighborhood, to reject the language, the style of social interaction, the connections in which identities are grounded. From the highly idealized viewpoint of youth, a career in sports does not appear to require these strategic detachments. Their heroes—players like Michael Jordan, Scottie Pippen, Dennis Rodman, Rickey Henderson, to name just a few—have achieved the highest reaches of success without disguising or eradicating their Blackness.

But these are only dreams, for the chances of getting drafted by professional teams are slim to nonexistent. The probability has been calculated as somewhere in the region of one in ten thousand that a youth will end up in pro football or basketball.[7] Based on these facts, a plethora of popular and scholarly literature, as well as fiction and documentary films, have underscored how unrealistic such ambitions are, making the point that few youths who pour their hearts, energy, and schooling into sports will actually make it to the professional teams where the glory lies and the money is made.[8] They point out this discouraging scenario in order to persuade young black males to rechannel their energies and ambitions into conventional school learning that allows for more "realistic" career options.

Yet, in reality, for these youth efforts to attain high-status occupations through academic channels are just as likely to fail, given the conditions of their schooling and the unequal distribution of resources across school systems.[9] Children attending inner-city public schools are more likely to end up in dead-end, minimum-wage, service sector jobs because they do not have the quality of education available in the suburban public or elite private schools. Today's dreams will be transformed into tomorrow's nightmares.

Nightmares

While I rejected the labeling practices of the school vice principal, in my opening [paragraph], I also reluctantly admitted that by the end of the school year I, too, had come to suspect that a prison cell might have a place in the future of many Rosa Parks students. In contrast to the vice principal, this foreboding was not by any means rooted in a conclusion I had come to about individual children's proclivity for a life of crime, nor was it grounded in any evidence that, as some labeling theories hold, individuals stigmatized as deviant come to internalize this identity and adopt delinquent behaviors at rates higher than other youth. Rather, it emanated from my increased awareness of the way that racial bias in institutions external to school, such as the media and criminal justice system, mirrored and converged with that of the educational system. This convergence intensifies and weights the odds heavily in favor of a young black male ending up in jail. School seems to feed into the prison system, but what exactly is the connection between the two? What are the practical links between the punishing rooms, jailhouses, and dungeons of educational institutions and the cells of local, state, and federal prison systems? There are both long-term causal links as well as visible, immediate connections.

There are serious, long-term effects of being labeled a Troublemaker that substantially increase one's chances of ending up in jail. In the daily experience of being so named, regulated, and surveilled, access to the full resources of the school are increasingly denied as the boys are isolated in nonacademic spaces in school or banished to lounging at home or loitering on the streets. Time in the school dungeon means time lost from classroom learning; suspension, at school or at home, has a direct and lasting negative effect on the continuing growth of a child. When removal from classroom life begins at an early age, it is even more devastating, as human possibilities are stunted at a crucial formative period of life. Each year the gap in skills grows wider and more handicapping, while the overall process of disidentification that I have described encourages those who have problems to leave school rather than resolve them in an educational setting.

There is a direct relationship between dropping out of school and doing time in jail: the majority of black inmates in local, state, and federal penal systems are high school dropouts.[10] Therefore, if we want to begin to break the ties between school and jail, we must first create educational systems that foster kids' identification with school and encourage them not to abandon it.

One significant but relatively small step that could be taken to foster this attachment would be to reduce the painful, inhospitable climate of school for African American children through the validation and affirmation of Black English, the language form that many of the children bring from home/neighborhood. As I pointed out earlier, the denigration of this form and the assumptions made about the academic potential of speakers of Ebonics pose severe dilemmas of identification for black students—especially for males. The legitimation of Black English in the world of the school would not only enrich the curriculum but would undoubtedly provide valuable lessons to all students about sociolinguistics and the contexts in which standard and nonstandard forms are appropriate. The necessary prerequisite for this inclusion would be a mandatory program for teachers and school administrators to educate them about the nature and history of Ebonics. This was of course the very change called for by the Oakland School Board in 1996. However, it is clear from the controversy that ensued and the highly racialized and obfuscatory nature of the national media's coverage of the Oakland Resolution that there is serious opposition to any innovations that appear to challenge the supremacy of English.[11]

There is also an immediate, ongoing connection between school and jail. Schools mirror and reinforce the practices and ideological systems of other institutions in the society. The racial bias in the punishing systems of the school reflects the practices of the criminal justice system. Black youth are caught up in the net of the juvenile justice system at a rate of two to four times that of white youth.[12] Does this mean that African American boys are more prone to criminal activity than white boys? There is evidence that this is not the case. A study by Huizinga and Elliot demonstrates that the contrast in incarceration statistics is the result of a different *institutional response* to the race of the youth rather than the difference in actual behavior. Drawing on a representative sample of youth between the ages of eleven and seventeen, they compare the delinquent acts individual youth admit to committing in annual self-report interviews with actual police records of delinquency in the areas in which the boys live. Based on the self-reports, they conclude that there were few, if any, differences in the number or type of delinquent acts perpetrated by the two racial groups. What they did find, however, was that there was a substantially and significantly higher risk that the minority youth would be apprehended and charged for these acts by police than the whites who reported committing the same kind of offenses. They conclude that "minorities appear to be at greater risk for being charged with more serious offenses than whites involved in comparable levels of delinquent behavior, a factor which may eventually result in higher incarceration rates among minorities."[13]

Images of black male criminality and the demonization of black children play a significant role in framing actions and events in the justice system in a way that is similar to how these images are used in school to interpret the behavior of individual miscreants. In both settings, the images result in differential treatment based on race. Jerome G. Miller, who has directed juvenile justice detention systems in Massachusetts and Illinois, describes how this works:

> I learned very early on that when we got a black youth, virtually everything—from arrest summaries, to family history, to rap sheets, to psychiatric exams, to "waiver" hearings as to whether or not he would be tried as an adult, to final sentencing—was skewed. If a middle-class white youth was sent to us as "dangerous," he was more likely actually to be so than the black teenager given the same label. The white teenager was more likely to have been afforded competent legal counsel and appropriate psychiatric and psychological testing, tried in a variety of privately funded options, and dealt with more sensitively and individually at every stage of the juvenile justice processing. For him to be labeled "dangerous," he had to have done something very serious indeed. By contrast, the black teenager was more likely to be dealt with as a stereotype from the moment the handcuffs were first put on—easily and quickly relegated to the "more dangerous" end of the "violent-nonviolent" spectrum, albeit accompanied by an official record meant to validate each of a biased series of decisions.[14]

Miller indicates that racial disparities are most obvious at the very earliest and the latest stages of processing of youth through the juvenile justice system, and African American male youth are more likely to be apprehended and caught up in the system in the very beginning. They are also more likely "to be waived to adult court, and to be adjudicated delinquent. If removed from their homes by the court, they were less likely to be placed in the better-staffed and better-run private-group home facilities and more likely to be sent into state reform schools."[15]

Given the poisonous mix of stereotyping and profiling of black males, their chances of ending up in the penal system as a juvenile is extremely high. Even if a boy manages to·avoid getting caught within the juvenile justice system through luck or the constant vigilance of parents, his chances of being arrested and jailed are staggeringly high as an adult. A 1995 report by the Sentencing Project finds that nearly one in three African Americans in his twenties is in prison or jail, on probation or parole, on any given day.[16]

The school experience of African American boys is simultaneously replicated in the penal system through processes of surveillance, policing, charges, and penalties. The kids recognize this; the names they give to disciplinary spaces are not just coincidence. They are referencing the chilling parallels between the two.

A systematic racial bias is exercised in the regulation, control, and discipline of children in the United States today. African American males are apprehended and punished for misbehavior and delinquent acts that are overlooked in other children. The punishment that is meted out is usually more severe than that for other children. This racism that systematically extinguishes the potential and constrains the world of possibilities for black males would be brutal enough if it were restricted to school, but it is replicated in other disciplinary systems of the society, the most obvious parallel being the juvenile justice system.

Open Endings

Whenever I give a talk about my research, I am inevitably asked what ideas or recommendations I have for addressing the conditions that I describe. What do I think should be done, listeners want to know? The first few times this happened I felt resentful partly because I knew my colleagues who did research on subjects other than schooling were rarely asked to come up with policy recommendations to address the problems they had uncovered. This request for solutions is made on the assumption that schools, unlike the family and workplace, are basically sound albeit with flaws that need adjusting.

My hesitation to propose solutions comes from a conviction that minor inputs, temporary interventions, individual prescriptions into schools are vastly inadequate to remedy an institution that is fundamentally flawed and whose goal for urban black children seems to be the creation of "a citizenry which will simply obey the rules of society." I stand convinced that a restructuring of the entire educational system is what is urgently required if we are to produce the thoughtful, actively questioning citizens that Baldwin describes in the epigraph to this chapter. To make the point, however, that small programs at Rosa Parks school such as PALS [Partners at Learning Skills]— always underfunded, always dependent on grants of "soft" money that required big promises of quick fixes—served always too few and would inevitably disappear entirely or be co-opted by the institution, was so disheartening, so paralyzing that I am forced to rethink my reply. Is it all or nothing? Can we eradicate forms of institutional racism in school without eliminating racism in the society at large? Are the alternatives either quick hopeless fixes or paralysis because small changes cannot make a difference in the long run? How can the proliferation of local initiatives that spring up, in hope and with enthusiasm, be sustained without taking on institutional goals and attitudes? How can emergent forms appear alongside and out of the old? Most important of all, will attention be paid to the counterdiscourse of the Troublemakers themselves?

When I asked the kids, Schoolboys and Troublemakers, how they thought schooling might be improved, they looked at me blankly. I think they shared my sense of despair. The responses that I wrung out of them seemed trivial, even frivolous. It was all about play, about recreation: a longer recess, bigger play areas, playgrounds with grass not asphalt—and so on. The list that I had dreamed up was the opposite of frivolous. It was all about curriculum: smaller classes, Saturday tutoring, year-round school, antiracist training for student teachers, mutual respect between adults and youth. One thing I am convinced of is that more punitive measures, tighter discipline, greater surveillance, more prisons—the very path that our society seems to be determined to pursue—is not the approach to take. Perhaps, allowing ourselves to imagine the possibilities—what could, should, and must be—is an indispensable first step.

ENDNOTES

[1] This research was assisted by an award from the Social Science Research Council through funding provided by the Rockefeller Foundation. The names of the city, school, and individuals in this ethnography are fictitious in order to preserve the anonymity of participants.

[2] Punishment resulted in suspension 20 percent of the time. Records show that in 1991–92, 250 students, or almost half of the children at Rosa Parks School, were sent to the Punishing Room by adults for breaking school rules, for a total of 1,252 journeys. This figure is based on my count of referral forms kept on file in the Punishing Room. However, it by no means represents the total number of students referred by teachers for discipline. I observed a number of instances where children came into the Punishing Room but the problem was settled by the student specialist on the spot and no paperwork was generated. This seemed especially likely to occur when the adult referring the child had written an informal note rather than on the official referral form, when a parent did not have to be called, or when the infraction was judged by the student specialist to be insignificant. So it is likely that a much larger number of children were sent to the Punishing Room over the year but no record was made as a result of the visit.

[3] "Survey: Schools Suspend Blacks More," *Detroit Free Press*, December 14, 1988, 4A; Joan Richardson, "Study Puts Michigan 6th in Student Suspensions," *Detroit Free Press*, August 21, 1990, p. 1A; Minnesota Department of Children, Families and Learning, *Student Suspension and Expulsion: Report to the Legislature* (St. Paul: Minnesota Department of Children, Families and Learning, 1996); Commission for Positive Change in the Oakland Public Schools, *Keeping Children in Schools: Sounding the Alarm on Suspensions* (Oakland, CA: The Commission, 1992), p. 1; and John D. Hull, "Do Teachers Punish According to Race?" *Time*, April 4, 1994, pp. 30–31.

[4] In Oakland, while 28 percent of students in the system were African American males, they accounted for 53 percent of the suspensions. See note 3 for racial imbalance in corporal punishment in Michigan schools ("Survey: Schools Suspend Blacks More") and the racial discipline gap in Cincinnati (Hull, "Do Teachers Punish?").

[5] It is interesting to note that the girls in the class all responded in a stereotypical way. The vast majority wanted to have "helping" careers in traditional female occupations: teachers, nurses, psychologists. None of the girls gave money as a reason for their choice.

[6] Survey reported in *U.S. News and World Report,* March 24, 1997, p. 46.

[7] Raymie E. McKerrow and Norinne H. Daly, "The Student Athlete," *National Forum* 71, no. 4 (1990): 44.

[8] For examples see Gary A. Sailes, "The Exploitation of the Black Athlete: Some Alternative Solutions," *Journal of Negro Education* 55, no. 4 (1986); Robert M. Sellers and Gabriel P. Kuperminc, "Goal Discrepancy in African-American Male Student-Athletes' Unrealistic Expectations for Careers in Professional Sports," *Journal of Black Psychology* 23, no. 1 (1997); Alexander Wolf, "Impossible Dream," *Sports Illustrated,* June 2, 1997; and John Hoberman, *Darwin's Athletes: How Sport Has Damaged Black America and Preserved the Myth of Race* (Boston: Houghton Mifflin, 1997).

[9] For a shocking demonstration of the difference between schools, see Jonathan Kozol, *Savage Inequalities: Children in America's Schools* (New York: Crown Publishing, 1991).

[10] United States Department of Justice, Profile of Jail Inmates (Washington, DC: U.S. Government Printing Office, 1980). Two-thirds of the black inmates have less than a twelfth-grade education, while the rate of incarceration drops significantly for those who have twelve or more years of schooling.

[11] For an excellent overview of the debate that ensued over the Oakland School Board's resolution and a discussion of Ebonics, see Theresa Perry and Lisa Delpit, eds., *The Real Ebonics Debate: Power, Language, and the Education of African American Children* (Boston: Beacon Press, 1998).

[12] Jerome G. Miller, *Search and Destroy: African-American Males in the Criminal Justice System* (New York: Cambridge University Press, 1996), p. 73.

[13] David Huizinga and Delbert Elliot, "Juvenile Offenders: Prevalence, Offender Incidence, and Arrest Rates by Race," paper presented at "Race and the Incarceration of Juveniles," Racine, Wisconsin, December 1986, quoted in ibid., p. 72.

[14] Ibid., p. 78.

[15] Ibid., p. 73.

[16] Sentencing Project, *Young Black Americans and the Criminal Justice System: Five Years Later* (Washington, DC: Sentencing Project, 1995). This unprecedented figure reflects an increase from the 1990 Sentencing Project findings that one in four black males in their twenties was under the supervision of the criminal justice system.

THE FAMILY

53

THE DEINSTITUTIONALIZATION OF AMERICAN MARRIAGE

ANDREW J. CHERLIN

This is the first of three readings that examine the social institution of the family. Similar to other social institutions we have investigated, the institution of the family is undergoing tremendous change. These changes are hotly debated in the media and by politicians who argue that the institution of the family is in moral decline. Many sociologists disagree with this debate about family values and instead are studying how the structure and social norms of the family are changing. This excerpt by Andrew J. Cherlin, the Griswold Professor of Public Policy and Sociology at Johns Hopkins University, argues that the institution of marriage is becoming deinstitutionalized, which is causing some instability with the family until new social norms become established.

A quarter century ago, in an article entitled "Remarriage as an Incomplete Institution" (Cherlin 1978), I argued that American society lacked norms about the way that members of stepfamilies should act toward each other. Parents and children in first marriages, in contrast, could rely on well-established norms, such as when it is appropriate to discipline a child. I predicted that, over time, as remarriage after divorce became common, norms would begin to emerge concerning proper behavior in stepfamilies—for example, what kind of relationship a stepfather should have with his stepchildren. In other words, I expected that remarriage would become institutionalized, that it would become more like first marriage. But just the opposite has happened. Remarriage has not become more like first marriage; rather, first marriage has become more like remarriage. Instead of the institutionalization of remarriage, what has occurred over the past few decades is the deinstitutionalization of marriage. Yes, remarriage is an incomplete institution, but now, so is first marriage—and for that matter, cohabitation.

By deinstitutionalization I mean the weakening of the social norms that define people's behavior in a social institution such as marriage. In times of social stability, the taken-for-granted nature of norms allows people to go about their lives without having to question their actions or the actions of others. But when social change produces situations outside the reach of established norms, individuals can no longer rely on shared understandings of how to act. Rather, they must negotiate new ways of acting, a process that is a potential source of conflict and opportunity. On the one hand, the development of new rules is likely to engender disagreement and tension among the relevant actors. On the other hand, the breakdown of the old rules of a gendered institution such as marriage could lead to the creation of a more egalitarian relationship between wives and husbands. . . .

The Deinstitutionalization of Marriage

Even as I was writing my 1978 article, the changing division of labor in the home and the increase in childbearing outside marriage were undermining the institutionalized basis of marriage. The distinct roles of homemaker and breadwinner were fading as more married women entered the paid labor force. Looking into the future, I thought that perhaps an equitable division of household labor might become institutionalized. But what happened instead was the "stalled revolution," in Hochschild's (1989) well-known phrase. Men do somewhat more home work than they used to do, but there is wide variation, and each couple must work out their own arrangement without clear guidelines. In addition, when I wrote the article, 1 out of 6 births in the United States occurred outside marriage, already a much higher ratio than at midcentury (U.S. National Center for Health Statistics 1982). Today, the comparable figure is 1 out of 3 (U.S. National Center for Health Statistics 2003). . . . Marriage is no longer the nearly universal setting for childbearing that it was a half century ago.

Both of these developments—the changing division of labor in the home and the increase in childbearing outside marriage—were well under way when I wrote my 1978 article, as was a steep rise in divorce. Here I discuss two more recent changes in family life, both of which have contributed to the deinstitutionalization of marriage after the 1970s: the growth of cohabitation, which began in the 1970s but was not fully appreciated until it accelerated in the 1980s and 1990s, and same-sex marriage, which emerged as an issue in the 1990s and has come to the fore in the current decade.

The Growth of Cohabitation

In the 1970s, neither I nor most other American researchers foresaw the greatly increased role of cohabitation in the adult life course. We thought that, except among the poor, cohabitation would remain a short-term arrangement among childless young adults who would quickly break up or marry. But it has become a more prevalent and more complex phenomenon. For example, cohabitation has created an additional layer of complexity in stepfamilies. When I wrote my article, nearly all stepfamilies were formed by the remarriage of one or both spouses. Now, about one fourth of all stepfamilies in the United States, and one half of all stepfamilies in Canada, are formed by cohabitation rather than marriage (Bumpass, Raley, and Sweet 1995; Statistics Canada 2002). It is not uncommon, especially among the low-income population, for a woman to have a child outside marriage, end her relationship with that partner, and then begin cohabiting with a different partner. This new union is equivalent in structure to a stepfamily but does not involve marriage. . . .

More generally, cohabitation is becoming accepted as an alternative to marriage. . . . A number of indicators suggested that the connection between cohabitation and marriage was weakening. . . .

The Emergence of Same-Sex Marriage

The most recent development in the deinstitutionalization of marriage is the movement to legalize same-sex marriage. . . .

Lesbian and gay couples who choose to marry must actively construct a marital world with almost no institutional support. Lesbians and gay men already use the term "family" to describe their close relationships, but they usually mean something different from the standard marriage-based family. Rather, they often refer to what sociologists have called a "family of choice": one that is formed largely through voluntary ties among individuals who are not biologically or legally related (Weeks, Heaphy, and Donovan 2001; Weston 1991). Now they face the task of integrating marriages into these larger networks of friends and kin. The partners will not even have the option of falling back on the gender-differentiated roles of heterosexual marriage. This is not to say that there will be no division of labor; one study of gay and lesbian couples found that in homes where one partner works longer hours and earns substantially more than the other partner, the one with the less demanding, lower paying job did more housework and more of the work of keeping in touch with family and friends. The author suggests that holding a demanding professional or managerial job may make it difficult for a person to invest fully in sharing the work at home, regardless of gender or sexual orientation (Carrington 1999).

We might expect same-sex couples who have children, or who wish to have children through adoption or donor insemination, to be likely to avail themselves of the option of marriage. (According to the United States Census Bureau [2003b], 33% of women in same-sex partnerships and 22% of men in same-sex partnerships had children living with them in 2000.) Basic issues, such as who would care for the children, would have to be resolved family by family. The obligations of the partners to each other following a marital dissolution have also yet to be worked out. In these and many other ways, gay and lesbian couples who marry in the near future would need to create a marriage-centered kin network through discussion, negotiation, and experiment.

Two Transitions in the Meaning of Marriage

In a larger sense, all of these developments—the changing division of labor, childbearing outside of marriage, cohabitation, and gay marriage—are the result of long-term cultural and material trends that altered the meaning of marriage during the 20th century. The cultural trends included, first, an emphasis on emotional satisfaction and romantic love that intensified early in the century. Then, during the last few decades of the century, an ethic of expressive individualism—which Bellah et al. (1985) describe as the belief that "each person has a unique core of feeling and intuition that should unfold or be expressed if individuality is to be realized" (p. 334)—became more important. On the material side, the trends include the decline of agricultural labor and the corresponding increase in wage labor; the decline in child and adult mortality; rising standards of living; and, in the last half of the 20th century, the movement of married women into the paid workforce.

These developments, along with historical events such as the Depression and World War II, produced two great changes in the meaning of marriage during the 20th century. Ernest Burgess famously labeled the first one as a transition "from an institution to a companionship" (Burgess and Locke 1945). In describing the rise of the companionate marriage, Burgess was referring to the single-earner, breadwinner–homemaker marriage that flourished in the 1950s. Although husbands and wives in the companionate marriage usually adhered to a sharp division of labor, they were supposed to be each other's companions—friends, lovers—to an extent not imagined by the spouses in the institutional marriages of the previous era. The increasing focus on bonds of sentiment within nuclear families constituted an important but limited step in the individualization of family life. Much more so than in the 19th century, the emotional satisfaction of the spouses became an important criterion for marital success. However, through the 1950s, wives and husbands tended to derive satisfaction from their participation in a marriage-based nuclear family (Roussel 1989). That is to say, they based their gratification on playing marital roles well: being good providers, good homemakers, and responsible parents.

During this first change in meaning, marriage remained the only socially acceptable way to have a sexual relationship and to raise children in the United States, Canada, and Europe, with the possible exception of the Nordic countries. In his history of British marriages, Gillis (1985) labeled the period from 1850 to 1960 the "era of mandatory marriage." In the United States, marriage and only marriage was one's ticket of admission to a full family life. . . .

But beginning in the 1960s, marriage's dominance began to diminish, and the second great change in the meaning of marriage occurred. In the United States, the median age at marriage returned to and then exceeded the levels of the early 1900s. In 2000, the median age was 27 for men and 25 for women (U.S. Census Bureau 2003a). Many young adults stayed single into their mid to late 20s, some completing college educations and starting careers. Cohabitation prior to (and after) marriage became much more acceptable. Childbearing outside marriage became less stigmatized and more accepted. Birth rates resumed their long-term declines and sunk to all-time lows in most countries. Divorce rates rose to unprecedented levels. Same-sex unions found greater acceptance as well.

During this transition, the companionate marriage lost ground not only as the demographic standard but also as a cultural ideal. It was gradually overtaken by forms of marriage (and nonmarital families) that Burgess had not foreseen, particularly marriages in which both the husband and the wife worked outside the home. Although women continued to do most of the housework and child care, the roles of wives and husbands became more flexible and open to negotiation. And an even more individualistic perspective on the rewards of marriage took root. When people evaluated how satisfied they were with their marriages, they began to think more in terms of the development of their own sense of self and the expression of their feelings, as opposed to the satisfaction they gained through building a family and playing the roles of spouse and parent. The result was a transition from the companionate marriage to what we might call the *individualized marriage*. . . .

During this second change in the meaning of marriage, the role of the law changed significantly as well. This transformation was most apparent in divorce law. In the United States and most other developed countries, legal restrictions on divorce were replaced by statutes that recognized consensual and even unilateral divorce. The transition to "private ordering" (Mnookin and Kornhauser 1979) allowed couples to negotiate the details of their divorce agreements within broad limits. . . .

Sociological theorists of late modernity (or postmodernity) such as Anthony Giddens (1991, 1992) in Britain and Ulrich Beck and Elisabeth Beck-Gernsheim in Germany (1995, 2002) also have written about the growing individualization of personal life. Consistent with the idea of deinstitutionalization, they note the declining power of social norms and laws as regulating mechanisms for family life, and they stress the expanding role of personal choice. They argue that as traditional sources of identity such as class, religion, and community lose influence, one's intimate relationships become central to self-identity. Giddens (1991, 1992) writes of the emergence of the "pure relationship": an intimate partnership entered into for its own sake, which lasts only as long as both partners are satisfied with the rewards (mostly intimacy and love) that they get from it. It is in some ways the logical extension of the increasing individualism and the deinstitutionalization of marriage that occurred in the 20th century. The pure relationship is not tied to an institution such as marriage or to the desire to raise children. Rather, it is "free-floating," independent of social institutions or economic life. Unlike marriage, it is not regulated by law, and its members do not enjoy special legal rights. It exists primarily in the realms of emotion and self-identity.

Although the theorists of late modernity believe that the quest for intimacy is becoming the central focus of personal life, they do not predict that *marriage* will remain distinctive and important. Marriage, they claim, has become a choice rather than a necessity for adults who want intimacy, companionship, and children. . . .

The Current Context of Marriage

Overall, research and writing on the changing meaning of marriage suggest that it is now situated in a very different context than in the past. This is true in at least two senses. First, individuals now experience a vast latitude for choice in their personal lives. More forms of marriage and more alternatives to marriage are socially acceptable. Moreover, one may fit marriage into one's life in many ways: One may first live with a partner, or sequentially with several partners, without an explicit consideration of whether a marriage will occur. One may have children with one's eventual spouse or with someone else before marrying. One may, in some jurisdictions, marry someone of the same gender and build a shared marital world with few guidelines to rely on. Within marriage, roles are more flexible and negotiable although women still do more than their share of the household work and childrearing.

The second difference is in the nature of the rewards that people seek through marriage and other close relationships. Individuals aim for personal growth and deeper intimacy through more open communication and mutually shared disclosures about feelings with their partners. They may feel justified in insisting on changes in a relationship that no longer provides them with individualized rewards. In contrast, they are less likely than in the past to focus on the rewards to be found in fulfilling socially valued roles such as the good parent or the loyal and supportive spouse. The result of these changing contexts has been a deinstitutionalization of marriage, in which social norms about family and personal life count for less than they did during the heyday of the companionate marriage, and far less than during the period of the institutional marriage. Instead, personal choice and self-development loom large in people's construction of their marital careers.

Why Do People Still Marry?

There is a puzzle within the story of deinstitutionalization that needs solving. Although fewer Americans are marrying than during the peak years of marriage in the mid-20th century, most—nearly 90%, according to a recent estimate (Goldstein and Kenney 2001)—will eventually marry. A survey of high school seniors conducted annually since 1976 shows no decline in the importance they attach to marriage. The percentage of young women who respond that they expect to marry has stayed constant at roughly 80% (and has increased from 71% to 78% for young men). The percentage who respond that "having a good marriage and family life" is extremely important has also remained constant, at about 80% for young women and 70% for young men (Thornton and Young-DeMarco 2001). What is more, in the 1990s and early 2000s, a strong promarriage movement emerged among gay men and lesbians in the United States, who sought the right to marry with increasing success. Clearly, marriage remains important to many people in the United States. Consequently, I think the interesting question is not why so few people are marrying, but rather, why so *many* people are marrying, or planning to marry, or hoping to marry, when cohabitation and single parenthood are widely acceptable options. . . .

The Gains to Marriage

The dominant theoretical perspectives on marriage in the 20th century do not provide much guidance on the question of why marriage remains so popular. The structural functionalists in social anthropology and sociology in the early- to mid-20th century emphasized the role of marriage in ensuring that a child would have a link to the status of a man, a right to his protection, and a claim to inherit his property (Mair 1971). But as the law began to recognize the rights of children born outside marriage, and as mothers acquired resources by working in the paid workforce, these reasons for marriage became less important.

Nor is evolutionary theory very helpful. Although there may be important evolutionary influences on family behavior, it is unlikely that humans have developed an innate preference for marriage as we know it. The classical account of our evolutionary heritage is that women, whose reproductive capacity is limited by pregnancy and lactation (which delays the return of ovulation), seek stable pair bonds with men, whereas men seek to maximize their fertility by impregnating many women. Rather than being "natural," marriage-centered kinship was described in much early- and mid-20th century anthropological writing as the social invention that solved the problem of the sexually wandering male (Tiger and Fox 1971). Moreover, when dependable male providers are not available, women may prefer a reproductive strategy of relying on a network of female kin and more than one man (Hrdy 1999). In addition, marriages are increasingly being formed well after a child is born, yet evolutionary theory suggests that the impetus to marry should be greatest when newborn children need support and protection. In the 1950s, half of all unmarried pregnant women in the United States married before the birth of their child, whereas in the 1990s, only one-fourth married (U.S. Census Bureau 1999). Finally, evolutionary theory cannot explain the persistence of the formal wedding style in which people are still marrying (see below). Studies of preindustrial societies have found that although many have elaborate ceremonies, others have little or no ceremony (Ember, Ember, and Peregrine 2002; Stephens 1963). . . .

From a rational choice perspective, then, what benefits might contemporary marriage offer that would lead cohabiting couples to marry rather than cohabit? I suggest that the major benefit is what we might call *enforceable trust* (Cherlin 2000; Portes and Sensenbrenner 1993). Marriage still requires a public commitment to a long-term, possibly lifelong relationship. This commitment is usually expressed in front of relatives, friends, and religious congregants. Cohabitation, in contrast, requires only a private commitment, which is easier to break. Therefore, marriage, more so than cohabitation, lowers the risk that one's partner will renege on agreements that have been made. In the language of economic theory, marriage lowers the transaction costs of enforcing agreements between the partners (Pollak 1985). It allows individuals to invest in the partnership with less fear of abandonment. For instance, it allows the partners to invest financially in joint long-term purchases such as homes and automobiles. It allows caregivers to make relationship-specific investments (England and Farkas 1986) in the couple's children—investments of time and effort that, unlike strengthening one's job skills, would not be easily portable to another intimate relationship.

Nevertheless, the difference in the amount of enforceable trust that marriage brings, compared with cohabitation, is eroding. Although relatives and friends will view a divorce with disappointment, they will accept it more readily than their counterparts would have two generations ago. As I noted, cohabiting couples are increasingly gaining the rights previously reserved to married couples. It seems likely that over time, the legal differences between cohabitation and marriage will become minimal in the United States, Canada, and many European countries. The advantage of marriage in enhancing trust will then depend on the force of public commitments, both secular and religious, by the partners. . . .

The Symbolic Significance of Marriage

What has happened is that although the practical importance of being married has declined, its symbolic importance has remained high, and may even have increased. Marriage is at once less dominant and more distinctive than it was. It has evolved from a marker of conformity to a marker of prestige. Marriage is a status one builds up to, often by living with a partner beforehand, by attaining steady employment or starting a career, by putting away some savings, and even by having children. Marriage's place in the life course used to come before those investments were made, but now it often comes afterward. It used to be the foundation of adult personal life; now it is sometimes the capstone. It is something to be achieved through one's own efforts rather than something to which one routinely accedes.

How Low-Income Individuals See Marriage

Paradoxically, it is among the lower social strata in the United States, where marriage rates are lowest, that both the persistent preference for marriage and its changing meaning seem clearest. Although marriage is optional and often foregone, it has by no means faded away among the poor and near poor. Instead, it is a much sought-after but elusive goal. They tell observers that they wish to marry, but will do so only when they are sure they can do it successfully: when their partner has demonstrated the ability to hold a decent job and treat them fairly and without abuse, when they have a security deposit or a down payment for a decent apartment or home, and when they have enough in the bank to pay for a nice wedding party for family and friends. Edin and Kefalas [2005], who studied childbearing and intimate relationships among 165 mothers in 8 low- and moderate-income Philadelphia neighborhoods, wrote, "In some sense, marriage is a form of social bragging about the quality of the couple relationship, a powerfully symbolic way of elevating one's relationship above others in the community, particularly in a community where marriage is rare."

Along with several collaborators, I am conducting a study of low-income families in three United States cities. The ethnographic component of that study is directed by Linda Burton of Pennsylvania State University. A 27-year-old mother told one of our ethnographers:

> *I was poor all my life and so was Reginald. When I got pregnant, we agreed we would marry some day in the future because we loved each other and wanted to raise our child together. But we would not get married until we could afford to get a house and pay all the utility bills on time. I have this thing about utility bills. Our gas and electric got turned off all the time when we were growing up and we wanted to make sure that would not happen when we got married. That was our biggest worry. . . . We worked together and built up savings and then we got married. It's forever for us. . . .*

. . . In sum, the demands low-income women place on men include not just a reliable income, as important as that is, but also a commitment to put family first, provide companionship, be faithful, and avoid abusive behavior. . . .

Alternative Futures

What do these developments suggest about the future of marriage? Social demographers usually predict a continuation of whatever is happening at the moment, and they are usually correct, but sometimes spectacularly wrong. For example, in the 1930s, every demographic expert in the United States confidently predicted a continuation of the low birth rates of the

Depression. Not one forecast the baby boom that overtook them after World War II. No less a scholar than Kingsley Davis (1937) wrote that the future of the family as a social institution was in danger because people were not having enough children to replace themselves. Not a single 1950s or 1960s sociologist predicted the rise of cohabitation. Chastened by this unimpressive record, I will tentatively sketch some future directions.

The first alternative is the reinstitutionalization of marriage, a return to a status akin to its dominant position through the mid-20th century. This would entail a rise in the proportion who ever marry, a rise in the proportion of births born to married couples, and a decline in divorce. It would require a reversal of the individualistic orientation toward family and personal life that has been the major cultural force driving family change over the past several decades. It would probably also require a decrease in women's labor force participation and a return to more gender-typed family roles. I think this alternative is very unlikely—but then again, so was the baby boom.

The second alternative is a continuation of the current situation, in which marriage remains deinstitutionalized but is common and distinctive. It is not just one type of family relationship among many; rather, it is the most prestigious form. People generally desire to be married. But it is an individual choice, and individuals construct marriages through an increasingly long process that often includes cohabitation and childbearing beforehand. It still confers some of its traditional benefits, such as enforceable trust, but it is increasingly a mark of prestige, a display of distinction, an individualistic achievement, a part of what Beck and Beck-Gernsheim (2002) call the "do-it-yourself biography." In this scenario, the proportion of people who ever marry could fall further; in particular, we could see probabilities of marriage among Whites in the United States that are similar to the probabilities shown today by African Americans. Moreover, because of high levels of nonmarital childbearing, cohabitation, and divorce, people will spend a smaller proportion of their adult lives in intact marriages than in the past. Still, marriage would retain its special and highly valued place in the family system.

But I admit to some doubts about whether this alternative will prevail for long in the United States. The privileges and material advantages of marriage, relative to cohabitation, have been declining. The commitment of partners to be trustworthy has been undermined by frequent divorce. If marriage was once a form of cultural capital—one needed to be married to advance one's career, say—that capital has decreased too. What is left, I have argued, is a display of prestige and achievement. But it could be that marriage retains its symbolic aura largely because of its dominant position in social norms until just a half century ago. It could be that this aura is diminishing, like an echo in a canyon. It could be that, despite the efforts of the wedding industry, the need for a highly ritualized ceremony and legalized status will fade. And there is not much else supporting marriage in the early 21st century.

That leads to a third alternative, the fading away of marriage. Here, the argument is that people are still marrying in large numbers because of

institutional lag; they have yet to realize that marriage is no longer important. A nonmarital pure relationship, to use Giddens' ideal type, can provide
much intimacy and love, can place both partners on an equal footing, and
can allow them to develop their independent senses of self. These characteristics are highly valued in late modern societies. However, this alternative
also suggests the predominance of fragile relationships that are continually
at risk of breaking up because they are held together entirely by the voluntary commitment of each partner. People may still commit morally to a relationship, but they increasingly prefer to commit voluntarily rather than to be
obligated to commit by law or social norms. And partners feel free to revoke
their commitments at any time.

Therefore, the pure relationship seems most characteristic of a world
where commitment does not matter. Consequently, it seems to best fit
middle-class, well-educated, childless adults. They have the resources to be
independent actors by themselves or in a democratic partnership, and without childbearing responsibilities, they can be free-floating. The pure relationship seems less applicable to couples who face material constraints
(Jamieson 1999). In particular when children are present—or when they are
anticipated anytime soon—issues of commitment and support come into
consideration. Giddens (1992) says very little about children in his book on
intimacy, and his brief attempts to incorporate children into the pure relationship are unconvincing. Individuals who are, or think they will be, the
primary caregivers of children will prefer commitment and will seek material support from their partners. They may be willing to have children and
begin cohabiting without commitment, but the relationship probably will
not last without it. They will be wary of purely voluntary commitment if
they think they can do better. So only if the advantage of marriage in providing trust and commitment disappears relative to cohabitation—and I
must admit that this could happen—might we see cohabitation and marriage on an equal footing.

In sum, I see the current state of marriage and its likely future in these
terms: At present, marriage is no longer as dominant as it once was, but it remains important on a symbolic level. It has been transformed from a familial and community institution to an individualized, choice-based achievement. It is a marker of prestige and is still somewhat useful in creating
enforceable trust. As for the future, I have sketched three alternatives. The
first, a return to a more dominant, institutionalized form of marriage, seems
unlikely. In the second, the current situation continues; marriage remains
important, but not as dominant, and retains its high symbolic status. In the
third, marriage fades into just one of many kinds of interpersonal romantic
relationships. I think that Giddens' (1992) statement that marriage has
already become merely one of many relationships is not true in the United
States so far, but it could become true in the future. It is possible that we are
living in a transitional phase in which marriage is gradually losing its
uniqueness. If Giddens and other modernity theorists are correct, the third
alternative will triumph, and marriage will lose its special place in the family system of the United States. If they are not, the second alternative will

continue to hold, and marriage—transformed and deinstitutionalized, but recognizable nevertheless—will remain distinctive.

ENDNOTE

Author's Note: I thank Frank Furstenberg, Joshua Goldstein, Kathleen Kieman, and Céline Le Bourdais for comments on a previous version, and Linda Burton for her collaborative work on the Three-City Study ethnography.

REFERENCES

Beck, U. and E. Beck-Gernsheim. 1995. *The Normal Chaos of Love.* Cambridge, England: Polity Press.
———. 2002. *Individualization: Institutionalized Individualism and Its Social and Political Consequences.* London: Sage.
Bellah, R., R. Marsden, W. M. Sullivan, A. Swidler, and S. M. Tipton. 1985. *Habits of the Heart: Individualism and Commitment in America.* Berkeley: University of California Press.
Bumpass, L. L., K. Raley, and J. A. Sweet. 1995. "The Changing Character of Stepfamilies: Implications of Cohabitation and Nonmarital Childbearing." *Demography* 32:1–12.
Burgess, E. W. and H. J. Locke. 1945. *The Family: From Institution to Companionship.* New York: American Book.
Carrington, C. 1999. *No Place Like Home: Relationships and Family Life among Lesbians and Gay Men.* Chicago: University of Chicago Press.
Cherlin, A. 1978. "Remarriage as an Incomplete Institution." *American Journal of Sociology* 84:634–50.
———. 1992. *Marriage, Divorce, Remarriage.* Rev. ed. Cambridge, MA: Harvard University Press.
———. 2000. "Toward a New Home Socioeconomics of Union Formation." Pp. 126–44 in *Ties That Bind: Perspectives on Marriage and Cohabitation,* edited by L. Waite, C. Bachrach, M. Hindin, E. Thomson, and A. Thornton. Hawthorne, NY: Aldine de Gruyter.
Davis, K. 1937. "Reproductive Institutions and the Pressure for Population." *Sociological Review* 29:289–306.
Edin, K. J. and M. J. Kefalas. 2005. *Promises I Can Keep: Why Poor Women Put Motherhood Before Marriage.* Berkeley: University of California Press.
Ember, C. R., M. Ember, and P. N. Peregrine. 2002. *Anthropology.* 10th ed. Upper Saddle River, NJ: Prentice-Hall.
England, P. and G. Farkas. 1986. *Households, Employment, and Gender: A Social, Economic, and Demographic View.* New York: Aldine.
Giddens, A. 1991. *Modernity and Self-Identity.* Stanford, CA: Stanford University Press.
———. 1992. *The Transformation of Intimacy.* Stanford, CA: Stanford University Press.
Gillis, J. R. 1985. *For Better or Worse: British Marriages, 1600 to the Present.* Oxford, England: Oxford University Press.
Goldstein, J. R. and C. T. Kenney. 2001. "Marriage Delayed or Marriage Forgone? New Cohort Forecasts of First Marriage for U.S. Women." *American Sociological Review* 66:506–19.
Hochschild, A. 1989. *The Second Shift: Working Parents and the Revolution at Home.* New York: Viking.
Hrdy, S. B. 1999. *Mother Nature: Maternal Instincts and How They Shape the Human Species.* New York: Ballantine Books.
Jamieson, L. 1999. "Intimacy Transformed? A Critical Look at the 'Pure Relationship'." *Sociology* 33:477–94.
Mair, L. 1971. *Marriage.* Middlesex, England: Penguin Books.
Pollak, R. A. 1985. "A Transaction Costs Approach to Families and Households." *Journal of Economic Literature* 23:581–608.
Portes, A. and J. Sensenbrenner. 1993. "Embeddedness and Immigration: Notes on the Social Determinants of Economic Action." *American Journal of Sociology* 98:1320–50.
Qian, Z. and S. H. Preston. 1993. "Changes in American Marriage, 1972 to 1987: Availability and Forces of Attraction by Age and Education." *American Sociological Review* 58:482–95.
Roussel, L. 1989. *La Famille Incertaine.* Paris: Editions Odile Jacob.
Statistics Canada. 2002. *Changing Conjugal Life in Canada.* No. 89-576-XIE. Ottawa, Ontario: Statistical Reference Centre.

Thornton, A. and L. Young-DeMarco. 2001. "Four Decades of Trends in Attitudes toward Family Issues in the United States: The 1960s through the 1990s." *Journal of Marriage and Family* 63:1009–37.

Tiger, L. and R. Fox. 1971. *The Imperial Animal.* New York: Holt, Rinehart and Winston.

U.S. Census Bureau. 1999. "Trends in Premarital Childbearing: 1930–1994." *Current Population Reports,* No. P23–97. Washington, DC: U.S. Government Printing Office.

———. 2003a. "Estimated Median Age at First Marriage, by Sex: 1890 to Present." Retrieved January 11, 2003 (http://www.census.gov/population/www/socdemo/hh-fam.html).

———. 2003b. "Married-Couple and Unmarried-Partner Households: 2000." *Census 2000 Special Reports,* CENSR-5. Washington, DC: U.S. Government Printing Office.

U.S. National Center for Health Statistics. 1982. *Vital Statistics of the United States, 1978,* vol. 1. *Natality.* Washington, DC: U.S. Government Printing Office.

———. 2003. "Births: Preliminary Data for 2002." Retrieved December 15, 2003 (http://www.cdc.gov/nchs/data/nvsr/nvsr51/nvsr51_11.pdf).

Weeks, J., B. Heaphy, and C. Donovan. 2001. *Same-Sex Intimacies: Families of Choice and Other Life Experiments.* London: Routledge.

Weston, K. 1991. *Families We Choose: Lesbians, Gays, Kinship.* New York: Columbia University Press.

54

UNMARRIED WITH CHILDREN

KATHRYN EDIN • MARIA KEFALAS

This reading by Kathryn Edin and Maria Kefalas is based on their critically acclaimed book *Promises I Can Keep: Why Poor Women Put Motherhood before Marriage* (2005). Edin, a professor of sociology at the University of Pennsylvania, and Kefalas, an associate professor of sociology at Saint Joseph's University in Philadelphia, spent five years talking with low-income mothers about their lives and how they perceive marriage and family. This excerpt is an example of sociological research that employs Mills' sociological imagination, specifically his distinction between personal troubles and public issues, and also the importance of social researchers using the lenses of both biography and history to understand social phenomena. As Edin and Kefalas illustrate, when a middle- or upper-class woman cannot have a child it is seen as a personal tragedy, but when groups of lower-income women are having children outside of marriage, their fertility becomes a matter of public concern. In order to explain why this raced and classed distinction occurs, Edin and Kefalas examine both the biographies and the larger social contexts of poor women who become single mothers.

Kathryn Edin and Maria Kefalas, "Unmarried with Children," *Contexts,* Vol. 4, pp. 16–22. May, 2005. Copyright © 2005, American Sociological Association. Reprinted by permission of Sage Publications, Inc.

Jen Burke, a white tenth-grade dropout who is 17 years old, lives with her stepmother, her sister, and her 16-month-old son in a cramped but tidy row home in Philadelphia's beleaguered Kensington neighborhood. She is broke, on welfare, and struggling to complete her GED. Wouldn't she and her son have been better off if she had finished high school, found a job, and married her son's father first?

In 1950, when Jen's grandmother came of age, only 1 in 20 American children was born to an unmarried mother. Today, that rate is 1 in 3—and they are usually born to those least likely to be able to support a child on their own. In our book, *Promises I Can Keep: Why Poor Women Put Motherhood Before Marriage,* we discuss the lives of 162 white, African American, and Puerto Rican low-income single mothers living in eight destitute neighborhoods across Philadelphia and its poorest industrial suburb, Camden. We spent five years chatting over kitchen tables and on front stoops, giving mothers like Jen the opportunity to speak to the question so many affluent Americans ask about them: Why do they have children while still young and unmarried when they will face such an uphill struggle to support them?

Romance at Lightning Speed

Jen started having sex with her 20-year-old boyfriend Rick just before her 15th birthday. A month and a half later, she was pregnant. "I didn't want to get pregnant," she claims. "*He* wanted me to get pregnant. As soon as he met me, he wanted to have a kid with me," she explains. Though Jen's college-bound suburban peers would be appalled by such a declaration, on the streets of Jen's neighborhood, it is something of a badge of honor. "All those other girls he was with, he didn't want to have a baby with any of them," Jen boasts. I asked him, "Why did you choose me to have a kid when you could have a kid with any one of them?" He was like, "I want to have a kid with *you.*" Looking back, Jen says she now believes that the reason he wanted me to have a kid that early is so that I didn't leave him.

In inner-city neighborhoods like Kensington, where childbearing within marriage has become rare, romantic relationships like Jen and Rick's proceed at lightning speed. A young man's avowal, "I want to have a baby by you," is often part of the courtship ritual from the beginning. This is more than idle talk, as their first child is typically conceived within a year from the time a couple begins "kicking it." Yet while poor couples' pillow talk often revolves around dreams of shared children, the news of a pregnancy—the first indelible sign of the huge changes to come—puts these still-new relationships into overdrive. Suddenly, the would-be mother begins to scrutinize her mate as never before, wondering whether he can "get himself together"—find a job, settle down, and become a family man—in time. Jen began pestering Rick to get a real job instead of picking up day-labor jobs at nearby construction sites. She also wanted him to stop hanging out with his ne'er-do-well friends, who had been getting him into serious trouble for more than a decade. Most of all, she wanted Rick to shed what she calls his "kiddie mentality"—his habit of spending money on alcohol and drugs rather than recognizing his growing financial obligations at home.

Rick did not try to deny paternity, as many would-be fathers do. Nor did he abandon or mistreat Jen, at least intentionally. But Rick, who had been in and out of juvenile detention since he was 8 years old for everything from stealing cars to selling drugs, proved unable to stay away from his unsavory friends. At the beginning of her seventh month of pregnancy, an escapade that began as a drunken lark landed Rick in jail on a carjacking charge. Jen moved back home with her stepmother, applied for welfare, and spent the last two-and-a-half months of her pregnancy without Rick.

Rick sent penitent letters from jail. *I thought he changed by the letters he wrote me. I thought he changed a lot,* she says. *He used to tell me that he loved me when he was in jail. . . . It was always gonna be me and him and the baby when he got out.* Thus, when Rick's alleged victim failed to appear to testify and he was released just days before Colin's birth, the couple's reunion was a happy one. Often, the magic moment of childbirth calms the troubled waters of such relationships. New parents typically make amends and resolve to stay together for the sake of their child. When surveyed just after a child's birth, eight in ten unmarried parents say they are still together, and most plan to stay together and raise the child.

Promoting marriage among the poor has become the new war on poverty, Bush style. And it is true that the correlation between marital status and child poverty is strong. But poor single mothers already believe in marriage. Jen insists that she will walk down the aisle one day, though she admits it might not be with Rick. And demographers still project that more than seven in ten women who had a child outside of marriage will eventually wed someone. First, though, Jen wants to get a good job, finish school, and get her son out of Kensington.

Most poor, unmarried mothers and fathers readily admit that bearing children while poor and unmarried is not the ideal way to do things. Jen believes the best time to become a mother is *after you're out of school and you got a job, at least, when you're like 21. . . . When you're ready to have kids, you should have everything ready, have your house, have a job, so when that baby comes, the baby can have its own room.* Yet given their already limited economic prospects, the poor have little motivation to time their births as precisely as their middle-class counterparts do. The dreams of young people like Jen and Rick center on children at a time of life when their more affluent peers plan for college and careers. Poor girls coming of age in the inner city value children highly, anticipate them eagerly, and believe strongly that they are up to the job of mothering—even in difficult circumstances. Jen, for example, tells us, *People outside the neighborhood, they're like, "You're 15! You're pregnant?" I'm like, it's not none of their business. I'm gonna be able to take care of my kid. They have nothing to worry about.* Jen says she has concluded that *some people . . . are better at having kids at a younger age. . . . I think it's better for some people to have kids younger.*

When I Became a Mom

When we asked mothers like Jen what their lives would be like if they had not had children, we expected them to express regret over foregone opportunities for school and careers. Instead, most believe their children "saved" them. They describe their lives as spinning out of control before becoming pregnant—struggles with parents and peers, "wild," risky behavior, depression, and school failure. Jen speaks to this poignantly. *I was just real bad. I hung with a real bad crowd. I was doing pills. I was really depressed. . . . I was drinking. That was before I was pregnant. I think,* she reflects, *if I never had a baby or anything, . . . I would still be doing the things I was doing. I would probably still be doing drugs. I'd probably still be drinking.* Jen admits that when she first became pregnant, she was angry that she *couldn't be out no more. Couldn't be out with my friends. Couldn't do nothing.* Now, though, she says, *I'm glad I have a son . . . because I would still be doing all that stuff.*

Children offer poor youth like Jen a compelling sense of purpose. Jen paints a before-and-after picture of her life that was common among the mothers we interviewed.

> *Before, I didn't have nobody to take care of. I didn't have nothing left to go home for. . . . Now I have my son to take care of. I have him to go home for. . . . I don't have to go buy weed or drugs with my money. I could buy my son stuff with my money! . . . I have something to look up to now.*

Children also are a crucial source of relational intimacy, a self-made community of care. After a nasty fight with Rick, Jen recalls,

> *I was crying. My son came in the room. He was hugging me. He's 16 months and he was hugging me with his little arms. He was really cute and happy, so I got happy. That's one of the good things. When you're sad, the baby's always gonna be there for you no matter what.*

Lately she has been thinking a lot about what her life was like back then, before the baby.

> *I thought about the stuff before I became a mom, what my life was like back then. I used to see pictures of me, and I would hide in every picture. This baby did so much for me. My son did a lot for me. He helped me a lot. I'm thankful that I had my baby.*

Around the time of the birth, most unmarried parents claim they plan to get married eventually. Rick did not propose marriage when Jen's first child was born, but when she conceived a second time, at 17, Rick informed his dad, *It's time for me to get married. It's time for me to straighten up. This is the one I wanna be with. I had a baby with her, I'm gonna have another baby with her.* Yet despite their intentions, few of these couples actually marry. Indeed, most break up well before their child enters preschool.

I'd Like to Get Married, but . . .

The sharp decline in marriage in impoverished urban areas has led some to charge that the poor have abandoned the marriage norm. Yet we found few who had given up on the idea of marriage. But like their elite counterparts, disadvantaged women set a high financial bar for marriage. For the poor, marriage has become an elusive goal—one they feel ought to be reserved for those who can support a "white picket fence" lifestyle: a mortgage on a modest row home, a car and some furniture, some savings in the bank, and enough money left over to pay for a "decent" wedding. Jen's views on marriage provide a perfect case in point.

> *If I was gonna get married, I would want to be married like my Aunt Nancy and my Uncle Pat. They live in the mountains. She has a job. My Uncle Pat is a state trooper; he has lots of money. They live in the [Poconos]. It's real nice out there. Her kids go to Catholic school. . . . That's the kind of life I would want to have. If I get married, I would have a life like [theirs].*

She adds, *And I would wanna have a big wedding, a real nice wedding.*

Unlike the women of their mothers' and grandmothers' generations, young women like Jen are not merely content to rely on a man's earnings. Instead, they insist on being economically "set" in their own right before taking marriage vows. This is partly because they want a partnership of equals, and they believe money buys say-so in a relationship. Jen explains,

> *I'm not gonna just get into marrying him and not have my own house! Not have a job! I still wanna do a lot of things before I get married. He [already] tells me I can't do nothing. I can't go out. What's gonna happen when I marry him? He's gonna say he owns me!*

Economic independence is also insurance against a marriage gone bad. Jen explains,

> *I want to have everything ready, in case something goes wrong. . . . If we got a divorce, that would be my house. I bought that house, he can't kick me out or he can't take my kids from me. That's what I want in case that ever happens. I know a lot of people that happened to. I don't want it to happen to me.*

These statements reveal that despite her desire to marry, Rick's role in the family's future is provisional at best.

> *We get along, but we fight a lot. If he's there, he's there, but if he's not, that's why I want a job . . . a job with computers . . . so I could afford my kids, could afford the house. . . . I don't want to be living off him. I want my kids to be living off me.*

Why is Jen, who describes Rick as "the love of my life," so insistent on planning an exit strategy before she is willing to take the vows she firmly believes ought to last "forever"? If love is so sure, why does mistrust seem so palpable and strong? In relationships among poor couples like Jen and Rick, mistrust is often spawned by chronic violence and infidelity, drug and alcohol abuse, criminal activity, and the threat of imprisonment. In these tarnished corners of urban America, the stigma of a failed marriage is far worse than an out-of-wedlock birth. New mothers like Jen feel they must test the relationship over three, four, even five years' time. This is the only way, they believe, to insure that their marriages will last.

Trust has been an enormous issue in Jen's relationship with Rick.

My son was born December 23rd, and [Rick] started cheating on me again . . . in March. He started cheating on me with some girl—Amanda. . . . Then it was another girl, another girl, another girl after. I didn't wanna believe it. My friends would come up to me and be like, "Oh yeah, your boyfriend's cheating on you with this person." I wouldn't believe it. . . . I would see him with them. He used to have hickies. He used to make up some excuse that he was drunk—that was always his excuse for everything.

Things finally came to a head when Rick got another girl pregnant. *For a while, I forgave him for everything. Now, I don't forgive him for nothing.* Now we begin to understand the source of Jen's hesitancy. *He wants me to marry him, [but] I'm not really sure. . . . If I can't trust him, I can't marry him, 'cause we would get a divorce. If you're gonna get married, you're supposed to be faithful!* she insists. To Jen and her peers, the worst thing that could happen is "to get married just to get divorced."

Given the economic challenges and often perilously low quality of the romantic relationships among unmarried parents, poor women may be right to be cautious about marriage. Five years after we first spoke with her, we met with Jen again. We learned that Jen's second pregnancy ended in a miscarriage. We also learned that Rick was out of the picture—apparently for good.

You know that bar [down the street?] It happened in that bar. . . . They were in the bar, and this guy was like badmouthing [Rick's friend] Mikey, talking stuff to him or whatever. So Rick had to go get involved in it and start with this guy. . . . Then he goes outside and fights the guy [and] the guy dies of head trauma. They were all on drugs, they were all drinking, and things just got out of control, and that's what happened. He got fourteen to thirty years.

These Are Cards I Dealt Myself

Jen stuck with Rick for the first two and a half years of his prison sentence, but when another girl's name replaced her own on the visitors' list, Jen decided she was finished with him once and for all. Readers might be asking what Jen ever saw in a man like Rick. But Jen and Rick operate in a partner market where the better-off men go to the better-off women. The only way for someone like Jen to forge a satisfying relationship with a man is to find a diamond in the rough or improve her own economic position so that she can realistically compete for more upwardly mobile partners, which is what Jen is trying to do now.

> *There's this kid, Donny, he works at my job. He works on C shift. He's a super-visor! He's funny, three years older, and he's not a geek or anything, but he's not a real preppy good boy either. But he's not [a player like Rick] and them. He has a job, you know, so that's good. He doesn't do drugs or anything. And he asked my dad if he could take me out!*

These days, there is a new air of determination, even pride, about Jen. The aimless high school dropout pulls ten-hour shifts entering data at a ware-house distribution center Monday through Thursday. She has held the job for three years, and her aptitude and hard work have earned her a series of raises. Her current salary is higher than anyone in her household commands—$10.25 per hour, and she now gets two weeks of paid vacation, four personal days, 60 hours of sick time, and medical benefits. She has saved up the necessary $400 in tuition for a high school completion program that offers evening and weekend classes. Now all that stands between her and a diploma is a passing grade in mathematics, her least favorite subject. *My plan is to start college in January. [This month] I take my math test . . . so I can get my diploma,* she confides.

Jen clearly sees how her life has improved since Rick's dramatic exit from the scene.

> *That's when I really started [to get better] because I didn't have to worry about what he was doing, didn't have to worry about him cheating on me, all this stuff. [It was] then I realized that I had to do what I had to do to take care of my son. . . . When he was there, I think that my whole life revolved around him, you know, so I always messed up somehow because I was so busy worrying about what he was doing. Like I would leave the [GED] programs I was in just to go home and see what he was doing. My mind was never concentrating.*

Now, she says,

> *a lot of people in my family look up to me now, because all my sisters dropped out from school, you know, nobody went back to school. I went back to school, you know? . . . I went back to school, and I plan to go to college, and a lot of people look up to me for that, you know? So that makes me happy . . . because five years ago nobody looked up to me. I was just like everybody else.*

Yet the journey has not been easy. *Being a young mom, being 15, it's hard, hard, hard, you know.* She says, *I have no life. . . . I work from 6:30 in the morning until 5:00 at night. I leave here at 5:30 in the morning. I don't get home until about 6:00 at night.* Yet she measures her worth as a mother by the fact that she has managed to provide for her son largely on her own. *I don't depend on nobody. I might live with my dad and them, but I don't depend on them, you know.* She continues,

> *There [used to] be days when I'd be so stressed out, like, "I can't do this!" And I would just cry and cry and cry. . . . Then I look at Colin, and he'll be sleeping,*

and I'll just look at him and think I don't have no [reason to feel sorry for my-self]. The cards I have I've dealt myself so I have to deal with it now. I'm older. I can't change anything. He's my responsibility—he's nobody else's but mine—so I have to deal with that.

Becoming a mother transformed Jen's point of view on just about every-thing. She says,

I thought hanging on the corner drinking, getting high—I thought that was a good life, and I thought I could live that way for eternity, like sitting out with my friends. But it's not as fun once you have your own kid. . . . I think it changes [you]. I think, "Would I want Colin to do that? Would I want my son to be like that. . .?" It was fun to me but it's not fun anymore. Half the people I hung with are either . . . Some have died from drug overdoses, some are in jail, and some people are just out there living the same life that they always lived, and they don't look really good. They look really bad.

In the end, Jen believes, Colin's birth has brought far more good into her life than bad.

I know I could have waited [to have a child], but in a way I think Colin's the best thing that could have happened to me. . . . So I think I had my son for a purpose because I think Colin changed my life. He saved my life, really. My whole life revolves around Colin!

Promises I Can Keep

There are unique themes in Jen's story—most fathers are only one or two, not five years older than the mothers of their children, and few fathers have as many glaring problems as Rick—but we heard most of these themes repeat-edly in the stories of the 161 other poor, single mothers we came to know. Notably, poor women do not reject marriage; they revere it. Indeed, it is the conviction that marriage is forever that makes them think that divorce is worse than having a baby outside of marriage. Their children, far from being liabilities, provide crucial social-psychological resources—a strong sense of purpose and a profound source of intimacy. Jen and the other mothers we came to know are coming of age in an America that is profoundly unequal—where the gap between rich and poor continues to grow. This economic real-ity has convinced them that they have little to lose and, perhaps, something to gain by a seemingly "ill-timed" birth.

The lesson one draws from stories like Jen's is quite simple: Until poor young women have more access to jobs that lead to financial independence—until there is reason to hope for the rewarding life pathways that their privi-leged peers pursue—the poor will continue to have children far sooner than most Americans think they should, while still deferring marriage. Marital standards have risen for all Americans, and the poor want the same things that everyone now wants out of marriage. The poor want to marry too, but they insist on marrying well. This, in their view, is the only way to avoid an almost certain divorce. Like Jen, they are simply not willing to make promises they are not sure they can keep.

RECOMMENDED RESOURCES

Kathryn Edin and Maria Kefalas. *Promises I Can Keep: Why Poor Women Put Motherhood Before Marriage* (University of California Press, 2005). An account of how low-income women make sense of their choices about marriage and motherhood.

Christina Gibson, Kathryn Edin, and Sara McLanahan. "High Hopes but Even Higher Expectations: A Qualitative and Quantitative Analysis of the Marriage Plans of Unmarried Couples Who Are New Parents." Working Paper 03-06-FF, Center for Research on Child Wellbeing, Princeton University, 2004. Online at http://crcw.princeton.edu/workingpapers/WP03-06-FF-Gibson.pdf. The authors examine the rising expectations for marriage among unmarried parents.

Sharon Hays. *Flat Broke with Children: Women in the Age of Welfare Reform* (Oxford University Press, 2003). How welfare reform has affected the lives of poor moms.

Annette Lareau. *Unequal Childhoods: Class, Race, and Family Life* (University of California Press, 2003). A fascinating discussion of different childrearing strategies among low-income, working-class, and middle-class parents.

Timothy J. Nelson, Susan Clampet-Lundquist, and Kathryn Edin. "Fragile Fatherhood: How Low-Income, Non-Custodial Fathers in Philadelphia Talk About Their Families." In *The Handbook of Father Involvement: Multidisciplinary Perspectives*, ed. Catherine Tamis-LeMonda and Natasha Cabrera (Lawrence Earlbaum Associates, 2002). What poor, single men think about fatherhood.

55

INVISIBLE INEQUALITY
Social Class and Childrearing in Black Families and White Families

ANNETTE LAREAU

In addition to gender inequality, the institution of the family produces and reproduces other forms of social inequality in family life. Numerous sociological studies have investigated the transmission of social class values and norms within families. In this selection, Annette Lareau shows how social class affects parenting styles among both white and black families. Lareau, a professor of sociology at the University of Maryland, observed and interviewed 32 children and most of their parents to learn the types of skills parents transmit to their children. This excerpt is from Lareau's prize-winning ethnography *Unequal Childhoods: Class, Race, and Family Life* (2003).

In recent decades, sociological knowledge about inequality in family life has increased dramatically. Yet, debate persists, especially about the transmission of class advantages to children. Kingston (2000) and others question whether disparate aspects of family life cohere in meaningful patterns. Pointing to a "thin evidentiary base" for claims of social class differences in the interior of family life, Kingston also asserts that "class distinguishes neither distinctive parenting styles or distinctive involvement of kids" in specific behaviors (p. 134).

One problem with many studies is that they are narrowly focused. Researchers look at the influence of parents' education on parent involvement in schooling *or* at children's time spent watching television *or* at time spent visiting relatives. Only a few studies examine more than one dynamic inside the home. Second, much of the empirical work is descriptive. For example, extensive research has been done on time use, including patterns of women's labor force participation, hours parents spend at work, and mothers' and fathers' contributions to child care. . . .

Third, researchers have not satisfactorily explained how these observed patterns are produced. Put differently, *conceptualizations* of the *social processes* through which families differ are underdeveloped and little is known about how family life transmits advantages to children. Few researchers have attempted to integrate what is known about behaviors and attitudes taught inside the home with the ways in which these practices may provide unequal resources for family members outside the home. . . .

Fourth, little is known about the degree to which children adopt and enact their parents' beliefs. Sociologists of the family have long stressed the importance of a more dynamic model of parent–child interaction, but empirical research has been slow to emerge. . . .

I draw on findings from a small, intensive data set collected using ethnographic methods. I map the connections between parents' resources and their children's daily lives. My first goal, then, is to challenge Kingston's (2000) argument that social class does not distinguish parents' behavior or children's daily lives. I seek to show empirically that social class does indeed create distinctive parenting styles. I demonstrate that parents differ by class in the ways they define their own roles in their children's lives as well as in how they perceive the nature of childhood. The middle-class parents, both white *and* black, tend to conform to a cultural logic of childrearing I call "concerted cultivation." They enroll their children in numerous age-specific organized activities that dominate family life and create enormous labor, particularly for mothers. The parents view these activities as transmitting important life skills to children. Middle-class parents also stress language use and the development of reasoning and employ talking as their preferred form of discipline. This "cultivation" approach results in a wider range of experiences for children but also creates a frenetic pace for parents, a cult of individualism within the family, and an emphasis on children's performance.

The childrearing strategies of white and black working-class and poor parents emphasize the "accomplishment of natural growth." These parents believe that as long as they provide love, food, and safety, their children will grow and thrive. They do not focus on developing their children's special talents. Compared to the middle-class children, working-class and poor children participate in few organized activities and have more free time and deeper, richer ties within their extended families. Working-class and poor parents issue many more directives to their children and, in some households, place more emphasis on physical discipline than do the middle-class parents. These findings extend Kohn and Schooler's (1983) observation of class differences in parents' values, showing that differences also exist in the *behavior* of parents *and* children.

Quantitative studies of children's activities offer valuable empirical evidence but only limited ideas about how to conceptualize the mechanisms through which social advantage is transmitted. Thus, my second goal is to offer "conceptual umbrellas" useful for making comparisons across race and class and for assessing the role of social structural location in shaping daily life.

Last, I trace the connections between the class position of family members—including children—and the uneven outcomes of their experiences outside the home as they interact with professionals in dominant institutions. The pattern of concerted cultivation encourages an *emerging sense of entitlement* in children. All parents and children are not equally assertive, but the pattern of questioning and intervening among the white and black middle-class parents contrasts sharply with the definitions of how to be helpful and effective observed among the white and black working-class and poor adults. The pattern of the accomplishment of natural growth encourages an *emerging sense of constraint.* Adults as well as children in these social classes tend to be deferential and outwardly accepting in their interactions with professionals such as doctors and educators. At the same time, however, compared to their middle-class counterparts, white and black working-class and poor family members are more distrustful of professionals. These are differences with potential long-term consequences. In an historical moment when the dominant society privileges active, informed, assertive clients of health and educational services, the strategies employed by children and parents are not equally effective across classes. In sum, differences in family life lie not only in the advantages parents obtain for their children, but also in the skills they transmit to children for negotiating their own life paths.

Methodology

Study Participants

This study is based on interviews and observations of children, aged 8 to 10, and their families. The data were collected over time in three research phases. Phase one involved observations in two third-grade classrooms in a public school in the midwestern community of "Lawrenceville."[1] . . .

Phase two took place at two sites in a northeastern metropolitan area. One school, "Lower Richmond," although located in a predominantly white, working-class urban neighborhood, drew about half of its students from a nearby all-black housing project. I observed one third-grade class at Lower Richmond about twice a week for almost six months. The second site, "Swan," was located in a suburban neighborhood about 45 minutes from the city center. It was 90 percent white; most of the remaining 10 percent were middle-class children.[2] . . . A team of research assistants and I interviewed the parents and guardians. . . . Thus, the total number of children who participated in the study was 88 (32 from the Midwest and 56 from the Northeast). . . .

Phase three, the most intensive research phase of the study, involved home observations of 12 children and their families in the Northeast who had been previously interviewed. Some themes, such as language use and families' social connections, surfaced mainly during this phase. . . .

Concerted Cultivation and Natural Growth

The interviews and observations suggested that crucial aspects of family life *cohered*. Within the concerted cultivation and accomplishment of natural growth approaches, three key dimensions may be distinguished: the organization of daily life, the use of language, and social connections. . . . These dimensions do not capture all important parts of family life, but they do incorporate core aspects of childrearing. Moreover, our field observations revealed that behaviors and activities related to these dimensions dominated the rhythms of family life. Conceptually, the organization of daily life and the use of language are crucial dimensions. Both must be present for the family to be described as engaging in one childrearing approach rather than the other. Social connections are significant but less conceptually essential.

All three aspects of childrearing were intricately woven into the families' daily routines, but rarely remarked upon. As part of everyday practice, they were invisible to parents and children. Analytically, however, they are useful means for comparing and contrasting ways in which social class differences shape the character of family life. I now examine two families in terms of these three key dimensions. I "control" for race and gender and contrast the lives of two black boys—one from an (upper) middle-class family and one from a family on public assistance. I could have focused on almost any of the other 12 children, but this pair seemed optimal, given the limited number of studies reporting on black middle-class families, as well as the aspect of my argument that suggests that race is less important than class in shaping childrearing patterns.

Developing Alexander Williams

Alexander Williams and his parents live in a predominantly black middle-class neighborhood. Their six-bedroom house is worth about $150,000. Alexander is an only child. Both parents grew up in small towns in the South, and both are from large families. His father, a tall, handsome man, is a very successful trial lawyer who earns about $125,000 annually in a small firm specializing in medical malpractice cases. Two weeks each month, he works very long hours (from about 5:30 A.M. until midnight) preparing for trials. The other two weeks, his workday ends around 6:00 P.M. He rarely travels out of town. Alexander's mother, Christina, is a positive, bubbly woman with freckles and long, black, wavy hair. A high-level manager in a major corporation, she has a corner office, a personal secretary, and responsibilities for other offices across the nation. She tries to limit her travel, but at least once a month she takes an overnight trip.

Alexander is a charming, inquisitive boy with a winsome smile. Ms. Williams is pleased that Alexander seems interested in so many things:

> *Alexander is a joy. He's a gift to me. He's a very energetic, very curious, loving, caring person, that, um . . . is outgoing and who, uh, really loves to be with people. And who loves to explore, and loves to read and . . . just do a lot of fun things.*

The private school Alexander attends has an on-site after-school program. There, he participates in several activities and receives guitar lessons and photography instruction.

Organization of Daily Life   Alexander is busy with activities during the week and on weekends (Table 55.1). His mother describes their Saturday morning routine. The day starts early with a private piano lesson for Alexander downtown, a 20-minute drive from the house:

> *It's an 8:15 class. But for me, it was a tradeoff. I am very adamant about Saturday morning TV. I don't know what it contributes. So . . . it was um . . . either stay at home and fight on a Saturday morning [laughs] or go do some-*

TABLE 55.1   Participation in Activities Outside of School: Boys

Boy's Name/ Race/Class	Activities Organized by Adults	Informal Activities
Middle Class		
Alexander Williams (black)	Soccer team	Restricted television
	Baseball team	Plays outside occasionally
	Community choir	with two other boys
	Church choir	Visits friends from school
	Sunday school	
	Piano (Suzuki)	
	School plays	
	Guitar (through school)	
Poor		
Harold McAllister (black)	Bible study in neighbor's house (occasionally)	Visits relatives
		Plays ball with neighborhood kids
	Bible camp (1 week)	Watches television
		Watches videos

thing constructive. . . . Now Saturday mornings are pretty booked up. You know, the piano lesson, and then straight to choir for a couple of hours. So, he has a very full schedule.

Ms. Williams' vehement opposition to television is based on her view of what Alexander needs to grow and thrive. She objects to TV's passivity and feels it is her obligation to help her son cultivate his talents.

Sometimes Alexander complains that *my mother signs me up for everything!* Generally, however, he likes his activities. He says they make him feel "special," and without them life would be "boring." His sense of time is thoroughly entwined with his activities: He feels disoriented when his schedule is not full. This unease is clear in the following field-note excerpt. The family is driving home from a Back-to-School night. The next morning, Ms. Williams will leave for a work-related day trip and will not return until late at night. Alexander is grumpy because he has nothing planned for the next day. He wants to have a friend over, but his mother rebuffs him. Whining, he wonders what he will do. His mother, speaking tersely, says:

You have piano and guitar. You'll have some free time. [Pause] I think you'll survive for one night. [Alexander does not respond but seems mad. It is quiet for the rest of the trip home.]

Alexander's parents believe his activities provide a wide range of benefits important for his development. In discussing Alexander's piano lessons, Mr. Williams notes that as a Suzuki student,[3] Alexander is already able to read music. Speculating about more diffuse benefits of Alexander's involvement with piano, he says:

I don't see how any kid's adolescence and adulthood could not but be enhanced by an awareness of who Beethoven was. And is that Bach or Mozart? I don't know the difference between the two! I don't know Baroque from Classical—but he does. How can that not be a benefit in later life? I'm convinced that this rich experience will make him a better person, a better citizen, a better husband, a better father—certainly a better student.

Ms. Williams sees music as building her son's "confidence" and his "poise." In interviews and casual conversation, she stresses "exposure." She believes it is her responsibility to broaden Alexander's worldview. Childhood activities provide a learning ground for important life skills:

Sports provide great opportunities to learn how to be competitive. Learn how to accept defeat, you know. Learn how to accept winning, you know, in a gracious way. Also it gives him the opportunity to learn leadership skills and how to be a team player. . . . Sports really provides a lot of really great opportunities.

Alexander's schedule is constantly shifting; some activities wind down and others start up. Because the schedules of sports practices and games are issued no sooner than the start of the new season, advance planning is rarely possible. Given the sheer number of Alexander's activities, events inevitably overlap. Some activities, though short-lived, are extremely time consuming.

Alexander's school play, for example, requires rehearsals three nights the week before the opening. In addition, in choosing activities, the Williamses have an added concern—the group's racial balance. Ms. Williams prefers that Alexander not be the only black child at events. Typically, one or two other black boys are involved, but the groups are predominantly white and the activities take place in predominantly white residential neighborhoods. Alexander is, however, part of his church's youth choir and Sunday School, activities in which all participants are black. . . .

Language Use   Like other middle-class families, the Williamses often engage in conversation that promotes reasoning and negotiation. An excerpt from a field note (describing an exchange between Alexander and his mother during a car ride home after summer camp) shows the kind of pointed questions middle-class parents ask children. Ms. Williams is not just eliciting information. She is also giving Alexander the opportunity to develop and practice verbal skills, including how to summarize, clarify, and amplify information:

> *As she drives, [Ms. Williams] asks Alex, "So, how was your day?"*
> Alex: *Okay. I had hot dogs today, but they were burned! They were all black!*
> Mom: *Oh, great. You shouldn't have eaten any.*
> Alex: *They weren't all black, only half were. The rest were regular.*
> Mom: *Oh, okay. What was that game you were playing this morning?. . .*
> Alex: *It was [called] "Whatcha doin?"*
> Mom: *How do you play?*
>
> *Alexander explains the game elaborately—fieldworker doesn't quite follow. Mom asks Alex questions throughout his explanation, saying, "Oh, I see," when he answers. She asks him about another game she saw them play; he again explains. . . . She continues to prompt and encourage him with small giggles in the back of her throat as he elaborates. . . .*

Not all middle-class parents are as attentive to their children's needs as this mother, and none are *always* interested in negotiating. But a general pattern of reasoning and accommodating is common.

Social Connections   Mr. and Ms. Williams consider themselves very close to their extended families. Because the Williamses' aging parents live in the South, visiting requires a plane trip. Ms. Williams takes Alexander with her to see his grandparents twice a year. She speaks on the phone with her parents at least once a week and also calls her siblings several times a week. Mr. Williams talks with his mother regularly by phone (he has less contact with his stepfather). With pride, he also mentions his niece, whose Ivy League education he is helping to finance.

Interactions with cousins are not normally a part of Alexander's leisure time. . . . Nor does he often play with neighborhood children. The huge homes on the Williamses' street are occupied mainly by couples without children. Most of Alexander's playmates come from his classroom or his organized activities. Because most of his school events, church life, and assorted activities are organized by the age (and sometimes gender) of the participants, Alexander interacts almost exclusively with children his own age, usually boys. Adult-organized activities thus define the context of his social life.

Mr. and Ms. Williams are aware that they allocate a sizable portion of time to Alexander's activities. What they stress, however, is the time they *hold back*. They mention activities the family has chosen *not* to take on (such as traveling soccer).

Summary   Overall, Alexander's parents engaged in concerted cultivation. They fostered their son's growth through involvement in music, church, athletics, and academics. They talked with him at length, seeking his opinions and encouraging his ideas. Their approach involved considerable direct expenses (e.g., the cost of lessons and equipment) and large indirect expenses (e.g., the cost of taking time off from work, driving to practices, and forgoing adult leisure activities). Although Mr. and Ms. Williams acknowledged the importance of extended family, Alexander spent relatively little time with relatives. His social interactions occurred almost exclusively with children his own age and with adults. Alexander's many activities significantly shaped the organization of daily life in the family. Both parents' leisure time was tailored to their son's commitments. Mr. and Ms. Williams felt that the strategies they cultivated with Alexander would result in his having the best possible chance at a happy and productive life. They couldn't imagine themselves not investing large amounts of time and energy in their son's life. But, as I explain in the next section, which focuses on a black boy from a poor family, other parents held a different view.

Supporting the Natural Growth of Harold McAllister

Harold McAllister, a large, stocky boy with a big smile, is from a poor black family. He lives with his mother and his 8-year-old sister, Alexis, in a large apartment. Two cousins often stay overnight. Harold's 16-year-old sister and 18-year-old brother usually live with their grandmother, but sometimes they stay at the McAllisters' home. Ms. McAllister, a high school graduate, relies on public assistance. Hank, Harold and Alexis' father, is a mechanic. He and Ms. McAllister have never married. He visits regularly, sometimes weekly, stopping by after work to watch television or nap. Harold (but not Alexis) sometimes travels across town by bus to spend the weekend with Hank.

The McAllisters' apartment is in a public housing project near a busy street. The complex consists of rows of two- and three-story brick units. The buildings, blocky and brown, have small yards enclosed by concrete and wood fences. Large floodlights are mounted on the corners of the buildings, and wide concrete sidewalks cut through the spaces between units. The ground is bare in many places; paper wrappers and glass litter the area.

Inside the apartment, life is humorous and lively, with family members and kin sharing in the daily routines. Ms. McAllister discussed, disdainfully, mothers who are on drugs or who abuse alcohol and do not "look after" their children. Indeed, the previous year Ms. McAllister called Child Protective Services to report her twin sister, a cocaine addict, because she was neglecting her children. Ms. McAllister is actively involved in her twin's daughters' lives. Her two nephews also frequently stay with her. Overall, she sees herself as a capable mother who takes care of her children and her extended family.

Organization of Daily Life   Much of Harold's life and the lives of his family members revolve around home. Project residents often sit outside in lawn chairs or on front stoops, drinking beer, talking, and watching children play. During summer, windows are frequently left open, allowing breezes to waft through the units and providing vantage points from which residents can survey the neighborhood. A large deciduous tree in front of the McAllisters' apartment unit provides welcome shade in the summer's heat.

Harold loves sports. He is particularly fond of basketball, but he also enjoys football, and he follows televised professional sports closely. Most afternoons, he is either inside watching television or outside playing ball. He tosses a football with cousins and boys from the neighboring units and organizes pick-up basketball games. Sometimes he and his friends use a rusty, bare hoop hanging from a telephone pole in the housing project; other times, they string up an old, blue plastic crate as a makeshift hoop. One obstacle to playing sports, however, is a shortage of equipment. Balls are costly to replace, especially given the rate at which they disappear—theft of children's play equipment, including balls and bicycles, is an ongoing problem. During a field observation, Harold asks his mother if she knows where the ball is. She replies with some vehemence, "They stole the blue and yellow ball, and they stole the green ball, and they stole the other ball."

Hunting for balls is a routine part of Harold's leisure time. One June day, with the temperature and humidity in the high 80s, Harold and his cousin Tyrice (and a fieldworker) wander around the housing project for about an hour, trying to find a basketball:

> *We head to the other side of the complex. On the way . . . we passed four guys sitting on the step. Their ages were 9 to 13 years. They had a radio blaring. Two were working intently on fixing a flat bike tire. The other two were dribbling a basketball.*

Harold: *Yo! What's up, ya'll.*
Group: *What's up, Har. What's up? Yo.*

> *They continued to work on the tire and dribble the ball. As we walked down the hill, Harold asked, "Yo, could I use your ball?"*

> *The guy responded, looking up from the tire, "Naw, man. Ya'll might lose it."*

Harold, Tyrice, and the fieldworker walk to another part of the complex, heading for a makeshift basketball court where they hope to find a game in progress:

> *No such luck. Harold enters an apartment directly in front of the makeshift court. The door was open. . . . Harold came back. "No ball. I guess I gotta go back."*

The pace of life for Harold and his friends ebbs and flows with the children's interests and family obligations. The day of the basketball search, for example, after spending time listening to music and looking at baseball cards, the children join a water fight Tyrice instigates. It is a lively game, filled with laughter and with efforts to get the adults next door wet (against their wishes). When the game winds down, the kids ask their mother for money, receive it, and then walk to a store to buy chips and soda. They chat with another young boy and then amble back to the apartment, eating as they walk. Another afternoon, almost two weeks later, the children— Harold, two of his cousins, and two children from the neighborhood—and the fieldworker play basketball on a makeshift court in the street (using the fieldworker's ball). As Harold bounces the ball, neighborhood children of all ages wander through the space.

Thus, Harold's life is more free-flowing and more child-directed than is Alexander Williams'. The pace of any given day is not so much planned as emergent, reflecting child-based interests and activities. Parents intervene in specific areas, such as personal grooming, meals, and occasional chores, but they do not continuously direct and monitor their children's leisure activities. Moreover, the leisure activities Harold and other working-class and poor children pursue require them to develop a repertoire of skills for dealing with much older and much younger children as well as with neighbors and relatives.

Language Use   Life in the working-class and poor families in the study flows smoothly without extended verbal discussions. The amount of talking varies, but overall, it is considerably less than occurs in the middle-class homes.[4] Ms. McAllister jokes with the children and discusses what is on television. But she does not appear to cultivate conversation by asking the children questions or by drawing them out. Often she is brief and direct in her remarks. For instance, she coordinates the use of the apartment's only bathroom by using one-word directives. She sends the children (there are almost always at least four children home at once) to wash up by pointing to a child, saying one word, "bathroom," and handing him or her a washcloth. Wordlessly, the designated child gets up and goes to the bathroom to take a shower.

Similarly, although Ms. McAllister will listen to the children's complaints about school, she does not draw them out on these issues or seek to determine details, as Ms. Williams would. . . .

Social Connections   Children, especially boys, frequently play outside. The number of potential playmates in Harold's world is vastly higher than the number in Alexander's neighborhood. When a fieldworker stops to count heads, she finds 40 children of elementary school age residing in the nearby rows of apartments. With so many children nearby, Harold could choose to play only with others his own age. In fact, though, he often hangs out with older and younger children and with his cousins (who are close to his age).

The McAllister family, like other poor and working-class families, is involved in a web of extended kin. As noted earlier, Harold's older siblings and his two male cousins often spend the night at the McAllister home. Celebrations such as birthdays involve relatives almost exclusively. Party guests are not, as in middle-class families, friends from school or from extracurricular activities. Birthdays are celebrated enthusiastically, with cake and special food to mark the occasion; presents, however, are not offered. Similarly, Christmas at Harold's house featured a tree and special food but no presents. At these and other family events, the older children voluntarily look after the younger ones: Harold plays with his 16-month-old niece, and his cousins carry around the younger babies.

The importance of family ties—and the contingent nature of life in the McAllisters' world—is clear in the response Alexis offers when asked what she would do if she were given a million dollars:

> Oh, boy! I'd buy my brother, my sister, my uncle, my aunt, my nieces and my nephews, and my grandpop, and my grandmon, and my mom, and my dad, and my friends, not my friends, but mostly my best friend—I'd buy them all clothes . . . and sneakers. And I'd buy some food, and I'd buy my mom some food, and I'd get my brothers and my sisters gifts for their birthdays.

Summary   In a setting where everyone, including the children, was acutely aware of the lack of money, the McAllister family made do. Ms. McAllister rightfully saw herself as a very capable mother. She was a strong, positive influence in the lives of the children she looked after. Still, the contrast with Ms. Williams is striking. Ms. McAllister did not seem to think that Harold's opinions needed to be cultivated and developed. She, like most parents in the working-class and poor families, drew strong and clear boundaries between adults and children. Adults gave directions to children. Children were given freedom to play informally unless they were needed for chores. Extended family networks were deemed important and trustworthy. . . .

Impact of Childrearing Strategies on Interactions with Institutions

I now follow the families out of their homes and into encounters with representatives of dominant institutions—institutions that are directed by middle-class professionals. Again, I focus on Alexander Williams and Harold McAllister. Across all social classes, parents and children interacted with teachers and school officials, health care professionals, and assorted government officials. Although they often addressed similar problems (e.g., learning disabilities, asthma, traffic violations), they typically did not achieve similar resolutions. The pattern of concerted cultivation fostered an *emerging sense of entitlement* in the life of Alexander Williams and other middle-class children. By contrast, the commitment to nurturing children's natural growth fostered an *emerging sense of constraint* in the life of Harold McAllister and other working-class or poor children.

Both parents and children drew on the resources associated with these two childrearing approaches during their interactions with officials. Middle-class parents and children often customized these interactions; working-class and poor parents were more likely to have a "generic" relationship. When faced with problems, middle-class parents also appeared better equipped to exert influence over other adults compared with working-class and poor parents. Nor did middle-class parents or children display the intimidation or confusion we witnessed among many working-class and poor families when they faced a problem in their children's school experience.

Emerging Signs of Entitlement

Alexander Williams' mother, like many middle-class mothers, explicitly teaches her son to be an informed, assertive client in interactions with professionals. For example, as she drives Alexander to a routine doctor's appointment, she coaches him in the art of communicating effectively in health care settings:

> *Alexander asks if he needs to get any shots today at the doctor's. Ms. Williams says he'll need to ask the doctor. . . . As we enter Park Lane, Mom says quietly to Alex: "Alexander, you should be thinking of questions you might want to ask the doctor. You can ask him anything you want. Don't be shy. You can ask anything."*

> *Alex thinks for a minute, then: "I have some bumps under my arms from my deodorant."*

> Mom: *Really? You mean from your new deodorant?*

> Alex: *Yes.*

> Mom: *Well, you should ask the doctor.*

Alexander learns that he has the right to speak up (e.g., "don't be shy") and that he should prepare for an encounter with a person in a position of authority by gathering his thoughts in advance. . . .

Middle-class parents and children were also very assertive in situations at the public elementary school most of the middle-class children in the study attended. There were numerous conflicts during the year over matters small and large. For example, parents complained to one another and to the teachers about the amount of homework the children were assigned. A black middle-class mother whose daughters had not tested into the school's gifted program negotiated with officials to have the girls' (higher) results from a private testing company accepted instead. The parents of a fourth-grade boy drew the school superintendent into a battle over religious lyrics in a song scheduled to be sung as part of the holiday program. The superintendent consulted the district lawyer and ultimately "counseled" the principal to be more sensitive, and the song was dropped.

Children, too, asserted themselves at school. Examples include requesting that the classroom's blinds be lowered so the sun wasn't in their eyes, badgering the teacher for permission to retake a math test for a higher grade, and demanding to know why no cupcake had been saved when an absence prevented attendance at a classroom party. In these encounters, children were not simply complying with adults' requests or asking for a repeat of an earlier experience. They were displaying an emerging sense of entitlement by urging adults to permit a customized accommodation of institutional processes to suit their preferences. . . .

Emerging Signs of Constraint

The interactions the research assistants and I observed between professionals and working-class and poor parents frequently seemed cautious and constrained. This unease is evident, for example, during a physical Harold McAllister has before going to Bible camp. Harold's mother, normally boisterous and talkative at home, is quiet. Unlike Ms. Williams, she seems wary of supplying the doctor with accurate information:

> Doctor: *Does he eat something each day—either fish, meat, or egg?*
>
> Mom, response is low and muffled: *Yes.*
>
> Doctor, attempting to make eye contact but mom stares intently at paper: *A yellow vegetable?*
>
> Mom, still no eye contact, looking at the floor: *Yeah.*
>
> Doctor: *A green vegetable?*
>
> Mom, looking at the doctor: *Not all the time.* [Fieldworker has not seen any of the children eat a green or yellow vegetable since visits began.]
>
> Doctor: *No. Fruit or juice?*
>
> Mom, low voice, little or no eye contact, looks at the doctor's scribbles on the paper he is filling out: *Ummh humn.*
>
> Doctor: *Does he drink milk every day?*
>
> Mom, abruptly, in considerably louder voice: *Yeah.*
>
> Doctor: *Cereal, bread, rice, potato, anything like that?*
>
> Mom, shakes her head: *Yes, definitely.* [Looks at doctor.]

Ms. McAllister's knowledge of developmental events in Harold's life is uneven. She is not sure when he learned to walk and cannot recall the name of his previous doctor. And when the doctor asks, *When was the last time he had a tetanus shot?* she counters, gruffly, *What's a tetanus shot?* . . .

[N]either Harold nor his mother seemed as comfortable as Alexander had been. Alexander was used to extensive conversation at home; with the doctor, he was at ease initiating questions. Harold, who was used to responding to directives at home, primarily answered questions from the doctor, rather than posing his own. Alexander, encouraged by his mother, was assertive and confident with the doctor. Harold was reserved. Absorbing his mother's apparent need to conceal the truth about the range of foods he ate, he appeared cautious, displaying an emerging sense of constraint.

We observed a similar pattern in school interactions. Overall, the working-class and poor adults had much more distance or separation from the school than their middle-class counterparts. Ms. McAllister, for example, could be quite assertive in some settings (e.g., at the start of family observations, she visited the local drug dealer, warning him not to "mess with" the black male fieldworker). But throughout the fourth-grade parent-teacher conference, she kept her winter jacket zipped up, sat hunched over in her chair, and spoke in barely audible tones. She was stunned when the teacher said that Harold did not do homework. Sounding dumbfounded, she said, *He does it at home.* The teacher denied it and continued talking. Ms. McAllister made no further comments and did not probe for more information, except about a letter the teacher said he had mailed home and that she had not received. The conference ended, having yielded Ms. McAllister few insights into Harold's educational experience.[5]

Other working-class and poor parents also appeared baffled, intimidated, and subdued in parent-teacher conferences. . . . Working-class and poor children seemed aware of their parents' frustration and witnessed their powerlessness. Billy Yanelli [a working-class boy], for example, asserted in an interview that his mother "hate[d]" school officials.

At times, these parents encouraged their children to resist school officials' authority. The Yanellis told Billy to "beat up" a boy who was bothering him. Wendy Driver's mother advised her to punch a male classmate who pestered her and pulled her ponytail. Ms. Driver's boyfriend added, "Hit him when the teacher isn't looking."

In classroom observations, working-class and poor children could be quite lively and energetic, but we did not observe them try to customize their environments. They tended to react to adults' offers or, at times, to plead with educators to repeat previous experiences, such as reading a particular story, watching a movie, or going to the computer room. Compared to middle-class classroom interactions, the boundaries between adults and children seemed firmer and clearer. Although the children often resisted and tested school rules, they did not seem to be seeking to get educators to accommodate their own *individual* preferences.

Overall, then, the behavior of working-class and poor parents cannot be explained as a manifestation of their temperaments or of overall passivity; parents were quite energetic in intervening in their children's lives in other spheres. Rather, working-class and poor parents generally appeared to depend on the school (Lareau 2000), even as they were dubious of the trustworthiness of the professionals. This suspicion of professionals in dominant institutions is, at least in some instances, a reasonable response.[6] The unequal level of trust, as well as differences in the amount and quality of information divulged, can yield unequal *profits* during a historical moment when professionals applaud assertiveness and reject passivity as an inappropriate parenting strategy (Epstein 2001). Middle-class children and parents often (but not always) accrued advantages or profits from their efforts. Alexander Williams succeeded in having the doctor take his medical concerns seriously.

Ms. Marshall's children ended up in the gifted program, even though they did not technically qualify. Middle-class children expect institutions to be responsive to *them* and to accommodate their individual needs. By contrast, when Wendy Driver is told to hit the boy who is pestering her (when the teacher isn't looking) or Billy Yanelli is told to physically defend himself, despite school rules, they are not learning how to make bureaucratic institutions work to their advantage. Instead, they are being given lessons in frustration and powerlessness.

Why Does Social Class Matter?

Parents' economic resources helped create the observed class differences in childrearing practices. Enrollment fees that middle-class parents dismissed as "negligible" were formidable expenses for less affluent families. Parents also paid for clothing, equipment, hotel stays, fast-food meals, summer camps, and fundraisers. In 1994, the Tallingers [a middle-class family] estimated the cost of Garrett's activities at $4,000 annually, and that figure was not unusually high.[7] Moreover, families needed reliable private transportation and flexible work schedules to get children to and from events. These resources were disproportionately concentrated in middle-class families.

Differences in educational resources also are important. Middle-class parents' superior levels of education gave them larger vocabularies that facilitated concerted cultivation, particularly in institutional interventions. Poor and working-class parents were not familiar with key terms professionals used, such as "tetanus shot." Furthermore, middle-class parents' educational backgrounds gave them confidence when criticizing educational professionals and intervening in school matters. Working-class and poor parents viewed educators as their social superiors.

Kohn and Schooler (1983) showed that parents' occupations, especially the complexity of their work, influence their childrearing beliefs. We found that parents' work mattered, but also saw signs that the experience of adulthood itself influenced conceptions of childhood. Middle-class parents often were preoccupied with the pleasures and challenges of their work lives.[8] They tended to view childhood as a dual opportunity: a chance for play and for developing talents and skills of value later in life. Mr. Tallinger noted that playing soccer taught Garrett to be "hard nosed" and "competitive," valuable workplace skills. Ms. Williams mentioned the value of Alexander learning to work with others by playing on a sports team. Middle-class parents, aware of the "declining fortunes" of the middle class, worried about their own economic futures and those of their children (Newman 1993). This uncertainty increased their commitment to helping their children develop broad skills to enhance their future possibilities.

Working-class and poor parents' conceptions of adulthood and childhood also appeared to be closely connected to their lived experiences. For the working class, it was the deadening quality of work and the press of economic shortages that defined their experience of adulthood and influenced their vision of childhood. It was dependence on public assistance and severe economic shortages that most shaped poor parents' views. Families in both classes had many worries about basic issues: food shortages, limited access to health care, physical safety, unreliable transportation, insufficient clothing. Thinking back over their childhoods, these parents remembered hardship but also recalled times without the anxieties they now faced. Many appeared to want their own youngsters to concentrate on being happy and relaxed, keeping the burdens of life at bay until they were older.

Thus, childrearing strategies are influenced by more than parents' education. It is the interweaving of life experiences and resources, including parents' economic resources, occupational conditions, and educational backgrounds, that appears to be most important in leading middle-class parents to engage in concerted cultivation and working-class and poor parents to engage in the accomplishment of natural growth. Still, the structural location of families did not fully determine their childrearing practices. The agency of actors and the indeterminacy of social life are inevitable. . . .

ENDNOTES

[1] All names of people and places are pseudonyms. The Lawrenceville school was in a white suburban neighborhood in a university community a few hours from a metropolitan area. The student population was about half white and half black; the (disproportionately poor) black children were bused from other neighborhoods.

[2] Over three-quarters of the students at Lower Richmond qualified for free lunch; by contrast, Swan did not have a free lunch program.

[3] The Suzuki method is labor intensive. Students are required to listen to music about one hour per day. Also, both child and parent(s) are expected to practice daily and to attend every lesson together.

[4] Hart and Risley (1995) reported a similar difference in speech patterns. In their sample, by about age three, children of professionals had larger vocabularies and spoke more utterances per hour than the *parents* of similarly aged children on welfare.

[5] Middle-class parents sometimes appeared slightly anxious during parent–teacher conferences, but overall, they spoke more and asked educators more questions than did working-class and poor parents.

[6] The higher levels of institutional reports of child neglect, child abuse, and other family difficulties among poor families may reflect this group's greater vulnerability to institutional intervention (e.g., see L. Gordon 1989).

[7] In 2002, a single sport could cost as much as $5,000 annually. Yearly league fees for ice hockey run to $2,700; equipment costs are high as well (Halbfinger 2002).

[8] Middle-class adults do not live problem-free lives, but compared with the working class and poor, they have more varied occupational experiences and greater access to jobs with higher economic returns.

REFERENCES

Epstein, Joyce. 2001. *Schools, Family, and Community Partnerships*. Boulder, CO: Westview.

Gordon, Linda. 1989. *Heroes of Their Own Lives: The Politics and History of Family Violence*. New York: Penguin.

Halbfinger, David M. 2002. "A Hockey Parent's Life: Time, Money, and Yes, Frustration." *New York Times*, January 12, p. 29.

Hart, Betty and Todd Risley. 1995. *Meaningful Differences in the Everyday Experience of Young American Children.* Baltimore, MD: Paul Brooks.

Kingston, Paul. 2000. *The Classless Society.* Stanford, CA: Stanford University Press.

Kohn, Melvin and Carmi Schooler, eds. 1983. *Work and Personality: An Inquiry into the Impact of Social Stratification.* Norwood, NJ: Ablex.

Lareau, Annette. 2000. *Home Advantage: Social Class and Parental Intervention in Elementary Education.* 2d ed. Lanham, MD: Rowman and Littlefield.

Newman, Kathleen. 1993. *Declining Fortunes: The Withering of the American Dream.* New York: Basic Books.

56

THE ATROPHY OF SOCIAL LIFE

D. STANLEY EITZEN

Social structures in the United States are dynamic and continually experiencing social change due to major structural and cultural trends. We need to understand that social change occurs on all levels in society, including the micro and macro levels. In this reading, the first of three to focus on social change, D. Stanley Eitzen, a professor emeritus of sociology at Colorado State University, examines how social change that occurs on the macro level of society can affect social experiences at the micro level of society. In particular, Eitzen argues that some types of social progress have led to a decrease in social interaction. Eitzen describes several social trends and the implications they have had for society and for increasing social isolation.

Harvard political scientist Robert Putnam has written a provocative book entitled *Bowling Alone,* in which he argues that we Americans are becoming increasingly disengaged from each other. That is, we are less likely than Americans of a generation or two ago to belong to voluntary associations such as the Rotary Club, to play bridge on a regular basis, to participate in a bowling league, to belong to the P.T.A., or to vote. In short, Putnam maintains that in the past 50 years or so social life has changed dramatically throughout the United States as various social trends isolate us more and more from each other. The effect, he suggests, is that the bonds of civic cement are disintegrating as we become increasingly separated from each other, from our communities, and from society. Consequently, the social glue that once held communities together and gave meaning to individual lives is now brittle, as people have become more and more isolated.

I am a sociologist. We sociologists focus on things social, the most fundamental of which is social interaction. This is the basic building block of intimate relationships, small groups, formal organizations, communities, and societies. I am concerned and I believe we should all be concerned by some disturbing trends in our society that hinder or even eliminate social interaction, and that indicate a growing isolation as individuals become increasingly separated from their neighbors, their co-workers, and even their family members.

Moving Away

Ours is a mobile society. We move, on average about every five years. We change jobs (14 percent of workers in a typical year leave their jobs voluntarily) or we lose jobs involuntarily (a recent survey indicated that 36 percent of Americans answered "yes" to the question "Has anyone in your immediate family lost a job in the last three years?"). It's important to note here that the bond between workers and employers is badly frayed as employees are no longer loyal to their employers and employers are clearly not loyal to their employees as they downsize locally and outsource their jobs and operations to low-wage economies.

We are also moving away from intimate relationships. With 1.25 million divorces occurring annually in the United States, 2.5 million move away from their spouses. Immigration has the same consequence, creating transnational families, where families are separated with some members living in the United States and one or more members back home in another country.

When we move out of relationships or to new geographical areas, or to new kinds of work, we leave behind our relationships with former neighbors, co-workers, and friends. If we anticipate moving, we act like temporary residents, not making the effort to join local organizations, to become acquainted with our neighbors, and invest our time and money to improve the community.

Living Alone

In 1930, 2 percent of the U.S. population lived alone. In 2000, some 10 percent (27.2 million) of the nation's 105 million households were occupied by single people without children, roommates, or other people. People are living longer and the elderly, especially older women, are most likely to live alone. Divorce, by definition, initiates living alone, with 2.5 million former spouses annually moving into separate living arrangements. Another source for living alone is the phenomenon of commuter marriage—an arrangement where wives and husbands maintain separate households as a way of solving the dilemmas of dual-career marriages.

Technology and Isolation

Modern technology often encourages isolation. Consider the isolating consequences of air conditioning, certainly a welcome and necessary technology in many places. Before air conditioning, people spent leisure time outside increasing the likelihood of interaction with neighbors and friends. Now they are inside their homes with doors and windows shut enjoying the cool air, but isolating themselves from their neighbors. Television, too, along with VCRs, DVDs, and video games entice us to stay in our homes more and more.

Before refrigerators, shopping was done every day. This meant that people would see the same shop proprietors and their fellow shoppers daily. This created a daily rhythm, a set of interactions, and the sharing of information, gossip, and mutual concerns. Thus, refrigerators, while reducing the spoilage of food and the necessity of going to the store every day, changed interaction patterns.

Because of computers and telecommunications there is a growing trend for workers to work at home. At last count, 28 million Americans worked out of their homes, using computers or telephones instead of face-to-face interaction. While home-based work allows flexibility and independence not found in most jobs, these workers are separated from the rich social networks that often give rise to numerous friendships and make working life enjoyable or at least tolerable.

With the new communications technology, you don't even have to go to a funeral to pay your respects. A new company is now broadcasting funerals on the Internet and you can even sign an electronic guest book and e-mail condolences to the family. Similarly, one can take college courses without attending classes, just using the Internet to communicate with their instructors. Missing, of course, is the face-to-face interaction with fellow students and professors.

Paradoxically, the current communications revolution increases interaction while reducing intimacy. Curt Suplee, science and technology writer for the *Washington Post,* says that we have seen tenfold increases in "communication" by electronic means, and tenfold reductions in person-to-person contact. The more time people spend online, the less they can spare for real-life relationships with family and friends. In effect, as we are increasingly alone before a computer screen, we risk what former U.S. Secretary of State Warren Christopher has called "social malnutrition." John L. Locke, a professor of communications, makes a convincing argument in his book, *The De-Voicing of Society,* that e-mail, voice mail, fax machines, beepers, and Internet chat rooms are robbing us of ordinary social talking. Talking, he says, like the grooming of apes and monkeys, is the way we build and maintain social relationships. In his view, it is only through intimate conversation that we can know others well enough to trust them and work with them harmoniously. Most face-to-face communication is nonverbal. Phone communication reduces the nonverbal clues, and e-mail eliminates them entirely. So the new information technologies only create the illusion of communication and intimacy. The result, according to Locke, is that we are becoming an autistic society, communicating messages electronically but without really connecting. In short, these incredible communication devices that combine to network us in so many dazzling ways also separate us increasingly from intimate relationships. Sometimes we even use the technology to avoid the live interaction for whatever reason. Jeffrey Kagan, a telecom industry analyst, sums up the problem: "We are becoming a society that finds it easier, and even preferable to hide behind our computer screens and chat with a raceless, nameless stream of words from across the country or across the globe rather than deal with people face to face and all the complexities, good and bad, of the human relationship."

Geography and Isolation

There is a strong pattern of social homogeneity by place. Cities are arranged into neighborhoods by social class and race. This occurs because of choice, economic means, and the discriminatory behaviors by neighbors, realtors, and lending institutions. Among multiracial societies, only South Africa exceeds our rate of segregation—a problem that concentrates poverty, social disorder, and dysfunctional schools as well as diminishing social cohesion. The degree of racial-ethnic segregation by neighborhood is higher now than in 1990. A Harvard University study found that about 2.3 million African American and Latino children attend "apartheid" schools, where virtually all students are minorities. Similarly, some neighborhoods are segregated by age. Some retirement communities, for example, limit their inhabitants to persons over 55 and those without minor children. Some 6 million households are in neighborhoods that have controlled-entry systems with guards and electric gates. These gated communities wall the residents off physically and socially from "others." Regarding this exclusiveness, sociologist Philip Slater said that we need heterogeneous neighborhoods: "A community that does not have old people and children, white-collar and blue-collar, eccentric and conventional, and so on, is not a community at all, but [a] kind of truncated and deformed monstrosity. . . ."

Even in non-gated communities, we isolate ourselves. One in three Americans has never spent an evening with a neighbor. The affluent often belong to exclusive clubs and send their children to private schools. Two million children are home schooled, which isolates them from their peers. Some people exercise on motorized treadmills and use other home exercise equipment instead of running through their neighborhoods or working out with others.

The suburbs are especially isolating. Rather than walking to the corner grocery or nearby shop and visiting with the clerks and their neighbors, suburbanites drive somewhere away from their immediate neighborhood to shop among strangers. Or they may not leave their home at all, working, shopping, banking, and paying their bills by computer. For suburban teenagers and children almost everything is away—practice fields, music lessons, friends, jobs, schools, and the malls. Thus, a disconnect from those nearby. Suburban neighborhoods in particular are devoid of meeting places. The lack of community and common meeting places in our cities and especially in the suburbs compounds the isolation of those who have experienced a divorce or the death of a spouse.

Isolation within Families

An especially disturbing trend is the separation of family members from each other. Many spouses are either absent or too self-absorbed to pay very much attention to their children or each other. A recent cover story in *Newsweek* noted that many dual-income couples no longer or rarely have sex because they are too exhausted and too stressed. On average, parents today spend 22 fewer hours a week with their children than parents did in the 1960s. Part of this is because both parents are working outside the home. But it also results from children being overscheduled with outside-the-home activities. These children have little time for play with other children and their activities replace parent–child interaction. To amplify the last point, American children spend more than half of their waking hours in supervised, child-centered environments. This causes economist Ellen Frank to ask: "What happens to parents, to children, and to the rest of us when children are stored out of sight?"

Although living in the same house, parents and children may tune each other out emotionally, or by using earphones, or by engaging in other solitary activities. A survey by the Kaiser Family Foundation found that the average child spends five and one-half hours a day alone watching television, on the Internet, playing video games, or reading. Some 30 percent of children under 3 have a television in their bedroom. Some older children even have their own rooms equipped with a telephone, television, VCR, microwave, refrigerator, and computer, which while convenient, isolates them from other family members. Many families rarely eat together in an actual sit-down meal. Family members are often too busy and too involved with their individual schedules to spend quality time together as a family. These homes may be full of people but they are really empty.

The Architecture of Isolation

Another contemporary trend—the increased number of megahouses in the suburbs—results in what we might call the architecture of isolation. These huge houses, built, ironically, at the very time that family size is declining, tend to isolate their inhabitants from outsiders and from other family members. They provide all of the necessities for comfort and recreation, thus glorifying the private sphere over public places. Moreover, the number and size of the rooms encourage each family member to have their own space rather than shared spaces. Thus, the inverse correlation between house size and family interaction.

Contemporary house and landscape design focuses interaction in the backyard, surrounded by privacy fences, some of which make our homes and lots resemble medieval fortresses. Back yards are inviting with grass and flowerbeds, barbeque pits, swimming pools, jungle gyms, and trampolines. The front of the house no longer has a porch. In the past, families spent time on the porch, relaxing and visiting with neighbors. The front yard, too, is less inviting than the back, often with rock instead of grass. It is important to note that the more affluent we are, the more likely our homes and consumer goods promote social isolation.

Consumerism and Isolation

Sociologist George Ritzer in his recent book, *The Globalization of Nothing*, argues that the social world, particularly in the realm of consumption, is increasingly characterized by "nothing," which he defines as a social form that is generally centrally conceived and controlled and comparatively devoid of distinctive substance. The "something" that is lost is more than likely, an indigenous custom or product, a local store, a familiar gathering place, or simply personalized interaction. Corporations provide standardized, mass-produced products for us to consume and become like other consumers in what we wear, what we eat, and what we desire. We purchase goods in chain stores and restaurants (Dillard's, McDonald's) that are efficient but devoid of distinctive content. A mall in one part of the world may be structured much the same in another location. We bank at ATMs anywhere in the world, but without social interaction. The same is true with shopping on the Internet.

Increasingly, Ritzer says, adults go through their daily routines without sharing stories, gossip, and analyses of events with friends on a regular basis at work, at a coffee shop, neighborhood tavern, or at the local grain elevator. These places of conversation with friends have been replaced by huge stores (Wal-Mart, Home Depot) where we don't know the clerks and other shoppers. The locally owned café has been replaced by chain restaurants. In the process we lose the intimacy of local stores, cafés, and hardware stores, which give their steady customers a sense of community and the comfort of meaningful connections with others. Sociologist Philip Slater said that "community life exists when one can go daily to a given location at a given time and see many of the people one knows."

Implications for Society

There are several important implications of increasing social isolation for society. First, the disengaged do not participate in elections, leaving a minority to elect our leaders as occurred in the 2000 presidential election when George Bush was elected with 24 percent of the votes of those eligible. This means that the voices of outsiders will be faint, if heard at all, while the voices of the affluent and their money are heard all the more. All of these consequences support the conservative agenda, as sociologist Paul Starr notes: "These trends could hardly please anyone who cares about the republic, but they have been particularly disturbing to liberals. The most intense periods of liberal reform during the past century—the Progressive era, the New Deal, and the 1960s—were all times when the public was actively engaged, and new forms of civic action and participation emerged. Reforms in that tradition are unlikely to succeed again without the same heightened public arousal, which not only elects candidates but also forces them to pay attention once they are in office."

Second, the breakdown in social connections shows up in everyday sociability, with pernicious effects for social relations as people are less and less civil in schools, at work, in traffic, and in public places.

Third, when people focus only on themselves and people like themselves, they insulate themselves from "others" and from their problems. Thus, we favor dismantling the welfare state and safety net for the less fortunate. We oppose, for example, equity in school funding, allowing rich districts to have superior schools while the disadvantaged have inferior schools. We allow this unraveling of community bonds at our peril; as the walls become thicker between the "haves" and the "have-nots," crime will increase and hostility and fear will reign.

Implications for Individuals

As for individuals, the consequences of this accelerating social isolation are dire. More and more Americans are lonely, bitter, alienated, anomic, and disconnected. This situation is conducive to alcohol and drug abuse, depression, anxiety, and violence. The lonely and disaffected are ripe candidates for membership in cults, gangs, and militias where they find a sense of belonging and a cause to believe in, but in the process they may become more paranoid and, perhaps, even become willing terrorists or mass murderers as were the two alienated adolescents who perpetrated the massacre at Columbine High School in a Denver suburb. At a less extreme level, the alienated will disengage further from society by shunning voluntary associations, by home schooling their children, and by voting against higher taxes for the public good. In short, they will become increasingly self-absorbed, caring only about themselves and ignoring the needs of their neighbors and communities. This translates into the substitution of accumulating things rather than cultivating relationships. In this regard, we should take seriously the admonition by David Wann, the coauthor of *Afluenza: The All-Consuming Epidemic*, who says "We need to acknowledge—as individuals and as a culture—that the best things in life really aren't things. The best things are people. . . ."

What to Do?

I am not a Luddite. I appreciate the wonders of technology. I welcome change. There are good reasons to move and to change careers and to live in nice houses. But we must recognize the unintended consequences of societal trends that deprive us of our shared humanity. Once we have identified the downside of these trends and our complicity in them, what can we do to reverse their negative effects? I don't have all the answers, but I believe that a few structural changes will help to reduce their negative consequences. As a start, we need to rethink urban design. We must reverse urban sprawl, increasing urban density so that people live near their work, near their neighbors, and within walking distance of stores and recreation. Second, as a society we need to invest in the infrastructure that facilitates public activities such as neighborhood schools, walking and biking trails, parks, the arts, libraries, and community recreation centers. Third, communities need to provide activities that bring people together such as public concerts, fairs, recreational sports for people of all ages, and art festivals. And, fourth, since U.S. society is becoming more diverse, we need to break down the structural barriers that isolate us from "others." We need to affirm affirmative action in legislation and deed, eliminate predatory lending practices and other forms of discrimination, and improve our schools so that equality of educational opportunity actually occurs rather than the present arrangement whereby school systems are rigged in favor of the already privileged. You will note that these proposals are opposite from current policy at the community, state, and federal levels, resulting in a descending spiral toward social atomization. We allow this to occur at our own peril.

At a personal level, we need to recognize what is happening to us and our families and work to counteract these isolating trends. Each of us can think of changes in our lives that will enhance human connections. To those changes, may I suggest the following: Engage in public activities. Have meaningful face-to-face conversations with friends on a regular basis. Get to know your neighbors, co-workers, and the people who provide services for you. Join with others who share a common interest. Work to improve your community. Become an activist, joining with others to bring about social change. And, most of all, we need to moderate our celebration of individualism and our tendency toward self-absorption and develop instead a moral obligation to others, to our neighbors (broadly defined) and their children, to those unlike us as well as those similar to us, and to future generations. If not, then our humanity is compromised and our quality of life diminished.

SUGGESTED FURTHER READINGS

Kane, Hal. 2001. *Triumph of the Mundane: The Unseen Trends That Shape Our Lives and Environment.* Washington, DC: Island Press.

Locke, John L. 1998. *The De-Voicing of Society: Why We Don't Talk to Each Other.* New York: Simon and Schuster.

Oldenburg, Ray. 1997. *The Great Good Place: Cafes, Coffee Shops, Community Centers, Beauty Parlors, General Stores, Bars, Hangouts, and How They Get You through the Day.* New York: Marlowe.

Putnam, Robert D. 2000. *Bowling Alone: The Collapse and Revival of American Community.* New York: Simon and Schuster.

Ritzer, George. 2004. *The Globalization of Nothing.* Thousand Oaks. CA: Pine Forge Press.

Slater, Philip. 1970. *The Pursuit of Loneliness: American Culture at the Breaking Point.* Boston: Beacon Press.

57

THE COSMOPOLITAN CANOPY

ELIJAH ANDERSON

The second reading in this section on social change is by Elijah Anderson, the Charles and William L. Day Distinguished Professor of the Social Sciences and a professor of sociology at the University of Pennsylvania. He is the author of several well-known urban ethnographies, including *A Place on the Corner: A Study of Black Street Corner Men* (2003); *Code of the Street: Decency, Violence, and the Moral Life of the Inner City* (1999); and *Streetwise: Race, Class and Change in an Urban Community* (1990). This article, written in 2004, builds on Anderson's earlier ethnographic work studying racial relationships in Philadelphia. Anderson illustrates well that not all interracial interactions are negative, and in fact, some public urban spaces dramatically alter the social distance and potential racial tensions that exist between people. These spaces Anderson calls "cosmopolitan canopies," where strangers from diverse backgrounds come together and interact on a day-to-day basis. The question here is whether these positive racial spaces are a potential model for social change.

In 1938, Louis Wirth published "Urbanism as a Way of Life," based on his observations of city life and drawing on Georg Simmel's (1950) earlier work in Europe, "The Metropolis and Mental Life" (Spykman 1925). What mainly concerned Wirth were the qualities that for him defined the city, particularly the variables of size, density, and heterogeneity. Especially striking to him was people's "blase" orientation as they traversed the urban spaces with an impersonal bearing that suggested an attitude of indifference.[1] In the sixty-five years since Wirth's groundbreaking formulations on urbanism, much has happened to big-city life. Of course, some conditions have remained constant, but many have changed profoundly. Strongly affected by the forces of industrialism, immigration, and globalism, the city of today is more racially, ethnically, and socially diverse than ever, with profound cleavages dividing one element from another and one social group from another (see Anderson 1990, 1999; Drake and Cayton 1945; Duneier 1999; Gans 1962; Goffman 1963; Hall 1966; Jacobs 1961; Sassen 2001; Suttles 1968; and Wilson 1987, 1996).

As the urban public spaces of big cities have become more riven by issues of race, poverty, and crime, much of what Wirth described as urbanites' blase

Elijah Anderson, "The Cosmopolitan Canopy," from *The Annals of the American Academy of Political and Social Science* 595, no. 1 (2004): 14–31. Copyright © 2004 by the American Academy of Political and Social Science. Reprinted with the permission of Sage Publications, Inc.

indifference seems to have given way to a pervasive wariness toward strangers, particularly anonymous black males (see Anderson 1990). In places such as bus stations, parking garages, and public streets and sidewalks, many pedestrians move about guardedly, dealing with strangers by employing elaborate facial and eye work, replete with smiles, nods, and gestures geared to carve out an impersonal but private zone for themselves. Increasingly, pedestrians are required to contend publicly with the casualties of modern urban society, not just the persistently poor who at times beg aggressively but also homeless people, street criminals, and the mentally disturbed. Fearful of crime, if threatened, many are prepared to defend themselves or to quickly summon help, if not from fellow pedestrians, then from the police. In navigating such spaces, people often divert their gazes, looking up, looking down, or looking away, and feign ignorance of the diverse mix of strangers they encounter. Defensively, they "look past" or "look through" the next person, distancing themselves from strangers and effectively consigning their counterparts to a form of social oblivion.

As anonymous pedestrians actively "see but don't see" one another, skin color often becomes a social border that deeply complicates public interactions; stereotypically, white skin color is associated with civility and trust, and black skin color is associated with danger and distrust—especially with regard to anonymous young males. Many ordinary pedestrians feel at ease with others they deem to be most like themselves; the more threatening the "other" is judged to be, the greater the distance displayed. Black strangers more often greet and otherwise acknowledge other strangers, particularly other blacks. But most other pedestrians seem simply to follow their noses, at times barely avoiding collisions with others. If they speak at all, they may utter a polite "excuse me" or "I'm sorry," and, if deemed appropriate, they scowl. In effect, people work to shape and guard their own public space.

Yet there remain numerous heterogeneous and densely populated bounded public spaces within cities that offer a respite from this wariness, settings where a diversity of people[2] can feel comfortable enough to relax their guard and go about their business more casually. A prime such location is Philadelphia's Reading Terminal Market. In this relatively busy, quasi-public setting, under a virtual *cosmopolitan canopy*,[3] people are encouraged to treat others with a certain level of civility or at least simply to behave themselves. Within this canopy are smaller ones or even spontaneous canopies, where instantaneous communities of diverse strangers emerge and materialize—the opportunities or openings provided by fascinating tidbits of eavesdropped (or overheard) conversation. Here, along the crowded aisle and eating places, visitors can relax and feel relatively safe and secure. Although they may still avoid prolonged eye contact or avert their glances to refrain from sending the "wrong" messages, people tend to positively acknowledge one another's existence in some measure. At times, strangers may approach one another to talk, to laugh, to joke, or to share a story here and there. Their trusting attitudes can be infectious, even spreading feelings of community across racial and ethnic lines.

Occupying a full city block in Center City Philadelphia, the Reading Terminal Market is composed of numerous shops, restaurants, and kiosks that offer an array of goods and services. It is a highly diverse setting wherein all kinds of people shop, eat, and stroll. Adjacent to the new convention center, it is centrally located among downtown office buildings and upscale condominiums but not far from white, working-class Kensington and black, North Philadelphia. The Terminal building itself, an enormous former train shed, has been part of Philadelphia for more than a century, since the days when trains arrived and departed through the space that became the market. In the 1990s, when the convention center complex was designed and built, the space for the market was kept more or less intact. Many long-time customers feared that it would become simply an upscale tourist attraction, a food court more than a market, but so far, the look of the place has more or less stayed the same, and it continues to draw residents from local neighborhoods, including professionals from Center City as well as Irish, Italian, Asian, and African Americans from Philadelphia's ethnic enclaves. Virtually all racial groups are well represented at Reading Terminal but not in even proportions. On average, about 35 percent of the people there are black, about 10 to 15 percent are Asian and other people of color, and the rest—somewhat more than half—are white, whether WASP or ethnic. The visual, impressionistic makeup of the place is that it is mostly white and middle-class with a healthy mixture of people of color.

The Terminal is a colorful place, full of hustle and bustle. Food is a major theme, and the smell of food is pervasive. The shops are bright and clean, and some are adorned with neon lights. Some of the craft shops have been carrying more expensive pieces aimed at tourists. But the grocery stalls still offer fresh produce and meat direct from Lancaster County farms, fish, seafood, and a wide array of fruits and vegetables; these stalls are interspersed with others selling flowers, health supplements, tea, coffee, spices, books, and crafts. A number of businesses are family owned. And Amish farm families are a strong historical presence in the market—their traditional dress adds an exotic element to the life of the marketplace. Their fresh produce, high-quality meats, and poultry are very inviting. Asian families are also well represented, selling all kinds of fresh fish and produce. Blacks own only a few businesses here, including an African crafts shop that sells masks, beads, and other adornments. Delilah's provides delicious African American cuisine, or "soul food." Other eateries, serving a great variety of tasty foods and drink, include a Thai place, an oyster bar, a French bakery, a Jewish bakery, a juice bar, a beer garden, and a cookie company, making the Terminal a particularly busy place at lunch time. Equally striking is the diversity of workers and the general comity with which they interact. For example, black stockmen work for the German butcher with apparent easygoing demeanor and attitude. Some of the white-owned businesses even have black cashiers, which would have been rare or nonexistent not too many years ago.

The customers, too, seem to be on their best behavior. People seem to be relaxed and are often seen interacting across the color line. Seeing a black woman with a walker wrestling with the heavy doors, two Irish men jump up from their meal at nearby Pearl's Oyster Bar to help her. The clientele at the many food counters represent various classes, races, and ethnicities. A black businessman can be seen talking on his cell phone. Hispanic construction workers are relaxing on their lunch break. This is a calm environment of equivalent, symmetrical relationships—a respite from the streets outside.

And it has been this way for years. The Terminal is an institution in Philadelphia and has always been known as a place where anyone could expect civility. In the days when blacks never knew what treatment they would be given in public, they could come to the Terminal and know they would not be hassled.[4] The ambience has always been comfortable and inviting. Perhaps the focus on food is a reason for this, suggesting a kind of festival of ethnic foods. On any given day, one might see a Chinese woman eating pizza or a white businessman enjoying collard greens and fried chicken or an Italian family lunching on sushi. When diverse people are eating one another's food, strangers in the abstract can become somewhat more human and a social good is performed for those observing. As people become intimate through such shared experiences, certain barriers are prone to be broken. The many lunch counters also help encourage strangers to interact, as they rub elbows while eating. At certain counters in particular, there seems to be a norm of talking with strangers. One woman told me you cannot get people to shut up. The Terminal is a neutral space in which people who behave civilly, whatever their ethnicity, usually will not be scrutinized, as would likely happen in the ethnic neighborhoods of the city if an unknown person were to pass through. In those neighborhoods, such keen notice of strangers is the first line of defense,[5] but the Terminal is not defended in this manner.

Multiple sets of doors on three sides of the market are used from morning to late afternoon, six days a week. Upon entering from any side, one is met by shoppers, diners, and others here to stroll and take in the ambience. One encounters a varied assemblage under the Terminal's canopy: unobtrusive security guards, both black and white; retired people; teenagers who gather with their friends to hang out; twenty-somethings who come to meet members of the opposite sex; homeless people who gravitate to the market for shelter, food, and the unhindered use of public bathrooms; and business executives and workers from nearby office buildings who make up the lunch crowd. Wholesome sandwiches or healthful, full-plate lunches can be purchased at a reasonable price and consumed quickly on the premises or taken out. At one buffet, you can get a hot meal of collard greens, chicken, sausage, roast, and salad for around $8. Working people and retirees on fixed incomes take advantage of this bargain, at times meeting their friends for sociability.

By the back wall, near the restrooms, black shoeshine men work and socialize, keeping up with one another. They share personal stories and seem always ready for a good laugh. Italians, Jews, Asians, and blacks sit nearby, snacking on baked goods and coffee while enjoying melodious piano sounds played for tips. The municipal courthouse is within a short walk, and occasionally, people appear for lunch with "juror" stickers affixed to their clothing. There is always a scene to be part of and to observe here.

As indicated above, immediately under the canopy, people relax their guard—not completely, but they do look more directly at others as they observe the goings on and move about with a greater sense of security. As they stroll up and down the aisles, stopping at the various shops and kiosks within the Terminal, they experience other people, and they generally seem to trust what they see. There is usually little cause for alarm. As people stop and purchase items or just walk around, sometimes they greet one another, verbally or nonverbally; there is a feeling of being involved with the others present.

When taking a seat at a coffee bar or lunch counter, people feel they have something of a license to speak with others, and others have license to speak with them.[6] Strikingly, strangers engage in spontaneous conversation, getting to know one another as they do. Testing others, trying things out on them, people are maybe seeing whether those different from themselves are for real. They find that they are. People leave such encounters with a good feeling about the other, as though recognizing that they have experienced something profound, as they have—they have made human contact across the putative barriers of race, ethnicity, and other differences. Here, race and ethnicity appear salient but understated. The following field notes are germane:

It was around 11 a.m. on a warm but overcast Sunday morning in March when an African American buddy and I walked into the Down Home Diner, just inside the Reading Terminal Market. The place always seems to be crowded on Sunday mornings with a remarkable diversity of people, locals and out-of-towners, because the Terminal caters to both the convention center crowd and the people from Philadelphia neighborhoods. The crowd that morning buzzed with small talk, resulting in a low-level conversational din, a dull roar. The overall tone was friendly. We walked in, took our seats at the counter, perused the menu, and ordered. He requested ham and eggs, and I ordered pancakes, ham, and milk. We caught up with each other over coffee while waiting for our food, occasionally looking up and checking out the scene. After a few bites of my pancakes and a drink of my milk, I felt a tap on my shoulder. I looked up to see a red-faced Irishman about forty-five years old. "Who won the game last night?" he asked expectantly. Without missing a beat, I replied, "The Sixers, 98–79." I shot him a smile, and he said, "Thanks," and moved on.

I was struck by the way this man assumed he could approach me about the score of a ball game, in part because of the race issue but also because of his assumption that I am a sports fan. I felt that he probably would not have approached me out on the street. But here, because of the apparently friendly atmosphere prevailing, he felt he could make such a request and was likely to get an answer. Does he presume that because I am a black male, I might be especially interested in basketball, that I would have followed the Sixers game the previous evening, and that I would not mind sharing the score with him? He was somehow colluding with me as an individual but also as a Philadelphia sports fan. At least he expected that I would be agreeable, and in fact, I did not disappoint him. And again [from my fieldnotes]:

On Saturday, I was to meet Rae at the Down Home Diner at 10 a.m. for break-fast. I arrived at the Terminal at about ten to the hour and walked around the area. . . .

On Saturdays, people seem especially relaxed, lazing about or doing their shopping in an unhurried way. The Down Home Diner was quite busy and crowded. There was a line of people waiting to be seated for the homemade pan-cakes, grits, eggs, sausages, and ham the place is known for—the smells wafting through the air, making people all the more hungry. The seating consists of four-and six-top tables, booths, and a counter for ten to twelve people.

I stood and waited for a bit, and when a seat at the counter became available, I took it. The stools are spaced quite close together, making for a certain coziness in which it is impossible not to literally rub shoulders with those seated on either side. As a result, upon sitting down, one is almost obliged to say "good morn-ing" to his or her neighbor. The waitstaff is exclusively female and racially mixed, reflecting the diversity of the city. The kitchen is visible through the pass-through, and the cooks, who too are black as well as white, are busy. . . .

While waiting for Rae, I ordered my coffee: it came quickly. In about five minutes, the stool next to mine became empty. I quickly covered it with my leather jacket and cap to reserve it. . . .

Minutes passed and still no sign of Rae. So I removed my coat and offered the man the seat. "Thanks. If she comes, I'll move," he said. We sat there elbow to elbow, shoulder to shoulder. I gathered that he was not from Philadelphia, and I asked him outright where he was from. "I'm from Sacramento. I've got a booth over at the convention center and nobody's there to watch it." He was in town for an exhibition on farm implements and equipment, and he ran a manufactur-ing business. He noted how good his food was and how efficient the service was. He also mentioned the diversity of people here at the Terminal and that this sit-uation was unusual for him, as he had little opportunity for this kind of interac-tion in Sacramento. Clearly, he was impressed. He revealed that he was from a pretty homogeneous background and that his water-skiing club was even more so. He told me that the club was white and male, including a couple of white supremacists, though he didn't share their views.

The man continued to tell me about his background, as I prompted him to talk about his work. It turned out that he employs a significant number of Mex-icans in his business and that he is firmly in favor of allowing driver's licenses to illegal immigrants ("they get licenses and Social Security cards anyway on the black market, so we may as well regulate them ourselves"). Also, he says, his business would fold without them. "I would not hire a man of my own race—they ain't worth a shit!" he stated. . . .

What is so striking about this episode is that in this setting, a white man with white-supremacist friends is able to have a frank conversation with me, a black man, in which he reveals his own feelings about race and diversity. It is the ambience of Reading Terminal that one can go there and take leave of one's particularism, while showing a certain tolerance for others. The Down Home Diner can be viewed as a version of the cosmopolitan canopy under which opportunities are provided, at least situationally, to connect across ethnic and racial lines. Outside, in a more impersonal public space, there is little chance for such interaction; the man would not have approached me, and there would have been no opportunity for the exchange described above. Of course, at least an occasional tension crops up in any human group, and the Terminal is no exception. Rarely, racial and ethnic tension does indeed occur, perhaps in relation to people's ethnic origins and their working out of their sense of group position. More often, due to the apparent large store of comity and goodwill manifested here, tension remains on the individual level. People come to this neutral and cosmopolitan setting expecting diverse people to get along.

This cosmopolitan canopy that seems to spread over and affect relations within the general space called Reading Terminal Market can be divided into subzones that might be seen as the quasi-public impersonal and the more intimate zones, the former being off-putting and the latter socially more encouraging. In the more intimate settings within the canopy, such as at one of the numerous lunch counters, people often feel welcome and secure enough to relax, even to the point of engaging complete strangers in conversation. In these circumstances, people carry on their business but also engage in *folk ethnography* and formulate or find evidence for their *folk theories* about others with whom they share the public space.[7]

In Philadelphia, the Reading Terminal Market is but one of many such locations that may be viewed, conceptually at least, as existing under this kind of "cosmopolitan canopy"; other examples with a similar ambiance are Rittenhouse Square park, 30th Street Train Station, the Whole Foods Market, the Italian Market, various fitness centers, hospital waiting rooms, the multiplex theater, indoor malls, and sporting venues, among other places.[8] . . .

Such neutral social settings, which no one group expressly owns but all are encouraged to share, situated under this kind of protective umbrella, represent a special type of urban space, a peculiar zone that every visitor seems to recognize, appreciate, and enjoy.[9] Many visit not only for instrumental reasons—to have a meal or just to be "out and about"—but also for the experience of being among the social types they believe they are likely to find here. The ambience is decidedly "laid-back," and in navigating the quasi-public spaces here, there is little sense of obligation to the next person other than common civility. Visitors leave with the memory of a good experience and are likely to return another day, perhaps to relive an otherwise uneventful and pleasant experience.

As people engage others in these public settings, they can do what I call both practical and expressive folk ethnography. Simply put, cosmopolitan canopies are interesting places to engage in the fine art of "people watching," for "all kinds" of folk are represented. The curious will sometimes gawk at strangers, but most often, people are polite and, from a safe distance, watch others unobtrusively, if indirectly. Others may be reluctant at first, only to find themselves unavoidably overhearing conversations that pique their interest; then they eavesdrop and collect stories, which they may either repeat to friends or keep to themselves.

In the more quasi-public areas, it is common for people to publicly interact with complete strangers, exquisitely expressing themselves through face and eye work; smiles and frowns are occasionally punctuated by a critical commentary of grunts and groans and outright talk. Through these various transactions, they legitimate a look here, discourage an advance there, and put "who they are" on public display. In time, their accumulating observations feed both prejudices and truths—affected by their own identities—about the others they encounter here.

With such frames in mind, they build on what they know, effectively "understanding" strangers they encounter and coming to "know" the public life of the canopy. They do all this with an eye to sorting out and making sense of one another, either for practical reasons or to satisfy a natural human curiosity. Later, among their friends, social peers, associates, people of their own ethnic communities, and others with whom they feel close enough, they share their observations, telling their stories and shaping them as they go.

This complex process affects how they view and define this place and other interesting aspects of the city for their local social networks, while inspiring folk notions about "how people are" and "how things work." At Reading Terminal, for instance, they casually observe and perhaps ponder the "Jewish butcher," the "Amish farmers stall," the "Asian fish counter," "the Italian bakery," or the "black shoeshine stand." The denizens learn to get along and deal effectively with life in this setting, all the while expressing their own identities with respect to others present.

While civility may rule and be taken for granted here, when people leave such zones, they may well be challenged in other ways that require different responses. The local neighborhoods from which they come and through which they must travel are publicly known for their racial and ethnic tensions. Because of this, the denizens of the most public spaces, spaces defined by civility as being within the cosmopolitan canopy, put an active, if unacknowledged, premium on up-close observations of others, including inadvertent eavesdropping and what are in effect informal studies of the local people. This kind of observation is never systematic or planned. And the collection of evidence as to what others are like is highly selective and might be seen as giving rise to or reinforcing persistent stereotypes, as well as uncovering unexpected truths about others they encounter.

In such urban social settings, passersby are often able and willing to sample sizable portions of other people's conversations. Such fragmentary data are like so many pieces of the jigsaw puzzle of social ambience or the ethnography of a given public place. People are inclined to fit these pieces together somehow, generally in a conscious manner with a grand design but also rather intuitively and inductively, creating a mental picture of the nature of the setting and of certain kinds of others. They may do this for no other reason than "to be in the know" or "not to make a fool of myself" in a given setting. They engage in folk ethnography to navigate uncertain terrain but also as naturally curious human beings inclined to make sense of their social habitat.

Naturally, a certain physical and social distance between people is common in the larger, more public settings such as Reading Terminal Market and Rittenhouse Square. And although the amount and quality of interaction are always a matter of person-to-person negotiation, numerous smaller quasi-public venues can be found all over the city where strangers coexist for a brief time with a kind of closeness bordering on intimacy. The more intimate the space, the more chance there is for up close "fieldwork," including direct and indirect observation and eavesdropping. Such places are important settings for diverse strangers to "learn" how to get along with one another, albeit at times superficially. The jazz bar Zanzibar Blue is an example of a setting that is both intimate and public.

After descending the steps off Broad Street down into Zanzibar Blue, one feels as though one has entered a dark inner sanctum, an underground world of live music, food, liquor, and a cosmopolitan mix of people who have in common a certain appreciation of jazz. On the left is a bar with a few people sitting around it, sipping their drinks, and nodding to the smooth beat wafting about and through space. As one's eyes slowly adjust to the gloom, little candlelit lamps suddenly become visible atop neat rows of four-top tables with blood-red tablecloths. One then encounters two hefty black bouncers in dark suits. They engage the visitor with small talk while checking him out to see what his business is, perhaps especially if he is a stranger dressed in dark clothes, though here everything has a dark hue.

Over in the corner sits a dark-skinned black man engaging his brown-skinned honey; his gold-rimmed glasses sparkle, capturing and reflecting the scarce light here. Nearer the bandstand, nine black women gather to honor a friend on her birthday—as becomes apparent later on when the waiter delivers a small cake with two candles on top. On the other side, facing the bandstand, another black couple enjoys their meal while waiting for tonight's sets to begin. The maitre d' shows another black man and me to a table, first a two-top but then a four-top that we accept more happily. . . .

The band is now set up—a cool-looking white man on guitar, a black Muslim with a coofee [cap] on sax, a small brown-skinned man on drums, and the leader, a muscular, bald-headed black man, on bass. The leader opens with the usual introductions. To start the first set, he makes fun of straying black men and their family responsibilities while pleading for the audience not to be too judgmental—"give a brother some slack because he always comes home." Chuckles come from the audience, the blacks perhaps "getting it" more than the whites. The combo plays. Naturally, the sounds are smooth, melodious, stark, and loud. People go into conscious listening and watching mode, as they are here to see the show, and a show it is.

But a show is being put on not just by the combo but by the clientele themselves. The people observe one another, watching how this or that person reacts to the sounds. When a player works especially hard to bring out an unusual or seemingly difficult but appealing sound, the audience collectively agrees to give the player some recognition—applause, that is. And when the guitar player makes a sound not commonly associated with the guitar, members of the audience clap spontaneously—almost on cue. It is especially interesting when the blacks clap enthusiastically for the white player. Everyone notices. People here are aware of each other but at the same time anonymous. They feel a sense of community while they are here, and then they move on.

One might say that places like Zanzibar Blue are a salve for the hustle and bustle of more fraught urban experience. While the jazz club is a special experience,[10] with complete strangers participating in a collective entertainment and artistic production, intimate spaces of a different sort proliferate with the boom of the franchise business. More generally, they include the Starbuckses and McDonaldses of the world, places where complete strangers congregate and observe one another but may not feel as connected as people do at a jazz club. Through people watching and eavesdropping in a tight space, they may leave with strong impressions and stories of other people's lives, truncated and fleeting as they may be, which serve to shape their gossip, not simply about individuals but about the groups these strangers seem to represent.

In the outpatient waiting room of the local university hospital, among computer screens, alcoves, plastic chairs, coffee wagon, and reception desk, people have slowed down as they kill time waiting for the bureaucracy to go through its motions. This is an ideal setting in which to observe more relaxed, quasi-public race relations. What one observes is that while some people might like to group themselves with others who are of a similar race, here, people sit where they can and tend not to go to the extra trouble of such racial sorting. Still, people like to be comfortable [from my fieldnotes]:

On this particular day, there are about forty people intermittently seated in rows of cushioned chairs facing each other. It is a somewhat busy setting, with diverse people moving to and fro doing their business. Staff people, who seem disproportionately African American, transport patients, equipment, and other materials. Every staff person is assumed to be engaged in critical work, a fact that garners certain respect, regardless of the worker's station, color, or perceived background.

Four no-nonsense, middle-aged black women handle paperwork at the various business windows, triaging outpatients. The patients are predominantly African American (about 70 percent), but whites (about 25 percent) and Asians and Latinos (about 5 percent) are being served as well. The black people, some of whom work for the university, are mostly poor to working class and from the nearby ghetto community, intermixed with a few middle-class people; the whites tend to be working to middle class as well. A younger black man and an older woman, who appears to be his mother, enter the setting and move slowly toward a couple of empty seats. Others present here, black as well as white, follow the couple with their eyes, momentarily, if inadvertently, making eye contact. They all take in the scene. A minor drama unfolds as the young man faces a seemingly difficult task of seating the heavy old woman. First, he relieves her of her bags and then helps her to remove her coat to make her comfortable, the object being to get her settled.

As this situation unfolds, a young, Irish, working-class man with stringy brown hair sitting in the next seat rises and offers assistance, which is soon shown to be unnecessary. But after seating his mother, the black man audibly thanks the young man anyway. The working-class white man nods. And things return to normal as people refocus their attention on their magazines, their children, or their partners. . . .

In a few minutes another scene develops. A rotund black man of about sixty-five in a motorized wheelchair, who has a hook for one hand, is clearly enjoying his conversation on his cell phone. He speaks at a voice level that allows many of those present to follow parts of his conversation. A few people are clearly annoyed by this, while others are perfectly tolerant in what is certainly a public place. It becomes clear that the man is speaking with a friend, apparently excited about the prospect of obtaining an artificial limb. Eyes follow the man as he moves across the room to be nearer the large window, perhaps for better reception on his cell phone. By the window, he continues his conversation, which is rather expansive, reflecting his cheerful mood. . . .

In this setting, the black people tend to be somewhat relaxed and at times even animated in their presentation of self (Goffman 1959). Most are of working-class status, but they outnumber the whites present. A perfunctory look might suggest that whites' attention is riveted on the blacks here, since this is a seemingly unique situation, but on close inspection, it is clear that people of both groups are curious and take this opportunity to observe each other closely. This is a relatively safe place, and people can look at others without feeling threatened, though some of the whites might feel somewhat awkward about being in the company of so many black people at one time.

Essentially, cosmopolitan canopies allow people of different backgrounds the chance to slow down and indulge themselves, observing, pondering, and in effect, doing their own folk ethnography, testing or substantiating stereotypes and prejudices or, rarely, acknowledging something fundamentally new about the other. . . .

Conclusion

Under the cosmopolitan canopy, whether quasi-public or intimate, people seem to have some special need to observe the social setting closely; for many, people watching is a common pastime, and for some, it has risen to an art form. They check others out, practicing a form of folk ethnography, making sense of what they observe while reserving the right to be highly selective in their sources of evidence. The resulting understandings may in fact be as much about themselves as about the others they come to know—a factor that helps them to remain "folk" in the sense that Redfield (1947, 1956) defined—not urban or pre-urban, despite the city's ever-growing size, density, and truly mind-boggling diversity. This kind of exposure to a multitude of people engaging in everyday behavior often humanizes abstract strangers in the minds of these observers.

The existence of the canopy allows such people, whose reference point often remains their own social class or ethnic group, a chance to encounter others and so work toward a more cosmopolitan appreciation of difference. As canopies, the Reading Terminal, Rittenhouse Square, Thirtieth Street Station, the Whole Foods Market, and sporting events certainly do not provide identical social experience. But they do all provide an opportunity for diverse strangers to come together and be exposed to one another. In these circumstances, they have a chance to mix, observe one another, and become better acquainted with people they otherwise seldom observe up close.

As urbanites, they encounter people who are strangers to them, not just as individuals but also as representatives of groups they "know" only in the abstract. The canopy can thus be a profoundly humanizing experience. People in these places are also inclined to express common civility toward others. For instance, families with children in tow enable adults to model for their children, and their children to model for still others, including both children and grown-ups. Some parents use such a setting as a teaching tool, at times making a point of having their children respect people who are in some way different from themselves. And when people exposed to all this return to their own neighborhoods, they may do so with a more grounded knowledge of the other than was possible without such experience. In this way, the generations establish new social patterns and norms of tolerance, while encouraging everyday common civility, if not comity and goodwill, among the various groups that make up the city.

To be sure, people may devolop new stereotypes or see fit to hold on to the ones they have previously formed. It is likely that they will opt to hold onto attitudes they are deeply invested in. Yet they will have been exposed to members of a heretofore unknown other (see Blumer 1958). If nothing more, through constant exposure, such environments can encourage common, everyday taken-for-granted civility toward others who are different from oneself.

As canopies proliferate, such neutral territories become an established element of the makeup of the city. Moving about through the major canopies such as the Terminal as well as the more intimate ones in restaurants and bars, people can have a sense of being out and about in a cosmopolitan setting. As they are exposed, others are exposed to them. And especially in the smaller settings, they can eavesdrop, look people over, and more closely observe people who are strange to them, whose behavior they previously could only imagine.

As the urban environment becomes increasingly diverse, the cosmopolitan canopy becomes ever more significant as a setting in which people of diverse backgrounds come together, mingle with strangers, and gain from their social experience a critical folk knowledge and social intelligence about others they define as different from themselves. In these circumstances, they may see profoundly what they have in common with other human beings, regardless of their particularity. A model of civility is planted in such settings that may well have a chance to sprout elsewhere in the city. People are repeatedly exposed to the unfamiliar and thus have the opportunity to stretch themselves mentally, emotionally, and socially. The resulting folk ethnography serves as a cognitive and cultural base on which denizens are able to construct behavior in public. And often, though certainly not always, the end result is a growing social sophistication that allows diverse urban peoples to get along.

ENDNOTES

[1] In Wirth's day, many wealthy people were concerned with moral contamination. Such people can be imagined strolling through the public spaces with their heads held high in an expression of disdain for those they considered beneath them. Today, the public issue more commonly is one of wariness and fear of crime.

[2] Gans (1962) has described these urban types as "cosmopolites," "urban villagers," "the deprived," and "the trapped."

[3] For a much earlier treatment of "cosmopolitans" and "locals" as a social types, see "Patterns of Influence: Local and Cosmopolitan Influentials," in Merton (1957).

[4] Traditionally, in certain segregated neighborhoods, outsiders were kept at bay, and this has kept these neighborhoods relatively homogenous. Since the end of de jure segregation, this situation has been slowly changing. See Massey and Denton (1993).

[5] See Suttles' discussion of "the defended neighborhood" in Suttles (1972:21–43).

[6] For an in-depth discussion of a similar phenomenon related to bar behavior see Cavan (1966).

[7] A distinction exists between Redfield's (1947) "folk society," which represents a "little tradition" in an enclosed folk setting, and the idea I am proposing of urban folk living in isolated ethnic communities within the context of the city (cf. Gans 1962). Philadelphia is quite an ethnic town, made up of neighborhoods that reflect its many ethnicities and that are rather particularistic. People from these neighborhoods carry along with them localized ideologies that tell them not only about their own situations but also about those of others. Some of these are clearly stereotypes they use in relating to others and in understanding how others relate to them. Yet this particularistic attitude is affected by class, education, and exposure to more cosmopolitan settings. So a tension forms between ethnic particularism and a more sophisticated understanding of diversity. When people leave their ethnic neighborhood or setting, it is imperative that they take on a more general perspective, especially as they move to more neutral territory where they encounter different kinds of people and the theme is one of general civility. It is in these settings that people can and do act civilly toward those who are different from themselves, even though it may be a challenge for them. Folk ideologies and orientation are challenged by the more sophisticated or tolerant signals of the more cosmopolitan situation. That is just the kind of place a cosmopolitan canopy is, and urban folk are challenged by the cosmopolitanism characteristic of these settings (cf. Wirth [1938] on urbanism and Hall [1966] on urban space and diversity).

[8] Other places are different from Reading Terminal as well as from one another, but they are similar as settings where people can come together and experience diverse others—they are places where diversity seems to congregate. The Terminal is unusual, however, in the amount of conversation that occurs between strangers, especially strangers of different races and ethnicities.

[9] For an example of a consciously constructed social setting of this type in Paris, France, see de la Pradelle and Lallement.

[10] See Grazian (2003).

REFERENCES

Anderson, Elijah. 1990. *Streetwise: Race, Class, and Change in an Urban Community*. Chicago: University of Chicago Press.

———. 1999. *Code of the Street: Decency, Violence, and the Moral Life of the Inner City*. New York: W. W. Norton.

Blumer, Herbert. 1958. "Race Prejudice as a Sense of Group Position." *Pacific Sociological Review* 1:3–7.

Cavan, Sherri. 1966. *Liquor License*. Chicago: Aldine.

Drake, St. Clair, and Horace R. Cayton. 1945. *Black Metropolis: A Study of Negro Life in a Northern City*. New York: Harper and Row.

Duneier, Mitchell. 1999. *Sidewalk*. New York: Farrar, Straus and Giroux.

Gans, Herbert. 1962. "Suburbanism and Urbanism as Ways of Life: A Re-evaluation of Definitions." In *Human Behavior and Social Processes*. Boston: Houghton Mifflin.

Goffman, Erving. 1959. *The Presentation of Self in Everyday Life*. Garden City, NY: Doubleday.

———. 1963. *Behavior in Public Places*. Glencoe, IL: Free Press.

Grazian, David. 2003. *Blue Chicago: The Search for Authenticity in Urban Blues Clubs*. Chicago: University of Chicago Press.

Hall, Edward T. 1966. *The Hidden Dimension*. New York: Doubleday.

Jacobs, Jane. 1961. *The Death and Life of Great American Cities*. New York: Random House.

Lofland, Lyn. 1973. *A World of Strangers: Order and Action in Urban Public Space.* New York: Basic Books.

Massey, Douglas and Nancy Denton. 1993. *American Apartheid: Segregation and the Making of the Underclass.* Cambridge, MA: Harvard University Press.

Merton, Robert K. 1957. *Social Theory and Social Structure.* New York: Free Press.

Redfield, Robert. 1947. "The Folk Society." *American Journal of Sociology* 52:293–308.

———. 1956. "The Social Organization of Tradition." In *Peasant Society/Little Community.* Chicago: University of Chicago Press.

Sassen, Saskia. 2001. *The Global City: New York, London, Tokyo.* Princeton, NJ: Princeton University Press.

Simmel, Georg. 1950. "The Metropolis and Mental Life." In *The Sociology of Georg Simmel,* edited by Kurt H. Wolff. Glencoe, IL: Free Press.

Spykman, J. Nicholas. 1925. *The Social Theory of Georg Simmel.* Chicago: University of Chicago Press.

Suttles, Gerald D. 1968. *The Social Order of the Slum.* Chicago: University of Chicago Press.

———. 1972. *The Social Construction of Communities.* Chicago: University of Chicago Press.

Wilson, William J. 1987. *The Truly Disadvantaged: The Inner City, the Underclass, and Public Policy.* Chicago: University of Chicago Press.

———. 1996. *When Work Disappears: The World of the New Urban Poor.* New York: Knopf.

Wirth, Louis. 1938. "Urbanism as a Way of Life." *American Journal of Sociology* 44:1–24.

58

GENERATIONS X, Y AND Z
Are They Changing America?

DUANE F. ALWIN

D. Stanley Eitzen, in the first reading in this section (Reading 56), argued that some types of social progress have led to a decrease in social interaction. Eitzen described several social trends and the implications they have had for society and for increasing social isolation. In this last reading on social change, Duane F. Alwin, the McCourtney Professor of Sociology and Demography at Pennsylvania State University, builds on Eitzen's arguments and claims that we need to carefully examine different explanations of social change, including whether changes in Americans' worldviews over time are due to an aging effect, a period effect, or a generational effect.

The Greatest Generation saved the world from fascism. The Dr. Spock Generation gave us rebellion and free love. Generation X made cynicism and slacking off the hallmarks of the end of the 20th century. In the media, generation is a popular and all-purpose explanation for change in America. Each new generation replaces an older one's zeitgeist with its own.

Generational succession is increasingly a popular explanation among scholars, too. Recently, political scientist Robert Putnam argued in *Bowling*

Duane F. Alwin, "Generations X, Y and Z: Are They Changing America?" *Contexts,* Vol. 1. pp. 42–51. November, 2002. Copyright © 2002, American Sociological Association. Reprinted by Permission of Sage Publications, Inc.

Alone that civic engagement has declined in America even though individual Americans have not necessarily become less civic minded. Instead, he argues, older engaged citizens are dying off and being replaced by younger, more alienated Americans who are less tied to institutions such as the church, lodge, political party, and bowling league.

Next to characteristics like social class, race, and religion, generation is probably the most common explanatory tool used by social scientists to account for differences among people. The difficulties in proving such explanations, however, are not always apparent and are often over-shadowed by the seductiveness of the idea. Generational arguments do not always hold the same allure once they are given closer scrutiny.

Changes in the worldviews of Americans result not only from the progression of generations but also from historical events and patterns of aging. For example, generational replacement seems to explain why fewer Americans now than 30 years ago say they trust other people, but historical events seem to explain why fewer say they trust government. Similarly, historical events in interaction with aging (or life cycle change) may explain lifetime changes in church attendance and political partisanship better than generational shifts.

Explaining Social Change

Some rather massive changes over the past 50 years in Americans' attitudes need explaining. Consider this short list of examples:

- In 1977, 66 percent said that it is better if the man works and the woman stays home; in 2000, only 35 percent did.
- In 1972, 48 percent said that sex before marriage is wrong; in 2000, 36 percent did.
- In 1972, 39 percent said that there should be a law against interracial marriage; in 2000, 12 percent did.
- In 1958, 78 percent said that one could trust the government in Washington to do right; in 2000 only 44 percent did.

Do changes in beliefs and behaviors reflect the experiences of specific generations, do they occur when Americans of all ages change their orientations, or do they result from something else? Although the idea of generational succession is promising and useful, it also has problems that may limit it as an all-purpose explanation of social change.

Some Preliminaries

Before we begin to deconstruct the idea of generational replacement we need to clarify a few issues. The first is that when sociologists use the term *generation* it can refer to one of three quite different things:

1. All people born at the same time.

2. A unique position within a family's line of descent (as in the second generation of Bush presidents).
3. A group of people self-consciously defined, by themselves and by others, as part of historically based social movement (as in the "hippie" generation).

There are many examples in the social science literature of all three uses, and this can create a great deal of confusion. Here I refer mainly to the first use, measuring generation by year of birth. Demographers prefer to use the term cohort. Either way the reference is to the historical period in which people grow to maturity. I use the terms cohort and generation more or less interchangeably.

When sociologists are discussing social change in less precise terms, they may refer to generations in a somewhat more nuanced, cultural sense. Generations in this usage do not necessarily map neatly to birth years. Rather, the distinction between generations is a matter of quality, not degree, and their exact time boundaries cannot always be easily identified. It is also clear that statistically there is no way to identify cohort or generation effects unequivocally. The interpretation of generational differences depends entirely on one's ability or willingness to make some rather hefty assumptions about other processes, such as how aging affects attitudes, but as we shall see, we can nonetheless develop reasonable conclusions.

Cohort Replacement

Cohort replacement is a fact of social life. Earlier-born cohorts die off and are replaced by those born more recently. The question is: do the unique formative experiences of cohorts become distinctively imprinted onto members' worldviews, making them distinct generations over the course of their lifetimes, or do people of all cohorts adapt to change, remaining pliable in their beliefs throughout their lives?

When historical events mainly affect the young, we have the makings of a generation. Such an effect—labeled a cohort effect—refers to the outcomes attributable to having been born in a particular historical period. When, for example, people describe the Depression generation as particularly thrifty, they imply that the experience of growing up under privation permanently changed the economic beliefs and style of life of people who grew to maturity during that time.

Unique events that happen during youth are no doubt powerful. Certainly, some eras and social movements, like the Civil Rights era and the women's movement, or some new ideologies (e.g., Roosevelt's New Deal) provide distinctive experiences for youth during particular times. As Norman Ryder put it, "the potential for change is concentrated in the cohorts of young adults who are old enough to participate directly in the movements impelled by change, but not old enough to have become committed to an occupation, a residence, a family of procreation or a way of life."

To some observers, today's younger generations—Generation X and its younger counterpart—display a distinctive lack of social commitment. The goals of individualism and the good life have replaced an earlier generation's involvement in social movements and organizations. Is this outlook simply part of being young, or is it characteristic of a particular generation?

Each generation resolves issues of identity in its own way. In the words of analyst Erik Erikson, "No longer is it merely for the old to teach the young the meaning of life. ... it is the young who, by their responses and actions, tell the old whether life as represented by the old and presented to the young has meaning; and it is the young who carry in them the power to confirm those who confirm them and, joining the issues, to renew and to regenerate or to reform and to rebel."

Such reasoning about generational replacement is not new. Eighteenth- and nineteenth-century social philosophers from David Hume to Auguste Comte linked the biological succession of generations to change in society. As early as 1835, the statistician Adolphe Quetelet wrote about the importance of taking year of birth into account when examining human development. In the 1920s, the German sociologist Karl Mannheim wrote an often-cited treatise on "the problem of generations," arguing that having shared the same formative experiences contributed to a generation's unique worldview, which remained a powerful force in their lives. In Mannheim's words, "Even if the rest of one's life consisted of one long process of negation and destruction of the natural worldview acquired in youth, the determining influence of these early impressions would still be predominant."

Before we accept this way of understanding change, however, we should consider other possibilities. One is that people change as they get older, which we call an effect of aging. The older people get, for example, the more intensely they may hold to their views. America, as a whole, may be becoming more politically partisan because the population is getting older—an age effect. Another possibility is that people change in response to specific historical events, what sociologists call period effects. The Civil Rights movement, for example, may have changed many Americans' ideas about race, not just the views of the generation growing up in the 1960s. The events of September 11, 2001, likely had an effect on the entire nation, not just those in the most impressionable years of youth.

A third possibility is that the change is located in only one segment of society. Members of the Roman Catholic faith, for example, may be the most responsive to the current turmoil over the sexual exploitation of youth by some priests in ways that hardly touch the lives of Protestants. Let us weigh these possibilities more closely, looking at the issues raised by Putnam in *Bowling Alone*.

Changes in Social Connectedness and Trust

It is often relatively easy to construct a picture of generational differences by comparing data from different age groups in social surveys and polls, but determining what produced the data is considerably more complex.

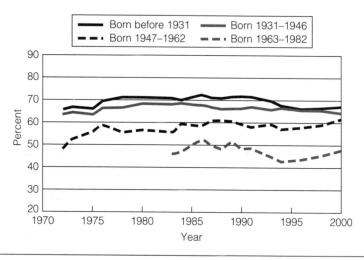

FIGURE 58.1 **Percent of U.S. Population Who Believe "Most People Try to Be Fair"**

Take, for example, one of the key empirical findings of Putnam's analysis: the responses people give to the question of whether they trust their fellow human beings. The General Social Survey (administered regularly to a nationwide, representative sample of American residents since 1972) asks the following question: "Do you think most people would try to take advantage of you if they got the chance, or would they try to be fair?" Figure 58.1 presents the percentage of respondents in each set of cohorts who responded that people would try to be fair. The results show that birth cohorts were consistently different from one another, the recent ones being more cynical about human nature. There has been little change in this outcome over the years except insofar as new generations replaced older ones. These results reinforce the Putnam thesis, that the degree of social connectedness in the formative years of people's generation shapes their sense of trust.

Still, I would note some problems with these conclusions. First, generational experiences are not the only factors that differentiate these four groups; they also differ by age. Second, these data do not depict the young lives of the cohorts born before 1930 (who were 42 years of age or older in 1972), so we have little purchase on their beliefs before 1972. Third, there is remarkable growth in trust among the Baby Boom cohorts—those born from 1947 to 1962—over their midlife period, and in 2000 they had achieved a level of trust on a par with earlier cohorts. Finally, even the most recent cohorts (the lowest line in the figure) show some tendency to gain trust in recent years. The point is that while the data appear to show a pattern of generational differences—less trust among more recent cohorts—age might be just as plausible an explanation of the differences: trust goes up as people mature.

There may be more than one way to explain changes in Americans' trust of people, but generations do not explain changes in Americans' trust of

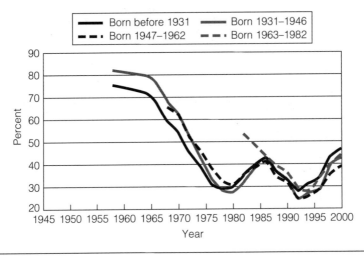

FIGURE 58.2 Percent of U.S. Population Who Believe "You Can Trust the Government in Washington to Do What Is Right"

government. In 1958 the National Election Studies (NES) began using the following question: "How much of the time do you think you can trust the government in Washington to do what is right—just about always, most of the time, or only some of the time?"

There are two important things to note about Figure 58.2. First, there are hardly any differences among birth cohorts who say most of the time or always in their responses to this question; the lines are virtually identical. Thus, generational replacement explains none of the very dramatic decline of trust in government. That decline may be better explained by historical events that affected all cohorts—the Vietnam War, the feminist movement, or the Watergate and Whitewater scandals—and there is little basis for arguing that more recent cohorts are more alienated from government than those born earlier. (Note that affirmations of trust in government rose dramatically right after 9/11.)

Trends in Church Attendance

Reports of attendance at religious services may provide the best example of the complexities of generational analysis. Regarding church attendance, Putnam states that "trends in religious life reinforce rather than counterbalance the ominous plunge in social connectedness in the secular community."

From 1972 through 2000, the General Social Survey has asked random samples of the American public to report how often they attend religious services. These data (not shown here) suggest some important cohort differences in attendance patterns. The Greatest Generation (those born from 1915 to 1930), as well as those born earlier, typically report attending church services something like 25 weeks per year or about half the time. By contrast, people born after the Second World War say they attend church substantially less often. Generation X members report attending services fewer than 15 weeks per year. Consequently, as the earlier cohorts of church attenders die off and are replaced by those less likely to attend church, it could be reasoned that society as a whole will become decidedly less observant. . . .

This interpretation matches the kind of conclusions drawn by Putnam and others who decry modern life as devoid of communal ties. However, these results might be explained, fully or partly, by aging. Typically, after a youthful period of church avoidance, people participate more regularly in religious activities. One common explanation, thus, is that levels of religious participation reflect the effects of aging or the life cycle rather than generation and that the higher levels of involvement reported by cohorts born earlier has as much to do with their age as it does with their generation.

Clearly, more recent generations report less church attendance than earlier ones, but within particular generations, reports of attendance increase over the years. The picture is clouded, however, by Catholic-Protestant differences. Members of the Roman Catholic faith (25 percent of the U.S. population) account for virtually all the decline in reported church attendance in American society between the 1970s and the 1990s. Typical Catholic attendance, some 35 weeks per year in the early 1970s, had declined to 23 weeks per year nearly 30 years later. Much of the decline was due to cohort replacement—younger, less active Catholics replacing the more active Catholics who had died. Most religion scholars attribute the change to the profound differences between Vatican policy on the reproductive rights of women and the views of many lay Catholics. Among Protestants, by contrast, the level of reported church attendance did not change significantly over this period; if anything, it increased. While less active youngsters replace more active older people among Protestant groups, too, that trend is entirely counterbalanced by more active attendance as each generation gets older.

These examples do not do justice to the complex and substantive issues Putnam has raised about civic engagement and social participation, but the case of church attendance points out the difficulties in making strong claims about cohort replacement.

Political Partisanship and the Aging of the Baby Boomers

There is yet another possible combination of generation and history: cohort differences may change over time. Take the example of whether or not people identify with a political party. Since 1952, the NES have asked the question: "Generally speaking, do you consider yourself a Republican, Democrat, Independent, or what?" Figure 58.3 presents data on the percentage of the American public who identify with either of the two major political parties. The earliest born cohorts—the top line—are clearly the most loyal to the major political parties. The two most recent generations—the Baby Boomers (those born 1947 to 1962) and the so-called Generation X (those born 1963 to 1980) are least likely to identify with the two major parties.

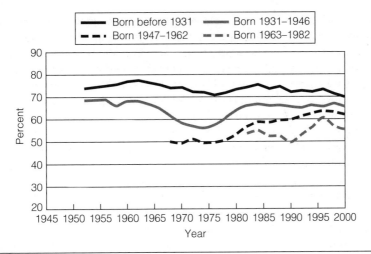

FIGURE 58.3 **Percent of U.S. Population Identifying with One of the Two Major Political Parties**

These trends, however, are not entirely stable. Throughout most of their lives, the Baby Boomers have been distinctively independent, but beginning in the early 1980s, they began a new trend, which might reflect the "aging of the Baby Boom generation." With time they have become much less independent and in fact more likely to affiliate with the Republican Party. What once appeared to be generational differences have gradually eroded.

Generations and Social Change

Society reflects, at any given time, the sum of its generations. Where one set of cohorts is especially large—like the Baby Boomers—its lifestyle dominates the society as it passes through the life course. Baby Boomers' taste in music and clothes, for example, disproportionately influences the whole culture. However, in cases where there are no major differences among generations (as in the example of trust in government), then generational succession cannot explain social change.

Where generations persistently differ, however, their succession will produce social change. Certainly, if the more recent generations have less affiliation and involvement with traditional religious groups, this will lead to social change, at least until they develop their own form of religiosity.

Because of the Baby Boomer generation's sheer size, its liberal positions on political and social issues will probably shape beliefs and behavior well into the new century, as Boomers replace the generations that came before. But even here, the Baby Boomers' distinctiveness may wane under the influence of historical events and processes of aging. Baby Boomers, for example, may be growing more conservative with age. This argues in favor of an alternative to the generational view: Generations do not necessarily differ in the same ways over time; individuals are not particularly consistent over their lives; and social change results as much from shifts in individual lives—due either to aging or historical events.

The most extensive effort to date to identify the presence of generational effects on social change is the work of James Davis, the founder of the General Social Survey. Analyzing how liberal or conservative survey respondents were across a range of social attitudes, Davis found a general trend in the liberal direction across cohorts—a broad turn he calls the "great 'liberal' shift since World War II." But Davis also found a different tendency within the generations, a "conservative trend between the early and late 1970s and a liberal 'rebound' in the 1980s." Generational change aside, there were historical changes, too. Sometimes those historical changes counterbalance the generational shifts.

The existence of generation effects may depend very much on when one takes the snapshot of generational differences, and how generations differ may depend on which groups in society one examines. All fair warnings for the next essay you read on Generations X, Y or Z.

Author Note: *The author wishes to acknowledge the support of funding from the National Institute on Aging (R01-AG4743-09).*

RECOMMENDED RESOURCES

Alwin, Duane F. "The Political Impact of the Baby Boom: Are There Persistent Generational Differences in Political Beliefs and Behavior?" *Generations* 22 (Spring 1998): 46–54. Uses the National Election Studies to document cohort change in political beliefs and behavior over the past 50 years.

Alwin, Duane F., and Ryan J. McCammon. "Generations, Cohorts, and Social Change." In *Handbook on the Life Course*, edited by Jeylan Mortimer and Michael Shanahan. New York: Kluwer Academic/Plenum Publishers, 2002. A recent detailed review of the scholarly literature on stability and change of individuals, cohorts and society from the perspective of life course theory.

Davis, James A. "Patterns of Attitude Change in the USA: 1972–1994." In *Understanding Change in Social Attitudes*, edited by B. Taylor and K. Thomson. Brookfield, VT: Dartmouth, 1996. The most exhaustive empirical examination of cohort effects and intracohort change on social attitudes and beliefs.

Erikson, Erik H. "Youth: Fidelity and Diversity." *Daedalus* 117 (1988): 1–24. A classic statement on the dilemmas and opportunities of youth.

Mannheim, Karl. "The Problem of Generations." In *Essays in the Sociology of Knowledge*; edited by P. Kecskemeti. Boston: Routledge & Kegan Paul, 1952. (Original work published in 1927.) A modern classic which examines the concept of generation and generational replacement.

Mason, William M., and Stephen E. Feinberg. *Cohort Analysis in Social Research: Beyond the Identification Problem*. New York: Springer-Verlag, 1985. A standard reference on the difficulties of drawing inferences about cohort effects in repeated cross-sectional research designs.

Putnam, Robert D. *Bowling Alone: The Collapse and Revival of American Community*. New York: Simon & Schuster, 2000. Argues on the basis of massive amounts of data that individual differences in social connectedness and trust depend heavily on cohort placement.

Ryder, Norman B. "The Cohort as a Concept in the Study of Social Change." *American Sociological Review* 30 (December 1965): 843–61. A carefully crafted demographer's perspective on the concept of cohort in understanding social change.